W. (William) Robinson

Hardy Flowers

Descriptions of upwards of thirteen hundred of the most ornamental Species

W. (William) Robinson

Hardy Flowers
Descriptions of upwards of thirteen hundred of the most ornamental Species

ISBN/EAN: 9783337106676

Printed in Europe, USA, Canada, Australia, Japan

Cover: Foto ©ninafisch / pixelio.de

More available books at **www.hansebooks.com**

HARDY FLOWERS.

DESCRIPTIONS OF UPWARDS OF THIRTEEN HUNDRED OF THE
MOST ORNAMENTAL SPECIES,

WITH

DIRECTIONS FOR THEIR ARRANGEMENT, CULTURE, ETC

> " Daffodils
> That come before the swallow dares, and take
> The winds of March with beauty: violets dim,
> But sweeter than the lids of Juno's eyes
> Or Cytherea's breath; pale primroses,
> That die unmarried, ere they can behold
> Bright Phœbus in his strength: . . . .
> . . . . bold oxlips and
> The crown-imperial; lilies of all kinds."
> SHAKESPEARE.

BY

W. ROBINSON, F.L.S.,

FOUNDER AND EDITOR OF "THE GARDEN;"
AUTHOR OF "ALPINE FLOWERS FOR ENGLISH GARDENS," "THE WILD GARDEN."

THIRD AND CHEAPER EDITION.

LONDON:
MACMILLAN AND CO.
1878.

CONTENTS.

Introduction 1

PART I.

CHAPTER I.

The Mixed Border for Hardy Flowers 5

CHAPTER II.

Hardy Flowers in the Mixed Shrubbery Border 7

CHAPTER III.

Beds and Groups of Hardy Perennials, etc. 11

CHAPTER IV.

Isolation of Hardy Plants 15

CHAPTER V.

Hardy Perennials and Alpines as Bedding Plants 17

CHAPTER VI.

Hardy Alpine and Perennial Plants in the Rock-garden, in the Wild-garden, in Water, and in Boggy Ground 20

CHAPTER VII.

Hardy "Florist's Flowers" 23

CHAPTER VIII.

Hardy Flowers in the Spring-garden. 25

CHAPTER IX.

The Culture of Hardy Flowers. 27

CHAPTER X.

The Propagation of Hardy Flowers 32

PART II.

Alphabetical Arrangement of the most Ornamental Hardy Flowers, with Descriptions, Culture, Suitable Positions, etc . . . 41 to 264

ADDENDA.

New Species, or those omitted in preceding Part . . . . . 265 to 274

PART III.

SELECTIONS OF HARDY FLOWERS FOR VARIOUS PURPOSES.

A Choice Selection of the very finest Herbaceous Perennials . . . 277
A Selection of the finest Hardy Bulbs, including Rhizomatous Plants like the Irises and Hardy Orchids 280
A Selection of Choice Alpine and Rock Plants suitable for the margins of Mixed Borders, etc. 281
A Selection of the most Ornamental Annual and Biennial Plants . 283
A Selection of the finest Hardy Flowers that Bloom in Spring . . 284

CONTENTS.

	PAGE
A Selection of Autumn-blooming Hardy Flowers	285
A Selection of Edging Plants	286
A Selection of Plants for forming " Carpets " beneath larger subjects	289
Hardy Plants with Silvery or Variegated Foliage	291
A Selection of Hardy Flowers suitable for Naturalization in Woods, Copses, Hedgerows, on Ruins, Rocky Banks, and in various other Wild or Half-wild Places	293
A Selection of Fragrant Hardy Plants	295
A Selection of Herbaceous Plants, etc., that will grow beneath the Shade of Trees, and in Copses, etc.	296
A Selection of Hardy Perennials, etc., suitable for Exhibition when Grown in Pots	297
A Selection of Ornamental Aquatic Plants	299
A Selection of Plants thriving in Marshy or Boggy Ground	299
Herbaceous and Alpine Plants, etc., that may with advantage be Raised from Seed	300
List of Dwarf Hardy Perennials and Alpine Plants with Fern-like or Graceful Leaves, and suitable for Association with those distinguished by Beauty of Flower in Borders, the Rock-garden, etc.	301
A Selection of Hardy Perennials affording the finest effects in the Picturesque or " Subtropical " Garden	302
A Selection of Hardy Plants of Vigorous Habit and Distinct Character, suited for Planting in Semi-wild places, in Pleasure-grounds, or near Wood-walks	302
A Selection of Ornamental Grasses	303
Selection of Alpine and Rock Plants of Prostrate or Drooping Habit suited for placing so that they may Droop over the Brows of Rocks and like Positions	304
Trailers, Climbers, etc., for Covering Bowers, Trellises, Railings, Old Trees, Stumps, Rockwork, Banks, etc.	305
Selection of Alpine and Rock Plants for Growing on Old Walls, Ruins, Chalk-pits, Stony Banks, etc.	306
List of Ferns that may be Grown with Advantage away from the Fernery Proper	307

HARDY FLOWERS CLASSED ACCORDING TO THEIR COLOURS.

	PAGE
A Selection of Hardy Plants with White Flowers	308
A Selection of Hardy Plants with Red, Crimson, Scarlet, or Pinkish Flowers	309
A Selection of Hardy Plants with Blue, Bluish, or Purplish Flowers	311
A Selection of Hardy Plants with Yellow Flowers, in Various Shades, or in which Yellow Predominates	311

Index to the Natural Orders of the Plants named in Part II. 313 to 322

A Concise Glossary of the Descriptive Terms used in this Work 323 to 332

Index to English Names . . . . 333 to 341

HARDY FLOWERS.

INTRODUCTION.

IN "Alpine Flowers" I treated of the most interesting classes of hardy plants, and the only ones with which there is the slightest difficulty as to cultivation, etc., but besides the true alpine flora there are many natives of the low hills, plains, and prairies which are not considered "alpine" either from a horticultural or a botanical point of view, and the best of these, with all the true alpine plants, are included here. The book comprises the cream of all the ornamental, hardy, herbaceous, alpine, and bulbous plants at every elevation, from sea shore to snowy peak, that are now to be had in cultivation. The descriptions are more technical than those in "Alpine Flowers," as it was thought desirable to give the reader some means of identifying any plant of which he might have doubts as to the name. Though the number of species selected is large (between thirteen and fourteen hundred), weedy subjects, or those unsuitable from any other cause, have been carefully excluded.

In the selection of these plants for ornamental purposes more care is required than is the case with any other class, and there is nothing more calculated to add beauty and interest of the highest order to the British garden than the spread of knowledge as to the really ornamental kinds.

That many perennials are very beautiful every person who knows a Pæony, or a Delphinium, or a Phlox must be aware; but that a vastly greater number of them are very ragged and weedy-looking is not less true; and it is this fact that explains why they have been so much driven from cultivation of late years. The variation in the aspects of plants, even of the same family, is as great as the contrast presented by their properties, which range from the deadliest of poisons to the most grateful, fragrant, and nourishing of products. Look through the vast and not odoriferous order Compositæ, and what a way you have to wade through groundsels and fetid and gawky weeds, before you meet a plant that can be called pretty. It is so all over the world. Doubtless many people think, from the fascinating banks of orchids shown at our floral exhibitions, that these favoured plants are gloriously beautiful wherever they are found; but, on the contrary, there are many unattractive plants in the family, many of them large-growing and noble looking, but bearing inconspicuous flowers, not half so beautiful as some of the poorest of our own little meadow orchids; and so it is with many a tropical family of plants of which only the gorgeous representatives are seen at our flower shows. But, of course, being tropical we have little opportunity of knowing the least ornamental kinds. Moreover, collectors do not bring them home, knowing them to be worthless, and if they are brought home by chance they are soon thrown away as useless. But in the case of the hardy plants of Europe and America it is very different. They are often seen—in fact, as often as we go among the fields, or hills, or wilds of those continents; often gathered and brought home, and once home they, like ill weeds, grow apace and soon become so conspicuous that the really beautiful hardy flowers are unseen among them, or exterminated by them. Most persons will understand what I mean when they remember the many mixed borders they have seen overgrown with weedy asters, Golden Rods, Lysimachia vulgaris, and like plants, which should never be planted except in rough and semi-wild places.

In garden books and garden journals it is not uncommon to see lists of those plants given, composed in some cases of the poorest weeds—the ground ivy and Moschatel, to wit. These are, of course, written by persons with a very slender knowledge of the subject, who supplement that little with the knowledge to be gained from lists in botanical books; and being unable to distinguish the kinds which are beautiful from those which are merely interesting in a botanical point of view, they have had considerable influence in retarding improvement in this direction.

It is to me a cause of surprise that while we find persons going to great expense to build a glass box wherein to preserve a little of the pretty vegetation of New Holland and other warm climates, and which is of necessity always in a condition less beautiful and less satisfactory than vegetation flourishing in the free air, we may seek in vain in their gardens for a group of the noble hardy Lilies, for the vividly-coloured and beautiful early spring flowers of northern and temperate climes, or for any interesting and beautiful hardy vegetation. We live in a country which is, on the whole, better calculated for the successful culture of the most beautiful vegetation of northern and temperate climes than any on the face of the earth, and at present we take as much advantage of it as if we lived in one where, from extremes of some sort, such vegetation could not exist, and where extraordinary and expensive artificial means were requisite for the enjoyment of a little vegetable beauty. That the natives of cool latitudes are of an inferior degree of beauty cannot be admitted. Travellers who love many aspects of vegetation give the palm, I believe, to that of the meadows, heaths, and uplands of cool countries and the high mountain sides near the line of perpetual snow, and certain it is that the finest Orchids of our stoves do not surpass in beauty Lilies and Irises, that are as easily grown as the common Seakale. The reason sometimes urged against the free use of hardy perennials, that they do not remain so long in flower as what are called bedding plants, is a groundless objection, or if not, why not apply it to the contents of the greenhouse and stove? There it would be sad to think that any one aspect of vegetation should prevail for months at a time, and why should not the same taste be exercised in some select spot in the open garden? The fact is that when rightly understood the very fugacity of the most transient kinds will not be considered objectionable; fortunately, however, a great number of species remain a sufficiently long time in bloom for their beauty to be thoroughly enjoyed.

The culture of the finest hardy perennials need not interfere in the slightest degree with that of bedding plants, or anything else—indeed, it would enhance the beauty of all; and in almost every garden there is, goodness knows, an abundance of room for improvement of this kind. To discuss the subject from the basis of the "mixed border," is completely to beg the question, and in most cases when people discuss this question, the old mixed border seems to represent their ideal of the highest beauty to be attained by the use of the hardy herbaceous and alpine flora of our gardens. To me it has a very different and a very much wider and nobler aspect. I have been somewhat surprised that people have spoken so encouragingly of the matter, considering their point of view. During the past eight or nine years I have sought after hardy plants of all kinds unremittingly, and previous to that I had seen a few good old-fashioned mixed borders; but at no time have I ever seen anything in this way that displayed a tithe of the beautiful plants which it might have had, or that was in any way worthy of a beautiful garden. Assuredly a well-arranged mixed border would be one of the most interesting things ever seen in a garden. But it is not alone in that way that the plants under discussion may be made available. Many combinations of the utmost beauty, and which have not yet been attempted in gardens, are quite possible with them, and very few have any idea of the many diverse ways in which they may be cultivated, so as to attain the happiest results. I will in the following chapters proceed to describe these various ways in which the flora of northern and temperate climes may be grown and arranged with best effect in our gardens, and by which we may, to a great extent, be delivered from the appalling monotony and vacant formality now displayed by the majority of them.

It is an every-day occurrence to see hardy plants placed in positions where there is no possibility of their surviving but for a very short time. Therefore at the risk of being a little monotonous at times, the culture and suitable positions for every species are given. This portion of the work is the result of my own observation of the plants in nearly all public and private gardens in these islands where a good collection is grown, and of their habitats in a wild state both on the continent of Europe and in America. By far the greater number of the plants have been described from personal knowledge of them in a living state.

I am greatly indebted to the owners of nearly all the good collections in the nurseries and private gardens near London, and in various other parts of the country, for specimens of a large number of the kinds named in the book. In a work dealing with such a number of plants from so many diverse climes, references to many books had to be made, principally to the following:—Walper's "Annales" and "Repertorium;" De Candolle's "Prodromus;" Grenier and Godron's "Flore de France;" Vilmorin's "Fleurs de pleine terre;" Duchartres' Jacques et Herincq's "Manuel des Plantes;" Gray's "Manual of the Botany of the Northern United States;" Pursh's "American Flora;" Torrey and Gray's "Flora of North America;" Wood's "Tourist's Flora;" Don's "System of Gardening and Botany;" Kunth's "Enumeratio Plantarum;" "Nouveau Jardinier;" Syme's "English Botany," and Miller's "Dictionary."

PART I.

CHAPTER I.

THE MIXED BORDER FOR HARDY FLOWERS.

THERE are several other ways of arranging hardy plants in a more beautiful, natural, and pleasing manner, but the mixed border forms a sort of reception room for all comers and at all times. On its front margin you may place the newest Sedum or silvery Saxifrage; at the back or in the centre the latest Delphinium, Phlox, or Gladiolus; and therefore it is, on the whole, the most useful arrangement, though it should as a rule be placed in a rather isolated part of the garden, where the extent of the place permits of that. Not that a mixed border is not sufficiently presentable for any position; but, having many more suitable things to offer for the more open and important surfaces of the garden, this had better be kept in a quiet, retired place, where indeed its interest may be best enjoyed. If no better situation be offered than the kitchen-garden, make a mixed border there by all means. The little nursery department, if there be one, will also suit; but best of all, in a large place, would be a quiet strip in the pleasure-ground or flower-garden, separated, if the garden be in the natural style, by a thin shrubbery, from the general scene of the flower-garden. It is vain to lay down any precise rules as to the position or arrangement of this or anything else; for, even if we succeeded in having them adopted, what a sad end would it not lead to—every place like its neighbour! That, above all others, is a thing to be avoided. In old times the borders on each side of the main walk of the kitchen-garden were mostly appropriated to herbaceous plants; and, if well done, this is a good practice, especially if the place be small. A border arranged in this way in a small villa garden will prove a very attractive feature, especially if cut off from the vegetable and fruit quarters by a trelliswork completely covered with good strong-growing varieties of Roses on their own roots.

The mixed border is capable of infinite variation as to plan as well as to variety of subjects. The most interesting variety is that

PLAN OF PORTION OF MIXED BORDER.

Trellis of galvanised wire covered with Roses growing on their own roots.

Hibiscus militaris. *	Lilium tigrinum Fortunei. *		Tritoma grandis. *				Iris, Victorine. *	
				Anemone Honorine Jobert. *				
Baptisia exaltata. *	Tall Delphinium. *	Phlox, tall kind. *						
			Eryngium amethystinum. *					
Echinops ruthenicus *		Rudbeckia Neumanni. *				Dielytra spectabilis. *		
Aster turbinellus. *	Pyrethrum roseum, var. *		Erigeron specioeus. *					Anemone fulgens. *
				Symphytum bohemicum. *		Gentiana asclepiadea. *		Phlox reptans. *
Pentstemon Hartwegi, var. *	Trollius napellifolius, *	Funkia grandiflora. *		Orobus vernus. *	Erica carnea. *	Aubrietia deltoidea. *	Gentiana acaulis. *	Iberis corifolia. *
Anemone sylvestris. *	Sempervivum californicum. *	Silene alpestris. *	Hepatica triloba. *					
Aster versicolor. *								
Saponaria ocymoides. *	Anthyllis montana. *							

Walk.

composed of choice hardy herbaceous plants, bulbs, and alpine plants. Another of a very attractive description may be made by the use of bedding plants only, from Dahlias and Gladioli to the smallest kinds, but in this case we will confine ourselves to the old-fashioned sort made with hardy plants alone. There is a symmetrical system, which must be entirely kept clear of—that of placing quantities of one thing, good or bad, as the case may be, at regular intervals from each other. The very reverse of that is the true system for the best and most interesting kind of mixed border. In a well-arranged one no six feet of its length should resemble any other similar space of the same border. Certainly it may be desirable to have several specimens of a favourite plant; but any approach to planting the same thing in numerous places along the same line should be avoided. I should not, for instance, place one of the neat Saxifrages along in front of the border at regular intervals, fine and well suited as it might be for that purpose, but, on the contrary, attempt to produce in all parts a totally distinct yet high type of vegetation. The Cannas may be used to diversify the mixed border, a plant here or there having a fine effect.

The accompanying plan shows a small portion of what I conceive to be an approach to a tastefully arranged mixed border, so far as size and quality of the plants are concerned. Each of the dwarf plants in front should be allowed to grow into a strong spreading tuft.

The borders should be deeply prepared, and of a fine free texture —in short, of good, rich, sandy loam. That is the chief point in the culture. It is a great mistake to *dig* among choice hardy plants, and therefore no amount of pains should be spared in the preparation of the ground at first. If thoroughly well made then, there will be no need of any digging of the soil for a long time, though it will require cleaning, and may with advantage be lightly forked from time to time.

CHAPTER II.

THE MIXED SHRUBBERY BORDER.

No practice is more general, or more in accordance with ancient custom, than that of digging shrubbery borders, and there is none in the whole course of gardening more profitless or worse. When winter is once come, almost every gardener, although animated with the best intentions, simply prepares to make war upon the roots of everything in his shrubbery border. The generally accepted practice is to trim, and often to mutilate, the shrubs, and to dig all over the surface that must be full of feeding roots. Delicate half-rooted shrubs are often disturbed; herbaceous plants, if at all delicate and not easily recognised, are destroyed; bulbs are often displaced and injured; and a sparse depopulated aspect is given to the margins, while the only "improvement" that is effected by the process is the annual darkening of the surface by the upturned earth. Walk through gardens in winter and spring, and observe the borders round masses of shrubs, choice and otherwise. Instead of finding the earth covered, or nearly covered, with vegetation close to the margin, and each individual developed into something like a respectable specimen of its kind, we find a spread of recently-dug ground, and the plants upon it with an air of having recently suffered from a whirlwind, or something or other that necessitated the removal of mutilated branches. Rough-pruners precede the diggers, and bravely trim in the shrubs for them, so that nothing may be in the way; and then come the delvers, who sweep along from margin to margin, plunging deeply round and about plants, shrubs, or trees. The first shower that occurs after this digging exposes a whole network of torn-up roots. There is no relief to the spectacle; the same thing occurs everywhere—in a London botanic garden as well as in our large West-end parks; and year after year the process is repeated. While such is the case, it will be impossible to have an agreeable or interesting margin to a shrubbery; albeit the importance of the edge, as compared to the hidden parts, is pretty much as that of the face to the back of a mirror. Of course all the labour required to produce this unhappy result is worse than thrown away, as the shrubberies would do better if left alone, and merely surface-cleaned now and then. By utilizing the power thus wasted, we might highly beautify the positions now so very objectionable.

If we resolve that no annual manuring or digging is to be permitted, nobody will grudge a thorough preparation at first. The planting should be so arranged as to defeat the digger. To graduate the vegetation from the taller subjects behind to the very margin of the grass is of much importance, and this can only be done thoroughly by the greater use of permanent evergreen and very dwarf subjects. Happily, there are quite enough of these to be

MIXED SHRUBBERY BORDER.

had suitable for every soil. On light, moist, peaty, or sandy soils, where such things as the sweet-scented Daphne Cneorum would spread forth their dwarf cushions, a better result would ensue than, say, on a stiff clay; but for every position suitable plants might be found. Look, for example, at what we could do with the dwarf green Iberises, Helianthemums, Aubrietias, Arabises, Alyssums, dwarf shrubs, and little conifers like the creeping cedar (Juniperus squamata), and the tamarix-leaved Juniper! All these are green, and would spread out into dense wide cushions, covering the margin, rising but little above the grass, and helping to cut off the formal line which usually divides margin and border. Behind them we might use very dwarf shrubs, deciduous or evergreen, in endless variety; and of course the margin should be varied also.

In one spot we might have a wide-spreading tuft of the prostrate Savin pushing its graceful evergreen branchlets out over the grass; in another the dwarf little Cotoneasters might be allowed to form the front rank, relieved in their turn by pegged-down Roses; and so on without end. Herbaceous plants, that die down in winter and leave the ground bare afterwards, should not be assigned any important position near the front. Evergreen alpine plants and shrubs, as before remarked, are perfectly suitable. But the true herbaceous type, and the larger bulbs, like Lilies, should be "stolen in" between spreading shrubs rather than allowed to monopolize the ground. By so placing them, we should not only secure a far more satisfactory general effect, but highly improve the aspect of the herbaceous plants themselves. The head of a white Lily, seen peeping up between shrubs of fresh and glistening green, is infinitely more attractive than when forming one of a large batch of its own or allied kinds, or associated with a mass of herbaceous plants. Of course, to carry out such planting properly, a little more time at first and a great deal more taste than are now employed would be required; but what a difference in the result. In the kind of borders I advocate, nearly all the trouble would be over with the first planting, and labour and skill could be successively devoted to other parts of the place. All the covered borders would require would be an occasional weeding or thinning, &c., and perhaps, in the case of the more select spots, a little top-dressing with fine soil. Here and there, between and amongst the plants, such things as Forget-me-nots and Violets, Snowdrops and Primroses, might be scattered about, so as to lend the borders a floral interest, even at the dullest seasons; and thus we should be delivered from digging and dreariness, and see our ugly borders alive with exquisite plants.

Assuming that one did not sufficiently esteem hardy flowers to go even to the trouble of adapting the margin of a shrubbery to them, it may not be amiss to point out that the beds of Rhododendrons and American plants generally offer the finest positions that can be desired for the making of the most charming and satisfactory kind of mixed borders.

The culture of Rhododendrons has for many years been so popular in this country that there are few places that do not possess beds or masses of them, or in which fertile masses of peaty soil have not been gathered for their reception. The Rhododendron bush, however fine in flower, has at all times a flattish, formal outline, and this is often disagreeably apparent where large masses are planted, as is now the custom in many places. The soil suited to the Rhododendron is also perfectly suited to the most beautiful and fastidious of all fine perennials. The bold and tall heads of Lilies standing above the flat green of the Rhododendrons in summer, sometimes, as in L. tigrinum Fortunei and L. superbum, in magnificent candelabra-like heads, are the very things to relieve these masses in the most effective way. Then again the Lilies themselves will be seen to much greater advantage; the bases of their stems, being hidden by their surroundings when withering, will not be an eyesore, as they often are when in a border, so that an impatient gardener might want to cut them down before their time, or have something else in their place. The very open spaces which long remain between Rhododendrons, &c., in consequence of their somewhat compact and slow-growing habit, encourage the kind of arrangement suggested. It would be desirable to treat various classes of plants in this way, as, for instance, the Lilies, the Gladioli, Sparaxis pulcherrima, Tritomas, Crocosmia aurea, &c., none of which need be disturbed after being planted, though tall and graceful subjects are undoubtedly best suited for it.

But even round the edge such comparatively dwarf subjects as the Solomon's Seal and the beautiful Lilium longiflorum might be placed with the happiest results. In the case of some of the American Lilies, like L. superbum, this plan is not merely a good one for growing the plants, but it is better than any hitherto pursued with them, the peat soil and the partial shelter enabling them to

BEDS AND GROUPS OF HARDY PERENNIALS. 11

attain their true dimensions and highest beauty, whereas as commonly grown they are starved, and rarely bloom. Another advantage of this mode is the succession of bloom from the same surface. As a rule, once the blush of early summer bloom has passed from the American plants, they present an uninviting surface for the season afterwards; whereas varied in the way described the beds would be most attractive at other seasons.

CHAPTER III.

BEDS AND GROUPS OF HARDY PERENNIALS, ETC.

THE forming of bold groups and beds of the finest perennials, not as part of the flower-garden scheme, but here and there on the quiet grassy bays of a shrubbery, or in any other quiet green or half-wild spot, is one of the most excellent ways of enjoying the nobler perennials, and one of which I hope the advantages will be clear to every reader of the following pages.

As, in the case of the properly made mixed border, one preparation is all that we require, no sensible person will begrudge the labour necessary in the first instance. Care should be taken that the far-searching roots of trees do not get to the soil of the beds and rob the plants of their nutriment. In a word, though the beds or groups will be the better for being associated with handsome shrubs and trees, they must never be so placed as to become mere troughs of rich food for trees with voracious appetites. As the kind of arrangements I recommend give little trouble after the first planting, they should get the best attention at first, and then they are finished for years. It is a most unsatisfactory and to some extent contemptible mode of gardening, that of continually "muddling" over the same ground, spring after spring and autumn after autumn. Doubtless it is necessary to do this for some subjects, and may always be so to some extent; but to have all the skill and labour thrown away upon fleeting things is really stupid, and totally opposed to any permanent or dignified work being done in the garden. The best and highest pleasure to be derived from our gardens will soon be found to lie in those things which, when once well done, we may leave alone for years, and in some cases for the course of our natural lives and the lives of those who come after us.

No. 1. First, then, for a noble circular bed in an isolated place, say on some little glade of grass where there is a recess in a shrubbery, and where you perhaps never thought of putting anything. Have a bed thoroughly well prepared in the first instance, say 8 ft., 10 ft., or 12 ft. wide, according to the size of your place, or the nook in which you plant. What I mean by well prepared is, that the soil should be rich, free, well drained, and 3 ft. deep, if possible. Place a good plant of the very tall and late-flowering Tritoma grandis, and then around it a circle of the excellent and somewhat smaller T. glaucescens. Follow that with a ring of the beautiful white Anemone Honorine Jobert and the showy and splendid Rudbeckia Newmanni, mixed plant for plant; and outside of that again place a circle of the fine herbaceous Sedum spectabile (sold and known as S. fabaria). This Sedum will form a grand edge to the bed, and flowers, like its companions, finely in autumn; while immediately outside of it, and between it and the grass, might be planted a line of Snowdrops, or Scilla bifolia, or both mixed. These would flower, ripen their leaves, and perish before the stronger margins started up. The above would form a grand autumn bed, and a noble object from any point of view—its aspect all through the spring and early summer being fresh, healthy, and in every way unobjectionable.

No. 2. This shall be a grand bed of Lilies. Unhappily, the fine hardy kinds of Lilies are anything but as plentiful as they should be, though in a free rich soil they increase readily enough. Few may have them sufficiently plentiful for some time to make beds of them, but when once people know how truly fine they are when seen well-arranged in a large bed in an isolated place, they will hardly rest content without such glorious garden ornaments. With such kinds as Lilium testaceum and tigrinum Fortunei in the centre, surrounded by the queenly candidum, burnished croceum, spotted canadense, pomponium, colchicum, vivid chalcedonicum, and gradually worked down to the edge with dwarf but beautiful kinds like eximium, longiflorum, and tenuifolium, a large circular or oval bed might be made on the grass, in some isolated spot, which, for the highest beauties of colour, form, and fragrance—for, in fact, almost every quality by which vegetable beauty endears itself to us—could not be surpassed by any arrangement of indoor or out-

BEDS AND GROUPS OF HARDY PERENNIALS. 13

door plants. The only precaution that need be mentioned is, that to grow Lilies well they should have three feet, or nearly that, of free loamy earth, with a good dash of vegetable mould in it. Even now such kinds as L. tigrinum, longiflorum, candidum, croceum, bulbiferum, &c., are to be had pretty cheap—although the chief thing that gardeners have been doing with the hardy Lilies for some time past has been to throw them on the rubbish heap, to make way for such glorious "stuff" as the yellow Calceolaria and the red Geranium.

No. 3. This shall be an evergreen bed, highly suited for a position near small clumps of choice shrubs, or indeed anywhere that a place may be found for it. In the centre a healthy, good young plant of Yucca gloriosa, and around it a ring of Yucca filamentosa and flaccida mixed. These two kinds flower regularly and well. If among them you could insert a few roots of Gladiolus in early summer, they would add very much to the effect of the white flowers of the Yuccas. Around the Yuccas place a ring of Iberis correæfolia, and around that a ring of that capital little spring plant, Erica carnea. Finally, if there be room—and if you have your bed in an isolated spot, you can of course make it as wide as you like—put a little cushion of the beautiful Aubrietia purpurea all round your Erica carnea; and if you have a few Crimean or common Snowdrops, or Scilla bifolia to spare, drop them here and there between the Erica and the Aubrietia, and the effect will be all the better.

No. 4. A mixed bed, carefully arranged as to the height, and tastefully as to the quality and disposition of the contents. In this kind of bed I should have no band or circle whatever, but simply a careful following out of the mixed principle. We could scarcely find a better centre for this type of bed than a good kind of Perpetual Rose, grown upon its own roots, or worked very low, or trained as a pyramidal bush, say 4 ft. high, more or less according to taste and the subjects to be grouped in the bed. No weedy subject should occur in a bed of this kind, but, on the contrary, everything of the most distinct beauty. You may employ in such a bed anything, from a tuft of Campanula carpatica bicolor on its outer edge to the choicest Pink, Phlox, or Picotee, the newest Delphinium, or the oldest spring flower. To specify a few choice things for such a bed, I may name—for the central parts and around the central subject, Platycodon autumnale, or P. grandiflorum, Delphiniums (some of the newer and better varieties), Aconitum variegatum, Achillea filipendulina,

Phloxes, Campanula persicifolia alba and C. coronata, Iris jacquesiana, pallida, and De Bergii, with a host of others equally good. For the middle region of the bed such plants as Dielytra spectabilis, Trollius napellifolius, Armeria cephalotes, Hoteia japonica, Pentstemon in its best forms, double Wallflowers, Achillea Ptarmica fl. pl., etc., would do charmingly; while near the margin such dwarf beauties as Cheiranthus alpinus, Ranunculus amplexicaulis, Achillea tomentosa, the Iberises, the dwarf Phloxes, a few of the better Sedums and Sempervivums, neat variegated or silvery plants, and even little tiny shrubs like the charming Gaultheria procumbens, will prove quite attractive. This kind of mixed bed admits of infinite variety and much interest.

No. 5. A bed of beautiful hardy foliage plants, interspersed with good bulbs or other spring-growing flowering things which will show above the foliage and amongst it. In this way we may have two distinct styles—one of dwarf, neat objects; and one of tall or strong-growing ones. In the centre of the bed, which need not be more than six feet wide or so, I would not put anything higher than a well-grown plant of Arundo Donax versicolor. This Arundo is fine when it is strong enough to make six or seven shoots, and has been protected through the winter by a little pile of cocoa fibre or something of the sort. It only pushes between two and three feet high, in consequence of its variegation, and therefore is very suitable for choice mixed beds. Around it I should place either a complete line of some pretty green-leaved plant like specimens of Rhus glabra laciniata, a little shrub with elegant leaves, or Achillea ægyptiaca or both mixed, the Achillea with the flowers pinched off; or say a line of the two Santolinas, viridis and Chamæcyparissus, mixed plant for plant, and outside of that one of the variegated Jacob's Ladders—the flower-stems of this last to be pinched off as soon as they show themselves, or rather to be nipped out altogether—and mixed with it the fern-like Thalictrum minus. There are dozens of both silvery-leaved and other plants which would edge such an arrangement charmingly—from young plants of the fine Salvia argentea to Alyssum spinosum, or Antennaria tomentosa; if, indeed, it would not be better to have a mixed planting of dwarf and elegant little plants all round. In most of the interspaces of such a bed the judicious cultivator might, if he chose, plant bulbs, &c.—say a sprinkling of Gladioli towards the centre, a few Tulips about the middle distance, and any choice and delicate spring bulbs about the

margin. These would in most cases come up and flower ere the foliage plants were vigorous. Where they do not do so early, as in the case of the Gladioli, the result is none the less beautiful, inasmuch as the effect in autumn of these magnificently coloured flowers among the rich and elegant foliage will prove simply superb.
Arrangements like these might be multiplied without end, wherever there is a stock of plants and a little taste. In forming combinations of this kind, and particularly in those in which no repetition or formal grouping is attempted, instead of having a formal margin to the bed or groups, it would be better to allow the turf to flow over, so to speak, and conceal it, and then carpet over the surface of the bed with the Lawn Pearlwort, a dwarf green Saxifrage, a Sedum, or some other dwarf carpeting plant. This brings us to an equally beautiful and very desirable way of arranging the nobler perennials.

CHAPTER IV.

ISOLATION OF HARDY PLANTS.

ONE of the most useful and natural ways of diversifying a garden, and one as yet almost unknown to our gardeners, consists in placing really distinct and handsome plants alone upon the grass, to break the monotony of clump margins and of everything else. To follow this plan is *necessary* wherever great variety and the highest beauty are desired in the ornamental garden, and among the very best materials for it are many of the finer perennials. Nothing, for instance, can look better than a well-developed tuft of the broad-leaved Acanthus latifolius, springing from the turf not far from the margin of the walk through a pleasure-ground; and the same is true of the Yuccas, Tritomas, and other things of like character and hardiness. We may make attractive groups of one family, as the hardiest Yuccas; or splendid groups of one species like the Pampas grass—not by any means repeating the individual, for there are about twenty varieties of this plant known on the Continent, and from these half a dozen really distinct and charming kinds might be selected to form a group. The same applies to the Tritomas, which we usually manage to drill into straight lines, but which, in an isolated group in a verdant glade, are seen for the first time to best advantage.

And what might not be done with these and the like by making mixed groups, or letting each plant stand distinct upon the grass, perfectly isolated in its beauty!

Let me again try to illustrate the idea simply. Take an important spot in a pleasure-ground—a sweep of grass in face of a shrubbery—and see what can be done with it by means of these isolated plants. If, instead of leaving it in the bald state in which it is often found, we try to place distinct things in an isolated way upon the grass, the margin of shrubbery will be quite softened, and a new and charming feature added to the garden.

If one who knew many plants were arranging them, and had a large stock to select from, he might have no end of fine effects. In the case of the smaller things, as Yucca filamentosa and the variegated Arundo, four or five good plants would be used to form an effective tuft, and, generally speaking, everything should be perfectly distinct and isolated, so that a person could freely move about amongst the plants without touching them. In addition to such arrangements, two or three individuals of a species might be placed here and there upon the grass with the best effect. For example, there is at present in our nurseries a great Japanese Polygonum (*P. cuspidatum*), which has never as yet been used with much effect in the garden. If anybody will select some open grassy spot in a pleasure-garden, or grassy glade near a wood—some spot considered unworthy of attention as regards ornamenting it—and plant a group of three plants of Polygonum cuspidatum, leaving fifteen feet or so between the stools, a distinct aspect of vegetation will be the result. The plant is herbaceous, and will spring up every year to a height of from six feet to eight feet if planted well; it has a graceful arching habit in the upper branches, and is covered with a profusion of small bunches of pale flowers in autumn. It is needless to multiply examples; the plan is capable of infinite variation, and on that account alone isolation should be welcome to all true gardeners. But the best way to show the beauty of any really fine and distinct hardy plant, is to isolate it on the turf, shaven or unshaven. It is a peculiarly useful method for the exquisitely graceful umbelliferous plants, many of which lose their leaves before the heats of summer are past. When planted in an isolated manner they are little missed when they fade away from before the margin of a shrubbery, whereas if grouped with subjects the foliage of which is more permanent, awkward gaps are left when they fade away.

CHAPTER V.

HARDY PERENNIALS AND ALPINES, AS BEDDING PLANTS.

THE desirability of using as many hardy plants as possible in our "bedding" arrangements is beginning to be fully recognised. That the practice will save horticulturists some trouble and much expense there can be no doubt, and still less of its adding much to the interest and variety of the flower garden. We have as yet merely dipped into the rich mine of hardy plants with a view to finding fit subjects for bedding-out; what has been done seems merely the result of chance, and doubtless a full examination of the qualities of the great number of hardy herbaceous and Alpine plants that may be grown with ease in our climate at all seasons, will yield a good result. There is one fact that I wish particularly to point out to all who are interested in hardy bedding plants (and who is not?), and that is, that not a few of them bloom much longer—much more like bedding plants, in fact—if fresh planted every year. The fact that a plant is quite hardy does not justify us in leaving it alone for years, if by a contrary course we may produce an end that many desire—long continued bloom. Much, or nearly all, of the continuity of bloom displayed by ordinary bedding plants, is the result of the fresh planting of young subjects every year. Suppose our climate suffered Geraniums, Calceolarias, &c., to live through the winter, would their second year's bloom be anything like what we are now accustomed to? I think not. Their bloom would "come to a head," and perish quickly, much like that of many herbaceous plants. Therefore, if we expect hardy plants to give us a long continued bloom, we must treat them, in a great number of instances, pretty much the same as tender "bedding plants," *i.e.*, plant afresh every season. This particularly applies to such things as Viola cornuta, which has proved itself so useful as an ornamental bedding plant. Of course it will best apply to subjects that grow and root quickly, and that flower in proportion to the vigour and continuity of their growth. Therefore the way to succeed with hardy perennial bedding plants is, as a general rule, to take them up when the tender bedding plants are removed in autumn, and divide and put them in stock in some snug nursery beds of finely-pulverized earth, where they may remain till the following spring, when they may be put in the positions designed for them. And what a luxury will it not prove to have one's best bedding plants so arranged during winter that a thought need not be bestowed upon them after being planted in their nursery. Of course such plants as the variegated Arabises, the beautiful Polemonium cæruleum variegatum, Dactylis glomerata variegata, the silvery Saxifragas, Gnaphaliums, and Cerastiums, the new Poa, the variegated Daisies, the dwarf Antennaria tomentosa, and the several kinds of Pansies, are among the best bedding plants in existence. By making free use of what hardy bedding materials we are already acquainted with, the judicious gardener may save himself much trouble. By the way, the Cliveden Pansies, so famous for the spring garden, will be found equally useful for the summer season, if propagated in autumn, and planted out in spring. The blue, for instance, will be found quite as good as Viola cornuta, and the other colours are equally valuable in their way. It is very likely the blue one would prove even better than cornuta during a dry season in ordinary soils. Of course there are hardy flower-garden plants that will not bear the annual removal that I advise for the free-growing and flowering kinds—the Tritomas, for instance, and some of those above enumerated when a particular end is desired; and the flowering kinds will require the change much more frequently than those grown for the beauty of their leaves. Others, again, will prove best during the second year of their blooming, and of these I may mention two of the finest plants in existence for autumal gardening—the fine white variety of Anemone japonica, and Rudbeckia Newmanni. These furnish a long-continued bloom, and on rich soils are truly fine for positions that require rather tall-growing subjects.

The hardy succulent alpine plants are capable of affording beautiful and distinct effects in the flower-garden from their neat foliage and habit alone, and the introduction of them is one of the most rapidly growing improvements now taking place in our flower-gardens. A few years ago they could only be found in very few gardens; now they may be seen in abundance in Battersea Park, and many other places about London where flower-gardening is well carried out; and, a demand having arisen for them, they may be seen in great variety in some of our London nurseries. The term "succulent" may not be familiar to every reader. It is applied to plants with stems or leaves of a very fat and juicy texture, and in which soft cellular tissue greatly predominates. Usually in botanic

PERENNIALS AND ALPINES, AS BEDDING PLANTS. 19

gardens the term is applied to the Cactuses, Aloes, Agaves, Mesembryanthemums, and plants of like character, so very different from the types of vegetation we are accustomed to in this country. Thus the house in which these plants, chiefly from South Africa, South America, Mexico, and various warm parts of the world, are gathered together at Kew, is called the "succulent house." It would be difficult to find anywhere a house more worthy of a visit or more remarkably striking than this, containing, as it does, a vast collection of the plants that to our eyes seem the most singular of all that exist on our world [at its present stage. But there are many other succulent plants besides those mostly well-armed and spiny monsters from hot countries. The little spider-webbed Sempervivum, that clothes the rocks on many a wild and cold alpine slope, is a succulent as well as the enormous cactus (*Cereus giganteus*) which, rising like a great branching pillar to a height of from forty to nearly sixty feet, gives such an "unearthly" character to the mountain ridges of New Mexico. Many of the dwarf plants with which the Alps and Pyrenees and other mountain chains are clothed are succulent. They are as hardy and as easily grown as the common Houseleek, which is an example of a northern succulent that must be familiar to all.

The way in which these plants have hitherto been found most useful in flower-gardens is in the making of edgings, borders, &c.; but when people begin to be more familiar with their curiously chiselled forms, they will use them abundantly for making small mosaic beds. Their great value as border and rock plants need not be spoken of here, as we are now merely considering them in relation to the bedding system, from which till very recently they were completely excluded. In addition to the making of neat little panels, borders, edgings, and beds, they may be employed for forming carpets to act as a setting for larger subjects—a very pretty way of using them.

The ways of arranging these plants so as to secure the most satisfactory effects vary much : they make the most exquisite little geometrical gardens yet seen, and may also be used with charming effect in the English or natural style of garden. As edgings these hardy succulents, from silvery Saxifrages to grey Houseleeks, may be considered the very jewellery of plant life.

A selection of suitable kinds is given at the end of the book.

CHAPTER VI.

HARDY ALPINE AND PERENNIAL PLANTS IN THE ROCK-GARDEN, IN THE WILD-GARDEN, IN WATER, AND IN BOGGY GROUND.

The rock-garden, the most interesting and beautiful of all known modes of enjoying hardy plants, has been the most misunderstood and neglected, not only in private but in public gardens. Are these plants not to be seen in our botanic gardens? They are to some slight extent, but, as a rule, they are stowed away in some old frame or pit, the whereabouts of which is only known to those in charge of it, or if not in an old frame, on a miserable stony bank, misnamed a rockwork. It is so in the Botanic Gardens of the United Kingdom. They are slightly protected in winter, and slightly shaded in summer. Is this necessary? About as much so as for an oak sapling. Those who have travelled in alpine countries well know that the dwarf and exquisite vegetation of such—the Gentians, and Primulas, and Androsaces, and hundreds of others—far surpasses in loveliness any other aspects of the earth's floral beauty. Would it not be possible to have a glint of this in some of our public gardens? Judging from present appearances, the majority of horticulturists could only answer this in one way—that it is impossible. And what else could they say when, if they searched them all, they could not find a healthy plant of Gentiana verna (which grows freely wild in England), or any of the very cream of the alpine flora? Why, even if they be grown to perfection in pots, the surroundings of such are generally sufficient to destroy all the wild native beauty that these plants exhibit when tastefully arranged on suitable rockwork; but the fact is they do twice as well when planted out in the open air, and could be grown to perfection in a London square.

In private gardens nearly everybody has attempted some sort of rockwork or other on a small scale; and it is certain that if the "rockworks" we are now in the habit of seeing satisfy the tastes of their owners, those constructed on a true and sensible principle will afford them the highest delight. Rockwork! why almost every absurd conglomeration of bricks and burrs and stones that one sees exposing its dry sides to the view, is dignified by the term! The object of a properly-constructed rockwork is, or ought to be, to provide a suitable soil and position for growing and exhibiting the beauties of tiny and interesting plants that in a wild state live in very rocky and stony places, seeking a subsistence where fat and leafy vegetation would have no chance; and of those beautiful mountaineers that grow away green and bright far above the limit of shrubby and herbaceous vegetation, where the fierce blast and bitter cold prevent them raising their tiny heads more than an inch or so from mother earth. Now such situations can of course only be imitated on a very lilliputian scale indeed in gardens, but the conditions in which the plants delight may be produced to perfection even in the suburban or the town garden; and they must be brought about by first demolishing all the notions about rockwork which have given birth to those half-wall, half-heap-of-rubbish abortions so prevalent in gardens.

Every person interested in rockwork, or alpine plants, should understand that, as a rule, high-pointed and loosely-thrown-together masses of rockwork with large surfaces exposed to evaporation, are much inferior to broad and less ambitious ones with comparatively slight exposure at the sides. In piling up loose mounds and almost wall-like banks of stone, we, instead of imitating the conditions in which plants are found in high, moist, and cool regions, simply make provision for drying winds quickly killing all the plants worth preserving on our " rockwork." A little rockery, four or five feet high and ten feet broad, is incomparably better for growing choice plants than one ten feet high and ten feet broad, and so on in proportion. And it should be distinctly borne in mind that the great majority of alpine plants will thrive much better on the level ground in ordinary sandy loam, than on the ugly banks on which they have been hitherto arranged.

This subject is, however, so extensive and interesting that space forbids its being fully dealt with here. In my " Alpine Flowers," everything in connexion with the subject will be found fully treated of and illustrated by numerous engravings.

HARDY FLOWERS NATURALIZED.—Many beautiful hardy plants besides the natives of our own country will thrive better and look better running wild in shrubberies, copses, and half-wild places than in gardens; and indeed, many perennials are only fitted for use in this way. I know of nothing more interesting than selecting and planting various sorts of those suitable to whatever rough spots may happen to be available. This subject is however fully discussed in my "Wild Garden," to which I refer all those who have opportunities for carrying out this system to any extent. In the descriptive part of the present volume it is always stated when a subject is useful in this way, and a selection of the most suitable kinds will be found at the end.

HARDY PERENNIALS, ETC. IN WATER AND IN BOGGY GROUND.—A great deal of beauty may be added to the margins, and here and there to the surface, of ornamental water, by the use of a good collection of hardy aquatics arranged with some taste, but, so far as I have seen, this has not yet been fairly attempted by any designer of a garden or piece of water. Usually you see the same monotonous vegetation all around the margin if the soil be rich; in some cases, where the bottom is of gravel, there is little or no vegetation, but an unbroken ugly line of washed earth between wind and water. In others, water-plants accumulate till they are a nuisance and an eyesore—I do not mean the submerged plants like Anacharis, but such as the Water Lilies, when they become matted. Where the soil is not such as will permit the growth of aquatics, a few loads of earth might be thrown in here and there, and in this way one could arrange to have the plants exactly in the positions one requires them, whereas, when there is a rich muddy bottom all round, the common kinds usually manage to crop up everywhere, and to produce a monotonous effect A carefully drawn up selection of aquatic plants is given in Part III., and the culture and arrangement of all the valuable kinds are described in the alphabetical arrangement.

Even more interesting than the culture of aquatic plants, but very rarely practised, is that of bog-plants. Varied as is the flora of the streamlet and lake margin, it is small indeed compared to that of the bogs and marshes, which to a great extent cover the surface of all wild countries, and indeed of old and long-cultivated ones. Although I had enjoyed such plants as Rhexia virginica grown to perfection in an artificial bog in a British garden and knew many of the beautiful plants worthy of a place with it, I had not the faintest conception of the enormous extent and importance of the marsh and bog Flora of northern countries till I visited America, where, in the northern parts, one sometimes travels for days through wet or boggy ground, often ornamented with very beautiful plants. A carefully compiled selection of bog-plants occurs in Part III., and the subject is exhaustively treated for the first time in the second edition of "Alpine Flowers," now in preparation; a carefully prepared illustration showing the effects that may be obtained.

CHAPTER VII.

HARDY FLORISTS' FLOWERS.

THESE are usually perennial or alpine plants that have varied much under the hand of man, and no lover of hardy flowers should fail to have a good supply of them. Like the herbaceous and alpine plants, they have been too much neglected of late years. We may assign some cause why many interesting plants and classes of plants have gone out of cultivation; but there is one thing that can hardly be accounted for, and that is, why the fragrant, beautiful, and neat classes of hardy florists' flowers—from elegantly laced Picotees to richly stained Polyanthuses—should have almost disappeared from our gardens, and be now in want of the least advocacy from me. In them we have flowers of unimpeachable merit, equally worthy of admiration in garden of peer or cottager. They are as hardy as our native plants, require no steaming in houses at any time of their lives, are generally pleasing in habit, whether in or out of flower, sometimes useful for the spring garden, and in nearly all cases among the very best plants which the gardener can grow for cutting from; and yet, with all these undoubted merits, where are they? Generally speaking, fallen into " the abyss of things that were."

There are enough of true florists yet left in the country to take care of the choicest of their favourites, but it is especially to be desired that people generally would grow free and vigorous kinds for the embellishment of borders, and many other positions in which they would not receive any but ordinary attention.

As for the choicer and newer kinds, the best way is to devote a special little department to them in a pleasant part of the kitchen or nursery garden; or, failing either of these, an isolated spot, where the flowers may be agreeably tended and enjoyed at all seasons. Such arrangements may be made a source of great enjoyment to owners and gardeners; but for all practical purposes they are unknown in our gardens, though there is scarcely a kitchen garden in which a capital one might not be made. The best way would be to select a border or strip with a good aspect, throw it into neat beds, edge them neatly, and, if a strip, surround it with a dwarf edge—say of Lavender Cotton, which bears clipping well. But anything like an approach to the farming system of growing such things should be avoided. Being somewhat more precious than mangold wurzel, they should not be treated on the same principle, or a dirtier one, as they are by some few gardeners, who are sagacious enough to employ them for cutting for indoor decoration—and for this purpose no flowers are better than Picotees, Carnations (from Cloves to the richest florist's or ordinary seedling variety), the Pinks, and not a few others. In such a place the cultivator might enjoy, in addition to the plants just named, his bed of good and distinct Pansies; the little groups of perpetual mule and clove-scented Pinks; the splendidly coloured perennial Lobelias, if no other place were found for them; the Mimulus, in its more beautiful varieties; the choicer Pentstemons, Phloxes, Pyrethrums, and choice Antirrhinums; bulbs of sorts a little too precious to use for general decoration; the Ranunculus, in its fascinating as well as rich and decided tints; the Anemones; the Gladiolus, for which there are, however, various more important uses; the Belladonna lily, in perfection if the place be warm and the soil good, deep, and light; the rich and pretty double Primulas, now very rarely seen in good condition; the Polyanthus, in its many lovely varieties; not to speak of various other flowers allied to these in interest, but for which a suitable place may not be found in the flower garden proper. In the same place small beds of the newer Geraniums and bedding and other plants might be planted out for trial; and, in fact, the whole affair made a most useful as well as most interesting thing. Here, also, some of the finer annuals, like the Stocks and everlasting flowers, might be grown; here such charming things as Clintonia pulchella might be employed for covering the beds containing plants that lose their leaves in early summer; here a selection of graceful ornamental grasses might be grown for indoor decoration. Many things requiring attention, noting, or collecting at a certain time, would be under the eye at all times, and the whole would prove one of the most enjoyable divisions ever added to a garden. In addition to it, we should fully employ all such plants for the general decoration of the pleasure and flower-garden wherever they could be introduced with correct taste—knowing well that the Carnation or Pink which is robust enough to take care of itself on rock or border, differs, after all, but very little from the choicest border variety, and is perhaps a more useful and beautiful plant for the gardening public generally.

CHAPTER VIII.

HARDY FLOWERS IN THE SPRING GARDEN.

THE garden depends as much for its beauty in Spring on hardy flowers as the Spring does for its life on the sun. How the earth is embellished with plant beauty at this season must be apparent to all who can get a glimpse at her where yet even a little free. For countless ages the flowers of Spring have been the joy of man. From the time of our first great poet, Chaucer, who forsook his book and his devotion to walk in the mead, to see the flowers "against the sunné spread," to Milton's "vernal flowers," and Shakspeare's "violets dim, but sweeter than the lids of Juno's eyes, or Cytherea's breath," "pale primroses," "lilies of all kinds," and the "flower de luce," their beauties have been sung by our greatest poets. But beautiful as are our own wildings, we may enjoy a host of continental, American, North Asian, and other plants, which being as hardy and as easily grown as our own, would make the margins, so to speak, of our gardens, paradisiacal enough to inspire a horticultural Burns. How snowy white, how thoroughly hardy, and how pretty and useful even as tiny evergreen shrubs, are the Iberises! How they live on or in anything—thrive on rockwork, and luxuriate on the level ground, even if wet and heavy enough to kill some of their pretty allies! Many and beautiful are the spring-flowering plants of the same order, which would thrive if only granted a spot in some outlying half-wild place, and would doubly repay in one spring day the very slight trouble of obtaining and planting them. Where will the Aubrietias not thrive if let alone, and what more beautiful? The numerous beautiful Narcissi—strong, rampant-growing too—how lovely are they, and how effective in Spring! How sweet is *odorus*, how pale and graceful *tortuosus*, how golden and showy *maximus!* Is there any spring-flower that can surpass in beauty or interest *poeticus* or *ornatus*, which is very like the Poet's Narcissus, but a week or two earlier in flower? These will all grow in the wildest of shrubbery margins if only permitted to develop their leaves in peace. In many other orders are there things of beauty suited for the sort of gardening I am advocating: however, it is needless to mention the many plants that may be used in the spring and early summer garden, as that is done in the body of the work. But is there any of this beauty to be seen in eight out of ten of the gardens of England—of the beauty of either choice British or exotic hardy plants? Very little! A chance spray here and there has escaped the incursions of the Vandals, and though people write and talk a good deal of spring flowers and spring gardening, yet, speaking generally, there is no such thing as spring-gardening to be seen in English gardens. I do not call the display of a few Forget-me-nots, Wallflowers, etc., stuck in in the autumn to produce a few faint and abortive flowers in spring, and perhaps to be torn up before they have time to open them fully, "spring gardening."

Leaving out all the fine hardy subjects introduced into botanic gardens during the last twenty years, where are the Anemones of sorts, the double Rockets, the pretty double white Ranunculus, the fine double Wallflowers of sorts, and the numerous "good things" with which our fathers used to make a garden pleasant during the sweetest months of the year? Frequently thrown away, or so neglected that persons with large gardens, and who spend much money on them, have, during the sweetest months of the year, not half so many floral charms around them as the peasant who happens to live in a good wild-flower district!

But, by the judicious use of the spring and early summer-flowering subjects described herein, the surroundings of almost every country or even suburban house, may be made delightfully attractive at these seasons. To this end they may be used in mixed borders, and in beds in the flower-garden proper, and removed in time to plant out the bedding subjects in early summer. In this way the dwarf Phloxes, Iberises, Daisies, Pansies, etc. are used with very good effect, and when removed in early summer, are taken to nursery beds, where they remain till the season arrives for placing them in the flower-garden again. It may, however, be well to tell those who have not proved it for themselves, that it is impossible to see our best spring and early summer hardy plants in all their beauty, if treated on the autumn-plant-and-spring-root-up principle, and perhaps, the prettiest way of all is to naturalize the numerous spring-flowering exotics in shrubberies, by wood-walks, etc., as pointed out fully in my book on the "Wild Garden." The rock-garden may also be easily rendered most attractive in spring and early summer, as many of the most brilliant rock and alpine plants flower in those seasons.

CHAPTER IX.

THE CULTURE OF HARDY FLOWERS.

THE only phase of the culture of the subjects embraced by this book that requires any elucidation from me, is the culture in pots, a way in which but few persons will grow them. But, for the reputation of these plants, it is very desirable that they should not be shown in the wretched condition in which they are usually seen at our shows. Anything that really requires to be stated as to the general culture of hardy perennials in the open air, in borders, etc., will be found under the head of the Mixed Border; while the culture of the fastidious alpine plants is fully described in "Alpine Flowers."

We are pre-eminently great at exhibiting; our pot-plants are far before those of other countries; specimens are to be seen at every show which are models not only as regards beauty, but as showing a remarkable development of plant from a very small portion of confined earth exposed to many vicissitudes; yet in one respect we have made no progress whatever, and that is, in the pot-culture of alpine and herbaceous plants for exhibition purposes.

Prizes are frequently offered at our flower-shows for these plants, and usually awarded, but the exhibitors rarely deserve a prize at all, for their plants are usually badly selected, badly grown, and such as never ought to appear on a stage at all. In almost every other class, the first thing the exhibitor does is to select appropriate kinds—distinct and beautiful, and then he makes some preparation beforehand for exhibiting them; but in the case of our hardy subjects, anybody who happens to have a rough lot of hardy miscellaneous rubbish, exhibits it, and thus it is that I have seen such beauties as the following more than once exhibited: a common Thrift with the unremoved dead flower-stems drooping over the green leaves; a plant of *Arabis albida* out of flower; the Pellitory-of-the-wall, which has as little beauty in flower as out of it: not to speak of a host of worthless things not in themselves ugly, but far inferior to others in the same families. What would become of our shows if the same tactics were carried out in other classes? Even the most successful exhibitors are apt to look about, a day or so before a show, for the best flowering cuttings of such things as *Iberis correæfolia*, and, sticking four or five of these into a pot, present that as a "specimen." Now, what is so easily grown into the neatest of specimens as an Iberis? By merely plunging in the ground a few six-inch pots filled with rich soil, and putting in them a few young cutting plants, they would, "left to nature," be good specimens in a short time, while with a little pinching, and feeding, and pegging-down, they would soon be fit to grace any exhibition. So it is with many other things of like habit and size—the dwarf shrubby *Lithospermum prostratum*, for example; a little time and the simplest skill will do all that is required. Such subjects as the foregoing, with tiny shrubs like *Andromeda tetragona* and *A. fastigiata*, the Menziesias and *Gaultheria procumbens*, the choicer Helianthemums and dwarf Phloxes, and many others enumerated in the selections of exhibition plants at the end of this volume, might be found pretty enough to satisfy even the most fastidious growers of New Holland plants.

The very grass is not more easily grown than plants like Iberises and Aubrietias, yet to ensure their being worthy of a place, they ought to be at least a year in pots so as to secure well-furnished plants. Such vigorous subjects, to merit the character of being well grown, should fall luxuriantly over the edge of the pots, and in all cases as much as possible of the crockeryware should be hidden. The dwarf and spreading habit of many of this class of plants would render this a matter of no difficulty. In some cases it would be desirable to put a number of cuttings or young rooted plants into six-inch pots, so as to form specimens quickly. Pots of six inches diameter suit well for growing many subjects of this intermediate type; and with good culture, and a little liquid manure, it would be quite possible to get a large development of plant in such a comparatively small pot; but if very large specimens were desired, a size larger might be resorted to.

To descend from the type that seems to present the greatest number of neat and attractive flowering plants to the cultivator, we will next deal with the dwarf race of hardy succulents, and the numerous minute alpine plants that associate with them in size—a class rich in merit and strong in numbers. These should, as a rule, be grown and shown in pans: they are often so pretty and singular

CULTURE OF HARDY FLOWERS.

in aspect, as in the case of the little silvery Saxifrages, that they will be very attractive when out of flower, while the flowers are none the less beautiful because the leaves happen to be ornamental in an unusual way. Many plants of a like size, as *Erpetion reniforme* and *Mazus Pumilio*, must be shown in good flower. All these little plants are of the readiest culture in pans, with good drainage and light soil. The quickest way to form good specimens of the most diminutive kinds is to dot young plants over the surface of the pot or pan at once.

Some few alpine plants are somewhat delicate or difficult to grow; and amongst the most beautiful and interesting of these are the Gentians, and certain of the Primulas. There are many who will of course be ambitious to succeed in cultivating them, but, in a general way, it would be better to avoid at first all such difficult subjects, since a failure with them is apt to be disheartening. I believe that a more liberal culture than is generally pursued is what is wanted for these more difficult kinds, and such as are usually considered impossible to cultivate. The plants are often obtained in a delicate and small state; then they are, perhaps, kept in some out-of-the-way frame, or put where they receive but chance attention; or, perhaps, they die off from some vicissitude, or fall victims to slugs, which seem to relish their flavour, considering how clean they eat off some kinds; or, if a little shaky about the roots, are interred by earth-worms, whose casts serve to clog up the drainage and thus render the pot uninhabitable. With strong and healthy young plants to begin with, good and more liberal culture, and plunging in the open air in beds of coal-ashes through the greater part of the year, the majority of those supposed to be unmanageable would soon flourish beautifully. I have taken species of Primula, usually seen in a very weakly and poor state, divided them, keeping safe all the young roots, put one sucker in the centre, and five or six round the side of a thirty-two-sized pot, and in a year made "perfect specimens" of them, with, of course, a greater profusion of bloom than if I had depended on one plant only. Annual or biennial division is an excellent plan to pursue with many of these plants, which in a wild state run each year a little farther into the deposit of decaying herbage which surrounds them, or it may be into the sand or grit which is for ever being carried down by natural agencies. In our long summer some of the Primulas will make a tall growth and protrude rootlets on the stem—a state for which dividing and replanting firmly, deep down to near the collar, is an excellent remedy.

There are many plants which demand to be permanently established, with which an entirely different course must be pursued, *Spigelia marilandica*, *Gentiana verna*, *G. bavarica*, and *Cypripedium spectabile*, for example. The Gentians are very rarely well grown, and yet few will fail to grow them if they procure in the first instance strong established plants; pot them carefully and firmly in good sandy loam, well drained, using bits of grit or gravel in the soil; plunge them in sand or coal-ashes to the rim, in a position fully exposed to the sun, and give them abundance of water during the spring and summer months, taking, of course, all necessary precautions against worms, slugs, and weeds. And such will be found to be the case with many other rare and fine alpine plants. The best position in which to grow the plants would be some open spot near the working sheds, where they could be plunged in coal-ashes, and be under the eye at all times. And as they should show the public what the beauty of hardy plants really is, so should they be grown entirely in the open air in spring and summer. To save the pots and pans from cracking with frost, it would in many cases be desirable to plunge them in shallow cold frames, or cradles, with a northern exposure in winter; but in the case of the kinds that die down in winter, a few inches of some light covering thrown over the pots, when the tops of the plants have perished, would form a sufficient protection.

Alpine and herbaceous plants in pots, and kept in the open air all the winter, are best plunged in a porous material on a porous bottom, and on the north side of a hedge or wall, where they would be less liable to change of temperature, or to be excited into growth at that season.

For growing the Androsaces and some rare Saxifrages a modification of the common pot may be employed with a good result. It is effected by cutting a piece out of the side of the pot, one and a half or two inches deep. The head of the plant potted in this way is placed outside of the pot, leaning over the edge of the oblong opening, its roots within in the ordinary way, among sand, grit, stones, &c. Thus water cannot lie about the necks of the plants to their destruction, which undoubtedly is an advantage for delicate tufted plants liable to perish from this cause. I first observed this method in M. Boissier's garden, near Lausanne, in 1868. The pots

CULTURE OF HARDY FLOWERS.

used there were taller proportionately than those we commonly use, so that there was plenty of room for the roots after the rather deep cutting had been made.

A yet more desirable mode than the preceding is that of elevating the collar of the plant somewhat above the level of the earth in the ordinary pot by means of half-buried stones, as shown by figures in my "Alpine Flowers."

In this way we not only raise the collar of the plant so that it is less liable to suffer from moisture, but, by preventing evaporation, preserve conditions much more congenial to alpine plants, and keep the roots firm in the ground; besides, the small plants look more at home springing from and spreading over their little rocks. It should, however, be distinctly understood that no such attention is required by the great majority of alpine plants.

No matter in what way these plants may be grown in gardens, it is desirable to keep the duplicates and young stock in small pots plunged in sand or fine coal-ashes, so that they may be carefully removed to the rockwork, or sent away at any time. It is impossible to keep up and increase an interesting collection of perennial and alpine plants without having small specimens in nursery beds for filling up blanks or effecting exchanges. In the bottom of beds of this kind there should be half a dozen inches of coal-ashes, so as to prevent worms getting into the pots, in which they always prove very injurious. Sand, or grit, or fine gravel, from its cleanliness and the ease with which the plants may be plunged in it, is to be preferred, but finely sifted coal-ashes will do if sand cannot be spared for this purpose.

Such beds should always be in the full sun, near to a good supply of water, and, if several or many are made, should be separated by gravelled alleys of about two feet wide. The watering is very important. In a large nursery it should be laid on and given with a fine hose. This certainly is the most convenient and economical way.

The larger type of alpine and herbaceous plants, beginning with such as the Aquilegias, and rising to the finer Phloxes, Pentstemons, &c., have not yet, any more than the preceding classes, been seen at our shows in anything approaching to proper condition, though the cultivator who can grow a good specimen of the Chrysanthemum should have no difficulty with them. The will, and a little timely preparation, are all the requisites; but as the grower of the most quickly-raised specimen of a soft-wooded plant must devote thought to his work at least twelve months before he stages his plant, so must he who wishes to succeed with the chief beauties of the hardy class prepare in time. Imagine an exhibitor busy at work the day before the show, putting flowering cuttings of Ixoras or Heaths into large pots. This is precisely what even our best growers do with many soft-growing perennials which are peculiarly adapted for growing into the neatest of specimens in a short time, and with but little trouble.

There is no class which offers to the tasteful exhibitor more beautiful or more varied subjects than the one under discussion—none that will better reward the enthusiastic cultivator. It is quite a new field, and almost an inexhaustible one. The judicious exhibiting of the finer alpine and herbaceous plants would really show to the million what treasures are within their reach, and help to spread more quickly the growing taste for them. There is no doubt that a more widely-spread knowledge of them would do more good than that of any other class of plants, because they may be grown by all, and enjoyed by all, more than any other known class of plants. Therefore, apart from any honour or pecuniary advantage to be had, those who would grow them and show them well, would be doing a real good.

Selections of the best kinds for exhibition are given in Part III.

CHAPTER X.

THE PROPAGATION OF HARDY FLOWERS.

A LARGE number of alpine and herbaceous plants may be raised from seed, and in every place where there is a collection, it is desirable to sow the seeds of as many rare and new kinds as are worth raising in this way. A good deal will depend on the appliances of the garden as to the precise way in which they are to be raised; but whether there be greenhouses on the premises or not even a glass hand-light, alpine plants and choice perennials may be raised there in abundance. Supposing we are supplied with a good selection of seeds in early spring, and have room in frames and pits to spare, some time might be gained by sowing in pans or pots, and by placing

PROPAGATION OF HARDY FLOWERS.

them in those frames, or by making a very gentle hotbed in a frame or pit, covering it with four inches or so of very light earth, and on that sowing the seeds. If this mode be adopted, they may be sown in March; and, thus treated, many will flower the first year. In gardens without any glass they may be raised in the open air. About the best time to sow in the open air is in April, choosing mild open weather, when the ground is more likely to be in the comparatively dry and friable condition so desirable for seed-sowing. But it should be borne in mind that they may be sown at any convenient time from April to August, as it is not till the year after they are sown that they display their full beauty or perhaps flower at all; and, therefore, should a packet or more of choice seed come to hand during the summer months, it is always better to sow it at once than to keep it till the following spring, as thereby nearly a whole season is lost. Those who already possess a collection of good hardy flowers may find a choice perennial ripening a crop of seed in May, June, or July—say, for instance, an evergreen Iberis, a Campanula, or a Delphinium. Well, suppose we want to increase it as much as possible, the true way is to sow it at once instead of keeping it over the winter, as is usually done. By winter the seedlings will be strong enough to take care of themselves, and be ready to plant out for flowering wherever it may be desired to place them.

But to the immediate subject of raising them in the open air. Well, the seeds we will suppose provided, and the month of April to have arrived. If not already done, a border or bed should be prepared for them in an open, airy, and warm position, and where the soil is naturally light and fine, or made so by artificial means. It would be as well to prepare and devote two, three, or more, little beds to this purpose of raising hardy flowers. They would form a most useful nursery-like kind of reserve ground, from which plants could be taken at any time to fill up vacancies, to exchange with those having collections, and to give away to friends; for assuredly it is one of the greatest pleasures of gardening to be able to give away a young specimen to a friend who happens to see and admire one of our "good things" in flower; and by raising them from seed we can always do this with ease. I have said that the seed-bed should be in a warm position, but let it, if possible, be in or near what is often called the reserve garden in large places, or, in smaller ones, in the kitchen-garden—anywhere but in the portion of the gardens devoted to ornament. If the ground happen not to be naturally fine, light, and open, make it so by adding plenty of sand and leaf mould, and then surface the ground with a few inches of fine soil from the compost-yard or potting-shed. The sifted refuse of the potting-bench will do well. Then level the beds nicely for the reception of the seed, and let them be each about four feet wide, with a little footway or alley between them about fifteen inches wide, and let them run from the back to the front of the border, not along it. Make the little drills across the beds, and, instead of making these drills with a hoe or anything of the kind, simply take a rake handle, a measuring rod, or anything straight that happens to be at hand, and, laying it across the little bed, press it gently down till it leaves a smooth impression from a quarter of an inch to one inch deep, according to the size of the seed to be sown. Do this at intervals of about six inches, and then your little nursery bed is ready for the seed. From these smooth and level drills the seedlings will spring up evenly and regularly.

Before opening the seed packets, it is necessary to have a number of wooden labels at hand on which to write the name of each species, so that there may be no confusion when the plants come up. These labels should be about eight or nine inches long, and an inch wide, and the name should be written as near the upper end as possible, so that it may not be soon obliterated by contact with the moist earth. The labelling process is usually performed at the time of sowing the seeds, but a very much speedier and better way is to lay out all the seeds on a table some wet day when out-of-door work cannot be done, and there and then arrange them in the order of sowing. Write a label for each kind, tie it to the packet of seeds with a piece of matting, and then, when a fine day arrives for sowing them, it can be done in a very short time. In sowing, put in at the outer end of the first little drill the label of the kind to be sown first, then sow the seed, inserting the label for the following kind at the spot to which the seed of the first has reached, and so on. Thus there can be no doubt as to the name of a species when the same plan is pursued throughout. Near at hand, during the sowing, should be placed a barrow of finely sifted earth; with this the seeds should be covered more or less heavily according to size, and then well watered from a very fine rose. Minute seed like that of Campanula will require but a mere dust of the sifted earth to cover it.

Once sown, the rest may be left to nature, save and except the keeping down of weeds, the seeds of which abound in the earth in

PROPAGATION OF HARDY FLOWERS.

all places, and will be pretty sure to come up among the young plants. But these being in drills, we can easily tell the plant from the weed, and nothing is required but a little persevering weeding. In these little beds the finest perennials will come up beautifully, and may be left exactly where sown till the time arrives for transplanting them to the rockery, spring-garden, or mixed border. This is a better way than sowing in pots, where they are liable to much vicissitude, and from which they require to be "potted off." Of course in the case of a very rare or admired kind, the seedlings might be thinned a little and the thinnings dibbled into a nursery bed, but by sowing rather thinly the plants will be quite at home where first sown till the time arrives for planting them out finally.

I am convinced that in finely pulverized earth, with, if convenient, an inch or so of cocoa fibre and sand between the drills to prevent the ground getting hard and dry, much better results will be obtained than by sowing in pots. In the open air they come up much more vigorously, and never suffer from transplantation or change of temperature afterwards. Nevertheless, as few will venture the very finest and rarest kinds of seed in the open air, how to treat them in frames is of some importance, and the following observations on this matter are by Mr. Niven, of the Hull Botanic Garden, one of the most successful cultivators of alpine plants, who possesses, chiefly in pots, one of the most complete collections ever made. They were communicated to the "Gardener's Chronicle."

"Much disappointment is often experienced in raising the seeds of perennial plants, and blame is attributed to the vendor of the seeds, that ought, in reality to be awarded nearer home. Presuming that the selection of the seeds is made, and that the seeds themselves are in the hands of the purchaser, the operation of sowing should take place as early as may be practicable in March. First of all, the requisite number of five-inch or six-inch pots should be obtained, so that each seed packet can have a separate pot for itself. Some nice light soil, with a fair amount of sand and leaf-mould therein (if obtainable), should be prepared and passed through a coarse sieve, keeping a sharp eye after worms, and at once removing them; the rough part which remains in the sieve should be placed above the drainage in the bottom of the pots to the extent of two-thirds of the depth, filling the remaining third with the fine soil; the whole should then be well pressed down, so that the surface for the reception of the seed should be half an inch below the brim of the pot, and tolerably even. Each packet of seed should then be sown, and covered with a sprinkling of fine soil, which is to be pressed down by means of a flat piece of wood, or, what will be perhaps more readily available, by the bottom of a flower-pot.

"The best guide as to the thickness of covering required is to arrange so that no seeds shall be seen on the surface after the operation. If the seeds are minute, a very small quantity will be required to attain this end; if they are large, more will be requisite. This completed, and each pot duly labelled with the name of the plant and height of growth, the pots should then be placed in a cold frame tolerably near the glass, taking care that each pot is set level or as nearly so as practicable.

"In preparing the frame for their reception, it is desirable to have a good thickness of lime rubbish in the bottom, say from nine to twelve inches, as a protection against worms.

"Many seeds come up a long time after others; in fact, seed-pots are often thrown away in the supposition that the seeds are dead, when they are perfectly sound; and some will come up a year or so after being sown. All that is necessary with the seeds that do not come up during the spring is to give them an occasional watering, and to guard against the growth of the Lichen-like Marchantia. This is frequently a great pest in damp localities, and is only to be kept in check by carefully removing it on its first appearance, for if allowed to make too much headway, any attempt at removal carries away the surface soil, and with it the seeds. In the month of October each pot should be surfaced with a sprinkling of fine soil, well pressed down; in fact, the process before described after sowing should be repeated. The pots may remain in the frame till the spring, nor should they be despaired of altogether till May or June, or in some instances later.

"To those who may not have the advantage of a cold frame to carry out the foregoing instructions, I would still recommend the use of flower-pots rather than sowing in the open ground; but under these circumstances I would say—sow one month later; place the pots in a warm, sunny corner, and arrange some simple contrivance so that you can shade with mats during hot sunshine, and also cover up at night, in order to keep off heavy rains; the same care in watering should be observed, and the same watchful eye after snails, woodlice, and other depredators, should be maintained.

"So much for the seeds in their seed-pots. Now a word or two

PROPAGATION OF HARDY FLOWERS.

as to the treatment of the plants afterwards. My practice is to pot off, as soon as they are sufficiently strong to handle, as many as are required, in three-inch or four-inch pots, say three in each pot. There they will grow well during the summer, and become thoroughly rooted, ready for consigning to their final habitat, be it rockery, border, or shrubbery, in the early part of spring, after the borders have been roughly raked over; thus giving them ample time to establish themselves before autumn arrives, and their enemy, the spade, is likely to come in their way. Failing a supply of pots sufficient for all, some of the stronger-growing ones may be planted in a sheltered bed of light soil, care being taken to shade them for a few days after being planted; or a few old boxes, five or six inches deep, may be used with even greater advantage for the same purpose, as they may readily be moved from the shady side of a wall to a more sunny locality after they have recovered sufficiently the process of transplanting; and, finally, they may receive the shelter of a cold frame as soon as winter sets in. This recommendation must not be considered as indicative of their inability to stand the cold weather, but as a precaution against the mechanical action of frost, which, in some soils especially, is apt to loosen their root-hold, and force the young plants, roots and all, to the surface.

" In the case of the smaller-growing alpines, such as the Drabas, Arabises, etc. I generally find that they stand the first winter best in pots of the smallest size, and in this form they may be the more readily inserted in the interstices of a rockery, where they will permanently establish themselves."

With by far the largest proportion of herbaceous and alpine plants, however, propagation is a matter of the very simplest kind, as they spread into masses of many crowns and roots. To increase these, all we have to do is to dig them up any time during the autumn, winter, or early spring, divide into as many pieces as are necessary, and replant at once. Where, in the case of rare plants, and those that may not be readily increased otherwise, it is necessary to resort to cuttings, these may be inserted under shaded lights, in the open air, or in cold frames. If inserted in early spring, a gentle heat will suit them best, or just such treatment as that given to ordinary bedding plants at that season. Some, however,—such as the dwarf Andromedas and Rhododendrons—the amateur gardener had better purchase in nurseries, as they are of much slower growth, and require much patience and special means of culture.

As regards the propagation of the rare and new plants that the cultivator will from time to time be glad to add to his collection, I should advise every amateur and every gardener to have a good rich border in which to plant his first stock of each. In this it would increase with rapidity, and become ready for any use that might be designed for it. Of course we may plant them in borders, and take them up and divide them; but much the best way is to have a border of rich and light, but deep sandy earth, in which they may be planted in rows, and where all the new and rare hardy plants may be looked after conveniently. Many a new subject gets an undeservedly bad character from being placed among established plants, which shade or otherwise injure it. When a new plant arrives, the grower should at once see if there be a possibility of dividing it, and in nine cases out of ten it will be found possible to do so. Then let him carefully pull the roots apart, save every shoot or division, however small, and place them in a line in a border of good soil, and thus get each bit to make a good plant, as quickly perhaps as the complete root would make one if planted undivided—indeed, often more so, for young plants of this kind frequently grow faster than old tufts.

PART II.

ALPHABETICAL ARRANGEMENT

OF THE

MOST ORNAMENTAL HARDY FLOWERS,

WITH

DESCRIPTION, CULTURE SUITABLE POSITIONS ETC.

HARDY FLOWERS.

Acæna microphylla (*Rosy-spined A.*) —Synonym, *A. Novæ Zealandiæ.*—A minute creeping evergreen herb, 1 to 2 in. high. *Flowers*, in summer; inconspicuous, in close heads furnished with long crimson spines so as to appear like globes of beautiful spines. *Leaves*, pinnate, 1 in. long; leaflets in from 2 to 6 pairs, about ¼ in. long, toothed. New Zealand.——Rockwork and margins of borders; best in very fine and cool sandy soil. Forming a dense low and compact turf it is well suited for carpeting the ground beneath taller plants. It is readily increased by division.

Acæna myriophylla (*Fern-leaved A.*) —A small fern-like herb, 6 to 8 in. high. *Flowers*, in summer and autumn; small and dull, in rounded spikes. *Leaves*, pinnate; the leaflets deeply cut into narrow pointed segments, slightly downy, light greyish, green beneath. Chili.——Edgings to flower-beds, or tufts on the margins of mixed borders, in ordinary soil. Division.

Acantholimon glumaceum (*Prickly Thrift*).—*Statice Ararati.*—A dwarf, tufted evergreen herb, 6 in. high. *Flowers*, in summer; rose, a little more than ½ in. across, in two ranks on spikes much longer than the leaves. *Leaves*, crowded, narrow, with sharp-pointed spines at the ends. Armenia.——Forms fine tufts on rockwork or slightly raised banks, and also on the front margin of the mixed border, in ordinary soil, but thrives best in light sandy loam. Careful division of tufts and by cuttings.

Acanthus latifolius (*Stately Bear's Breech*).—This is a noble variety of *A. mollis*, larger in all its parts, with leaves more leathery, rigid, broader, and less cut; the flowers on stems sometimes 5 ft. high; when in rich ground more intense in colour, and the leaves, when well established, forming noble tufts of deep glossy green a yard high and several ft. in diameter. ——Fine as isolated tufts in warm sheltered parts of the flower-garden, pleasure-ground, or subtropical garden, and also as a border plant, thriving best in very rich, deep, and moist ground.

Acanthus longifolius (*Long-leaved A.*) —A fine distinct and new species, 3 to 4½ ft. high. *Flowers*, in June and July; wine-red, in the axils of bracts which are oval, acuminate, spiny, veined with green and of a reddish hue on the top; forming a spike of about 14 in. long. *Leaves*, radical, very long (2½ ft.), narrow (4 or 4½ in.), numerous, erect, then inclining and forming a sheaf of fine effect; bright green, smooth above, paler and rather pubescent underneath; pinnatifid with lozenge-shaped oval lobes. *Roots* abundant, but not running; distinguished from *A. mollis* (to which it is allied) chiefly by the length and narrowness of its leaves.

ACANTHUS — ACHILLEA.

Native of forests of Dalmatia and S. Europe.——Borders, margins of shrubberies, and isolation in semi-wild places, in deep ordinary soil, the richer the better. Division and seed.

Acanthus mollis (*Common Bear's Breech*).—A well known vigorous perennial 3 to 4 ft. high. *Flowers*, in summer; white, rose, or lilac, sessile in the axils of deeply toothed bracts, the inflorescence forming a remarkable looking spike half the length of the stem. *Leaves*, large, nearly 2 ft. long by 1 ft. broad, heart-shaped in outline, cut into angular toothed lobes. S. Europe.——Same positions and uses as for the preceding. Increased by division of roots in early spring.

Acanthus spinosissimus (*Armed Bear's Breech*).—A handsome and distinct plant, about 3½ ft. high when in bloom. *Flowers*, late in summer; rosy flesh-colour, stalkless, arranged in a very handsome spike, and accompanied with acute, recurved, and very spiny bracts. *Leaves*, growing in a tuft, pinnatifid, leathery, almost smooth, excessively spiny on all parts, and with deeply pinnatifid divisions. Native of S. Europe.——Much less common in gardens than *A. mollis*. Thrives equally well in the worst and coldest kind of soil, but as the plant depends for its attractions a good deal on its leaves, it is best to secure the development of these by planting in rich warm ground. Division in early spring.

Acanthus spinosus (*Spiny Bear's Breech*).—Another ornamental kind, 2 to 4 ft. high. *Flowers*, in summer; purplish, in spikes; calyx spiny. *Leaves*, pinnatifid, deeply and regularly cut, each division terminated by a sharp spine. S. Europe.——Borders, tufts isolated on grass, among hardy fine-leaved plants, by woodwalks, or on the margins of shrubberies, in good garden soil. Increased readily by division.

Achillea ægyptiaca (*Egyptian Yarrow*). — A very silvery fern-like plant, 12 to 18 in. high. *Flowers*, in summer; fine yellow, in corymbs at the top of the stalks. *Leaves*, pinnate; leaflets obtusely lance-shaped, serrate-toothed. Egypt and Greece.—— Rockwork, among the taller plants in sunny sheltered positions; as an edging to beds of subtropical plants, on warm borders and dryish banks. This plant is not fastidious as to soil, but thrives best in a deep and well-drained sandy loam. Division.

Achillea asplenifolia (*Asplenium-leaved A.*)—*Flowers*, in summer; small, rose-coloured, in a compound corymb; involucrum obovate-oblong, smooth, the scales having a very narrow reddish-brown margin. *Leaves*, lower ones stalked, pinnatifid, with pinnate lobes; upper ones pinnate; segments of the leaves more obtuse than in the rose-coloured var. of the common yarrow. Long cultivated under the name of *A. Millefolium* var. *rosea*. Native country unknown.——Borders and naturalization, in any soil. Division.

Achillea Clavennæ (*Silvery Yarrow*). —A dwarf, white-leaved, distinct plant, 6 to 10 in. high, not rampant like some of the other kinds. *Flowers*, in early summer; white, in neat heads standing well above the foliage. Scales of the calyx rather hairy. *Leaves*, pinnatifid; segments linear, obtuse, slightly toothed at the tip, and, like the whole plant, hoary. Alps of Switzerland, Austria, and Carinthia.——A good and easily grown rock plant, and also an excellent subject for the front rank of the mixed border, where the soil is not too cold and stiff. On congenial soils it might be used as an edging plant for the sake of variety. Increased by division of the tufts.

Achillea filipendula (*Noble Yarrow*). —A noble and showy perennial, 3 to 5 ft. high. *Flowers*, in summer; yellow, in dense, convex, compound corymbs of many heads. *Leaves*, pinnate, pubescent, somewhat rough. A variety, *A. Eupatorium*, has bright yellow flowers in broad flat corymbs. Native of the eastern parts of the Caucasus.——Mixed borders and in groups of the most showy herbaceous plants, in ordinary soil. It is quite strong enough to be well able to take care of itself in woods and semi-wild spots. Division and seed.

Achillea Millefolium (*Common Yarrow*).—A native herb, attaining a height of from 1 to 3 ft. in garden soil. *Flowers*, in summer; white or pink, in numerous small ovoid heads. *Leaves*, strap-shaped in outline, finely divided into very narrow segments. Europe, Asia, and America. —— The fine rose-coloured variety is the only one worth cultivation, and it is useful as a border plant, growing freely in any kind of soil. Division at any season.

Achillea Ptarmica (*Sneezewort*).— *Ptarmica vulgaris.*—A well known British plant, 1 to 2 ft. high. *Flowers*, in summer; white, in terminal corymbs, flower-heads not numerous. *Leaves*, strap-shaped, regularly toothed. The double variety, *A. Ptarmica* fl. pl., is a very handsome border plant. —— In ordinary soil. It is very useful for cutting where white flowers are much in demand. Division.

Achillea serrata (*Serrate-leaved Achillea*).—A handsome plant, with an erect simple stem nearly 2 ft. high. *Flowers*, in summer; large, white, numerous, in small corymbose clusters forming a somewhat spreading terminal panicle. *Leaves*, sessile, partially clasping, ascending, lance-shaped, with the margins deeply serrated: the double kind only is worthy of culture. European Alps. ——Borders, margins of shrubberies, and naturalization in any soil. Division.

Achillea tomentosa (*Woolly Yarrow*).—A handsome and showy mountain herb, 6 to 12 in. high. *Flowers*, all summer; bright yellow, in repeatedly compound corymbs. Calyx smooth, rather shining. *Leaves*, woolly, bipinnatifid; segments crowded, linear, acute. Europe.——Rockwork, margins of borders or on bare banks, in ordinary soil. Easily increased by division.

Achillea umbellata (*Dwarf Silvery Yarrow*).—*Ptarmica umbellata* (*Sibth.*) —A very neat, silvery herb, 4 in. or 5 in. high. *Flowers*, in June; white, about the size of those of *A. Ptarmica*, 6 or 8 in a simple umbel. Scales of involucrum membranous, with a green line through the middle and a blackish margin, inner scales largest. *Leaves*, clearly and regularly lobed, small, chiefly about the lower part of the stem; divisions obovate, entire, covered, as are the stem and pedicels, with very short, fine, whitish wool. Said to be allied to *A. Clavennæ*. Mountains of Greece. —— Edgings, tufts on rockwork, or margins of mixed borders, in ordinary sandy garden soil. Division or cuttings.

Acis autumnalis (*Autumn Acis*).— *Leucojum autumnale.*—A pretty little autumn-flowering bulb, 3 to 4 in. high. *Flowers*, white, delicate pink at the base, 2 to 3 on a stem, appearing before the leaves. *Leaves* few, very slender, sheathing the stems at the base, sometimes not appearing till spring. *Bulb* thick for the size of the plant, covered with a whitish membrane. Southern Europe.——Rockwork or raised borders, always in a warm, well-drained, and carefully shaded position, and in very sandy soil. Increased by division every second or third year.

Aconitum autumnale (*Autumn Monkshood*).—A fine species, about 3½ ft. high. *Flowers*, from August to November;

large, of a pale blue tinged with lilac. *Leaves*, alternate, palmate-3-cleft, pale underneath. Southern Europe. Resembles *A. japonicum*, but is something taller in habit, and its flowers are of a lighter hue.——Borders, and fringes of shrubberies, in ordinary light garden soil. Division.

Aconitum chinense.—A large and stately species, 4 ft. to 6 ft. high. *Flowers*, in summer; large, showy, of an intense and very bright blue, in large compound racemes; pedicels slightly hairy above; upper flowers with small bracts. *Leaves*, lower ones large, deeply cut into three wedge-shaped segments tapering at the base; upper leaves sessile, gradually becoming more entire. China.——Warm borders in sandy loam. Division.

Aconitum japonicum (*Japan Monkshood*).—A noble late-flowering kind, 2½ ft. to over 3 ft. high. *Flowers*, in autumn; large, of a deep blue or lilac, in a dense short spike rarely branching; helmet with a small point; upper petals with a broad, swollen tube; spur thick, bent, almost rolled. *Leaves*, alternate, somewhat thick, of a pale green underneath, palmate-3-cleft; lateral lobes 2-cleft, middle lobe 3-cleft, all obtuse, toothed; teeth rounded with a point. Japan.——Borders, and here and there among rather low shrubs in fine, deep, sandy soil, or in peat. Division.

Aconitum lycoctonum (*Wolf's-bane Aconite*). — An interesting and vigorous perennial, with a stout, twisted, and angular branching stem 3 ft. to 4 ft. high. *Flowers*, late in summer; pale creamy yellow, in dense elongated clusters at the ends of the branches. *Leaves*, palmate, with from 5 to 7 deeply incised and toothed segments; lower leaves nearly 10 in. across, almost reniform in outline, long-stalked; stem, branches, and leaf-stalks covered with very fine, soft, short down. Alps of Europe.——Margins of shrubberies, and naturalization in woods and semi-wild places in any soil. Division.

Aconitum Napellus (*Common Monkshood*). — A very common plant in gardens, 2 to 4 ft. high. *Flowers*, in summer; dark blue, on erect stalks, forming a handsome terminal raceme 1 to 2 ft. long. *Leaves*, darkish green, smooth or slightly downy, divided to the base into 5 or 7 deeply-cut, narrow, pointed segments. There are several varieties. Britain, Europe, and Virginia. —— Borders, or naturalization by wood-walks and in wild places; but it is such a frightfully poisonous plant that many will rather destroy than cultivate it. It should never be grown in a vegetable garden of any sort. Thrives in ordinary soil, and is very easily increased by division.

Aconitum paniculatum (*Panicled Monkshood*).—A tall and handsome kind, 3½ to 5 ft. high. *Flowers*, late in summer; blue or variegated with white; end of the helmet greenish-blue; spur short and recurved; arranged in wide-spreading and branching panicles; sepals smooth or slightly downy. *Leaves*, smaller than those of *A. Napellus*, palmate, with segments twice 3-cleft, incised-dentate, lozenge-shaped. *Root* tubercular; stem frequently bent zigzag, always more or less branching at the top. South of France.——Borders and groups of the bolder and handsomer herbaceous plants. It prefers peat. Division.

Aconitum septentrionale (*Northern Monkshood*).—A distinct late-flowering kind, about 3¼ feet high. *Flowers*, late in summer; reddish lilac or wine-coloured, arranged in panicled clusters at the summit of the stems. *Leaves*, alternate, of a deep green. Siberia. —— Borders and fringes of shrubberies. It prefers peat soil. Division.

ACONITUM — ADENOPHORA.

Aconitum variegatum (*Variegated-flowered A.*)—A handsome, and when well grown, stately perennial, about 4 ft. high. *Flowers*, late in summer; large, closely-packed, sky-blue variegated with white, in an irregular panicle. *Leaves*, alternate, glistening, deeply divided. Native of most parts of Europe.——Borders, groups of the finer herbaceous plants, and naturalization. This plant is excellent for forcing, and is readily increased by division in autumn, winter, or spring.

Acorus Calamus (*Sweet Acorus*).—A very hardy marsh plant, supposed to have been originally introduced from India, but now naturalized in most parts of Europe. *Flowers*, in midsummer; small, of a greenish yellow, insignificant in appearance, borne on a cylindrical spadix 4 to 6 inches long. *Leaves*, sword-shaped, erect, striated, about 3¼ ft. in length. Rhizome cylindrical, channelled and very fragrant. A variety has gold-striped leaves (*A. japonicus foliis aureo-striatis*). —— *A. Calamus* is fond of rather stiff moist soil, and may be planted either on the margins of pieces of water, or in the water itself. Easily multiplied, like the Iris, by division. The variegated variety deserves pot culture in cool houses.

Acorus gramineus (*Grass-leaved A.*) —A species with a slender, creeping rhizome covered with numerous narrow linear leaves, and a slender stem nearly as long as the leaves, which are from 4 to 6 in. in length. *Flowers* small, numerous, sessile, and of a pale yellow. China and Japan. A variety with white-streaked leaves (*A. g. variegatus*) is more tender than the type, and enjoys protection in winter.——Thrives out of as well as in the water, but requires a cool and even moist soil, peat being the most suitable. Both kinds are propagated by division, and are useful for edgings to beds with a north or half-shady aspect. They also look pretty on the margins of fountain-basins, etc.

Adenophora denticulata (*Toothed A.*) —A somewhat showy herb, 1 to 1½ ft. high. *Flowers*, in early summer; dark blue, in a branched leafy panicle; segments of the calyx ovate, sharply toothed; style hardly appearing beyond the tube. *Leaves*, of stem somewhat ovate; of root, heart-shaped, deeply serrated. Siberia. —— Borders, in dry open positions, in sandy loam. Division or seed, which does not ripen readily unless the seed vessel is fertilized artificially.

Adenophora Lamarckiana (*Lamarck's A.*)—An interesting perennial, about 1 ft. high. *Flowers*, in summer; pale sky-blue, bell-shaped, with pointed divisions, about ¼ in. across, and a long protruding style, in loose spikes. *Leaves*, irregularly alternate, those of the stem oval, pointed, serrate, nearly sessile; radical leaves reniform, coarsely toothed. Siberia.——The rock-garden, or mixed borders, in sandy loam. Seed or division.

Adenophora liliifolia (*Lily-leaved A.*) —*Campanula liliifolia*.—An interesting and pretty perennial, 1 to 1½ ft. high. *Flowers*, in summer; pale blue, numerous, sweet-scented, in loose pyramidal panicles; lobes of the calyx somewhat erect, triangular, slightly toothed; style half as long again as the corolla. *Leaves*, alternate; of root stalked, somewhat heart-shaped, crenately toothed; of stem stalkless, ovate-lanceolate, coarsely serrated. Europe, Siberia. —— Borders and slightly raised banks, in good warm loam. Division or seed.

Adenophora suaveolens (*Sweet A.*)—A handsome perennial, about 2¼ ft. high. *Flowers*, in summer; bell-shaped or funnel-shaped, numerous, pale blue, arranged in a pyramidal panicle. *Leaves*, alternate, smooth or slightly hairy; the radical leaves stalked, roundish-oval, cordate, dentate; stem leaves stalkless, oval-lanceolate, largely-toothed. Native of Siberia.——Similar treatment and positions to preceding kinds.

Adonis vernalis (*Spring Adonis*).— A very showy plant, with finely-cut leaves, and from 8 to 15 in. high. *Flowers*, in spring; yellow, solitary at the tops of the stems, 2 to 4 in. across; petals 10 to 12, oblong. *Leaves*, lower ones abortive or reduced to somewhat sheathing scales; upper ones stalkless, much divided, lobes entire. There are several varieties. Southern Europe and Siberia.—— Rockwork, sunny spots on borders, margins of shrubberies, or naturalization on bare banks, or in thin woods. Grows in almost any soil, but thrives best in a rich and moist sandy loam. Division in autumn or winter.

Æthionema coridifolium (*Iberis jucunda*).—*Lebanon Candytuft*.—A little novelty in leaf and flower, distinct from any other kind hitherto in cultivation. *Flowers*, early in summer; rather large, of a pleasing flesh-colour prettily veined with rose, in small dense clusters. *Leaves*, numerous, oblong-linear, or linear obtuse, ending in a minute brownish point, and attenuated at the base, a little more than ⅛ in. long, and about a line broad. When in flower it resembles *Æthionema pulchellum*, but is distinguished by the greater size of its flowers, the shortness of its leaves, and its boat-shaped narrowly-winged seed-vessels. Mount Lebanon, in calcareous soil.—— This class does not possess the rude vigour of our evergreen *Iberises*, among which it is placed by some authors, but it is none the less valuable for being unlike them, and is fitted for association with a dwarfer and more select class of subjects. It should be planted on warm and sunny parts of the rock-garden, in well-drained sandy loam. Increased by cuttings or seed.

Æthionema membranaceum (*Broad-podded Æ.*)—A neat alpine plant, with wiry prostrate simple stems, 6 to 8 in. high. *Flowers*, late in summer; handsome rose, in small, dense, terminal heads. *Leaves*, oblong-linear, obtuse, of various sizes, clothing the stem rather thickly from the base up. *Pods* overlapping each other, roundish, with a very broad membranous margin deeply notched at the top. Mountains of Persia.——The rock-garden or the margin of borders, in a sandy loam. Seed.

Æthionema saxatile (*Rock Æ.*)—A plant much resembling the preceding, 6 to 10 in. high. *Flowers*, in summer; lilac-rose, in flat, crowded racemes terminating the round, thread-like stems. *Pods*, 2-celled, many-seeded; style very short. *Leaves*, lance-shaped, obtuse, upper ones pointed. S. Europe.——The rock-garden and the margins of mixed borders, in sandy loam. Seed.

Agapanthus umbellatus (*African Lily*).—A beautiful old border and green-house plant, 2½ to 3 ft. high. *Flowers*, late in summer; delicate blue, tubular bell-shaped, divided into 6 reflexed segments, arranged in a magnificent umbel of from 30 to 120 blossoms, borne on pedicels about 2 in. long. At the base of the umbel is a spathe with two scarious bracts. *Leaves*, all radical, linear, narrow, smooth, flat, reflected, of a deep green colour. *Root-stock*, oblique, tuberous, with numerous fleshy roots. Cape of Good Hope.——Borders, raised banks, the lower flanks of rockwork, etc., in deep, well-drained light soil with plenty of peat or leaf mould. In the S. and Mid. parts of England and Ireland only; and even in these parts the

AGROSTEMMA — ALLIUM.

roots require to be protected by a few inches of leaf mould or like material in winter. Division.

Agrostemma coronaria (*Rose Campion*).—*Lychnis Coronaria*.—A woolly-leaved herb, 1 to 2 ft. high; biennial in some soils. *Flowers*, in summer; red-crimson; stems erect, forked; peduncles lengthened, 1-flowered; calyx somewhat bell-shaped; petals notched. *Leaves*, lance-shaped, very broad, and of a leathery texture. There are two varieties of this plant sometimes met with in cultivation, one having white and the other double red flowers. S. Europe.——Borders or banks, in common soil. It is long-lived and gayest in flower on dry hill-sides, and in such places is worthy of being naturalized on wild banks and in thin copses.

Ajuga genevensis (*Geneva Bugle*).—A dwarf, hairy herb, without runners, 6 to 12 in. high. *Flowers*, in summer; blue, in whorls forming handsome spikes; calyx very hairy; tube of corolla straight, projecting. *Leaves*, oblong, hairy, narrowed at the base, coarsely toothed. *A. pyramidalis* is a variety of the preceding, found in Britain, not at all ornamental, but curious from the floral leaves being crowded into quadrangular or pyramidal leafy spikes. Europe.——Borders and fringes of shrubberies, in ordinary light soil. Division.

Ajuga reptans (*Creeping Bugle*).—A smooth, creeping herb, with runners, 4 to 8 in. high. *Flowers*, nearly all summer; blue, rarely white, in whorls in the axils of the leaves, on erect stems. *Leaves*, entire, ovate. Common everywhere in Britain.——The variegated and darkest leaved forms of this plant are not unfrequently used as edging and rock plants under various false names. They are easily grown in any ordinary soil and quickly increased by division.

Alfredia cernua (*Nodding A.*)—A vigorous, thistle-like perennial herb, 4 to 7 ft. high. *Flowers*, in summer; yellowish; the stem sending out several small branches, each terminated by one large head of flowers. *Leaves*, of root 1 ft. long and 6 in. wide in the middle, heart-shaped at the base, tapering gradually to a point; the stalks margined, the margins cut, and ending in spines; deep green on the upper side, and white beneath, sharply serrate; lower stem-leaves heart-shaped, half clasping; those near the top long and narrow, sharp-pointed. Siberia.——Among vigorous perennials, by wood-walks or in wild places, in ordinary soil. Division or seed.

Allium azureum (*Azure A.*)—Distinguished at once by its handsome deep blue heads, 1 to 2 ft. high. *Flowers*, in summer; deep sky-blue, with a dark line through the middle of each division, arranged in a dense, almost globular umbel, longer than the spathes which envelop them before expanding. *Leaves*, triangular, from 6 to 12 in. long. Siberia.——Borders. A little tender, and requires a warm, well-drained soil. Division or seed.

Allium flavum (*Yellow A.*) — A slender, somewhat delicate-looking species, with grass-like and rather greyish leaves, about 1 ft. high. *Flowers*, in summer; yellow, bell-shaped and somewhat drooping, in pretty umbels; scape leafy at base. *Leaves*, round, not hollow, flattish above the base. Italy, Tyrol, and S. Europe generally.——Borders, in collections of hardy bulbs, or on warm, dry banks, in light sandy soil. Division.

Allium fragrans (*Sweet-scented A.*)—*Nothoscordon fragrans*. — A tall and vigorous species, with slightly glaucous leaves, 15 to 24 in. high. *Flowers*, in summer; white, with a bar of very pale lilac on the outer side of each petal, in umbels of from 6 to 20 flowers, *Leaves*, linear-lance-shaped. *Bulb* ovate, whitish tinged with buff. N. America, Africa, and E. Indies. ——— Naturalization in semi-wild places, and also on borders, for which however it is scarcely attractive enough, though not disagreeably scented like other Alliums. Division.

Allium Moly (*Golden A.*)—A showy old border plant, 10 to 15 in. high. *Flowers*, in early summer; bright yellow, numerous, in compact umbels; stem sub-cylindrical. *Leaves*, few, lance-shaped. Hungary and the Pyrenees.——Borders, or bare banks, or naturalization among hardy bulbs, in any soil. Division.

Allium neapolitanum (*Daffodil A.*) —A stout and very handsome kind, with bloom resembling that of a pure white Narcissus; 15 to 20 in. high. *Flowers*, in early summer; white, with green stamens, numerous, in a loose umbel, on stems longer than the leaves; pedicels much longer than the flowers. *Leaves*, 2 or 3, sheathing the flower-stem, strap-shaped, sometimes more than an inch across, but usually smaller. S. Europe.——Under south walls, on borders, and naturalization, in warm soils. Division in autumn or winter.

Allium nigrum (*Black A.*) — *A. magicum*.—Remarkable for the vigour of its habit and luxuriance of its inflorescence; 2½ to 3¼ ft. high. *Flowers*, in summer; very numerous, dull violet, rose, or whitish, with a green vein, in a large umbel. *Leaves*, thick, broadly lance-shaped, acute, ciliated, toothed at the edges, at first erect and glaucescent, afterwards green and spreading, much shorter than the stem; bulb large, egg-shaped, with tawny coats. South of France.——Borders and semi-wild places in ordinary sandy garden soil; most fitted for the botanical or curious collection. Separation of the bulbs and by seed.

Allium paradoxum (*Quaint A.*)—An odd-looking but rather pretty plant, 9 to 14 in. high. *Flowers*, in spring; paper white, gracefully pendulous, borne on long footstalks springing from little nests of yellow bulbils. *Leaves*, 1, sometimes 2, as long as the scape, linear-lanceolate, acute, keeled, striated, smooth, ¼ in. broad, drooping and recurved; bulb roundish, whitish. Caucasus and Siberia.—— Borders and banks, in ordinary soil. It increases very rapidly from the bulbils.

Allium roseum (*Rose-coloured A.*)— Another interesting kind, bearing bulbils at the base of the umbels, 12 to 16 in. high. *Flowers*, in summer; pale lilac-rose, large, in umbels of 10 or 12; stamens white and very short, petals notched; stems round, rather longer than the leaves. *Leaves*, strap-shaped, channelled, rolled inwards at the top, not hairy. S. Europe.——Warm borders, or sunny nooks on the flanks of rockwork, in deep sandy loam. Division.

Allium triquetrum (*Keeled A.*)—A pleasing kind, with the leaves keeled in such a marked manner that they seem triangular, 9 to 12 in. high. *Flowers*, in summer; white, somewhat bell-shaped, with a narrow streak of pure green down each petal, in a loose slightly drooping umbel, on erect triangular stems shorter than the leaves. *Leaves*, green, broadly strap-shaped, somewhat like those of the Bur-reed, folded and keeled, sometimes very long. Mediterranean region from Spain to Greece, and in the Channel Islands. —— Borders, and naturalization on warm banks, in ordinary soil. Division.

Alstræmeria aurantiaca (*Orange A.*) —*A. aurea.*—A vigorous species, 2 to 4 ft. high. *Flowers*, in summer and autumn; orange, two upper petals lanceolate, streaked with red, arranged in a 5 to 6-stalked umbel, bearing 10 to 15 blooms. *Leaves*, numerous, linear-elliptical, glaucous, twisted and turned back at the base, about 4½ in. long. Native of Chili and the Island of Chiloe.——Capital plant to naturalize wherever a vegetable soil occurs. I have seen it running through shrubberies and thriving there as luxuriantly as the Willowherb. Division.

Alstræmeria chilensis (*Chili A.*)— *A. hæmantha.*—A handsome and much varied kind, 2 to 3 ft. high. *Flowers*, in summer and autumn; large, blood-red, the 2 upper interior petals longer and narrower, variegated with yellow lines, in pairs on a 5- to 6-stalked umbel. *Leaves*, scattered, obovate, spathulate; upper ones lanceolate, twisted at the base, minutely fringed on the edges, glaucescent. *Roots* very long, thread-like, with oblong, soft, white tubercles. There are many varieties, varying in colour from a rosy white to a deep orange.—— Warm banks and borders in sheltered positions, in deep, light, sandy loam or peaty soil thoroughly drained. The roots should be planted at least a foot deep, which will render them less likely to suffer from frost, and if in congenial soil and situation they need not be disturbed oftener than every fourth year. Careful division in early spring, or by seeds sown in spring or early summer.

Alstræmeria versicolor (*Variously-coloured A.*)—A valuable species, and among the hardiest; 6 in. high. *Flowers*, late in summer; yellow with purple marks, lowest petal the broadest; in an umbel of 2 to 3 blooms. *Leaves*, linear-lanceolate, stalkless, scattered. *Root* with oblong, greenish-white, very soft tubercles. On dry, lofty hills in Chili.—— Similar positions and treatment to those recommended for *A. chilensis*.

Althæa ficifolia (*Fig-leaved A.*)—A stout and vigorous herb, 6 to 10 ft. high, with hand-shaped leaves. *Flowers*, in summer; red or orange-coloured, large, in terminal spikes. *Leaves*, deeply cut into 6 or 7 lobes or parts; lobes oblong, obtuse, irregularly toothed. Double varieties are sometimes met with. Siberia.——In shrubberies, or naturalization in woods or copses, in ordinary soil. Division or seed.

Althæa narbonnensis (*Narbonne A.*) —A vigorous herb, 4 to 6 ft. high, with leaves somewhat downy on both sides. *Flowers*, late in summer; pale red; peduncles axillary, many flowered, loose, longer than the leaves. *Leaves*, alternate, stalked, serrate; lower ones bluntish, 5- or 7-parted; upper ones acute, 3-parted, with the lobes lance-shaped. France and Spain. ——Naturalization in woods, or copses, in ordinary soil. Division or seed.

Althæa rosea (*Common Hollyhock.*)— A well-known plant, 6 to 12 ft. or more high, the parent of the cultivated Hollyhocks. *Flowers*, late in summer; various colours, axillary, somewhat spiked at the top. *Leaves*, rough, heart-shaped, cut at the extremity into 5 or 7 angles. There are, as everybody knows, numerous varieties. —— Borders or shrubberies, in rich cool soil. Cuttings or seed.

Alyssum · alpestre (*Alpine A.*)—A neat, greyish, evergreen plant, 3 to 5 in. high. *Flowers*, in early summer; yellow, in corymbose racemes at the ends of the branches. *Leaves* roundish, attenuated at the base silvery white beneath; stems woody at the base. High Alps of Europe. ——Exposed sunny spots on rockwork, or on the margins of borders, in rather dry, sandy loam. This would do well in chinks in old ruins, etc. Division or seed.

Alyssum montanum (*Mountain A.*)—A spreading, tufted, evergreen alpine plant, 2 to 6 in. high. *Flowers*, in early summer; rich yellow, in simple racemes. *Leaves*, alternate, small, green, or but slightly hoary, rough with stellate hairs, dotted; stems pubescent, spreading. Alps and Pyrenees.——Rockwork, borders, or naturalization on dry and bare sunny banks, in well-drained soil. Seed, cuttings, or careful division.

Alyssum olympicum (*Hort.*)—(*Fragile A.*)—An interesting alpine herb, 2 to 3 in. high, with slender, wiry, decumbent branches. *Flowers*, in summer; small, deep yellow, in roundish corymbose heads. *Leaves* greyish, very small, spoon-shaped, sessile. Northern Greece.—— The rock-garden, in any soil not saturated. Division or cuttings.

Alyssum saxatile (*Golden Tuft.*)—A showy alpine herb, somewhat shrubby at the base, about 1 ft. high. *Flowers*, in April or May; bright yellow, freely produced, in loose panicles. *Leaves*, numerous, lance-shaped, entire, hoary. *A. saxatile variegatum* is a variegated form, sometimes used as an edging plant, and also useful for the rock-garden, or for borders. Southern Russia.——Rockwork, borders, beds and vases in the spring garden; naturalization on ruins, rocky places, or bare banks, in ordinary soil. Seed or cuttings.

Alyssum spinosum (*Spiny A.*)—A minute silvery bush, 4 to 8 in. high. *Flowers*, in early summer; small, white, and inconspicuous, in small clusters at the ends of the branches. *Leaves*, lance-shaped, very small and hoary. Branches spiny when old. Southern Europe.——Rockwork, edgings, or margins of borders, in ordinary soil. Scarcely ornamental in flower, but pleasing from its silvery leaves. Seed and cuttings.

Alyssum Wiersbeckii (*Wiersbeck's A.*)—A hardy herbaceous perennial, about 1½ ft. high, with rigid, erect, unbranching stems. *Flowers*, in summer; deep yellow, in large close corymbose heads, about 1½ in. across. *Leaves*, 2 in. long, oval-oblong-pointed, sessile, attenuated at the base, covered with rough prominences and fine hairs, almost erect and overlapping, densely covering the stem from the base to the top. Asia Minor. —— Rough borders, margins of shrubberies, and naturalization. Seed.

Amaryllis Belladonna (*Belladonna Lily*).—A noble hardy bulb, 1½ to 3 ft. high. *Flowers*, late in summer, or in autumn; delicate silvery rose, very sweet, 5 to 12 issuing from a two-cleft sheath, each as large as a white lily bloom, in 6 divisions, on naked stems. *Leaves*, smooth, channelled, obtuse, 10 to 12 in. long, appearing in spring. Bulbs very large, pear-shaped, with brownish coats. Cape of Good Hope.——In borders on the sunny side of glass-houses and walls, and on the southern flanks of rockwork, in deep sandy and well-drained loam, the bulbs to be planted a foot deep. Propagated by division of the roots every fifth or sixth year, replanting them immediately, not nearer than a foot to each other, and so deep that from 4 to 6 in. of soil may be left above the apex of the bulbs.

Amaryllis blanda is a variety of the preceding, with much larger bulbs and general development, bearing noble umbels of white blossoms, turning to pale rose, not scented, blooming in summer. There are several other varieties all worthy of cultivation in similar positions. Where the ground is not naturally suitable for their growth, it is well worth while to prepare a deep bed of loam, peat, leaf-mould and sand, in which they would attain a fine development, if placed in sunny sheltered spots. Division.

Ammobium alatum (*Winged A.*)— A handsome "everlasting," covered with soft, silky, silvery hairs, 20 to 40 in. high. *Flowers*, from May to September; white, with a yellow conical disk about an inch across, very numerous, in loose corymbose panicles. *Leaves*, oblong - lance-shaped; those of the root in a tufted rosette; stem-leaves narrower. Stems winged. New Holland.——Borders, in sandy dry soil, in which it becomes perennial. On some heavy clay soils it must be treated as an annual or biennial. Seed.

Amsonia salicifolia (*Willow-leaved A.*) — An interesting but not showy perennial, 20 to 32 in. high. *Flowers*, in summer; light blue, in terminal corymbose cymes; corolla small, funnel-shaped, with a rounded tube; throat whitish, bearded; limb divided into 5 spreading, almost oblique, segments. *Leaves*, smooth, alternate, lance-shaped, acute. Carolina.——Borders, in peaty soil, in a half-shady position in borders or fringes of shruberies. It is scarcely suited for any but large or botanical collections. Division.

Amsonia Tabernæmontana (*Erect A.*) —A plant of more erect habit than *A. salicifolia*, 20 to 32 in. high. *Flowers*, in summer; pale blue, in cymes; corolla with lance-shaped, acute segments, slightly hairy on the outside; sepals also lance-shaped, acute. *Leaves*, oval-lance-shaped, acute, slightly pointed at the base. Carolina.——Same soil and position as for *A. salicifolia*. Division.

Anchusa hybrida (*Hybrid Alkanet*). —A showy perennial, 1 to 3 ft. high. *Flowers*, in summer; purple, in axillary spikes a foot or more long; pedicels shorter than the bracts; tube longer than the calyx; calyx divided to about the middle. *Leaves*, lance-shaped, unevenly toothed, stiff, rough, 6 or 7 in. long, ⅜ in. broad at the top, and about 2 in. broad at the base. Italy.——Borders, margins of shruberies, or naturalization in semi-wild places, in ordinary soil. Division.

Anchusa italica (*Italian Alkanet*).— A handsome vigorous and showy plant, 3 to 4 ft. or more high. *Flowers*, in summer; beautiful blue or purple, in panicled racemes; calyx divided nearly to the base; lobes acute, shorter than the tube of the corolla, spreading when in fruit. *Leaves*, lance-shaped, entire, shining; those of root sometimes 2 ft. long. France and Italy. ——Borders and margins of shruberies, or naturalization in copses, in any soil. Seed and division.

Anchusa sempervirens (*Evergreen A.*)—A British plant, 1½ to 2 ft. high. *Flowers*, in summer; rich blue, in short axillary spikes, generally leafy at the base; calyx very hairy. *Leaves*, broadly ovate, stalked; stem ascending or erect. Britain and Western Europe. ——Scarcely attractive enough for general culture as a border plant, but worthy a position in woods and semi-wild places. Seed and division.

Andromeda fastigiata (*Himalayan A.*)—*Cassiope fastigiata.*—A remarkably neat little shrub, with its leaves closely imbricated along the stems. *Flowers*, in summer; of a waxy white, produced at the top of each little branchlet, and turning down bell-fashion. *Leaves*, small, closely overlapping each other, and having a white, thin, chaffy margin, terminating in a small point (which distinguishes it from *A. tetragona*), and with a deep and broad keel. Himalayas.——Rockwork, in a deep, moist, but well-drained peat or very sandy loam, but carefully guarded against drought in the warm season. It also thrives in beds and borders of silvery peat in moist districts. Cuttings, careful division, or seed.

Andromeda hypnoides (*Mossy Andromeda*).—*Cassiope hypnoides.*—A minute, spreading, moss-like shrub, with wiry, much divided branches, 1 to 4 in. high. *Flowers*, in summer; white, 5-cleft, with reddish calyces, drooping, on slender reddish flower-stems, one on each. *Leaves*, bright green, flat and needle-like. N. Europe and N. America.——On rockwork, in elevated, cool and moist districts, in sandy or gritty, moist, but well-drained peat, freely exposed to the sun and air, but kept thoroughly moist in dry weather. Seed or cuttings. As yet very rarely grown or increased in this country.

Andromeda tetragona (*Square-stemmed A.*)—*Cassiope tetragona.*—A neat and diminutive shrub, rarely growing more than 6 to 12 in. high. *Flowers*, in spring; white, bell-shaped, somewhat contracted near the mouth, and resembling those of the lily of the valley; they are produced singly, but rather freely. *Leaves*, opposite, imbricated, in four rows, the margins rolled back, minutely ciliated, blunt. N. Europe and America.——Rockwork, or margins of beds of choice dwarf shrubs, in fine and moist sandy peat. Division, wherever it grows freely.

Androsace carnea (*Rose-coloured A.*)—A brilliant little evergreen alpine plant, distinguished from its fellows by its small pointed leaves not being produced in rosettes, but regularly clothing a somewhat elongated stem, 3 in. high. *Flowers*, in early spring; of a lively pink or rose, with a yellow eye, produced in umbels of from 3 to 7, on hairy stalks. *Leaves*, awl-shaped, smooth. Summits of the Alps and Pyrenees, in exposed positions.——It succeeds on rockwork, and should have a mixture of sandy loam and peat at least a foot deep, so that the roots may descend and be less likely to suffer from vicissitudes. Thorough watering should be given in the dry season. Seed, sown as soon as gathered, or careful division in early spring.

Androsace Chamæjasme (*Rock Jasmine*).—A beautiful alpine plant, 2 to 5 in. high. *Flowers*, in early summer; white at first, with a yellow eye, which eventually changes to deep crimson, the outer part becoming a delicate rose; in umbels, borne on stout little stems; divisions of calyx linear-lanceolate. *Leaves*, fleshy, lance-shaped, acute, attenuated towards the base, and arranged in large rosettes, not forming dense cushions as the other kinds often do, but often a little distance from each other. Plant covered with long spreading hairs. Tyrolese and Swiss Alps.——Rockwork, in deep and well-drained rich light loam, the surface to be covered with pieces of broken rock or stone, to prevent evaporation and to preserve the plant from injury. It may also be grown in pots plunged in sand in an exposed position. Division or seed.

Androsace ciliata (*Ciliated A.*)—A very handsome species, forming dense cushions, 2 or 3 in. high. *Flowers*, in early summer; pink or rose-coloured, with crimson throat, rising a little above the leaves; divisions of calyx 5, lanceolate-linear acute, pubescent. *Leaves*, lanceolate-oblong, smooth on both sides, and fringed with hairs on the edges, imbricated or overlapping each other, but not so closely set as to give the stem a columnar or cylindrical appearance. Pyrenees.——On fully exposed parts of the rock-garden, in gritty or sandy soil, deep and moist. Division and seed.

Androsace cylindrica (*St. Bertrand A.*)—A very rare kind, confined to one locality, where it is found growing from the rocks in large pendent tufts 2 to 6 in. in length. *Flowers*, in July and August; small, white, solitary, on long slender footstalks, covered with hairs, which are often hooked and stellate; sepals lanceolate-acute, with a prominent green vein. *Leaves*, narrowly linear-lanceolate, more or less obtuse, very closely set in deep somewhat cylindrical rosettes, and covered with simple and stellate hairs. Central Pyrenees, on the calcareous rocks of St. Bertrand.——Same treatment and positions as those recommended for *A. pubescens*.

Androsace glacialis (*Glacier A.*)— *A. alpina*.—A rather rare species, growing in compact sheets, about 2 in. high. *Flowers*, in June; pale purplish-rose, with yellow throat and tube, solitary, on stalks about ⅔ in. long; divisions of the calyx acute, longer than the tube of the corolla. *Leaves*, closely crowded, small, tongue-shaped, narrowed at the base, pubescent, as are the flower-stalks and calyces, with very short, scattered, stellate hairs, and forming small rosettes at the ends of the stems; main stems slender, tinged with red. Alps of Switzerland, the Tyrol, Styria, and Carinthia.——The same treatment and the same positions as those for *A. pubescens*.

Androsace helvetica (*Swiss Androsace*).—A very attractive kind, forming dense cushions of diminutive ciliated leaves, about 1 in. high, compact and hard to the touch. *Flowers*, in spring and early summer; white, with a yellowish eye, almost twice as large as the little rosettes of leaves on each stalk, nearly sessile; segments of calyx somewhat acute; valves of ripe capsules erect. *Leaves*, closely imbricated, lance-shaped, obtuse. Alps and Pyrenees, on very high rocks.—— It requires considerable nicety of cultivation, and should have a fully exposed well-drained position on rockwork, and be placed between and tightly pressed by stones about the size of the fist; in rich sandy loam and peat. Seed and careful division.

Androsace imbricata (*Silvery A.*) *A. argentea*. — A species differing from the other Pyrenean and Swiss Androsaces by having the rosettes of a beautiful silvery white instead of greenish; 1 to 2 in. high. *Flowers*, in summer; white, stalkless, so' freely produced as often to overlap each other; divisions of calyx acute; valves of capsules at last spreading or reflexed. *Leaves*, densely imbricated, lance-shaped, oblong, covered, especially at the tip, with short hairs. Pyrenees, Alps of Dauphiny, Switzerland, and North Italy.——Rockwork, in narrow well-drained fissures, in rich loamy soil with grit or sand. Seed and division.

Androsace lactea (*Milk-white A.*)— Rather a free-growing kind, 2 to 4 in. high. *Flowers*, in summer; large, pure white with yellow throat and heart-shaped petals; arranged in an umbel; scales 10. *Leaves*, numerous, narrow, almost linear, of a lively green, arranged in rosettes, sometimes scattered along the elongated branches, and frequently fringed at the end and on the sides with short hairs; the old leaves of a deep red. Alps and Pyrenees.——On rockwork in deep calcareous soil. Seed or division.

Androsace lanuginosa (*Himalayan A.*) —A beautiful and very distinct kind at once easily distinguished by its spreading and, when in good health, long stems, 6 to 9 in. high. *Flowers*, in summer; delicate rose, in umbels. *Leaves*, nearly an inch long clothed with long silky hairs. Himalayas.—— On rockwork in ledges in a mixture of sandy peat and loam, and in warm positions. I have seen it grow into vigorous wide-spreading tufts, in borders of moist and deep sandy loam on the sunny side of one of the hothouses in the College Gardens of Dublin. Cuttings and seed. Where it perishes in winter it is worthy of being annually propagated.

Androsace obtusifolia (*Blunt-leaved A.*) — Allied to *A. Chamæjasme*; 2 to 6 in. high. *Flowers*, in spring; white or rose, with yellow eye, in umbels; stems numerous, covered with short down; divisions of calyx oval, lanceolate and pointed. *Leaves*, in rosettes, larger and firmer than those of *A. Chamæjasme*, lance-shaped, or somewhat spoon-shaped, blunt, stalkless, smooth. Widely distributed over the European Alps.——Similar treatment to that for *A. Chamæjasme*.

Androsace pubescens (*Downy A.*) —Distinguished from its fellows by a small swelling on the stem close to the flower. *Flowers*, in spring or early summer; white with yellow centre, on stalks shorter than the leaves, the unopened buds looking like pearls set in tiny five-cleft cups, and scarcely rising above the dense cushion of foliage. *Leaves*, spoon-shaped, ciliated, the surfaces clothed with simple or (rarely) forked hairs, and forming densely packed hoary rosettes. Pyrenees and Alps.——Not difficult to cultivate in sunny fissures planted in sandy or gritty peat mixed with fibry loam.

Androsace pyrenaica (*Pyreneean A.*) — Resembling *A. helvetica*, often less than an inch high. *Flowers*, in summer; white with yellow eyes, on smooth incurved stems, longer than the leaves; segments of calyx blunt. *Leaves*, downy, having a keel at the back, recurved, narrow-oblong, ciliated, forming diminutive pincushion-like tufts. Very high mossy rocks on the Pyrenees.——Rockwork, in fissures between large stones, with plenty of sandy loam and peat between them, or on level exposed parts with small stones on the surface. Division or seed.

Androsace villosa (*Shaggy A.*) — A very pretty kind, with the flowers in umbels and the little stems inclined to creep a good deal, 2 to 4 in. high. *Flowers*, in early summer; white or pale rose, with purplish or yellowish eyes, in umbels. *Leaves*, narrow, oblong, covered with soft white hair or down, mostly on the under side. Alps, Pyrenees, and mountains of Dauphiny.—— Ledges in the rock-garden, or on level spots, planted between pieces of limestone. Careful division and seed.

Androsace Vitaliana (*Yellow A.*)— *Aretia Vitaliana*. — Distinguished at once by its clear yellow flowers, and rarely growing more than an inch high, except in rich moist soil, where it sometimes reaches two inches or a little more. *Flowers*, in summer; rich yellow, large for so small a plant, scarcely rising above the leaves, the throat much more dilated than in the other kinds, and the tube elongated. *Leaves*, very narrow, sharp pointed, greyish; stems numerous. Alps of Europe.—— Rockwork, where it should be abundantly supplied with water during the dry months, or on the level border in suitable districts, surrounded by stones half plunged in the ground, to prevent evaporation, in free, sandy, and moist soil. Careful division or seed.

Androsace Wulfeniana (*Wulfen's A.*) —A very rare dwarf free-growing species, forming dense rigid tufts of deep green leaves 2 in. high. *Flowers*, in summer; vivid rosy or purplish crimson, larger than those of any other species. *Leaves*, oval, pointed, in close rosettes. Styria. —— Rockwork in peaty loam and grit. Seed or division.

Andryala lanata (*Woolly A.*)—Like a woolly *Hieracium*, 1 ft. high. *Flowers*, in summer; yellow, like those of a *Hieracium*, stems having a leaf at each joint. *Leaves*, thick, very woolly, oblong-ovate, entire or slightly toothed near the base; lower ones stalked and blunt; upper ones stalkless, pointed. Southern Europe.——In collections of woolly-leaved and variegated plants, in ordinary soil. Seed and division.

Anemone alba (*White A.*)—Resembling *A. sylvestris*, but dwarfer, 4 to 6 in. high. *Flowers*, in summer; white, like those of *Clematis montana*, rising 1 to 2 in. above the leaves, on single stalks; sepals 5, obovate, concave. *Leaves*, ternate or quinate, purple on the under side, close to the ground; segments deeply toothed at top; those of the involucre stalked. Roots creeping and fibrous. Dauria, Russian Asia, and the Crimea.——Borders, or among the stouter plants on rockwork, in deep fibry loam. Division or seed.

Anemone alpina (*Alpine Windflower*). —A noble species, 6 to 18 in. or 2 ft. high, distinguished at a glance by its large and much-cut leaves, and the very soft down on the exterior of its flowers. *Flowers*, in early summer; white or yellowish, sometimes bluish or purple at the back, erect; sepals 6, spreading, very variable in size, sometimes but not always as large as those of *A. coronaria*. *Leaves*, biternate; segments pinnate and deeply serrated; bracts like the leaves, stalked, sometimes smooth and sometimes sparingly pilose. *A. sulphurea* is a variety with yellow flowers, paler on the outside, and with the leaves clothed with long loose hairs. Sloping pastures and mountains in Central Europe, and on the Rocky Mountains in North America.——Amongst low shrubs and the largest alpine plants on rockwork, or borders, in sandy loam. Propagated either by division or by seed, which should be sown as soon as possible after it is gathered.

Anemone angulosa (*Large Hepatica*). —*Hepatica angulosa.*—A beautiful plant allied to the *Common Hepatica*, but fully twice the size of that species in all its parts, 6 to 12 in. high. *Flowers*, in spring; of a fine sky-blue, more than 2 in. across, with numerous black anthers surrounding a tuft of yellow styles. *Leaves*, 3 in. broad, distinguished by their 5 lobes from *A. Hepatica;* the lobes coarsely notched. Transylvania.——Rockwork, border, margins of beds of shrubs, and naturalization in copses, etc. Division.

Anemone apennina (*Apennine Windflower*).—A well-known old favourite, 4 to 9 in. high. *Flowers*, in spring; bright sky-blue, 1½ to 2 in. across, 1 on each stem; style linear, and equalling the younger seed-vessels in length; sepals more or less rough on the outside with adpressed hairs. *Leaves*, of stem in whorls of 3, ternate, with long blunt lobes, all somewhat pubescent; root-leaves biternate. *Roots* tuberous, irregular, elongated, blackish. The double variety is not so ornamental as the single one. South Europe.——Rockwork, naturalization in half-shady places, in pleasure-grounds, by wood-walks, and borders in any soil, but best in a sandy loam or peat, and in a somewhat shady position. Division.

Anemone blanda (*Blue Winter A.*)— Very like the last species. *Flowers*, in early spring; deep sky-blue; sepals 9 to 14, oblong-linear, smooth on the outside; seed-vessels pubescent, tipped with a short black pointed style. *Leaves*, 3-parted or cut; segments stalked or sessile, 3-parted, cut or slashed; those of the involucre stalked, deeply cut. Southern Europe and Asia Minor.——Rockwork, or warm and sunny banks and borders, or naturalization on sheltered banks among short grass. Thrives in sandy loam, or peat and loam, and is increased readily by division.

Anemone coronaria (*Poppy A.*)—The most popular and varied of cultivated Anemones, 6 to 9 in. high. *Flowers*, in spring, early summer, and often throughout the winter; red, white, and purple in variety; sepals 6, oval, rounded. *Leaves* ternate, deeply cut; segments numerous, narrow, pointed; bracts stalkless, divided. There are a great many varieties both double and single. S. Europe.—Rockwork, the spring garden, or borders, or naturalization in semi-wild places, in a rich deep loam. Propagated by seed or division. The roots of the more select named kinds should be taken up when the leaves die down, and planted at intervals to secure a continuity of bloom. The best bloom is obtained by planting in September or October.

Anemone elegans (*Pale Japan A.*)—This plant differs from *A. japonica* in being less pubescent, being generally taller (2½ ft. to 3½ ft.), having broader leaves, and particularly in having flowers of a paler rose-colour, more than 3 in. across. It also seems to grow more in a tuft, and to run rather less at the root than the common *A. japonica*, of which it is probably a variety or sub-species. Japan.— Similar treatment and positions to those for the *Japan Windflower*.

Anemone fulgens (*Scarlet Windflower*).—A noble kind, about 1 ft. high, conspicuous for its brilliant scarlet flowers. *Flowers*, early in summer; large, solitary, of a dazzling vermilion or scarlet, sometimes with a light-coloured ring round the stamens, which form a jet-black centre. *Leaves*, 3-lobed, incised-dentate, of a lively green. Native of the South of Europe.

——Borders, rockwork, beds in the spring garden, and when sufficiently plentiful may be scattered about in half-wild places, in calcareous clay, or rich loam. Propagated by division or by seed.

Anemone Hepatica (*Common Hepatica*) — *Hepatica triloba*. — A well-known old spring-flower, 3 to 6 in. high, with 3-lobed leaves. *Flowers*, February to April; usually blue, 1 on each stalk; stalks numerous and hairy; involucre consisting of 3 entire leaves. *Leaves*, heart-shaped, 3-lobed; lobes entire, ovate, acute. There are many varieties of this plant; the principal of which are the single blue, double blue, single white, single red, double red, single pink (*carnea*), single mauve purple (*Barlowi*), crimson (*splendens*), and *lilacina*. The double varieties continue longer in bloom than the single. A native of many hilly parts of Europe. —— Borders, edgings to beds of American plants, or rockwork. It grows freely in good garden soil, but loves best a rich stiff loam, and a half-sheltered position. Propagated by division or seed, the double ones by division only.

Anemone japonica (*Japan Windflower*) —A noble perennial, about 3 ft. high. *Flowers*, in autumn; numerous, rosy-carmine and downy on the inside, pale rose without, 2 to 2½ in. across, on long footstalks which spring from a whorl of 3 or 4 leaves; anthers, golden yellow. *Leaves*, ternate, with unequally lobed, toothed segments. Native of Japan.—— Borders, and naturalization in almost any position, the plant having a vigorous constitution. Division of root, almost every particle of which is capable of forming a plant. A noble variety with pure white flowers is known in gardens as *Anemone Honorine Jobert*; it is one of the finest perennials we

ANEMONE. 57

have, and is suitable for the same positions as *A. japonica.*

Anemone montana (*Mountain Pasqueflower*)—Differs from *A. Pulsatilla* only in having its leaves less finely cut, and its flowers more drooping, less open, and of a black and velvety violet, which looks red when seen against the light. On the seacoast near Trieste, and in S. Tyrol near Botzen.——Rockwork and borders, in light well-drained soils.

Anemone narcissiflora (*Narcissusflowered A.*)—A distinct looking kind, 8 in. to 1 ft. high. *Flowers*, in early summer; whitish, sometimes purple on the outside, in umbels. *Leaves*, stalked, palmately divided; the lobes deeply toothed; leaves of the root somewhat hairy. In calcareous mountain pastures in many parts of Europe, and Siberia.——Borders, rockwork, or on banks in a calcareous or sandy soil. Division.

Anemone nemorosa (*Wood A.*)—A well-known native plant, 4 to 8 in. high. *Flowers*, in spring; white, solitary; sepals 6, oval, veined, silky outside; involucre consisting of 3 stalkless leaves, deeply cut into narrow segments. *Leaves*, of root on long stalks, covered with silky hairs when young, and divided 2 or 3 times into long narrow segments. There are double varieties, and occasionally flowers of lilac, blue, reddish and purplish tones are to be met with. Common in woods throughout Europe and North America from Canada to Carolina.——In England this is best seen in a wild state, but some of its varieties are desirable for the rock-garden and the border.

Anemone palmata (*Cyclamen-leaved A*).—A remarkable and showy kind, 6 to 8 in. high. *Flowers*, in early summer; glossy golden-yellow, only opening in sunshine; bracts trifid, stalkless; sepals 10 to 12, oblong, blunt. *Leaves*, heart-shaped, roundish, blunt, 3 to 5-lobed, slightly toothed and hairy. *Roots*, tuberous. There is a double variety, *A. palmata, fl. pl.*, and a white one, *A. palmata alba*, both now rare. North Africa, Spain, and other places on the shores of the Mediterranean.——On rockwork, planted in deep turfy peat, or light fibrous loam and leaf-mould, with plenty of moisture in summer. Division or seed.

Anemone pavonina (*Peacock A.*)—Closely allied to the common garden *Anemone*, but having very acute petals; 6 to 8 in. high. *Flowers*, in early summer; rich red, smaller than those of the common garden *Anemone*, usually very double from the great number of petals filling up the centre of each blossom; central petals green, lance-shaped, and very acute. *Leaves*, 3-parted; lobes wedge-shaped, deeply toothed. S. Europe. —— Borders, rockwork, or edgings for beds of spring and early summer flowers, in light, warm, and well-drained soil. Division or seed.

Anemone Pulsatilla (*Pasque-flower*). —A well-known old native border plant, 3 to 12 in. high. *Flowers*, in spring; purple, solitary, slightly drooping, spreading; segments 6, pointed, clothed with long silky hairs on the outside. *Leaves*, 2-pinnate; leaflets deeply cut, with linear lobes; involucre deeply cut into numerous linear segments. There are several varieties, red, lilac, and white; also a double one. Dry hills and exposed places throughout Europe and Siberia. ——Rockwork or borders, in a well-drained light, but deep, soil. Division.

Anemone ranunculoides (*Yellow Wood A.*)— A dwarf species, with flowers somewhat resembling those of the lesser Celandine (*Ficaria ranunculoides*), 4 to 6 in. high. *Flowers*, in spring; clear golden yellow, either solitary or in pairs; sepals 6, elliptical. *Leaves*, of root 3 to 5-parted; leaflets somewhat trifid, deeply toothed;

those of the involucre scarcely stalked, 3-parted, deeply toothed. There are two varieties, one with purple, and the other with white flowers. Middle and Northern Europe. ——Rockwork and borders, and naturalization in calcareous soil, or well-drained, sandy loam. Division.

Anemone stellata (*Star A.*)—*A. hortensis.*—A pretty kind, with star-like flowers springing from the much dissected leaves; 8 to 10 in. high. *Flowers*, in early summer; red, purple, rose, or whitish; sepals 10 to 12, oblong, bluntish. *Leaves*, 3-parted; lobes wedge-shaped, deeply toothed, of the involucre stalkless, oblong, entire, or a little toothed. Southern Europe.—— On rockwork, borders, and in the choice spring-garden in warm and sheltered positions, and sandy, well-drained soil. Division.

Anemone sylvestris (*Snowdrop Anemone.*)—A handsome species, with drooping flower-buds, 6 to 18 in. high. *Flowers*, in early summer; pure white, solitary, sometimes as large as a crown piece when opened; sepals 6, elliptical. *Leaves*, ternate or quinate, hairy beneath; segments deeply toothed at top; those of the involucre stalked. Europe and Siberia.—— Borders, on the lower parts of rockwork, by wood-walks and in half-wild spots, shrubberies, etc., in ordinary soil. Division.

Anemone trifolia (*Three-leaved A.*)— Nearly allied to the *Wood Anemone*; 4 to 6 in. high. *Flowers*, in spring or early summer; white; sepals 5, elliptical, blunt. *Leaves*, all stalked, ternate; segments ovate-lance-shaped, acute, toothed. On woody hill-sides of Piedmont, the Tyrol, and Siberia. —— Borders, or naturalization with our own Wood Anemone. It grows in any soil. Division.

Anemone vernalis (*Shaggy Anemone*). —A singular and interesting kind, 2 to 8 in. high. *Flowers*, early in summer; solitary, terminal, bell-shaped, with 5 to 6 almost erect, oval divisions, whitish inside, violet and covered with silky down outside. *Leaves*, small, downy, winged, with one or two pairs of leaflets, oval-rounded, or wedge-shaped at the base, 2- to 3-cleft at the point. Whole plant covered with long tawny hairs. Alps and Pyrenees.——Rockwork and borders in well-drained, moist, sandy soil or peat; in borders surround the plant with stones. Division and seed.

Anemone vitifolia (*Vine-leaved Windflower*). — Resembles the *Japan Windflower* in habit; 8 to 10 in. high. *Flowers*, in summer; few, white, each blossom 2 in. or more across; petals oval; sepals oval-oblong, thickly covered with silvery down on the outside. *Leaves*, almost all radical, stalked, 3- or 5-lobed; lobes unequally incised-dentate. Whole plant velvety. ——Borders and the rougher parts of the rock garden, thriving best in peat soil. Where it thrives it is worthy of naturalization, but it is not so vigorous as the *Japan Windflower*.

Anomatheca cruenta (*Bloody A.*)—A pretty and distinct little bulbous plant, 6 to 12 in. high. *Flowers*, in summer; rich carmine-crimson, three lower segments marked at the base with a dark spot; tube of flower long and whitish. *Leaves*, two-ranked, narrow, sword-shaped, spreading above; bulb ovate, rather large. Native of S. Africa.——Warm slopes of rockwork, in very sandy dry soil, or on warm borders among the smaller and choicer bulbous plants; the bulbs to be planted rather deep. Increased by separating the bulbs, or by seed.

Antennaria dioica(*Mountain Everlasting*).—*Gnaphalium dioicum.*—A dwarf greyish herb, 4 to 8 in. high. *Flowers*, in summer; whitish, inconspicuous, in heads, several together in a corymb.

Leaves, mostly smooth on the upper, silvery on the under side, lower ones spoon-shaped; stem - leaves lance or strap-shaped. Britain, Northern Europe, and America. The varieties called *A. dioica rosea* and *A. d. minima* with rose-coloured flowers, are by far the best worthy of cultivation.—— Rockwork and tufts on the margin of the mixed border, also as an edging plant to beds of alpines, in well-drained sandy soil. Increased by division of the tufts in early spring.

Antennaria tomentosa (*Hort.*) (*Silvery A.*)—A very dwarf and very silvery plant, scarcely 1 in. high. *Flowers*, in summer; small, insignificant, in corymbs like those of a *Gnaphalium*. The chief attraction of the plant is its foliage, which is dwarf, dense, spreading, and of a silvery whiteness, forming a carpet of rare and exquisite beauty. Native of the Rocky Mountains.—— Rockwork, borders, edgings, or forming silvery carpets in the flower-garden. It thrives in most garden soils, but perishes on cold clay ones in winter. Division.

Anthemis Chamomilla fl. pl. (*Chamomile*). — A dwarf perennial, 6 to 10 in. high. *Flowers*, late in summer; white, double, nearly 1 in. across. *Leaves*, much divided into linear, almost thread-like segments; stem slightly downy. Garden variety.—— Borders, in which it will prove as ornamental as the other double-flowering composites. Division.

Anthericum Hookeri (*Hooker's A.*)—*Chrysobactron Hookeri*. — A showy perennial, with fleshy fibrous roots, 1 ft. to 20 in. high. *Flowers*, in early summer; bright yellow, nearly ½ in. across, freely produced in racemes, 3 to 5 in. long. *Leaves*, linear, sheathing at the base, 8 to 12 in. long, and ⅓ in. to rather more than 1 in. broad. New Zealand.——Borders; thriving in ordinary soil, but only forming fine specimens in that which is deep and moist. Division and seed.

Anthyllis erinacea (*Rushy A.*)— A singular-looking, much branched, tufted, spiny, almost leafless shrub, about 1 ft. high. *Flowers*, in summer; few, purplish, closely set, so as almost to form heads, stalked, and furnished with bracts. *Leaves*, very few, oval or oblong, scattered. Spain and Barbary. —— Borders and rockwork, in ordinary sandy or calcareous soil. Division or seed.

Anthyllis montana (*Mountain A.*)— A dwarf, prostrate and very ornamental rock plant, about 6 in. high. *Flowers*, in early summer; pink, in close heads, on long stalks, with a leafy involucre. *Leaves*, pinnate; leaflets 15 to 19 pairs, oval-oblong, acute, small and entire, silky and hoary on both sides. There is a variety with white flowers, but it is rare. Southern Europe.——Borders, rockwork, and naturalization on bare banks, thriving in the worst and coldest soils, though it grows more freely in deep sandy loam. Division and seed

Antirrhinum Asarina (*Heart-leaved A.*)—A greyish clammy herb, with the trailing habit of some of the *Linarias*, and the spurless flowers of the *Antirrhinums*; 3 or 4 in. high. *Flowers*, in summer; pale yellow, tube longer than in the Greater Snapdragon; segments of the calyx, linear-lance-shaped, acute, hairy. *Leaves*, on long stalks, 5-nerved, opposite, heart-shaped, crenated. S. Europe.——Sunny borders, or sunny sheltered spots on rockwork, in warm well-drained sandy loam. It is scarcely ornamental enough for the select collection. Seed.

Antirrhinum majus (*Great Snapdragon*).—A well-known old plant, the companion of the wallflower on old walls and ruins; 1 to 3 ft. high. *Flowers*, nearly all summer; varying from white to deep red or purple, in a many-flowered raceme; peduncles short and very hairy; corolla above an inch long. *Leaves*, narrow, lance-shaped, smooth, entire. There are many beautiful varieties. Mediterranean regions, and abundantly naturalized elsewhere.——Borders, margins of shrubberies, or naturalization on old walls, ruins, and rocky or stony places, in common soil. Seed or cuttings.

Antirrhinum rupestre (*Linaria*).—(*Rock Snap-dragon*).—A pretty and interesting prostrate kind, 6 to 12 in. high. *Flowers*, in summer; dull rosy-lilac, in few-flowered loose racemes; spur awl-shaped, nearly straight, shorter than the corolla. *Leaves*, scattered, somewhat linear, acute. Native of the Caucasus.——Rockwork or borders, in light soil. Seed.

Aphyllanthes monspeliensis (*Montpellier A.*)—A rush-like plant, forming dense, erect tufts, 1 ft. or more high. *Flowers*, in summer; deep blue, about ¾ in. across, with a membranous imbricated brown calyx, solitary, on slender scapes as long as the leaves. *Leaves*, very slender, pointed, with membranous sheaths at the base; root fibrous. South of France.——Borders, in light soil. Division and seed.

Apios tuberosa (*Tuberous A.*)—An interesting climbing perennial, with a tuberous root. *Flowers*, late in summer; dull brownish purple, sweet-scented, in axillary racemes; corolla like that of the Pea; calyx bell-shaped. *Leaves*, unequally pinnate. Pennsylvania to Carolina.——So far as I have seen, this is only suited for a botanic garden, but my experience with it has been on very cold soil. Separation of the tubers.

Apocynum androsæmifolium (*Border Fly-trap*). — A pretty and curious plant, 2 to 3 ft. high. *Flowers*, late in summer; pale red with darker stripes, freely produced in terminal and lateral cymes; tube of the corolla much longer than the calyx. The flowers emit a grateful odour and entrap numbers of flies. *Leaves*, opposite, ovate, smooth on both sides pale beneath. North America.——Borders and margins of shrubberies, or naturalization in moist, slightly boggy spots in woods. It does not like a dry soil. Division.

Aponogeton distachyon (*Floating A.*) —A very ornamental water-plant, the leaves and flowers of which float on the surface. *Flowers*, in spring, summer, and autumn; deliciously fragrant. The petals are wanting, but are replaced by oval, entire, whitish bracts, arranged in a forked spike from 2 to 4½ in. long. At the base of each bract are produced from 6 to 12 stamens and 2 to 5 pistils; anthers of a purple brown. *Leaves*, entire, oblong, of a lively green, on stalks long in proportion to the depth of the water. It is a native of the Cape of Good Hope.——To establish it, pot some plants in a small rough basket allowing them to become strong in a fountain, basin, tank, or water in which they will not meet with accidents. In spring these baskets should be dropped into the desired positions in ornamental water, if at first near a spring, so much the better, in water about 18 in. or 2 ft. deep. They will soon root through the baskets into the soil beneath. This plant is a lovely object in a greenhouse or conservatory tank, flowering abundantly during the winter months.

Aquilegia alpina (*Alpine Columbine*). —A beautiful mountain perennial from 9 in. to 2 ft. high. *Flowers*, in early summer; blue; stem leafy, two or three flowered; spur slightly incurved, half as long as the petals. *Leaves*, biternate, segments deeply divided into linear lobes. It is handsomest when the centre of the flower is white. Higher parts of the

AQUILEGIA. 61

Alps of Europe.——Rockwork, borders, or among the choice alpine plants in pots; in light sandy and moist loam. Careful division, or seed.

Aquilegia cærulea (*Rocky Mountain A.*)—A beautiful and singular kind, 9 to 15 in. high. *Flowers*, in summer; blue and white, spurs green-tipped, slender, about 2 in. long, with a tendency to twist round each other; styles and stamens shorter than the corolla. *Leaves*, biternate. Rocky Mountains.——Margin of the mixed border, or on rockwork, in a well-drained sandy loam. Seed or division.

Aquilegia canadensis (*Canadian Columbine*). — A showy herb, 12 to 18 in. high. *Flowers*, early in summer; scarlet outside, yellow inside, drooping; spur straight, much longer than the limb; sepals ovate or oblong, a little longer than the petals. *Leaves*, mostly biternate; leaflets wedge-shaped, crenately lobed, smooth. North America.—— Mixed borders and rough rockwork, in rich light loam. Seed.

Aquilegia fragrans (*Sweet Columbine*). — A handsome, much branching, bushy kind, 2 to 2½ ft. high. *Flowers*, in summer; large, light flesh-colour, or lilac, agreeably fragrant, slightly downy; sepals ovate-lance-shaped, acute; spur curved inwards, twice as long as the truncated petals. *Leaves*, upper ones downy, somewhat glandular, as are also the ovaries; lower ones 3-cleft, with segments reaching beyond the middle. Himalayas.——The rock-garden, in moist, sandy, well-drained soil. Seed and division.

Aquilegia glandulosa (*Glandular Columbine*).—One of the most beautiful of alpine perennials, 8 to 12 in. high. *Flowers*, in early summer; fine blue, tips of the petals white; sepals dark blue, large, nearly oval, with a long footstalk; spur much shorter than the limb. *Leaves*, biternate, leaflets having numerous lobes. Altai Mountains. ——Rockwork, or borders, in well-drained sandy loam. Seed, or very careful division in spring.

Aquilegia pyrenaica (*Pyrenean Columbine*).—Allied to *A. alpina*, but smaller in all its parts; 6 to 9 in. high. *Flowers*, in early summer; blue, smaller than those of *A. alpina*; spur nearly equalling the petals in length; stem 1 to 3-flowered, nearly naked. *Leaves*, 1 or 2-ternate; segments linear. Pyrenees.——Rockwork, front margin of the mixed border, or cultivated in pots, in a moist sandy loam. Seed or division.

Aquilegia Skinneri (*Skinner's Columbine*).—A noble species 2 to 3 ft. high. *Flowers*, in summer; red, with the tips of the petals golden yellow; spurs straight, spreading, about 2 in. long; sepals lance-shaped, twice as long as the limb of the petals; stamens projecting. Entire plant glabrous. Pacific coast of the southern parts of N. America.——Borders, or beds of the finer perennials, in warm sandy loam. Division and seed.

Aquilegia truncata (*Large Scarlet Columbine*). — *A. californica.* — *A. eximia.*—A noble kind, 2 to 3½ ft. high. *Flowers*, late in summer and early in autumn; of an orange-scarlet throughout; petals truncate, almost wanting; sepals oblong-lanceolate, reflexed, spreading; spur straight, thick, ⅜ in. long. *Leaves*, in tripartite segments, somewhat obtuse at the ends, incise-dentate. California.—— Borders, in fine deep and well-drained sandy loam. I have never seen this plant in such perfection as in the Edinburgh Botanic Gardens. Seed and careful division.

Aquilegia vulgaris (*Common Columbine*).—A well-known inhabitant of gardens, 1 to 3 ft. high. *Flowers*, in early summer; variously coloured, single or double; spurs incurved; stem leafy, many-flowered. *Leaves*, biternate, nearly smooth. *A. Vervaineana* is a variety with variegated or mottled leaves; and there are many other forms. A native of Britain and most parts of Europe and Japan.——Borders, margins of shrubberies, and naturalization in ordinary soil. Seed or division.

Arabis albida (*White Rock Cress*).—A dwarf free-flowering tufted evergreen herb, very common in gardens, 6 to 9 in. high. *Flowers*, in favourable seasons, soon after Christmas, continuing in bloom till March, April, or May; pure white, in terminal racemes; petals two or three times larger than calyx; stalks longer than calyx. *Leaves*, hoary, few-toothed; of root obovate-oblong, of stem heart-shaped, clasping. Tauria and Caucasus.——Rockwork, borders, on bare banks, or naturalized in rocky or stony places. The variegated forms are often used as edging plants. In ordinary soil. Seed, cuttings, or division.

Arabis Androsace (*Rosette A.*)—A neat species, growing in very dense tufts, and resembling an *Androsace;* about 2 in. high. *Flowers*, in summer; white, with ovate petals 2½ times longer than the calyx, in corymbose racemes. *Leaves*, small, entire; those of the root linear-oblong, or lanceolate-obtuse, in compact rosettes; those of the stem sessile, linear, or linear-ovate, sometimes feebly toothed. Pods erect, about ⅓ in. long, compressed, attenuated at the end into the short style; seeds wingless. Asia Minor on Mt. Taurus, at an elevation of 7500 ft. to 8000 ft.——Rockwork, or margin of the mixed border, in sandy or calcareous soil, and associated with dwarf and compact alpine plants. Seed and division.

Arabis blepharophylla (*Rosy Rock Cress*).—Like the *White Rock Cress* in leaves and habit, but with very showy rosy purple bloom; 3 to 4 in. high. *Flowers*, in early summer; rosy-purple, petals roundish, narrowing to the base, with slender claws. *Leaves*, naked, except the margins, which are fringed with very stiff hairs; root-leaves spoon-shaped, stem-leaves oblong, stalkless. California.——The rock-garden or the raised border, in sandy loam; as it often perishes in winter, the plant should be raised annually and put out in spring.

Arabis lucida (*Shining-leaved A.*)—A dwarf, shining-leaved evergreen herb, 4 to 6 in. high. *Flowers*, in summer; white, in terminal corymbs; petals entire, narrowed at the base, twice as long as the calyx. *Leaves*, clasping the stem, obovate, thickish. There is a variegated variety which is extensively used as a winter edging plant. Hungary.——The green form is not at all ornamental, but the variegated one is worthy of a place among silvery-leaved and variegated plants, in moist and very sandy loam. Division.

Arabis procurrens (*Spreading A.*)—A creeping, tufted, evergreen herb, with shining leaves, 3 to 6 in. high. *Flowers*, in summer, densely produced; white, not ornamental; petals double the length of the calyx; the limb obovate or wedge-shaped. *Leaves*, smooth, ovate, quite entire, those of root narrowing into the stalk; stem-leaves stalkless, pointed. Hungary.——Rough parts of rockwork, or on bare banks, in any soil. There is a brilliant variegated variety which is useful as an edging, or for association with variegated plants. Division and seed.

Aralia edulis (*Edible A.*)—A stately herbaceous plant, 4 to 6 ft. high. *Flowers*, in summer; numerous, white, in globose umbels, which spring from the axils of the leaves, and the summit of the stem, and are united into simple or compound racemes. *Lower leaves*, simply pinnate, with 5 leaflets, or 3-pinnate, with divisions of 3 to 5 leaflets. *Upper leaves* more frequently simple, with stalked leaflets, having a roundish or heart-shaped base, ovate, acute, finely-toothed, downy; stem herbaceous, pubescent, spineless. Native of Japan.——Associated with perennials grown for the effect of their foliage, or isolated by wood-walks, always in rich deep soil. Division.

Aralia nudicaulis (*Naked-stalked A.*) —A vigorous perennial, 3 ft. to 4 ft. high. *Flowers*, in summer; greenish-white; stems bearing three round umbels; the pedicels slender. *Leaves*, radical, the divisions pinnately 5-foliate; leaflets oblong-oval, with a long tapering point, serrate; root very long, horizontal. N. America. ——Rich deep loam. Similar positions and treatment to those for *Aralia edulis*. Division.

Aralia racemosa (*Spikenard*). — A vigorous, widely spreading perennial, 3 to 6 ft. high. *Flowers*, in summer; small, greenish-white, in numerous small umbels, forming doubly compound racemose panicles; fruit small, dark purple. *Leaves*, very large, decompound; leaflets heart-shaped-ovate, with a long tapering point, doubly serrate, slightly pubescent; root large and thick; the plant is strongly aromatic. N. America.—— Isolated tufts by wood-walks, or grouped with vigorous perennials, in rich deep loam. Division.

Arctostaphylos Uva-ursi (*Bearberry*). —A neat evergreen mountain shrub, 1 ft. high. *Flowers*, in early summer; delicate rose, in clusters at the ends of the branches, of an oval-conical shape and divided into five blunt segments; producing berries about the size of those of the Holly, and red when ripe in autumn. *Leaves*, resembling those of Box, leathery, entire, obovate. Abundant in hilly places in Europe and N. America. —— Borders and rough rockwork, especially for hanging over the brows of rocks. It grows in any soil, but prefers a moist one. Division or layers.

Arenaria balearica (*Balearic Sandwort*).—A fragile creeping evergreen herb, 1 to 3 in. high. *Flowers*, in early summer; white, freely produced, 1 on each stalk; sepals ovate, bluntish, much shorter than the petals. *Leaves*, ovate, rather fleshy, shining, with scattered hairs on the edges. Corsica and the Balearic Islands.——The rock-garden, in which it runs over the faces of the stones and rocks. Division.

Arenaria ciliata (*Fringed Sandwort*). —A procumbent, tufted, evergreen herb, 2 or 3 in. high. *Flowers*, in summer; white, usually solitary, on slender stalks ¼ to ½ in. long; petals obovate, much longer than the sepals. *Leaves*, small, ovate, fringed with a few stiff hairs near the base. High mountains of Europe and Britain.—— Rockwork, in sandy loam. Division or seed.

Arenaria graminifolia (*Grass-leaved A.*)—A tufted, evergreen, grass-like plant, 6 to 10 in. high. *Flowers*, in summer; white, on erect stems; petals obovate, five or six times longer than the blunt sepals. *Leaves*, long, thread-like, rough on the edges. Caucasus. ——Rougher parts of rockwork, or on bare banks, in sandy loam. Division.

Arenaria laricifolia (*Larch-leaved A.*) —A dwarf evergreen perennial, 6 in. high. *Flowers*, in summer; white, 1, 3, or 6 borne on rather rough ascending stems; sepals linear-oblong, 3-nerved; petals twice as long as sepals. *Leaves*, awl-shaped, denticulately ciliated.

ARENARIA — ARMERIA.

Alps of Switzerland and France.—— Borders, rougher parts of rockwork, or naturalization on bare banks, in sandy loam. Division.

Arenaria montana (*Mountain Sandwort*).—A handsome spreading plant, 3 to 6 in. high. *Flowers*, in early summer; white, large, 1 on each stalk; sepals ovate, acute, shorter than the petals. *Leaves*, oblong-lance-shaped, very narrow, on wiry, slightly downy, procumbent stems. France.——Rockwork, front margin of the mixed border, or on bare banks, in sandy soil. Seed and division.

Arenaria purpurascens (*Purplish-flowered A.*)—A closely tufted dwarf evergreen herb, 2 or 3 in. high. *Flowers*, in summer; purplish, abundantly produced. *Leaves*, smooth, ovate-lance-shaped, acuminate, stalkless. Abundant on the Pyrenees.—— Among free-growing dwarf-plants on rockwork, or on borders or naturalized on bare banks, in sandy loam. Division or seed.

Arenaria tetragona (*Square-stemmed A.*)—A singular-looking evergreen tufted herb, with the leaves disposed in four rows; 6 in. high. *Flowers*, in summer; white, in heads, with narrow leaves between them; sepals stiff, acute, about the same length as the petals. *Leaves*, ovate, with a white cartilage along the margin, fringed at the base. France and shores of the Mediterranean.—— The rock-garden, or borders. Seed and division.

Arenaria verna (*Vernal Sandwort*).— A prostrate, tufted evergreen herb, 1 to 3 in. high. *Flowers*, in spring; white, with greenish centres, abundantly produced; sepals shorter than the petals. *Leaves*, awl-shaped, rather stiff, upper ones shorter and broader. A native plant, and widely distributed over Europe, Asia, and America.——Rockwork or borders, associated with very dwarf plants. Division.

Argemone grandiflora (*Large-flowered A.*)—A handsome poppy-like plant, but very delicate in colour, 2 to 3 ft. high. *Flowers*, in summer; white, large, in numerous-flowered panicles; petals 4 to 6; calyx smooth; capsules bluntly 4-angled. *Leaves*, large, smooth, wavy, spiny-toothed, nerves smooth. A native of Mexico.——Borders, in well-drained sandy loam. I have not seen this plant live more than a year, but it is said to be a true perennial. Seed.

Aristolochia Sipho (*Siphon A.*)—A vigorous, climbing, deciduous, large-leaved shrub, attaining a height of 20 feet or more in this country. *Flowers*, in early summer; yellowish-brown, 1½ in. long, and nearly 1 in. broad at the base; tube shaped like a siphon. *Leaves*, heart-shaped, stalked, about 6 in. across, and tapering to a point, entire. *A. tomentosa* is a variety with the mouth of the tube of a deep purple, and border of the corolla much more deeply divided. North America. —— Excellent for covering bowers, stumps, railings, cliffs, etc. Suckers, or seeds, which last are rarely produced in this country.

Armeria cephalotes (*Great Thrift*).— A very handsome perennial, 4 to 20 in. high. *Flowers*, in summer; deep rose, in a large roundish head on round, erect stalks; petals obtuse. *Leaves*, broadly lance-shaped, smooth, entire, pointed, on channelled petioles sheathing at the base. North Africa and Southern Europe.——In warm positions among the taller plants on rockwork, and the mixed border, in well-drained, deep sandy loam. Seed and careful division.

Armeria vulgaris (*Common Thrift*)— *Statice Armeria—Armeria maritima*.— A well-known evergreen herb, with tufted grass-like leaves, 3 or 4 in. high.

Flowers, in early summer, and continuing a long time; lilac, white, or deep rose, in a roundish head, on stems 3 to 6 in. or more high. Found on the shores of the British Isles, and on the tops of the Scotch mountains and the Alps of Europe.——The deep rose is the best variety, and it is useful as an edging in the spring garden, for bare banks or margins of shrubberies, and for rockwork, in ordinary soil. Increased by division, which is desirable every two or three years, as old plants do not bloom so freely as young ones.

Aronicum scorpioides (*Scorpion A*).—A somewhat showy but not very ornamental perennial, 6 in. to 1 ft. high. *Flowers*, in summer; yellow, large, solitary, 1 to 3 on a stem. *Leaves*, pale green, toothed; radical leaves on long stalks, broadly oval; the lower stem-leaves shortly stalked, stem-clasping, with two incise-dentate lobes, the upper ones sessile. South of France and the Pyrenees.——Rockwork and borders, in ordinary garden loam. Seed and division.

Artemisia alpina (*Alpine Wormwood*).—A dwarf, very tufted kind, 6 to 10 in. high. *Flowers*, in summer; solitary, yellow, button-like, on long, slender stalks; scales of the involucrum lanceolate. *Leaves*, covered with whitish silky hairs, pinnate; the lobes linear, entire, seldom divided. Southern Italy, in gravelly places on mountains.—— The rock-garden and borders, in ordinary soil. Division.

Artemisia anethifolia (*Dill-leaved A*).—A graceful perennial, with a simple stem, branching at the top, from 3 to 4½ ft. high. *Flowers*, late in summer; small, whitish, very numerous, in an immense panicle nearly 2 ft. long. *Leaves*, very much divided into fine, thread-like segments of a greyish green colour, and growing chiefly on the upper part of the stem; stem woody at the base, nearly smooth. Siberia. ——Among fine-foliaged hardy plants. Division.

Artemisia cana (*Hoary A.*)—A distinct-looking and rapid growing perennial, 2 to 3 ft. high. *Flowers*, not ornamental, ovate, small, in a close spiky panicle; stem ascending; branches erect. *Leaves*, silky, hoary; root-leaves wedge-shaped, sharply 3-cleft; stem-leaves, linear-lanceolate, 3-nerved. Rocky Mountains, and in plains near the Columbia River.—— Desirable only from the silvery tone of its foliage and stems. Borders, and naturalization, growing in the commonest soil. Division.

Artemisia frigida (*Silky Wormwood*). —A very silvery, dwarf, creeping herb, 6 to 12 in. high. *Flowers*, in summer; dull yellow, not ornamental; heads small, roundish, racemose-paniculate. *Leaves* pinnately divided; segments narrow. North America.—— Rockwork or margins of borders, in ordinary soil; only worthy of a place for its foliage. Division.

Artemisia gracilis (*Graceful Wormwood*).—A tall and graceful perennial, 3 to 5 ft. high. *Flowers*, in autumn; small, whitish, very numerous, in a dense broad panicle, about 1½ ft. long. *Leaves*, very much divided into very fine hair-like segments; lower branches of the stem very slender.——Useful in the subtropical garden, or in borders in ordinary garden soil. Seed and division.

Artemisia maritima (*Sea Wormwood*).—A dwarf native undershrub, with much branched decumbent or erect stems, which with the leaves are more or less downy, 1 to 2 ft. high. *Flowers*, in autumn; yellowish, erect, or drooping. *Leaves*, 2-pinnate, oblong in outline, sometimes kidney-shaped, leaflets narrow, linear. There are varieties differing in stem, leaves, branches, and flowers. Europe, generally near the sea-coast.——Borders, rough rockwork, fringes of shrubbery, or arid banks. Division and cuttings.

Artemisia Stelleriana (*Steller's A.*)—A hoary vigorous herb, 1¼ ft. to 2 ft. high. *Flowers*, in summer; yellowish, in hemispherical, somewhat erect heads, not at all ornamental. *Leaves*, silvery white, (lower ones spathulate-incised, those of the middle of the stem pinnatifid with obtuse lobes, the end lobes often confluent), few, scarcely 2 in. long including the leaf-stalk, covered with white wool underneath; stem also woolly. Siberia.——Rough rockwork and borders, or fringes of shrubberies, in any soil. Division or cuttings.

Artemisia tanacetifolia (*Tansy-leaved A.*)—An interesting perennial. 18 in. high. *Flowers*, in summer; yellowish, in terminal, simple racemes; stem sometimes branching at the base, herbaceous. *Leaves*, bipinnate, somewhat downy, with the lobes linear-sublanceolate, pointed, entire, forming handsome fern-like foliage. S. Europe.——Borders and banks, in ordinary light garden soil.

[A few other species of *Artemisia* are in cultivation, for the most part not ornamental, scarcely so much so as the *Common Wormwood* and *Southernwood*.]

Arum crinitum (*Dragon's Mouth*).—A very remarkable plant, 12 to 20 in. high. *Leaves*, pedate; lateral segments lanceolate, intermediate one hastate. Flowers much larger than those of *A. Dracunculus;* also remarkably fetid, and quite startling in their aspect; spadix and inside of the spathe covered with hairs. Native of Balearic Islands, Sardinia, Syria, and Mesopotamia.——In borders and warm banks, among low shrubs in warm good soil. Separation of tubers. I have not seen it seed in this country.

Arum Dracunculus (*Dragon's A.*)—*Dracunculus vulgaris.*—An old and very curious plant, nearly 3 ft. high. *Flowers*, in summer. *Leaves*, pedate, in 5 lanceolate segments, broadly veined, the middle ones the largest; stem and petioles marbled with black like the belly of a viper; spathe furrowed on the inside, slightly ventricose at the base, with a widely dilated limb of a pale green externally, and a deep dull violet purple on the inside; spadix smooth on the top. Native of S. Europe and the Canary Islands.——At the warm side of walls, in borders, or among low shrubs in half-shady spots, growing best in light sandy soil or peat. Separation of tubers.

Arum italicum (*Italian A.*)—Remarkable for its strikingly variegated leaves, 9 to 15 in. high. *Flowers*, in spring. *Leaves*, appearing in the preceding winter, with long stalks, cordate-hastate, acute, the lobes at the base large and spreading, shining dark green, veined and often spotted with white, sometimes also spotted with black. Spathe greenish, very much dilated above, shorter than the leaves; spadix club-shaped, yellowish. Native of Europe and N. Africa.——Borders, banks, rough rockwork, or the margins of shrubberies, thriving in almost any soil, but attaining greatest size and beauty in that which is rich, light, and deep. Division.

Arundo conspicua (*Silvery Arundo*).—A noble plant, the largest of the New Zealand grasses, with some resemblance to *Gynerium argenteum*, 3 to 8 ft. high.; growing in dense tussocks, from which rise a profusion of long curving leaves, and erect, slender culms, with large white, silky panicles, from 1 to 2 ft. long; branches drooping. *Leaves*, leathery, narrow, smooth, or slightly rough. Northern and middle islands of New

Zealand.——This plant, though not so hardy as the Pampas grass, does well in the southern counties of England in warm sheltered positions. Grown in small tubs or large pots, richly fed and freely watered, it will flourish luxuriantly, and prove one of the most distinct and beautiful ornaments of the winter-garden, or large conservatory. Seed or division.

Arundo Donax (*Great Reed*).—A noble and giant grass, 7 to 13 ft. high, sometimes more. *Flowers*, in autumn; in numerous spikelets, forming a large compact panicle, 1 ft. to 16 in. long, at first of a reddish colour, afterwards becoming whitish. *Leaves*, large and handsome, alternate, ribbon-like, lanceolate-acute, smooth on the edges, of a glaucous green, gracefully arching. The variegated form *A. Donax versicolor*, is an exceedingly handsome plant, and is somewhat tenderer than the ordinary form. Native of Southern Europe.——Isolated tufts in the pleasure-ground, or grouped with other striking hardy plants in deep thoroughly drained sandy loam. It often perishes in winter on the London clay. The variegated form should be slightly protected in winter with coal-ashes or some like material. Increased by division of well-established plants; the variegated form, by the stems, which, if cut off and thrown into water, send out young plants freely from the joints.

Asarum europæum (*Asarabacca*).—A very dwarf plant, with roundish heart-shaped leaves 1 to 3 in. broad. *Flowers*, in summer; of a greenish-brown colour, and about ¼ in. long, on very short stalks close to the ground, under the leaves. The Virginian and Canadian species are also in cultivation, but none worthy of a place, except in botanical collections or perhaps occasionally as edgings. They grow in ordinary soil, and are easily increased by division.

Asclepias Cornuti (*Silk-weed*).—*A. syriaca*.—A vigorous herb, with stout simple stems 3 ft. to 5 ft. high. *Flowers*, in summer; pale purple or light rose, sweet scented, numerous, in dense umbels; hoods of the crown ovate, obtuse, with a lobe, or tooth, on each side of the short and stout claw-like horn. *Leaves*, opposite, oval-oblong, 4 to 8 in. long, contracted at the base into a short footstalk, pale, covered with a fine down underneath, as are also the flower-stalks; pods ovate, and woolly, covered with weak spines. Native of N. America in rich ground everywhere.——Borders, and naturalization in moist, rich soil, also in tufts in shrubberies and copses. Division.

Asclepias Douglasii (*Douglas's Asclepias*).—A vigorous-growing, handsome plant, with thick, woolly, simple stems, 2 to 3 ft. high. *Flowers*, in summer; large, waxy, purplish-lilac, sweet-scented, in many-flowered umbels. *Leaves*, opposite, oval-heart-shaped, pointed, 6½ in. long by 5 in. or more in width, smooth above, downy underneath, on short stalks. N. America.——Borders, and naturalization, in sandy loam. Seed and division.

Asclepias incarnata (*Flesh-coloured A.*)—A showy and stout perennial, with erect stems, branching at the top, 2 to 4 ft. high. *Flowers*, in summer; deep rose, or purple, having a delicious scent, in umbels usually in pairs, terminating each branch. *Leaves*, opposite, lance-shaped, slightly woolly on both sides. Swamps and river-banks in North America.——Borders, or margins of shrubberies, or naturalization on river banks, in a deep and moist soil. Division.

Asclepias tuberosa (*Orange A.*)—A handsome tuberous-rooted perennial,.

with erect hairy stems, branched at the top, 1 to 2 ft. high. *Flowers*, in summer; bright orange, in umbels, disposed in a terminal sub-corymb. *Leaves*, scattered, oblong-lance-shaped, hairy. North America.—— Borders, or margins of shrubberies, in peaty, or light sandy soil. Division or seed, which sometimes ripens in this country.

Asparagus Broussoneti (*Giant A.*)— A climbing asparagus, 10 ft. high. *Flowers*, in summer; inconspicuous, followed by small red berries; stem tapering, streaked, shrubby. *Lower leaves* solitary, the others ternate, an inch long, needle-shaped, persistent, distant from each other, glaucescent: stipules with reflected spines at the base; root fasciculate, with oblong, white tubers. Canary Islands and North Africa.—— For rustic bowers, stumps, poles, etc., in deep soil. Division.

Asperula odorata (*Sweet Woodruff*). —A dwarf perennial, with erect stems, 6 to 12 in. high. *Flowers*, in summer; white, small, in terminal corymbs. *Leaves*, mostly 8 in a whorl, (sometimes, but rarely, 6, 7, or 9,) lance-shaped, smooth, slightly rough at the edges. Fruit roundish, and very hairy. The plant has a delicious hay-like odour when dried. Europe, Siberia, and plentiful in Britain.——Margins of shrubberies, in ordinary soil. Division in autumn or winter.

Asphodelus luteus (*Yellow A.*)—Probably the finest of its family, 2 to 4 ft. high. *Flowers*, in summer; yellow, fragrant, in a dense, very long, straight, slender cluster, in the axils of buff-coloured bracts, nearly as long as the flowers. *Leaves*, numerous, awl-shaped, triangular, furrowed, smooth, glaucescent, dilated at the base into a membranous sheath; root-leaves united in a tuft. *Root*, fibrous, yellowish.

Native of S. Europe and N. Africa. There is a variety with double flowers. ——Borders and fringes of shrubberies, in ordinary good garden soil, but best and strongest in deep and dry sandy loam.

Asphodelus ramosus (*Great A.*)—A bold and striking tuberous-rooted perennial, 3 to 5 ft. high. *Flowers*, in summer; large, white, with a reddish-brown line in the middle of each petal, springing from the axils of oval-lanceolate bracts, and in very long dense clusters. *Leaves*, sword-shaped, stiff, keeled, spreading, of a dull green, about 2 ft. long. *Root*, fasciculate, tuberous. Native of S. Europe, N. Africa, and the Canary Islands. —— Similar positions and treatment to those for the preceding kind.

Aster alpinus (*Blue Daisy*).—A pubescent or hairy minute species, the single blue heads of which scattered over the grass in high alpine meadows look like blue daisies. In gardens it grows larger, and forms vigorous leafy tufts from 6 to 10 in. high. *Flowers*, in early summer; blue, 1 to 2 in. across. *Leaves*, entire, somewhat spoon-shaped, rough with hairs. Alpine ranges of northern hemisphere. There is a white var.——Mixed borders and rockwork; it is occasionally used as a bedding plant on the Continent. An interesting subject for naturalization in an upland meadow. Division and seed.

Aster altaicus (*Great-flowered Aster*). A dwarf, very pubescent species, with mauve-coloured flowers, nearly 2 in. across, and with a yellow disk ¾ in. in diameter. *Flowers*, in early summer; few, in partial or imperfect corymbs. Upper *leaves* linear-lanceolate, entire, ciliated. Native of the Siberian part of the Altai Mountains.——Borders and rough rockwork, or banks, in ordinary soil. Division and seed.

ASTER. 69

Aster Amellus (*Italian Starwort*).—A handsome kind, 15 to 24 in. high, with stems growing in large clusters from the root, branching at the top, each terminated by a single flower. *Flowers*, in late summer and autumn; blue with yellow disk. *Leaves*, oblong-lance-shaped, entire, rough. The variety *bessarabicus* very much resembles the type, but has oblong-obtuse leaves, narrowed at the base, and obtuse scales of the involucrum. Europe.——Borders and banks, in any soil. Division.

Aster cabulicus (*Indian Aster*).—A tall, fine species, very handsome and free-flowering, with a stem about 3 ft. high, branching above. *Flowers*, in autumn; ¾ in. across, blue with bright yellow centre, in a large branching panicle. *Leaves*, entire, lance-shaped, smooth, sessile, clasping; the lower ones 4 in. long, gradually diminishing in size towards the top of the stem. N. India.——Borders, and naturalization in ordinary soil. Division.

Aster cordifolius (*Heart-leaved Starwort*).—A tall, graceful kind, with stems often zigzag below, and inflorescence slightly drooping, 3 to 4½ ft. high. *Flowers*, in summer and autumn; pale violet, or nearly white, turning deeper; heads small, mostly crowded into racemes on the short spreading branches. *Leaves*, heart-shaped, acute, often hairy beneath, rough above; root and lower stem-leaves gradually pointed, sharply serrate, on slender stalks, the upper ones egg-shaped or lance-shaped, stalkless, or with short margined stalks, often entire. North America and Northern Asia. —— Borders, shrubberies, and naturalization. Division.

Aster (Galatella) dracunculoides.—A very pleasing kind, with light green stems and branches, 2 ft. or more in height, branching above; branches nearly erect. *Flowers*, in autumn;

1 in. or more across, purplish-blue, with dull yellow centre, in dense cymose, level clusters. *Leaves*, linear, pointed, sessile, about 1 in. long, chiefly on the upper part of the plant. South of Russia. —— Borders, by wood-walks, and naturalization, in common soil. Division.

Aster dumosus (*Bushy Aster*).—A very dense bushy species, forming thick branching tufts, 9 to 12 in. high. *Flowers*, in autumn; pale lilac-blue, about ¼ in. across, in broad clusters on the tops of the branches. *Leaves*, about 2 in. long, lance-shaped, pointed, sessile; upper ones much smaller. N. America. —— Borders, rockwork, and naturalization on bare slopes, etc., in ordinary soil. Division.

Aster elegans (*Elegant Starwort*).— A tall and graceful kind, with slightly drooping inflorescence, 3 to 5 ft. high. *Flowers*, in autumn; pale purple or approaching to white, small, in a contracted corymb. *Leaves*, narrow, lance-shaped, stalkless, pale, rather rough, particularly at the margins, somewhat 3-nerved; stems clothed with erect leaves, 1 to 2 in. long, and ½ to ¼ in. wide, becoming gradually smaller towards the top. Plains of Oregon, and on the Blue Mountains, N. America.—— Excellent for borders, and for associating with large autumn-flowering subjects; ordinary soil. Division.

Aster fragilis (*Fragile Starwort*).— A bushy kind, with numerous brittle stems, 2 ft. to 2½ ft. high. *Flowers*, in autumn; small, white at first, with a yellow disk, changing afterwards to light flesh-colour, then to rosy white with a purplish disk. *Leaves*, alternate; lower ones oblong-lance-shaped; upper ones smaller, often tinged with red. N. America. ——Borders and banks, in any soil. Division.

ASTER.

Aster grandiflorus (*Christmas Daisy*). —A peculiarly handsome-flowered species, with somewhat stiff and wiry stems, but with little of the vigour or coarseness of the other kinds ; 2½ to 3 ft. high. *Flowers*, in October, November, and December ; large, violet, terminating the branches. *Leaves*, of the branches alternate, lance-shaped, hairy and rough to the touch, about the size of those of Hyssop ; lower ones 1 to 2 in., those of the branches often less than ¼ in. long. Southern United States, in elevated parts, and in warm soils.—— Except on very warm soils and favourable situations this plant should be trained against a low south wall, on which the flowers would be seen to perfection. Division.

Aster lævis, var. **lævigatus** (*Smooth Aster*).—A variable and elegant kind, smooth throughout, 1½ to 2 ft. high. *Flowers*, in autumn ; about 1 in. across, purplish-blue with yellow centre, in a large, close panicle. *Leaves*, thickish, oblong-lance-shaped, pointed, scarcely, if at all, glaucous, the upper ones more or less clasping by an auricled or heart-shaped base ; scales of the involucrum lance-shaped or linear, with narrow and acute green tips tapering down on the mid-nerve. The variety *cyaneus* is glaucous, has thicker leaves, and the scales of the involucrum are broader and more leathery, with shorter and abrupt tips. N. America.——Borders, naturalization, and margins of shrubberies, in any soil. Division.

Aster laxus (*Loose-branched Aster*). —A very fine and pleasing species, with a slender stem upwards of 2 ft. high. *Flowers*, early in autumn ; pale purplish-blue, about 1 in. across, in loose, irregular clusters. *Leaves*, oval-lance-shaped, pointed, sessile, partially clasping ; the lower leaves about 3 in. long. N. America.——Borders and naturalization by wood-walks, etc., in any soil. Division.

Aster longifolius (*Long-leaved A.*)— A very variable and showy species, with smooth, branched stems, 1 to 5 ft. high. *Flowers*, in autumn ; bright purplish-blue, nearly 1 in. across, in dense corymbose panicles. *Leaves*, lance-shaped or linear, taper-pointed, shining above, entire or sparingly serrate in the middle. The varieties of this species are multiform. N. America.——Borders and naturalization, in ordinary soil. Division.

Aster multiflorus (*Many-flowered Starwort*).—*A. ericoides*.—A densely bushy species, 3½ to nearly 4 ft. high. *Flowers*, in autumn ; numerous, small ; florets of the ray pure white ; disk very small, yellowish-white ; arranged in an elongated corymb, forming a very large bouquet. *Leaves*, alternate, small, linear, like the leaves of certain heaths ; those at the top of the branches reflected. N. America. ——Borders and naturalization, in any soil. Division.

Aster Novæ-Angliæ (*New England Starwort.*)—A very tall and robust perennial, 5 to 8 ft. high, with purpled, hairy stems, and usually covered with a viscid pubescence in the upper parts. *Flowers*, late in summer and autumn ; violet - purple, sometimes rose-coloured ; heads in a thyrsus or corymb, or compound somewhat paniculate corymbs. *Leaves*, numerous, lance-shaped, auriculate, clasping, entire, sharp-pointed, clothed with a rough pubescence. North America.——Among the tallest plants at the back parts of the mixed border, in warm soils and positions. It grows anywhere but in cold soils and positions —often blooms only in time to be destroyed by frosts. Naturalized in sunny sheltered positions in woods and copses, it would probably be seen to greater perfection than in a garden, and it would form a good covert. Division.

Aster Novi-Belgii (*New Belgium Starwort*.)—A smooth herb, with stout stems; the branches upright, racemose, or somewhat corymbose, 3 to 5 ft. high. *Flowers*, in autumn; blue, either solitary on short branchlets, or in crowded racemes at the tops of axillary branches. *Leaves*, thickish, pale, and smooth, or slightly rough on the margins and upper surface, somewhat lance-shaped, serrate, tapering to each end, acute, the lower ones partly clasping by the narrow base, the others short, clasping by a broader base, often entire. North America.——Position, soil, etc., the same as recommended for *A. Novæ Angliæ*.

Aster obliquus (*Oblique Starwort*.)—A plant deserving of notice for its luxuriant and prolonged flowering, and growing in immense tufts, nearly 5 ft. high. *Flowers*, in autumn; numerous, florets of the ray white, disk purplish. *Leaves*, alternate, lower ones linear-lance-shaped, oblique; upper stem-leaves much smaller. North America.——Borders and semi-wild places in any soil. Division.

Aster patens (*Spreading A.*)—A very fine kind, with procumbent stems, 1 to 2 ft. long. *Flowers*, in autumn; purplish-blue, about 1 in. across, solitary, on long spreading stalks, clothed with very minute clasping leaves. *Leaves*, over 1 in. long, rough, oval, pointed, with a broad, clasping base. North America.—— Borders, rockwork, and naturalization on bare banks, etc., in ordinary soil. Division.

Aster pendulus (*Pendulous Aster.*)—A pretty kind, about 2½ ft. high. *Flowers*, in autumn; small, very handsome, pure white at first, becoming rose-coloured afterwards; disk small and changing in colour, like the florets of the ray. *Leaves*, oval, lance-shaped, those at the top of the stem much smaller. North America.——Border or shrubbery margins, in any soil. Division.

Aster puniceus (*Purple-stemmed A.*)— A very tall and stout species, with rough, hairy stems, 3 to 6 ft. high, usually purple below, panicled above. *Flowers*, late in autumn; lilac-blue, with yellow centre, an inch across, in a very large pyramidal panicle. *Leaves*, oblong-lance-shaped, clasping at the base, sparingly serrate in the middle, rough above, nearly smooth underneath, pointed. North America.—— Borders, naturalization, and shrubberies, in any soil. Division.

Aster pyrenæus (*Pyrenean Starwort.*)—A very large, handsome, and early autumn-flowering kind, 2 to 3 ft. high. *Flowers*, large, lilac-blue with yellow disk, in a short corymb of 3 to 5 heads, sometimes solitary. *Leaves* numerous, rather firm, but not fleshy, rough on both sides with small hairs, which issue from glands; those of the stem, oblong-lanceolate, acute, half embracing the stem, sharply toothed on the upper part. Pyrenees.——Borders, fringes of shrubberies, and naturalization on banks, copses, etc., in any soil. Division.

Aster Reevesi (*Hort.*) *Reeves's A.*— A dwarf species, with slender, branching stems, 9 to 12 in. high. *Flowers*, in autumn; small, white, with yellow centre, very numerous, forming a dense pyramidal panicle. *Leaves*, very small, linear, acute. North America.——Borders and rockwork, in ordinary soil. Division.

Aster rubricaulis (*Red-stemmed Starwort*).—A very distinct species, 3½ to nearly 4 ft. high. *Flowers*, in autumn; few, large; florets of the ray narrow, of a lilac-blue; disk yellow. *Leaves*, alternate, oblong-lance-shaped, of a glaucous green colour; stems of

a reddish hue. North America.——
Borders and banks, in common soil.
Division.

Aster sericeus (*Silky Starwort*).—
A greyish herb, with numerous slender stems, 1 to 2 ft. high. *Flowers*, late in summer and in autumn; deep blue, about 1½ in. across, usually terminating the short branchlets. *Leaves*, lance-shaped, silky, about an inch long, obscurely 3-nerved, crowded on the branches, those of the root about 3 in. long, distinctly 3-nerved. North America.——Borders, in warm, well-drained soil, or on sunny banks. Division.

Aster Shortii (*Short's Aster*).—A very pretty species, with a slender, spreading, nearly smooth stem, 2 to 4 ft. high. *Flowers*, in autumn; purplish-blue, about 1 in. across, numerous, in long racemose panicles. *Leaves*, lanceolate, or ovate-lanceolate, elongated, gradually tapering to a point, 3 to 5 in. long, all but the uppermost more or less heart-shaped at the base. N. America.——Borders, and naturalization, in ordinary soil. Division.

Aster tardiflorus (*Late Starwort*).—
A very free-flowering kind, about 3 ft. high. *Flowers*, in autumn; florets of the ray light rosy lilac; disk at first yellow, afterwards purplish. *Leaves*, alternate, oblong-lance-shaped, of a deep green; upper stem-leaves very small. N. America.——Borders, in any soil. Division.

Aster Tradescantii (*Michaelmas Daisy*).—A very late-flowering kind, 3 to nearly 5 ft. high. *Flowers*, in October; florets of the ray white; disk at first yellow, afterwards purplish. *Leaves*, alternate, oval-lance-shaped, acute, of a handsome green, sometimes tinged with red; the lower ones often toothed in the middle. N. America. —— Naturalization in semi-wild places, in any soil. Division.

Aster turbinellus (*Mauve Starwort*).
—A fine showy kind, with smooth stem and paniculate branches, 2 to 3 ft. high. *Flowers*, late in summer and in autumn; delicate mauve, in panicles; involucre top-shaped, scales overlapping each other. *Leaves*, lance-shaped, smooth, entire, with fringed margins, tapering to each end, slightly stem-clasping, those of the thread-like branchlets awl-shaped. North America.——Borders, with groups of handsomer autumn-flowering perennials, and naturalization. Grows freely anywhere, but is worthy of good soil. Division.

Aster versicolor (*Various-coloured Starwort*).—A dwarf neat species, the branches often prostrate from the crowd of flowers at their apex, 9 to 15 in. high. *Flowers*, in summer; very showy, white at first, changing into pink or purple. *Leaves*, smooth, oblong-lance-shaped, tapering to a point; lower ones serrate in the middle, upper ones stem-clasping, entire. Said to have been found in N. America, but not recorded by recent American botanists.——Front of the mixed border, in sandy loam; on the rougher part of rockwork, or on banks in sandy loam, and in sunny positions. Division.

Astilbe rivularis (*Rivulet A.*)—A vigorous, handsome *Spiræa*-like perennial, 3 to 4 ft. high. *Flowers*, in summer; greenish-yellow, in spiked racemes. *Leaves*, biternate; leaflets ovate, doubly serrate, hairy beneath, as are also the stalks. Nepal.——As isolated specimens in the subtropical garden or pleasure-ground, among vigorous herbs, by wood-walks or margins of shrubberies, in sandy loam. Division.

Astilbe rubra (*Red Astilbe*). — An ornamental species; as yet rare in gardens, 4 ft. to 6 ft. high. *Flowers*, late in summer and in autumn; rose-coloured, numerous, on short pedicels, in short dense panicles arranged in a long spike. *Leaves*, biternate, with adnate, half-sheathing stipules; leaflets 1 to 2 in. long, oblique, cordate, serrate. N. America, Japan, and Mountains of N. India.——Grouped with hardy subtropical plants, or in isolated tufts on banks, and in semi-wild places in good deep soil. Division.

Astragalus alpinus (*Alpine A.*)—A prostrate hairy herb, with branching stems varying from a few inches to a foot in length. *Flowers*, in summer; bluish-purple, sometimes whitish, drooping, in short racemes about ½ in. long. *Leaves*, divided into from 8 to 12 pairs of ovate or oblong leaflets, with an odd one. Mountains of Northern Europe and Russian Asia, also in Britain, though rare.—— Rockwork, or margins of borders, in ordinary soil. Division.

Astragalus dasyglottis (*Clover A.*)— A low and pleasing species, nearly allied to *A. hypoglottis*, but not so tall nor so hairy, with the stipules united, and oblong-obovate bracts nearly as long as the tube of the calyx. *Flowers* purple, resembling those of a Clover. *Leaflets*, elliptical-oblong, sometimes emarginate. Flower-stems a little longer than the leaves; root creeping. The Siberian parts of the Altai Mountains.——Rockwork and borders, in sandy loam. Division.

Astragalus hypoglottis (*Purple A.*) —A hairy prostrate herb. *Flowers*, in summer; bluish-purple, in large roundish heads on stalks longer than the leaves; calyx covered with black and white hairs. *Leaves*, composed of 8 to 10 pairs of oblong dark-green leaflets. There is a white-flowered variety. Europe, Britain, and North America.——Level spots on rockwork, in well-drained sandy loam, or a chalky soil. Seed or division.

Astragalus galegiformis (*Galega-like A.*)—A hardy plant of large size, resembling *Galega officinalis*, 3 ft. or upwards in height. *Flowers*, in summer; very numerous, yellowish-white, in long axillary clusters. *Leaves*, resembling those of *Galega officinalis*, with lanceolate pointed leaflets. Siberia and the East.——Association with the coarser perennials in wild or rough places. Division.

Astragalus monspessulanus (*Montpellier A.*)—A vigorous prostrate species with leaves a span long. *Flowers*, in early summer; deep crimson before opening, and pale rosy-lilac when open, with bars of white on the upper petals, in racemes from 2 to 5 in. long, on stalks 6 to 12 in. high, according to the strength of the plant. *Leaves*, composed of 12 to 20 pairs of ovate-acute leaflets, the outer ones the smallest. South of France.——Front of borders or rougher parts of rockwork, or planted so that the shoots may droop over the edge of banks, etc. It thrives in common soil, and is increased by seed and careful division.

Astragalus Onobrychis (*Saintfoinlike A.*)—A very showy pubescent species, in some varieties dwarf and spreading, in others erect and growing to a height of 18 in. *Flowers*, in early summer; purplish-crimson, in oblong-ovate spikes, on stalks longer than the leaves. *Leaves*, of 7 to 12 or more pairs of oblong leaflets. There are several varieties, *alpinus*, *moldavicus*, and *microphyllus*, all of which are prostrate in habit, and *major*, an erect growing one. There are also white forms of all the varieties. Europe and Siberia.—— The dwarf varieties are admirably adapted for rockwork, and the tall one for borders, or the rougher parts of the rockwork, in a good sandy loam. Division or seed.

Astragalus pannosus (*Shaggy Milk Vetch*).—A singular and attractive kind, from its very silvery and woolly pinnate leaves, growing in compact tufts about a span high. Attracted by its appearance, when I saw the plant in cultivation in Switzerland, I brought home some seeds, from which plants have been raised by Mr. W. Bull and Mr. Jas. Backhouse. I have not yet seen it in flower, but from the beauty of its leaves alone it is likely to prove an excellent rock-garden plant, and probably a valuable bedding and edging one. It is easily increased from seed.

Astragalus ponticus (*Pontic A.*)—A very stout perennial, 2 to 3 ft. or more high, with erect hairy stem and large handsome leaves. *Flowers*, in summer; yellow, sessile, in roundish heads; segments of the calyx linear, much shorter than the tube of the corolla. *Leaves*, smoothish; leaflets oblong; stipules lance-shaped. Tauria and Bessarabia——Among vigorous perennials on margins of shrubberies and in wild places, in any soil. Division or seed.

Astragalus Tragacantha (*Goat's Thorn A.*)—A dwarf spiny shrub, 1 to 3 ft. high. *Flowers*, in summer; pale violet, sessile, 2 to 5 together in the axils of the leaves; calyx downy, cylindrical. *Leaves*, hoary, having 7 to 11 pairs of leaflets; stalks becoming spiny when old. Native of the Levant.——Rockwork, among dwarf shrubs or on banks. It grows in any soil, but does not flower so freely in stiff soils as in fine sandy ones, and is more fitted for the botanic garden than the select collection. Seed or cuttings.

Astragalus vaginatus (*Sheathed A.*)—A handsome species with erect, pubescent stem, about 1 ft. high. *Flowers*, in summer; rosy-purple, with white-tipped wings; calyx somewhat inflated, tinged with rose-colour, and thickly covered with soft white and black hairs; flowers each about an inch long, arranged in dense spikes on stalks longer than the leaves. *Leaves*, of 7 or 8 pairs of leaflets and an odd one; leaflets elongated-oblong, with a very short point at the apex, and covered on both sides with short, silvery, adpressed hairs, distinctly arranged in the direction of the length of the leaflet; young stipules joined together and opposite the leaves. Siberia and N. America.——Borders or rockwork, in sandy loam. Seed or division.

Astragalus vimineus (*Silvery A.*)—A very handsome plant, 6 to 8 in. high. *Flowers*, in May; standard purplish rose, 1¼ times longer than the wings, which are of a pure white, as is also the keel, arranged in short spikes, which are nearly capitular in form, on stalks longer than the leaves. *Leaflets*, linear-lance-shaped, acute, marked with 5 or 6 ridges. Native of Iberia, the Caucasus, and the neighbourhood of Odessa. —— Rockwork and select borders, in very sandy loam, thoroughly drained, and in a sunny position. Seed and division.

Astrantia major (*Greater A.*)—One of the most distinct and ornamental of hardy umbelliferous plants, 1 to 2 ft. high. *Flowers*, in summer; pinkish, striped, in umbels. *Leaves* of root, 5-partite, segments ovate-lance-shaped, toothed; those of involucre linear-lance-shaped, entire, 15 to 20 in number, about the same length as the umbel. Europe and Caucasus.—— Borders, rough rockwork or banks, shrubberies and naturalization in copses in any soil. Division.

Athamanta Matthioli (*Matthioli's A.*) —A dwarf graceful perennial, 1 to 2 ft. high, with finely-cut fennel-like leaves. *Flowers*, in summer; white, 12 to 25 in an umbel. *Leaves*, 3- to 4-ternate; leaflets narrow, thread-like; both stem and leaves smooth. Alps of Carinthia and Carniola.——Among fine-leaved plants, in borders, or groups, or naturalization on banks, in ordinary soil. Division or seed.

Aubrietia deltoidea (*Deltoid A.*)— A very valuable dwarf, slightly hoary, evergreen herb, 2 to 4 in. high. *Flowers*, in early spring; lilac or purplish, in clusters of 3 or 4 blooms, so freely produced as to nearly hide the leaves; petals twice the length of the calyx, with long claws. *Leaves*, obovate-lance-shaped, nearly entire, with 1 or 2 teeth, rough with short hairs. Southern Europe.——Front margin of the mixed border, rockwork, ruins, or sloping bare banks, in dry soil. Division, seed, or cuttings which root readily.

Aubrietia purpurea (*Purple A.*)— Closely allied to *A. deltoidea*, but somewhat taller, flowering a fortnight later in spring, and continuing longer in bloom. *Flowers*, larger, and of a fine violet. *Leaves*, broader, with from 2 to 5 teeth. Stems more leafy, branching, and erect. Asia Minor.——To this species (the *A. macrostyla* of Boissier) belong *A. grandiflora*, *A. græca*, and the fine variety *A. Campbelli*. These are all well worthy of culture, as are the variegated forms. Similar positions and soil to those for the preceding.

Bahia lanata (*Woolly Bahia*).—A greyish herb, mostly much branched from the base of the stem, 6 to 15 in. high. *Flowers*, in summer; one on each stalk, yellow, in great abundance. *Leaves*, slightly downy beneath, alternate, lower ones sometimes opposite, deeply divided, often strap-shaped and entire. America.——Borders or banks, in light, sandy, well-drained loam, on which, flowering much more abundantly, it is a much more ornamental plant than when on cold clay soils. Seed, or more readily by division.

Bambusa aurea (*Yellow-stemmed Bamboo*).—A shrubby perennial, hardy and graceful, 6½ to 10 ft. high, differing but slightly from *B. viridi-glaucescens* in size, habit, and elegance. *Stem*, light green when young, changing into a yellowish hue, and finally becoming of a straw yellow when fully grown. The leaves differ from those of *B. viridi-glaucescens* in having their under surface less glaucescent; and the sheath is always devoid of the long silky hairs. China.——In sheltered and warm but not shady spots in the pleasure-ground, and, till more plentiful, usually as an isolated specimen. It delights in well-drained, deep, and good loamy soil, enriched with vegetable matter, and with plenty of moisture in summer. Careful division of strong established tufts.

Bambusa falcata (*Common Hardy Bamboo*).—The only kind at present much planted with us; 7 to 20 ft. high. *Stem* woody, twisted, smooth, of a yellowish-green or straw-colour, knotty, bearing on one side of each of the knots a bundle of small branches equally knotty and twisted. *Leaves*, linear-acute, alternate, in two rows, sheathing, ribbon-like, of a fine, delicate green, from 4 to 6 in. long, on short stalks. Native of the Himalayas, at elevations of from 7500 to 10,000 ft., where, according to Royle, "its annual stems are yearly beaten down by the falls of snow, which protect its perennial roots from excessive frost."——It is hardy over the greater part of England and Ireland, but only attains full development in the south and west. I have seen it attain great luxuriance in Devon, and nearly 20 ft. high in Mr. Smith-Barry's place near Cork, where I had the pleasure of seeing a large plantation of it a few days before Christmas, 1870.——In sheltered nooks in the pleasure-ground, with best effect as an isolated

BAMBUSA — BAPTISIA.

specimen. Where it thrives it might be used in the flower-garden with fine effect; where it does not thrive freely, it is not worth planting. It loves a deep, sandy, and rich soil, and plenty of moisture when growing fast, and is propagated by careful division of established plants.

Bambusa Fortunei (*Fortune's Bamboo*). —A pretty dwarf variegated species, of which I have not seen the green form in cultivation, with a half shrubby, very dwarf, slender, branching, hollow stem, with very short internodes, and seldom growing more than 18 in. high. *Leaves*, linear-lanceolate, abruptly pointed, somewhat rounded at the base, on very short hairy stalks, serrated and often fringed with long hairs on the margin, downy on both sides, and distinctly variegated, the transverse veins being often of a bottle-green colour. Native of Japan.——This has proved hardy in our gardens; but it has not the charm of grace possessed by the taller kinds, and is chiefly desirable in collections of variegated and edging plants.

Bambusa japonica (*Metake Bamboo*) —*B. Metake.*— A large-leaved and rather dwarf species, 4 to 7 ft. high. *Stem*, entirely concealed by the sheaths of the leaves, thickly tufted, with erect branches. *Leaves*, lance-shaped, dark green, persistent, with a very sharp point, narrowed into a short leafstalk, and nearly a foot long. Spikes with from ten to twenty flowers, narrow, often somewhat cylindrical. Japan.——I have seen this thrive very freely in the late Mr. Borrer's garden in Sussex, and in one or two other places; but, unfortunately, it, unlike many of the other kinds, goes to seed so freely that it is rarely ornamental. Loves a peat soil or a very free moist and deep loam, and runs a good deal at the root.

Bambusa nigra (*Dark-stemmed Bamboo*).—A rather compact-growing kind. *Stems*, smooth, bushy, about 7 ft. high, of a light green, dotted and striped with purple when young, changing to a glistening black when fully grown; branching very much at the top, and sometimes from the base up. *Leaves*, shortly stalked, oval-oblong-acute, with a hard, dry, persistent sheath. China.——As isolated specimens near the margins of shrubberies in the pleasure-ground, in warm, sunny, and sheltered positions, in deep, sandy, and well-drained soil.

Bambusa viridi-glaucescens (*Greyish Bamboo.*)—This has been proved very hardy and free in the Paris gardens, and will probably make a more vigorous growth, and prove a more beautiful object than any other kind, in warm parts of our islands. *Stems*, 7 to 12 ft. high, of a light yellowish green, branching from the base, each branch again branching very much. *Leaves*, pale green, bluish underneath, sheathing the stem for a considerable length. China.——As isolated specimens in sheltered warm glades in the pleasure-ground, or in snug, open spots near wood-walks, in very deep, rich, and light, well-drained soil.

The following kinds are also known in French gardens : *B. edulis, B. Simonii, B. mitis, B. scriptoria, B. verticillata, B. graminea, B. violacea, B. Duquilioi.* Of these, some are not yet sufficiently proved; the first two are the best, and would, like the others, thrive well in the South of England and Ireland.

Baptisia alba (*White B.*)—An interesting perennial, 2 to 3 ft. high. *Flowers*, in early summer; white, in racemes about a foot long, on stalks springing from the root. *Leaves*, stalked, smooth, somewhat like those of the *Laburnum*. North America.——Borders, in deep loamy soils. Seed or division.

Baptisia australis (*Southern B.*)—A handsome plant, with spreading, branched, smooth stems, 2 to 3 ft. high. *Flowers*, in summer; dark-blue or purple, in few-flowered racemes shorter than the branches; calyx with 4 divisions, lower one blunt. *Leaves*, stalked, smooth; leaflets oblong-wedge-shaped, blunt. Banks of rivulets in North America.——Borders, margins of shrubberies, or naturalization in any soil. Division or seed.

Baptisia exaltata (*Tall B.*)—A fine, showy perennial, with erect stem, 3 to 4 ft. high. *Flowers*, in summer; deep blue, scattered in many-flowered racemes, longer than the branches; calyx with 4 divisions, lower one acute. *Leaves*, ternate; leaflets lance-shaped-obovate. North America. ——Borders, by wood-walks, margins of shrubberies, or naturalization in ordinary soil. Division or seed.

Barnardia scilloides (*Squill-like B.*) —A pretty squill-like bulbous plant, about 6 in. high. *Flowers*, in summer; pale blue, green on the outside, with yellow anthers, numerous in dense terminal racemes. *Leaves*, linear, channelled, pointed, 6 in. long; bulb tunicated. Macao.——Rockwork, in light sandy loam, and on warm borders. Division.

Begonia Veitchii (*Veitch's B.*)—A brilliant and large-flowered, hardy kind, resembling *Saxifraga ciliata* in habit, 8 in. to 1 ft. high. *Flowers*, in autumn; 2 to 2½ in. across, of a vivid vermilion cinnabar-red, usually 2 on each stem. *Leaves*, of a rich, glossy, dark green, nearly circular, about 3 in. across. Found near Cuzco, in Peru, at an elevation of upwards of 12,000 feet, and proved in this country sufficiently hardy to withstand seven degrees of frost without the least injury.——Rockwork, or slightly raised, choice borders, in rich, light, and very well-drained soil. Division and seed.

Bellis perennis (*Daisy.*)—It is needless to describe this well-known native plant, but the handsome double varieties, from the quilled white and the double red, to the singular aucuba-leaved one, with its leaves so richly stained and veined with yellow, and the quaint hen-and-chicken variety, are among the most effective and easily-managed subjects we can use for the spring and early summer garden.——They grow best in rich garden soil, and may be increased rapidly by dividing them into small pieces in April.

Betonica grandiflora (*Large-flowered B.*)—A dwarf, hairy, erect perennial, 12 to 18 in. high. *Flowers*, in summer; purplish, in whorls of from 10 to 20; corolla 3 times as long as the somewhat bell-shaped calyx. *Leaves*, stalked, broadly-ovate, blunt, heart-shaped at the base; floral ones stalkless, stem-clasping. Siberia.——Borders, margins of shrubberies, or naturalization in common soil. Division.

Bocconia cordata (*Heart-shaped B.*) — *Macleya*. — A stately perennial, 4 to 8 ft. high. *Flowers*, in summer; brownish, in large panicles. *Leaves*, roundish-heart-shaped, whitish beneath, shortly lobed. China.——In borders or in isolated tufts in the turf of the pleasure-ground. This attains greatest vigour and beauty in deep, warm, sandy loam, and in a sheltered and sunny position. Division of well-established plants.

Borago orientalis (*Early Borage*)— *Borago cordifolia*. — A somewhat coarse but pleasing herb, 8 in. to 15 in. high. *Flowers*, early in spring; bluish, with five reflected ovate-obtuse divisions longer than the tube, in panicled clusters; stamens projecting very far from the mouth of the flower. *Leaves*, nearly all radical, heart-shaped, set with rigid hairs. This runs very much at the root, which is thick and blackish on the outside. Found about Constantinople.——Naturalization in lanes, on banks, etc., in any soil, but best in sunny spots, as it is an early flowerer. Division.

Boussingaultia baselloides (*Trailing B.*)—A very luxuriant trailing plant, 16 to nearly 20 ft. long, sometimes more. *Flowers*, late in autumn; small, white, fragrant, becoming black as they fade, disposed in clusters 2 to 4 in. long, which spring from the axils of the leaves at the ends of the branches. *Leaves*, of a fine green, alternate, cordate, smooth, shining, fleshy, slightly wavy; stems very twining, tinged with red, growing with extraordinary rapidity, and producing numerous tubercles. Root fibrous and long. Native of Quito. ——Prefers a rich vegetable soil and sunny aspect, although it will grow in almost any soil and position. It is only suited for dry banks and chalkpits, associated with climbing and trailing plants. Propagated with the greatest facility by means of the tubercles of the stem; these are extremely brittle, and break with the least shock, but the smallest fragment will vegetate as well as the entire tubercle.

Briza media (*Common Quaking-grass*). —An erect-growing ornamental grass, 9 to 15 in. high. *Flowers*, in early summer; in loose panicles 2 to 4 in. long; spikelets two on each slender branch, roundish at first, heart-shaped afterwards, smooth, shining, usually variegated with green and purple, but sometimes white. *Leaves* flat, 2 to 4 in. long, and ¼ in. broad, few, except at the bottom of the stem. Asia, Europe, and Britain. —— Borders, and naturalized on bare banks and slopes. Seed and division.

Brodiæa coccinea (*Crimson-flowered B.*)—A very beautiful bulbous plant of the lily family, with a flower-scape from 2 to 3 ft. in height. *Flowers*, in summer; about 1¼ in. long, tubular-campanulate, with six recurved segments of a pea-green colour, the remainder of the flower being of a rich magenta crimson. The three exterior stamens are petal-like and greenish-white. The flowers are nodding, and borne in a terminal umbel of from 5 to 12, or even 15 to 20 flowers, when established and vigorous. *Leaves*, linear, channelled, lax, nearly as long as the flower-scape. Trinity Mountains, California. —— Select warm spots on rockwork, and mixed border among select plants, in warm sandy loam. Division and seed.

Brodiæa congesta (*Allium-like B.*)— A rather handsome Allium-like bulb, 8 to 20 in. high. *Flowers*, in summer; of a fine blue, with the crown paler; in an umbel of 6 to 8 blooms; petals cleft at the top. *Leaves* few, long, slender, and grooved on the inside. *Bulb*, small, roundish, and much wrinkled. Native of the N.W. coast of N. America. A peculiarity of the flowers of the plants of this species is that some of the stamens are metamorphosed into fleshy scales, which adhere to the mouth of the corolla, and in this state bear anthers.——Borders in light soil. Division.

Brodiæa grandiflora (*Large-flowered B.*)—A handsome bulbous plant, 8 in. to 1 ft. high. *Flowers*, in summer; bluish-purple, with entire pointed petals, in an umbel of 2 to 7 flowers. *Leaves*, 2 or more, linear, pointed, slender, grooved on the inside, furnished with a few membranous scales. *Bulb*, small, roundish, dry and wrinkled. Native of N.W. coast of N. America.——Choice borders, rockwork and bulb-garden, in light, sandy, deep and well-drained soil. Division.

Bromelia sphacelata (*Hardy B.*)—A rough plant, forming tufts of harsh, rigid, spiny leaves 1 ft. to 2 ft. high. *Flowers*, in summer; purple, sessile, crowded and overlapping each other, in axillary spikes. *Leaves*, numerous, erect, sword-shaped, long-pointed, fringed with stiff spines pointing upwards. Chili.—— The rock-garden and warm borders, in light, perfectly-drained soil. This plant has stood out of doors for several winters past, and will probably prove quite hardy on rockwork in the southern counties.

Bryanthus erectus (*Hybrid B.*) — A dwarf evergreen bush, 8 in. to 1 ft. high. *Flowers*, in April; pinkish, about ¼ in. across, cup-shaped with 5 broad pointed segments, arranged on thin, wiry, hairy stalks about 1 in. long, in erect corymbose groups on the tops of the stems; style twice as long as the flower, projecting; calyx of 5 broad oval-acute segments, tinged with red, and with a very narrow membranous margin. *Leaves*, linear-lanceolate, obtuse, keeled, with reflexed margins, smooth, leathery, erect, crowded densely and overlapping on the upper parts of the branches, few and scattered on the lower parts of the stem; stem and branches very rigid. Said to be a hybrid between *Rhododendron Chamæcistus* and *Kalmia glauca*.—— Rockwork and choice border, in sandy peat soil. Division and cuttings.

Bulbocodium vernum (*Spring Meadow Saffron*).—A very early handsome bulb, 4 to 6 in. high. *Flowers*, very early in spring; whitish at first, changing to purplish-violet, with a white spot on the claw, long, tubular, funnel-shaped, 2 or 3 from each bulb, appearing before the leaves. *Leaves*, generally three in number, strap-shaped, broad, concave, and surrounded at the base by well-developed membranous sheaths. *Bulb*, black, oblong, resembling that of a *Colchicum*. Native of Switzerland, Hungary, and S. transalpine Europe generally.—— Borders, the rock-garden, the bulb-garden, and naturalization on bare slopes and banks, with a good aspect. It thrives in almost any soil, best in a moist loam perhaps, and is increased by separation of the bulbs.

Calamagrostis argentea (*Silvery C.*) —A rather ornamental grass, forming tufts of long glaucous leaves, and sending up flower-stems about 3 ft. high. The inflorescence consists of close spiked panicles, 8 or 9 in. long; the spikelets presenting a feathery appearance from the extreme narrowness of the glumes and paleæ. *Leaves*, upwards of 1 ft. long and about ¼ in. across, finely channelled on the back, and rough with very minute teeth. South of Europe.——Borders, in ordinary soil. Division.

Calamintha glabella (*Tom Thumb Calamint*).—A very charming minute herbaceous plant, forming compact and neat little tufts about 3 in. high. *Flowers*, in summer; lilac-purple, tubular, scented, very numerous and large for the size of the plant. *Leaves*, linear-lance-shaped, sessile. —— The rock-garden, in sandy loam, and among the very dwarfest plants. Division and seed.

Calandrinia umbellata (*Brilliant C.*) —A very dwarf evergreen herb, with much-branched stems, half shrubby at the base, 3 to 4 in. high. *Flowers*, in summer; magenta-crimson, in a terminal corymb, on erect, naked stems. *Leaves*, very narrow, hairy, acute. Chili. —— Rockwork, margin of the mixed border, small beds, or edgings; always in a fine sandy or peaty soil. It is better to sow it every year, as young plants flower more continuously than old established tufts.

Calceolaria Kellyana (*Kelly's C.*)—A handsome hardy hybrid, with twice-branching downy stems, 6 in. to 9 in. high. *Flowers*, in summer; nearly ¾ in. across, deep yellow with numerous small brown dots, two or three together on the top of the stems. *Leaves*, all radical, in a rosette, almost spathulate in shape, with an irregular toothed margin, and more or less covered on both sides with soft white hairs.——Rockwork and borders, in well-drained sandy loam. Division.

Calla palustris (*Bog Arum*).—A very interesting and ornamental trailing bog-plant, 3 to 8 in. high. *Flowers*, in summer; spadix yellow, half as long as the spathe, which is persistent, flat, oval-obtuse, with a terminal point, pure white on the inside, and greenish externally. *Leaves*, all radical, oval or heart-shaped, stalked, the stalks sheathing the stem at the base. *Rhizome*, thick, creeping, jointed. Marshes in the N. E. of France, N. Europe, N. Asia, and N. America. ——Grows freely in every kind of bog, natural or artificial, and by the margins of ponds and lakes. I have never seen it so luxuriant as on beds of rich soft mud. Easily increased to any extent by division of the long creeping rootstock.

Calliprora lutea (*Yellow C.*) — A rather pretty bulbous plant. *Flowers*, in early summer; yellow; divisions purplish-brown in the middle on the outside. *Leaves*, linear-sword-shaped, pointed, grooved, longer than the flower-stem; bracts sheathing, scarious, much shorter than the pedicels. Native of N. California.——The bulb border, or a well-drained spot on the lower flanks of rockwork, in dry sandy soil. Separation of the bulbs.

Callirhoe digitata (*Finger-leaved C.*) —A glaucous herb, 2 to 3 ft. high. *Flowers*, in summer; reddish purple; peduncles long, axillary, 1-flowered. *Leaves*, subpeltate, 6 to 7-parted; segments, linear, entire or 2-parted; upper ones more simple. North America. —— Borders, or rough rockwork, in rich fibry loam. Seed, or careful division.

Callirhoe involucrata (*Crimson Malva*).—A very handsome procumbent herb, 6 in. high. *Flowers*, in summer, crimson, 1½ to 2 in. across, in a loose panicle; sepals lance-shaped, very hairy; stalks erect, 1½ to 2 in. long. *Leaves*, divided nearly to the base, 3 to 5-parted; segments narrow, lance-shaped, 3 to 5-toothed, hairy on both sides; stem clothed with spreading hairs. Valley of the Loup, Fork of the Platte, N. America.——Sunny borders, or rockwork, in good sandy loam. Seed.

Calluna vulgaris (*Common Ling*).—*Erica vulgaris.*—A well-known spreading evergreen shrub, 1 to 2 ft. high or more. *Flowers*, in summer; purplish-pink, small, in long, terminal, spiked racemes. *Leaves*, 3-cornered, small and short, opposite, blunt at the point, arrow-shaped at the base.—— Few of us would think of giving a place to the common Ling, but several of its dwarf and highly-coloured forms deserve a place on the rougher parts of the rockwork, or in beds in tufts, or as edgings, in a peat soil.

Calopogon pulchellus (*Pretty C.*)—A very attractive tuberous-rooted orchidaceous plant, about 1 ft. high. *Flowers*, late in summer; purple, with a handsome pale-yellow beard or tuft of hairs growing from the lip. *Leaves* few, radical, grassy. Native of all parts of the United States, in wet prairies, or the edges of pine woods. ——Well suited for a good position on the rockwork, or for an open spot in the hardy fernery. I have had no experience of the mode of propagating it.

Caltha palustris (*Marsh Marigold*). --A well-known native plant with slightly branched stems, 6 to 12 in.

high. *Flowers*, in spring, continuing until early summer; bright golden-yellow, large; peduncles furrowed. *Leaves*, roundish, kidney-shaped, roundly crenate, on long stalks. There is a double variety and a smaller-flowered one, the double one excellent for gardens. Marshy places, moist meadows and margins of rivers, brooks, etc., throughout Europe, Western Asia, and North America. —— The double var. is a first-class plant for moist soils and the artificial bog: the single one always looks well by the side of ponds and streams. Division.

Calypso borealis (*Northern C.*)—A handsome and very interesting orchid, about 1 ft. high. *Flowers*, in summer; rose-coloured, resembling those of a *Cypripedium*, solitary on the end of a slender, sheathed stem. *Leaves*, one only, thin, many-nerved, either ovate or cordate. Native of the Northern parts of Europe, Asia, and America, in woods, especially of Firs. The plant appears to be nearly related to *Cœlogyne*, and particularly to the section *Pleione*.——Half-shady spots on the margins of the rock-garden or artificial bog, or in a select spot in shrubberies, in light, moist vegetable soil mulched with cocoa fibre or other material to keep the surface open.

Calystegia dahurica (*Dahurian C.*) — *Convolvulus dahuricus* — A very showy twining perennial. *Flowers*, in summer; rosy purple; peduncles axillary, 1-flowered; sepals, lance-shaped, 2 outer ones broadest. *Leaves*, somewhat heart-shaped, smooth; margins and veins of the under surface downy; stems downy. *Roots*, creeping. Caucasus. —— Excellent for covering bowers, railings, stumps, cottages, etc., and also for naturalization in hedgerows and copses. It grows in almost any kind of soil, and, like its relation the bind-weed, is readily increased by division of the root.

Calystegia pubescens plena (*Double C.*—A handsome twining plant, 3 to 6½ ft. high. *Flowers*, in summer and autumn; large, of a flesh rose-colour, changing to bright rose, very double, on stalks from 2½ to 3½ in. long. *Leaves*, alternate, hastate, downy. China.——Likes a light soil and warm aspect, and is useful for the same positions as the preceding though not so vigorous. Grown in large pots and tubs, I have seen it used with good effect in London for forming small bowers, etc. on balconies. Division of the root, which runs very much.

Camassia esculenta (*Quamash-root*). —A handsome and distinct bulbous perennial, 1 to 2½ ft. high. *Flowers*, in summer; dull violet-blue, 6 to 10 in. a lax spike. *Leaves*, linear, grooved on the inside, streaked, sometimes glaucescent. *Bulb*, of moderate size, egg-shaped, whitish. Native of N. W. America and the valleys of the Rocky Mountains. —— Borders and bulb-garden, attaining greatest vigour and beauty in free and deep sandy loam, well drained. Separation of the bulbs every third or fourth year.

Campanula alpina (*Alpine Harebell*). —A dwarf herb, covered with stiff down, and with nearly simple, furrowed stems, 5 to 10 in. high. *Flowers*, in summer; deep blue, scattered in a pyramidal manner along the stems; lobes of the calyx nearly as long as the corolla. *Leaves*, oblong-linear, woolly, those of the root crowded and narrowed at the base. Transylvania and the Carpathian Mountains.—— The front margin of the mixed border, or rockwork, in sandy loam. Division or seed.

Campanula autumnalis (*Autumn C.*) —*Platycodon autumnale.*—A handsome perennial, 20 in. to 2 ft. high. *Flowers*, in autumn; of a vivid blue, glistening

CAMPANULA.

on the outside, arranged in a lengthened panicle. *Leaves*, alternate, oval-acute, toothed, often tinged with red. There are several varieties: one with single white flowers, another with double blue, another with double light-blue or lilac, and another with double white. China.——This kind differs from *C. grandiflora* by its pyramidal habit, its stem being more branching, with slenderer branches, and covered with leaves up to the top.——Mixed borders, in warm sandy loam, and in a warm position, or as isolated clumps near the fringes of shrubberies, in the picturesque garden. Division and seed.

Campanula barbata (*Bearded Harebell.*)—A distinct kind, with rough, shaggy leaves, and round, nearly simple stems, 6 to 18 in. high. *Flowers*, in summer; pale sky-blue, nearly 1¼ in. long, drooping gracefully, and with a long beard at the mouth, in a few-flowered raceme, 1 on each stalk; calyx hairy, about one quarter of length of corolla. *Leaves*, nearly entire; radical ones crowded, lance-shaped; stem-leaves few, strap-shaped. France, Switzerland, North Italy, and Austria.—— Mixed borders, or the rougher parts of rockwork in sandy soil. Seed.

Campanula cæspitosa (*Tufted Harebell*).—*Campanula pumila*, *Hort.*—A very dwarf alpine herb, long known in our gardens, 3 to 6 in. high. *Flowers*, in summer; deep blue, 1 to 4 on each stem, drooping; divisions of the calyx narrow, erect, one-third the length of the corolla. *Leaves* of root crowded, on short stalks, obovate or kidney-shaped, those of stem narrower, toothed. There is a white variety, equally common. Central Europe, on mountains.——Front margin of the mixed border, rockwork, or as edging to beds, growing in almost any soil, but thriving best in a moist one. Division.

Campanula carpatica (*Carpathian Harebell*).—A dwarf, but noble kind, 6 to 15 in. high. *Flowers*, in summer; large and handsome, blue, about the size of those of the Peach-leaved Campanula, in loose panicles, on long stalks; divisions of the calyx nearly erect, two-thirds shorter than the broadly bell-shaped corolla. *Leaves*, smooth; lower ones somewhat kidney-shaped, toothed, and on long stalks; upper ones on short stalks, ovate-acute. There is a variety with white flowers, *C. carpatica alba*, and a light blue and white one, *C. carpatica bicolor*.——The rock-garden, mixed border, as an edging and bedding plant, and for naturalization in any soil. Seed and division.

Campanula cenisia (*Mont Cenis Harebell*).—A very dwarf tufted perennial, a few inches high, running much at the root. *Flowers*, in summer; blue, solitary, somewhat funnel-shaped, but open, and cut nearly to the base into 5 divisions; divisions of the calyx about half as long as the corolla. *Leaves*, entire; radical ones in rosettes, obovate, obtuse; stem-leaves ovate-oblong. Alps of Europe, at high elevations.—— Rockwork, in gritty or sandy soil. I have no experience of this as a border plant. In its native haunts it did not seem a very attractive kind. Division and seed.

Campanula Elatines (*Elatine Harebell*).—A dwarf downy kind, with ascending branching stems, 3 to 6 in. high. *Flowers*, in summer; pale bluish-purple, freely produced in loose racemes or panicles; divisions of calyx spreading, linear-lanceolate, about half as long as the corolla. *Leaves*, lower ones roundish; upper ones heart-shaped and more pointed all coarsely toothed. In shady rocky places on the Mountains of Italy.—— Rockwork, borders, old ruins, etc., in

CAMPANULA.

dryish or calcareous soils. Seed and division.

Campanula fragilis (*Fragile Harebell*).—A free-blooming and valuable dwarf kind, 3 to 6 in. high. *Flowers*, in summer; pale blue, in loose corymbs, or panicles; corolla broadly bell-shaped, about as long as the divisions of the calyx. *Leaves*, of root roundish-heart-shaped, toothed, on long stalks; stem-leaves smaller, somewhat lance-shaped, and on shorter stalks. *C. fragilis hirsuta* is a variety clothed with long hairs on all parts. South of Italy.——Rockwork, borders, stony banks, old ruins, etc., in lightish soil, dry in winter. Seed and division.

Campanula garganica (*Gargano Harebell*).—Another excellent dwarf species, with somewhat of the habit of the *Carpathian Harebell*, but smaller, 3 to 6 in. high. *Flowers*, in summer; bluish-purple with whitish centres, in loose racemes; corolla flat, 5-parted; divisions of calyx spreading, unequal. *Leaves*, of root kidney-shaped; of stem heart-shaped, all toothed and downy. Italy.——In interstices of the most vertical parts of rockwork, or borders in warm and well-drained positions; in a deep sandy loam. Seed or division.

Campanula glomerata (*Clustered C.*) —A showy native perennial, 1 to 2 feet high or more. *Flowers*, in summer; blue or violet, sessile, in terminal clusters on the branches and stem; corolla funnel-shaped, ½ in. or more long; divisions of calyx awl-shaped, obtuse, half the length of corolla. *Leaves*, ovate or heart-shaped; lower ones stalked; upper stem-leaves sessile. There are several varieties, the best being *C. glomerata alba*, a white one, and *C. glomerata plena*, a double one. Europe, Asia, and Britain.——Borders, margins of shrubberies, by walks, in any soil. Division or seed.

Campanula grandiflora (*Noble Hare bell*).— *Platycodon grandiflorum.*—A stately, smooth, glaucous plant, 20 in. to 2 ft. or more high. *Flowers*, late in summer; large, cup-shaped, deep blue, glistening as if varnished, in a very long panicled cluster, containing a few flowers, each flower 2 to 2½ in. across, erect, solitary, on a long naked stalk. *Leaves*, alternate or nearly opposite, stalkless, rather long, oval-acute, coarsely serrated; upper ones much the smallest. Siberia. —— Borders, and warm banks, in deep sandy loam. Careful division, or seeds, which do not ripen readily in this country.

Campanula grandis (*Great Bellflower*).—A very distinct and handsome species, with a simple, furrowed stem, 1½ to 2 ft. high. *Flowers*, early in summer; pale violet-blue, broadly bell-shaped, with large pointed divisions, axillary and alternate on the upper part of the stem. *Leaves*, long, sessile, lance-shaped, pointed, finely serrate, attenuated towards the base, and most numerous in the middle part of the stem. Siberia and Asia Minor. ——Mixed border, margins of shrubberies, and naturalization among the medium-sized herbaceous plants, long grass, etc. Division and seed.

Campanula hederacea (*Ivy Harebell*). —*Wahlenbergia hederacea.*—A very small, graceful, creeping kind, with almost thread-like branchlets. *Flowers*, in summer and autumn; faint bluish-purple, less than ½ in. long, on long slender stalks, drooping in the bud, and nearly erect when fully open; corolla 5-lobed, four times as long as the divisions of the calyx. *Leaves*, on long stalks, roundish-heart-shaped in outline, 5 to 7-lobed. Europe, America, and Britain in moist and boggy places.——In the artificial bog, or in moist spots near the rockwork or hardy fernery. Division.

G 2

CAMPANULA.

Campanula isophylla (*Ligurian Harebell*).—*C. floribunda.*—A free-flowering and showy dwarf kind, 3 to 6 in. high. *Flowers*, in summer; pale bright blue, with whitish centres, very numerous, erect, disposed in corymbs; style protruding; corolla flat, twice as long as the divisions of the calyx. *Leaves*, stalked, roundish-heart-shaped, crenately toothed, all about the same size. Italy.——The rock-garden, borders in light and calcareous soil, old chalk-pits, ruins, etc., in sunny spots. Seed or division.

Campanula lactiflora (*Milk-flowered C.*)—A vigorous and handsome herb, with branching stems, 2 to 4 ft. high. *Flowers*, in summer; milk-white, tinged with blue, rather large, and produced in loose leafy panicles; divisions of the calyx very broad, acute, half as long as the corolla, which opens wide, and has a short tube. *Leaves*, sessile, ovate-lanceolate, sharply serrated, pale underneath. Caucasus and Siberia.——Borders, fringes of shrubberies, or naturalization in any soil. Division.

Campanula latifolia (*Broad-leaved C.*)—A large and handsome native species, 3 to 6 ft. high, with simple stems and leaves, often 6 in. long and 2 in. broad. *Flowers*, in summer; blue, axillary, forming a leafy raceme; peduncles erect, 1-flowered; divisions of the calyx, tapering, broad at the base, 3 times shorter than the large bell-shaped corolla. *Leaves*, ovate-lance-shaped, pointed and toothed; root leaves stalked, upper ones stalkless, all narrowed at the base. *C. macrantha* is a variety with larger flowers, and with stem and leaves more hairy. There is also a white-flowered variety. Europe, Britain, and Central Asia.——Among the taller plants in the mixed border, on the margins of shrubberies, and by wood-walks, in any soil. Division.

Campanula muralis (*Wall Bell-flower*).—A very distinct and charming dwarf species, 6 to 9 in. high. *Flowers*, in summer; pale violet-blue, ¾ in. long and ½ in. across, abundantly produced in racemes; corolla funnel-shaped, three times as long as the divisions of the calyx. *Leaves*, nearly equal in size, roundish-heart-shaped, toothed, stalked. On walls in Dalmatia.—— The rock-garden, in positions where it may spread, like ivy, up the face of a steep part of the stone-work. In such a position only it is seen to best advantage. Division and seed.

Campanula nitida (*Shining Harebell*). —A slow-growing, stiff, and dwarf kind. *Flowers*, in summer; blue or white, resembling those of the Peach-leaved Campanula, but smaller and on very stiff stems, from 3 to 9 in. high. *Leaves*, in rosettes, leathery, very dark and shining green, oblong, crenate; those of the stem lance-shaped, almost entire. There is a double variety. North America. ——Borders and the rock-garden in free and open, but moist and firm soil. Division.

Campanula nobilis (*Long-flowered Harebell*).—A very noble and large-flowered species, 1 to 1½ ft. high. *Flowers*, whitish or reddish, crowded towards the ends of the branches, pendent, of an elongated bell-shape, smooth on the outside, hairy within. *Leaves*, hairy, serrate, green on both sides; the radical leaves on long stalks, deeply heart-shaped-ovate; the stem-leaves sessile, lanceolate. China.—— Borders and the rougher parts of rockwork, and naturalized on banks or slopes. Division and seed.

Campanula persicifolia (*Peach-leaved C.*)—One of our handsomest tall perennials, 1 to 3 ft. high. *Flowers*, in summer; blue, glistening, very large, broadly bell-shaped, terminal and axillary, 1 on each stalk. *Leaves*, smooth, stiff, 3 or 4 in. long and about ⅙ in. broad ; root-leaves lance-shaped, obovate ; those of the stem linear-lance-shaped, stalkless. There are several varieties double and single, both blue and white. Europe and Siberia.——Borders, fringes of shrubberies, and naturalization in ordinary soil. Division.

Campanula pulla (*Dark-coloured C.*) — A very charming dwarf alpine plant, 3 to 6 in. high. *Flowers*, in summer ; very dark purple, terminal ; corolla bell-shaped, large for the size of the plant. *Leaves*, smooth ; lower ones on short stalks, ovate-roundish ; upper ones stalkless, ovate-acute. Alps of Central Europe.—— The rock-garden in small carpets near the eye, margins of the choice mixed border, or in pans in light sandy loam or peaty soil. Division or seed.

Campanula pyramidalis (*Pyramidal Harebell*).—A noble and remarkable kind, 4 to 6 ft. high. *Flowers*, in summer ; pale blue, the stem sending out numerous flowering - branches from the bottom to the top, and forming quite a pyramidal raceme ; corolla bell-shaped. *Leaves*, glandularly toothed, smooth ; lower ones somewhat heart-shaped, on long stalks ; upper leaves stalkless, ovate lance-shaped. There is a white variety. Carniola and Dalmatia.——Borders, among the most stately and ornamental perennials, in sandy loam ; it is also grown largely in pots. Seed.

Campanula Raineri (*Rainer's Harebell*).—A very pretty, and as yet rare dwarf Harebell, 2 to 4 in. high. *Flowers*, in early summer ; blue, erect, 1 to 3 on each branch ; corolla funnel-shaped. *Leaves*, almost stalkless ; lower ones the smallest, obovate ; upper ones ovate, remotely serrated. Alps of Southern Europe.——The rock-garden on warm ledges, or the margin of the choice mixed border, in fine sandy soil, and in a warm position. Division or seed.

Campanula rotundifolia (*Harebell*). —A beautiful and well-known native plant, 6 to 18 in. high. *Flowers*, in summer ; deep blue, on stalks either one- or few-flowered, in a loose raceme or panicle ; corolla bell-shaped, gracefully drooping. *Leaves*, of root roundish-heart-shaped, toothed, mostly dying away by the time of flowering ; of stem narrow, lance-shaped, entire. There is a white variety also well worthy of cultivation. Common in most Northern regions.——Borders, the rougher parts of the rock-garden, slopes, and banks in any soil. Division and seed.

Campanula soldanellæflora (*Soldanella-flowered C.*) — A pretty and curious kind, with simple slender stems about 1 ft. high. *Flowers*, in summer ; semi-double, pale-blue, turbinate, with shallow marginal divisions very acutely pointed, axillary on thread-like stalks near the top of the stem. *Leaves*, long, linear, acute, sessile, distant.——The rock-garden, or borders in ordinary free soil. Division or cuttings.

Campanula speciosa (*Showy Harebell*).—Somewhat like the clustered Harebell, but with larger flowers, and 9 in. to 2 ft. high. *Flowers*, in summer ; deep blue, or purplish, sometimes reddish outside, funnel-shaped, in large clustered heads. *Leaves*, of root heart-shaped, on long stalks ; those of stem stalkless ; stem hairy, square, two sides grooved. Siberia.——Borders, fringes of shrubberies, and naturalization in ordinary soil. Division and seed.

Campanula Trachelium (*Nettle-leaved C.*)—A vigorous and handsome species, with coarsely-toothed leaves, which when young resemble those of the common Nettle, and angled stems, 3 or 4 ft. high. *Flowers*, in summer ;

blue, large, in terminal leafy racemes, 2 or 3 together, sometimes solitary; calyx very hairy. *Leaves*, lower ones heart-shaped, on long stalks; upper ones oblong, stalkless. There are three desirable varieties in cultivation—*C. Trachelium alba*, single white, *C. Trachelium alba plena*, double white, and *C. Trachelium plena*, the double variety of the common form. Europe, Britain, and Asia.——Borders and shrubberies, in any soil. Division and seed.

Campanula turbinata (*Vase Harebell*).—A sturdy little kind, 3 to 8 in. high with very handsome flowers, huge for the size of the plant. *Flowers*, in summer; deep purple, nearly 2 in. across, cup-shaped. *Leaves*, rigid, of a greyish green, toothed and pointed, with heart-shaped bases, in stiff tufts, 2 to 3 in. high. Mountains of Transylvania.——The rock-garden, margins of mixed borders, and naturalization on bare sunny banks and slopes in light soil. Seed and division.

Campanula Wanneri(*Wanner's Harebell*).—A distinct and handsome Harebell, 6 to 10 in. high. *Flowers*, in May; handsome dark blue, tubular-bell-shaped, 1½ in. long, drooping, with very short, apiculate segments; peduncles long, 1-flowered, axillary and terminal; sepals ¼ in. long, widely separated, triangular, pointed, ciliated. *Leaves*, lanceolate, unequally toothed, the lower ones decurrent on long leaf-stalks. Native of Transylvania and the Banat Alps.——The rock-garden till more plentiful; at present it is very seldom seen. It will probably prove an excellent border plant. Seed and division.

Campanula Zoysii (*Zoysi's Harebell*).—A small tufted herb, with erect stems, 4 to 9 in. high. *Flowers*, in summer; pale blue, bell-shaped, drooping, 1 to 3 on each stem. *Leaves*, entire, those of the root crowded, stalked, ovate blunt, stem-leaves obovate-lance-shaped and linear. Alps of Styria, Carniola and Carinthia.——The rock-garden and borders, in sandy soil. Seed and division.

Cardamine latifolia (*Broad-leaved C.*) —Resembling our Cuckoo Flower; 8 to 16 in. high. *Flowers*, in summer; large, lilac, in corymbs; sepals oval, loose, one-third the length of the petals. *Leaves*, rather thick, usually fringed, pinnate, all having a very large, roundish, terminal segment, sinuated, and frequently heart-shaped at the base; lateral segments oval or rounded, gradually diminishing, 6 or 8 in number on the leaves of the middle of the stem, and only 2 on the upper leaves. Pyrenees and South of France, on the banks of streams.—— The bog-bed, moist spots near rockwork, and on borders. Division and seed.

Cardamine pratensis (*Cuckoo Flower*). —One of our commonest and most admired wild-flowers, 9 to 18 in. high. *Flowers*, in spring and early summer; pink, white, or purplish, in a terminal cluster. *Leaves*, pinnate; divisions of the lower ones roundish; of stem ones narrow, lance-shaped, entire. There is a double variety. Europe, Northern Asia, and America, also common in Britain. —— The single kind is too common to need cultivation; the double kind is a pretty subject for the spring garden and for borders. Division.

Cardamine rotundifolia (*Round-leaved C.*)—Six inches high. *Flowers*, in early summer; white, small, in a terminal raceme. *Leaves*, smooth, roundish, slightly toothed, stalked; stems procumbent. On rocks by rivulets on the high mountains of North America.——Borders, in any soil. Division and seed.

Cardamine trifolia (*Three-leaved C.*) —A dwarf plant, with neat trifoliate leaves and creeping runners, 3 to 6 in. high. *Flowers*, in spring; white, in a terminal cluster, on nearly naked stems. *Leaves,* smoothish, ternate; leaflets, rhomboid-roundish, toothed. On shady parts of mountains in Central Europe.——Borders, the rougher parts of the rock-garden, and naturalization on bare banks. It thrives anywhere, but flowers best in a moist peaty or fine sandy soil. Division.

Carduus acaulis (*Dwarf Thistle*)— *Cnicus acaulis.* — A nearly stemless thistle. *Flowers,* in summer; purple, in large heads, stalkless, or rarely on stalks a few inches long. *Leaves,* very prickly, smooth, pinnatifid. Europe and Britain. —— Margins of shrubberies, or bare banks in semi-wild places, in ordinary soil. Seed.

Carduus eriophorus (*Woolly Thistle*). —A noble thistle, growing 3 to 4 ft. high, very stout and much-branched. *Flowers,* in summer; purple, in very large and handsome globular heads. *Leaves,* downy and cottony underneath, hairy and green above, the narrow lobes fiercely armed with prickles; lower ones, 1 to 2 ft. long. A native of Southern England and many parts of Europe.——In open spots in woods, by wood-walks, margins of shrubberies, or among vigorous herbs in the subtropical garden, in any soil. Seed and division.

Carlina acanthifolia (*Stemless C.*)— Resembling the Dwarf Thistle, but differing from that species by being quite stemless, and with leaves larger, more cottony, and less cut. *Flowers,* in summer; yellow, very large, solitary. *Leaves,* stalked, pinnatifid; segments spiny, toothed. Alps of Carniola.——By wood-walks, margins of shrubberies, or naturalization on warm sunny banks, in sandy loam. Seed.

Cassia marilandica (*American Senna*). — A noble-looking herbaceous plant, 3¼ ft. to 6 ft. high. *Flowers,* in autumn; bright yellow, in axillary clusters; petals 5, narrowly-obovate, about ½ in. long; sepals 5, unequal, nearly free; stamens 10. *Leaves,* alternate, pinnate; leaflets opposite equal, oval-oblong, acute. N. America.——The back portions of borders among the taller perennials, and in isolated tufts in the pleasure-ground, thriving best in a deep warm loam. Seed or division.

Catananche cærulea (*Blue C.*)—A handsome border-plant, about 2 ft. high. *Flowers,* in summer; fine blue, each stalk being terminated by a single head; rays indented at the ends; scales of the involucre ovate. *Leaves,* hoary, narrow, lance-shaped, with one or two little teeth on each side, sometimes pinnatifid at the base. South of France and Italy.——Borders, margins of shrubberies, or naturalization, in a well-drained warm soil. Seed.

Centaurea babylonica (*Babylonian C.*).—A very tall and stately perennial, with silvery leaves, growing from 6 to 10 ft. high. *Flowers,* in summer; yellow, close to the tall stem. *Leaves,* as white as those of *C. ragusina;* of root, lance-shaped-ovate, stalked and with a few small teeth; stem-leaves narrower, lance-shaped, decurrent. The Levant. —— Borders and margins of shrubberies, or in groups of silvery-leaved plants. It is chiefly valuable for the effect of its large silvery leaves, and it may be well, to improve these, to prevent it from flowering. Allowed to flower, it is fitted for association with the tallest and most vigorous perennials; in half-wild places. Seed.

Centaurea dealbata (*Whitened C*).— A very hardy perennial with graceful and somewhat silvery leaves, 15 to 18 in. high. *Flowers,* in summer; rose-coloured. *Leaves,* smooth above and covered with white hairs underneath; radical leaves stalked, pinnate, with obovate lobes, coarsely toothed, often auricled at the base; stem-leaves pinnate, with oblong-lanceolate lobes. Mountain pastures of the Caucasus.——Borders, or naturalization in any soil. Division.

Centaurea macrocephala (*Great-headed C.*) —Rather a coarse perennial. *Flowers*, late in summer; yellow, larger than a hen's egg; scales of involucrum jagged. Stem simple, hollow and thickened under the flower. *Leaves*, oblong-lanceolate, shortly decurrent, undivided, rough, somewhat serrated, ending in a short abrupt sharp point. Iberia, on hills and mountains.—— Naturalization in any soil. Division or seed.

Centaurea montana (*Mountain C.*)— A handsome border plant, 1 to 2½ ft. high, with slightly cottony leaves, and flowers resembling those of the Corn blue-bottle (*C. Cyanus*), but larger. *Flowers*, in early summer; blue, large and handsome; florets deeply cut into 4 or 5 segments, 12 or 13 in each head. *Leaves*, lance-shaped, entire, decurrent; stem mostly simple, but sometimes with a branch or two. There is a white and a red variety in cultivation. Europe. —— Borders, margins of shrubberies, or naturalization in any soil. Division and seed.

Centaurea uniflora (*One-flowered C.*) —A distinct and ornamental mountain plant, as yet not common in our gardens, 9 to 15 in. high. *Flowers*, in summer; purple, roundish, terminal, nearly sessile among the upper leaves, the unopened heads seeming covered with a dark net-work, from being overlapped with the hairy points of the scales. *Leaves*, small, white and downy; lower ones oblong-lanceolate, toothed; upper ones, lanceolate, entire. Mountain pastures in S. Europe —— Borders and the rock-garden, or naturalization on slopes, in sandy or gritty soil. Division and seed.

Centranthus ruber (*Red Valerian*).— A showy and useful perennial, 1 to 3 ft. high. *Flowers*, in summer; red, in dense cymes forming a handsome corymbose panicle. *Leaves*, lance-shaped, smooth, entire, and of a glaucous hue; stem somewhat shrubby at the base. There is a variety with white flowers. S. Europe.——Banks, on which the plant lives long and flowers freely, on borders, margins of shrubberies, stony places, etc., in any soil. Seed.

Cerastium alpinum (*Alpine C.*)—An interesting native alpine plant, with stems 2 to 4 in. high. *Flowers*, in summer; white, rather freely produced on somewhat hairy stalks, 1 or 2 on each; calyx hairy; petals twice as long as the calyx. *Leaves*, ovate, small, nearly smooth, or clothed with long woolly hairs. A very variable species, sometimes green, and at others quite hoary. Pyrenees and Britain. ——Rockwork, and among the smallest flowers in borders, in ordinary free garden soil. Division.

Cerastium Biebersteinii (*Bieberstein's C.*) — A silvery-foliaged mountain plant, now pretty well known in gardens, 6 in. high. *Flowers*, in early summer; white, larger than those of *C. tomentosum;* stalks erect, dichotomous. *Leaves*, woolly, ovate-lance-shaped; stems branching. The higher mountains of Tauria. —— Borders, edging, rootwork, rough rockwork, and naturalization on banks and slopes, in any soil. Division.

Cerastium Boissieri (*Boissier's C.*)— A handsome new silvery kind, 4 in. to 1 ft. high. *Flowers*, large, arranged in a rather regular dichotomous cyme on the top of the stem; anthers yellow; bracts oblong-lanceolate, scarious on the margin, often ciliated. *Leaves*, all sessile, generally ovate-lanceolate (more rarely linear), acute, entire. *Rhizome*, creeping extensively, emitting numerous roots from the under side of its joints, and stems from the upper side. A species containing many forms, and found in hilly parts of Spain.——Useful for the same purposes as our now common silvery *Cerastiums*, but till plentiful it should be grown in the rock-garden, or choice border, in well-drained soil. Division.

Cerastium grandiflorum (*Large-flowered C.*)—Like *C. tomentosum*, but less hoary, and with leaves narrower and more acute, and a profusion of flowers; stems 6 in. high. *Flowers*, in summer; white, large, and showy, 7 to 15 on erect stalks. *Leaves*, narrow, acute, hoary, or woolly, with somewhat revolute margins. Hungary and Iberia.—— Rough rockwork, borders, naturalization on banks, and among dwarf vegetation in open spaces, in any soil. Division.

Cerastium tomentosum (*Common Woolly C.*)—A silvery plant, very well known in gardens; 6 in. high. *Flowers*, in early summer; white, in forked cymes, on erect stalks. *Leaves*, oblong-spathulate, upper ones lance-shaped. Southern Europe.——Largely used in many places as an edging to the summer flower-beds, and highly useful for borders, running over rough rockwork, bare banks, or naturalization amongst dwarf vegetation, in any soil. Division.

Cheiranthus Cheiri (*Common Wallflower*).—A sweet old plant long cultivated in our gardens, and naturalized on old ruins, walls, etc., 1 to 2 ft. high. *Flowers*, in spring and early summer; variable in colour. *Leaves*, lance-shaped, quite entire. Abundant in many parts of Europe, on old walls, and stony places.—— Borders, banks, slopes, etc., particularly the various handsome double kinds, which become shrubby on banks and dry slopes. Seed or cuttings, the choice double kinds by cuttings.

Cheiranthus Marshallii (*Marshall's C.*)—A half-shrubby plant, with erect, angular branches, clothed, like the leaves, with adpressed forked hairs, 1 to 1½ ft. high. *Flowers*, in spring or early summer; nearly ¾ in. across, deep clear orange at first, becoming rather paler, rather freely produced in a terminal raceme; petals, with a roundish spreading limb. *Leaves*, crowded at the lower part of the stems, more distant upwards, and on the flowering stems; upper ones narrowly lance-shaped, with a few teeth; lower ones tapering downwards into a narrowly-winged, stalk-like base, becoming more or less spoon-shaped. This is said to be a hybrid between *Cheiranthus ochroleucus* and *Erysimum Peroffskianum*.——Borders and the rock-garden, in light, well-drained soil. It is increased by cuttings, and a young stock should be kept up as it is not perennial, and is apt to perish in winter.

Chelidonium japonicum (*Japan C.*) —A poppy-like plant, handsomer than our allied Greater Celandine, 1 to 2 ft. high. *Flowers*, in early summer; yellow, large, axillary, stalked; calyx smooth; corolla rather larger than the calyx. *Leaves*, pale underneath, ovate, pinnate; leaflets ovate-oblong, acute, on very short stalks. Japan.—— Borders, margins of shrubberies, or naturalization, in ordinary soil. Division and seed.

Chelidonium majus (*Greater Celandine*).—A well-known native plant, 1 to 2 ft. high. *Flowers*, throughout the summer; yellow, 3 to 6 together in a loose umbel; peduncles hairy with a roundish bract at the base. *Leaves*, thin, pale underneath, pinnate; leaflets roundish, coarsely toothed. There is a cut-leaved variety very distinct in aspect from the common one. Britain and Europe generally. ——Only worthy of a place among wild plants, on the margins of ditches, stony places, etc. Division or seed.

Chelone Lyoni (*Lyon's C.*)—A very showy perennial, allied to *C. obliqua*, and differing chiefly by being slightly covered with hairs, with an erect, slightly-branched stem, 3 to 4 ft. high. *Flowers*, in summer; purple, in dense terminal spikes. *Leaves*, stalked, cordate-ovate, serrated, slightly ciliated at the margin. Upper Carolina and Georgia.——A fine plant for borders, in sandy loam. Division.

Chelone obliqua (*Oblique C.*) — Another handsome plant, but not so vigorous as *C. Lyoni*, 2 to 3 ft. high. *Flowers*, in summer; purple, large, in close terminal spikes. *Leaves*, stalked, opposite, ovate-lance-shaped, unequally serrated, very smooth. Banks of rivers and swamps in North America.——Similar uses and treatment to the preceding.

Chimaphila maculata (*Spotted C.*)— A dwarf, and handsome, little shrubby evergreen, with leathery, shining leaves pleasingly variegated, 3 to 6 in. high. *Flowers*, in summer; whitish, on slender red stems, bearing 2 or 3 flowers. *Leaves*, stiff, lance-shaped, 2 to 3 in. long, and ½ in. broad at the base, ending with acute points, the margins rigidly serrate, red on the under side, and beautifully veined with white on the upper one. In shady, sandy, or gravelly woods, from Canada to Carolina.——Half shady and moist nooks, in or near the rock-garden or hardy fernery, in moist, fibry, vegetable earth. Careful division.

Chimaphila umbellata (*Umbellated C.*)—A dwarf, slightly shrubby evergreen, 3 to 6 in. high. *Flowers*, in summer; greenish-white, tinged with red, 5 or 6 in an umbel; stems pubescent. *Leaves*, opposite, or in whorls, wedge-shaped, or lance-shaped, narrow at the base, serrate, shining, stiff, dark green on the upper, and pale green on the under side. Europe, Asia, and North America.——The same positions and treatment as for *C. maculata*.

Chrysocoma latifolia (*Broad-leaved C.*)—A vigorous-growing plant, with an angular, furrowed, downy stem, 3½ ft. high, branching above. *Flowers*, in autumn; bright golden-yellow, numerous, in large terminal corymbose clusters. *Leaves* of the stem oval-oblong, pointed, rough, sessile; radical leaves very large, oval-oblong, obtuse, on long, furrowed stalks, which overlap each other at the base. S. Africa. —— Borders, and naturalization in ordinary soil. Division.

Chrysopsis Mariana (*Golden Aster*).— A showy composite, 6 in. to 1 ft. high. *Flowers*, late in autumn; aster-like, of a rich, deep yellow, arranged in a simple corymb. *Leaves*, sessile, oblong-elliptical, the lower ones nearly ovate, obtuse, distantly toothed, covered with a loose, somewhat silky down, growing in dense tufts. Found in dry, sandy places in Carolina and Georgia in the United States.—— Borders, in sandy loam. Division and seed.

Cichorium Intybus (*Chicory*.)— A well-known native plant, a good deal used in commerce and as a salad, 2 to 5 ft. high. *Flowers*, in July and August; numerous, handsome, bright blue, axillary, sessile, 1 to 1¼ in. across, growing in pairs, or three together. *Leaves*, lower ones oblanceolate, runcinate, pinnatifid, or dentate; upper stem-leaves lanceolate, half stem-clasping, broadly toothed or entire, all glandular, ciliated. Britain and various parts of Europe, in waste places, on a gravelly or chalky soil.——Is worth introducing as a wild plant in districts where it is not found native. Division and seed.

Cineraria macrophylla (*Great-leaved C.*) — *Ligularia macrophylla*. — A stately plant, 4 to 6 ft. high. *Flowers*, in summer; yellow, numerous, in an elongated, crowded, leafless, branching panicle; florets of the ray 2 to 3; florets of the disk 6 to 7; pedicels rather scaly. Lower *leaves* elliptical, narrowed into an ovate, margined footstalk, from 1½ to 2 ft. long including the footstalk, and 5 to 9 in. broad, indented with cartilaginous teeth; upper leaves clasping the stem, glaucous. Altai Mountains.——Associated with the finer and stronger hardy foliage-plants in rich, deep soil; also as an isolated specimen in the turf, by wood-walks. Seed and careful division.

Cineraria maritima (*Silvery C.*)— A half-shrubby, silvery plant, 18 in. to 2½ ft. high. *Flowers*, late in summer; yellow, in compound panicled corymbs; involucrum with a few small bracts at the base. *Leaves*, stalked, smooth above, covered with white down underneath, pinnatifid, with from 4 to 6 oblong, obtuse, three-lobed segments on each side. Stem downy, like the under side of the leaves. South of France. A new variety with broader foliage (*C. acanthifolia*), is now in cultivation.—— Borders, fringes of shrubbery, rough, rocky places, etc.; it is much used as an edging and bedding plant. Cuttings and seed.

Clematis calycina (*Winter Clematis.*) —*C. balearica.*— A very elegant, hardy climber, attaining a height of 12 ft. or more. *Flowers*, cream-colour, about 2 in. across, very numerous, growing in pairs from the axils of the many-jointed stems, and appearing in mild districts, through the winter and spring. *Leaves*, trifoliate, stalked, in partial whorls at the joints of the stem; leaflets variously lobed. Island of Minorca.——

Bowers, trellises, clambering over rough shrubs and hedges, and also on rough rockwork. Division, cuttings, or seed.

Clematis campaniflora (*Bell-flowered C.*) — A free and graceful climbing plant, growing 6 to 12 ft. high. *Flowers*, in early summer; delicate light purple; sepals half-spreading, widening at the base; peduncles 1-flowered. *Leaves*, biternately decompound, leaflets entire or 3-lobed. Portugal.——Creeping over old stumps, bowers, arches, and naturalization in hedgerows, on banks, and in very rough rocky places, in any soil. Seed and division.

Clematis erecta (*Erect C.*)—An herbaceous perennial, with a straight, erect, furrowed, light-green stem, about 3 ft. high. *Flowers*, in summer; large, white, on long fine stalks, in terminal umbel-like clusters. *Leaves*, opposite, large, pinnate; leaflets stalked, oval-acute, with downy petioles. Austria.——Borders, margins of shrubberies, naturalization in semi-wild places, in any soil. Division.

Clematis Flammula (*Sweet C.*)—A vigorous climbing shrub, the stems attaining in cultivation a length of from 12 to 30 ft. *Flowers*, in summer and autumn; white, very fragrant, in panicles; peduncles sometimes simple and sometimes branched. *Leaves*, pinnate, smooth; leaflets, entire or 3-lobed, roundish, oval, or linear, somewhat acute. Southern Europe and Northern Africa.—— Similar positions to the preceding, and worthy of universal culture. Seed or layers.

Clematis integrifolia (*Entire-leaved C.*)—A very ornamental dwarf herb, with entire leaves, 1 to 2 ft. high. *Flowers*, in summer; purple; peduncles long, terminal, usually 1-flowered, sometimes branched in the upper axils; sepals leathery; anthers long, yellow; stamens forming a kind of pitcher-shaped centre. *Leaves*, opposite, smooth, ovate - lance-shaped; margins hairy; stem slightly fistulose. Hungary and Germany.——Borders, banks or slopes, in good sandy loam. Seed or division.

Clematis lanuginosa (*Woolly C.*)— A noble species, 3 to 6½ ft. high. *Flowers*, early in summer; of a lilac-blue, 6 to 7 inches across, with 4 to 6 spreading sepals. *Leaves*, simple or with three almost leathery leaflets, quite woolly when young, and continuing so on the under side when fully grown. The flower-stalks and buds are also woolly. There is a variety, *C. l. pallida*, with paler and still larger flowers. China.——Against south walls, on sunny banks, and in the rock-garden, planted so that its shoots may fall over the faces of sunny rocks, in rich light and deep but thoroughly-drained soil. Seed and layers.

[The numerous fine hybrids lately raised rival this (from which most of them are descended) in size, and are worthy of universal culture, placed and treated as recommended for *C. lanuginosa*. They may be most effectively used as bedding plants, and trained over supports of various kinds, but they will be seen to greatest advantage in the large rock-garden and on slopes and banks in very deep, good soil, the shoots being allowed to trail freely and naturally down.]

Clematis montana (*Mountain C.*)— A very ornamental, free-flowering, climbing shrub, with stems 10 to 20 ft. long. *Flowers*, in early summer; white, large, resembling in size and form those of *Anemone sylvestris*, several borne together, or one upon each slender upright stalk. *Leaves*, ternate or trifid, smooth; leaflets oblong, pointed, toothed. Himalayan Mountains.——For covering walls, bowers, old stumps, trailing over rude wigwams with a framework of rough branches, and naturalization on wild slopes, hedgerows, etc. Layers, and seed. Easily obtained in nurseries.

Clematis tubulosa (*Tubular C.*)—A singular kind, 2 ft. to 32 in. high. *Flowers*, in autumn; blue, with a long slender tube, of a deeper colour than the divisions of the flower, very much resembling in shape the flower of a common Hyacinth. *Leaves*, broad, with three broadly oval - rounded leaflets; stem erect, almost woody. Native of China.——Borders, or margins of shrubberies; of most interest in the botanical or curious collection. Multiplied only by division or cuttings.

Clematis Viorna (*Leathery-flowered C.*) —A climbing shrub, attaining a height of 8 to 12 ft. *Flowers*, in summer; dark blue, or purple outside, yellow within, large, drooping, bell-shaped; peduncles 1-flowered; sepals leathery, pointed, and turned back at the apex; stamens scarcely appearing beyond the sepals. *Leaves*, smooth, pinnate; leaflets entire, oval - lance-shaped, 3-lobed or ternate; floral ones entire. Hedges and copses, Virginia and Carolina.——Borders, rockwork, etc., also naturalization in copses, hedge-rows, and on wild banks. Seed and division.

Clematis Viticella (*Vine-bower C.*)— A climbing shrub, with very slender branching stems, growing to a length of 12 or 15 ft. *Flowers*, in summer; blue or purple; peduncles longer than the leaves, 1-flowered; sepals blunt, thin. *Leaves*, entire, or ternately decompound; leaflets entire. There are several varieties in cultivation, the white one and the double one being the most distinct from the ordinary form. S. Europe.——Similar uses, etc. to those for the preceding kind.

Colchicum alpinum (*Alpine Meadow Saffron*).—An interesting and pretty alpine bulb, a little over 1 in. high. *Flowers*, in autumn; bell-shaped, of a deep rose-colour, one bloom from each bulb. *Leaves*, linear, erect, 2 to 2½ in. long, narrowed at the base, appearing in February and March. *Bulb* small. Alps of Europe.——The rock- and choice bulb-garden, in deep sandy loam; also for the margins of the mixed border, and as edgings in the spring garden, when sufficiently plentiful. Separation of the bulbs, and seed.

Colchicum Bivonæ (*Bivona's C.*)—A pretty and at present uncommon kind. *Flowers*, in autumn; radical, elegantly marked with alternate chequers of white and purple, chess-board fashion; petals elliptical-oblong. *Leaves*, linear, grooved, not wavy at the edges. Native of Sicily, the kingdom of Naples, Greece, and Portugal.——The rock- and choice bulb-garden, at least till more plentiful, and in deep sandy loam. Separation of the bulbs, and seed.

Colchicum autumnale (*Meadow Saffron.*)—A well-known plant. *Flowers*, in autumn; numerous, bright purple, with very long tubes, appearing before the leaves. *Leaves*, erect, lanceolate, dark green, smooth, 1 ft. long, and often an inch or more broad. *Bulb*, large, egg-shaped, dark brown on the outside. There are numerous varieties of this plant. Many parts of Europe, in moist meadows.——Borders, and as edgings to beds of autumn flowers, and occasionally dotted over the grass; it may be often seen in a wild state. It does best in a moist soil, but thrives in all ordinary garden soils. Separation of bulbs.

Colchicum byzantinum (*Byzantine C.*) —A fine species. *Flowers*, in autumn; larger than those of *C. autumnale*, of a pale rose-colour, with elliptical-oblong segments, 12 to 15 from each bulb. *Leaves*, broad, undulating, plaited, dark green, 4 or 5 in number. *Bulb*, very large, roundish, depressed. The Levant, in the vicinity of Constantinople. —— Borders, and the bulb- and rock-garden, in good deep soil. This, like the preceding and following kinds, is very suitable for association with the autumn-blooming crocuses and other plants flowering at that season. Separation of the bulbs, and seed.

Colchicum variegatum (*Variegated Meadow Saffron*).—*C. Agrippinæ.*—A prettily chequered kind. *Flowers*, in autumn; rose-colour, marked with purple-violet chequers like *C. Bivonæ*; petals lanceolate, acute. *Leaves*, oblong-lanceolate, grooved, wavy on the edges. *Bulb* similar to that of *C. autumnale*. Native of the Islands of the Archipelago, and also found in Asia Minor, in the neighbourhood of Smyrna.——Borders, edgings, and the lower parts of the rock-garden. This thrives everywhere as freely as the common *Meadow Saffron*. Separation of the bulbs.

Commelina cœlestis (*Blue Spiderwort*).—A very pretty vividly-coloured plant, 1½ to 2 ft. high. *Flowers*, in summer; small, of a deep sky-blue, grouped on the ends of axillary footstalks, and enveloped by a rather inflated leafy spathe, from which they issue in succession; the unequal petal oval or roundish, almost sessile, and frequently falling before the other two. *Leaves*, oval-lanceolate-acute, sheathing at the base, sessile, fringed at the edges. *Root*, tuberous, swollen, fasciculate. There are two pretty varieties, *C. c. alba* and *C. c. variegata*. Mexico.——Sunny borders, in very light, warm soil, or on slopes and banks having the same advantages. Division and seed.

Convallaria bifolia (*Two-leaved C.*) —*Smilacina bifolia.*—A pretty and

CONVALLARIA — CONVOLVULUS.

interesting little plant, 6 to 8 in. high. *Flowers*, in summer; small, with reflexed segments, white, fragrant, on long pedicels, in a rather dense, terminal raceme, resembling a spike. *Leaves*, 2, on short stalks, oval, deeply heart-shaped, pointed, marked with a fine tracery of nerves and veins. *Berries*, yellow, with brown spots. Native of most parts of Europe, in low meadows and damp woods.——Borders, or the rock-garden, in almost any kind of soil. Occurring only in one or two places in Britain, it is well worthy of being naturalized in our pleasure-grounds and woods, either in open shady or half-shady places. Division.

Convallaria majalis (*Lily of the Valley*).—A well-known and favourite old plant, 6 in. to 1 ft. high. *Flowers*, in spring; small, white, bell-shaped, very fragrant, hanging in a graceful raceme at the end of an arching flower-stem. *Leaves*, 2, radical, on long stalks, elliptical-oblong, marked with a delicate tracery of nerves and veins. Native of most parts of Europe, Siberia, Caucasus, and N. America, in woods and thickets. The principal varieties are, one with gold striped leaves, one with pink, and one with double flowers.——Borders, fringes of shrubberies, etc., best in sandy loam. The Lily of the Valley is worthy of being abundantly planted in our pleasure-grounds and woods, where it does not already occur wild, and in all sorts of positions. Division.

Convolvulus althæoides (*Mallow Bindweed*). — A climbing perennial, with stems about 3 ft. long, and silvery leaves. *Flowers*, in summer; pale rose; peduncles 2-flowered. *Leaves*, heart-shaped, lower ones entire, upper deeply cut into narrow spreading segments, shining and soft. S. Europe.——Naturalized on dry sandy slopes and banks, as a border plant trained over stakes, or on rootwork or rough rockwork; always in light soil. Division.

Convolvulus bryoniæfolius (*Bryony-leaved Bindweed*).—A climbing perennial, with leaves very hairy on both sides. *Flowers*, in summer; dark rose or reddish purple, large; peduncles axillary, 1-flowered; sepals ovate, acute. *Leaves*, varying in shape but mostly heart-shaped, divided into 7 unequal lobes, the centre one the largest; the stalks usually as long as the leaves and channelled on the upper side. China.——Similar uses and positions to those for the preceding kind. Division or seed.

Convolvulus cantabricus (*Cantabrian Bindweed*.)—A graceful kind, 1 ft. to 16 in. high. *Flowers*, in summer; numerous, rose, pale pink, or flesh-coloured, silky on the outside, on long, leafy, loosely-panicled stalks. *Leaves*, sessile, linear-lanceolate, acute, 1 to 1¼ in. long. Stem ascending, not twining, branching, covered with long, spreading, whitish hairs; seed vessel hairy. South of France. Scarcely hardy on cold soils——Borders, warm banks, or in the wilder parts of the rock-garden, in sandy, light, dry soil. Seed.

Convolvulus Cneorum (*Silvery Bindweed*.)—A white-leaved, small, evergreen shrub, 1 to 3 ft. high. *Flowers*, in summer; pale rose, hairy outside, produced in clusters at the ends of the short stalks. *Leaves*, silky, lance-shaped-obovate, blunt, about 2 in. long, and ¼ in. broad. Southern Europe.——Sunny parts of the rock-garden, and on warm banks, or old chalkpits, always in light, warm soil. This pleasing plant perishes in winter, on cold soils. Seed and cuttings.

Convolvulus lineatus (*Pigmy Convolvulus*).—A very diminutive and pretty plant, 3 to 6 in. high. *Flowers*, in summer; deep rose or flesh-coloured, more than an inch across; stalks axillary, solitary, mostly 2-flowered. *Leaves*, lance-shaped, stalked, acute, very silky. Southern Europe.—— The rock-garden, in level spots, near or beneath the eye, the margins of the mixed border, or naturalization on very bare banks. It will live in the coldest clays, but thrives and flowers best in a very free sandy loam. Division.

Convolvulus mauritanicus (*Blue Rock Bindweed.*)—A prostrate, twining plant, with very slender, almost thread-like stems. *Flowers*, in summer; small, blue, with a white throat and yellow anthers, handsome, about an inch across, borne one to three on each flower-stalk; calyx villous, with 5 linear oblong divisions, two of them a little smaller than the rest. *Leaves*, nearly round, or ovate, especially the lower ones, never cordate, 1 to 1½ in. long, alternate, in two rows, on very short stalks; whole plant covered with soft white hairs, scarcely perceptible to the naked eye. North Africa, near Constantine.——The rock-garden, and raised borders, always in sunny, somewhat raised positions, and in sandy, well-drained soil. Division or cuttings.

Convolvulus Soldanella (*Sea Bindweed.*)— A distinct - looking, trailing kind, with roundish fleshy leaves. *Flowers*, in summer; pale red, large, handsome, and freely produced on angled stalks. *Leaves*, small, thick, broadly rounded, or kidney-shaped, entire, or slightly angled. Europe, Britain and Tauria.—— The rock-garden, planted so that its shoots may droop over the brows of rocks. It will also thrive and look very well in borders, in ordinary soil. Division.

Coptis trifolia (*Goldthread.*) — A dwarf, neat and pretty evergreen bog-plant, 3 to 4 in. high. *Flowers*, early in summer; white, 1 on each slender stalk, springing from the root. *Leaves*, trifoliate, shining; leaflets wedge-shaped, rounded at the end, about 1 in. long, toothed, obscurely 3-lobed. It derives its common name from its long, bright-yellow, fibrous roots. Northern parts of Europe, Asia, and America.——Moist peat or very sandy, moist soil, on the margins of beds of American plants; in moist spots on rockwork, or in the artificial bog. Propagated by division.

Coreopsis auriculata (*Eared C.*)—A showy perennial, 16 in. to 2 ft. high. *Flowers*, in summer; solitary, on long stalks; florets of the ray yellow, marked with a few purple or reddish-brown spots on the claw, toothed; disk yellow. *Leaves*, sometimes entire, sometimes 3-lobed, the two lower lobes being auricled; the flower-stems are also furnished with a circlet of small, oval, acute, spreading leaves. N. America.—— Borders in ordinary good garden soil. Division or seed.

Coreopsis grandiflora (*Large-flowered C.*)—A showy perennial, with deeply cut leaves, 3 to 4 ft. high. *Flowers*, in summer; bright yellow, 1 on each lengthened peduncle; florets of the ray, 5-toothed, so deeply cut as to give them a fringe-like appearance. *Leaves*, opposite, connate, nearly stalkless, fringed with hair at the base. North America.——Borders, in ordinary soil. Division or seed.

Coreopsis lanceolata (*Lance-leaved C.*)—A handsome kind, 1 to 3 ft. high. *Flowers*, nearly all the summer; bright yellow, 2 to 3 in. across, mostly one on each long stalk; florets of the ray 4-toothed. *Leaves*, lance-shaped, entire, fringed with hairs; upper ones slightly connate at the base; stem sometimes branched at the base. N. America. ——Borders, or margins of shrubberies, in light, well-drained soil. Division or cuttings.

Coreopsis præcox (*Early C.*)—A very charming plant, seldom seen in cultivation, 2 ft. or upwards in height. *Flowers*, in summer; large, orange-yellow, arranged in a corymbose panicle. *Leaves*, opposite, entire or ternate, with narrow linear leaflets of a vivid green colour. N. America.——Borders, in good free soil. Division and seed.

Coreopsis tenuifolia (*Slender-leaved C.*)—A very graceful and ornamental plant, with a furrowed branching stem, from 1 to 2 ft. high. *Flowers*, in summer; rich golden yellow, 1¼ in. across, numerous, terminal, erect, solitary on the ends of the many subdivisions of the branches. *Leaves*, very much divided into narrow linear segments, and produced in whorls at the joints of the stem and branches. N. America.——Borders, and margins of shrubberies, in sandy loam. Division or seed.

Coreopsis verticillata (*Whorled-leaved C.*)—A slender but showy species, 2 to 4 ft. high. *Flowers*, in summer; bright yellow, 2 to 3 in. across; florets of the ray entire. *Leaves*, slender, in whorls, stalkless, divided into three very narrow, linear segments. N. America.——Borders, in sandy loam. Division.

Coris monspeliensis (*Montpellier C.*)—A rather pretty dwarf branching plant, about 6 in. high, usually biennial in our gardens. *Flowers*, in summer; bright lilac, with orange anthers, in elongated terminal heads. *Leaves*, linear, acute, with revolute margins, sessile, patent, rather close together, and clothing the stem from the base to the top. South of France.——Dry and sunny parts of rockwork, in dry sandy soil, and among dwarf plants. Seed.

Cornus canadensis (*Dwarf Cornel*).—A pretty miniature shrub, the shoots of which are tipped with white bracts, tinted with rose at the points, 4 to 6 in. high. *Flowers*, in early summer; purplish-white, in an umbel much shorter than the leaves of the involucre. *Leaves*, about 1½ in. long and 1 in. broad, nearly stalkless, ovate, acuminate, entire, veined, in whorls of 4 or 6 at the top of each stalk, Berries globose, red, ripe in July.—— The rock-garden, mixed border, and bog-bed, in almost any soil, but thriving best in a moist sandy, or peaty one. Division.

Cornus suecica (*Dwarf Cornel*).—An interesting British plant, with simple stems, 4 to 6 in. high. *Flowers*, in early summer; purple, small, 20 or more in a simple terminal umbel, surrounded by an involucre, consisting of 4 large white petal-like leaves, tinged with red. *Leaves*, opposite, stalkless, ovate, entire, veined almost from the base, about 1 in. long. Berries small, red when ripe, sweetish. Britain, N. Europe and Asia.——The rock-garden, in moist, sandy, or peaty soil. Scarcely worthy of culture except in a botanical collection. Division.

Coronilla iberica (*Iberian C.*)—A smooth, dwarf, showy, but tiny shrub, with ascending stems, 6 or 8 in. high. *Flowers*, in summer; yellow, large, seven or eight in an umbel. *Leaves*, pinnate; leaflets 9 to 11, obcordate, ciliate. Iberia and Cappadocia.——The rock-garden, and among the dwarfest plants in the mixed border, in sandy loam. Division.

Coronilla juncea (*Rush-stemmed C.*)—A low evergreen shrub of rather pleasing aspect, forming a neat bush with branching stems, from 1 to 3 ft. high. *Flowers*, in summer; clear yellow, small, in terminal and axillary clusters. *Leaves*, trifoliate, few, and distant. Stem striated. France.—— Among neat shrubs on the rougher parts of rockwork, in warm sandy loam. Division and seed.

Coronilla minima (*Least C.*) — A diminutive evergreen, a few inches high. *Flowers*, in summer; small, rich yellow, freely produced, 6 to 12 in each head. *Leaves*, pinnate; leaflets 7 to 13, ovate-roundish, obtuse or retuse; stipules opposite the leaves, 2-toothed at the apex. France and Southern Europe. —— The rock-garden and among the smallest subjects in the mixed border; in sandy soil. Division or seed.

Coronilla montana (*Mountain C.*) — An erect, free-flowering, slightly glaucous perennial, 15 to 18 in. high. *Flowers*, in summer; yellow, 15 to 20 in each umbel. *Leaves*, pinnate; leaflets 7 to 9, ovate, mucronate. Brightly-coloured forms frequently occur. Mountains of Southern Europe. —— Mixed border, rougher parts of the rock-garden, margins of shrubberies, and naturalization, in ordinary garden soil. Division or seed.

Coronilla varia (*Rosy C.*) — A very handsome, free, and graceful trailing herb, bearing a profusion of rose-coloured flowers. The shoots sometimes attain a length of 4 or 5 ft. *Flowers*, in summer; from 16 to 20 in each umbel, on stalks about as long as the leaves. *Leaves*, pinnate; leaflets 9 to 13, small, oblong, mucronate. The flowers vary in colour from deep rose to nearly white. Europe and Tauria, in fields and meadows. —— Behind some bare rock, so that it may hang down over the face of it; in borders, on chalky banks, running amongst trailing shrubs, or for naturalization in semi-wild places, in ordinary soil. Seed.

Cortusa Matthioli (*Alpine Sanicle*). — Resembling *Primula cortusoides*, with large leaves like those of the tender *Primula mollis*. *Flowers*, in early summer; deep purplish-crimson, on stems from 9 to 15 in. high, arranged in a loose umbel; corolla funnel-shaped. *Leaves*, roundish-heart-shaped, lobed, sharply toothed. Alps of Piedmont and Germany.——Sheltered nooks in the rock-garden, in moist loam or peat, or on sheltered borders. Division and seed.

Corydalis lutea (*Yellow C.*)—*Fumaria lutea.*—A graceful perennial, with fern-like but somewhat glaucous leaves, forming close tufts abundantly dotted with yellow flowers, 12 to 18 in. high. *Flowers*, most of the summer; yellow, in racemes; bracts linear awl-shaped, one-third the length of the pedicel. *Leaves*, 3-ternate; leaflets, wedge-shaped with roundish lobes. A native of Southern Europe, and naturalized on old walls in various countries. ——Borders, old ruins, walls, stony places or bare banks, in any soil. Division.

Corydalis Marschalliana (*Marschall's C.*)—A dwarf tuberous-rooted perennial, 8 to 10 in. high. *Flowers*, in April or May; sulphur-coloured, in short racemes; spur straight or scarcely incurved, blunt. *Leaves*, 2, situated above the middle of the stem, 2-ternate; lobes oval, entire, or bifid. Tauria and the mountains in the Ukraine, under trees. —— Borders, and the rougher parts of the rock-garden, in sandy loam. Division.

Corydalis nobilis (*Noble C.*)—The stoutest and handsomest kind in cultivation, 10 to 12 in. high. *Flowers*, in spring and early summer; rich yellow when opened; the unopened ones at the apex forming a light green rosette; borne in massive heads on stout leafy stems, double the size of those of *C. solida*, all turned the same way; spur long, blunt and incurved at the point. *Leaves*, bipinnate; segments wedge-shaped, cut at the top; bracts acute, entire or cut. Siberia. —— Borders, or the lower flanks of rockwork, in deep sandy loam. Division.

H

Corydalis solida (*Solid C.*)—*Fumaria bulbosa.*—A compact, free-flowering kind, now becoming popular among spring flowers, 4 to 6 in. high. *Flowers*, in spring; purplish-rose, a little whitish underneath, borne in a dense, somewhat one sided cluster, which becomes elongated as the flowering advances, each flower springing from the axil of a much-divided bract. *Leaves*, few, twice-ternate, with glaucous, wedge-shaped leaflets, divided at the end; stems scaly at the base; bulb or tubercle roundish, solid, about the size of a small hazel-nut, with fibrous rootlets issuing from the lower part only. Europe and Asia.——Borders, edgings, the spring garden, and naturalization among dwarf plants in bare places. Division.

Corydalis tuberosa (*Tuberous C.*)—*C. cava.*—Resembling *C. solida*, but with the small floral leaves quite entire, 4 to 6 in. high. *Flowers*, in spring; white, in a loose, slightly unilateral cluster, each flower springing from the axil of an entire bract. *Leaves*, much cut, twice-ternate, with wedge-shaped segments; stem not scaly; bulb or tubercle egg-shaped, hollow, with rootlets issuing from every part of its surface. France and the Pyrenees.——Borders, naturalized among spring and early summer flowers, in almost any position. Division of established tufts.

Cotyledon Umbilicus (*Wall C.*)—*Umbilicus erectus.*—A distinct-looking plant, with creeping fleshy roots and erect flower-stems, 6 to 12 in. high. *Flowers*, in summer; yellowish-green, in a longish raceme; corolla about ¼ in. long, cylindrical. *Leaves*, fleshy, roundish, more or less peltate, dentately crenated, on long stalks. Britain and Southern and Western Europe, in damp places.—— The rougher parts of rockwork and in hardy ferneries. Division or seed.

Cousinia Hystrix (*Spring C.*)—A singular plant. *Flowers*, purplish, about the size of those of the Cotton-thistle, in solitary, somewhat globose, woolly heads. *Leaves*, pinnatifid or pinnate, with spiny teeth, covered on both sides with a cobweb-like down; those of the stem decurrent; stem branching at the top. Mountain pastures in the eastern parts of the Caucasus, and adjoining regions of Persia.——Borders, or banks, in well-drained sandy soil. Division and seed.

Crambe cordifolia (*Heart-leaved C.*)—A noble perennial with huge leaves and small honey-scented flowers, appearing in dense multitudes; 4 to 6 ft. high. *Flowers*, in summer; white, in much-branched, smooth, leafless panicles; stamens forked. *Leaves*, stalked, toothed; lower ones heart-shaped; upper ones ovate, nearly smooth, as is the stem. Caucasus. ——Isolated, near the margin of shrubberies in the picturesque garden, or grouped with hardy plants having fine leaves, or naturalized in glades in almost any position or soil. It is, however, worthy of a very deep and good soil, in which it becomes much larger and handsomer. Division or seed.

Crambe juncea (*Rushy C.*)—Smaller than the preceding kind, 3 to 4 ft. high. *Flowers*, in summer; whitish. *Leaves*, lyrate, with toothed lobes, the terminal lobe the largest; leaf-stalks and stem rough with recurved hairs. Native of Iberia, near Tiflis. Not so fine a species as *C. cordifolia*, having smaller and less divided leaves; those of the stem very few and small, and scarcely any on the branches.——Similar uses to the preceding, but being inferior, it is suited chiefly for botanic gardens. Division or seed.

Crepis aurea (*Golden C.*)—A pretty little composite plant, 4 in. to 1 ft.

CRINUM — CROCUS.

high. *Flowers*, late in summer; orange, seldom more than one bloom on each stem; involucrum and stem covered with long black hairs, mingled with a few small, white, woolly ones. *Leaves*, all radical, ½ or ¼ as long as the stem, spoon-shaped, oblong, dentate, or runcinate, of a lively green, smooth and shiny, disposed in a rosette. Root fibrous, without runners or tubercles. Elevated pastures on the Alps of Southern Europe.——Borders, and naturalized on bare banks and slopes, in any common sandy soil. Division and seed.

Crinum capense (*Cape Crinum*).—A noble, fragrant, and perfectly hardy bulb, from 2 to 3 ft. high. *Flowers*, late in summer; very large and funnel-shaped, white, sometimes tinged with red, in a terminal umbel of ten to fifteen blooms, producing large heads of curious, fleshy, irregularly-sized seeds, by which the plant is readily increased. *Leaves*, ribbon-like, long and narrow, grooved, rough on the margins, glaucous. There are several varieties, the most remarkable being *riparium*, *fortuitum*, and *striatum*—the first has dark purple, the second fine white, and the third striped flowers. Cape of Good Hope.——As isolated tufts or small beds in the pleasure-ground, arranged with groups of hardy fragrant plants, or with the nobler herbaceous subjects, particularly those that flower in late summer and early autumn; also, for grouping and massing on small islands or parts of islands on which a distinct and choice type of vegetation is sought, and near the margin of water. Few plants repay better for a sheltered and warm position, and deep, very rich soil, with abundance of water in summer, though it exists in ordinary soil. In very cold situations a little pile of leaves may be desirable over the roots in winter, but I have known the plant withstand the most intense frosts, and by planting the top of the bulbs half a foot beneath the surface there need not be any fear of injury from this cause. Separation of the bulbs and from seed.

Crocosmia aurea (*Golden C.*)—*Tritonia aurea*.—A bulbous perennial, 2 ft. high. *Flowers*, late in summer or in autumn; few, brilliant orange-red, in a loose spike. *Leaves*, sword-shaped, pointed, about a foot long and ½ in. broad, sheathing the base of the stem for about a foot. Stem slightly winged. South Africa.——Borders, margins of beds of Rhododendrons, etc., in peaty or very sandy soil. Division.

Crocus Boryanus (*White Autumn C.*) —A very pretty autumn-flowering Crocus, as yet rare in gardens, 3 to 4 in. high. *Flowers*, late in autumn; creamy white, throat orange-yellow, the base of the segments sometimes marked externally with dull purple lines; anthers white; stigmas orange-scarlet. *Leaves*, narrow, smooth, appearing a little earlier than the flowers. *Corm* covered by two smooth, soft, persistent, reticulated coats. Asia Minor, the Morea, and the Greek Islands. —— The rock-garden, bulb garden, and choice borders, in fine deep sandy soil. Separation of the bulbs and from seed.

Crocus Cartwrightianus (*Cartwright's C.*) — A very dwarf free-flowering species, about 3 in. high. *Flowers*, in autumn; fragrant, usually white, more or less stained inside with purple lines, sometimes pure white, often of a pale and sometimes a pretty rich purple; the throat is never yellow. *Leaves*, appearing before the flowers, narrow, with the reflexed margin and the dorsal rib densely ciliate; veins very slightly grooved. *Corm* covered with softly-membranous, reticulated fibrous coats. Greek islands,

H 2

Teno and Scyro.——The positions and treatment recommended for *Crocus Orphanidis* will also suit this.

Crocus Imperati (*Imperati's Crocus*). —Nearly allied to *C. versicolor*, but much handsomer, 3 to 6 in. high. *Flowers*, in very early spring; sweet-scented, of a lilac-purple on the inside; external divisions 1¾ in. long and ¾ in. broad, of a creamy white on the outside, marked with three longitudinal dark purple lines, of which the two outer ones and the end of the middle one are feathered with short lines of the same colour. *Leaves*, appearing before the flowers, longer than the flower-stem, linear, thick, recurved, with a distinct white line in the middle of the concave inner side, and enveloped for 2 or 3 in. from the base with a series of three or four opposite, deeply furrowed, obtuse, membranous sheaths. *Corm* roundish, irregular, about the size of a small nutmeg, partially covered at the base and sides with brown fibres. Found on the mountains of Calabria at 3000 to 6000 ft. of altitude.——Borders, the rock-garden, edgings, and naturalization, on warm, sunny banks and slopes, in ordinary soil. Separation of the bulbs.

Crocus luteus (*Common Yellow C.*)—The common yellow Crocus of our gardens. *Flowers*, early in spring, appearing at the same time as the leaves; of a bright yellow, two on a stem. *Leaves*, linear; sheaths wide. *Corm* covered with veined tunics. Native country uncertain, but supposed to have been introduced from the Levant.——Borders, edgings, or naturalized in grass, in almost any position and in any soil. Separation of the bulbs.

Crocus nudiflorus (*Naked-flowered C.*) —*C. multifidus.* — A beautiful late blooming species. *Flowers*, in autumn; pale bright purple, with the tube 3 to 10 in. long, and the segments 1½ to 2 in. long. *Leaves*, appearing very early in spring, very slender, with a narrow white line in the centre. *Corm* flowers when about the size of a pea, sending out stolons in spring, the thickened apices of which form fresh corms. S. W. Europe, but abundantly naturalized in meadows about Nottingham, Derby, Halifax, and Warrington.——Borders, edgings to beds of autumnal flowers, the lower parts of the rock-garden, or naturalized in the grass, in open sunny spots near wood-walks, in ordinary soil. Separation of the bulbs.

Crocus Orphanidis (*Orphanides' C.*) —A rare and recently introduced kind. *Flowers*, in autumn; soft lilac-blue with yellow throat, 2¼ in. in diameter. *Leaves*, appear with the flowers, exceeding them in length and getting much longer afterwards. *Corms* unusually large, nearly 2 in. long, closely covered with a bright chestnut-brown tissue. A native of Greece. —— The rock-garden and choice border, in deep sandy loam, and in sunny, warm, and sheltered positions. When more plentiful it will doubtless prove useful in various other ways. Separation of the bulb every second year, soon after the leaves have died down, replanting the bulbs at once, and rather deeply.

Crocus pulchellus (*Mount Athos C.*) —A rare and pretty late-blooming kind, 4 to 5 in. high. *Flowers*, in autumn; large and showy, pale bluish-pearl colour, with darker veins, the throat orange-yellow; anthers white. *Leaves*, broad, smooth, green with a white streak. *Corm* covered with a membranous coat, having a ring at the base ciliated with fibres. Native of Belgrade, the east side of the Bosphorus, and Mount Athos.—— The positions and treatment recommended for the preceding will suit this.

Crocus reticulatus (*Cloth of Gold C.*) —*C. susianus.*—A very early bloomiing kind. *Flowers*, early in spring; of a rich golden colour, brownish-black on the outside. *Leaves*, very narrow, smooth, grooved and veined on both sides, appearing with the flowers. *Corm* covered with a reticulated tunic. Levant.—— Commonly used in the spring garden and in borders, and well worthy of naturalization, on very bare and sunny banks, where its flowers would prove very attractive in early spring. Separation of the bulbs.

Crocus sativus (*Saffron Crocus*).— The plant from which the saffron of commerce is obtained, which consists, in fact, of the dried filaments of the flowers. *Flowers*, in autumn; of a pale violet with deeper coloured veins, the tube of the flower long, exhaling a sweet and delicate odour. *Leaves*, very narrow, slightly ciliated, appearing soon after the flowers. *Corm* rather large, globular, usually depressed, covered with a fibrous greyish tunic. Native country uncertain, but probably comes from the Eastern shores of the Mediterranean. ——Sunny sheltered nooks in the rock-garden, or on slightly raised warm and sunny banks or slopes, always in perfectly drained and very sandy soil. It is very shy of blooming in cold soils. Separation of the bulbs every third or fourth year, soon after the leaves have withered.

Crocus speciosus (*Large Autumn C.*) —Perhaps the handsomest and largest of the late - blooming kinds. *Flowers*, in autumn; bluish violet, striped internally with deep purple lines, which are deeper at the base of the divisions. *Leaves*, appearing almost with the flowers, very narrow, erect. *Corm* of medium size, nearly round, with tunics formed of reticulated fibres.

Native of the Caucasus. ——The rock-garden, borders, edgings to beds of autumn flowers, clumps on warm fringes of shrubberies, and naturalization on sunny banks and slopes. Separation of the bulbs every second or third year, and about the period when the leaves decay.

Crocus vernus (*Spring Crocus*).—The parent of most of the blue, white, and striped kinds generally cultivated in our gardens. *Flowers*, in spring; lilac, violet, white, bluish, or streaked with white and violet; inside of the throat hairy. *Leaves*, grooved with veins, appearing soon after the flowers. *Corm* solid, fleshy, generally roundish, depressed, sometimes slightly pear-shaped or elongated, covered with reticulated coats. Alps and Apennines. —— Edgings, borders, beds in the spring garden, naturalization, etc. The beautifully striped varieties are well worthy of being naturalized in the grass on warm slopes, in the rougher parts of pleasure-grounds and parks. Separation of the bulbs.

Crocus versicolor (*Various-coloured C.*)—*Flowers*, in spring; white, richly striped with purple, the throat sometimes yellow, sometimes white, smooth on the inside, by which it can be readily distinguished from *C. vernus*, which has the inside of the throat hairy. *Leaves*, grooved, with a double opaque spathe, without nerves, appearing at the same time as the flowers. Native of the South of France. —— Similar positions and treatment to those for *C. Imperati*.

Crucianella stylosa (*Long-styled C.*) —A pretty dwarf procumbent herb, with leaves arranged in whorls, 9 to 12 in. high. *Flowers*, in summer; pale rose, small, but freely produced in dense terminal heads; style much protruding. *Leaves*, 8 to 9 in a whorl, hispid, as are also the stems. Rocks and barren places in Persia and the

Caucasus. —— Borders, rockwork, or bare banks, in sandy or calcareous soil. Division or seed.

Cucurbita perennis (*Perennial Cucumber*).—A remarkable-looking trailing plant, with large hoary leaves. *Flowers*, in summer; pale yellow; lobes of calyx awl-shaped; fruit roundish, smooth, almost sessile. *Leaves*, triangularly heart-shaped with undulating margins. —— Associated with fine-leaved hardy plants, gourds, etc., in very deep and rich soil, in which it will attain great vigour. It may be trained over stakes or stumps, or allowed to trail over undulating banks; but it is chiefly valuable for the botanical or curious collection. Seed and careful division.

Cyananthus lobatus (*Lobed C.*) — A brilliant and remarkable Himalayan rock plant, about 4 in. high. *Flowers*, in August and September; purplish-blue with a whitish centre, few, solitary, usually terminal, about an inch across, funnel-shaped, with 5 spoon-shaped lobes; throat covered with numerous soft, long, whitish hairs; calyx 5-cleft, large, roundish, thickly set with short blackish hairs. *Leaves*, lozenge-shaped, small, fleshy, alternate, deeply and irregularly notched or lobed, greyish underneath. Stems branching but little, procumbent or ascending, spreading loosely about. Himalayas.—— The rock-garden in sunny chinks. It grows best in a mixture of sandy peat and leaf-mould, with plenty of moisture during the growing season. Increased freely by cuttings. The seed requires a dry, favourable season to ripen it; in wet weather the large, erect, persistent calyx becomes filled with water, which remains and rots the included seed vessel.

Cyclamen coum (*Round-leaved C.*)— Distinguished by its rounded leaves. *Flowers*, December to March; reddish purple, darker at the mouth, where there is a white circle; inside striped with red; corolla short, closed at the mouth. *Leaves*, roundish-heart-shaped, divided at the base, the lobes overlapping. *C. vernum* of Sweet ("Brit. Fl. Gard.," vol. i. t. 9), is a variety with the leaves marked, or zoned, with an unequal band of white between the margin and the centre, and flowers similar to the best varieties of *C. coum*. Tuber round, depressed, fibres issuing from underside only. *C. coum album* is a variety raised by Mr. Atkins, of Painswick, with white flowers, having a dark mouth. Greek Archipelago.——The rock-garden, or choice warm sheltered borders, in fibry vegetable soil. Seed.

Cyclamen europæum (*European C.*) —*Flowers*, from June to November, or if slightly protected till the end of the year; reddish-purple, very fragrant; petals rather short and stiff; mouth of the corolla pentagonal, not toothed. *Leaves*, appear in early summer, and remain the greater part of the year; they vary considerably in outline, the markings of the surface, and the colour beneath; but they are always more or less toothed, those from more northern habitats more so than those from localities south of the Alps, where they assume, in a measure, the rounder form and more delicate markings of *C. persicum*. Tuber of medium size and very irregular form, sometimes roundish, depressed, or knotted, at others lengthened out sometimes more than a foot. The rind is thin, smooth, yellowish, sometimes "scabby." The southern varieties have flowers much longer and of a more delicate colour, often approaching peach-colour; pure white ones are rare, but pale ones not uncommon. Central Europe.——The rock-garden, or warm borders in rich light earth. This, like the *Ivy-leaved C.*, may be naturalized in parks and pleasure-grounds amidst short grass, mosses, and other small plants. Seed.

Cyclamen hederæfolium (*Ivy-leaved C.*).—A beautiful tuberous perennial, happily perfectly hardy. *Flowers*, in late summer and autumn; purplish red, frequently with a whitish stripe down the petals; mouth or base of the corolla 10-toothed, pentagonal. *Leaves*, variously marked, the greater number appearing after the flowers, 4 to 6 in. long and 4 to 5½ in. in diameter. *Tuber* not unfrequently a foot in diameter, covered with a brownish rough rind, which cracks irregularly, so as to form little scales. There is a pure white variety and one white with pink base or mouth of corolla, both of which come true from seed. There are also, according to Mr. Atkins, valuable and distinct varieties from the Greek Isles, that flower later and continue longer in bloom. Their leaves are thick, shining, and wax-like, rising with or before the majority of the flowers, being both stronger and larger than the ordinary type, with more decided difference of outline and markings on the upper surface, the under surface being frequently of a beautiful purple. *C. græcum* is a very near ally if more than a variety; the foliage is more after the *persicum* type, the shape of the corolla and toothing of the mouth the same. South of Europe and Northern Africa.——The rock-garden, borders, or naturalization in half-shady bare places, in light vegetable earth. Seed.

Cyclamen vernum (*Spring C.*) — *C. repandum*.— A valuable kind. *Flowers*, from April to end of May; from a delicate peach to deep red purple, the last-named colour being very rare; corolla long; petals somewhat fleshy, twisted; mouth round, not toothed. *Leaves*, appearing before the flowers, generally more or less marked with white on the upper surface, and often purplish beneath, semi-transparent when young. *Tuber* round, somewhat depressed, rough or russety on outer surface; fibres issuing from one point on the under side only. Southern Europe.——The rock-garden and sheltered mixed border, in sunny sheltered spots, in light, rich, well-drained soil. Seed.

Cynara Scolymus (*French Artichoke*). —A noble plant, 3 to 6 ft. high. *Flowers*, in autumn; purple, very large, surrounded by an involucrum of oval-obtuse, sometimes emarginate, downy scales. *Leaves*, long, somewhat spiny, nearly pinnatifid, covered underneath with white cottony down. South of Europe.——Well known in the vegetable garden. This is one of the most striking plants when seen isolated on the grass, in the picturesque flower garden, or occasionally in the shrubbery. It loves rich soil, and sometimes perishes if not protected in winter. Seed and division.

Cypripedium Calceolus (*Lady's Slipper*).—Our largest-flowered British orchid, now nearly or quite exterminated, 1 to 1½ ft. high. *Flowers*, in summer; usually solitary, or two, large; sepals 1 to 1½ in. long, dark brown; petals dark brown, narrower than sepals; lip 1 in. long, inflated, yellow, netted with darker veins. *Leaves*, large, ovate, pointed, veined, generally 3 or 4 in number. Native of N. Europe, in dense woods; very rare.——The rock-garden, in sunny nooks sheltered by small bushes, etc., in calcareous soil. Careful division of established tufts.

Cypripedium candidum (*White Lady's Slipper*).—A small-flowered kind, the lip of which reminds one of a small bird's egg; 8 to 15 in. high. *Flowers*, in May and June; solitary; lip about the size of a sparrow's egg, white, marked with rose-coloured dots on the inside, flattish laterally, convex above; petals and sepals greenish, not much longer than the lip; sepals ovate-lanceolate, two of them united into one piece under the lip. *Leaves*, lanceolate-oblong, acute, slightly pubescent. Bogs of Central and W. New York (rare) to Kentucky and Wisconsin.——The artificial bog, or in moist peaty spots near the rock-garden. Best suited for the botanical or the curious collection. Careful division.

Cypripedium guttatum (*Spotted C.*)—A very handsome, rare kind. *Flowers*, in summer; rather small, but beautiful, of a purplish-violet tint, spotted with white, the lip also edged with white; the upper sepal very large, pointed; the lower one cleft; petals oval, abruptly pointed; lip longer than the sepals, nearly round, with the orifice expanded and flattened. *Leaves* 2, alternate, oval-elliptical, pointed, fringed. Native of Canada, N. Europe, near Moscow, N. Asia, in dense forests (dry in summer) amongst the roots of trees, in black, moist vegetable mould, in parts completely shaded from the sun.——Of the successful culture of this plant little is as yet known. It is best to try it in shady and half-shady situations, in vegetable soil. Division.

Cypripedium spectabile (*Noble Lady's Slipper*).—Perhaps the handsomest of this handsome family, from 15 in. to 2½ ft. high. *Flowers*, in summer; large, handsome, white, slightly tinged with rose; lip of a bright rosy carmine, longer than the petals, inflated, slightly furrowed; sepals oblong, obtuse, undivided, longer and broader than the petals which are lanceolate and flat; 1 or 2 blooms on a stem. *Leaves*, oval - pointed, pubescent, veined. Native of N. America from Canada to Carolina, in marshy places.——The artificial bog, moist borders, at the foot of north walls, among low shrubs, etc., always in deep moist peat or vegetable soil. Division of well-established tufts.

Daphne Cneorum (*Garland Flower*)—A very neat evergreen shrub, bearing a profusion of rosy-lilac flowers, the unopened buds being crimson, 6 to 12 in. high. *Flowers*, often twice a year, in April and September; in dense terminal umbels, deliciously fragrant. *Leaves*, smooth, lance-shaped, mucronate. A native of most of the great mountain chains of Europe.——Rockwork, front margin of the mixed border, or as edging to beds of choice low shrubs. Thrives best in sandy peaty soil, kept rather moist in summer. Layers.

Datisca cannabina (*Hemp-like D.*)—A tall and graceful perennial, 3 to 6 ft. high. *Flowers*, in summer; yellow, in long, loose, axillary spikes at the tops of the stems. *Leaves*, pinnate, alternate; leaflets in 3 pairs and an odd one, about 2 in. long and ½ in. broad, acutely pointed, deeply serrate. Both the male and female forms should be grown, as, though both are graceful, the fertilized female plant is the most so, and continues much the longest in a green state. Candia.——Associated with fine-leaved hardy plants, or as isolated specimens in the pleasure-ground, in deep good soil. Seed and division of well-established plants.

Delphinium elatum (*Bee Larkspur*).—*D. exaltatum.*—A stately perennial, 4 to 6 ft. high in gardens. *Flowers*, in summer; blue or white, middle size, in straight racemes; spur straight, as long as the calyx; limb of lower petals bifid. *Leaves*, flat, hairy when young, but becoming smooth when old, cleft beyond the middle into 3, 5, or 7 parts: lobes wedge-shaped, trifid or jagged, acuminated at the apex; stem, smooth, somewhat branching. Mountains of Virginia and Carolina.——Borders and fringes of plantations, in good rich soil. Division and seed.

Delphinium elegans (*Elegant Larkspur*).—A neat border plant, 1 to 2 ft. high. *Flowers*, in summer; dark blue, smaller than those of *D. grandiflorum*, in loose, few-flowered racemes; petals shorter than the calyx; spur curved, shorter than the sepals; limb of lower petals bifid. *Leaves*, smooth, 5-parted, with 3- to 5-cleft lobes, and linear-lance-shaped acute lobules; stalks scarcely widening at the base. There is a double variety. N. America.——Borders in good soil. Division and seed.

Delphinium formosum (*Showy D.*)—A very handsome kind, 18 in. to 3¼ ft. high. *Flowers*, in summer and autumn; a fine azure blue, shaded with indigo; spur of a violet blue, rather long, two-cleft, and having a rumpled appearance; petals shorter than the sepals. *Leaves*, alternate, of a greyish-green, palmate with unequal segments, the lower ones stalked, the upper ones sessile and simply tripartite. Native country unknown.——Borders and fringes of shrubberies in good soil. Division and seed.

Delphinium grandiflorum (*Large-flowered D.*)—One of the handsomest kinds, 1 to 3 ft. high. *Flowers*, in summer; from June to September, blue, very large, in spreading few-flowered racemes; petals shorter than the calyx; limb of lower ones entire, somewhat orbicular. *Leaves*, smooth, light green above, hoary beneath, palmately divided into many narrow lobes. There is a fine double variety (*D. g. plenum*). *D. sinense*, is a variety differing chiefly in having a stiffer and more erect stem than the species, and the two lower petals bearded with yellow hairs. There are several other varieties, both double and single, varying in colour from deep blue to white. The best of these are one with white flowers (*D. g. fl. alb.*), another dwarf kind (*D. g. pumilum cœruleum*) with blue flowers, and one (*D. g. pumilum album*) with white flowers. Siberia and Dauria.——Borders and fringes of shrubberies in good soil. Division and seed.

Delphinium intermedium (*Intermediate D.*)—4 to 8 ft. high. *Flowers*, in summer; in glaucous racemes; sepals blue; petals very hairy, almost black, the limb of the lower ones bifid; pedicels, bracts, calyx, and ovaries smooth. *Leaves*, heart-shaped, 5- to 7-cleft, upper ones 3-lobed, all deeply serrated. There are several varieties of this species. Europe.——Borders, in good soil. Division or seed.

Delphinium nudicaule (*Dwarf Red D.*)—A singularly brilliant and recently introduced dwarf kind, 10 to 18 in. high. *Flowers*, early in summer, in a loose raceme; vivid red, inclining to orange, the petals clear yellow, lower ones spoon-shaped, with a 2-cleft, fringed limb; upper ones elongated, prominent, hairy at the ends; spur nearly twice as long as the smooth calyx. *Leaves*, fleshy, somewhat peltate, 3-parted, with numerous subdivisions, which in the lower leaves are obcordate with notched lobes, and in the upper ones oblong entire. California.——On warm flanks of the rock-garden, or on warm banks or borders till plentiful, in light, well-drained, sandy loam. Increased by seeds. This plant is as yet rare, and few have had any experience of its culture, but as it grows on the hills and plains near San Francisco, in gravelly and very sandy places, it certainly will be the better of a sandy and thoroughly drained loam in this country.

[Hybrids and varieties of *Delphinium*, of the highest order of beauty, have been raised in such abundance that they are now of greater importance than the species. Additions are being yearly made to the number by nurserymen who cultivate florists' flowers, and have usually a good selection of fine kinds. These *Delphiniums* are of the highest importance in the flower-garden, where they may be used in lines and in mixtures, in the mixed border of which they are some of the finest ornaments, and, in a word, for every use to which the most beautiful perennials may be put. They thrive best in rich light soil; and if, after flowering in summer, they are cut down to near the ground, they will again bloom vigorously by autumn. All are easily increased by division in winter, or early spring. The following are excellent kinds:— *Alopecuroides, Belladonna, Barlowii, Hendersoni, La Belle Alliance, Schamyl, Wheeleri, William Pfitzer. Ranunculæflorum, Delight, Hyacinthiflorum, Magnificum, Keteleeri, Reine des Delphiniums, Madame Chaté, Hebe,* and *Bicolor grandiflorum*.

Dentaria bulbifera (*Bulb-bearing D.*) —An interesting perennial, bearing bulbils in the axils of its leaves, as in *Lilium bulbiferum;* 1 to 2 ft. high. *Flowers,* in spring; purple, sometimes nearly white, rather large, produced in a raceme at the top of the stem. *Leaves,* lower ones pinnate, with 5 or 7 segments; upper ones undivided or with few segments; segments 1 to 2 in. long, lance-shaped, toothed or entire, tapering at the base. Europe, Asia, and Britain.——Borders, and fringes of shrubberies in half-shady positions, and in sandy vegetable soil. Division and seed.

Dentaria digitata (*Showy Toothwort.*) — A very handsome dwarf kind, about 12 in. high. *Flowers,* in April; rich purple, in flat racemes at the top of the stem. *Leaves,* stalked, palmately cut into 5 oblong-lanceolate, pointed, deeply serrated segments.

France, Italy, and Switzerland, in shady woods.——Half-shady borders, margins of beds of American plants, or among low shrubs near rockwork, in rich light and moist soil. Division.

Dentaria pinnata (*Pinnate D.*)—A stout species at once distinguished by its pinnate leaves; 14 to 20 in. high. *Flowers,* from April to June; large, pale purple, lilac, or white, in a terminal cluster. *Leaves,* few, near the top of the stem, alternate, stalked, pinnate; leaflets 5 to 7, lance-shaped, acute, smooth, irregularly toothed, pale underneath. Switzerland, in mountain and sub-alpine woods.—— Fringes of shrubberies and half-shady spots, in rich light earth. Careful division of the thick scaly roots.

Dianthus alpinus (*Alpine Pink*).—A rare and beautiful mountain pink, 3 or 4 in. high. *Flowers,* in summer; deep rose spotted with crimson, large, solitary on each stem, so freely produced as to hide the leaves; petals crenated. *Leaves,* green, oblonglinear, obtuse. Alps of Austria.—— The rock-garden, in exposed spots, in light, fibry, gritty, or sandy loam. Where plentiful enough, and where it thrives freely, it should be used on the margin of the choice border. I have seen it attain great beauty as an edging to small beds of American plants, in sandy peat. Seed and careful division.

Dianthus barbatus (*Sweet William*). —One of our most popular old garden flowers, 1 to 2 ft. high. *Flowers,* in summer; variously coloured, from dark purple to white, in dense cymes; petals bearded; scales of the calyx ovate, awl-shaped, about equalling the tube. *Leaves,* broadly-lance-shaped, nerved. There are many varieties, both single and double. Various parts of Central and Southern Europe.—— Borders, margins of shrubberies; the finer kinds in beds, with the florists' flowers. It is a biennial in cold soils, but a perennial in warm ones. Seed.

Dianthus cæsius (*Cheddar Pink*).—A dwarf, very glaucous, densely tufted kind, 6 to 8 in. high. *Flowers*, in early summer; delicate rose, very fragrant, generally solitary; scales of calyx roundish, short; petals crenated, pubescent. *Leaves*, very glaucous, short, with rough margins. On mountains in Europe, and in England on limestone rocks at Cheddar, in Somersetshire. —— The rock-garden, old walls and ruins, and dry, sandy, or calcareous borders. Seed and careful division.

Dianthus Caryophyllus (*Carnation*). —The parent of our Carnations, Picotees, and Clove Pinks; 1 to 3 ft. high. *Flowers*, in summer; all colours except blue, solitary; scales of the calyx 4, very short, ovate, rather mucronate; petals, broad and beardless; stem branched. *Leaves*, linear-awl-shaped, channelled, glaucous. Europe and England. —— The finer named kinds in beds, with the florists' flowers; in the kitchen-garden, grown for the sake of their cut flowers, or in borders, in various ways. It prefers a sound loam, with sharp sand, and decomposed manure. Where there are old ruins and the like, the single forms might be established upon them with good effect. Layers, cuttings, and seed.

Dianthus cruentus (*Blood-scarlet Pink*).—A slender kind, with deeply coloured flowers, many in a head; 1 to 2 ft. high. *Flowers*, in summer, small, numerous, of a bloody-scarlet colour, arranged in contracted, many-flowered, somewhat globose cymes; petals, ¼ in. long, toothed, bearded towards the base with scattered reddish-violet hairs; calyx tubular, reddish-violet above, streaked, and ending in 5 very acute teeth. *Leaves*, linear-lanceolate, very acute, those of the stem in 3 or 4 pairs, connate for the space of ⅛ in., 3-nerved underneath, much shorter than the internodes; lower leaves growing in tufts; all smooth, and scarcely glaucescent; stems slightly squared in the upper part. Native country unknown. —— Borders, banks, or the rougher parts of rockwork, in free soil. Seed.

Dianthus deltoides (*Maiden Pink*).— Forms dense, almost grassy tufts, with flowering-stems 6 to 9 in. high. *Flowers*, in summer; bright pink with a dark circle, sometimes white; scales of the calyx 4, ovate-lance-shaped, acute; stem ascending, branched, 1-flowered. *Leaves*, lower ones oblong, obtuse; upper ones narrower, acute, pubescent. *D. deltoides glaucus* is a variety with the stem and leaves slightly glaucous, and white flowers with a dark circle. Europe, Asia, and Britain, but not found in Ireland.—— Borders and rockwork in ordinary garden soil. Division and seed.

Dianthus dentosus (*Amoor pink*).— A dwarf but sturdy and large-flowered species, 5 or 6 in. high. *Flowers*, in summer; more than an inch across, of a fine violet-lilac, with a regular dark spot formed of purple streaks at the base of each petal, producing a dark eye in the centre of the flower; the petals toothed at the margin, and bearded at the base. *Leaves*, linear, rather broad, sometimes slightly undulated, glaucous, tinged with a reddish hue, especially in autumn, spreading into broad tufts. Southern Russia and E. Siberia.——The rock-garden and borders, in sandy well-drained loam. Seed.

Dianthus Fischeri (*Fischer's Pink*.)— A beautiful kind, as yet rare, 7 to 10 in. high. *Flowers*, in summer; light rose, with the petals much cut or feathery at the edges, numerous, in closely-set fascicles; scales oval, pointed, twice as long as the tube of the calyx. *Leaves*, lance-shaped, stiff, with a single vein on the upper side. Russia.——The rock-garden, at least till more plentiful, and in moist sandy or gritty loam. Seed.

Dianthus glacialis (*Glacier Pink*).— A brilliant kind, allied to *D. neglectus*, 2 or 3 in. high. *Flowers*, in summer; solitary, rose-coloured; petals notched, one and a half times longer than the calyx; divisions of the calyx lance-shaped, awned; awn linear, awl-shaped, herbaceous, longer than the tube. *Leaves*, linear, obtuse, 1-nerved, attenuated towards the base. Granitic Alps of the Tyrol, Salzburg, and Carinthia.—— The rock-garden, in exposed spots, in moist sandy loam. Seed and division.

Dianthus neglectus (*Grass Rose*).— Resembling the Alpine Pink in its large and handsome blossoms, but with narrower and more pointed grass-like leaves; 2 to 4 in. high. *Flowers*, in summer; deep rose; calyx striped, scales of the calyx 2, as long as the tube; petals serrated; stems erect, tufted, short, generally 1-flowered. *Leaves*, green, linear, acute, serrulated. Alps of Dauphiny, Pyrenees, Switzerland, and North of Italy.——The rock-garden, in exposed spots, and the margin of the choice mixed border, in fine sandy loam. It is much more easily grown than the Alpine Pink, and in many soils will thrive in any exposed spot, the plant or group of plants being surrounded by a few half-buried stones. Seed and division.

Dianthus petræus (*Rock Pink*).— Forms compact tufts, in poor soil, little more than 1 in. high; flower-stems about 6 in. high. *Flowers*, in summer; fine rose, usually solitary on the stems, which are very freely produced; scales of the calyx obovate, mucronate; petals beardless, multifid. *Leaves*, smooth, awl-shaped, entire, nerved. Hungary.—— The rock-garden, or borders, in ordinary light soil. This is easy to grow and much less liable to suffer from wire-worm than most of the other kinds. Division or seed, but if grown near other kinds the seedlings are apt to vary very much.

Dianthus plumarius (*Garden Pink*). —This is considered the parent from which all our varieties of pinks have sprung. *Flowers*, in early summer; white, purple, spotted, or variegated, double or single; stems 2- or 3-flowered; scales of calyx ovate, short; teeth obtuse; petals bearded, jagged. *Leaves*, linear, margins rough. Europe. ——The finer named kinds in beds of rich sandy loam, with the florists' flowers, or in borders, fringes of shrubberies, or on banks. The wild single kind thrives best on old walls and ruins, and also in the rock-garden and borders, frequently however perishing in winter in cold soils. Cuttings or seed.

Dianthus ramosissimus (*Bush Pink*). —A hardy, dwarf, free-flowering species, forming dense and branching tufts; about 6 in. high. *Flowers*, late in summer; purplish-rose, very numerous, solitary, on wiry stems. *Leaves*, linear, pointed, flat, sessile. Tartary.——The rock-garden, and the margin of the mixed border, in sandy, well-drained loam. Seed.

Dianthus suavis (*Sweet Pink*).—A pretty and sweet kind, 6 in. high. *Flowers*, in summer; pink, petals bearded, deeply serrated; scales of the calyx 4, acute, short. *Leaves*, linear, spreading, glaucous; stem generally 1-flowered. Native country unknown. —— The rock-garden and borders, in light soil. Seed and division.

Dianthus superbus (*Fringed Pink*).—A handsome and fragrant species, distinguished by its petals being cut into lines or strips for more than half their length; 9 to 18 in. high. *Flowers*, after midsummer; rose-coloured or reddish; petals divided beyond the middle, feathery, bearded at the base; scales of the calyx short, ovate, mucronate. *Leaves*, resembling those of a narrow-leaved Sweet William, bright green, linear-lance-shaped, acute, entire; stem smooth, many-flowered. The plant is a biennial in some soils, but a perennial in light, well-drained ones. Many parts of Europe.—— Borders, and the less important parts of the rock-garden. It will grow in any kind of soil for a time, but thrives best in light, rich ones, well drained. Seed.

Diapensia lapponica (*Lapland D.*)—A sturdy, but very dwarf, evergreen shrub, 1 to 2 in. high. *Flowers*, in early summer; white, salver-shaped, about ⅓ in. across; mostly solitary, on erect stalks; stamens yellow. *Leaves*, very narrow, closely packed, linear-spoon-shaped, smooth. Northern Europe and North America.——The rock-garden, in moist sandy peat, and in well exposed positions. As yet, this plant has been but very rarely seen even in our best collections. Careful division of well-established tufts.

Dicentra (*Dielytra*) **chrysantha**.—(*Yellow-flowered D.*)—A very ornamental, bushy, herbaceous plant, 3 to 5 ft. high. *Flowers*, in autumn; full golden yellow, in erect racemes. *Leaves*, very finely cut, glaucous, resembling those of the Rue. California.——Borders, in rich, deep, and well-drained loam. Seed.

Dicentra cucullaria (*Hooded D.*)—*Fumaria cucullaria*.—A graceful and interesting, but not very conspicuous little plant, about 3 in. high.

Flowers, in early summer; white, with yellow tips; produced in simple racemes on naked stalks; spurs 2, straight, acute. *Leaves*, tri-ternate, smooth, slender. *Root*, tuberous, about the size of a large hazel nut. North America.——The rock-garden, in quiet, half-shady nooks, amid dwarf plants, or on the margins of beds of shrubs, in peat soil. It is very uncommon in gardens, and is not likely to be popular, not being so ornamental as the following kinds. Division.

Dicentra eximia (*Plumy Dielytra*).—Combines the grace of a fern with the blooming qualities of a first-class perennial; 9 to 18 in. high. *Flowers*, in spring and throughout the summer; reddish purple, drooping, oblong, in a compound raceme; spurs short, blunt, somewhat incurved; wings of the inner petals projecting beyond the summit; stigma 2-angled. *Leaves*, 3 to 8, or more, growing from the crown of the roots; stalks channelled, widened at the base; divisions of the blades variable, but mostly oblong. Clefts of rocks on the mountains of Virginia and North Carolina.——Borders, or rockwork; grows in any soil, but thrives best in a deep, sandy loam. Division.

[*D. formosa*, of Nuttall, is by some considered a distinct species, known by the "wings of the inner petals scarcely projecting, the stigma triangular and entire, the flowers broadly ovate, and the spurs short, and very obtuse." The plants grown under this name in gardens are, from a horticultural point of view, not distinct from the preceding, require the same treatment, and are suitable for the same positions.]

Dicentra spectabilis (*Dielytra*).—One of our most beautiful and graceful hardy flowers; 9 in. to 2 ft. high. *Flowers*, in spring and early summer;

large, rosy-crimson, about an inch long, produced in a graceful raceme on a leafy stem ; spurs 2, short, very blunt. *Leaves*, stalked, much divided; segments obovate-wedge-shaped, cut. There is a pale variety. Siberia and China. —— Borders, and margins of shrubberies, mixed groups, rough rockeries or banks in a half-naturalized state. It grows in any soil, but perhaps attains greatest vigour in a deep peat or fine sandy soil. Division.

Dictamnus Fraxinella (*Fraxinella*). —A showy border-plant, covered with glandular hairs exuding a strongly scented and inflammable oily resin; 1 to 2 ft. high. *Flowers*, in early summer; pale purple, in long terminal racemes; petals 5, unequal. *Leaves*, pinnate, resembling those of the Ash; leaflets in 4 or 5 pairs, heart-shaped at the base, acute at the apex, finely serrulated. There is a white variety. Southern Europe.——Borders, in any soil, but usually best in a dry one. Where it grows vigorously, it would be worth placing in isolated tufts, in the grass near the margins of shrubberies, in unmown spots. Division or seed, which should be sown when gathered.

Digitalis grandiflora (*Large-flowered Foxglove*).—3 to 4 ft. high. *Flowers*, in summer ; very large (nearly 2 in. long and ½ in. broad), yellow, bell-shaped, pubescent, glandular, very open at the mouth (which is streaked with lines of a deeper tint) and arranged in a long unilateral spike. *Leaves*, lanceolate, or oval-lanceolate, pubescent on the margin and on the prominent nerves, the lower leaves narrowed into a short winged leaf-stalk; the upper ones sessile, half clasping the stem ; the whole plant more or less set with soft jointed hairs. There are two varieties, *D. acutiloba* and *D. obtusiloba;* the former has the lower lip of the corolla acute, and the latter has the same part obtuse. France, Alps, and Pyrenees.——Borders and naturalization, in ordinary soil. Seed.

Digitalis lanata (*Woolly D.*)—This species, *D. lutea*, and *D. ochroleuca*, are perhaps scarcely brilliant enough for very select ornamental collections ; 2 to 3 ft. high. *Flowers*, in summer; white, delicately veined with pinkish lines, in dense, terminal, many-flowered racemes ; corolla roundish-ventricose, downy; lip ovate, naked, sometimes purplish. *Leaves*, oblong, deep green, ciliated with woolly hairs. Hungary. —— Borders and naturalization in almost any soil. Seed.

Digitalis lutea (*Yellow Foxglove*).— 1½ to 3 ft. high. *Flowers*, in summer; pale yellow, small, produced in dense racemes; corolla funnel-shaped, smooth or downy towards the top; segments ovate, bearded ; lower bracts longer than the flowers. *Leaves*, lance-shaped, toothed, smooth; stem simple, angular. There are several varieties. Southern Europe. —— Borders, and naturalization, in ordinary soil. Seed.

Digitalis mariana (*Sierra Morena D.*) —A handsome plant resembling our common Foxglove; 1½ ft. high. *Flowers*, in summer ; rose-coloured, bearded on the lower part inside with long white hairs, and marked in the same place with brownish-red white-edged spots; in a unilateral raceme of 10 to 20 blooms. *Leaves*, mostly radical, covered on both sides with a very soft greyish down, ovate or ovate-oblong; stem-leaves smaller, acute, nearly sessile. Sierra Morena in S. of Spain. ——Borders, fringes of shrubberies, and naturalization in copses, etc., in light or well-drained soils. Seed.

Digitalis ochroleuca (*Cream-coloured D.*)—A rather showy herb, with both stem and leaves villous; 2 to 3 ft. high. *Flowers*, in summer; yellow reticulated with brown, in a terminal raceme; corolla, oblong-ventricose, villous; segments ovate, acute; lip bearded. *Leaves*, ovate-lanceolate, acuminated, toothed. Central Europe. —— Borders, and naturalization in ordinary soil. Seed.

Digitalis purpurea (*Common Foxglove*).—Our well-known native Foxglove; 2 to 5 ft. high. *Flowers*, in summer; large, purple, marked inside with deep spots which are edged with white, in a dense terminal raceme, all nodding in the same direction; segments ovate-oblong; peduncles straight, about equal in length to the calyces. *Leaves*, very rough, oblong, crenate, on short winged stalks. There are many beautifully spotted forms as well as a white one. Britain and many other parts of Europe.——The prettily spotted varieties deserve to be abundantly grown in shrubberies and copses. Seed.

Digitalis Thapsi (*Mullein-like D.*)— A handsome plant allied to the common Foxglove, but somewhat smaller, and a true perennial; 2 to 3 ft. high. *Flowers*, in summer; purple, with pale throat dotted with blood-red spots, smaller than those of *D. purpureum*, and like them produced in a dense raceme; peduncles arched, much longer than the calyx. *Leaves*, oblong, rough, crenated, undulated, decurrent. S. Europe. ——Borders, fringes of shrubberies, and naturalization in copses, etc., in light, well-drained soil. Seed.

Diotis maritima (*Sea Cottonweed*).— A dwarf cottony herb, with hard, almost woody, stems branching at the base; 8 to 10 in. high. *Flowers*, in late summer or autumn; bright yellow, in dense terminal corymbs. *Leaves*, alternate, oblong, or almost spoon-shaped, entire, or slightly toothed, sessile, about 1 in. long, quite white on both sides with cottony down. On sea-shore sands of the southern half of Great Britain, in St.

Ouen's Bay, Jersey, and also S. Europe.——Borders, grouped with plants having silvery and variegated foliage, or as a rock plant, in sandy soil. Cuttings and seed.

Diphylleia cymosa (*Cymose-flowered D.*)—A smooth herb with somewhat the habit of *Podophyllum*, 1 ft. high. *Flowers*, in early summer; white, in large loose heads or cymes; petals 6, naked on the inside; stamens 6; berries roundish, bluish-black. *Leaves*, 2, very large, alternate, umbrella-like, glaucous, kidney-shaped, usually 2-cleft. Native of North America, on the borders of rivulets and on mountains.——Peat borders and fringes of beds of American plants in the moistest spots. Propagated by division in spring.

Diplopappus rigidus (*Rigid D.*)—A dwarf hardy Aster-like shrub with prostrate stems, and ascending flower-bearing branches; about 1 foot high. *Flowers*, in autumn; 1¼ in. across, sky-blue with yellow centre, terminal, solitary. *Leaves*, numerous, linear-acute, sessile, rigid, with a prominent dorsal keel. N. America.——Borders, in ordinary free soil. Seed and division.

Dodecatheon integrifolium (*Entire-leaved D.*)—Allied to the American Cowslip, but dwarfer and more brilliant in bloom; 4 to 6 in. high. *Flowers*, in early summer; deep rosy crimson, smaller than those of *D. Meadia*, and produced in small few, flowered umbels; the base of each petal white, springing from a yellow or dark orange cup. *Leaves*, oval or spoon-shaped, entire. In shady woods near rivers, on the Alleghany Mountains, and also the Rocky Mountains in N. America.——The rock-garden, in rich soil. Seed.

Dodecatheon Jeffreyanum (*Hort.*)(*Jeffrey's American Cowslip*).—A very vigorous kind, easily recognised when above ground by its large leaves, with very thick reddish midribs; 15 in. to 2 ft. high. *Flowers*, in early summer; purplish-rose, the petals 4 in number, reflexed as in the other species, and with a yellowish spot at the base. *Leaves*, 4 to 10 in., sometimes more, in length, narrowly-spoon-shaped, tapering very much towards the base of the very thick midrib. Rocky Mountains.——Borders, low and sheltered portions of the rock-garden, or here and there amid dwarf shrubs, always in rich, light, and deep soil. It would also thrive very well in the drier parts of the bog-bed, associated with such plants as *Trillium grandiflorum* and *Cypripedium spectabile*. Easily increased by careful division of the root in autumn.

Dodecatheon Meadia (*American Cowslip*).—A beautiful perennial, 10 to 16 in. high. *Flowers*, in April or May; purple, inclining to the colour of the peach-blossom, freely produced in a loose umbel on smooth naked stems, each blossom drooping elegantly. *Leaves*, oblong-oval, smooth, unevenly toothed, waved, 6 or 7 in. long and from 2 to 3 in. broad, erect when first appearing, but afterwards spreading. There are several varieties, all of which are worthy of cultivation. Rich woodlands in N. America.——Borders, and the rock-garden, thriving best in light, sandy or vegetable, earth. Division, or seed sown soon after being gathered.

Dondia Epipactis (*Epipactis*). — *Hacquetia Epipactis*.—A singular and pleasing little herb, 3 to 6 in. high. *Flowers*, in spring; greenish-yellow, in a simple umbel; involucre of 5 or 6 ovate leaves, toothed at the apex, exceeding the umbel. *Leaves*, radical, ternate or 3-parted, serrated. *Root* black on the outside. Carinthia and Carniola.——Margins of borders, in the spring-garden, or occasionally in the rock-garden, or naturalized on

very bare banks and slopes, where such a small and unobtrusive plant may be seen. Division.

Doronicum austriacum (*Austrian D.*) —A very showy-flowered and neatly-tufted perennial; 1 to 1½ ft. high. *Flowers*, in spring and early summer; yellow, large, 1 to 5 on each stem. *Leaves*, dentate, those of the root heart-shaped, stalked; lower stem-leaves ovate-spoon-shaped, abruptly narrowed at the base; upper ones lance-shaped, cordate, clasping the stem. Whole plant rather hairy. Sub-alpine woods of Hungary, Bohemia, Austria, Carinthia, Central France, and the Pyrenees. —— Borders, or naturalized on rough rocky ground, or banks. It thrives in any soil, and is readily increased by division.

Doronicum caucasicum (*Caucasian Leopard's-bane*). — A showy perennial, about 1 ft. high. *Flowers*, in spring; yellow, 1¾ in. across, solitary, terminal and axillary. *Leaves* of the stem, oval, pointed, with a broad clasping base and toothed margin; radical leaves reniform, with deeply - toothed margins. Neck of the rhizome more or less covered with silky down; seed-vessels of the ray quite smooth, without pappus. Caucasus. —— The same positions and treatment as for the last. Division.

Doronicum Columnæ (*Columna's D.*) Very like the preceding; 1 to 1½ ft. high. —*Flowers*, early in spring and summer; yellow, large. *Leaves*, dentate, softly and shortly downy; those of the root almost kidney-shaped, stalked; lower stem-leaves auricled; middle ones cordate-spoon-shaped, or simply cordate; upper ones ovate-lance-shaped, clasping the stem. Distinguished from *D. caucasicum* by the absence of silky down at the neck of the rhizome, and by the seed-vessels of the ray being slightly downy. S. Europe. —— Similar positions

DORONICUM — DRABA.

and treatment to those recommended for *D. austriacum*. Division.

Doronicum Pardalianches (*Leopard's-bane*).—A coarse perennial, 1½ to 3 ft. high. *Flowers*, in spring and early summer; yellow, usually 3 to 5 on each stem; rays numerous, very narrow. *Leaves* of root heart-shaped, hairy, stalked; of stem, few, ovate, lower ones stalked, upper sessile and clasping. *Roots* fleshy, forming at intervals small tubers about the size of a bean. Central Europe.— Suitable for rough and wild places only, under trees or otherwise, and in any soil. Division.

Doronicum plantagineum (*Plantain D.*)—A vigorous herb allied to the previous species, but with larger flowers, and leaves not heart-shaped, but varying, either entire or irregularly toothed; 2 to 3 ft. high. *Flowers*, in spring and early summer; yellow, usually solitary on a terminal peduncle, sometimes, though very rarely, 2 or 3 on a stem. *Leaves* of root, ovate or oval, stalked, unevenly toothed; stem-leaves nearly entire, lance-shaped, narrower than those of the previous species. Central and Southern Europe.——Like the preceding, not desirable for any but semi-wild spots. Division.

Draba aizoides (*Seagreen D.*)—A brilliant dwarf rock plant, 2 to 3 in. high. *Flowers*, in spring; bright yellow, in terminal racemes; stamens about as long as the petals; scapes naked, smooth. *Leaves*, narrow, lance-shaped, keeled, ciliate, arranged in neat rosettes. It rarely ripens seeds. Found in one locality in South Wales, and on rocky and gravelly spots on mountains in Central Europe. ——The rock-garden, in gritty soil, crevices in mossy old walls and ruins; occasionally, in very fine and well-drained sandy soils, it thrives very well in borders, but in this case it ought to be protected from the encroachments of coarser plants. Division and seed.

Draba Aizoon (*Evergreen D.*)—Allied to the previous species, but a more vigorous grower, with the leaves broader and of a darker green, arranged so as to form a large and complete rosette, from which spring the flower-stems, about 5 or 6 in. high. *Flowers*, in spring; pale yellow, produced in terminal racemes; scape naked, villous. *Leaves*, linear, acutish, keeled, stiff, ciliated. It ripens seed freely. Mountains of Carinthia.—— The positions and treatment recommended for the preceding species will suit this also.

Draba alpina (*Alpine D.*)—An arctic species, 2 to 3 in. high. *Flowers*, in spring; yellow, rather smaller than those of *D. aizoides*, in terminal racemes; scape naked, pubescent. *Leaves*, lance-shaped or ovate, dark green, flat, smooth. N. Europe and N. America.——A somewhat delicate subject, and best adapted for pot culture, or well-drained chinks in rockwork, in sandy loam. Seed or division.

Draba ciliaris (*Large Yellow D.*)— One of the largest-flowered and finest of the yellow Drabas, 3 to 4 in. high. *Flowers*, in spring and early in summer; yellow. *Leaves*, densely clothed with soft spines, in rosettes. Probably a variety of *D. cuspidata*. Alps.— Rockwork. Seed or division.

Draba ciliata (*Ciliated Draba*).— One of the finest of the white-flowered kinds, and resembling a miniature plant of *Arabis albida*; 2 in. high. *Flowers*, early in summer; white, few, closely set; sepals, green, oval. *Leaves*, somewhat leathery, smooth, with a cartilaginous margin, slightly toothed and fringed with stiff hairs; those of the rosette obovate, shortly pointed; those of the stem oblong, usually two or three in number. Pods linear;

I

stems and flower-stalks very smooth. Croatia and Carniola.——The rock-garden, among the dwarfest plants, in tufts or small sheets near the level of the eye, in light, moist soil. Seed and division.

Draba cinerea (*Grey D.*)—The most effective, perhaps, of the white-flowered species; 3 to 6 in. high. *Flowers*, in early spring; white, in terminal racemes, on simple, leafy, somewhat pubescent stems. *Leaves*, oblong-linear, entire; stem-leaves 5 or 6 in number, scattered. Siberia.—Rockwork in well-drained sandy loam. Seed or division.

Draba cuspidata (*Pointed-leaved D.*)—A pretty dwarf species, 3 in. high, with a thick woody stem, and closely resembling *D. ciliaris*. *Flowers*, in spring; yellow, in terminal racemes; scapes naked, villous. *Leaves*, linear, acutish, keeled, ciliated, in dense rosettes. Mountains in Tauria and Spain.——Rockwork, old walls and ruins, and front margin of mixed border, in warm sandy loam. Seed, which is sparingly produced.

Draba glacialis (*Glacier D.*)—A very minute kind, forming dense little cushions, 1 to 2 inches high. *Flowers*, in earliest spring; yellow. *Leaves*, linear, pointed, smooth, stiff, fringed on the edges with rigid hairs. Very much resembling a small specimen of *D. aizoides*, and considered by Koch to be merely a variety of that species growing at a higher elevation. It differs from it by having a few-flowered stem, pedicels shorter than the pod, and a short style. Granitic Alps of Switzerland.——The rock-garden in exposed spots, in moist and very gritty or sandy soil, and associated with the dwarfest alpine plants. Seed or very careful division.

Draba rupestris (*Rock D*).—A dwarf, compact-growing species, 2 to 3 in.

high. *Flowers*, in summer; white, few, small, on almost leafless stems. *Leaves*, crowded, lance-shaped, almost entire, pilose. Norway, Scotland, and North America.——Rockwork, in sandy loam. Seed.

Draba tridentata (*Three-toothed-leaved D.*)—Easily distinguished by its 3-toothed leaves; 2 to 4 in. high. *Flowers*, in spring; golden yellow, in terminal racemes; scapes naked, smooth. *Leaves*, dark green, obovate, narrowed at the base into the stalk, hairy. Mountains of Southern Russia.——The rock-garden, in light moist soil. Seed and division.

Dracocephalum argunense (*Argunsk D.*)—A handsome perennial allied to *D. Ruyschianum*, but with larger flowers, and smooth calyces; 1 to 1½ ft. high. *Flowers*, in summer; blue, in whorled spikes; calyx quite smooth; upper lip semi-trifid, lower one narrowly bipartite. *Leaves*, linear-lanceolate, entire, smooth, nearly sessile, 2 or 3 in. long; floral ones wedge-shaped-elliptic, acute; stems smooth. Dahuria.——A fine border plant, especially in warm soils. In cold ones it would be better on raised borders, or on the rockwork. Seed or division.

Dracocephalum austriacum (*Austrian D.*)—Another fine kind, with the habit of *D. Ruyschianum*, but with divided leaves; about 1 ft. high. *Flowers*, in summer; blue, in whorled spikes, each bloom being more than ½ in. long; upper teeth of calyx ovate, lower ones lance-shaped; corolla about 3 times as long as the calyx. *Leaves*, 3- or 5-parted; segments linear; margins revolute; floral ones trifid, and with long fine spines; stems rather pilose. Most of the great mountain chains of Europe.——Positions and treatment the same as for the preceding.

Dracocephalum grandiflorum (*Betony-leaved D.*)—A very dwarf and distinct species, somewhat resembling a *Betonica* in habit, 3 to 12 in. high. *Flowers*, in summer; fine blue, in whorled oblong spikes, 2 or 3 in. long; segments of calyx equal; corolla nearly 2 in. long, 3 times the length of calyx. *Leaves*, of root, oblong, obtuse, heart-shaped at the base, on long stalks; stem-leaves ovate, on short stalks; floral leaves oblong, deeply toothed. Siberia, frequent on the Altaian Alps.——The rock-garden or the margins of borders, always in good sandy loam, and in a thoroughly well-drained soil. This plant is now, and has long been, very uncommon in gardens, and deserves a favourable position till sufficiently increased. Careful division and seed.

Dracocephalum peregrinum (*Twin-flowered D.*)—A decumbent species, with bracts and leaves furnished with sharp-pointed teeth; about 1 ft. high. *Flowers*, in summer; blue, 1 to 1½ in. long, in pairs both turned the same way, in few-flowered whorls; corolla about 3 times as long as the calyx. *Leaves*, lance-shaped, resembling those of Hyssop or Rosemary, somewhat hoary beneath, about an inch long, deeply toothed; floral leaves linear-lanceolate, somewhat spiny. Siberia.——Borders, and the rougher parts of the rock-garden, in light well-drained soil. Seed and division.

Dracocephalum Ruyschianum (*Hyssop-leaved D.*)—A handsome species, 12 to 18 in. high. *Flowers*, in summer; purplish, blue, about an inch long; about 6 flowers at the top of each stem; calyx pubescent, half as long as the corolla. *Leaves*, linear-lanceolate, entire, smooth, 1 to 2 in. long; floral leaves ovate-lanceolate; stems branched from the base, pubescent. Europe and Russian Asia. ——Borders, and the rock-garden, in light warm soil. Seed and division.

Dryas Drummondi (*Drummond's Avens*). — A dwarf, hardy, evergreen trailer, with flower-stems from 3 to 8 in. high. *Flowers*, in summer; golden yellow, about 1 in. across; calyx densely covered with blackish glandular hairs. *Leaves*, oval, scalloped on the margin, stalked, white and downy underneath. North America.—— A pretty rock plant, easily grown in any free soil, and also suited for the margins of borders, edges of beds of American plants, etc. It is very uncommon in gardens, but thrives quite as well in sandy soil as the common *Mountain Avens*. Division.

Dryas octopetala (*Mountain Avens*). —A prostrate or creeping evergreen herb, forming dense spreading tufts. *Flowers*, in summer; white, with yellow stamens, an inch or more across, on erect peduncles, 3 to 8 in. high; fruit with a feathery appendage an inch long, like those of *Anemone*. *Leaves*, oblong, green, smooth and shining above, white and downy beneath, deeply crenate, about ½ in. long. Europe, Britain, and North America.——Borders and edgings, in peaty or very sandy soil, or on rockwork, in somewhat moist spots. It looks very pretty, drooping over the brows of rocks. Division.

Dyckia rariflora (*Hardy Dyckia*).— An interesting plant of a tropical family (*Bromelia*), which, Major Trevor Clarke informs me, has lived out of doors and flowered in his garden for some years; 2 ft. high. *Flowers*, in summer; orange-coloured, and very showy, in panicles, with spiny bracts. *Leaves*, radical, lance-shaped, pointed, narrow, marked with longitudinal lines, whitish underneath, and disposed in a rosette. Brazil.——Warm, sheltered, and dry nooks of the rock-garden, in well-drained, sandy loam. Seed.

Echinacea angustifolia (*Narrow-leaved E.*)—A perennial of distinct aspect, 2 to 4 ft. high. *Flowers*, in summer; light purple or rose, 4 to 6 in. across. *Leaves*, lance - shaped, hairy, entire, 3-nerved, 4 to 8 in. long, and about ½ in. broad; stem hairy below, nearly smooth above the middle. *Root* perpendicular. North America.——The positions and treatment, etc. recommended for *E. purpurea* will suit this perfectly.

Echinacea purpurea (*Purple E.*)—*Rudbeckia purpurea.*—A rigid, stout, and remarkable-looking perennial, 3 to 4 ft. high, or more, in very rich, warm soils. *Flowers*, late in summer and in autumn; dull purple, 4 or 5 inches across. *Leaves* of root oval-lance-shaped, on reddish stalks; stem-leaves more lance-shaped, tapering into a winged stalk, or nearly stalkless; all somewhat rough. Stem smooth. *E. serotina* is a variety of this, with hairy and rougher leaves; the rays usually shorter and broader. Southern and Western United States of America.——Associated with the Tritomas, Eryngium amethystinum, or plants of like stature and merit, in mixed borders, or as strong, isolated tufts, in warm spots in the subtropical garden or pleasure-ground, always in rich, deep soil. Propagated by seed or division of the root in autumn, or very early spring; the plants not to be often disturbed for this purpose.

Echinops bannaticus (*Hungarian E.*) — A plant of stiff, slightly branching habit, 2 to 3 ft. high or more. *Flowers*, in summer; blue, in spherical heads. *Leaves*, roughish, pubescent above, downy underneath; radical ones pinnate, upper ones pinnatifid; lobes oblong, acuminate, spiny, somewhat sinuated, and having a spinous fringe. Hungary and Southern Tauria. —— Borders and edges of woods, naturalization in copses, or in groups with the bolder perennials, in any soil. Division.

Echinops exaltatus (*Tall E.*)—A vigorous species, 5 to 7 ft. high. *Flowers* in summer; whitish, in large spherical heads; stem rather simple, covered with glandular hairs and cobweb-like down. *Leaves*, pinnatifid, rough on the upper side with thinly-set hairs, covered underneath with ash-coloured down, and set with small spines on the margin; scales of the involucrum smooth, pointed, shortly ciliated; pappus crown-shaped. Austria.——Scarcely worthy of a position in the borders, not being nearly so ornamental as the following species, but worthy of being naturalized amongst the most vigorous perennials in half-wild places, in any soil. Division.

Echinops ruthenicus.— The handsomest species I am acquainted with, 3¼ to 4 ft. high; the heads of bloom being of a fine blue. *Flowers*, late in summer; blue, collected in spherical clusters on the tops of the branches, those on the summit of the clusters opening first, and all resting on a common receptacle; each flower-head is surrounded by an oblong, angular involucrum, formed of linear-awl-shaped bluish scales. *Leaves*, alternate, leathery, pinnatifid, with toothed and spiny divisions, like those of some Thistles, of a dull green above, white and cottony underneath; stem also covered with a cottony down of silvery whiteness. Southern Russia. ——A first-rate border plant; also excellent for groups, and for naturalization in open glades, near wood-walks; in ordinary soil. Division.

Edraianthus Pumilio (*Silvery Harebell*).—A singularly pretty and minute rock-plant, allied to the Campanulas, with foliage resembling that of a dwarf tufted Pink; about 3 in. high. *Flowers*, early in summer; of a pure, purplish blue, about 1 in. long, terminal, solitary, barely rising above the leaves, cup-shaped, cut into segments for about one-third of their length; tube of the calyx obconical, smooth. *Leaves*, linear, entire, hoary and silvery, with adpressed hairs on the upper side, very finely ciliated at the edges, and quite smooth on the under side, which is of a dark, shining green. Dalmatia, on elevated parts of Mount Biocovo.——A gem for the rock-garden, thriving in moist loam, with abundance of sand or grit; well suited for association with the alpine Forget-me-not, and other dwarf, choice May-flowering rock-plants. Seed.

Empetrum nigrum (*Black Crowberry*).— A small, creeping, much branched, heath-like shrub, forming thick tufts, 1 ft. high. *Flowers*, in spring; purplish, small, with a whitish calyx, sessile, axillary, near the ends of the branches. *Leaves*, crowded, linear-oblong, about ¼ in. long; margins rolled back so as to nearly meet. Berries black, clustered, resembling those of the Juniper. N. Europe and Britain.——This may occasionally be thought worthy of a place in the rock-garden, or in collections of dwarf shrubs, in peaty or very sandy soil. Division.

Epigæa repens (*Ground Laurel*).—A very handsome, creeping, tufted, evergreen shrub; 6 in. high. *Flowers*, in early summer; white, tinged with red, in small clusters, exhaling a sweet and spicy fragrance; corolla cylindrical. *Leaves*, roundish-heart-shaped, quite entire, covered with russety hairs; margins waved. North America.——Peat borders, or the rock-garden, in half-shady spots, in sandy peat, or naturalized in sandy woods or copses, in which it would look as much at home as in its native woods, Careful division of established tufts.

Epilobium angustifolium (*French Willow*).—Perhaps the most showy perennial that blooms in the middle of summer 3 to 6 ft. high. *Flowers*, crimson, in spiked racemes, each flower with a bract. *Leaves*, lance-shaped, undulated, nearly stalkless, smooth; stems erect, nearly simple. There is a pure white variety. Mountain woods and pastures in Europe and Siberia, and in many parts of Britain.——This fine plant, which runs so quickly in a border as to soon become a most troublesome weed, is magnificent when allowed to run wild in a rough shrubbery or copse, where it may bloom along with the Foxgloves, etc. Division.

Epilobium angustissimum (*Narrow-leaved E.*)—A medium-sized perennial, with a reddish stem, from 1 to 2 ft. high. *Flowers*, late in summer; rose-coloured, more than an inch across; flower-buds covered with a white mealy bloom. *Leaves*, lance-shaped, sessile, attenuated at both ends. European Alps.——Borders, in ordinary soil. Division.

Epilobium Dodonæi (*Dodonæus's E.*) —A showy herb, with rosemary-like leaves; 1 to 1½ ft. high. *Flowers*, in summer; deep rose, terminal. *Leaves*, very narrow, lance-shaped, nearly entire, smooth; stem almost smooth, ascending, branched at the apex. Piedmont and Dauphiny.—— Borders, fringes of shrubberies, or naturalization in open copses, in ordinary soil. Division or seed.

Epilobium hirsutum (*Hairy E.*)—A handsome and common species, 3 to 6 ft. high. *Flowers*, in summer; purple or flesh-coloured, somewhat bell-shaped, in a leafy, corymbose cluster; petals cloven, twice the length of calyx. *Leaves*, lower ones opposite; upper ones alternate, ovate-lance-shaped, hairy, toothed; stems branched, hairy. Britain, Europe and Siberia, in wet places.——Only useful by the margins of streams, ponds, etc., associated with the Loosestrife and like plants, in any soil. Division or seed.

Epilobium rosmarinifolium (*Rosemary French Willow*). — A graceful plant growing in bushy tufts, 2 to 3 ft. or more in height. *Flowers*, in summer; purplish-rose, about 1 in. across, in a loose spike; petals obovate; tube of calyx 4-sided. *Leaves*, alternate or opposite, linear, of a lively green, very closely set, often crowded together at the joints of the stem, not veined, narrowed for a short distance at both ends, entire or faintly wavy, denticulated, and terminated by a pointed and deciduous callosity. Europe.——Borders, and fringes of shrubberies, in ordinary soil. A first-rate and easily grown perennial, not at all sufficiently cultivated. Division, seed, or cuttings.

Epimedium alpinum (*Alpine Barren-Wort*).—A dwarf evergreen herb, with handsome foliage and slender creeping rootstock, which scarcely penetrates the ground; 6 to 9 in. high. *Flowers*, in spring; purplish, yellow on the inside, in a loose terminal raceme, about 6 in. long; petals 4; stamens 4; sepals red, 4 to 6. *Leaves*, bi-ternate; leaflets heart- or lance-shaped, acuminated, serrated. Woods and coppices in the North of England, France, and Southern Europe.——The rock-garden, borders, or fringes of beds of shrubs, planted in peat soil. Division.

Epimedium diphyllum (*Two-leaved E.*)—*Aceranthus diphyllus*. — Seldom exceeds 3 or 4 in. in height. *Flowers*, in April and May; numerous, small, white; rootstock running a little. This species is distinguished from all the others by its dwarfness, and especially by the absence of the spur from the corolla, and by the flower-stalks branching only once, and bearing only two lozenge-shaped leaflets, smaller, and narrower than those of the other species. Japan.——The rock-garden, in sheltered nooks, and in tufts towards the margins of beds or groups of minute shrubs, in moist sandy peat. Division.

Epimedium Muschianum (*Muschi's E.*)—A tufted erect and compact-growing kind, 1 ft. high. *Flowers*, in May; few, of a dull white; nectaries longer than the petals; style thread-like, almost central; stigma somewhat lobed. *Leaves*, ternate. Japan.——Not of much beauty or interest in the presence of the other kinds, but worthy of a place where there is much room, in peat borders for plants of this kind. Division.

Epimedium macranthum (*Large-flowered E.*) — *E. grandiflorum*. — A handsome species, 10 to 15 in. high. *Flowers*, in late spring or early summer, and occasionally in autumn; large, white, drooping, numerous, in panicles not branching much; stamens yellow; spurs straight, about ½ in. long; flower-stems with 1 to 3 leaves on each; lobes at the base of the leaflets rounded, while the margins are fringed with hairs. *E. niveum* is a var. of *E. macranthum*, from which it differs in having much smaller leaves and flowers. Japan.——Peat borders and the less exposed and less important parts of the rock-garden. Division.

Epimedium pinnatum (*Large Yellow E.*)—So far as I have seen, the strongest grower and the handsomest species; 8 to 24 in. high. *Flowers*, late in spring, or early in summer; large, bright golden yellow, in an elongated cluster. *Leaves*, all radical, stalked, tripinnate, with stalked, oval-acute, toothed segments, pubescent when young, leathery when mature; stem also pubescent, creeping. Persia.——Borders, the rougher parts of the rock-garden, the fringes of shrubberies.

and beds of American plants. It thrives well in ordinary sandy loam, but attains its greatest dimensions and beauty in a deep, moist, and very sandy loam or peat. It is the kind best suited for naturalization, and forming in sheltered nooks dense tufts of handsome foliage, and is peculiarly well suited for associating with the smaller shrubs. Division.

Epimedium purpureum (*Purple E.*)—*Flowers*, in May; purplish on the outside, brownish-yellow within, twice as large as those of *E. alpinum*, from which it is also distinguished by its rootstock not running so much, and by the larger divisions of its leaves. Japan.——Fringes of shrubberies, and beds of American shrubs, borders, rockwork, or banks; always in peat soil. Division.

Epimedium violaceum (*Violet E.*)—Resembles *E. macranthum* in habit and stature. *Flowers*, in May; large, numerous, violet. *Rootstock* not running. Japan. Seems to differ from *E. macranthum* only in the colour of its flowers, and its leaflets not being regularly fringed with hairs; the spurs of the petals also are not half as long as those of that species, being, in fact, not longer than the sepals.——Similar positions and treatment to those recommended for the preceding kind will suit this. Division.

Epipactis palustris (*Marsh E.*)—A somewhat showy orchid, 1 to 1½ ft. high. *Flowers*, late in summer; drooping; arranged in a loose spike of 6 to 12 on a stem; petals and lip white, tinged with purple; calyx purplish-green. *Leaves*, lanceolate, erect, sheathing the stem at their base, 5-nerved. *Stem*, pubescent in the upper part. Native of all parts of temperate and southern Europe, in moist grassy places.——The artificial bog, or moist spots near a rivulet, in soft peat. In moist districts it thrives very well in peat beds away from the water. Division of established tufts.

Equisetum scirpoides (*Dwarf Horsetail*).—A minute and interesting kind, 2 to 6 in. high. *Flowers*, in spring. *Stems*, in very dense tufts, almost thread-like, not rigid but somewhat contorted, usually 6-grooved; sheaths 3-toothed. North America.——Peat borders, among minute plants, on the rockwork in moist peaty spots, or in the hardy fernery. Division.

Equisetum sylvaticum (*Wood Horsetail*).—A little plant of the most exquisite grace when well grown; 8 to 15 in. high. *Flowers*, in spring; spike blunt. Sterile and fertile stems similar, 12 to 18 in. high, with about 12 furrows, and many whorls of slender, compound, spreading or deflexed, solid branches; sheaths lax, ending in 3 or 4 blunt lobes. Sheaths of the branches with 3 long acute teeth, each 1-ribbed up to its tip. North European and Britain, in wet shady places.——In the hardy fernery, in shady moist spots near the rock-garden, rocky fringes of rivulets or cascades. It also looks very graceful grown in pots in cold frames. Division.

Equisetum Telmateia (*Giant Horsetail*).—A plant of much nobility of port as well as grace of character when well-developed; 2 to 6 ft. high. *Flowers*, in spring. Sterile stem 3 to 6 ft. high, occasionally bearing a small terminal spike, furnished from top to bottom with whorls of slender branches which have 4 angles, each with a longitudinal furrow and 4-toothed sheaths, the lowest joint and sheath exceeding the stem-sheath. Fertile stem stout, 1 ft. or more high, with many pale-brown sheaths with 30 to 40 teeth each; spike large. Europe and Britain, in wet places. —— In the hardy fernery, artificial bog, shady peat border, near cascades, or among shrubs growing in moist hollows, in vegetable soil. Division.

Equisetum variegatum (*Variegated Horsetail*).—A simple-stemmed and somewhat slender species, 8 to 20 in. high. *Spike*, short, egg-shaped, pointed. *Stems*, simple or slightly branched, growing in tufts, of a pale green, very rough, with 4 to 10 furrows; sheaths slightly enlarged upwards, green below, black above; teeth blunt, each tipped with a deciduous bristle, persistent, ovate, black in the centre, with a white membranous margin. Europe and Britain.——In wet places or in water, by the margins of ponds or streams. Division.

Eranthis hyemalis (*Winter Aconite*).—A small plant, with yellow flowers, surrounded by a whorl of shining-green divided leaves, and a short, blackish underground stem, resembling a tuber; 3 to 8 in. high. *Flowers*, from January to March; calyx of from 5 to 8 oblong, petal-like sepals; petals 6 to 8, very short and tubular; stamens numerous. *Leaves*, deeply divided; involucre composed of 3 deeply-cut leaves growing together. Europe.——This is seen to best advantage in a wild state, under deciduous trees or shrubs, on slopes in half-wild places, etc., though it is occasionally worthy of a place among the earliest border flowers. It grows in any soil and is most easily increased by division.

Eremostachys laciniata (*Jagged E.*) —A very distinct-looking subject, 12 to 30 in. high. *Flowers*, in summer; purplish, in whorls of from 10 to 20; calyx downy, widely tubular-campanulate, with 5 prominent ribs. *Leaves*, pinnate; leaflets oblong-lance-shaped or linear, deeply jagged; root-leaves 6 in. long or more; stem-leaves the same shape but smaller; stems nearly simple. Levant and Eastern Caucasus.——Borders, in warm sandy loam. It is also useful in groups of the bolder perennials, and in warm soils might be naturalized on sunny banks or slopes, amidst other tall perennials. Division or seed.

Eremostachys iberica (*Iberian E.*) — *Phlomis iberica*. — Differs from *E. laciniata* in having leaves less hairy, and flowers yellow, with the limb not so open or gaping. Georgia, near the Caucasus. —— Similar positions and treatment to the preceding.

Erica carnea (*Winter Heath*).—A brilliant, dwarf, very early-flowering shrub, 6 to 9 in. high. *Flowers*, from March to May; red, axillary, drooping, disposed in racemes; corolla conical, ¼ to ⅓ in. long; bracts remote from the calyx. *Leaves*, linear, smooth, 3 to 4 in a whorl. Stems and branches prostrate. Germany, Switzerland, and Britain.——Borders of all kinds, in tufts or as edgings, the rock-garden, or naturalized among our own wild heaths. It thrives in ordinary garden soil, but, like most of its family, grows best in peat or in fine moist sandy soil. Division.

Erica ciliaris (*Ciliated Heath*).— A somewhat straggling evergreen shrub, readily known by its very showy racemes of flowers, as large as those of St. Daboec's Heath; 1 ft. high. *Flowers*, in early summer; pale red; corolla ovate, oblique at the mouth, nearly ½ in. long; sepals small, ciliated. *Leaves*, 3 in a whorl, ovate, glandular, ciliated, spreading. Western Europe. —— Beds, with the smaller shrubs, on the margins of shrubberies, and in the rougher parts of the rock-garden in peat soil. Division.

Erica cinerea (*Scotch Heath*).—A dwarf evergreen shrub, allied to *E. Tetralix*, but easily distinguished by its flowers not being in terminal heads, and by its deep green hue; 6 to 12 in. high. *Flowers*, in summer and autumn; purple, changing to blue when fading, in showy terminal racemes; corolla ovate-urceolate, about ¼ of an inch long. *Leaves*, usually 3 in a whorl, linear. There are several varieties, one being white. Britain and Northern Europe.——Similar treatment and positions to those recommended for the preceding kind.

Erica Tetralix (*Cross-leaved Heath*). —A species with leaves shorter and less pointed than those of the Scotch Heath; 6 to 12 in. high. *Flowers*, rather late in summer; pale red, about the size of those of the Scotch Heath, in terminal heads or umbels; corolla ovate-globose, downy at top. *Leaves*, 4 in a whorl, ciliated. The plant is often of a greyish hue, from a short whitish down that clothes the branches and upper leaves. Northern Europe, and plentiful in Britain.——There are several varieties, some of them very pretty. The treatment and positions advised for *E. ciliaris* will suit this.

Erica vagans (*Cornish Heath*).—A neat bushy kind, not so ornamental in bloom as some of the preceding; 1 ft. or more high. *Flowers*, in summer; pinkish, rather small, but very numerous, on slender pedicels, usually in pairs, forming terminal oblong racemes; corolla bell-shaped when it first expands, but afterwards nearly globular. *Leaves*, 3, 4, or 5 in a whorl, linear, smooth; stems smooth. There are several varieties enumerated in catalogues. Southern Europe and Britain (in Cornwall), and on the south coast of Ireland.——Peat beds and fringes of shrubbery. Cuttings or layers.

Erigeron grandiflorus (*Large-flowered Fleabane*).—A small rigid herb, 4 to 6 in. high. *Flowers*, late in summer; purple or whitish, very large for the size of the plant, on stems bearing one head each. *Leaves*, of root, oblong-spoon-shaped; of stem oval-lance-shaped. Summits of the Rocky Mountains, North America.——Margins of mixed borders, or the rock-garden, in ordinary moist but well-drained soil. Division and seed.

Erigeron Roylei (*Royle's Fleabane*). —A very ornamental species, 4 to 8 in. high. *Flowers*, in summer; large, 2 in. across, bluish purple, with yellow disk, arranged in a loose corymb. *Leaves*, oblong-spathulate, smooth, ciliated. Stems hairy, glandular. Himalayas. —— The same treatment and positions as for the preceding kind.

Erigeron speciosus (*Showy Fleabane*). —*Stenactis speciosa.*—A tall showy perennial with erect stem, smooth below, much branched and slightly hairy above, leafy to the summit; about 2 ft. high. *Flowers*, in summer; violet-purple, 2 in. or more across, in corymbose heads, terminating the leafy branchlets. *Leaves*, lance-shaped, acute, entire, slightly stem-clasping, often somewhat smooth except at the margins, 2 to 4 in. long; root-leaves spoon-shaped and tapering into a stalk. North America.——Borders, or naturalization in shrubberies or on banks. It thrives in any soil and is easily increased by division.

Erinus alpinus (*Alpine E.*)—A beautiful mountain plant, 3 to 6 in. high. *Flowers*, early in summer; small, purple-violet, in sub-corymbose racemes; corolla funnel-shaped, with the limb divided into 5 segments, notched at the end; calyx bell-shaped; sepals 5, lanceolate-acute. *Leaves*, about ½ in. long, and ⅛ in. broad, oblong, toothed, obtuse at the end, those of the root in rosettes; stem-leaves alternate. *E. hirsutus* is a variety larger and more vigorous in all its parts than the type, and covered with a long whitish pubescence. There is also a white variety. Alps of Switzerland, the Tyrol, and the Pyrenees.——Walls, ruins, or the rock-garden, in any soil. No plant is more easily established on walls or ruins, or more beautiful and long-lived on them. Seed.

Eritrichium nanum (*Fairy Borage*).—A dwarf Alpine gem, growing in dense tufts; 2 or 3 in. high. *Flowers*, in summer; of a brilliant sky-blue with small yellow eye, very much resembling those of *Myosotis alpestris*, but larger and of a lighter hue, just appearing above the foliage. *Leaves*, oblong, or oblong-obovate, covered, as are the flower-stalks and calyx, with long, silky, white hairs; the lower leaves forming dense rosettes above the withered and persistent foliage of former years; the upper ones smaller and not so closely set. *Root* woody, simple, blackish, generally of extraordinary length. Granitic Alps of Switzerland and France.——The rock-garden, in the most select spots, and among the choicest and dwarfest alpine plants, in moist, sandy, or gritty loam, deep, and kept thoroughly moist in summer. The plants should be in a fully exposed position, and closely surrounded by half-buried stones, if not planted immediately against the sides of rocks or stones. Seed.

Erodium alpinum (*Alpine E.*)—This has the habit and general character of *E. Manescavi*, but is smaller; 6 to 8 in. high. *Flowers*, continuously from spring to autumn; of a handsome violet reddish or carmine, about an inch across, arranged in umbels of 6 to 10 flowers each; petals obtuse; calyx small, with long-pointed sepals. *Leaves*, smooth, twice pinnatifid, with a toothed midrib. South of Europe.—The rock-garden and borders in sandy loam. Seed or division.

Erodium caruifolium (*Caraway-leaved E.*)—A hardy, herbaceous perennial, with erect, leafless flower-stems; 6 to 10 in. high. *Flowers*, in spring and early summer; red, about ½ in. across; in umbels of 9 or 10 blossoms. *Leaves*, very graceful, 8 or 9 in. long, alternately pinnate; leaflets very deeply cut, twice divided; midrib and under side of leaves covered with soft, white, downy hairs. Spain.——The rock-garden, or margins of borders in light or calcareous soil. In this kind of soil it might also be naturalized in bare places. Division or seed.

Erodium hymenodes (*Pelargonium E.*)—Somewhat like a cut-leaved *Pelargonium* in appearance; 6 to 15 in. high. *Flowers*, all spring and summer; pinkish, the upper petals having a reddish-brown spot at the base; stalks many-flowered. *Leaves*, somewhat 3-lobed, very blunt, deeply-toothed; stipules and bracts ovate; stem shrubby at the base, erect, branched, clothed with soft hairs. In fissures of rocks on Mount Atlas.——Borders, very rough rockwork, or naturalization in chalk-pits, etc., in any dryish soil. It is scarcely worthy of a place in any but a botanical collection. Seed or cuttings.

Erodium macradenum (*Black-eyed E.*)—Nearly allied to *E. petræum*; 2 to 6 in. high. *Flowers*, in summer; of a delicate flesh-colour, veined with purplish rose; the two upper petals marked with a large, blackish spot; 2 to 6 blooms on each stem. *Leaves*, twice divided, forming graceful little tufts, and possessing a peculiar and aromatic fragrance. Pyrenees. —— The rock-garden, in dry chinks and ledges, or in borders, where the soil is dry and warm. Division or seed.

Erodium Manescavi (*Showy Heron's-bill*).—A very large and handsome species, 10 in. to 2 ft. high, with numerous long, much-divided leaves, and flower-stems bearing 5 to 15 handsome flowers, each more than an inch across. *Flowers*, in summer; and in young plants for a long time in succession, purplish-red, in umbels; bracts few, broad. *Leaves*, pinnate; leaflets oblong, deeply cut; rachis without teeth; lower leaflets opposite and rather larger than the others. Pyrenees.——Borders and the rock-garden, in good soil. It is also a fine plant for naturalization on banks or slopes. Seed and division.

Erodium petræum (*Rock Heron's-bill*).—A graceful and pretty little rock-plant; 3 to 6 in. high. *Flowers*, in early summer; lively rose, or white and veined, but not spotted; peduncles many-flowered, and with the pedicels hairy; petals retuse, twice as long as the calyx. *Leaves*, smoothish, pinnate, with deeply divided segments, and lance-shaped or linear lobes; rachis-toothed; lower leaflets opposite, and rather larger than the others. Pyrenees, on rocks.—— The rock-garden, in dry warm fissures or ledges, in sandy well-drained loam. Seed or careful division.

Erodium Reichardi (*Fairy Heron's-bill*).—A minute, tufted, stemless herb, with little heart-shaped leaves, that rest upon the ground, and flower-stems that attain a height of only 2 or 3 in. *Flowers*, from early summer often till autumn; white, faintly veined with pink; solitary, rather large for the size of the plant; petals larger than the calyx. *Leaves*, small, heart-shaped, crenated, obtuse, smoothish. Majorca.—— The rock-garden, in tufts, or carpets, in any soil. It is also a neat subject for growing in pans. Division.

Erodium romanum (*Roman Heron's-bill*).—A species with gracefully-cut leaves, allied to the British *E. cicutarium*, but differing by having larger flowers, and by being a perennial; 6 to 9 in. high. *Flowers*, in spring or early summer; purplish; peduncles many-flowered; petals equal, longer than the calyx; bracts numerous.

Leaves, pinnate; leaflets ovate, deeply cut; rachis without teeth. *Root* thick, red within. South Europe——Borders, in ordinary dry soils. Seed.

Erodium trichomanefolium (*Fern-leaved E.*)—A very graceful little kind, with leaves so deeply cut as to resemble a fern; 4 to 6 in. high. *Flowers*, in early summer; flesh-coloured, with darker veins; peduncles 4-flowered; petals blunt, a little longer than the calyx. *Leaves*, bipinnate, hairy; lobules oblong-linear. Mount Lebanon. ——The rock-garden, in warm chinks and ledges, in well-drained very sandy loam. I have not yet seen this species with us, but noticed it thriving in the botanic garden at Geneva, a year or two since. Seed or careful division.

Erpetion reniforme (*New Holland Violet*).—*Viola hederacea.*—A charming, but somewhat tender little plant; about 2 in. high. *Flowers*, throughout the summer; blue and white, one on each stalk; petals reflexed, the two side ones furnished with a beard on the upperside; sepals lance-shaped. *Leaves*, small, crowded, kidney-shaped, unevenly toothed, dotted. New Holland about Port Jackson.—— The rock-garden, and occasionally as a carpet plant in beds or borders. Except in very mild districts, it will perish in winter, but even if it did so everywhere, it is worthy of being annually propagated, to plant out every May. In light soil. Division.

Eryngium alpinum (*Alpine Eryngo*). —An interesting and handsome perennial, the flowers of which are surrounded with an azure blue involucre; 1½ to 3 ft. high. *Flowers*, in summer; blue, sometimes white, with green anthers, in oblong heads; bracts 12 to 20, soft, rather longer than the head of flowers; outer ones pinnatifid; inner deeply serrato-ciliate. *Leaves*, root and lower stem ones on long

ERYNGIUM — ERYSIMUM.

stalks, heart-shaped, toothed, undivided; stem-leaves clasping, palmately lobed. Mountains of Central and Southern Europe.——A noble border plant, thriving in almost any soil. This would prove a fine subject for naturalization among our choicer perennials, as it is so very distinct in port. Division and seed.

Eryngium amethystinum (*Amethystine E.*)—A very handsome species, with the upper part of the stem and the heads of flowers of a beautiful amethystine blue; 1 to 2½ ft. high. *Flowers*, in summer; heads globose; bracts 7 or 8, lance-shaped, with a few teeth at the base, exceeding the heads in length. *Leaves*, heart-shaped in outline; root-leaves divided into several segments; segments cut, spiny; stalks sheathing, entire at the base; stem-leaves smaller, and more divided; stems smoothish, corymbose. Dalmatia and Croatia.——Borders, in ordinary soil. Division and seed.

Eryngium Bourgati (*Bourgati's E.*)—An interesting glaucous kind; 1 to 2 ft. high. *Flowers*, in summer; light blue, in large heads; bracts 10 to 12, lance-shaped, prickly, exceeding the ovate head, with 1 or 2 teeth on each side. *Leaves*, of root nearly circular, on long stalks, 3-parted; lobes cut, the lower part of each quite entire; stalk of lower stem-leaves short, not sheathing; stems simple, a little branched at the apex. Pyrenees.——Borders, rough rockwork or banks, in sandy loam. Careful division.

Eryngium bromeliæfolium (*Pine-Apple-leaved E.*)—This has Yucca-like leaves, spiny at the margins; 2 ft. high or more. *Flowers*, in summer; white; bracts 10, lance-shaped, acute, exceeding the heads. *Leaves*, with parallel veins, bearing large awl-shaped teeth; root-leaves very long, broadly lance-shaped or linear. Native of Mexico.

——Dry borders, or warm banks, in deep sandy loam. Seed and division.

Eryngium giganteum (*Giant Eryngo*).—The largest kind; 3 to 4 ft. high. *Flowers*, in summer; blue; heads ovate, surrounded by 8 or 9 large, ovate or lance-shaped, deeply-cut, spiny bracts. *Leaves*, heart-shaped; lower ones entire, roughish, pubescent or smooth beneath, with reticulated veins, crenate-toothed, and with long stalks; stem-leaves clasping, deeply lobed, spiny; stems dichotomously branched, blue at the top. Caucasus, Armenia, and Iberia. —— Borders, in good sandy loam. Division.

Eryngium maritimum (*Sea Holly*).—A well-known coast plant, with grey, roundish, leathery leaves, spiny at the edges; 1 to 1½ ft. high. *Flowers*, in summer; whitish-blue; heads roundish; bracts 5 to 7, ovate, stiff, spiny or toothed. *Leaves*, of root stalked, nearly circular, heart-shaped at the base, more or less 3-lobed, veined and bordered by prickly teeth; upper stem-leaves clasping. On sandy shores of Britain, and many parts of Europe.——Borders, in any soil. Division.

Eryngium planum (*Flat-leaved E.*)—1 to 2 ft. high. *Flowers*, in summer; blue; heads round; bracts 6 or 7, blue, lance-shaped, remotely spiny-serrated, about equalling the heads in length. *Leaves*, of root oval, heart-shaped at the base, flat, crenated, undivided, on long stalks; stem-leaves stalkless, middle ones undivided, upper 5-parted, serrated; stem whitish, bluish at top. Eastern Europe.——Warm borders, in deep sandy soil. Division.

Erysimum Barbarea (*Yellow Rocket*).—*Barbarea vulgaris.*—In its ordinary form not a very attractive object; 9 to 18 in. high. *Flowers*, in spring; yellow, crowded, in erect terminal racemes; pedicels bractless; calyx green; petals longer than the calyx. Leaves of root, lyrate, terminal lobe roundish; upper ones obovate, toothed. This is only mentioned here on account of its double variety, *E. Barbarea*, fl. pl., which is a pretty border plant. Moist waste places nearly throughout Europe and common in Britain.——Borders, in ordinary soil. Division.

Erysimum ochroleucum (*Alpine Wallflower*).—*Cheiranthus alpinus*.—A beautiful dwarf evergreen perennial, 4 to 12 in. high. *Flowers*, in summer; large, fragrant, pale-yellow. *Leaves*, green, linear-lanceolate, narrowed for some distance into the footstalk, covered with small hairs; lower leaves entire, upper ones slightly and distantly toothed. Alps and Pyrenees. ——Borders and the rock-garden, in sandy loam, on level ground. This plant is the better of frequent division, at least in some soils. Division.

Erysimum pumilum (*Fairy Wallflower*).—Nearly allied to *E. ochroleucum*, but much dwarfer, and with more fragrant flowers; 1 to 3 in. high. *Flowers*, in summer; pale sulphur, nearly as large as those of *E. ochroleucum*, appearing just above the foliage. *Leaves*, narrow, linear-lanceolate, entire, of a dull greyish green, the lower ones closely set around the base of the flower-stems; stem-leaves 3 to 5 in number; stem of a brownish colour, not branching, rather thick for the size of the plant. Eastern Pyrenees.—— The rock-garden, associated with the dwarfest and choicest alpine flowers, in moist sandy or gritty loam. Seed and careful division.

Erythræa littoralis (*Sea-shore E.*)— A very dwarf, handsome biennial, forming neat dense tufts, 2 to 4 in. high. *Flowers*, in summer; pure and brilliant lilac-rose, very numerous, covering the plant with a mass of bloom. *Leaves*, opposite, lance-shaped, obtuse, sessile; lower leaves somewhat broader. Britain.——The rock-garden. Seed.

Erythronium americanum (*Yellow E.*) — A pretty bulb; 3 to 6 in. high. *Flowers*, in spring; of a bright yellow; the divisions of the flower oblonglanceolate, obtuse; anthers yellow, dotted at the base. *Leaves*, ellipticallanceolate, turned inwards at the top, dotted and marbled with violet and white; style club-shaped, threecornered. A variety has brown spots at the base of the flower. North America, plentiful in the Central Park, New York. —— The rockgarden, beds in the spring garden, the mixed border and bulb-garden, in deep loam or peat. Separation of the bulbs every third or fourth year.

Erythronium Dens-canis (*Dog'stooth Violet*).—A beautiful old border plant; about 6 in. high. *Flowers*, in spring; large, solitary, drooping, purplish rose-colour on the outside, white or pale-rose within. *Leaves*, radical, stalked, broadly-oval, rounded at the base, pointed at the tip, marbled with spots of a brownish red. *Bulbs* oblong, solid, white, elongated, somewhat resembling teeth. There are two or three varieties with white, rose, and flesh-coloured flowers. Native of S. Europe and also of Siberia.——The same positions and treatment as recommended for the preceding.

Eupatorium ageratoides (*Nettleleaved E.*) — A vigorous branching perennial; 3 to 4 ft. high. *Flowers*, in summer; pure white, very numerous, in compound corymbs, 12 to 20 in each head, emitting a somewhat unpleasant odour. *Leaves*, opposite, on long stalks, rounded at the base, ovate, sometimes slightly heart-shaped, 3-

nerved, coarsely toothed. North America.——Borders, naturalization in woods, margins of shrubberies, or by wood-walks, in any soil. Division.

Eupatorium aromaticum (*Aromatic Hemp Agrimony*). — Another stout kind, 3 to 4 ft. high. *Flowers*, late in summer ; pure white, in loose corymbs, 8 to 20 in a head, mostly 12 to 15. *Leaves*, opposite, on short stalks, sometimes almost stalkless, rounded, narrowed towards the stalk, with blunt teeth, 3-nerved. There is usually considerable variety in the form of the leaves, length of stalks, etc., of this species. North America. ——Borders, margins of shrubberies, or naturalization in copses, etc., in any soil. Division.

Eupatorium purpureum (*Purple Hemp Agrimony*).—A stout, usually simple stemmed kind, 3 to 6 ft. high. *Flowers*, late in summer ; purplish, in a corymb, 5 to 9 in each head. *Leaves*, 3 to 6 in a whorl, rough, of a very dark green, somewhat ovate or lance-shaped, more or less stalked, pointed, slightly downy beneath, unequally toothed. North America.——Moist borders, and naturalization by the banks of rivulets, etc. Division.

Euphorbia Cyparissias (*Cypress Spurge*).—A distinct and pleasing-looking perennial, 1 to 1½ or 2 ft. high. *Flowers*, in spring or early summer; yellow, produced in umbels ; rays once or twice forked; leaves of the involucre about twenty, semi-circular, broader than long, often yellow ; glands of the involucre somewhat heart-shaped and rather pointed. *Leaves*, linear, quite entire, somewhat crowded; those of the branches very narrow. Barren fields and roadsides in Central and Southern Europe.—— Borders, banks, and fringes of shrubberies, or naturalized on rough rocky ground or wild slopes, in any soil. Division.

Euphorbia Myrsinites (*Glaucous Spurge*).—A prostrate kind, with handsome, whitish, fleshy leaves. *Flowers*, in early summer ; yellow, in an umbel of from 5 to 9 rays, surrounded by an involucre of as many ovate, sharp leaflets narrower than the leaves; calyces serrate about the edges. *Leaves*, concave, sea-green, stalkless; the upper ones turned back. Southern Europe.——Borders, and occasionally in the rock-garden, in almost any soil. Seed.

Euphorbia portlandica (*Portland Spurge*).—A dwarf species with stems rather shrubby, ascending or decumbent, cylindrical, smooth, and red, especially in winter ; from a few inches to a foot high. *Flowers*, in summer; in terminal umbels of 5 forked rays ; leaves of the involucre broadly heart-shaped. *Leaves*, pale green or glaucous, linear-obovate, pointed, smooth, crowded, spreading ; stem-leaves narrower. Europe and Britain.——Worth a place in the wild garden for the sake of its coloured stems. Propagated by division or seed.

Ferula asparagifolia (*Asparagus-like F.*)—An elegant perennial, with very graceful and finely-cut leaves ; 4 to 5 ft. high. *Flowers*, in summer ; yellow, borne in umbels, of which the central one is rather shortly stalked. Radical leaves, 1 ft. to 2 ft. long (including the leaf stalk), broadly ovate in outline, 4 times pinnate, the divisions very narrow, linear, pointed, and set with hairs ; upper stem-leaves reduced to short sheaths, the lowest of them bearing a short pinnate limb, the upper ones oblong, hooded ; leaves, both of the partial and the general involucrum numerous, oblong-lanceolate, acute, reflexed. Asia Minor, near Smyrna, Budja, and Magnesia. ——Borders, groups of fine-foliaged

FERULA. 127

perennials, and isolated in the grass near the margins of shrubberies. It and all the species grow in ordinary soil, but attain greatest perfection in deep, rich, and sandy ones. Seed, to be sown soon after it is gathered, or careful division of well-established tufts.

Ferula communis (*Common Giant Fennel*).—A noble species, with much-divided, spreading, shiny green leaves; 6 to 10 ft. high or more. *Flowers*, in summer; yellow, in a large compound terminal umbel, the central umbel nearly sessile; the side ones stalked; involucre wanting. *Leaves*, repeatedly subdivided; segments linear-setaceous, flaccid; sheaths of upper ones very large; lower ones spreading more than two feet each way. Hills on the Mediterranean coast.—— The same positions and treatment as for the preceding. This, however, being much more easily procured, should be naturalized here and there, as its foliage, starting up before the earliest spring flowers, produces a finer effect than the choicest ferns.

Ferula Ferulago (*Broad-leaved F.*) —This has leaflets nearly as broad as those of *F. tingitana*, but longer and of a darker green; stems striped, 6 to 8 ft. high. *Flowers*, in early summer; yellow, in a large terminal umbel. *Leaves*, many times divided; leaflets pinnatifid, spreading; segments linear, somewhat acute. Hills and exposed places in the Mediterranean Islands.—— The cultural remarks, etc., applied to *F. asparagifolia*, suit this equally well.

Ferula glauca (*Glaucous Giant Fennel*).—Another valuable and imposing kind, 4 to 6 ft. high or more. *Flowers*, in summer; yellow, in a terminal compound umbel; central umbel stalked; side ones on longer stalks; involucre wanting. *Leaves*, supra-decompound, shining above, glaucous beneath; segments linear, lengthened, flat; stalks of upper leaves widened. Southern Europe.——The same treatment and positions as for *F. asparagifolia*.

Ferula persica (*Persian Asafœtida*). —Like the other species mentioned, has very handsome foliage, but with a very powerful asafœtida-like odour; 3 to 6 ft. high. *Flowers*, in early summer; in umbels; the involucre and involucels wanting. *Leaves*, ternately supra-decompound; leaflets rather distant; segments lance-shaped, widening and cut at the apex; stem tapering gradually upwards, glaucous. Persia and the Caucasus. ——This may be used for the sake of its leaves, like the other kinds, while it is also interesting for the medicinal garden. I only remember seeing it in cultivation in the College Botanic Gardens at Dublin. Division.

Ferula sulcata (*Furrowed F.*)—A somewhat slender species with an angular, furrowed stem, 2 ft. high. *Leaves*, supra-decompound; segments pinnatifid; lobes linear, pointed; leaflets of involucrum very numerous, oblong-linear, reflexed. On sunny hills of Genoa, Naples, Sicily, and North Africa.—— Borders, and on grassy banks, in warm sandy soil. Division.

Ferula tingitana (*Tangier F.*)— Another noble hardy "foliage plant," 6 to 8 ft. high. *Flowers*, in summer; in umbels, the terminal ones on short stalks; side ones few, on longer stalks; involucre wanting. *Leaves*, repeatedly subdivided, shining; segments broader than in any other kind, oblong or lance-shaped, deeply toothed. Spain and North Africa. ——Like *F. glauca* and *F. communis*, this would form a splendid object naturalized in half wild places, where its great fern-like vegetation would look superb among the earlier flowers, while it may be used in the garden proper in the same manner as *F. asparagifolia*.

Ficaria grandiflora (*Great Pilewort*). —*Ranunculus calthæfolius.* — Allied to our common Pilewort or Lesser Celandine, but much larger and finer; 8 in. to 1 ft. high. *Flowers*, early in spring; large, solitary, of a glistening yellow, nearly 2 in. across. Petals oblong; sepals 3 to 5, of a yellowish white, marked with veinings, oval, concave; scale of the petals oval, emarginate, covering the nectary. *Leaves*, broad, all stalked, oval-rounded, heart-shaped at the base, where the lobes meet and sometimes cross each other in the lower leaves. *Root* formed of oblong or club-shaped tubers, arranged in a bundle mixed with fibres. Native of South of France, near Toulon, Hyères Islands, Nizza. ——I brought this plant from the Paris garden a couple of years ago. It is as yet very scarce in this country, and till more common, should have a place on the rockwork or choice border, in light loam. Division or seed.

Ficaria ranunculoides (*Lesser Celandine*).—*Ranunculus Ficaria.*— A very common British herb, with smooth shining leaves, and stems bearing a single flower and one or two small leaves; 3 to 6 in. high. *Flowers*, in early spring; golden yellow; petals 8 or 9; sepals 3. *Leaves*, heart-shaped, mostly springing from the root. *Rootstock* small, knotted. It is so very common that it would not have been mentioned here but for its double and white varieties, which are very desirable little plants. Europe and Western Asia. —— Borders, in any soil. Division.

Fragaria indica (*Rock Strawberry*).— An interesting little trailer, bearing an abundance of deep red berries. *Flowers*, late in summer; yellow, small, axillary; segments of calyx flat, with tridentate bracts at the points. *Leaves*, alternate, hairy, three-lobed; lobes oboval, indented, on stalks with lance-shaped stipules. *Stem* rooting, emitting very long runners. *Fruit* not fleshy, red, without odour or taste. Nepaul.——Borders, and rough rockwork, in any (not over wet) soil. Division.

Frankenia lævis (*Sea Heath*). — A prostrate, much-branched, evergreen herb, with crowded smooth leaves. *Flowers*, in summer; pink, either in little terminal heads or short axillary spikes, sessile among the upper leaves; petals small, wedge-shaped. *Leaves*, small, fleshy, linear, appearing almost cylindrical from the edges being rolled down. *Stems* rooting. Marshes by the seaside in many parts of Europe, the Canary Islands, and on the eastern coast of England.——The rock-garden or occasionally in borders, in dry light soil. The flowers being very small, it is chiefly of interest in botanical or very full collections. Division.

Funkia albo-marginata (*White-margined F.*) — A variegated perennial. 16 to 20 in. high. *Flowers*, in summer; lilac, streaked with white and purplish-red, funnel-shaped, drooping, accompanied with oval silver-edged bracts about twice as long as the pedicels of the flowers, which grow in a long loose cluster. *Leaves*, broadly-oval-lanceolate, of a lively green edged with white, on long foot-stalks; those of the root numerous, somewhat concave in the middle and wavy at the edges; stem-leaves small. Japan.—— Borders and edgings, in ordinary garden soil. Division.

Funkia cærulea (*Blue Funkia*).— *Hemerocallis cærulea.* — *F. ovata.*—A handsome perennial, 16 in. to 20 in. high. *Flowers*, in summer; violet-blue, in an arching group of unilateral blossoms, which become pendent after expansion. *Leaves*, in tufts, of a deep and shining green, especially on the underside; radical leaves on long stalks, broadly oval, somewhat heart-shaped at the base, pointed at the tip, regularly folded, and decurrent on the stalk, which is grooved; stem-leaves alternate, small, and nearly sessile. Native of Japan. —— Borders and edgings, in ordinary soil. Division.

Funkia japonica (*Sweet F.*)—*Hemerocallis japonica* — *F. grandiflora*. — A beautiful and delightfully fragrant plant, 1 ft. to 16 in. or more in height. *Flowers*, from July to September, numerous, large, funnel-shaped, curved, milk-white, with an odour like that of orange-blossoms, slightly inclining to one side, nearly 4 in. long and 2 in. across, accompanied by oval leafy bracts longer than the pedicels. *Leaves*, of a lively or light green, glistening, especially on the upper-side, large, oval-heart-shaped, pointed, with marked parallel veins. The young leaves are a favourite prey of slugs and snails. Japan.——Borders of all kinds, the rock-garden, and naturalized in groups on sunny slopes and banks where there is a warm soil. About Paris this plant is grown in vast quantities as an edging plant, etc., but with us it does not appear to flower regularly unless in sunny spots and in warm, well-drained, and very sandy loam. Division.

Funkia Sieboldi (*Siebold's F.*) — A graceful and noble plant, remarkable for the elegance of its foliage; 1 ft. to 16 in. high. *Flowers*, in summer; large, bluish, or light lilac, in a crowded group of unilateral pendent blossoms growing from the axils of lanceolate bracts, of which the lower ones are longer than the accompanying flowers. *Leaves*, large, broadly-ovate-acute, heart-shaped; at the base glaucous, slightly waved, elegantly and regularly veined or figured. Japan.——Borders, groups or beds of fine perennials, and even as isolated specimens on grass when fully developed. It thrives best in, and is well worthy of, a deep peat soil or a free loam well enriched with vegetable matter. Division.

Gaillardia aristata (*Bristly Gaillardia*).—A handsome perennial, growing from 1 to 3 ft. high. *Flowers*, in summer; yellow, 1 to 3 in. across. *Leaves*, 4 to 6 in. long; lower ones lance-shaped, tapering into slender stalks, sinuately pinnatifid; upper ones stalkless, entire. North America.——Borders, in well-drained soil. Seed or division.

Gaillardia lanceolata (*Lanceolate G.*) —*G. perennis.*—1 ft. to 1½ ft. high. *Flowers*, late in summer; about 2 in. across; disk purplish; florets of the ray saffron-yellow marked with a purplish spot at the base; scales of the head hairy on the outside. *Leaves*, alternate, lanceolate, sometimes entire, sometimes cut. *Stem*, branching, tufted. A variety, sometimes called the *Golden-fleece G.*, has very large slightly fragrant blooms, with florets of the ray of an almost uniform yellow with faint reddish furrows towards the claw; florets of the disk orange-yellow changing into red. North America.——Borders, in ordinary soil. Division.

Gaillardia Loiseli (*Loisel's G.*)—A hardy herbaceous perennial, with a simple, furrowed, woolly stem, about 1¼ ft. high. *Flowers*, in summer; 3½ in. across; petals trifid, brilliant orange-red for three-quarters of their length, the extremities clear yellow. *Leaves*, lance-shaped, pointed, with a very broad base, sessile, rough, striated, and covered with a fine down. North America.——Borders, in good well-drained soil. Division.

Galanthus Imperati (*Imperati's Snowdrop*)—*G. plicatus*, Tenore.—Resembles *G. nivalis*, but is double the size in all its parts, and flowers later; external divisions of the flower ovate-oblong,

K

one of them larger than the other. *Fruit*, roundish (in *G. nivalis*, oblong or obovate). Native of mountains in the kingdom of Naples.——I am not sure if this plant is in cultivation; I failed to obtain it from Italy. Till more plentiful it ought to have a place with the choicest and rarest ornaments of the bulb- or rock-garden, in deep sandy soil.

Galanthus nivalis (*Snowdrop*).—The common Snowdrop; 4 to 6 in. high. *Flowers*, early in spring; solitary; external divisions pure white, oval, concave; internal divisions much shorter, cleft at the top, with a small green wavy mark at the ends on the outside, and longitudinal green ridges on the inside, surrounded by a narrow white margin, gracefully pendent from a membranous spathe at the summit of the stem. *Leaves*, 2, rarely 3, linear, obtuse, of a glaucous green, shorter than the stem, and sheathing it at the base. *Bulb*, small, egg-shaped, black or brown. Native of the temperate and southern parts of Europe in thickets.——It is needless to mention here the many positions in gardens which this plant is fitted to adorn; but its fitness for naturalization in grass, and even grass that must be mown very early in the year, cannot be too much spoken of. Division.

Galanthus plicatus (*Crimean Snowdrop*). — Similar to *G. nivalis*, but larger in all its parts, except the flower, which is sometimes even smaller and of a more greenish hue. The leaves also have a longitudinal fold on both sides near the edge, from which the specific name is derived. The Crimea, Caucasus, and neighbouring countries.——Till more plentiful this should be in positions where it may be free from accident, and in deep loam, where it will increase rapidly. When plentiful it will be found to suit much the same positions as the common one, and it is easily naturalized in free soil and in half-shady positions. It must not be supposed, however, that it is so pretty as the common Snowdrop, though more than this has often been claimed for it. Division.

Galatella hyssopifolia (*Hyssop-leaved G.*)—A pretty Aster-like plant; 1½ ft. high. *Flowers*, in autumn; florets of the disk yellow; of the ray elongated, white tinged with purple. *Leaves*, lanceolate-linear, acute, entire, three-nerved, rough; those of the branches linear-awl-shaped; scales of the involucrum pointed. North America from New Jersey to Carolina, in sandy fields and woods.——Borders, or naturalization, in any soil. Division.

Galega officinalis (*Officinal Goat's-rue*).—A very handsome and abundantly blooming perennial; 3 to 4 ft. high. *Flowers*, in summer; pink, or white, in axillary, simple racemes; stipules broad, lance-shaped. *Leaves*, imparipinnate; leaflets in 5 to 7 pairs or more, lance-shaped, mucronate, smooth. *G. officinalis alba* is a showy white variety, and there is a variety with a closer truss of lilac flowers, better than either the ordinary or the white form, and which, but very seldom seeding, flowers much longer. This form I have only seen in cultivation about Paris. Southern Europe, Barbary, and Tauria, in stony places. ——Borders, groups, or beds, associated with the largest and handsomest perennials, or naturalized in any position or soil. Division and seed.

Galega orientalis (*Oriental Goat's-rue*).—An ornamental plant, though not so much so as the preceding, and easily distinguished by its simple zigzag stem and creeping roots; 2 to 4 ft. high. *Flowers*, in summer; purplish, small, but freely produced in axillary simple racemes; stipules broad-ovate. *Leaves*, imparipinnate; leaflets ovate, acuminated, smooth; roots creeping. Caucasus and all the Eastern mountains.—— The same positions and treatment as for the preceding kind.

Gaultheria procumbens (*Creeping Wintergreen*).—A very small and neat evergreen shrub, with gaily coloured berries; 4 to 6 in. high. *Flowers*, in summer; white, drooping, solitary, terminal, succeeded by red berries about the size of peas. *Leaves*, smooth, leathery, obovate, acute at the base, finely ciliated. *Stems*, procumbent; branches erect, naked at the bottom, crowded with leaves at the top. In sandy places and cool damp woods, from Canada to Virginia.—— The rock-garden, borders, or as edgings to beds of small American plants. It is said to prefer peat, but I have seen it thrive perfectly in moist clay soils, fully exposed to the sun. Division.

Gaura Lindheimeri (*White Gaura*).—A slender perennial, 3 to 4½ ft. high. *Flowers*, in summer and autumn; pure white and rose, slightly drooping, numerous, arranged in long, slender spikes. *Leaves*, alternate, oval-lanceolate, toothed, often spotted with reddish-purple, those of the stem linear-lanceolate; stems branching, slender, tapering, erect. Texas.——Borders, in sandy loam. Division and seed.

Genista pilosa (*Hairy Genista*).—A dwarf British shrub, with numerous procumbent, branched, striped, knotted, leafy stems. *Flowers*, in early summer; bright yellow, smaller than those of *G. tinctoria*, solitary, axillary, on short stalks; calyx and stalks silky; legumes pubescent, 3 or 4-seeded. *Leaves*, lance-shaped, obtuse, clothed with silky down beneath. Europe and Britain.——On sandy slopes and banks, or occasionally as a border plant, or in collections of British wild flowers. Seed or cuttings.

Genista prostrata (*Prostrate Genista*). —A prostrate shrub with spreading stems, and angular, striped, and hairy branches. *Flowers*, in early summer; yellow, axillary, on erect stalks, three times the length of calyx; corolla smooth; legumes hairy; calyx and stalks covered with spreading hairs. *Leaves*, ovate-oblong, somewhat hairy beneath. Alps of Jura and Burgundy.——The rougher parts of the rock-garden, or on banks or borders. In the last position it looks well planted on the tops of small mounds. Seed or cuttings.

Genista sagittalis (*Arrow-pointed Broom*).—A curious-looking kind, the winged branches of which at first sight remind one of a diminutive *Epiphyllum*; 6 in. high. *Flowers*, in early summer; yellow, in an ovate, terminal, leafless spike; corolla smooth, with a villous line on the back of the keel. *Leaves*, ovate-lance-shaped, sessile, placed singly at the joints of the stem and branches. Native of mountain pastures of Europe.——The rougher parts of the rock-garden, or borders, in any soil. Also well fitted for naturalization in unmown places, with any aspect, and either on slopes or the level ground. Seed, cuttings, and division.

Genista tinctoria (*Dyer's Genista*).— A neat native shrub, with nearly upright spreading stems, that form compact tufts; 12 to 18 in. high. *Flowers*, in early summer; yellow, smooth, in terminal spiked racemes, each flower springing from the axil of a small leaf or bract; legumes smooth. *Leaves*, lance-shaped, sessile, usually smooth and shining; branches upright, striped, round. Europe, not uncommon in England, but rare in Scotland or Ireland.——Banks, slopes, rough rocky ground, or grouped with the smaller shrubs in beds or borders, in any soil. Seed or division.

Gentiana acaulis (*Gentianella*). — One of the noblest of its brilliant

K 2

GENTIANA.

family, with great vase-like flowers opening on a carpet of shining leathery leaves; 1 to 3 in. high. *Flowers*, in summer; fine blue, with dotted throat, often 2 in. long, solitary, bell-shaped, 5 to 10-cleft; segments obtuse, mucronate. *Leaves*, of root in rosettes, ovate-lance-shaped. *Stem* short, quadrangular, with one or two pairs of leaves. *Gentiana alpina* is a variety with shorter but broader leaves, and there are several other varieties. Alps and Pyrenees.—— The rock-garden, borders, edgings; preferring a moist deep loam. It is also well suited for naturalization in moist and somewhat bare upland pastures. Division or seed. All the Gentians may be grown from seed, but are raised very slowly and with difficulty in this way. The seed should always be sown soon after being gathered.

Gentiana Andrewsii (*Andrews's G.*) An erect and peculiar kind, with handsome deep blue clusters; about 1 ft. high. *Flowers*, in autumn; dark blue, about 1 in. long, closed at the top, in clusters near the head of the stem. *Leaves*, ovate-lanceolate, acute, narrowed at the base, rough at the edges. North America, from Carolina to Lake Huron.—— Borders, and with the choicer medium-sized perennials, such as the finer Aquilegias, in the rougher parts of the rock-garden, in ordinary sandy garden soil. Division.

Gentiana asclepiadea (*Asclepias-like G.*)—A handsome herbaceous kind, with simple, willow-like, erect stems swollen at the joints, from 15 in. to 2 ft. high., and bearing numerous flowers for a considerable portion of their length. *Flowers*, in summer; rather large, purplish-blue, with dark dots inside, arranged in numerous pairs, axillary, nearly sessile; corolla bell-shaped, 5-cleft. *Leaves*, ovate-lanceolate, 5-nerved, about 2 in. long and ¾ in. broad at the base, sessile. European Mountains.—— Borders, or fringes of shrubberies, in almost any soil, but best in a very fine deep and moist sandy loam. Division.

Gentiana bavarica (*Bavarian G.*)— An exquisite kind, resembling the Vernal Gentian in size and flowers, but with blunter and smaller box-like leaves of a yellowish-green tone; 3 in. high. *Flowers*, in summer; beautiful blue, large, and freely produced, on simple 1-flowered stems; corolla 5-cleft, tube long, cylindrical; throat naked; segments ovate, not fringed. *Leaves*, small, obovate, very blunt, attenuated; lower ones crowded. High Alps of Europe.—— The rock-garden, in very moist, deep loam, in very wet ground, near the margin of a rivulet, or in pots of loam, plunged nearly to their rims in a tank of water. Careful division.

Gentiana lutea (*Yellow G.*)— A robust perennial, with somewhat the habit of a *Veratrum*; 3 to 4 ft. high or more. *Flowers*, in summer; yellow, in whorls at the upper joints; corolla rotate, veined and spotted, 5 or 6-parted; segments lance-shaped, acuminate. *Leaves*, large; root-leaves ovate-oblong, with 5 large veins on the back; stem-leaves sessile, ovate, acute, a pair at each joint. Alps of Middle Europe.—— Scarcely ornamental enough for the border, it will grow as well in rough grassy places with us as it does on the high meadows of the Alps. It grows finest in a deep loam and should have a place in all botanical collections. Division of established tufts.

Gentiana Pneumonanthe (*Marsh G.*) —A lovely dwarf kind, as beautiful in the lowland marsh as the Vernal and Bavarian species are on the uplands and Alps; 6 to 12 in. high. *Flowers*, in summer; tubular, 1¼ in. long or more; deep-blue within, with greenish dotted belts without; the lobes of the mouth short and spreading; blossoms in opposite pairs in the axils of the upper leaves. *Leaves*, smooth, 1½ in. long, and ¼ in. broad; linear or spoon-shaped, obtuse, sessile; all rather thick; the lower ones shorter and broader. There is a variety with white flowers. Siberia, Europe, and Britain.——The artificial bog, rock-garden, or the choice border, in deep soil, and in very moist spots. Careful division.

Gentiana pyrenaica (*Pyrenean G.*)— Allied to the Vernal Gentian, but differing by the corolla being nearly regularly 10-cleft, and by its narrow, sharp-pointed, imbricated leaves; 1 to 3 in. high. *Flowers*, in early summer; terminating the branches, solitary; corolla funnel-shaped, pale-green outside, deep-blue within; calyx half as long as the corolla, 5-cleft; segments lance-shaped, acute, edges pale. *Leaves*, lanceolate-linear; stem procumbent, branching at bottom; sterile branches densely leafy. Pyrenees.—— Suited for the same positions, and requiring the same treatment as *Gentiana verna*.

Gentiana septemfida (*Crested G.*)— A curious species, with erect, simple stems; 6 to 12 in. high. *Flowers*, in early summer; in clusters, cylindrical, blue and white inside, greenish-brown outside, and having, between each of the larger roundish segments, a smaller one finely cut. *Leaves*, ovate-lanceolate, 3-nerved, decussate, crowded. Caucasus.——The rock-garden and choice borders, in fine sandy loam. Division.

Gentiana verna (*Vernal G.*)—One of the most brilliant, and perhaps the most admired by travellers of all alpine flowers; 1 to 3 in. high. *Flowers*, in spring; beautiful blue, solitary, on simple terminal stems; corolla salver-shaped, 5-cleft, with five small, bifid, accessory segments.

Leaves, ovate, somewhat acute; those of the root crowded; stem-leaves in about 3 pairs. Mountain pastures on the Alps of Southern and Central Europe, and in one or two places in the British Isles. —— The rock-garden, choice borders, and in pots, or deep pans, plunged in sand in the open air. Sandy or gritty loam, with abundance of water in summer, and full exposure, are the essential conditions of success. In borders, the plant should be surrounded by half-buried stones. It might be easily naturalized in moist, upland pastures. Careful division.

Geranium argenteum (*Silvery Crane's-bill*).—A beautiful, dwarf, alpine perennial, with silvery-white leaves, and large handsome flowers on stalks, rarely more than 2 in. high, usually nearly prostrate. *Flowers*, in early summer; pale rose, with darker veins, 1 to 2 in. across; petals notched; stalks 2-flowered, almost springing from the roots. *Leaves*, on long stalks, hoary, or silky on both surfaces, 5 to 7-parted; segments linear. Alps of Dauphiny and the Pyrenees.—— The rock-garden, and margins of borders, in light friable loam. This might, with advantage, be grown in pots, wherever it is an object to show alpine or herbaceous plants in pots. Propagated by division or seed, which is sparingly produced.

Geranium cinereum (*Grey Crane's-bill*).—A very beautiful plant, allied to the silvery Crane's-bill, but with leaves less·silvery and not so deeply divided, and attaining a height of 5 or 6 in. *Flowers*, in summer; pale red, with darker stripes; petals notched; stalks 2-flowered, almost springing from the root. *Leaves*, stalked, almost all radical, clothed with a slightly glaucous pubescence, 5 to 7-parted; lobes trifid, wedge-shaped. Pyrenees.—— Treatment and positions the same as for *G. argenteum*. Seed or division.

GERANIUM.

Geranium ibericum (*Iberian Crane's-bill.*)—A very showy large-flowered kind, with deeply-cut leaves and villous, erect, forked stems; about 1 ft. high. *Flowers*, in summer; violet, large, very handsome; petals obcordate; calyces very villous. *Leaves*, villous, 5 to 7-parted, with deeply-cut lobes, and toothed minor divisions. Iberia.——Borders and naturalization in any soil. This and some of the other free-growing and showy kinds would grow very freely on rough rockwork, which, however, should, as a rule, be reserved for subjects that do not thrive so well in ordinary soil on the level ground. Division.

Geranium Endressii (*Endress's Crane's-bill*).—A plant of greyish-green aspect, covered with a feeble pubescence; 1 ft. to 16 in. and upwards in height. *Flowers*, in summer; of a light rose, veined and streaked with a darker shade, borne two on each flower-stalk; flower-stalks axillary; petals, oblong-obovate, entire, fringed at the base; filaments densely feathery; calyx downy, ⅓ the length of the petals. *Leaves*, opposite, stalked, palmate-lobed; the upper ones 3-lobed, lower ones 5-lobed; lobes acute, incised-serrate. *Root-stock* elongated, very much branched, almost running. Pyrenees.——Borders in any ordinary garden soil. Division.

Geranium Lamberti (*Lambert's Crane's-bill*).—A handsome Crane's-bill, about 18 in. high. *Flowers*, early in summer; bright lilac, nearly as large as those of *G. ibericum*. *Leaves*, heart-shaped in outline, deeply 5-cleft; lobes wedge-shaped, with yellowish spots near the margin, and clothed with soft woolly hairs; stems of a reddish colour. Nepaul.——Borders, and fringes of shrubberies, banks in pleasure-grounds, etc., in good ordinary soil. Division and seed.

Geranium macrorrhizum(*Long-rooted G.*)—A dwarf species, with large, thick, permanent stems; 1 ft. high. *Flowers*, in early summer; deep-red or bright-purple; stalks 2-flowered; petals entire, a little turned back; calyces globose. *Leaves*, on long stalks, 5-parted; deeply and irregularly-lobed; lobes toothed at the apex, the margins on both sides being of a reddish-brown colour. There is a variegated variety. Italy and Southern Europe.—— Borders, or naturalization on warm sunny banks. Division.

Geranium platypetalum (*Broad-petalled G.*)—One of the handsomest plants of its family; 1½ to 2½ ft. high. *Flowers*, in summer; numerous, more than 1 in. across, deep violet, with streaks of a darker, almost reddish, hue; petals lobed; calyx rough with hairs. *Leaves*, alternate or opposite, long-stalked, with 5 to 7 deeply-cut, irregularly-fringed, incised-dentate lobes. Georgia near the Caucasus.——Borders, or naturalization, in ordinary soil. Division.

Geranium pratense (*Meadow G.*)—A handsome native kind, 2 to 3 ft. high. *Flowers*, in early summer; blue-purple, large, somewhat corymbose; petals entire, twice as long as the sepals. *Leaves*, palmately 7-lobed; lobes sharply cut, linear; stems round, erect, downy. A rather common native plant, mentioned here for its double varieties, *G. pratense fl. pl.*; the double blue, and *G. p. fl. pl. alba* the double white one, both of which are handsome. Europe and Britain.—— Borders, in any soil. Division.

Geranium sanguineum (*Blood-red G.*)—A native species with roundish, deeply-out leaves, forming neat, spreading tufts; 1 to 2 ft. high. *Flowers*, in summer; deep crimson-purple, about 1½ in. across, freely produced on one-

GERANIUM — GILLENIA. 135

flowered stalks; petals notched, twice as long as the sepals. *Leaves*, kidney-shaped in outline, 5- to 7-parted; segments divided into linear lobes. *G. lancastriense* is a variety of this, with pink flowers veined with red.——Borders, and fringes of shrubberies; also in semi-wild places here and there. It is perhaps on the whole the handsomest species we have, and were it not a common native, would probably have a prominent place on every rockwork. The var. *lancastriense* is not so free as the common form, and should have better and lighter soil. Division.

Geranium striatum (*Striped G.*)—A pretty old kind; 12 to 18 in. high. *Flowers*, in early summer; white, finely striped with small red veins; stalks 2-flowered; petals obtuse, deeply indented at top. *Leaves*, broad, yellowish-green, each of the divisions having a blackish spot at the base; lower leaves 5-lobed, upper ones 3-lobed. Southern Europe.——Borders, rough rockwork or rootwork, and naturalization, in any soil but a cold clay. Division and seed.

Geranium subcaulescens (*Dwarf Crane's-bill*). — *G. asphodeloides*. — A short-stemmed and very ornamental kind. *Flowers*, in summer; few, purplish-violet, sometimes, but rarely, of a pale hue; petals obovate, often truncate, twice as long as the calyx; sepals shortly pointed, covered with close adpressed down interspersed with longer hairs. *Leaves*, roundish, divided into five wedge-shaped, 3-cleft segments; those of the root long-stalked, all covered with closely adpressed down, and frequently ash-coloured underneath; stems sometimes leafless. This plant varies very much in the division of its leaves, the shape of the lobes, and in its downy covering. Mount Parnassus, and other mountains of Greece, also in Dalmatia.——The rock-garden, and margin of the choice border, in free and well-drained soil. Seed and division.

Geum chiloense (*Chiloe Avens*).—A very showy perennial, 1 to 2 ft. high. *Flowers*, in early summer; scarlet, in erect panicles. *Leaves*, downy, pinnate; leaflets crenate-serrated, terminal one large, roundish-heart-shaped, lobed and crenated; stem-leaves 3-parted, deeply cut. Native of Chiloe.——Borders, in good ordinary soil, also suitable for naturalization on warm open spots. Seed or division.

Geum montanum (*Mountain Geum*). —A dwarf, compact, and showy kind, with large flowers, and simple erect stem; 9 to 18 in. high. *Flowers*, in summer; yellow, solitary, 1½ in. across; petals obcordate, notched; segments of calyx undivided, shorter than the petals. *Leaves* of root, interruptedly pinnatifid; terminal leaflet ovate, obscurely lobed and veined, 2 or 3 in. long and broad, the others becoming gradually smaller; stem-leaves undivided, stalkless. Alps of Europe. ——The rock-garden and borders, in ordinary free soil. It would be easy to naturalize this on high hills or mountains. Seed or division.

Geum reptans (*Creeping Avens*).-·· Another valuable dwarf kind, with the barren stems creeping, the flowering ones erect; about 6 in. high. *Flowers*, in summer; yellow, larger than those of *G. montanum*, solitary on the top of the stem; segments of the calyx lengthened, usually trifid at the apex. ·*Leaves* of root, uninterruptedly pinnate, larger leaflets obovate, toothed at the apex, smaller ones ovate, entire or 3-toothed at the apex, the terminal one not much larger than the others; stem-leaves 3-lobed. Alps of Europe. —— Similar positions to those for the preceding kind. Division.

Gillenia trifoliata (*Three-leaved G.*) —A rather pretty but not showy perennial, 1 to 2 ft. high. *Flowers*, in early summer; whitish-red, in loose terminal or axillary panicles, on slender stalks; petals 5, linear-lanceolate, rather unequal, spreading; calyx tubular or bell-shaped. *Leaves*, mostly trifoliate, sometimes single or in pairs; leaflets stalked, serrated, about 1½ in. long, and ½ in. broad, acutely pointed, bright green above, pale beneath. In shady woods and bogs, from Florida to Canada.——Borders, chiefly in medicinal or botanical gardens, in any free soil. Division.

Gladiolus communis (*Foxglove G.*)— A pretty old inhabitant of our gardens; 16 to 20 in. high. *Flowers*, in summer; bright rose, flesh-coloured, or even white in some varieties, 6 to 8 in a unilateral spike; tube short; limb almost two-lipped, with the upper segments approaching, larger than the lower ones, the three internal segments being almost of equal size, oblong-spoon-shaped; anthers half the length of the filaments; seeds flat or angular, winged. *Leaves*, sword-shaped, stiff, smooth. *Bulb*, roundish or depressed, with reticulated tunics. Native of the South of France and South of Europe, in fields.——Borders, and naturalized, in any light soil. Separation of the bulbs.

Gladiolus segetum (*Cornfield Gladiolus*). — This is often confounded with *G. communis*, but is distinguished from it by having its rose-coloured flowers in two rows; the lower segments unequal, each marked with a long, narrow, white spot; the anthers longer than the filaments, and finally by its seeds being nearly round and not winged. Native of France and Southern Europe.——This, like *Gladiolus communis*, will grow freely in borders or rough places in all rich soil. Separation of the bulbs.

Glechoma hederacea (*Ground Ivy*). —*Nepeta Glechoma*. — A well-known, much-creeping British plant, almost too common to deserve notice here, but that it has one or two varieties finely variegated that are quite worthy of a place. *Flowers*, in summer; blue, nearly an inch long, in axillary whorls. *Leaves*, roundish, crenated, heart-shaped at the base. Abundant in Britain, and throughout Europe.—— In beds of plants with variegated leaves, on the edges of raised borders, rockwork, etc. The variegated forms only are worth growing; the common green form has been recommended for cultivation, but is best seen in its native hedge-banks. Division.

Globularia cordifolia (*Heart-leaved G.*)—A neat and very trailing shrub; 6 in. high. *Flowers*, in early summer; blue; heads small, globular, solitary at the ends of the branches, on stalks that are nearly naked. *Leaves*, stalked, heart-shaped, small, gradually widening from the base, notched at the apex, sometimes with a little tooth there. *Stems* shrubby, prostrate, much branched. Central and Southern Europe.——The rock-garden, in light soil. Division.

Globularia nana (*Thyme-leaved G.*) — A dense trailing, dwarf shrub, forming a fine mass of thyme-like verdure; 1 to 2 in. high. *Flowers*, in summer; numerous, bluish-white, in globular heads nearly half-an-inch across, barely rising above the foliage. *Leaves*, fleshy, glistening, narrowly-obcordate-wedge-shaped, forming rosettes at the base of the flower-stalks. *Stems* very branching and woody, creeping and rooting, lying close to the ground. It is by some considered a variety of *G. cordifolia*, but is sufficiently distinct. Eastern Pyrenees. ——The rock-garden, in moist free soil; or as a dwarf border plant in moist districts. Division.

Globularia nudicaulis (*Naked-stalked G.*)—An interesting perennial, not devoid of beauty when well-developed

6 in. high. *Flowers*, in summer; blue; heads larger than those of *G. cordifolia*, on naked stalks. *Leaves*, oblong, crenate, round at top, thickish, larger than those of *G. cordifolia*; stems herbaceous. Alps and Pyrenees. ——Margins of borders, and the rock-garden, in light soil. This and its family are rarely seen to advantage in cold clay soil. Division or seed.

Globularia trichosantha (*Hair-flowered G.*)—A species distinguished by its glaucescent foliage, and finely-divided petals; from 6 to 8 in. high. *Flowers*, in summer; flower-heads sky-blue, large, many-flowered, very similar in shape to those of *Erigeron alpinus*: divisions of the corolla thread-like, twice the length of the tube; divisions of the calyx four times as long as the tube. Radical leaves 1-nerved, spathulate, sometimes tridentate; stem-leaves nearly linear, mucronate; stem herbaceous, leafy, bearing one head; root many-crowned; entire plant very glabrous and glaucescent. Asia Minor.——The same positions and treatment as for the preceding kind.

Gnaphalium margaritaceum (*Pearl Cudweed*).—The well-known old border Everlasting. *Flowers*, in summer; white with yellow disk, numerous, in flat terminal corymbs. *Leaves*, numerous, sessile, linear-lanceolate, entire, dark green above, white and cottony beneath, and often on both sides. *Stems*, extremely downy, branched at top. North America.——Borders, in any soil. Division.

Gymnadenia conopsea (*Fragrant Orchis*).—A sweet-scented orchid, 6 in. to nearly 2 ft. high. *Flowers*, late in summer; pale purple, in a dense, cylindrical, tapering spike, 1 to 4 in. long, not unilateral. *Leaves*, oblong-strap-shaped, or strap-shaped-lanceolate, acute, 2 to 6 in. long or more; folded down the middle and keeled on the back; more or less recurved, the lower ones much larger than those on the upper part of the stem. *Root-knobs*, two, palmately cleft, compressed. Britain and Ireland.——In grassy places, drier parts of the bog-bed, or borders; worth growing for its fragrance only. Separation of the root-knobs.

Gynerium argenteum (*Pampas grass*). — The noble and now well-known Pampas grass, 4 ft. to 14 ft. high, according to the strength of the plant. *Flowers*, in autumn; in a very large dense panicle, from 1 to 2 ft. long; formed of spikelets of about six flowers each, distant, covered with silky silvery hairs. *Leaves*, very long, linear, very rough on the edges, of a glaucous green, forming huge dense tufts, 4 to 6 ft. high, and as much or more across. The Pampas, or prairies, of S. America, chiefly in Paraguay. ——Isolated specimens in the pleasure-ground, flower-garden, or woods; or grouped with other fine perennials. It will be found to attain greatest vigour in light rich deep loam, and where sheltered. Division and seed.

Gypsophila arenaria (*Sand G.*)—A neat perennial, 1 ft. high. *Flowers*, in summer; pale red, in dense long corymbs; petals rarely notched. *Leaves*, linear, flat, smooth, rather fleshy. Sandy or gravelly soil in Hungary and Volhynia. —— Borders, in ordinary soil. Seed and division.

Gypsophila paniculata (*Panicled G.*) —A very handsome herbaceous plant, forming a dense compact bush, 3 ft. or more in height and as much across. *Flowers*, from midsummer to the end of August; small, white, exceedingly numerous, arranged on thread-like stalks in much-branched panicles, with the light, airy, graceful effect of certain ornamental grasses. *Leaves*, few, linear-lanceolate, opposite, sessile. *Stems* knotty, smooth and glistening, very much branched, slender, fragile, spreading. Siberia and Sicily.—— Borders, and naturalization in any dryish soil. Seed or division.

Gypsophila repens (*Creeping G.*)—A dwarf and neat species; 3 to 6 in. high. *Flowers*, in summer; reddish, few, on bifid or trifid stalks; segments of the calyx with a dark green purple line along the middle, and a white edge; petals flat, slightly narrowed towards the base and notched. *Leaves*, glaucous, lanceolate-linear-acute, thick, stalkless, not quite an inch long, and narrow. *Stems* creeping, branched; with simple, erect branches, reddish at the joints. Alps of Europe.——Borders, the rock-garden, or ruins, in ordinary soil. Seed and division.

Gypsophila scorzoneræfolia (*Scorzonera-leaved G.*)—1 to 3 ft. high. *Flowers*, from July to August and sometimes later; numerous, white, a little larger than those of *G. paniculata*, and in less diffuse panicles, the ramifications of which are slightly viscid. *Leaves*, lanceolate-acute, half stem-clasping, with 3 to 5 veins. The Crimea.——Borders, or naturalization, in any dryish soil. Seed or division.

Gypsophila Steveni (*Steven's G.*)— Somewhat resembling *G. paniculata*, but of much smaller dimensions, and of a rather glaucous hue; 1 ft. to 20 in. high. *Flowers*, from July to August, and sometimes later; white, somewhat larger than those of *G. paniculata*, but not so numerous, in a slightly spreading, almost corymbose, panicle. *Leaves*, almost all radical, linear-lanceolate. *Stems* branching chiefly at the top. Germany.——Borders, in ordinary soil. Division.

[Other hardy species of interesting habit, and producing a profusion of small white flowers, are:—*G. dichotoma*, *G. glauca* (*acutifolia*), *G. saligna*, and *G. sabulosa*. All flourish in ordinary, dry, light or calcareous soil.]

Hedysarum coronarium (*French Honeysuckle*).—A handsome and popular old garden plant; 3 to 4 ft. high. *Flowers*, in summer; fine red, in ovate spikes, crowded; legumes smooth, with prickly joints. *Leaves*, imparipinnate; leaflets in 3 to 6 pairs, roundish, downy beneath and on the margins. *Stems* spreading, hollow, smooth. There is a white form.—— Borders, in ordinary soil. It is usually a biennial, but comes up abundantly from self-sown seed. Seed.

Hedysarum obscurum (*Creeping-rooted H.*)—A brilliant and compact perennial; 6 to 12 in. high. *Flowers*, in summer; showy, purple, about ¾ in. long, on short stalks, produced in racemes; bracts longer than flower-stalks; legumes pendulous, smooth. *Leaves*, imparipinnate; leaflets in 5 to 9 pairs, ovate, smooth, on short stalks. *Stems* erect. Alps from Austria to Provence.——The rock-garden, borders, and naturalization, amongst vegetation not more than a foot high, chiefly on banks and slopes, in sandy loam. Division or seed.

Helenium atropurpureum (*Dark-purple H.*)—A richly-blooming perennial; 2½ to 3½ ft. high. *Flowers*, late in summer; of a purplish black, variegated, somewhat like those of *Calliopsis tinctoria marmorata*, loosely arranged in heads of medium size, exhaling an agreeable odour. *Leaves*, alternate, linear - lanceolate. Texas. —— Borders, or in beds or groups of the finer perennials, in light, rich well-drained soil. Division or seed.

Helenium autumnale (*Smooth H.*)— A showy perennial, 4 to 6 ft. high. *Flowers*, in August, continuing till destroyed by frost; yellow, resembling those of a Sun-flower, but smaller; rays long, deeply cut into 4 or 5 segments. *Leaves*, smooth, lance-shaped, on sub-decurrent or winged stalks, 3 or 4 in. long and ½ in. broad in the centre.

HELENIUM — HELIANTHEMUM. 139

Stem branching at top. On the banks of rivers, ponds, and ditches in North America.——Borders, and naturalization in woods and copses, or by the margin of streams. Division or seed.

Helenium Hoopesii (*Hoopes's H.*)—A showy but somewhat coarse perennial, with a simple stem; about 2½ ft. high. *Flowers*, early in summer; bright orange, about 2 in. across; segments of involucre long, narrow, and pointed. *Leaves*, lance-shaped, pointed, smooth, clasping the stem; upper part of stem slightly downy.——Rough borders, in any soil. Division or seed.

Helianthemum formosum (*Beautiful H.*)—A very attractive rock-rose; 1 to 3½ feet high. *Flowers*, in summer; yellow, large and handsome, with a dark spot at the base of each petal; sepals 3; calyces and peduncles villous. *Leaves*, tomentosely-villous, younger ones hoary, on short stalks, lance-shaped, 3-nerved. Stems erect, branched. Portugal.——The rock-garden, on sunny warm slopes, or raised and warm borders, in light sandy or calcareous soil. Seed or cuttings.

Helianthemum ocymoides (*Basil-like H.*)— *Cistus algarvensis*.— Another fine kind, with hoary branches; 1 to 3 ft. high. *Flowers*, in summer; bright yellow, with a dark purple eye, nearly 1¼ in. across; sepals 3, much pointed; peduncles long, branched, paniculate; pedicels opposite, somewhat umbellate. *Leaves*, from 1 to 1½ in. long, narrow and pointed; stem-leaves obovate, 3-veined, almost stalkless, green; those of the branches stalked, turned back at the top, and hairy on both sides. Dry rocky hills, in Spain and Portugal.——Similar positions and treatment to those for the preceding. Seed or cuttings.

Helianthemum Pilosella (*Downy H.*)—An interesting dwarf kind with a woody prostrate stem and ascending branches; about 6 in. high. *Flowers*, in summer; small, yellow, in short terminal clusters. *Leaves*, oval-elliptical, entire, downy on both sides, whitish underneath, with a prominent dorsal vein. Pyrenees.——The rock-garden and margins of dry borders, in ordinary soil. Seed and cuttings.

Helianthemum rosmarinifolium (*Rosemary-leaved H.*)—A neat erect little bush; about 1 ft. high. *Flowers*, in summer; white, on very short axillary stalks, bearing each from one to three flowers. *Leaves*, linear-oblong, rolled back at the margin, dark green, whitish underneath. North America.——The rock-garden and borders, in sandy well-drained loam. Cuttings and seed.

Helianthemum Tuberaria (*Truffle Sunrose*).—This differs completely in aspect from the shrubby species, and is second to none in beauty; 6 to 12 in. high. *Flowers*, in summer; resembling a single yellow rose, with dark centre, 2 in. across, drooping when in bud; pedicels disposed in something like a panicle, furnished with bracts at the base; calyx smooth, shining. *Leaves*, of root, ending in the foot-stalk, ovate-oblong, tomentosely hairy, greyish; under surface nerved, upper surface furrowed; stem-leaves lance-shaped, stalkless, almost smooth. Southern Europe.——The rock-garden on warm ledges, in well-drained sandy or calcareous soil. When sufficiently plentiful it should be used in the mixed border. Seed and careful division.

Helianthemum venustum (*Showy Sunrose*).—A hardy evergreen trailer, with ascending stems, about 6 in. high. *Flowers*, in summer; deep red, about ¾ in. across, in terminal clusters. *Leaves*, opposite, oval-oblong, short-stalked, slightly reflexed, and finely toothed on the margin. South of Europe.——The rougher parts of the rock-garden, and on borders or fringes of shrubbery, best in a light or calcareous soil. Division, cuttings, and seed.

Helianthemum vulgare (*Common Sunrose*).—A dwarf spreading evergreen undershrub, with much-branched stems and numerous flowers, 8 to 15 in. high. *Flowers*, nearly all summer; bright yellow, produced in loose racemes; petals spreading, about ⅜ in. long and broad. *Leaves*, shortly stalked, ovate-lanceolate, green above, and somewhat hoary beneath, smooth or slightly hairy. Europe and Britain in dry hilly places.——There are many very pretty varieties of this in various colours, sometimes supposed to be distinct species. The finer varieties, which may be raised from seed in abundance, are excellent for rough rockwork, banks, edgings, etc., growing in any soil, but showing to greatest advantage in a calcareous one. Seed or division.

Helianthus atrorubens (*Dark-red Sunflower*).—A vigorous perennial with dull purple stems, rough from whitish hairs, 2 to 3 ft high or more. *Flowers*, in autumn; disk dark red or purple; rays yellow, marked with a few lines, pointed and entire; flowering branches scattered. *Leaves*, of root flat, hairy; stem-leaves twisted and waved, rough with hairs (the lower ones particularly so) and small tubercles. Pennsylvania to Carolina.——Borders, in sandy loam. Division and seed.

Helianthus multiflorus (*Many-flowered H.*)—A fine showy perennial, 4 to 6 ft. high. *Flowers*, late in summer and autumn; yellow, at the end of the branches, the largest sometimes 8 to 9 in. in diameter; the side ones gradually smaller. *Leaves*, alternate, sometimes opposite, lower ones heart-shaped, upper ones ovate, rough. *H. multiflorus fl.pl.* is a double variety oftener met with than the single form. Said to be a native of America, but American botanists say they have not found it there.——Borders, associated with the taller plants, and in a semi-wild state in shrubberies, in any soil. May be seen flowering abundantly in some of the London squares.

Helianthus orgyalis (*Graceful Sunflower*).—A tall graceful, somewhat willow-like herb, 6 to 8 ft. high. *Flowers*, in autumn; yellow, on long stalks. *Leaves*, alternate, rather small, stalkless, 3 to 6 in. long, and about 1 in. across, very numerous and narrow, much recurved, so as to give the tips of the shoots a very graceful appearance, lower ones slightly toothed. North America.——Among groups of fine-leaved hardy plants in the sub-tropical garden or pleasure-ground, margins of shrubberies, or wood-walks. The tips of the shoots for a length of 15 in. or so, cut off and placed in water indoors, are as ornamental as the most graceful or delicate young Palm or Dracæna. As the plant throw up a great number of shoots, they should be thinned out when young. Division.

Helianthus rigidus (*Rigid Sunflower*).—*Harpalium rigidum.*—A remarkably showy and rapidly-growing perennial, 3 to 4 ft. high. *Flowers*, in summer; a pleasing golden yellow, 3 to 4 in. across; disk darkish brown about an inch in diameter. *Leaves*, of stem opposite, very thick, lance-shaped; root-leaves oval, blunt, 3-nerved; stem rough, sometimes exuding a small quantity of resin. *Root* spreading about very much. North America. ——Borders, in which from its rapidly-spreading habit, it will require annual division. It is a capital plant for naturalization among the finer perennials in almost any position or soil. Division.

Helichrysum arenarium (*Yellow Everlasting*).—*Gnaphalium arenarium.*

HELICHRYSUM — HELLEBORUS.   141

—A bright and lovely plant, with leaves quite white with down on both sides; 4 to 10 in. high. *Flowers*, in summer; bright golden yellow, in a compound corymb. They are much used on the Continent for *Immortelles* and ornaments. *Leaves*, lance-shaped, entire, nearly stem-clasping, blunt and recurved at the points, with revolute edges; stem upright, downy, not branching, clothed with leaves to the top. Central and Southern Europe. —— Excellent for rockwork and the margins of borders, always in very sandy, warm, and well-drained soil. Division.

Helichrysum Stœchas (*Stœchas H.*) — A neat perennial, with very branching spreading stems, about 1 ft. high. *Flowers*, in summer; yellow, in terminal corymbose heads, closely crowded together, on short stalks. *Leaves*, sessile, linear, obtuse, silvery underneath; stems and branches covered with silvery down. South of Europe. —— Margins of borders, and the rock-garden, in lightish soil. Division.

Heliopsis lævis (*Smooth H.*) — A vigorous smoothish herb, 3 to 6 ft. high. *Flowers*, late in summer; yellow; heads about 3 in. across, on long stalks, terminating the stem. *Leaves*, oval-lance-shaped, abrupt at the base, or tapering abruptly into the stalks, coarsely serrate. *H. gracilis* is a variety of this species, with a slender stem, clothed with fine down at the top, and much smaller in all its parts, with lance-shaped, rough leaves, acute at the base. *H. scabra* is another variety with stem and leaves rough, and the involucre slightly downy. United States of North America. —— Naturalization among strong herbs in common soil. Division and seed.

Helleborus abchasicus (*Abchasian Christmas Rose*).—An interesting but uncommon kind of Christmas rose, about 1 ft. high. *Flowers*, in spring; green, usually nodding; anthers yellowish-white; petals 18 to 24 in number; sepals obovate-oblong, pointed, waved at the margin, not overlapping each other, of a purplish hue. *Leaves*, mostly radical, somewhat pedate, with 5 to 7 spathulate-lanceolate, widely-spreading, smooth, distantly-toothed leaflets, continuing through the winter. Region between the Caucasus and the Black Sea. —— Sheltered and sunny banks, or borders, in warm well-drained soil. Division.

Helleborus atrorubens (*Dark-purple H.*)—Stem about 18 in. high, producing branches with 2 or 3 series of forkings. *Flowers*, in March or April; deep purple in bud, when first expanded violet purple, the edges and centre green, afterwards changing to dull purple. *Leaves*, pedate, variable in form, 5- to 9-parted, never assuming the lobed condition of *H. purpurascens*, nor are the lobes united half way up, but distinct almost to the base, except in the side ones. Woods and thickets in Southern Europe. —— Sheltered borders, banks, and fringes of shrubberies, in deep good loam. Division.

Helleborus fœtidus (*Fetid H.*)—A hardy native plant, very distinct and striking in habit, and well worthy of cultivation for the sake of its handsome winter foliage. In a wild state it forms luxuriant tufts, about 2 ft. high, and in gardens has attained a height of 3 ft. or more. *Flowers*, early in spring; globose, greenish, tipped with purple, drooping, in panicled cymes. *Leaves*, alternate, persistent, leathery, of a dull green colour, the lower ones divided into from 7 to 11 lance-shaped serrated segments, pedately arranged. Britain and Europe. —— Borders, or fringes of shrubberies, in ordinary soil. Division.

Helleborus niger (*Christmas Rose*). —A well-known old garden plant; G to 15 in. high. *Flowers*, 1, 2 or 3 on a stem, the unopened buds suffused with faint rose, gracefully curved downwards; when fully expanded pure white, 3 to 4½ in. in diameter, with a bunch of yellow stamens an inch or more across; usually with two concave, shell-like, heart-shaped bracts just behind the flower. *Leaves*, pedate, quite smooth; leaflets 5 to 10, lance-shaped, serrate in the upper part, stout and leathery. *H. niger maximus* is a variety much larger in all its parts, flowering considerably earlier; attaining, when well-grown, a height of 2 ft., and bearing 2 to 7 flowers, from 3½ to 5½ in. across, on branched stems; the leaflets more oblique and irregular in outline. *H. niger minor* is a variety much smaller than the type, with leaflets distantly and irregularly toothed, the teeth resembling small lobes, and with sepals narrower and more pointed. Europe.——Perhaps the best positions for the Christmas Rose and its varieties are on warm and sheltered grassy banks, where they would have better drainage, and where the flowers would be kept from splashing by the surrounding grass; but they are so excellent that they may with advantage be used in almost any other position in which they may be desired in ordinary soil. They should be naturalized where there is space for this interesting phase of gardening. Division.

Helleborus odorus (*Sweet H.*)—A rare and interesting kind, 1 ft. high. *Flowers*, in March and April, sometimes in February; greenish, sweet-scented, drooping, nearly 2 in. across; 3 to 5 flowers on the top of each stem. *Leaves*, pale green, veined with white; those of the root stalked, pedate, with 6 to 8 lanceolate, regularly toothed divisions; near the top of the stem there is a single, almost sessile, leaf with from 3 to 5 divisions. Hungary.

——Does best on declivities with a shady northern aspect, in substantial loam, mixed with peat. Division.

Helleborus olympicus (*Olympian H.*) —A handsome species; 12 to 15 in. high. *Flowers*, in spring; purplish; petals about 13 in number; anthers of a yellowish white; 2 or 3 blooms on each stem. *Leaves*, digitate-pedate, or palmate, with 5 to 7 linear-oblong, smooth, dentate-serrate lobes rather close together. Mount Olympus, in Greece.——Warm sheltered borders and banks, the margins of beds of early-flowering shrubs, or in sunny nooks on the lower flanks of the rough rockwork, in good soil. Division.

Helleborus orientalis (*Oriental Hellebore.*)—A very fine kind, allied to the Christmas Rose, but distinguished from it by its leaves, which are annual and appear with the flowers; 8 in. to 2 ft. high. *Flowers*, from February to April; large, rose-coloured. *Leaves*, very much divided, large, somewhat downy when young; stem-leaves sessile and palmate. Greece and Syria.——A number of intermediate varieties have been obtained by crossing this plant with the Christmas Rose, and also perhaps with *H. purpurascens*. These varieties are generally more vigorous than either of the types, and bear large open flowers with slightly waved petals more or less white or rose-coloured. The most remarkable of them is *H. atrorubens hybridus*.——Borders, fringes of shrubberies, grassy banks and slopes, etc., in good garden soil. Division.

Helleborus purpurascens (*Purple-flowered H.*)—A dwarfer species than *H. atrorubens*, with violet-coloured stems, 6 to 10 in. high, surrounded at the base by a membranous sheath. *Flowers*, in March; purplish-red, with white stamens; broadly vase-shaped, nearly 2 in. across, drooping, 1 to 2 on each stem. *Leaves*, of a greyish-green colour, with from 6 to 9 oval-lance-shaped, toothed divisions; the floral leaf nearly sessile, with 5 or 6 divisions. Native of Hungary.—— Similar positions and treatment to those given for preceding kinds.

Helonias bullata (*Spiked H.*) — *H. latifolia.*—A distinct and handsome bog perennial; 12 to 16 in. high. *Flowers*, in summer; small, very handsome, purplish-rose, arranged in an oval spike, the lower blossoms only accompanied by linear-lanceolate bracts. *Leaves*, all radical, oblong-lanceolate, acute, veined, much shorter than the flower-stems. *Root* tuberous, fleshy. Native of marshy places in N. America.—— In the artificial bog, or in moist ground near a rivulet. In fine sandy and very moist soils it thrives well as a border plant. I have never seen it so fine as at Edinburgh, except in the bogs of New Jersey. Division.

Hemerocallis disticha (*Two - rowed Day-lily*).— A handsome tuberous perennial; 1 to 2 ft. high. *Flowers*, in summer; large, yellowish on the outside, reddish within; segments lanceolate, wavy, acute, spreading or reflected, the three external ones broader. *Leaves*, linear, arranged in two rows, keeled. There is a variety with double flowers. Native of Japan, China, and Nepaul. —— Borders, fringes of shrubberies, and naturalized in ordinary free soil. Division.

Hemerocallis Dumortieri (*Dumortier's Day-lily*).—Resembles *H. graminea*; 1 ft. to 16 in. high. *Flowers*, in May and June, and sometimes again at the end of summer; large, reddish-orange, tinged with brown on the outside, usually 1 to 3 on each stem. At the base of each flower is a keeled bract, of a brownish or reddish-green tinge. *Leaves*, very narrow, in two rows, similar to those of *H. graminea*, from which plant it is not easily distinguished. Japan.——Borders and fringes of beds of American shrubs in peat, or the rougher parts of the rock-garden. Division.

Hemerocallis flava (*Yellow Day-lily*).—A showy and vigorous kind; 2 to 3 ft. high. *Flowers*, in summer; orange-yellow, very fragrant, erect, with 6 flat pointed divisions, resembling those of a Lily. *Leaves*, numerous, narrow, 2 to 2½ ft. long, keeled, of a shining green, in a strong tuft. *Root* fasciculate, half-fibrous and half-tuberous. Native of Hungary, Illyria, Carniola, and Switzerland.——Borders and shrubberies, or groups of perennials, or in isolated tufts in the grass, or naturalization, in any soil. Division.

Hemerocallis fulva (*Tawny Day-lily*).—Another strong and showy kind; 2½ to 4 ft. high. *Flowers*, in summer; large, about 4 in. wide, very open, of a buff-yellow, scentless, arranged in a lax cluster; segments almost obtuse. *Leaves*, broad, very long, keeled, numerous, in a large tuft. France, about Pau, Tarbes, and Bordeaux.——Similar positions and treatment to those for the preceding kind.

Hemerocallis graminea (*Grass-leaved H.*)—A small and graceful kind; 8 to 14 in. high. *Flowers*, in summer; yellow, slightly tinged with green; smaller and less fragrant than those of *H. flava*, with the 3 internal segments wavy. *Leaves*, very narrow, keeled through their entire length, pointed, of a lively green. Native of Siberia. ——Borders, the rock-garden, or naturalized where the vegetation is not too strong, in peat or very sandy loam. Division.

Heracleum flavescens (*Austriacum*). (*Yellowish Cow-parsnip*).—A vigorous perennial, with deeply-furrowed hispid stems, and convex green leaves; 5 to 6 ft. high. *Flowers*, in summer; yellowish, in large umbels; petals bent in, not notched; pedicels rough. Leaves, rough from hairs, pinnate; leaflets ovate or oblong, serrate. Dauphiny to Siberia.——Banks of rivers and ponds, where effective foliage is desired, in ordinary soil. Seed, to be sown as soon as ripe; most of the kinds come freely from self-sown seeds.

Heracleum persicum (*Persian Cow-parsnip*).—6 ft. high and upwards. Flowers, in summer; small, whitish, numerous, in regular umbels of enormous size; the upper ones being 16 in. across, and sometimes more; petals very small, oboval, faintly notched. Leaves, of the root very large, slightly downy underneath, smooth above, pinnate, with 3 to 4 pairs of lanceolate-acute distant segments, of a dark-green hue, afterwards brownish; stem-leaves smaller, with broadly-sheathing stalks. Persia.——Similar positions to those for the preceding, but in drier soil. Seed.

Heracleum pubescens (*Downy Cow-parsnip*).—Still larger in its proportions than the foregoing kinds; 6½ ft. to nearly 10 ft. high. Flowers, in summer; small, yellowish-white, in umbels, about 1 ft. in diameter. Leaves, very large, smooth above, somewhat rough underneath, pinnate, with oval, pointed, closely-placed segments; the intermediate segments 3-lobed. Caucasus and Tauria.——In rich bottoms, or by margins of water, or wherever very imposing foliage is desired. Seed and division.

Heracleum Wilhelmsii (*Wilhelm's Cow-parsnip*).—An imposing kind, 6½ ft. and upwards in height. Flowers, in summer; whitish, in large umbels, 10 in. to 1 ft. in diameter. Leaves, very large, downy and wrinkled when young, pinnate; lateral segments lanceolate-acute, distant; terminal one entire and larger. Siberia.——Similar uses to the preceding.

Hesperis matronalis (*Dame's Violet*) —A popular old garden plant, with spear-shaped leaves indented at their edges, and erect, slightly-branched stems, 1 to 2 ft. high or more. Flowers, in early summer; deep purple, sweet-scented, produced in terminal racemes; petals roundish, notched at the tops. Leaves, 2 or 3 in. long, ovate-lanceolate, toothed. There are several double kinds, white, purple, and streaked, all sweet and very handsome border-flowers. Europe, and said to be a native plant, but probably not truly so.——The single kind is only fitted for naturalization, and will grow anywhere; the double ones are among the most valuable ornaments of the mixed border; they love a good sandy moist loam, and will be found to thrive best if divided and carefully replanted in fresh soil every second year soon after flowering. The single kind grows very freely from seed; the double ones are increased by careful division and cuttings.

Hesperis tristis (*Night-scented Rocket*).—A quaint-looking, interesting kind; 9 in. to 2 ft. high. Flowers, in spring or early summer; varying from a dirty-white to a dull dark-purple, sweet-scented in the night, in terminal racemes; petals oblong, oblique; pedicels long, spreading, rigid. Leaves, of root, stalked; stem-leaves sessile, ovate, acute, entire or toothed, smooth or pubescent, pale-green, 2 to 4 in. long. Austria, Hungary, Russia, and Tauria. ——This may be established on old ruins, in chalk-pits, etc., by sowing the seed in mossy or earthy chinks; on the level ground it is tender.

Heuchera glabra (*Smooth H.*)— A dark-foliaged dwarf perennial, 12 to 18 in. high. Flowers, in summer; small and not ornamental. Leaves, roundish-heart-shaped, acutely 5- to 7-lobed, toothed; stalks smooth,

HEUCHERA — HIPPOCREPIS. 145

root-leaves on long-stalks; stem-leaves more deeply lobed, and on shorter stalks. North America.—See cultural remarks, etc. on following kind.

Heuchera ribifolia (*Currant-leaved H.*)—Panicle oblong-conoidal; limb of calyx oblique, lobes nearly triangular; petals obtuse, and about as long as the calyx. *Leaves*, obtuse, 5-lobed, smooth above; leaf-stalks smooth, polished; stems rough, with very short muricated points, 1- to 3-leaved. North America.—Borders, and as edgings, the peculiarly dark tone of its leaves making it of some value for the last-named use. In bloom, the *Heucheras* are not attractive; they thrive on any soil, and are readily increased by division.

Hibiscus militaris (*Showy H.*)—A splendid perennial, 3 to 4 ft. high. *Flowers*, in summer; rose with a darker centre; in a lengthened few-flowered raceme; corolla about 2½ in. long, hairy on the outside near the base. *Leaves*, smooth, hastate-lobed, somewhat heart-shaped, tapering to a point, serrate, 3 to 5 in. long. North America.—Borders, groups of tall perennials, or as isolated specimens in the subtropical garden or pleasure-ground, in deep sandy loam, and in warm and sheltered positions. Division.

Hibiscus Moscheutos (*Mallow Rose*).—A vigorous perennial with stems 3 to 5 ft. high. *Flowers*, late in summer; light rose-colour, sometimes nearly white, with a crimson centre; as large as those of the common Hollyhock; petals inverted-ovate, the tips slightly hollowed, style projecting. *Leaves*, about 5 in. long and 3 wide, ovate, tapering to a point, usually 5-nerved, serrate, clothed with whitish down beneath and rough pubescence above, somewhat remarkable from the flower often springing from the leaf-stalk. United States, by the borders of marshes.—Moist borders, among bog-plants, or in isolated tufts by the sides of lakes, in ordinary soil. Division or seed.

Hibiscus palustris (*Marsh H.*) — This plant has often been confounded with *H. Moscheutos*, but is quite distinct; grows 3 to 5 ft. high. *Flowers*, late in summer; large, purple, on long axillary stalks. *Leaves*, broadly-ovate, obtusely serrated, faintly 3-lobed, 3-nerved, downy and whitish underneath. Swamps and marshes from Canada to Virginia.—Similar positions and treatment to those directed for *H. Moscheutos*. Seed or division.

Hibiscus roseus (*Rosy H.*)—Another very attractive kind, 4 to 6 ft. high. *Flowers*, late in summer; showy rose, 4 in. across; petals with straight deeply-coloured veins; pedicels axillary, 1-flowered, jointed about the middle. *Leaves*, heart-shaped, toothed, somewhat 3-lobed, clothed with down beneath. France, on the banks of the river Adour.—See cultural remarks, etc., for *H. Moscheutos*.

Hieracium aurantiacum (*Orange H.*) —A pleasing and easily grown perennial, distinct among dwarf composite plants from its deep orange colour; 1 to 1¼ ft. high. *Flowers*, in early summer; orange-red, 8 or 10 borne in a panicle; pedicels short. *Leaves*, grass-green, obovate-lanceolate, quite entire, obtuse, narrowing into the stalk; those of the stem sessile; stem simple, bearded with slender hairs, which are black in the upper part. Western Europe.—Borders, in any soil. Division.

Hippocrepis comosa (*Horse-shoe Vetch*). — A minute, prostrate, Coronilla-like British evergreen herb, about 6 in. high. *Flowers*, in spring and summer; yellow, 5 to 8 being borne together in a crown, and resembling those of the common Bird's-foot Trefoil, but

L

paler and rather smaller; legume curved, uneven on both sides. *Leaves*, composed of from 9 to 15 pairs of small, oblong or linear, smooth leaflets. Europe.——The rock-garden; and borders, in any soil. Seed and division.

Hoteia japonica (*White H.*) — *Spiræa japonica*.—A fine herbaceous plant of tufted habit, covered, especially at the base of the stems and leafstalks, with long, scattered, semi-transparent, reddish hairs; 1 ft. to 16 in. high. *Flowers*, early in summer; numerous, silvery white, in a panicled cluster, the ramifications of which, as well as the pedicels and bracts of the flowers, are also white. *Leaves*, of the root numerous, in tufts, with 3-cleft footstalks, which are swollen at the commencement of the first forking: those of the stem alternate, stalked, thrice-pinnate; divisions oval, toothed and fringed, of a glistening green on the upper side. Japan.—— Warm borders, fringes of shrubberies, rough rockwork, etc., in peat or sandy soil. It is now much grown in pots for forcing. Division.

Hottonia palustris (*Water Violet*).—A beautiful British water-plant, with bright green, deeply cut, submerged leaves and stems; from 9 in. to 2 ft. high. *Flowers*, in early summer; pink or pale lilac with a yellow eye, in whorls at intervals one above the other, forming a handsome spike; calyx and corolla divided into five segments; pedicels short, with a small bract at the base of each. *Leaves*, pinnatifid; leaflets linear, narrow. Europe.—— Lakes, ponds, and fountain-basins; also on the soft and wet muddy banks of streams. Division, or seed, which should be sown in autumn.

Houstonia cærulea (*Bluets*).—A very minute and charming evergreen herb, with small pointed leaves, forming low cushions on the ground, from which spring the slender stems about 2 in. high. *Flowers*, in early summer; beautiful blue or white; the stems dividing into 2, or sometimes 3, thread-like branches or peduncles, each being terminated by a single flower. *Leaves*, of root spoon-shaped; stem-leaves, somewhat lance-shaped. North America, from New England to Florida.——The rock-garden, on well-drained spots in very fine sandy or peaty soil. It frequently perishes in winter, and should be grown in small pans in cold frames in peat soil. Careful division or seed.

Humulus Lupulus (*Common Hop*).— A very common, well known, and vigorous twining perennial. *Flowers*, in summer; greenish yellow, the males in loose panicles in the axils of the upper leaves; females in shortly-stalked, axillary, roundish spikes or heads. *Leaves*, opposite in pairs, stalked, broadly heart-shaped, deeply 3- or 5-lobed, sharply toothed, rasplike to the touch. Europe, Asia, and Britain.—— Admirable for covering bowers, etc., especially where vegetation that disappears in winter is desired; also when allowed to run wild among shrubs, etc., in almost any soil. Division.

Hutchinsia alpina (*Alpine Hutchinsia*) —A very pretty and diminutive alpine plant, with shining green leaves and hosts of small white flowers; 2 or 3 in. high. *Flowers*, in spring, and, when planted in spring, for a long period; pure white, abundantly produced, in clusters. *Leaves*, smooth, shining, deeply cut into comb-like lobes, and resembling pinnate leaves. Mountain chains of Central and Southern Europe.——The rock-garden, and the margin of choice borders, in sandy soil. Division or seed.

Hyacinthus amethystinus (*Amethyst H.*)—A beautiful bulb, 4 in. to 1 ft. high. *Flowers*, in early summer; handsome blue, drooping, nearly unilateral, arranged in a loose cluster of 4 to 12 blooms, accompanied with bracts as long as the pedicels. *Leaves,* narrow, linear, smooth, longer than the flower-stem. Native of S. Europe, and especially of the Pyrenees.——Borders, the rock-garden, and the bulb-garden; best in deep sandy soil. Separation of the bulbs.

Hyacinthus orientalis (*Common Hyacinth*).—The parent of our popular Hyacinths; 8 in. to 1 ft. high. *Flowers,* in spring; very fragrant, blue in the original type, but varying much in colour under cultivation, in a cluster of 6 to 15 blooms. *Leaves,* lanceolate, grooved, of a dark green. *Bulb* round, of medium size. Native of S. Europe and the Levant. —— The varieties deserve to be much more commonly grown in the open air, as they are perfectly hardy. Planted deeply, the crown of the bulb 6 or 8 inches or more under the surface, they flower strongly year after year if in good sandy loam.

Hypericum calycinum (*Great-flowered H.*)—A well known and very showy low trailing shrub; about 1 ft. high. *Flowers,* nearly all summer; bright yellow, 3 or 4 in. across, 5 or 6 in a corymb; sepals about ¼ in. long, roundish; stamens long and slender. *Leaves,* nearly stalkless, large, ovate or oblong, blunt, smooth, when young they are of a pale green, but when old of a very dark green, and somewhat glaucous at the back. Southern Europe, naturalized in several parts of Britain.——Best suited for naturalization; it grows freely and increases rapidly in any ordinary soil.

Hypericum Coris (*Heath-leaved H.*) —A dwarf evergreen shrub with a slender branching stem; 4 to 6 in. high. *Flowers,* in summer; bright yellow, ¾ in. across; margin of calyx dotted with small black prominences. *Leaves,* very small, linear, with revolute edges, sessile, in closely-set whorls. Cape of Good Hope.——The rock-garden, in well-drained soil. Cuttings and division.

Hypericum nummularium (*Moneywort H.*)—A diminutive perennial, forming neat, compact tufts, with very slender stems; 3 in. high. *Flowers,* in summer; yellow, ¾ in. across; margin of calyx toothed and tinged with purplish red. *Leaves,* opposite, nearly round, almost sessile, about ¼ in. broad, close together. *Root* long and wiry, much branched and very fibrous. South of Europe. ——The rock-garden, in well-drained soil. Division and seed.

Iberidella rotundifolia (*Round-leaved I.*)—*Thlaspi rotundifolium.*—A dwarf evergreen herb, with prostrate or ascending stems, and smooth, thick, leathery leaves of a glaucous olive green; 3 to 6 in. high. *Flowers,* in early summer; rosy-lilac, sweet-scented, freely produced, in terminal racemes. *Leaves,* somewhat fleshy, quite entire; lower ones stalked, obovate; those of the stem almost stalkless, ovate-oblong. A native of the Alps of Switzerland, Savoy, and Austria. —— The rock-garden, among the dwarfest alpine plants, in any lightish soil. Seed or division.

Iberis Bubani (*Buban's Candytuft*).— A neat dwarf plant, forming compact tufts, nearly 6 in. high. *Flowers,* in summer; pink, in corymbose clusters. *Leaves,* spathulate, lobed, very deep glossy green, forming dense rosettes, covered with a profusion of branching flower-stems. Pyrenees. —— The rock-garden, in well-drained soil, and among dwarf plants. Division or seed.

Iberis corifolia (*Coris-leaved I.*) — The neatest and dwarfest of the Iberises, very near or perhaps a dwarf form of *I. saxatilis,* 3 or 4 in. high. *Flowers,* in early spring; white, in corymbs. *Leaves,* linear, entire, blunt, smooth; stems decumbent; tufts very dwarf and densely-cushioned. A native of Sicily.—— Borders, the rock-garden, or edgings, in ordinary soil. Division, cuttings, or seed.

Iberis corræfolia (*Late White Iberis*). —*I. gibraltarica* (*Hort.*)—*I. coriacea.*— The finest kind we have, more shrublike than *I. saxatilis*; 6 to 15 in. high. *Flowers*, in May, later than the other common evergreen Iberises; large, pure white, in close corymbs. *Leaves*, oblong - spathulate, entire, almost sessile, about 1 in. long and ¼ in. broad at the widest part, gradually attenuated towards the stem. Seeds produced very sparsely. This plant is probably a hybrid, between *I. semperflorens* and the Rock Iberis or one of its forms, and was first distributed from the Botanic Garden at Bury St. Edmunds. One of the most valuable of all plants for rockwork, borders, or banks, growing freely in any soil or position, but preferring spots well exposed to sun and air. Cuttings, seed, and division.

Iberis gibraltarica (*Gibraltar I.*)— The largest, showiest and most straggling kind, 1 to 2 ft. high. *Flowers*, in early spring; large, white, often suffused with red, in close heads. *Leaves*, about 2 in. long, and ½ in. wide, oblong-spoon-shaped, fleshy, distinctly toothed at the top, slightly ciliated. Southern Spain.—— The rock-garden, borders, and banks, in well-drained sandy loam. Seed or cuttings.

Iberis saxatilis (*Rock Candytuft*).— A small evergreen shrub, the commonest and one of the most useful of the evergreen Candytufts; 6 to 12 in. high. *Flowers*, in spring or early summer; white, in corymbose heads. *Leaves*, linear, entire, rather fleshy, acute, ciliated. Native of Southern Europe.——Borders, the rock-garden, edgings, and naturalization on rocky places or bare banks in any soil. Division, seed, or cuttings.

Iberis semperflorens (*Window Candytuft*). — A fine kind, common in Southern France and Italy; 12 in. to 2 ft. high. *Flowers*, from October to May; very numerous, large, and of a pure and dazzling white. *Leaves*, broad, thick, spathulate, of a fine green colour. A native of Persia.—— It seldom seeds in this country, and must be propagated by cuttings, for which summer is the best time. Succeeds as a rock plant only in mild parts, and in those near the sea. I have seen it thrive well on the rockwork in the College Botanic Garden at Dublin, but our winters prevent it from blooming as early as it does in the south of Europe.

Iberis Tenoreana (*Tenore's I.*)—A showy species, resembling *I. gibraltarica*, but smaller, with rather fleshy, toothed leaves, and ascending stems, shrubby at the base; 3 to 6 in. high. *Flowers*, in early summer; white, changing to purple, freely produced, in close heads. *Leaves*, lower ones obovate, narrowed at the base; upper ones oblonglinear, both leaves and stem hairy. This plant does not survive our winters on heavy soils, but is quite hardy on light well-drained ones. Naples.—— The rock-garden, or borders, in very sandy dry soil. It is rarely healthy or long-lived on clay. Seed.

Inula Helenium (*Elecampane*).— A vigorous native herb, with the lower leaves a foot long, and 4 in. broad in the middle, narrowing into a stalk; 2 to 4 ft. high. *Flowers*, in summer; yellow, in large solitary heads, terminating the branches; rays linear, about 1½ in. long, with three sharp teeth at the end. *Leaves*, of root oblong, stalked; of stem ovate or oblong, clasping, almost smooth above, clothed with soft whitish hairs beneath; those of involucre bluntly-ovate, downy; stem

INULA — IRIS.

striped, downy, branching at the top. Europe, Caucasus, Japan.——This inmate of the kitchen-garden is worth a place among perennials, grown for the sake of the effect of their foliage, in ordinary soil. Division.

Inula Oculus Christi (*Hoary I.*)—A hardy herbaceous perennial, 1½ to 2 ft. high. *Flowers*, in summer; orange, 3½ in. across; petals very narrow; divisions of the involucrum covered with a thick, soft, dark-brown down. *Leaves*, broadly lance-shaped, obtuse, almost entire, or with a few small and distant teeth, and covered, as is the stem, with a feeble whitish down. Austria.——Borders, or naturalization, in warm sandy soil. Division or seed.

Iris amœna (*Pleasing I.*)—A delicately tinted and elegant species, 1½ to 2 ft. high. *Flowers*, in summer; whitish at the base, rayed and veined with pale violet outside; the upper part and internal divisions white, tinged with blue, and veined with violet; yellowish at the base inside, dotted and rayed with violet; lamina of the stigma white. Central and South Europe.——Borders, or beds of Irises and other fine perennials that flower in early summer, in light, deep, sandy soil. Division.

Iris cristata (*Crested Iris*).—A charming and very dwarf kind, 6 in. high, somewhat like *I. pumila*, but easily recognised by its rhizome creeping well above the ground, looking as if it had grown too far out of it. *Flowers*, in May; generally solitary, erect, pale purplish-blue; external divisions drooping, obtuse, blue, with deeper blue spots, and three elevated wavy ribs, variegated with orange and yellow; internal divisions narrower, pointed, erect, uniform in colour. *Leaves* numerous, short, equitant, swordshaped, curved at the top, with a pale membranaceous margin; stem very slender, small at the base, and gradually thickening as it ascends. N. America. ——On margins of borders, edges of beds of mixed flowers, or flat, low parts of the rock-garden, always in light, rich, sandy soil. Division.

Iris flavescens (*Yellowish I.*)—This plant resembles *I. germanica* in its habit, leaves, and rhizome. *Flowers*, early in summer; external divisions yellow, reticulated with purplish-red on the lower half, spathulate-oboval, with a beard of bright yellow; internal divisions deep yellow, wedge-shaped, obovate, very obtuse, having the claw furnished with yellow hairs; limb of the stigma yellow, spathulate-oblong. Native country uncertain.——Borders, beds, or naturalization, in any soil. Division.

Iris florentina (*Florentine I.*)—A delicately-coloured and very desirable kind, very like *I. germanica* in its rhizome, stem, and leaves; 1½ to 3 ft. high. *Flowers*, in spring; very fragrant, white slightly tinged with blue, with a bright yellow beard; exterior divisions wedge-shaped-spathulate, indented, covered with yellow hairs; internal divisions oboval, indented at the top, wavy at the edges, a little wider than the exterior divisions. Native of Italy and S. Europe.—— Mixed borders, margins of shrubberies, or naturalization, in almost any kind of soil. Division.

Iris fœtidissima (*Gladdon*).—A well-known but undeservedly neglected British plant; 1½ to 2 ft. high. *Flowers*, in summer; lead-coloured or bluish, rarely yellow; exterior divisions marbled with violet on the claw, and having an oval wavy limb veined with the same colour; interior divisions streaked with faint blue. *Leaves*, lance-shaped, stiff, dark-green, when bruised emitting an odour somewhat like that of cold roast beef. Britain and most parts of Europe, in damp woods and thickets.——A variety with variegated leaves forms a very pleasing addition to our list of variegated border plants, and is also an excellent house plant. A graceful-leaved and pleasingly striped plant, seen in many Parisian houses, is perhaps rarely suspected to be this variegated form. The common green form is well worthy of being grown in semi-wild places for the sake of the effect of its brilliant coral-red seeds. Division.

Iris germanica (*Common Iris*).—The well-known large violet Iris, which may be seen blooming abundantly in small gardens in some parts of London; 1½ to 3 ft. high. *Flowers*, early in summer; large, irregular, and fragrant, four or five on each stem; exterior divisions deep violet, broad, spathulate - wedge - shaped, blunt, curved backwards, with a yellowish beard; internal divisions same colour, very broadly spathulate, erect, elliptical or oblong, blunt, with wavy edges; limb of the stigma streaked with lilac and rosy-white. *Leaves*, in two rows, sword-shaped, slightly arching, of a glaucous green, shorter than the stem. Rhizome creeping, fleshy and knotty. Native of Southern Europe.——A variety, named *I. germanica alba*, has the external divisions bluish-white; internal, pure white. Another (*I. g. cærulea*) has the external divisions violet; internal, sky-blue.——Borders or naturalization in semi-wild places. It does best in well-drained soil in a warm aspect, but will thrive in almost any soil or position. There are many beautiful varieties, all readily increased by division.

Iris gramineus (*Grass-leaved I.*)—Intermediate in stature between the dwarf and the tall kinds, and with distinct-looking foliage. *Flowers*, early in summer; solitary, slightly fragrant; external divisions with a claw 2 in. long, of a violet-lilac veined with blue, and a yellow band in the middle; limb half the length of the claw, nearly round, obtuse, wavy, streaked and veined with white, yellow, and blue; internal divisions of a uniform violet-blue, lanceolate - oblong, indented. *Leaves*, nearly linear, streaked, straight, stiff, and erect, of a bright green, glossy on one side only. Rhizome slender. Native of South Europe.——Borders, and fringes of shrubberies, in any soil. Division.

Iris iberica (*Iberian I.*)—*Oncocyclus ibericus.*—A remarkably striking Iris, reminding one of *I. susiana*, but quite distinct in leaf and flower; 4 to 16 in. high. *Flowers*, in summer; solitary; external divisions roundish, clawed, of a dull-red, marked with tawny streaks, with a few hairs on the upper part, and an oval, velvety, black, purple-edged spot in the middle, recurved, and with slightly reflected edges; internal divisions roundish, clawed, larger, erect, spreading, of a very pale purple, with streaks of a darker hue, veined and spotted about the base; blade of the stigma, yellowish, dotted with purple. *Leaves*, linear, arched, almost curled, folded lengthwise. Iberia, on hills near Tiflis. ——On the warm flanks of the rock-garden, or in choice beds in good sandy soil, at least till more plentiful. It is but recently introduced.

Iris junceus (*Rush I.*)—*I. lusitanica.* —A brilliant kind in the way of the Spanish and English Irises; 1 ft. to 2 ft. high. *Flowers*, in spring; usually one on a stem; external divisions of a bright yellow, streaked and veined with violet on the claw; internal divisions spathulate-oblong, pointed, indented, of the same length and colour as the external divisions; limb of the stigma yellow, about 2 in. long. *Leaves*, longer than the flower-stem, linear-lanceolate, narrow, glaucous, rather flaccid. Native of Spain, Portugal, Barbary.——-Warm sandy borders, or grouped in beds with the English and Spanish Irises. Separation of the bulbs every second or third year.

Iris longipetala (*Long-petalled I.*)— A very distinct and fine species, 2 to 3 ft. high. *Flowers*, in summer; white, and regularly flaked throughout their whole length with rather broad and even bands of bluish-lilac. *Leaves*, sword-shaped. California.—— Borders, fringes of shrubberies, etc., in sandy loam. Division.

Iris Monnieri (*Golden I.*)—A bright and noble-flowered kind, quite distinct from any other in cultivation; 2 to 3 ft. high. *Flowers*, in summer; large, fragrant, bright orange yellow; tube short; external divisions 3 in. long, roundish, indented, wavy; internal divisions spathulate-oblong, 2-lobed at the top, shorter than the external divisions; limb of the stigma of a brilliant golden yellow. *Leaves*, lance-shaped, about 2½ ft. long. Native of the Levant. —— Borders, margins of shrubberies, and in tufts in open glades by wood-walks, in rich and rather moist soil. Division.

Iris nudicaulis (*Naked-stemmed I.*) —A very dwarf, sturdy, and handsome kind, 4 to 10 in. high. *Flowers*, in early summer; 4 to 7 on each stem, violet-blue, large; external divisions spathulate-oboval, blunt, seldom wavy; internal divisions oval, a little longer than the external divisions; limb of the stigma violet. *Leaves*, lanceolate, arching; stem-leaves very short, resembling spathes. Native of Southern Europe.——Suited for association with the dwarf Flag, the crested Iris, and other select plants on level parts of the rock-garden, in the front rank in the choice mixed border, and as edgings or tufts on margins of beds of choice dwarf shrubs. Division.

Iris ochroleuca (*Yellowish I.*) — A tall, erect, distinct-looking sort; 1½ to 3½ ft. high. *Flowers*, in summer; with a short greenish tube; external divisions 2 in. to 4½ in. long, white, marked on the claw with a yellow band and yellow veins; limb oval, indented, yellow at the base; internal divisions much longer than the external ones, and of a deeper yellow on the upper side, spathulate-oblong, indented; limb of the stigma white; *Leaves*, straight, stiff, striated, 1½ to 2 ft. long. Native of South Russia. ——Borders, among the taller herbaceous plants, and in tufts two or three feet within the margin of shrubberies; best in rather moist soil; only when sheltered in the last position have I seen it attain a growth of over three feet high. Division.

Iris pallida (*Pale-flowered I.*) — A tall, and noble species, 2 to 3½ ft. high. *Flowers*, in early summer; pale blue; external divisions wedge-shaped, oboval, obtuse, with a whitish yellow beard; internal divisions rather longer than the external, oboval-roundish, obtuse, or indented; five to nine on each stem, with the odour of orange-blossoms. *Leaves*, shorter than the stem, very glaucous. Central and South Europe. —— Mixed borders, fringes of shrubberies, in strong tufts by wood-walks, and any position in which the common *I. germanica* may be found useful. Division.

Iris Pseudacorus (*Marsh I.*) — *I. Pseudo-Acorus.*—The common Flag, 3 to 4 ft. high. *Flowers*, in summer; large, almost without odour; external divisions yellow, with a round spot at the base of a brighter yellow, veined with violet; internal divisions pale yellow. *Leaves* green, erect, sword-shaped, about 2½ ft. in length. Native of most parts of Europe.——Margins of ponds, etc.; the variegated form is the only one likely to be required for garden use, as the green one is found on the margin of almost every piece of water.

Iris pumila (*Dwarf Flag*).—The best known of the smaller Irises, though far from being as common as it deserves; 1½ to 8 in. high. *Flowers*, in spring, and frequently a second time in autumn; small, of a deep violet, one or two on each stem; external divisions broad, oblong: internal divisions spathulate, and wavy on the edges; *Leaves*, narrow. There are varieties with light blue, whitish, and yellowish flowers. Southern Europe.——Well adapted for edgings, rockwork, and tufts on the margins of borders, and thrives best in rich, light, and well-drained soil. The finest plants I have seen were on very sandy, deep, well-drained peat. Readily increased by division.

Iris reticulata (*Early Bulbous I.*)—One of the most singularly beautiful of early flowers; 4 to 6 in. high. *Flowers*, in spring; one on each stem, deliciously fragrant, about 3 in. long; external divisions concave, oblong-spathulate, of a rich violet-purple, veined and reticulated with a darker shade of the same colour, and a deep and brilliant orange stain in the middle; internal divisions blunt, 2 in. long, of a uniform violet hue, narrower than the limb of the stigma. *Leaves*, erect, slender, pointed, hollow, irregularly four-angled, glaucous, 5 to 18 in. long. *Bulb*, small, egg-shaped, brownish. Caucasus.——In select sunny nooks in the rock-garden, in a deep and thoroughly drained bed of rich and light soil, or in the same description of soil on a bank or slightly raised border, always in a sunny, warm position. I have seen this plant thrive when fully exposed, where the soil was of a fine sandy character and well drained, but recommend positions which will encourage its early-blooming character, and also, as it is scarce, prevent its suffering from the destruction of its leaves by storms. Separation of the bulbs, every second or third year when the stems are nearly withered.

Iris ruthenica (*Russian I.*) — A very small kind, with grassy leaves; 1½ to 4 in. high. *Flowers*, in spring, fragrant; external divisions spathulate-obtuse, yellowish above, streaked underneath with yellow, white, and violet; internal divisions linear-spathulate, indented, bluish or violet, half the length of the external divisions; limb of the stigma violet-blue. *Leaves*, 8 to 13 in. long, lanceolate-linear, some erect, others curving a little, streaked, green and shining on one side, glaucous on the other. South Russia and Siberia.——Borders, in fine free moist soil. Division.

Iris sambucina (*Elder-scented I.*) — A vigorous and rather tall kind, 1½ to 3¼ ft. high. *Flowers*, in summer; large, with the odour of Elder-flowers; external divisions spathulate-oblong, rounded and somewhat jagged above, yellow, with brown or violet rays and veins, and a dense bright yellow beard; internal divisions elliptical-oblong, very obtuse, wavy, of a buff yellow tinged with violet, turned back underneath. *Leaves*, curving, glaucous. Native of South Europe.——Mixed borders or beds, margins of shrubberies, or naturalization, in any rich soil. Division.

Iris sibirica (*Siberian I.*)—A tall kind with slender leaves; 1¼ to nearly 3 ft. high. *Flowers*, in summer; external divisions 2 in. long, spathulate-obovate; limb rather wavy, variegated with white and blue, veined with violet; claw of a brownish yellow streaked with violet, having a wide white band in the middle; internal divisions lanceolate-oblong, nearly blunt, entire, violet-blue, with a whitish claw veined with violet; limb of the stigma streaked

IRIS. 153

with lilac and violet, 2 to 6 on each stem, having a faint scent of Hyacinths. *Leaves,* straight, erect, 6 to 13 in. long; stem hollow. Vars. *I. s. longifolia,* with long leaves; *I. s. flexuosa,* with white flowers; *I. s. ochroleuca,* with yellowish flowers; *I. s. hæmatophylla* (or *sanguinea*), with purplish-violet leaves. Siberia, Austria, and Switzerland.——Naturalization, or borders, in any soil. It thrives vigorously in the worst clay soils, where most of the other kinds grow badly or perish. Division at any season.

Iris spuria (*Spurious I.*)—An elegant kind, 1½ to 2 ft. high. *Flowers,* in summer; large; external divisions with a roundish bright blue limb, veined at the base with violet, and a whitish claw veined with violet, and having a broad yellow band in the middle; internal divisions of a deep blue, inclining to violet, wavy, rather concave. *Leaves,* sword-shaped, very pointed, glaucous; lower stem-leaves much shorter than the stem, upper ones inflated. *Rhizome* tolerably thick, covered with rusty - brown scales. South Europe.——Borders, or beds, in good rich loam. Division.

Iris squalens (*Squalid I.*) — Very closely allied to *I. sambucina,* of which it may be a variety; 1½ to 2½ ft. high. *Flowers,* in summer; external divisions spathulate - obovate, very obtuse, erose above, of a violet blue, with a bright yellow beard; internal divisions pale blue, tinged with yellow, elliptical, very obtuse, rather wavy, indented; limb of the stigma streaked with yellow and dull violet. *Leaves,* similar to those of *I. sambucina.* South Europe. —— Similar positions, etc., to those for the Elder-scented I.

Iris subbiflora.—A sturdy, rather dwarf, and stout species, 10 to 15 in. high. *Flowers,* in summer; large, violet, with a yellow beard;

external divisions 2½ in. long, spathulate - oboval, slightly undulating at the margin; internal divisions elliptical-oboval, roundish above, indented, and as if gnawed on the wavy margin, a little longer and broader than the external divisions; limb of the stigma spathulate-oblong, 2 in. long, violet. *Leaves,* straight, those of the stem short, and resembling sheaths. Native of Portugal. —— Mixed borders, or beds of herbaceous plants, or the rougher parts of the rock-garden, also for naturalization, though not amidst vigorous vegetation, in sandy loam. Division.

Iris susiana (*Mourning I.*)—One of the most singular of all the flowers of temperate and northern climes; 1½ to 2½ ft. high. *Flowers,* in early summer; very large, densely spotted and striped with dark purple on a grey ground; external divisions oval, wavy, with a violet beard; internal divisions wedge-shaped-obovate; limb of the stigma violet. *Leaves,* narrow, lanceolate-acute, glaucous. Native of Asia Minor and Persia.——In sunny nooks in the rock-garden, or on sheltered banks or borders, always in light, warm, and thoroughly drained soil. In mild and warm parts of the south and west it may be easier to cultivate than about London; in any case it is one of the most interesting plants grown in the open garden, and deserves our best attention. In cold districts or on heavy soil the protection of a handlight would be desirable in winter. Increased by division.

Iris Swertii (*Swert's I.*)—1 to 2 ft. high. *Flowers,* in summer; very fragrant, milk-white, veined with violet on the edges, with a beard yellow at the base and bluish at the ends; external divisions spathulate - obovate, indented, obtuse; internal divisions obovate, indented, truncate at the ends, wavy, glabrous. *Leaves,* usually straight, glaucous; spathes whitish, tinged with violet. Native of South Europe.——Borders, in ordinary rich soil. Division.

Iris tuberosa (*Snake's Head*).—An interesting but dull-coloured kind, 12 or 13 in. high. *Flowers*, in spring; small; external divisions brownish-green, streaked with yellow, with a purplish-brown tinge on the upper part, round and entire; internal divisions yellowish, very small, covered with hairs. *Leaves*, 4-angled, pointed, longer than the stem, of a pale green; tubers usually two, white, sending out runners. South Europe.——Not worthy of a place in the garden, but where admired it may be naturalized in light soil. Division.

Iris variegata (*Variegated I.*)— A handsome richly-toned kind, 1 to 2 ft. high. *Flowers*, in summer; slightly fragrant; external divisions spathulate - oblong, roundish, and rather indented and wavy above, yellow, streaked with brown or violet, with a dense bright yellow beard; internal divisions elliptical - oblong, very obtuse, wavy, of a bright yellow finely veined with violet, folded back underneath; limb of the stigma bright yellow, not veined. *Leaves*, straight, turned inwards at the point, glaucescent. *I. De Bergii*, supposed to be a variety of this, is a richly-coloured and very ornamental kind. Austria and Hungary.——Borders or beds, in ordinary garden soil. Division.

Iris Xiphioides (*English I.*)—*I. Anglica*.—A handsome popular plant, long grown in our gardens, 1 ft. to over 2 ft. high. *Flowers*, in June and July; 2 to 3 on each stem, large, sky-blue, veined with a darker shade of same colour, with a broad yellow spot or band in the middle of the external divisions, which are deflected at the base, and abruptly narrowed there into a broad concave claw, and have a roundish, indented, emarginate limb; internal divisions rather shorter, wedge-shaped-oboval, wavy. *Leaves*, long, linear, channelled, glaucous. *Bulb*, of an elongated egg-shape, with brownish coats. Many varieties exist, differing chiefly in shades of colour, from which however the yellow hue is absent in a remarkable degree. Spain and the Pyrenees.——Borders and groups of the finer perennials, thriving best in deep sandy soil. Separation of the bulbs.

Iris Xiphium (*Spanish I.*) — Another handsome bulbous Iris, 1½ to 2½ ft. high. *Flowers*, in May and June; fragrant; external divisions 2 in. long, pale blue veined with violet, with a roundish limb shorter than the claw; internal divisions usually of a violet-blue, not veined, lanceolate-oblong, acute, wavy, a little longer than the external divisions. *Leaves*, longer than the stem, linear-lanceolate, narrow, awl-shaped at the end, rather flaccid. *Bulb*, egg-shaped, yellow or brown, narrowed and often compressed at the base. Spain and Portugal.——The same treatment and positions as for the preceding kind. There are numerous varieties.

Isopyrum thalictroides (*Meadow-rue I.*) — A graceful plant, with leaves resembling those of a *Thalictrum*, the stems attaining a height of from 10 to 14 inches. *Flowers*, in early summer; white, with a faint green tinge, stalked; sepals blunt; petals 5, sometimes 6, obtuse. *Leaves*, ternate, stalks widening at the base into membranous ears; leaflets 3-lobed or cut, stalked. Pyrenees and Mountainous parts of Greece, Italy, and Carniola.——Borders, in any soil, and as a graceful fern-like edging plant, the flower-stems in this case to be pinched off as they appear. Division.

Jasione humilis (*Small Jasione*).—A modest and pretty-looking minute alpine herb, 1 to 3 in. high. *Flowers*, in summer; blue, in heads ⅝ to ¾ in. across; calyx hairy, with linear, hairlike segments. *Leaves*, linear-obovate, bluntish, flat, entire; radical ones set closely together in rosettes; stem-leaves scattered; bracts ovate-acute, entire or dentate; whole plant downy. Elevated pastures of the Pyrenees.——The rock-garden, in moist, gritty, or sandy loam. Division.

Jasione perennis (*Perennial J.*)—A pleasing-looking perennial, 6 to 12 in. high. *Flowers*, in early summer; blue, in terminal, large, roundish heads, ½ to ¾ in. across, on naked stalks. *Leaves*, narrow, rather hairy; those of root obovate; stem-leaves oblong-linear, flat; stems smooth or hairy, erect, simple, or branched from the base, clothed with leaves to about half their height. Pyrenees and Dauphiny.——Borders, in sandy soil. Division or seed.

Jeffersonia diphylla (*Twinleaf*).—A very interesting dwarf plant, allied to the Blood-root and the Duck's-foot; 3 to 10 in. high. *Flowers*, in early spring; white, about 1 in. across, with 8 yellow stamens in the centre; petals 8, stalks 1-flowered; the seed-vessel after the petals have fallen, resembling that of the Poppy. *Leaves*, distinctly divided into 2 lobes. Moist places in Tennessee and Virginia.——Margins of beds of shrubs in peat soil, or in peaty places in the rock-garden, or the drier portions of the artificial bog. Division and seed, which should be sown as soon as ripe.

Kitaibelia vitifolia (*Vine-leaved K.*)—A vigorous, robust, Mallow-like herb, with dark-green leaves; 6 to 8 ft. high. *Flowers*, late in summer; small, white, with yellow stamens, axillary; calyx 5-parted; involucels 7- or 9-parted. *Leaves*, 5-lobed, acute, toothed, shaped like those of the Vine. Hungary.—— Naturalization in rough places in any soil. Propagated by division.

Lachenalia serotina (*Late-flowering L.*)—*Uropetalum serotinum*.—A somewhat singular-looking bulbous plant, 1 to 1½ ft. high. *Flowers*, in summer; external divisions of a dirty-brown, marked with a purplish streak; internal divisions of the same colour tinged with red, and whitish on the inside, arranged in spike-like, many-flowered racemes, nearly secund. *Leaves*, linear, pointed, channelled, erect, nearly the length of the flower-stem. Native of Spain, Portugal, Teneriffe, and North Africa.—— Mixed borders, or lower parts of rockwork, in sandy loam; in severe frosts it will require to be covered; scarcely ornamental enough for the choice collection. Division.

Lactuca sonchifolia (*Blue Dandelion*).—An interesting and uncommon perennial, with smooth, erect stem, 1 ft. to 20 in. high. *Flowers*, late in summer; sky-blue, larger than those of *L. perennis*, in racemose panicles, with bracts on the flower-stalks. *Leaves*, runcinate - pinnatifid, with lance - shaped, somewhat recurved, finely-toothed lobes. South of Russia, and about Constantinople.—— Borders, in sandy soil. Seed or division.

Lamium garganicum (*Gargano Dead Nettle*).—A pretty Dead Nettle, 1 ft. to 16 in. high. *Flowers*, in summer; purplish, in dense, imperfect whorls of 10 to 20 blossoms each; corolla four times the length of the calyx; tube straight, smooth inside, velvety without; throat very wide; upper lip broadly notched; side lobes angular, or forming two very short teeth; anthers very hairy; calyx villous, with awl-shaped pointed teeth; bracts very short. *Leaves*, heart - shaped, wrinkled, covered on both sides with soft down; stems ascending, clothed with dense, long, white hairs. Found on Mount Gargano, in the southeast of Italy.——Naturalization, or borders, in any soil. Division.

Lamium maculatum (*Spotted L.*)—A native plant, common in gardens, with leaves veined or blotched with white; about 1 ft. high. *Flowers*, in spring and early summer; purplish-red, about 10 in a whorl; tube of corolla recurved; upper lip oblong. *Leaves*, heart-shaped, acute, doubly toothed, or slightly cut, hairy and blotched. *L. maculatum album* is a variety with showy white flowers. Europe, North Africa, and Middle Asia.——The white variety is a neat and pretty plant for borders, and naturalization on banks, thriving in any soil. Division.

Lamium Orvala (*Red Dead Nettle*).—A large and distinct Dead Nettle, with erect stems, 1 to 3 ft. high. *Flowers*, in early summer; deep red, in axillary whorls from 6 to 14 flowers in each; corolla about 1½ in. long; tube straight, with a ring of hairs inside. *Leaves*, large, broadly-ovate, unequally serrated, stalked, smooth and shining above, often red beneath. France and Italy.——Borders, in ordinary soil, and only in large or botanical collections. Division.

Lathyrus californicus (*Californian Everlasting Pea*).—A handsome climbing perennial, from 2 to 4 ft. high. *Flowers*, in summer; with a lilac-purple standard, and white keel and wings, in many-flowered clusters, as long as the leaves. *Leaves*, of from 6 to 10, oval-oblong, mucronate, glaucous leaflets; stipules half-arrow-shaped. California.——Borders, and the rougher parts of the rock-garden, in sandy loam. Division and seed.

Lathyrus grandiflorus (*Large-flowered L.*)—A very handsome, hairy, climbing herb, with blooms larger than those of the common Everlasting Pea; 4 ft. high. *Flowers*, in summer; very large, rose-coloured; stalks axillary, 2- or 3-flowered, longer than the leaves. *Leaves*, with 1 pair of large ovate, blunt leaflets; stems 4-angled, winged. Southern Europe.——Banks and hedges, in which it will run freely through low bushes, etc.; also in borders on low trellises, on rootwork, or large rockwork; allowed to fall over precipices in isolated tufts, or planted beneath low specimen trees and shrubs, and allowed to run through their foliage. It prefers a deep sandy loam, or warm soil. Division.

Lathyrus latifolius (*Everlasting Pea*). —A beautiful climbing plant, common in gardens; 6 ft. high. *Flowers*, nearly all the summer; bright-rose; stalks many-flowered, axillary, longer than the leaves. *Leaves*, with 1 pair of elliptic, slightly glaucous, 3- to 5-nerved, mucronate leaflets; stipules broadly-ovate; stems winged. There is a fine white variety. Europe, in woods, and naturalized in some parts of Britain.——Suitable for the same purposes as *L. grandiflorus*. The white variety is very fine. Not seeding so freely as the common forms, it blooms longer, and nothing can look finer than strong isolated specimens of it allowed to grow untrained and unsupported on banks. Division and seed.

Lathyrus palustris (*Marsh Vetchling*).—A seldom seen but very graceful native plant, 2 to 3 ft. high. *Flowers*, in June and July; bluish-purple, in clusters of 3 to 5 flowers on each peduncle. *Leaves*, composed of two or three pairs of linear-lanceolate, acute leaflets; stipules small, lanceolate, half-arrow-shaped, and sharp-pointed at both ends; stem winged; pods linear-oblong compressed. Britain and other parts of Europe in boggy meadows, rare.——Allowed to trail among American and other shrubs, in moist soil. Seed and division.

Lathyrus rotundifolius (*Round-leaved Vetchling*).—A small but handsome Everlasting Pea, 1½ ft. high. *Flowers*, from June to August; bright rosy-purple, arranged in long clusters rising above the leaves. *Leaves*, composed of a single pair of greyish-green oval-roundish leaflets with from 3 to 5 nerves; stipules half-arrow-shaped, sometimes toothed. *Stem*, narrowly-winged, branching. The Caucasus and South Russia.——Borders, at the foot of walls or houses, or naturalized, where its somewhat delicate but very free-blooming shoots may trail over low shrubs, etc. It thrives best in sandy loam, but is not fastidious as to soil. Division and seed.

Lathyrus tuberosus (*Tuberous L.*)—A pretty small Everlasting Pea, 2 ft. high. *Flowers*, in early summer; rose-coloured; stalks 3- to 6-flowered, 2 or 3 times the length of the leaves. *Leaves*, with one pair of oblong-elliptic, slightly pointed leaflets; stipules nearly arrow-shaped, narrow; stems 4-angled; roots creeping, throwing out irregular brown tubers. Europe and Britain.——Borders, rough rockwork, and copses, or fringes of shrubberies, in ordinary soil. Division and seed.

Lavatera unguiculata (*Samian L.*)—A vigorous-growing perennial with a dark-green, woody, branching stem, about 4 ft. high. *Flowers*, in autumn; light rosy-lilac, about 3 in. across, showy, nearly sessile, solitary, axillary. *Leaves*, slightly downy, large, the upper ones with 3-pointed lobes; the lower ones 5-lobed. Island of Samos.——Borders, or naturalization, in light or calcareous soil. Seed and cuttings.

Leiophyllum buxifolium (*Sand Myrtle*). — *Ledum thymifolium*. — A pretty dwarf evergreen shrub, forming compact bushes 4 to 6 in. or more high. *Flowers*, in May or June; pinkish-white, when open; the un-opened buds a delicate pink; freely produced in terminal corymbs. *Leaves*, small, oval, smooth, shining. Sandy pine-barrens in New Jersey, and the Mountains of Carolina.——Among dwarf shrubs in peat beds, and occasionally in the rock-garden in similar soil, and as an edging. Layers.

Leontopodium alpinum (*Lion's-foot*). —A very hoary alpine herb, with simple stems, 4 to 8 in. high. *Flowers*, in summer; pale yellow; inconspicuous, in a crowded head; surrounded by an elegant star-like whorl of oblong, spreading, densely woolly leaves. *Leaves*, oblong, very woolly. High sloping pastures on many of the great Continental mountain ranges.——Rockwork on exposed spots, in moist sandy soil. Careful division.

Leptinella scariosa (*Creeping L.*)—A very dwarf composite plant, 1 or 2 in. high. *Flowers*, in summer; small, yellow; peduncle scape-like, shaggy. *Leaves*, rather smooth, linear at the base, lyrate-pinnatifid in the upper part. *Stem*, prostrate, rooting, leafy, shaggy. Native country unknown.——Suited for creeping about on rockwork, in any soil. Division.

Leucanthemum arcticum (*Arctic L.*) —*Chrysanthemum arcticum.*—A dwarf smooth alpine herb, 6 to 12 in. high. *Flowers*, in summer; white, sometimes reddish, with yellow centre, 1 to 2 in. across. *Leaves*, lower ones wedge-shaped, toothed at the apex; upper ones mostly strap-shaped and entire. Northern Europe and America.——Rockwork, or borders, in ordinary soil. Division.

Leucojum æstivum (*Summer Snowflake*).—A handsome and graceful plant, somewhat like a tall and vigorous Snowdrop; 1 to 1½ ft. high. *Flowers*, in spring and early summer; later than *L. vernum* or *L. Hernandezii*; pure white, the tip of each petal being marked with green both inside and out, drooping, in a cluster of four to eight blooms, each about an inch long. *Leaves*, daffodil-like, shorter than the flower-stem, appearing in winter before the flowers. A native of Central and South Europe, but naturalized in Britain.——This plant, found on the banks of the Thames about Woolwich and Greenwich, and in a few other places, is deserving of a place in every garden, either as a border plant or naturalized with the more vigorous kinds of daffodils in grassy places. It grows freely in almost any soil, and is easily increased by separation of the bulbs.

Leucojum Hernandezii (*Small Summer Snowflake*).—This is the kind commonly grown in gardens as *S. pulchellum*. It grows from 1 to 1½ ft. high, and blooms in summer, three weeks or a month earlier than *L. æstivum*. *Flowers*, white, with oblong-obtuse divisions, having the tips marked with a green spot, and about half an inch long, or half the size of those of *L. æstivum*, 1 to 3 on each stem. *Leaves*, linear, about ¼ in. broad, flat, blunt at the end, nearly as long as the flower-stem. Native of mountains near Lluch, in Majorca; found also in Minorca.——This plant, which has been supposed by some to be a form of *L. æstivum*, differs from it in having leaves one-third narrower, flowers only half the size, spathe with only from 1 to 3 flowers, germen oblong, and in flowering three or four weeks earlier. Not being so handsome as the Summer Snowflake, nor very distinct from it in appearance, it is not worthy of a place except as a naturalized plant in rough places.

Leucojum vernum (*Spring Snowflake*).—A very handsome spring flower, resembling the Snowdrop in stature, and somewhat in grace, but larger in all its parts; from 4 to 6 in. high. *Flowers*, in spring; white with a green spot on the tips of the petals, solitary, drooping, and fragrant. *Leaves*, few, linear, ribbon-like. Native of Central Europe; lately discovered to be a native of Britain also, "on the Greenstone heights in the neighbourhood of Britford."——Grows freely in any good sandy loam, but till more plentiful should be treated well, *i.e.*, planted in deep and very sandy loam, in a sheltered sunny position. It deserves to be made almost as plentiful as the Common Snowdrop, being admirably suited for the rock-garden, borders, and naturalization on grassy banks in the pleasure-ground, or in semi-wild spots in sandy loam. Separation of the bulbs; where scarce, its seed should be saved and sown.

Liatris elegans (*Button Snake-root*). — A showy herb, 2 to 4 ft. high. *Flowers*, late in summer; purplish, in spikes a foot or more long. *Leaves*, spotted, smooth; root-leaves spoon-shaped, 3- to 5-nerved; upper stem-leaves strap-shaped, short, often having a short spine at the points. North America.——Borders, or margins of shrubberies, in sandy loam. Division or seed.

Liatris pycnostachya (*Dense - spiked L.*)—A stout species with very leafy stems, and thick and dense spikes, 3 to 5 ft. high. *Flowers*, late in summer; pale purple, in a dense cylindrical spike, about 2 ft. long, somewhat leafy below. *Leaves*, rigid, stalkless, partly clasping at the base; lower ones narrow, lance-shaped, blunt, 5- to 7-nerved; upper ones usually short and much crowded, narrowly-strap-shaped, pointed. North America. ——Borders, or grouped with the bolder perennials, in ordinary soil. Division.

Liatris spicata (*Spiked Button Snake-root*).—A handsome perennial, 3 to 4 ft. high. *Flowers*, in summer; pale purple, almost stalkless, in spikes, 6 to 15 in. long; involucre somewhat resinous, the scales oblong or oval adpressed. *Leaves*, strap-shaped, acute, fringed at the base, the nerves frequently hairy. North America.—— Borders, or margins of shrubberies, in moist, deep loam. Division.

Liatris squarrosa (*Scaly Button Snake-root*).—A showy herb, 2 to 3 ft. high. *Flowers*, late in summer; bright purple, in rough heads, with short stalks, on downy stems, having many alternate leaves; the scales of the involucre with elongated and leaf-like spreading tips. *Leaves* of root, long, ½ in. wide, 3- to 5-nerved; those of stem strap-shaped, rigid. *Root*, tuberous. North America.——Borders and margins of shrubberies, in ordinary soil. Division.

Libertia ixioides (*Tall L.*)—A tall perennial, with somewhat the aspect of a narrow-leaved Iris, but of a very dark-green hue; 3 to 4 ft. high. *Flowers*, in summer; white, with pale-yellow stamens, numerous, arranged in closely-packed heads one above another. *Leaves*, sword-shaped, about ½ in. broad, 18 to 24 in. long, in close tufts. Native of Chili. —— Grows freely in peaty soil or sandy loam, but is not on the whole, a pretty, effective, or first-class plant, and should therefore be confined to unimportant positions. Careful division.

Libertia magellanica (*Dwarf L.*)— An attractive species, 15 to 18 in. high. *Flowers*, in summer; pure white, arranged in heads much closer together than those of *L. ixioides*. *Leaves*, 12 to 15 in. long, narrow, sword-shaped. Native of the southern part of South America.——Very suitable for cutting for bouquets of white flowers, and pretty in borders, or in rockwork, in peaty or fine sandy soil, and in warm positions. Division.

Lilium auratum (*Gold-striped Lily*). —One of the noblest of its race, with enormous flowers on very slender stems, from 3 to 7 ft. high. *Flowers*, late in summer; 4 in. or more in length, 7 to 10 in. across; white, with a golden stripe running longitudinally through each petal on the inside, which is also more or less densely marked with oval purplish spots; 1 to 100 blooms on each stem, according to age of plant, exhaling a powerful and peculiar odour. *Leaves*, narrow, lanceolate, on short stalks. Various forms, differing much in colour, are now in our nurseries. Native of Japan or the Corea.——Borders, or in tufts among shrubs, in peat or light, sandy, well-drained soil. Increased by separation of the small bulbs, and also by stem-scales and bulbils. This Lily is perfectly hardy.

Lilium Brownii (*Brown's Lily*).—A noble Lily resembling *L. longifolium*, but attaining a height of 3 or 4 ft. *Flowers*, in summer; bell-shaped, very large, somewhat long and drooping, 1 to 4 on a stem; pure white on the inside, dashed or streaked on the outside with lines of a dark violet or purple; with reddish-brown anthers. *Leaves*, of stem reflected, the upper ones wider, and lance-shaped, on stems rigid, erect, and spotted with purple, especially towards the base. *Bulb*, rather large, top-shaped, with numerous scales, which are acute, loosely-overlapping; the external ones as high as the internal, all of a rosy hue on the inside. Probably from the Corea or Japan, but native country uncertain. —— Among low shrubs, where it will be sheltered, in deep sandy well-drained peat, or in a collection of choice lilies, on a warm sheltered border. The bulbs should be planted not less than 7 in. deep. Propagated by separation of the small bulbs given off by the matured ones.

Lilium bulbiferum (*Bulb-bearing Lily*). — A sturdy, richly-coloured species, 2½ to 4 ft. high. *Flowers*, early in summer; large, deep saffron-yellow or bright orange-red, with one large spot of a paler colour and numerous brown dots; arranged in an umbellated panicle, 2 to 10 on each stem. *Leaves*, alternate, linear-lanceolate, almost quite smooth, bearing in their axils the bulbils whence the plant derives its specific name. *Bulb*, large, pear-shaped, with very fleshy compressed scales, white on the outside, rosy within. Central and Southern Europe.——Isolated plants and small groups in beds of dwarf evergreens, in mixed borders, and grouped with other kinds, in deep sandy loam. Increased by the bulbils and by separation of the bulbs.

Lilium canadense (*Canadian Lily*).—A prettily-spotted medium-sized kind, with whorled foliage; 2 to 4 ft. high. *Flowers*, in summer; of an orange-yellow at the top, yellow spotted with purple in the middle, with lanceolate divisions curving backwards a little; 1 to 10 on each stem. *Leaves*, numerous, in distant whorls, ovate-lanceolate, smooth above, slightly villous underneath. *Bulb* resembling that of *L. Martagon*, but smaller and whiter. Native of N. America.——Suitable for beds of lilies and mixed borders, in very sandy soil. Separation of the bulbs.

Lilium candidum (*White Lily*).—The well-known White Lily of our cottage gardens, 3 to 5 ft. high. *Flowers*, in summer; pure white with yellow anthers, of an elegant bell-shape, smooth on the inside, standing nearly erect or horizontal, emitting an agreeable but powerful odour; 4 to 20 on a stem. *Leaves*, gradually diminishing in size from the base upwards; those of the base wedge-shaped, the upper ones linear-lance-shaped. *Bulb*, large, pear-shaped, with loose scales of a greenish-white on the outside, and a light flesh-colour within; in autumn the external scales develop themselves into small leaves. A very fine variety, *L. candidum striatum*, has the flowers handsomely spotted and striped with purplish-red. A double white variety is often sold, but it has none of the beauty, grace, or purity of colour of the ordinary single form, and is not worthy of cultivation. There is also a variety with variegated leaves. Syria and Persia.——Borders, margins of shrubberies, or naturalization, in ordinary soil, the deeper and lighter the better. Increased by separation of the bulbs.

Lilium carniolicum (*Lily of Carniola*).—At present an uncommon kind, 1 to 2 ft. high. *Flowers*, in summer; scarlet-red or orange-yellow, with greenish base, marked on the lower part with a great number of prominent tawny-purple lines, the divisions being turned back as in the Turban Lily, pendulous, 1 to 6 on each stem. *Leaves*, almost patent, at regular distances from each other, lanceolate-acute, rough and downy on the edges, diminishing in size as they approach the top of the stem. Carniola.——Among the dwarf and medium-sized kinds, in light soil. Separation of the bulbs.

Lilium carolinianum (*Carolina Lily*).—Allied to *L. superbum*; 2 to 3 ft. and upwards high. *Flowers*, in summer; of an orange-yellow spotted with deep purple in the throat, generally in threes, on thick flower-stalks bent downwards. *Leaves*, for the most part in whorls, wedge-shaped-lanceolate, or oboval. Divisions of the perianth lanceolate, very acute and very much reflected. Native of North America.——In beds or groups, in moist deep peat. Separation of the bulbs.

Lilium Catesbæi (*Southern Red Lily*).—A very distinct kind; 16 in. to 2 ft. high. *Flowers*, in summer; open bell-shaped, erect, usually solitary, sometimes 2, 3, or 4, growing from the same point on the top of the stem, scarlet, spotted with dark purple, greenish-yellow outside, and yellow within, long-clawed, wavy on the margins, and recurved at the summit. *Leaves*, linear-lanceolate, scattered. North America.——Borders and beds, in deep peaty, or very sandy soil. Associated with the dwarfer Lilies. Separation of the bulbs.

Lilium chalcedonicum (*Scarlet Martagon*). — The well - known Scarlet Martagon, 2½ to 4 ft. high. *Flowers*, in summer; the colour of a thoroughly ripened Tomato, the inside rough with small blackish protuberances, pendulous, with revolute petals; seldom more than 6 on each stem. *Leaves*, smooth, twisted, linear-lanceolate, blunt at the point, rough at the edges, suddenly diminishing in size about the middle of the stem, and becoming very narrow towards the top. *Bulb*, large, round, with pointed, closely - overlapping scales, yellowish on the outside. Asia Minor.——In beds of lilies grouped with the taller kinds, borders, and small groups on margins of shrubberies, in ordinary garden soil. Increased by separation of the bulbs.

Lilium croceum (*Orange Lily*).—A well-known plant, with numerous gay flowers on a stiff, furrowed stem, from 1½ to 3¼ ft. high. *Flowers*, in summer; of a deep saffron or orange, with numerous very small black spots, arranged in a kind of panicle, 3 to 15 on each stem, over a whorl of 3 to 5 leaves larger than the rest. *Leaves*, scattered, numerous, of a bright green, spreading or arched, rarely upright, linear-lanceolate. *Bulb*, large, round, broader than deep. There are, under the name of *Lilium umbellatum*, some varieties of this plant, varying chiefly in tone from a more or less orange or ochre-yellow to a deep vermilion-red, and with brown punctuations on the divisions of the flowers. Italy. —— Borders, beds, margins of shrubberies, or naturalization in copses, etc., in common soil, though the more highly manured it is the finer will be the blooms and the larger the bulbs. Increased by separation of the bulbs; when growing in gardens, it should be raised every three years, as the flowers from the crowded bulbs are small.

Lilium eximium (*Transparent Trumpet Lily*).—Closely allied to *L. longiflorum*, probably a variety of it; 10 to 18 in. high. *Flowers*, in summer; resembling those of *L. longiflorum*, but with wider, thicker, and less reflected divisions of a transparent white colour. The midrib is also white throughout; in *L. longiflorum* it is greenish at the base of the divisions inside the flower. Native of Japan.——For culture, etc., see *Lilium longiflorum*.

Lilium giganteum (*Giant Lily*).—A huge Lily, quite different in aspect from any other in cultivation; 7½ to 9½ ft. high. *Flowers*, in summer; greenish-white outside, tinged with violet on the inside, large, 6 to 7 in. long, funnel-shaped, with divisions slightly reflected, fragrant, pendulous, 8 to 15 (sometimes 20) on each tall and stout stem. *Leaves*, very broad, those of the root and lower part of stem stalked, oval-acute, with a heart-shaped base; the upper stem-leaves nearly stalkless, with a rounded base, and diminishing in size. *Bulb*, very large, conical, with scales which are very broad at the base and narrow at the top, very fleshy, not compressed, of a greenish-white colour. Native of Nepaul. —— Occasionally grown in greenhouses, but hardy, though only flowering under favourable conditions in the open air. I have seen it flowering vigorously on deep and fine sandy soil in mild districts. A well-drained position, good, deep, and very

M

sandy soil, are indispensable. The best position for it is isolated a few feet within the margin of a shrubbery, with a warm exposure. Also suitable for association with hardy subtropical plants and the like. Separation of bulbs.

Lilium japonicum (*Japan Lily*).—Allied to *L. longiflorum*—About 2 ft. high. *Flowers*, in summer; whitish inside, purplish outside, very large, funnel-shaped, about 8 in. long, standing horizontally, terminal, solitary. *Leaves*, alternate, few, and distant from each other; very long, lanceolate, pointed, smooth. Native of Japan, China, Nepaul.——Similar positions etc. to those for *L. longiflorum*.

Lilium kamtchatcense (*Black Lily*).—*Fritillaria kamtchatcensis*.—A very singular species, though not brilliant or ornamental like the other kinds; 8 to 16 in. high. *Flowers*, in summer; solitary, bell-shaped, with oval-lanceolate divisions of a deep dull purplish-red, paler towards the base, which is marked with small purplish dots. Sepals furnished with a nectary at the base. *Leaves*, lanceolate, the lower ones whorled, the upper opposite or solitary. *Bulb*, used as food by the poor inhabitants of Kamtchatka, by whom it is called *serenna*, or *sarana*. This plant varies much in the number of its leaves and flowers. Native of Kamtchatka. —— Chiefly interesting for botanical or curious collections. It should be planted in sandy and deep moist loam. Separation of the bulbs.

Lilium longiflorum (*Trumpet Lily*).—Combines dwarfness of habit, purity and size of flower, and sweetest odour, more than any other known lily; 10 to 20 in. high. *Flowers*, in summer; funnel-shaped, 4 to 6 in. long, with the extremities of the divisions turned back, pure white, with greenish stamens terminated by handsome yellow anthers, and a greenish stigma; exceedingly fragrant; 2 to 5 on each stem, set almost horizontally. *Leaves*, scattered, lanceolate-acute, narrowed towards the foot-stalk, spreading or bent downwards, of a bright green. *Bulb*, of medium size, top-shaped, with fleshy yellowish-white scales. Japan. ——In small clumps on the margins of beds and masses of shrubs, as an edging to beds of lilies in borders, or in beds or groups of fragrant flowering plants, and among the larger and more vigorous subjects on the lower flanks and outskirts of the rock-garden; in all cases in deep, thoroughly drained fine sandy earth; the bulbs to be planted rather deeply. Increased by separating the young bulbs from the matured one.

Lilium Martagon (*Martagon Lily*).—A kind frequently seen, not brilliantly coloured like most cultivated lilies, but graceful and attractive in some of its forms; 1 to 3½ ft. in height. *Flowers*, in summer ; dull rosy-violet, deeply marked on the inside, and particularly towards the base, with carmine dots, with 6 oblong-lanceolate thick divisions, villous on the outside, arching backwards, exhaling a disagreeable odour, drooping, 3 to 20 on each stem. *Leaves*, in whorls or alternate, lanceolate-elliptical, acute. *Bulb*, of medium size, nearly pear-shaped, with yellowish scales, not fleshy, lanceolate-acute. There are numerous varieties with white, yellow, red, and double flowers. Native of Central and Southern Europe and Siberia. —— Naturalization in the wilder parts of the pleasure-grounds, in copses, etc., in any soil.

Lilium monadelphum. — An ornamental species very rarely seen in our gardens; 3 to 5½ ft. high. *Flowers*, in summer; citron-yellow marked with red dots, in size and form resembling those of *L. album*, pendulous, 2 to 6 on each stem. The stamens are united at the base, whence the specific name

LILIUM. 163

of the plant. *Leaves*, lanceolate, pubescent underneath, veined, the lower one wider. *Bulb*, pear-shaped or oval-oblong, large, covered with very numerous loose, whitish-yellow, or flesh-coloured scales. The Caucasus.——On warm borders, in beds of lilies, and in open spots on the sunny fringes of the choice shrubbery, in deep, well-drained, very sandy soil. Well grown in the Botanic Garden at Edinburgh. Separation of the bulbs.

Lilium Pomponium (*Turban Lily*).—Somewhat like the Martagon Lily in shape; 1 to 2 ft. high. *Flowers*, early in summer; red, orange, or vermilion, dotted with black inside, and covered with protuberances for nearly half their length, with long lanceolate-acute divisions rolled back like a turban; 4 to 6 on each stem. *Leaves*, scattered, numerous, three-veined, the lower ones linear-lanceolate, acute; the upper linear, standing close together, almost in whorls, all much fringed, ciliated on the margin and on the midrib underneath. *Bulb*, the size of a large walnut, with scales of a yellowish white. There is a variety with yellow flowers, called the Yellow-flowered Martagon Lily, or Yellow Duke. Siberia.——Borders, among the dwarfer kinds in beds, and in beds of American plants, in deep sandy peat. Separation of the bulbs.

Lilium speciosum (*Spotted Lily*).—*L. lancifolium.* — A beautifully-marked Lily, often grown in pots, but perfectly hardy; 2 to 4 ft. high, sometimes more. *Flowers*, late in summer and autumn; large, 4 to 5 in. in diameter, rosy-white, spotted with carmine-red or purple, and covered on the internal surface with irregular protuberances which are frequently of a deeper purplish-red, pendulous or inclining, very fragrant, 1 to 10 on each stem. *Leaves*, scattered or alternate, rather wide, narrowing to a point, and rounded at the base. *Bulb*, almost round, sometimes rather depressed, at others somewhat elongated, with very fleshy scales, of a blood-red hue. There are many varieties, chiefly differing in colour, some of them not uncommon in our greenhouses. Native of the Corea and Japan.——In the open air this may be associated with the finest autumn-flowering herbaceous plants; also planted in very small groups in isolated beds, near the margin of masses of shrubs, and towards the outer edge of beds of mixed kinds of lilies, always in well-drained sandy soil, and in as sheltered a position as is convenient. Separation of bulbs.

Lilium superbum (*Great American Lily*).—A very tall kind, 5 to 9 ft. high, with slender stems and leaves, and a profusion of flowers. *Flowers*, late in summer; in a pyramidal raceme, very numerous, according to the strength of the plant, with divisions curving backwards, of a light mahogany-red or cochineal on the outside, yellow, spotted with violet-purple on the inside, in a pyramidal cluster of from 10 to 40 on each stem. *Leaves*, linear-lanceolate, the lower ones in whorls, the others alternate. *Bulb*, white, rather large, with whitish scales. North America.——In groups here and there between tall American shrubs, always in deep sandy peat. I have never seen this plant so finely developed as in Mr. Antony Waterer's nursery at Woking, under and at the very base of Magnolia trees. It is seen to greatest perfection when growing among shrubs from 6 to 10 ft. high, which will also help to shelter it. Probably a form of this is the plant grown in the Dublin Botanic Garden under the name of *Lilium Michauxii.* Increased by separation of the bulbs.

Lilium tenuifolium (*Tomb Thumb Lily*).—A very dwarf and slender-leaved kind, but with all the glory of

M 2

colour of the Scarlet Martagon; 8 to 16 in. high. *Flowers*, in summer; very deep scarlet-red without spots, pendulous, 1 to 6 on each stem. *Leaves*, scattered, linear, almost grass-like. *Bulb*, pear-shaped, of the size of a walnut, with rather compressed white scales. Native of the Caucasus.—— On the warm flanks of rockwork, on the margins of very select borders, or in the little nursery or warm border devoted to choice bulbs; in all cases in fine sandy loam thoroughly drained. Increased by seed, by separation of the bulbs, and also from the scales.

Lilium testaceum (*Buff Lily*).—*L. excelsum*.—A tall and very stout kind, 4½ to 6⅓ ft. high, at once distinguished by its colour and the vigour of its stems. *Flowers*, in summer; of a nankeen or very bright buff, with small dots of orange-red and a few protuberances, on very long flower-stalks, 1 to 5 on each stem. *Leaves*, shining, of a fine green, slightly undulating, edged with a whitish down; the lower ones in clusters, lanceolate; the upper, or stem-leaves, linear-lanceolate. *Bulb*, large, roundish, with oblong-obovate or oblong-acute scales loosely overlapping each other, the exterior as long as the interior ones, all of a rosy flesh-colour. Native country uncertain, but believed with good reason to be a hybrid between the common White Lily and *L. chalcedonicum*.—— Somewhat within the margins of shrubberies, or on borders, in deep good soil. Propagated by separation of the bulbs.

Lilium tigrinum (*Tiger Lily*).—The well-known Tiger Lily, 3 to 5½ ft. high. *Flowers*, in summer; orange-scarlet, and dotted with dark purple on the inside, the divisions curving backwards and covered with brownish protuberances, villous on the outside; 2 to 18 on each stem. *Leaves*, scattered or alternate, linear-lanceolate, of a dull green, the upper or floral leaves solitary, oval-heart-shaped. *Bulb*, rather large, pear-shaped, with compressed, fleshy-white scales, overlapping each other in a very regular manner. Native of the Corea and Japan.——Fringes of shrubberies, borders, mixed beds of lilies, and groups of the finer summer-flowering plants, in sandy loam.

Lilium tigrinum Fortunei (*Fortune's Tiger Lily*).——A magnificent variety of the preceding, or perhaps a distinct species, has been lately introduced into our gardens under the name of *L. tigrinum Fortunei*. It differs from the common type in growing very much taller, attaining a height of from 6 to 10 ft.; in bearing a superb branched pyramid of flowers (often 40 on one stem), and in being much more hairy. No plant yet introduced presents a more noble appearance when seen growing singly or in small groups amidst shrubs about 6 ft. high. It is sufficiently hardy and vigorous for naturalization in half-wild places, and is so easily propagated from the bulbils, which appear in great numbers on the stems, as well as by separation, that those who have it should soon be able to spare some bulbs of it for trial in this way. A noble subject for the centre of a bed of lilies.

Lilium venustum (*L. Thunbergianum*).—Allied to the Orange and Bulb-bearing lily, but very dwarf; 1¼ to 2 ft. high. *Flowers*, in summer; very numerous, of an orange-red, bell-shaped, very open, with the edges slightly turned outwards, arranged in a pyramidal cluster, 1 to 10 on each stem. *Leaves*, linear-lanceolate, smooth; floral leaves shorter, sub-ovate. *Bulb* small, nearly conical, with compressed scales, rosy on the outside, white or light flesh-colour on the inside. Native of Japan.——Associated with the dwarf kinds on the margins of beds of lilies, in borders, or in the rock-garden, in sandy loam.

Linaria alpina (*Alpine Toadflax*).— A pretty dwarf plant, forming dense tufts of a bluish silvery tone; 6 in. high. *Flowers*, in summer; bluish-violet with a rich golden centre, in form, like those of the Snapdragon, but much smaller, in a close raceme at the top of the stems. *Leaves*, smooth, glaucous, linear-lanceolate, entire, ¼ to ¾ in. long; the lower ones in whorls of 4. Alps and Pyrenees. ——The rock-garden and the margins of borders, in sandy or fine gravelly soil. It may be naturalized in moist districts, in bare, or nearly bare, sandy or gravelly places. Seed or division.

Linaria crassifolia (*Thick-leaved Toadflax*).—A small and pretty, though not very showy species, 3 to 6 in. high. *Flowers*, in summer; fine blue, with a yellow deeply-channelled throat; upper lip erect, with rounded lobes; lower lip roundish-wedge-shaped, with flat, close, emarginate divisions; in loose racemes. *Leaves*, fleshy, ovate, narrowed into the leaf-stalk, without veins; stem branching at the base, glandular-pubescent. Southern Spain, near the town of Chiva.——This plant resembles *L. origanifolia*, and, in the dried specimen, is hardly to be distinguished from it, but the living plants present a marked difference. The rock-garden, walls, ruins, borders, or in pans, in light, sandy soil. Division and seed.

Linaria Cymbalaria (*Ivy L.*)— A very common and elegant trailer, with small, roundish, or kidney-shaped leaves, in outline somewhat resembling those of Ivy. *Flowers*, all summer; pale blue or lilac, small, with short spurs, on recurved stalks. *Leaves*, stalked, shining, broadly 5-lobed; slightly marked with hand-shaped veins; lobes rounded or wedge-shaped. There is a variety with white flowers, and another with variegated leaves, both very pretty, and well worthy of culture. On old walls and stony places, in several parts of Europe, and apparently wild in Britain, but probably only naturalized.——Walls and rough rockwork or rootwork, in any soil, or without soil on dry walls. It usually establishes itself. Seed.

Linaria dalmatica (*Large Yellow L.*)— A vigorous-growing perennial, 3 to 5 ft. high. *Flowers*, in summer; large, handsome, light-yellow, in branching spikes. *Leaves*, sessile, oval, pointed, entire, glaucous; leaves of the branches much smaller, narrower, and more pointed; stem smooth. Dalmatia and Levant. —— Borders, in well-drained, ordinary soil. Seed and division.

Linaria genistæfolia (*Broom-leaved L.*)—A tall, smooth, erect, glaucous herb, with branching stems; 2 to 4 ft. high. *Flowers*, in summer; pale yellow, a little smaller than those of *L. vulgaris*, in loose racemes; mouth of corolla yellow; spur nearly straight, equal in length to the corolla. *Leaves*, somewhat clasping, 1 to 2 in. long, lance-shaped, acute, 3- or 5-nerved. Central Europe and Caucasus.—— Borders, in sandy soil, and naturalized in stony or gravelly places, or on old walls or ruins. Seed.

Linaria origanifolia (*Marjoram-leaved L.*)—A dwarf kind, allied to *L. crassifolia*. *Flowers*, in summer; bluish-violet, with yellow throat; rather small, in the axils of the upper leaves forming a loose raceme. *Leaves*, oblong, on short stalks, lower ones opposite; upper ones alternate. Pyrenees and South of France, on walls and rocks.——The rock-garden, old walls, in pans, or on the margin of the mixed border, in sandy loam. Propagated by seed or division.

Linaria purpurea (*Purple L.*)—An erect, rather tall kind, 1 to 3 ft. high

Flowers, in summer; in long loose racemes, purplish-blue; mouth of corolla bearded with white hairs; tube striped with purple; spur arched, as long as the corolla. *Leaves*, slightly glaucous, 1 to 1½ in. long, linear; lower ones in whorls of from 4 to 9; upper ones 3 in a whorl; stems purplish-green. Southern Europe.—Ruins, walls, or stony places. Seed.

Linaria vulgaris (*Common Toadflax*). — A handsome native herb, with smooth glaucous stems, 1 to 3 ft. high. *Flowers*, in summer and autumn; pale yellow; large, in a handsome terminal panicle; mouth of corolla bright orange or copper-coloured; spur long and pointed. *Leaves*, crowded, narrow, lance-shaped, 1 to 1½ in. long. *L. vulgaris Peloria* is a singular variety, with a 5-spurred corolla. Found throughout Europe, and plentiful in Britain. —— The variety *Peloria* is the only one generally worthy of garden culture, in consequence of the prevalence of the common form, which thrives in any soil. Division or seed.

Lindelofia spectabilis (*Long-flowered L.*) — *Cynoglossum longiflorum.* — A rather showy perennial, 1½ ft. high. *Flowers*, in early summer; sky-blue, with obtuse petals, and a purplish tube, nearly ¼ in. long, without bracts, in racemes; lobes of calyx oval-obtuse. *Leaves*, oblong, pointed; the radical ones narrowed into a footstalk, those on the middle of the stem sessile, and those on the upper part clasping. Northern India.——Borders, in sandy loam. Division.

Linnæa borealis (*Twinflower*).—A very graceful and interesting native trailing evergreen, with opposite, roundish leaves. *Flowers*, in summer; pale pink, gracefully drooping, fragrant, bell-shaped, 5-parted, about ¼ in. long, borne in pairs. *Leaves*, small, round-oval, tapering into the stalks, slightly toothed at the top; the plant more or less clothed with a minute down, sometimes smooth. Europe and America, and also in Scotland and the north of England.——Shady moist parts of the rock-garden and hardy fernery, and in the artificial bog, or in pans or pots of moist peat. Division.

Linosyris vulgaris (*Goldilocks*). — *Chrysocoma Linosyris.* — A showy native herb, with smooth, erect, stiff stems, 1 to 2 ft. high, densely clothed with long, narrow, pale green leaves. *Flowers*, in late summer and autumn; bright yellow, in a compact terminal head; florets tubular, 5-cleft. *Leaves*, linear, entire, dotted, smooth. Native of Europe and the Caucasus, and of the western and southern coasts of England.——Rough places or borders, in any soil. Division.

Linum alpinum (*Alpine Flax*).—A handsome dwarf blue flax, 3 to 8 in. high. *Flowers*, in summer; dark blue, large, slightly corymbose; sepals oval, outer ones acutish; inner ones blunt. *Leaves*, awl-shaped, entire, stalkless, the upper ones nearly upright. Alps, Pyrenees, and hilly parts of Europe.——Borders, and the rock-garden, in sandy loam. It is also desirable for naturalization among small plants, on sandy banks, slopes, or rather bare grassy places. Seed and division.

Linum arboreum (*Evergreen Flax*). —A handsome, low-spreading, evergreen shrubby species, with smooth, grey-green leaves; 1 ft. high. *Flowers*, in early summer; clear yellow, large, 1½ in. across; sepals oval or lance-shaped, finely pointed. *Leaves*, wedge-shaped, obtuse, alternate, recurved. A native of hilly parts of South-east Europe, Asia Minor, and South Africa. —— The rock-garden, borders, and fringes of beds of dwarf shrubs, in any lightish soil. Cuttings.

Linum flavum (*Yellow herbaceous*

LINUM — LITHOSPERMUM.

Flax). — A showy perennial, with stems slightly woody at the base; 1 to 1½ ft. high. *Flowers*, in summer; golden-yellow, in corymbs, opening most in the morning when the sun shines; petals blunt, 3 times as long as the calyx. *Leaves*, narrow-lance-shaped, acute, stalkless, about 1½ in. long, smooth, thickish. Austria and Hungary.——Borders, in sandy loam. Division or seed.

Linum narbonnense (*Narbonne Flax*). — A beautiful and large kind, generally continuing a long time in flower, with erect stems, 1 to 1½ ft. or more high. *Flowers*, in summer; light sky-blue, with violet-blue veins, large, in a kind of umbel; sepals tapering to a long point; anthers 3 times as long as broad. *Leaves*, alternate, distant, narrow-lance-shaped, very acute, rather stiff; stems branching almost from the bottom, glaucous. S. Europe. ——Warm borders, in well-drained and deep sandy loam. Division or seed.

Linum perenne (*Perennial Flax*). — A pretty native species, forming tufts 12 to 18 in. high. *Flowers*, in summer; bright cobalt-blue; more than 1 in. in diameter; sepals blunt, petals overlapping each other at the edges. *Leaves*, small, narrow-lance-shaped, entire. There is a white variety, and one with the flowers variegated with white, known in gardens as *L. Lewisii variegatum*, but this marking is not conspicuous nor constant. Found in the eastern counties of England.——Borders and banks, in ordinary soil. Division and seed.

Linum salsoloides (*Heath L.*) — A hardy, dwarf, half-shrubby kind, somewhat like a dwarf Heath, with the stem twisted at the base; 3 or 4 in. high. *Flowers*, in summer; white with a slight tinge of blue, nearly ½ in. across. *Leaves*, linear, smooth, scattered, the lower ones shorter and almost imbricated. South of Europe.

——The rock-garden, in sandy soil, and on the margins of well-drained borders where sufficiently plentiful. Seed or cuttings.

Linum viscosum (*Viscid Flax*).— A neat kind, with half-shrubby, slightly branching downy stems; about 1 ft. high. *Flowers*, in summer; rich lilac, with deeper veins, nearly 1 in. across. *Leaves*, alternate, lance-shaped, acute, covered with viscous glands, and a feeble whitish down. Pyrenees. ——The rock-garden, in moist sandy loam. Seed, and division.

Lithospermum Gastoni (*Gaston's L.*) —A rare and beautiful species, with erect, herbaceous stems; 1 to 1½ ft. high. *Flowers*, in summer; bright sky-blue, twice the size of those of *L. prostratum*, in terminal clusters. *Leaves*, obovate-lance-shaped, numerous, slightly rough with adpressed hairs. Central Pyrenees.——Borders, or the rougher parts of rockwork, in rich, well-drained loam. Seed or division.

Lithospermum petræum (*Rock Grom-well*).—A charming dwarf rock-shrub, 6 to 8 in. high. *Flowers*, in summer; tubular, funnel-shaped, violet-blue, with protruded anthers of a deep orange-red, in dense, small, oblong heads; lobes of calyx silky, lanceolate-acuminate. *Leaves*, linear-oblong, obtuse, somewhat turned back at the edges, and covered with very short, silky, whitish, adpressed hairs. Dalmatia and Southern Europe.—— Sunny warm ledges in the rock-garden, in well-drained sandy soil. Cuttings, and seed if obtainable.

Lithospermum prostratum (*Gentian L.*) — A dwarf, brilliantly-blooming, trailing evergreen, with prostrate spreading stems slightly shrubby at the base. *Flowers*, in early summer; fine blue with reddish-violet stripes, axillary, stalkless, freely produced, about ¼-in. across; corolla with a straight tube and a shortly 5-lobed limb. *Leaves*, small lance-shaped, or linear, stalkless and hispid; stems pilose, branched. Spain and South of France.——The rock-garden, borders, fringes of shrubberies, and among dwarf shrubs; best in a deep and sandy loam. Cuttings.

Lithospermum purpureo-cæruleum (*Creeping Gromwell*).—A pretty British perennial, with barren stems creeping, flowering ones erect; 1 to 1½ ft. high. *Flowers*, in early summer; reddish at first, afterwards blue, in short, twin, terminal racemes. *Leaves*, dark green, rough, lance-shaped-acute, gradually tapering at the base, with the margins rolled back, 1 to 2 in. long, stalkless, or nearly so. Woods and bushy places on chalk and limestone, from Southern England to Sicily, Phrygia, and the Caucasus.—— Borders, and rougher parts of rockwork, ferneries, etc., or in a semi-wild state in shrubberies, copses, and half-shady positions. I have not found this plant to thrive on clay soil; indeed it seems to quite die out on the London clay. Division and seed.

Lobelia cardinalis (*Cardinal-flower L.*)—A brilliant perennial, long cultivated in our gardens; 1 to 3 ft. high. *Flowers*, in summer; fine scarlet, in one-sided terminal racemes; corolla tubular, divided on the upper side; limb 5-parted; segments of the lower lip obtuse. *Leaves*, smooth, oblong-lance-shaped, toothed, about 3 in. long and 1¼ broad, purplish beneath; stems erect, smooth. Native of N. America. ——Borders, in rich moist soil. Generally this plant will require to be taken up and stored during the winter, though in some districts it survives it. Division.

Lobelia fulgens (*Glowing L.*) — Closely resembling the previous one, but differing chiefly by being more downy; 1 to 2 ft. high. *Flowers*, in summer; splendid scarlet, in a terminal raceme; corolla about 1 in. long, downy outside; segments of the lower lip lance-shaped. *Leaves*, 3 to 6 in. long, lance-shaped, toothed, downy, the margin turned back; stems downy, reddish. Mexico.—— The same treatment, etc., as for the preceding kind.

Lobelia syphilitica (*Tall-blue L.*) — A large species, 1 to 2 ft. high. *Flowers*, in summer; blue, forming a long leafy raceme; corolla angular, with almost equal segments; stalks hairy. *Leaves*, stalkless, rather rough, ovate or oblong, tapering at both ends, unequally serrated; stems erect, simple, hairy. There is a white-flowered variety. North America.——In tufts round the margins of shrubberies, in moist soil, or naturalized near the margins of rivulets or in wet soil. In America it seemed to me much more ornamental and vigorous when in wet places. Division.

Lobelia Tupa (*Tupa L.*)—*Tupa Feuillei.* — A noble kind, very rarely seen; 4 to 5 ft. high. *Flowers*, late in summer; reddish, in a terminal spiked raceme; corolla large, and with the stalks and calyces downy. *Leaves*, ovate-lance-shaped, stalkless, covered with soft white down; stems erect, simple, thick, somewhat shrubby at the base, leafy. Native of Chili and Peru.——A magnificent plant in rich light soil in mild districts, and fine for association with the Tritomas and finer herbaceous plants, but not hardy in cold inland districts or on heavy cold soils. Division.

Loiseleuria procumbens (*Trailing L.*) —*Azalea procumbens.*—A very small trailing evergreen shrub, from 1 to 6 in. high. *Flowers*, in spring; reddish, small, in short terminal clusters; corolla short, bell-shaped, 5-lobed. *Leaves*, about ¼ in. long, opposite, numerous, smooth, oblong, the margins rolled back. Europe, America, and Britain, on mountains.—— The rock-garden, in peat beds, among diminutive shrubs; always in moist sandy peat. Layers.

Lophanthus urticæfolius (*Nettle-leaved L.*)—A hardy herbaceous perennial, 3 or 4 ft. high, with an almost smooth, square stem. *Flowers*, late in summer; purple (sometimes white, with pink sepals), with long protruding stamens and petals, in dense oblong spikes, more than 2 inches long. *Leaves*, opposite, oval-heart-shaped, broadly crenate on the margin, stalked, pointed. North America.——Borders, or naturalization, in ordinary soil. Division.

Lotus corniculatus (*Common L.*) — A well-known native herb, with creeping stems. *Flowers*, all summer; bright yellow, the upper part often red on the outside, 5 to 12 in an umbel, on axillary stalks much longer than the leaves. *Leaves*, pinnate; leaflets differing in form from bluntly-ovate to narrow-lance-shaped; stipules resembling the leaves but more pointed; stem and leaves both glaucous. There are several forms of this species. Abundant throughout Europe and Asia, also in Australia. —— Too common to be much used in gardens, yet few plants are more beautiful. Plants allowed to become fully developed on slopes, etc., are very fine. Seed and division.

Lunaria rediviva (*Perennial Honesty*). —A vigorous hairy herb, with erect branching stems, 2 to 3 ft. high. *Flowers*, in early summer; purplish, sweet-scented, large, showy, in terminal racemes; petals nearly entire. *Leaves*, heart-shaped, deeply-toothed, on long stalks, 8 or 9 in. long, and 3 or 4 in. broad; lower ones opposite; upper alternate. Native of mountain woods in Europe.——Borders in half-shady places, in light soil. Division or seed.

Lupinus macrophyllus (*Large-leaved Lupine*).—A tall and robust hairy herb, allied to *L. polyphyllus*, but larger in all its parts; 3 or 4 ft. high. *Flowers*, in summer; purplish-blue, 10 to 15 in a whorl, forming a dense raceme 9 to 12 in. long; calyx with both lips entire, lower one lance-shaped, acute, as long again as the upper one. *Leaves*, large, on large slender stalks, composed of from 12 to 15 lance-shaped acute leaflets; stem straight, cylindrical. Native of North America.——Cultivation and position the same as for *L. polyphyllus*, but, being much scarcer, it deserves good rich soil.

Lupinus polyphyllus (*Perennial L.*) —A fine showy perennial, 2 to 4 ft. high. *Flowers*, in summer; bluish-purple, arranged in whorls on a handsome spike; lips of calyx quite entire. *Leaves*, pinnate, with from 11 to 15 lance-shaped leaflets, hairy beneath; stems hairy. There is a white form and various others distinct in colour from the common one. North America. —— Borders, in ordinary garden soil. A fine plant for naturalization. Seed or division.

Lychnis alpina (*Alpine L.*) — A diminutive form of *Lychnis Viscaria*, but smooth and not viscid, and attaining a height of only a few inches. *Flowers*, in spring and early summer; pink, in close heads; petals narrow, deeply bifid; calyx short. *Leaves*, narrow-lance-shaped, slightly fringed; lower ones in a tuft. Found in Cumberland, and on the summit of Little Kilrannock in Forfarshire, and in various parts of Northern Europe. —— The rock-garden, in sandy or gritty soil, in well-drained chinks. Division and seed.

Lychnis chalcedonica (*Scarlet L.*) —A well-known old border plant, 1½ to 3½ ft. high. *Flowers*, in summer; scarlet, in corymbose clusters; calyx, round, clubbed, ribbed.

LYCHNIS.

Leaves, lance-shaped, slightly heart-shaped at the base. pilose, clasping the stem; the plant somewhat clammy. There are the following varieties in cultivation, the single white, double white, and double scarlet; the best is the double scarlet. S. Russia and Japan. —— Borders, in light rich loam. Division and seed.

Lychnis diurna (*Red Campion*).— *Silene diurna.*—A common hedge plant, 1 to 3 ft. high. *Flowers*, in summer; purplish - rose; calyx very hairy. *Leaves*, opposite; lower ones obovate-spoon-shaped, middle ones oval-elliptical, acute; upper ones lanceolate. Whole plant covered with long, soft hairs, not glandular. Britain, and other parts of Europe.——The double variety is a handsome border plant, increased by division, and thriving best in rich deep soil. Division.

Lychnis Flos-cuculi (*Ragged Robin*). —*Agrostemma Flos-cuculi.* — A well-known British plant, 1 to 2 ft. high. *Flowers*, early in summer; red, scentless, in loose terminal panicles; petals cut into 4 narrow lobes, the middle ones the longest; calyx bell-shaped, with 10 ribs, and 5 short teeth. *Leaves*, few, narrowly lance-shaped; those stem connate, of root stalked. The plant is so abundant in Britain that it would not have been mentioned here, were it not for its double variety *L. Flos-cuculi, fl. pl.*, which is a very ornamental border plant. Europe and Russian Asia. —— Borders, and in moist spots, in ordinary soil. Division.

Lychnis Flos-Jovis (*Umbellate L.*)— *Agrostemma Flos-Jovis.* — A whitish-leaved species, 12 to 15 in. high. *Flowers*, in summer; purple or scarlet, in umbellate heads; calyx cylindrical, clubbed; petals 2-lobed. *Leaves*, lance-shaped, stem-clasping, clothed with a white silky down. Switzerland. —— Borders, rockwork, or on bare banks, in sandy loam. Seed.

Lychnis fulgens (*Brilliant L.*)—A very showy plant, 6 in. to 1 ft. high. *Flowers*, in early summer; brilliant vermilion, large and handsome, in corymbs; petals 2-divided, outer divisions awl-shaped; calyx cylindrical, woolly. *Leaves*, ovate - lanceolate, greyish; stems hairy. Siberia. ——Borders, in sandy loam. Seed and division.

Lychnis grandiflora (*Large L.*)—*L. coronata.* — A remarkably handsome plant, 8 in. to 1 ft. high. *Flowers*, from June to August; of a brick-red or scarlet colour, sometimes nearly 2 in. across; limb of the petals elegantly cut and spreading, 1 to 3 flowers at the top of each flower-stem; calyx swollen, marked with longitudinal lines. *Leaves*, almost sessile, opposite, oval-acute, smooth, of a delicate green. China. —— Warm borders, in sandy loam. Seed and division.

Lychnis Haageana (*Shaggy L.*) — Remarkable for its very large and brilliant flowers and shaggy stems, 1 to 1¾ ft. high. *Flowers*, in summer; of a splendid scarlet, nearly, and sometimes quite, 2 in. across, 2 or 3 on each of the very shaggy stems; petals broadly obovate, indented on the top and furnished with 2 long teeth at the side; calyx shaggy, inflated and angular. *Leaves*, large, lanceolate, acuminate, hairy and purplish-brown below. Native country unknown, probably a hybrid. ——Borders, in sandy soil. Seed and division.

Lychnis Lagascæ (*Rock L.*)—A brilliant alpine plant, about 3 in. high. *Flowers*, early in summer; bright rose-colour, with white centres when young, each about ¾ in. across. *Leaves*, obovate or oblong, somewhat leathery, and slightly glaucous. Sub-alpine region of the Western Pyrenees.—— The rock-garden, in any position. A few specimens should be on high points as it is effective a long way off; it is also a capital border plant, and for growing in pots or pans for exhibition. Seed and division.

Lychnis Preslii (*Presl's L.*)—An interesting and little known kind, with glabrous foliage and tufted habit, 1 ft. to 20 in. high. *Flowers*, in summer; purplish or carmine-rose, nearly 1 in. across, numerous, scentless, opening in the daytime, arranged in forking panicled clusters, and accompanied by reddish bracts; corona fringed, of a satiny rose-white, not closing the throat; calyx reddish, very much swollen, with five short teeth, closely adpressed against the tube of the corolla, and shorter than it. *Leaves*, of the root numerous, stalked or narrowed into a stalk, oval-lanceolate or obovate, pointed, decurrent, arranged in rosettes; stem-leaves oval, abruptly pointed, all entire, and very much veined, smooth, and of a lively dark green colour. Poland.——Rockwork or borders in half-shady positions, in light well-drained soil. Division and seed.

Lychnis pyrenaica (*Pyrenean L.*)— A small and pretty, but not showy kind, 3 or 4 in. high. *Flowers*, in early summer, pale flesh-colour, more than ¼ in. across, in forked bundles, with a single flower in each fork, which stands on a long stalk; petals slightly notched; calyx bell-shaped, lobes short. *Leaves*, glaucous, opposite, leathery those of the root on long stalks. spoon-shaped; of the stem heart-shaped, stalkless. Pyrenees.——The rock-garden, in ordinary soil. Seed.

Lychnis Sieboldi (*Siebold's L.*)—A handsome kind, about 1 ft. high. *Flowers*, in summer; large, pure white, few, in a contracted terminal cyme; limb of the petals wedge-shaped, irregular, jagged on the margin, slightly 2-lobed. *Leaves*, sessile, lower ones very closely set, spathulate-oblong; middle and upper ones ovate-oblong, acute, entire, slightly undulating, soft and downy on both sides. Japan.——Warm borders, in sandy loam. Seed and division.

Lychnis vespertina (*White L.*)— *Silene pratensis*. — A common native perennial, with loosely branched stems, 1 to 3 ft. high. *Flowers*, in summer; white, slightly scented, in loose panicles, opening in the evening; petals bifid; calyx nearly ¾ in. long, hairy, ribbed, with 5 lance-shaped teeth. *Leaves*, opposite, connate, oval-oblong, pointed, tapering at the base, hairy, slightly nerved, upper ones without stalks, lower ones stalked; stems purplish, swelling at the joints, the upper branches forked; plant more or less glutinous. There is an ornamental double variety. Abundant in Britain and throughout Europe.——The double variety, generally known as *L. dioica fl. pl.*, is a handsome border flower, thriving well in rich, free soil. Division.

Lychnis Viscaria (*German Catchfly*). —A showy and gracefully tufted ever-green herb, with erect stems, very viscid in the upper parts, 10 to 18 in. high. *Flowers*, in early summer; rosy-red, in close, showy heads; petals slightly bifid; calyx tubular, narrow, about ½ in. long, purplish. *Leaves*, opposite, grass-like, about 3 in. long, and scarcely ¼ in. wide, with a reddish tip. There are several varieties, the most worthy of cultivation being *splendens*, a variety with brighter flowers; *alba*, a charming white one, and the double ones, which have fine rocket-like flowers. Found in Wales and near Edinburgh, and freely distributed over Europe and Asia.—— Arid rough slopes of the rock-garden, in any soil, or in borders, or in a semi-wild state on slopes or banks. Division or seed.

Lycopodium dendroideum (*Ground Pine*).—A club-moss, in habit like a Lilliputian pine-tree. The stems, growing to a height of 6 to 9 in. from a creeping root, are much branched and clothed with small, bright, shining green leaves. Fruit-cones yellow, long, cylindrical, and, like the stem, erect. A native of moist woods in North America, and high mountains of the Southern United States.—— Well adapted for the embellishment of rockwork, where it should be established in a deep bed of moist, sandy peat, fully exposed to the sun. Careful division and spores, which should be sown in a moist spot, in a half-shady position, the soil being made level and firm, and surfaced with a little silver sand.

Lysimachia angustifolia (*Narrow-leaved L.*)—A graceful kind (a variety of *L. lanceolata*), with smooth, branching stems, 12 to 18 in. high. *Flowers*, in early summer; pale yellow, small, drooping, in short terminal racemes; divisions of the corolla oblong. *Leaves*, dotted, long, linear. North America.——Borders, in sandy soil. Division.

Lysimachia Ephemerum (*Willow-leaved L*).—A distinct kind, of graceful habit, and with sea-green leaves; 2 to 3 ft. high. *Flowers*, in summer; white, in handsome upright racemes; corolla wheel-shaped, divisions blunt, spreading; stamens projecting. *Leaves*, linear-lance-shaped, stalkless, smooth, entire. *Stem* smooth, round, hollow. A native of several parts of Southern Europe.——Naturalized in copses or woods, or occasionally in borders in light soil. Division.

Lysimachia Leschenaultii (*Carmine L.*)—A very interesting kind, about 1 ft. high. *Flowers*, late in autumn; of a brilliant carmine. *Leaves*, lanceolate, acute, sometimes opposite or ternate, sometimes alternate. *Stem*, herbaceous, branching, tufted. Malabar.——This is too tender to be recommended for general cultivation, but is worth a place in the rock-garden, in sandy soil, in warm spots in the southern counties. Division.

Lysimachia Nummularia (*Creeping Jenny*).—A well-known creeping plant. *Flowers*, in summer and autumn; bright yellow, large and very handsome, freely produced on axillary stalks shorter than the leaves; corolla rotate, nearly 1 in. across, deeply divided into 5 ovate, pointed lobes. *Leaves*, opposite, roundish, on short, broad stalks, smooth, somewhat veined. There is a variety with the leaves blotched with yellow.——Ditch banks, etc., borders, vases, and rockwork, in any soil. Division.

Lysimachia thyrsiflora (*Tufted L.*) —A semi-aquatic kind, with erect stems, 1 to 2 ft. high. *Flowers*, in summer; yellow, smaller than those of the Common L., in dense racemes; stalks many-flowered, shorter than the leaves; corolla wheel-shaped, deeply divided into narrow lobes; segments of calyx narrow. *Leaves*, about 3 in. long, and nearly ¾ in. broad at the base, lance-shaped, acute, entire, slightly pubescent beneath, stalkless, many together at the top of the stem. Britain, Europe, and Northern Asia and America.——Margins of streams and ponds. Division.

Lysimachia vulgaris (*Common L.*)— A British plant, with erect branching stems, 2 to 3 ft. high. *Flowers*, in summer; yellow, in short terminal leafy panicles; peduncles many-flowered; corolla bell-shaped, lobes broad; calyx 5-divided; divisions lance-shaped, varying in breadth, ciliated at the edges. *Leaves*, rather large, mostly in whorls of 3 or 4, ovate, pointed, entire, but slightly waved at the edges; stems rather hairy at top, smooth below.——England, Ireland, and Scotland, but less frequent in the latter; also in other parts of Europe and Asia. Best suited for wild places, though it is not unfrequently seen in borders, in moist ordinary soil. Division.

Lythrum alatum (*Winged-stemmed L.*)—An elegant half-shrubby, smooth herb, 2 to 4 ft. high. *Flowers*, in summer; fine purple, small, solitary in the axils of the leaves, almost stalkless; petals 6; stamens 6. *Leaves*, opposite, ovate-oblong, acute, slightly heart-shaped at the base, stalkless, or on very short stalks; branches twiggy, tetragonally winged. Southern parts of N. America.——Borders and fringes of shrubbery, in sandy soil. Division.

Lythrum Salicaria (*Loosestrife*).— A vigorous native herb, with erect, slightly - branched, reddish stems; smooth, 4-angled below, pubescent, and 5-angled above; 2 to 5 ft. high. *Flowers*, in summer; reddish-purple, almost stalkless, in whorls in the axils of the leaves, forming a handsome, long, leafy, terminal spike; petals 6–7 oblong, about ½ in. long, stamens 12–14. *Leaves*, about 3 in. long, lance-shaped, entire, Willow-like, opposite, 3 or sometimes 4 in a whorl, clasping the stem at the base. Europe and Britain.——The finely-coloured variety known in gardens as *L. roseum-superbum* is well-worthy of a place by the margin of every stream and lake; it also thrives in borders, in any soil. Division.

Lythrum virgatum (*Twiggy Purple L.*) —Allied to the previous species but smoother, of a looser habit, and with the flowers in threes; 2 to 3 ft. high or more. *Flowers*, in summer; purple, in spikes about the same size as those of the common *L*. *Leaves*, opposite, entire, smooth, lance-shaped, gradually tapering at the base, 1½ to 2 in. long. Austria, Germany, Siberia, Russia, and North America.——Borders, in sandy loam. Division.

Malva Alcea (*Hollyhock Mallow*).— A vigorous-growing perennial, upwards of 3 ft. high. *Flowers*, in summer; pale rosy-purple, about 2 in. across, in terminal and axillary clusters. *Leaves*, palmate, with incised divisions, long - stalked, light green, thinly overspread, as are the stem and leaf-stalks, with a short roughish down. France.——Borders, margins of shrubberies, and naturalization, in sandy loam, or ordinary calcareous dry soil, in almost any position. Seed or division.

Malva campanulata (*Bell - flowered Mallow*). — An interesting kind, with ascending stems from 1 to 1¼ ft. high. *Flowers*, late in summer; small, about ¾ in. across, bell-shaped, light purplish rose-colour, in a long, lax, terminal spike. *Leaves*, large, irregular in outline, deeply lobed; lobes twice subdivided; both leaves and stem covered with very short thin down. Chili.——The rock-garden, or banks, in well-drained sandy soil. It perishes on the level ground in winter, and is probably only hardy in the mildest parts of Southern England. Seed or cuttings.

Malva Morenii (*Moren's Mallow*).— An herbaceous perennial, 2 to 3 ft. high. *Flowers*, in summer; very large (nearly 2½ in. across); pink-rose, axillary, solitary, and in terminal and axillary clusters. *Leaves*, 3-lobed, variously cut and toothed, for the most part resembling the leaves of the common Oak in appearance and colour. Italy.——Borders, or naturalization, in ordinary soil. Seed or division.

Malva moschata (*Musk Mallow*).—A vigorous native perennial, 2 to 2½ ft. high. *Flowers*, in summer; showy, delicate rose-colour (sometimes white), about 2 in. across, in terminal and axillary clusters. *Leaves*, of the lower part of the stem roundish, incised; the upper ones much divided, all with a strong musky odour. The white variety is very fine. Britain and Europe in calcareous and gravelly soil.——Same positions and treatment as for *M. Alcea*.

Mazus Pumilio (*Dwarf M.*)—A very dwarf herb, creeping underground, quickly forming dense tufts that rarely reach more than an inch in height. *Flowers*, in summer; pale violet, with white centres, 1 to 6 on slender stems, scarcely rising above the leaves; corolla about ½ in. across; lower lip, 3-cleft; upper one 2-cleft; calyx bell-shaped, 5-parted. *Leaves*, bundled, spreading, 1 or 2 in. long, stalked, narrow-spoon-shaped, obtuse, entire or lobulate, smooth or slightly hairy. Australia and New Zealand.——The rock-garden, and borders, in ordinary soil. Division.

Meconopsis aculeata (*Prickly Poppy*).—A beautiful species, with an erect, furrowed, prickly stem, from 1½ to 2 ft. high. *Flowers*, in summer; fine purple, like shot-silk, solitary or terminal in panicles. *Leaves*, on long stalks, oblong, decurrent, somewhat pinnate, with obtuse divisions. Seedvessels oblong, sharp on both sides, densely covered with prickles. Himalayas.——The lower and sunny flanks of the rock-garden, in well-drained sandy soil. Seed.

Meconopsis cambrica (*Welsh Poppy*).—A handsome Poppy-like herb, forming, when established, large pale green tufts of rather hairy, divided leaves; 1 ft. high. *Flowers*, in early summer; sulphur-yellow, largish, erect, drooping in bud, on long smoothish stalks. *Leaves*, pinnate, glaucous beneath; leaflets ovate or lance-shaped, toothed, lower ones on long stalks, upper ones smaller and on shorter stalks. Europe and some of the Western counties of England, Wales, and Ireland.—— On rocky places or banks in peaty soil this plant usually grows and looks best, taking care of itself in a semi-wild state. Seed or division.

Medicago falcata (*Sickle Medick*).—A vigorous British herb, with trifoliate leaves and prostrate stems, 2 to 4 ft. long. *Flowers*, in summer; yellow, in short, close, axillary racemes, on stalks longer than the leaves. *Leaves*, pinnate, on short stalks; leaflets oblong or linear, smooth, toothed at top, entire at base; stipules awl-shaped, entire. Europe, Asia, and the Southern and Eastern counties of England. —— Banks or slopes, on which its wide-spreading masses may be seen to advantage, borders, or very rough rock or rootwork, so planted that its long shoots may fall over the brows of rocks. It thrives in any soil. Division or seed.

Melianthus major (*Large Honeyflower*).—A half-shrubby plant, with very handsome and distinct grey, pinnate leaves; 4 to 6 ft. high. *Flowers*, in summer; chocolate-brown, in longish spikes springing from the axils of the upper leaves. *Leaves*, clasping the stem, having broadish stipules sheathing the petiole, smooth on both sides; leaflets, 4 or 5, large, deeply cut into acute divisions; stems hollow, woody at base. Cape of Good Hope.——Hardy in sunny nooks on sheltered banks, in well-drained soil. The stems are usually cut down by frost, but the plants look all the better for this when they come up the following summer. Seed and division.

Melissa officinalis (*Common Balm*).—A well-known old garden plant, with a very grateful odour when bruised; 2 to 3 ft. high. *Flowers*, in summer; white or pale yellow, in 3- to 6-flowered whorls; corolla twice the length of calyx. *Leaves*, broadly-ovate, blunt or heart-shaped at the base, hairy above and smooth beneath; lower ones on longish stalks. There is a variegated variety. Southern Europe and Caucasus. —— The variegated form is sometimes used as an edging plant, and the common kind might be naturalized in any position or soil by those who admire fragrant plants. Division.

Melittis Melissophyllum (*Balm M.*) —*M. grandiflora*.—A very ornamental native plant ; 1 to 2 ft. high. *Flowers*, in early summer ; reddish-purple and white, 2 to 6 in axillary whorls, on hairy stalks, scarcely so long as leaves ; corolla with a broad tube, nearly 1½ in. long ; upper lip slightly concave ; lower one the largest, spreading, 3-lobed. *Leaves*, about 2 in. long, heart-shaped, stalked, opposite, toothed, clothing the stem to the apex, slightly hairy. Europe, Asia, and Southern England.——Margins of shrubberies, in a wild state, among shrubs, etc., in peaty soil. Division.

Mentha Requieni (*Requien's Pennyroyal*). — *Thymus corsicus*. — A very minute creeping herb, quite smooth, having the odour of Peppermint. *Flowers*, in summer ; pale purple, in loose, few-flowered whorls ; calyx somewhat 2-lipped, smooth ; throat villous inside. *Leaves*, small, stalked, roundish, almost entire ; stems spreading at the base, much branched ; branches thread-like, ascending. Native of Corsica.——The rock-garden, allowed to trail about among the Pearlworts and other minute plants which usually make themselves at home on all parts of this structure. Division.

Mentha rotundifolia variegata. — A variegated variety, about 1 ft. high. *Flowers*, late in summer ; very small, whitish, numerous, in dense cylindrical spikes. *Leaves*, opposite, sessile, roundish, notched, wrinkled on the upper surface, covered with a cobweb-like down underneath, elegantly variegated with green and light yellow, which becomes darker with age. Europe.——Edgings, in ordinary soil. Division.

Menyanthes trifoliata (*Buckbean*).— A beautiful British aquatic herb, with trifoliate leaves. *Flowers*, in early summer ; corolla white inside, tinged with red outside, beautifully bearded, bell-shaped, 5-lobed ; segments narrow, pointed. *Leaves*, on long stalks, consisting of 3 oblong leaflets, 1 to 2 in. long, smooth, veined, edges wavy. Common in Europe and North America.——Margins of lakes, ponds, and streams, or in the artificial bog. Division.

Menziesia cærulea (*Yew-leaved M.*) —A small prostrate, evergreen, Heath-like, much-branched shrub ; 4 to 6 in. high. *Flowers*, in late summer and autumn ; pinkish-lilac, in small terminal, umbellate clusters, on glandular stalks ; corolla between ¼ and ½ in. long, bell-shaped with a contracted 5-toothed mouth ; divisions of the calyx 5, tapering to a point. *Leaves*, crowded, linear, obtuse, with very minute teeth at the margins. Native of northern and arctic parts of Europe, Asia, and America, and on the Sow of Atholl Perthshire, Scotland. —— The rock-garden, in moist peat. Division of healthy tufts, or cuttings.

Menziesia empetriformis (*Empetrum-like M.*)—A small creeping Heath-like evergreen shrub, allied to the previous species ; seldom exceeding 6 in. high. *Flowers*, in early summer ; brilliant rosy-purple, in clusters, on slightly glandular stalks ; corolla bell-shaped ; divisions of calyx ovate, obtuse. *Leaves*, linear, obtuse ; margins toothed. North America, on the Rocky Mountains, and near the mouth of Columbia River.——The rock-garden, in moist, sandy peat, or in choice borders, where it thrives on the level ground. Careful division of established tufts, or layers.

Menziesia polifolia (*St. Daboec's Heath*). —A spreading, bushy, evergreen, Heath-like shrub ; 12 to 20 in. high.

Flowers, in summer; crimson-purple, in a graceful, one-sided, drooping raceme; corolla oval, inflated, about ¼ in. long; mouth 4-toothed; divisions of calyx 4. *Leaves*, small; lower ones elliptic, upper ones narrow, clothed with white down beneath; margins rolled back when young, but becoming flat when older. There is a white variety sold sometimes under the name of *M. globosa*, more rare than the common form, and equally beautiful. France, Spain, England, Ireland, and Scotland.——In beds of low shrubs, fringes of shrubberies, among the bolder plants in the rock-garden, in peat soil, or naturalized in heathy places. Division, layers, or cuttings.

Merendera Bulbocodium (*Autumn M.*)—*Colchicum montanum.*—Very like *Bulbocodium vernum*, but flowering in autumn. *Flowers*, in autumn; large and handsome, of a pale pinkish-lilac, with narrow, oblong segments. The flower-stem remains under ground during the period of flowering, then commences to grow, and ultimately bears the seed-vessel at a height of about 4 in. *Leaves*, 4 or 5, appearing soon after the flowers, linear, channelled, without veins, 5 to 6 in. long, arching and finally spreading on the ground. *Bulb*, nearly round, brownish, the size of a hazel-nut. Native of alpine meadows in the Central Pyrenees.——The rock-garden and bulb-garden, till plentiful enough to be used in borders, and for naturalization, in deep sandy loam. Separation of the new bulbs, and seed.

Mertensia maritima (*Oyster Plant*). —*Pulmonaria maritima.*—A trailing evergreen, smooth, glaucous herb, with branching stems; 3 or 4 in. high. *Flowers*, in spring and summer; beautiful purplish-blue, erect, in a terminal raceme; corolla 2 or 3 times the length of the calyx; limb nearly bell-shaped; pedicels about ¼ in. long. *Leaves*, ovate, bluntish, fleshy, entire; lower ones stalked, upper ones stalkless. Found on the sea-shore in several parts of Britain, and also in Northern Europe.——An open spot in the rock-garden, protected from snails and slugs which are very fond of the plant, and will quickly destroy it if permitted, in free sandy or gritty earth (sea sand, if obtainable, to be preferred). Increased by seeds, gathered and sown as soon as they ripen.

Mertensia virginica (*Virginian Cowslip*).—*Pulmonaria virginica.*—A handsome and graceful perennial, with smooth, slightly glaucous leaves; 10 to 18 in. high. *Flowers*, in April, May, and June; a beautiful purple-blue, tubular, about 1 in. long, in clusters rather gracefully drooping. *Leaves*, lanceolate-ovate; lower ones 4 to 6 in. long, and 2 to 3 in. broad, on short footstalks; upper ones of the same shape, gradually diminishing in size, stalkless. In its native country it is said to vary with white and flesh-coloured flowers, but I have not seen any but the blue form in cultivation. North America, on mountains, and gravelly shores of rivers.——Mixed borders, margins of clumps of American plants, the lower parts of the rock-garden, associated with the Aquilegias and other taller alpines, or naturalized in wood or copse; in all cases in a sheltered position, and in light, rich, and well-drained soil. Division in autumn, and seeds sown soon after they ripen.

Meum athamanticum (*Spignel*).—A very graceful British plant, with finely divided Fennel-like leaves; 1 to 2 ft. high. *Flowers*, in summer; white, tinged with green, in not very large compound, terminal umbels; petals entire. *Leaves*, deep green, much cut into thread-like segments; those of the root in a tuft; of the stem, few, smaller, less cut; stems channelled, slightly branching. Found in the Highlands of Scotland, North of England and Wales, and in various parts of Western Europe.——Borders, banks, and the rougher parts of the rock-garden, used for the sake of its graceful leaves, in any soil. Division.

Michauxia campanuloides (*Harebell-like M.*)—A remarkable Campanula-like plant; 3 to 8 ft. high. *Flowers*, in summer ; white, tinged with purple on the outside, drooping, in a panicle ; corolla wheel-shaped, 8-parted, 3 or 4 inches across, the petals curled back, showing the broad filaments; calyx and stigma 8-parted. *Leaves*, 3 to 5 in. long, clothed with stiff hairs; root-leaves heart-shaped, irregularly lobed, stalked; stalks margined and lobed; stem-leaves lance-shaped, acute, half embracing ; stems branching at top, clothed with stiff hairs. Native of the Levant.—— Borders, in deep sandy loam. Seed.

Mimulus cardinalis (*Cardinal M.*)— A showy perennial, clothed with long, whitish, glutinous hairs, allied to the common Musk ; 1 to 1½ ft. high. *Flowers*, in summer ; red or scarlet ; corolla large, lobes notched at the ends ; calyx tubular, scarcely plaited, sharply toothed. Native of California. ——Borders, in moist soil. Division or seed.

Mimulus cupræus (*Coppery Monkey-flower*).—A dwarf, very free-blooming kind ; 8 in. to 1 ft. high. *Flowers*, in summer ; coloured, both on the inside and out, with yellowish - copper, or reddish-brown—almost bordering on crimson, with reflexed, velvety, and somewhat transparent margins ; lower lip prominent and plaited near the throat, which is dotted with purplish crimson. *Leaves*, opposite, usually tinged with red ; the lower ones stalked, attenuated towards the stalk, oval-lance-shaped, toothed; the upper ones sessile. Andes of Chili.

——Borders, or the margins of beds of American plants, in light moist loam and peat. Division or seed, from which it varies much.

Mimulus luteus (*Yellow Monkey-flower*).—A smooth herb, with coarsely-toothed leaves ; 6 to 10 in. high. *Flowers*, in summer ; yellow ; calyx ovate, when in a fruiting state bell-shaped, teeth ovate, acute, upper one largest. There have been numerous hybrids raised from this species, with flowers varying much in size and colour. A native of Chili.——Naturalization, in moist or boggy places. Division or seed.

Mimulus moschatus (*Common Musk*). —One of our most popular plants. *Flowers*, in summer ; yellow, small, corolla spreading; upper lip 2-lobed, lower one trifid; calyx tubular. *Leaves*, somewhat clammy, hairy, on little stalks, ovate, or ovate - lanceolate, slightly toothed, rounded at the base. Found near the Columbia River on the north-west coast of America. ——Borders, and naturalization in moist places. Division.

Mirabilis Jalapa (*Marvel of Peru*). —A handsome bushy herb ; 2½ to 3½ ft. high. *Flowers*, late in summer ; funnel - shaped, nearly 2 in. long ; of various colours, red, white, or yellow, 3 to 6 in a terminal cluster, opening only at night ; each blossom is surrounded by a tubular, bell-shaped calyx, with five divisions, which continues to grow after the flower has fallen. *Leaves*, alternate, smooth, or finely ciliated, oval, acute, with an obtuse, or almost heart-shaped base. Native of Peru.—— Borders, or in beds with the finer perennials, in warm, deep, sandy loam. The tuberous roots frequently perish in winter, and should therefore be taken up in autumn and stored, as we store Dahlias in winter. Seed and division.

Modiola geranioides (*Geranium-like M.*)—A hardy, tuberous-rooted, trailing Malvaceous plant, 4 or 5 in. high. *Flowers*, late in summer; rich rosy-purple, marked with a dark line in the centre, solitary, 1 in. or more across, supported on very long and slender flower-stalks, springing from the axils of the leaves. *Leaves*, cut into three very deep lobes, which are again deeply cut, on stalks about 1 in. long, distant from each other. North America.——The rock-garden, and easily grown in the margins of borders in well-drained sandy soil. Division.

Mœhringia muscosa (*Mossy M.*)—A very dwarf evergreen herb, 2 or 3 in. high, with prostrate, thread-like stems, clothed with very narrow leaves, like those of an *Arenaria*. *Flowers*, in early summer; white, small, axillary, solitary; divisions of calyx flat, lance-shaped, acute. *Leaves*, linear, connate. Europe, on the margins of woods, in humid parts of mountains.—— The rock-garden and borders, in fine, very sandy loam. Division and seed.

Molopospermum cicutarium (*Cicuta-like M.*)—A large and handsome Fern-like plant, with dark-green shining leaves; 3 to 4 ft. high. *Flowers*, in summer; yellowish-white, in umbels; terminal ones large, fertile; side ones small, sterile. *Leaves*, large, of a lively green, ternately decompound; leaflets lance-shaped, lengthened, deeply cut into acute points; stems large, hollow. There is a form with leaves variegated with yellowish-white and green. S. Europe.——In groups of fine-leaved hardy plants, isolated in the grass, in the picturesque garden, in borders, or naturalized in half-wild places. Where used in groups, or isolated in the kept portion of the ground, it will be better to pinch off the flowering-stems as they appear. In good and deep soil. Seed sown when ripe, and division.

Monarda didyma (*Bee Balm*).— A fine strong perennial, with smooth, acutely 4-angled stems; 2 to 3 ft. high. *Flowers*, in summer; bright scarlet, in distinct whorls, either solitary or in pairs; corolla widened, quite smooth; lips nearly equal, upper one erect, entire, or notched; lower one spreading, mostly with three short teeth at the apex; calyx tubular, 5-toothed, incurved, striped, scarlet, throat almost naked; bracts coloured. *Leaves*, smooth, 2 to 4 in. long, broadly lance-shaped, deeply serrate. North America.——Borders and naturalization in copses, or anywhere in the spaces among low shrubs, etc. Division.

Monarda fistulosa (*Wild Bergamot*). —Allied to *M. didyma*, but with hairy, obtuse-angled stems; 2 to 4 ft. high. *Flowers*, in summer; pale red or purple, mostly in solitary whorls; corolla villous; calyces rather incurved, scarcely coloured; throat hispid inside; bracts slightly coloured. *Leaves*, oblong-lance-shaped, serrate, flat, villous, green or greyish, on long ciliated stalks. Common in hedges and woods from Canada to Carolina. ——The same positions and treatment as for *M. didyma*.

Morina longifolia (*Whorl Flower*).— Singular in aspect and ornamental both in leaf and flower; 2 to 3 ft. high. *Flowers*, in summer; white in the bud and when first opening, afterwards changing to a handsome rose-colour, which passes into a lively carmine, in crowded whorls in the axils of the upper leaves; corolla long, tubular, spreading. *Leaves*, about a foot long, 1½ in. wide, pinnatifid, with wavy margins, somewhat spiny-ciliated; stem tapering, not furrowed. Nepaul.——Borders, and in groups or beds of the finer perennials, in good deep soil. Seed.

Mulgedium alpinum (*Blue Sow-thistle*).—A tall blue composite plant, 3 to

4 ft. high. *Flowers*, late in summer; deep blue, arranged in a corymb-like cluster. *Leaves*, alternate, those of the root lyrate-toothed, on long stalks which are widely dilated at the base; stem furrowed almost simple. Alps. ——Among tall perennials by wood-walks and in semi-wild places, in dry soil. Division.

Mulgedium Plumieri (*Plumier's M.*) —Like the preceding but larger; 6 ft. high. *Flowers*, in summer; purple, in panicles almost like corymbs, with short bracts. *Leaves*, broad, pinnatifid-runcinate, glaucous underneath. South of France.——Similar uses, etc. to those for the preceding.

Muscari botryoides (*Sky - blue Grape Hyacinth*).—A charming bulb, 6 in. to 12 in. high. *Flowers*, in spring; of a lovely deep sky-blue, with six diminutive white teeth or segments, arranged in a short, dense, almost globose cluster, afterwards elongated on short drooping pedicels, which become horizontal as the fruit ripens. *Leaves*, linear, channelled, stiff, erect, slightly glaucous. Southern Europe.——Borders, in all sorts of positions, in sandy loam. It is readily increased by division, and will be the better for being raised and divided every third or fourth year.

Muscari commutatum (*Changeable Grape Hyacinth*).—Nearly allied to *M. racemosum*, 6 in. to 10 in. high. *Flowers*, in spring; pitcher-shaped, at first bluish, afterwards changing to reddish-purple, in a very short raceme; teeth of corolla inflexed, approaching. *Leaves*, linear, channelled, flaccid, longer than the flower-stem. Native of Sicily and Apulia. —— Borders, in sandy soil. Division.

Muscari comosum monstruosum (*Feathery Hyacinth*).—*Hyacinthus monstruosus*.— A singular and ornamental plant, 12 to 18 in. high. *Flowers*, in early summer; bluish - violet or amethyst-blue, all-sterile, composed of slender, twisted, wavy, frizzled and scaly divisions or filaments, and arranged in a large cluster 5 or 6 in. long or more; the clusters frequently becoming so heavy, in proportion to the sustaining power of the stem, that they fall to the ground and require to be propped up. *Leaves*, linear, ribbon-like, channelled, toothed at the edges, longer than the flower-stem. *Bulb*, of medium size, covered with light flesh-coloured or rosy, sometimes brownish, coats. Southern Europe. The variety named *plumosum*, differs only in having the divisions of the petals finer and more feathery. —— Borders, fringes of shrubbery, or beds in the spring-garden; best in peat or sandy loam. Division.

Muscari Heldreichii (*Greek Grape Hyacinth*).—A beautiful long-spiked, and as yet rare, kind. *Flowers*, in spring; of a fine blue, somewhat like those of *M. botryoides*, but nearly twice as large, and arranged in a longer spike. *Leaves*, flat, like those of *M. commutatum*, but not open at the top like those of that plant. Greece. ——The rock-garden and choice borders, at least till more plentiful, and in deep sandy soil. Division.

Muscari luteum (*Yellow G. Hyacinth*). —A large yellow and fragrant kind, about 6 in. high. *Flowers*, in spring; large, deliciously fragrant, of a dull, dirty purple as they open, and changing slowly to a clear waxy sulphur; about 20 blooms to a stem. *Leaves*, channelled, 8 to 10 in. long. —— Borders, and sunny banks, or the bulb-garden, in sandy soil. Division.

Muscari moschatum (*Musk Hyacinth*). — Inconspicuous and dull-coloured but very sweet; 8 to 10 in. high. *Flowers*, in spring; purplish when they first appear, but gradually becoming of an unattractive greenish-yellow, slightly tinged with violet, deliciously fragrant and arranged in a dense, nearly globose cluster about 2½ in. long. *Leaves*, alternate, linear, concave, about as long as the flower-stem, of a tender green, spreading on the ground. *Bulb*, of medium size, elongated, yellowish. The Levant.——Borders, or naturalized on warm sunny banks among the violets and early spring flowers, in sandy soil. Division.

Muscari racemosum (*Grape Hyacinth*).—The commonest kind, frequent in cottage and old gardens, 4 to 8 in. high. *Flowers*, in spring; deep blue, whitish at the ends, smelling strongly of plums, arranged in a close cylindrical cluster. *Leaves*, few, linear, rush-like, spreading, about 8 to 10 in. long. *Bulb*, egg-shaped, small, whitish. Southern and Central Europe and Britain.——Borders, or naturalized in any bare positions, in any soil. Division.

Myosotis alpestris (*Alpine Forget-me-not*).—*M. rupicola*.—An exquisite alpine plant, 2 or 3 in. high. *Flowers*, in early summer; handsome blue, with a very small yellowish eye, sweet-scented in the evening. *Leaves*, dark green, hairy, alternate, sessile, oblong-lance-shaped, in very dense tufts close to the earth. North of England and Scotland. It is distinct from the *Myosotis alpestris* of Continental botanists.——The rock-garden, or the margins of the choice mixed border, among the choicest plants, either in fully exposed or somewhat shady positions, in sandy or gritty loam, kept moist in summer. Seed.

Myosotis azorica (*Azorean Forget-me-not*).—A beautiful kind, known at once by its deep blue blooms not having an "eye" of another colour in the centre; 6 to 10 in. high. *Flowers*, in summer; rich purple when they first open, afterwards of a fine indigo-blue throughout; about ¼ in. across, in dense racemes without bracts; throat yellow; calyx deeply divided;

Leaves, hairy, upper ones oblong-obtuse; lower ones oblong-spoon-shaped. Azores Islands.——Warm and moist nooks in the rock-garden, or half-shady spots in borders, in moist peat or sandy loam with leaf-mould. It does not long endure, and is somewhat tender, so that some seed should be sown every year in spring or summer, some of the seedling plants to be kept over the following winter in frames. Seed.

Myosotis dissitiflora (*Early Forget-me-not*).—*M. montana*.—A very early-flowering beautiful plant, 6 in. to 1 ft. high. *Flowers*, very early in spring; large, handsome, deep sky-blue, numerous, continuing to bloom till the middle of summer; resembling those of *M. sylvatica* more than any other, but standing more apart from each other on the spike. *Leaves*, oblong-lanceolate, gradually pointed. Alps, near the Vogelberg.——Borders, the rock-garden, beds in the spring-garden, or naturalized here and there in copses, woods, or shrubberies, in any (not too cold or heavy) soil. In some moist districts it sows itself abundantly; and it may be readily increased by division and cuttings.

Myosotis palustris (*Forget-me-not*).—The well-known Forget-me-not; 6 to 12 in. high or more. *Flowers*, all the summer, in one-sided racemes, either simple or forked; corolla rather large, bright blue with a yellow throat, limb flat, longer than the tube, calyces 5-parted, not below the middle, obtuse, spreading, on pedicels about twice their length. *Leaves*, smooth or hairy, obovate-lance-shaped, obtuse; stems creeping at base. Common in wet ditches, and by the sides of streams and canals throughout Britain.——Although a common wild plant, this well deserves a place in the garden, among shrubs in peat beds, or even as edgings, or used as a carpet beneath taller subjects; or in small beds or borders in moist soil. Division.

Myosotis sylvatica (*Wood Forget-me-not*). — Now popular in consequence of being used for flower-beds in spring; 1 ft. high. *Flowers*, in spring and early summer; blue, with yellow throat, as large as those of *M. palustris*, in long loose racemes; limb of corolla spreading out flat, longer than the tube; calyx rather shorter than pedicels, cut nearly to the base into narrow segments. *Leaves*, oblong-lanceolate, bluntish, clothed with soft hairs. There is a white, a rose-coloured, and a striped variety. Europe, and in the North of England and Scotland. ——In beds in the flower-garden in spring, and should be grown in a wild state abundantly by wood-walks in copses, etc. It sows itself freely in woods; for garden-use it should be sown in beds in August every year.

Myrrhis odorata (*Sweet Cicely*).—A graceful-looking plant with a peculiar but grateful odour, and with sweet-tasted stems; 2 to 3 ft. high. *Flowers*, in spring and early summer; white, in terminal compound umbels; involucre wanting; leaves of involucels lance-shaped, finely ciliated. *Fruit* from ½ to nearly an inch long, with 5 very prominent ribs, often clothed with minute stiff hairs. *Leaves*, rather villous beneath, ternately decompound; leaflets deeply divided and toothed. Root fusiform. Britain and several parts of Middle and Southern Europe.——By wood-walks, and in semi-wild places in any soil, or occasionally used among fine-leaved perennials. Division.

Narcissus bicolor (*Two-coloured Daffodil*).—Somewhat like the Common Daffodil, but handsomer and distinguished from it by having the tube of the flower of the same length as the ovary, and the limb of the petal of a pure white, expanding nearly horizontally, the crown being of a handsome yellow, with 6 very short lobes, notched at the edges, and swollen at the base. *Flowers*, in early spring. Southern Europe, chiefly in the Pyrenees.——Borders, fringes of shrubberies, and naturalization, in grassy places. Division.

Narcissus Bulbocodium (*Hoop-petti-coat Narcissus*).—A very beautiful and distinct Daffodil, now too seldom in our gardens; 4 to 10 in. high. *Flowers*, in spring; 1 on each stem; rich golden yellow, with the crown or cup usually erect, gradually and regularly widening from the base to the margin and longer than the divisions. *Leaves*, erect, half round, dark green, and somewhat rushy-looking, in tufts. Native of Southern France, Spain, and Portugal. There are two varieties, viz., *lobulatus* and *serotinus*. ——On sunny spots in the rock-garden, or warm borders devoted to choice hardy flowers. It is not sufficiently plentiful, or I should recommend it to be naturalized on snug banks in the pleasure-ground. It should always have well-drained and free sandy soil. Division.

Narcissus incomparabilis (*Incomparable Daffodil*).—A fine showy kind, most frequently seen in the double form, in which it is often called "butter and eggs;" 12 to 16 in. high. *Flowers*, in spring; solitary, slightly fragrant; outer divisions spreading, slightly overlapping, 1 in. long, ½ or ¾ in. broad, usually of a paler hue than the crown, which is orange yellow, about ¼ in. deep and ¾ in. wide, nearly erect, much plaited at the throat, and furnished with 6 deep imbricated lobes. *Leaves*, 3 or 4 to each flower-stem, about 1 ft. long and ¼ in. broad, bluntly keeled, greyish. Bulb pear-shaped, 1 to 1½ in. thick, with light brown coats. Southern Europe.—— Borders, fringes of shrubberies, and naturalized by wood-walks in ordinary soil. Division.

Narcissus Jonquilla (*Jonquille*).—A favourite old plant, slenderer and more delicate than the other garden kinds, and with blooms almost as sweet as orange-blossoms ; 9 to 15 in. high. *Flowers*, in spring; 2 to 6 on a stem; outer divisions a bright yellow, spreading horizontally when fully expanded, ⅜ in. to ½ in. long, slightly imbricated, lance - shaped, broader towards the end and pointed ; crown saucer-shaped, not more than a line deep, about the same colour as the outer divisions, the edge faintly and bluntly notched, about ⅜ in. across. *Leaves*, 1 to 2 to each flower-stem, deep glossy green, 8 to 12 in. long, rush-like, semi-cylindrical, channelled down the face, about a line in thickness. *Bulb* roundish, pear-shaped, but variable, less than 1 in. thick. There is a variety with double flowers. Native of S. Europe.——On warm sunny borders, and sheltered nooks in the rock-garden ; always in sandy and thoroughly drained soil. Division.

Narcissus juncifolius (*Rush-leaved Daffodil*).—A beautiful little Daffodil, recently introduced into cultivation ; about 6 in. high. *Flowers*, in spring ; outer divisions bright yellow, spreading ⅜ to ½ in. long, ¼ in. broad, pointed, overlapping each other ; crown same colour as divisions, narrowing towards the base, slightly notched, about ¼ in. deep, and nearly ½ in. across the mouth ; one, two, rarely three, to a stem. *Leaves*, 3 to 4 to each flower-stem, of a bright green, quite cylindrical and rush-like in shape, 4 to 6 in. long. *Bulb* egg-shaped, about ¼ in. thick. Native of Spain and the South of France.——Level spots in the rock-garden in very sandy soil, also in select borders; or for naturalization in very bare and rocky places, when sufficiently plen-

tiful to be spared for this purpose. Division.

Narcissus maximus (*Golden Daffodil*).—A noble, hardy plant, by some not considered a species, but the finest variety of the Common Daffodil ; 12 to 16 in. high. *Flowers*, late in spring ; of a very bright golden-yellow, with spreading, somewhat wavy, outer divisions ; crown very large and deep, with deeply - notched spreading lobes, uniform in colour with the outer divisions. *Leaves*, nearly flat. *Bulb* of medium size, elongated pear-shaped, of a light brown colour. Native of S. Europe and some parts of France.——Borders, fringes of shrubberies, and naturalization on grassy slopes and in glades in half-wild places, in ordinary soil. Division.

Narcissus minor (*Least Daffodil*).— A most interesting and diminutive kind ; 4 to 6 in. high. *Flowers*, in spring; outer divisions sulphur-yellow; crown orange-yellow, bell - shaped, with 6-toothed, fringed lobes, much longer than the outer divisions, one bloom on each stem. *Leaves*, erect, greyish, strap - shaped, about 4 in. long. *Bulb* very small, round, dark-brown, with thin coats. Native of the Pyrenees and other parts of Spain and Portugal. —— Select borders among dwarf plants, or among like subjects in level parts of the rock-garden, always in fine, sandy, well-drained soil. In consequence of its dwarfness, it is better to allow a carpet of some very diminutive plant, like the Lawn Pearlwort, or *Sedum glaucum*, to spread over the spot where it grows. This will prevent the flowers from being soiled by earthy splashings. Division.

Narcissus odorus (*Large Jonquille*). —A fragrant, beautiful, and distinct Daffodil, 12 to 15 in. high. *Flowers*, in spring, sweet-scented ; outer divisions bright yellow, oblong - lance-shaped, acute, very slightly paler than the crown, which is about ½ in. deep, slightly plaited; usually two blooms on a stem. *Leaves*, 3 to 4 to each stem, nearly 1 ft. long; not flat or strap-shaped like most of the common kinds, but concave on the face and convex on the back, and usually bright green. *Bulb* egg-shaped, generally more than 1 in. thick. Native of S. France, Spain, Italy, and Dalmatia. —— Borders, fringes of beds of shrubs, the rougher parts of the rock-garden, in sandy well-drained soil. Also suitable for naturalization on sunny sheltered banks in half-wild places. Division.

Narcissus poeticus (*Poet's Narcissus*). — A beautiful and well-known garden flower, sold abundantly in the streets of London in May; 12 to 16 in. high. *Flowers*, late in spring and in early summer; one, rarely two, blooms to a stem; outer divisions pure white, broadest towards the point, slightly overlapping each other; crown about a line deep, saucer-shaped, very much crisped, with a bright scarlet edge. *Leaves*, flat, with a blunt keel, greyish, of about the same length as the flower-stem. *Bulb* egg-shaped, more than 1 in. thick when well grown. Southern Europe, from France to Greece. *N. angustifolia*, and one or two other kinds resemble this; *N. poetarum* is the larger variety. —— Suitable for borders, fringes of shrubberies, and any position in which the Common Daffodil will grow, in almost any soil. This plant deserves to be abundantly naturalized in grassy places, by wood-walks, and on sunny banks and slopes where the grass is not mown till late in summer, or not at all. Division.

Narcissus tenuior (*Slender Narcissus*). — A slender species, about 8 in. high. *Flowers*, late in spring; 1¼ in. across, light yellow, usually in pairs, with a shallow deep orange cup; tube 1 in. long. *Leaves*, few, grass-like, about 7 in. long. Native country unknown. —— Rockwork and front margin of borders, in sandy soil. Division.

Narcissus tortuosus (*Twisted Daffodil*). — A graceful, distinct kind; 9 to 12 in. high. *Flowers*, early in spring; external divisions, whitish, nearly 1 in. broad, and twisted or wavy; crown lemon-colour, fading late and imperfectly to sulphur white, and longer than the exterior divisions. In other respects it does not differ much from *N. bicolor*. The Pyrenees. —— Borders and naturalization on slopes, banks, etc., in light deep soil. Division.

Narcissus triandrus (*Three-stamened N.*). — A charming kind; from 6 to 9 in. high. *Flowers*, late in spring; solitary or in pairs, pale yellow, with a bell-shaped cup of the same colour, and reflexed petals. *Stem* tolerably thick. *Leaves*, few, grass-like, 8 to 10 in. in length. Portugal. —— Rockwork and front margin of mixed borders, in well-drained sandy soil. Division.

Nepeta Mussini (*Bedding N.*) — A somewhat downy plant, of a whitish-green colour, and having a powerful aromatic odour; about 1 ft. high. *Flowers*, in summer; small, of an azure blue, the lower lip being of a deeper shade, in a long loose spike or cluster; calyx velvety, and tinged with violet. *Leaves*, opposite, stalked, oval-obtuse, crenate. Caucasus. —— A very free and vigorous plant, in any soil. It is best suited for naturalization in rough places, not being quite ornamental enough for the choice border, though much used in bedding. Division.

Nertera depressa (*Fruiting Duckweed*). — A minute plant, resembling a duckweed in the aspect of its leaves, but with numbers of small round orange fruit. *Flowers*, in summer; white, very small and inconspicuous, sessile, solitary in the axils of the leaves, succeeded by a profusion of bright red berries. *Leaves*, broadly ovate, blunt or acute, from ¼ to ½ in. long, rather fleshy; stems 4-angled, tufted, creeping and rooting, 6 to 12 in. long. New Zealand, and the Andes of South America. —— The rock-garden in moist spots, or in pans. Division.

Nierembergia frutescens (*Tall N.*) —A very elegant plant, naturally of somewhat shrubby habit, but with us usually cut down by frosts in winter; 12 to 18 in. high. *Flowers*, in early summer; delicate blue shading to white at the edges, about 1 in. across when well-grown, densely produced on the much-branched, flax-like stems. *Leaves*, linear, 1½ to 2 in. long. Easily distinguished from all other cultivated species by its tall and half-shrubby habit. Chili.——On warm borders or banks, or lower parts of the flanks of the rock-garden, in perfectly-drained, light, rich soil. Very quickly increased by cuttings put in a gentle hot-bed.

Nierembergia rivularis (*White Cup*). —A handsome plant, with slender, smooth, creeping, rooting stems, much branched and matted; 4 or 5 in. high. *Flowers*, in July; bell-shaped, white, with a yellowish, and sometimes a rosy tinge; corolla about 1 in. across with 5 broadly-obtuse, spreading lobes, and a very slender tube, from 1 in. to 2½ in. long; calyx ¼ to ¾ in. long, cylindrical, with 5 slightly spreading, oblong-lanceolate, pointed lobes. *Leaves*, very variable in size, 1 to 3 in. long, including the stalk, which is long and slender; blade of leaf oblong or oblong-spoon-shaped, obtuse, membranous, almost without nerves. La Plata.——The rock-garden, and the margins of borders, in moist, sandy loam. Division.

Nuphar advena (*Yellow American Water-lily*). — *Nymphæa advena*. — A noble aquatic plant, with heart-shaped leaves, rising considerably above the surface of the water. *Flowers*, in summer; yellow, with red anthers, large, on round stalks, rising above the surface of the water; petals numerous, small, never exceeding the stamens; calyx of 6 sepals, purple within, and green without. *Leaves*, erect, heart-shaped-oblong, more narrowed towards the top than those of *N. lutea*, on half-round stalks. Native of lakes, ponds, and ditches, from Canada to Carolina. —— Lakes and ponds, associated with our White and Yellow Water-lilies, and other fine aquatic plants. Division.

Nuphar Kalmiana (*Small Yellow Water-lily*). — A small-flowered species. *Flowers*, in summer; yellow, floating. *Leaves*, heart-shaped, slightly margined; lobes nearly meeting; leaf-stalks almost round; calyx with 5 divisions. N. America. —— Quiet clean bays in lakes or ponds, or fountain basins. Division.

Nuphar lutea (*Common Yellow Water-lily*).— A well-known inhabitant of our rivers and ponds. *Flowers*, nearly all the summer; yellow, on stalks rising a little above the surface, much smaller and less expanding than those of the White Water-lily, emitting a brandy-like scent; petals very numerous; sepals 5, roundish, blunt, erect, about twice the length of the petals. *Leaves*, oval or heart-shaped, smooth, flat, turning up a little at the margins, 8 to 12 in. across, on smooth 3-sided stalks. *N. pumila* is a variety smaller in all its parts, found in a few localities in Scotland. Europe and Britain in slow streams, pools, and ditches.——Lakes, ponds, or streams, associated with the White Lily, *Villarsia*, and other good aquatic plants. Division.

Nuttallia pedata (*Bird's-foot-leaved N.*)—An erect, bushy, glabrous, branching plant; 2 to 4 ft. high. *Flowers*, late in summer; handsome reddish-violet with a white centre, in panicles. *Leaves*, alternate, laciniately-pedate, toothed, upper ones trifid. North America.——By wood-walks, margins of shrubberies, or naturalization, in ordinary soil. Division, or seed.

Nymphæa alba (*White Water-lily*).—One of the most beautiful of all hardy plants. *Flowers*, in summer; white, scentless, lying on the surface of the water, 4 to 6 in. across; sepals 4, smaller than the outer petals, about 2 in. long and 1 in. wide, smooth, yellowish-green outside, white within; petals from 16 to 24, in two or three rows, the outer ones having a green streak along the back. *Leaves*, deeply heart-shaped, entire, smooth, larger than those of the Yellow Water-lily; stalks round. Europe.——In lakes, ponds, or streams. It looks much better as an isolated plant or group than when the whole surface of the water is covered densely with its crowded leaves, as is not unfrequently the case. Division.

Nymphæa odorata (*Sweet-scented Water-lily*). — A fine sweet-scented kind. *Flowers*, in summer; white, nearly 6 in. across when fully expanded, very sweet-scented, opening at early morn and closing in the afternoon; petals blunt. *Leaves*, roundish, entire, cut at the base into blunt spreading lobes, 6 to 9 in. across, notched at the apex. This species varies with reddish or pink-tinged flowers. *N. minor* is a variety with much smaller leaves and flowers. In ponds, North America.——In ponds, fountain basins, and slow - flowing waters. Division.

Œnothera fruticosa (*Sundrops*).— One of the most ornamental species, 1 to 3 ft. high. *Flowers*, in summer; pale yellow, scarcely fragrant, erect before expanding; petals broadly obcordate; corymb peduncled, naked below, lengthened in fruit; tube of the calyx much longer than the ovary. *Leaves*, lance-shaped, or oblong-lance-shaped, unevenly toothed, sessile or slightly stalked; stem simple, or branching above, erect, purplish, stiff but not shrubby. *Œ. serotina* is a variety having sessile leafy corymbs. North America.——Borders, margins of shrubberies, or naturalization in thin woods or copses, in sandy loam. Division and seed.

Œnothera Jamesii (*James's Œ.*)—A vigorous and showy species about 3 ft. high with a decumbent stem. *Flowers*, in summer; very large, fine yellow, in panicles at the ends of the branches; petals not much longer than the drooping stamens. *Leaves*, oblong-lance-shaped, acute, dentate. Canada, by river-sides.——Borders, in sandy loam. Seed or division.

Œnothera linearis (*Narrow-leaved Œ.*)—A neat kind, 10 to 15 in. high or sometimes more. *Flowers*, in summer; yellow, somewhat corymbose, on the tops of the branches, scarcely fragrant, erect before expansion, unchanged in fading; tube of the calyx slender, longer than the ovary but scarcely exceeding the segments. *Leaves*, linear or narrowly-lance-shaped, rather blunt, remotely toothed or entire, sometimes linear-oblong, tapering at the base, and slightly stalked; stem slender, often branched. N. America.——Borders, margins of shrubberies, and bare banks, in sandy loam. Division.

Œnothera marginata (*Large Evening Primrose*). — A magnificent kind; 9 to 12 in. high. *Flowers*, in summer; very large and handsome, whitish turning to rose-colour, deliciously fragrant; petals large; tube of the calyx longer than the segments. *Leaves*, lance-shaped, on long stalks, deeply jagged or toothed towards the base, about the length of the calyx-tube. North America.——Borders, beds, and the rock-garden, in light rich soil. Seed.

Œnothera missouriensis (*Missouri Œ.*)—*Œnothera macrocarpa.*—A handsome prostrate species, 9 to 12 in. high. *Flowers*, in summer; light yellow, with orange veins, axillary, very large; corolla 4 to 6 in. across; petals, roundish-fan-shaped; tube of the calyx often more than 4 in. long. *Leaves*, thick, lance-shaped, acute, tapering into a short stalk, greyish when young, obscurely toothed. Missouri, on dry hills, and on the Canadian River. —— Borders, or rockwork, in sandy loam. Seed, division, or cuttings.

Œnothera riparia (*Rock Evening Primrose*).—A showy useful kind, 2 to 3 ft. high. *Flowers*, in summer; large, yellow,in a somewhat leafy lengthened raceme; scarcely fragrant, erect before expansion, unchanged in fading; petals slightly obcordate. *Leaves*, linear-lance-shaped, remotely toothed or entire, rather thick, mostly blunt, 2 to 4 in. long, and pubescent along the midrib and margins; stems slender, often twiggy, branched. North America.——Borders, or margins of shrubberies, in ordinary soil. Division or seed.

Œnothera speciosa (*Tall White Evening Primrose*).—A very distinct, handsome, erect-growing kind, varying from 6 in. to 2 ft. high. *Flowers*, in summer; white, large, fragrant, drooping before expansion, turning to rose when fading; in a lengthened spike. *Leaves*, lance-shaped or oblong-lance-shaped, tapering at the base; root- and lower stem-leaves twice divided or pinnately toothed near the base, the uppermost ones denticulate or remotely toothed, varying considerably in the degree of division, as well as in the pubescence; stems often slightly woody at the base, erect or ascending, branching. South parts of North America.——Borders, in sandy soil. Division and seed.

Œnothera taraxacifolia (*Dandelion-leaved Œ.*)—A popular and beautiful prostrate plant. *Flowers*, in summer; large, white, changing to red when fading; tube very long, petals large, obovate, entire, 5-nerved; tube of calyx cylindrical, widened at the apex. *Leaves*, pubescent, alternate, pinnatifid, sinuately toothed, but entire at the apex; stem lengthened, branched, prostrate. Chili.——Borders,in good soil. Some of this should be annually raised from seed, as it is useful for surfacing beds containing larger subjects.

Omphalodes verna (*Creeping Forget-me-not*). — Resembling a handsome Forget-me-not, but with creeping shoots; 6 in. high. *Flowers*, in early spring; blue, in shape like those of Borage, but smaller, about ¼ in. across, in few-flowered racemes, on erect, simple, smooth stems emitting stolons at their base. *Leaves*, on long slender stalks, bright green; root-leaves heart-shaped; stem - leaves broad - lance-shaped, or oval; rhizome creeping underground. Southern Europe, in woods.——Naturalized in woods and shrubberies, and also in borders or on rockwork, in sandy loam. Division.

Omphalodes Luciliæ (*Rock O.*)—An exquisite perennial, with glaucous leaves; 4 to 6 in. high. *Flowers*, in summer; broadly-funnel-shaped, fine lilac-blue, nearly ¼ in. across; twice, or more than twice, as large as those of *O. verna*. *Leaves*, oblong-obtuse, those of the root narrowed into a long footstalk, those of the stem sessile, the upper ones ovate. Asia Minor. ——The rock-garden, in warm spots, in fine sandy soil, and in beds of dwarf shrubs, etc. Seed and division.

Onobrychis montana (*Mountain O.*) —A pleasing, almost decumbent, rock-plant; 6 to 12 in. high. *Flowers*, in summer; purplish-rose-coloured, in short compact heads; keel longer than the standard; wings shorter than the calyx; back of the pod toothed, sides wrinkled, downy. *Leaflets*, lanceolate-wedge-shaped, obtuse, mucronate, smooth; stipules united. Elevated pastures of the Alps and Pyrenees.——The rock-garden, and the margins of the mixed border, in sandy loam. Division and seed.

Ononis arvensis (*Hairy Rest-harrow*).—A variable perennial, sometimes 1 ft. or 18 in. high, but generally a low, spreading, much-branched undershrub, thinly clothed with soft hairs, more or less glutinous. *Flowers*, in summer and autumn; pink, the upper ones deeper, either solitary on short axillary stalks, or forming a short leafy raceme; corolla rather longer than the calyx. *Leaves*, pinnately trifoliate; leaflets oblong, side ones smallest; branches often ending in a thorn. There is a variety smoother, more thorny and erect, sometimes called *O. campestris;* and *O. arvensis alba* is a white variety. Very common in Britain and throughout Europe. —— The white variety is a pretty border plant, and the other kinds, if too common in some parts to permit of their garden use, look very pretty naturalized in rough places. Division or seed.

Ononis fruticosa (*Shrubby Rest-harrow*).—A very ornamental low shrub, 1 to 2 ft. high. *Flowers*, in early summer; purple, nodding, mostly on 3-flowered stalks, forming a handsome raceme; calyx 5-parted; segments equal, linear. *Leaves*, trifoliate; leaflets stalkless, smooth, lance-shaped, shining, unequally serrated. Hills and mountains in Southern Europe. —— Beds of dwarf shrubs, isolated specimens on grass, or on the lower and rougher parts of the rock-garden. Seed.

Ononis Natrix (*Ram Rest-harrow*).-- A downy viscid plant, exhaling an unmistakeably rammish odour; about 20 in. high. *Flowers*, in summer, and sometimes a second time in autumn; yellow, veined with red; standard almost round, notched at the top; keel elongated, as long as the wings; calyx bell-shaped, irregular, with 5 divisions, of which the lower one is the largest. *Leaves*, alternate, trifoliate, with oval-oblong or oboval toothed leaflets; the upper leaves sometimes simple, all accompanied with lanceolate-acute stipules. South of Europe.——Banks and borders, in sandy soil. Division or seed.

Ononis rotundifolia (*Round-leaved Rest-harrow*).—A somewhat shrubby species, readily distinguished by its roundish leaflets; 12 to 20 in. high. *Flowers*, in early summer; rose-coloured, with the standard veined with crimson, usually in pairs, in the axils of the upper leaves. *Leaves*, trifoliate; leaflets toothed, margined with triangular teeth, and thickly clothed with gland-tipped, slightly viscid hairs. The Pyrenees and Alps of Europe.——Margins of shrubberies, and naturalized, in sandy soil. Seed and division.

Ononis viscosa (*Clammy Ononis*). A handsome perennial with downy-viscid stems from 15 in. to 3 ft. high. *Flowers*, in summer; yellow, the back of the standard striped with purple, numerous, in long panicled spikes. *Leaves*, of the lower part of the plant trifoliate, the middle leaflet larger than the others; upper leaves simple, ovate, toothed, all with pointed stipules. South of France.——The rock-garden or border, in ordinary free soil. Described as an annual plant, but is certainly perennial in some soils. Division or seed.

Onosma taurica (*Golden Drop*).— A fine evergreen perennial, quite distinct in appearance from anything else in cultivation; 6 to 8 in. high. *Flowers*, in spring and early summer; fine yellow, arranged in clustering cymes; corolla wide above, twice as long as the calyx. *Leaves*, linear-lance-shaped, acute, hispid, rolled back at the edges. Caucasus.——Borders and the rock-garden, in warm positions and in well-drained sandy loam. Seed and cuttings.

Ophiopogon spicatus (*Spiked Snake's Beard*).—A fibrous-rooted herbaceous perennial, about 1½ ft. high. *Flowers*, late in summer and in autumn; very numerous, small, lilac; in spikes from 2 to 5 in. long, with a tendency to branch at the end. *Leaves*, flat, thin, and furrowed underneath, about 2 ft. long, by ⅙ in. broad. China.——Borders or margins of shrubberies, in sandy loam. Scarcely ornamental. Division.

Ophrys apifera (*Bee Orchis*).—An interesting native Orchid, the bloom of which resembles the body of a bee; 6 in. to 1 ft. or more high. *Flowers*, in early summer; few, large, rather distant; sepals whitish, tinged with purple; lip velvety-brown with yellow markings, convex, bearing some resemblance to a bee. *Leaves*, few, glaucous near the ground. Native of various parts of England and Ireland, on calcareous soils.——This interesting plant may be grown without difficulty in the rock-garden or border, or in a small bed devoted to Orchids in calcareous well-drained soil. The only way we can add to the stock in our gardens is by gathering the plant in a wild state, taking up the roots very carefully.

Ophrys muscifera (*Fly Orchis*).—Smaller than the Bee Orchis, 1 ft. high. *Flowers*, in early summer; petals very narrow, purple; sepals green; lip brownish-purple, with a somewhat square, bluish, central spot. *Leaves*, elliptical, 2 to 5 in. long;

fewer and narrower at the base than those of any other species. Native of damp calcareous thickets and pastures in England and Ireland.——Easily grown with the treatment advised for the preceding kind.

Opuntia Rafinesquiana (*Hardy O.*)—A dwarf spreading *Cactus*, forming clusters of thick, ovate, very green stems, each 3 or 4 in. long, and about 3 in. broad, studded with small tufts of minute, sharp-pointed, reddish, hair-like spines. *Flowers*, in summer; bright sulphur-yellow. *Fruit* said to be edible "like a gooseberry." North America.——This has been proved hardy in England. Its most appropriate positions are on dry banks or borders, rough rock-work, old walls, or ruins. Division and cuttings.

Orchis foliosa (*Leafy O.*) — A showy handsome Orchid, from 1½ to 2½ ft. high. *Flowers*, in May; numerous, purple, in an ovate or oblong-ovate spike, about 9 in. long and 3 in. broad; sepals erect, ovate, obtuse, palish-purple; petals similar in form, but narrower and smaller, nearly erect, dark purple; lip pendent, very broad, roundly-wedge-shaped, 3-lobed (middle lobe smallest), purple, with darker blotches of same colour; spur much shorter than the lip; bracts leafy, generally shorter than the flowers. *Leaves*, unspotted, oblong, lower ones blunt. Madeira, on rocky banks.——The rock-garden, in sheltered nooks in deep, light soil, or grown in pots, in which way it has been frequently shown in London.

Orchis latifolia (*Marsh O.*)—A very ornamental native kind; 1 to 1½ ft. high. *Flowers*, in summer; sepals dull purplish-crimson; lip of the same colour, paler at the base, and spotted and lined purple; the middle lobe usually not longer than the lateral ones. *Leaves*, oblong-elliptical, broadest near the middle, usually spotted with purplish-black. Bogs and marshes in most parts of Great Britain and Ireland. There is a fine large variety recently introduced into cultivation. —— The bog-bed, associated with *Cypripedium spectabile*, and like plants. This may be increased by division of established tufts.

Orchis laxiflora (*Guernsey O.*)—A showy-flowered species, 1 to 3 ft. high. *Flowers*, in summer; of a very rich crimson-purple, in a very lax spike 3 to 9 in. long; bracts 3- to 5-nerved, generally tinged with crimson. *Leaves*, lance-shaped, or linear-lance-shaped, 3 to 6 in. long, not collected in a radical rosette, but distributed over the stem. Root-knobs globular, undivided, from the size of a blackcurrant to that of a damson plum. Channel Islands, in meadows and bogs.——The rock-garden in a moist spot, or the artificial bog; it may also be naturalized. Division.

Orchis maculata (*Spotted Hand O.*) — A delicately-coloured native species; 1 to 1½ ft. high. *Flowers*, in summer; in an ovate spike, afterwards elongated, pale purple, more or less streaked with a darker hue. *Lip* usually flat, deeply 3-lobed; lateral lobes rounded; middle lobe longer and narrower. *Leaves*, usually spotted with purple; lower ones blunt or rarely acute, broadest towards their top; upper ones linear-lanceolate, resembling bracts. Europe and Britain.——This plant does thoroughly well if carefully placed in moist deep loam, in a somewhat shady border, forming large and very handsome tufts. It may also be grown with the other hardy Orchids in almost any position. Division.

Ornithogalum narbonnense (*Narbonne O.*)—*Star of Bethlehem.*—A handsome bulbous plant; 12 to 16 in. high. *Flowers*, early in summer; milk-white, marked with a narrow green stripe on the outside of each petal, very numerous, arranged in a cluster 4 to 8 in. long, lax at the base and dense at the top. *Leaves*, broadly-linear or sword-shaped, deeply channelled, longer than the flower-stem. *Bulb*, egg-shaped. S. Europe, N. Africa, and the Caucasus.——Borders, or naturalization in sandy soil. Division.

Ornithogalum pyramidale (*Tall Star of Bethlehem*).—A tall and noble kind; 1½ to 2 ft. high. *Flowers*, in summer; of a pure white, marked with a green stripe on the back of each petal, accompanied with coloured bracts, and arranged in a conical cluster, 6 to 8 in. long. *Leaves*, linear, flat, of a soft tissue, generally withering before the plant has ceased to flower. *Bulb* tolerably large, pear-shaped, slightly flattened, somewhat resembling a Hyacinth-bulb. Native of the South of Europe.——Although this will grow in almost any soil, its spikes will be very much finer in deep, rich loam. It is a fine border-bulb, and might be planted here and there in shrubberies with advantage. Division.

Ornithogalum umbellatum (*Star of Bethlehem*).—A popular cottage-garden plant; 4 to 12 in. high. *Flowers*, early in summer; of a satiny white on the inside, and green striped with white without, arranged in an umbel on long stalks. *Leaves*, broadly-linear, channelled, with a whitish streak through the middle, usually withering at the time of flowering. *Bulb*, under the medium size, white, pear-shaped, rather irregular in figure. South Europe, North Africa, and the Caucasus.——The flowers of this species exhibit the peculiarity of opening about 11 o'clock, a.m., and closing about 3 o'clock p.m., whence the French popular name of *Dame d'onze heures*. Borders, in any soil. Division.

Orobus aurantius (*Orange O.*)—From 18 in. to 2 ft. high. *Flowers*, early in summer; orange-yellow; peduncles shorter than the leaves; calyx hairy, with 5 teeth, 2 very short, the lower one very long. *Leaves*, of 4 or 5 pairs of broadly-oval pointed leaflets, with divergent veins. *Stems* angular. Iberia. —— Borders, in ordinary soil. Division.

Orobus atropurpureus (*Dark-purple O.*)—A Vetch-like herb; 1 to 1½ ft. high. *Flowers*, in early summer; purple, drooping; stalks many-flowered, 1-sided, forming a dense raceme at the top; corolla lengthened; teeth of calyx short, nearly equal, blunt. *Leaves*, with one or several pairs of smooth, narrow, acute leaflets; stipules semi-arrow-shaped, very narrow, awned; stems nearly simple, striped. Mediterranean region.——Borders, in sandy loam. Division or seed.

Orobus cyaneus (*Blue Bitter Vetch*). —*Platystylis cyaneus* — A handsome dwarf Vetch-like herb; 6 to 12 in. high. *Flowers*, in spring; blue when first opening, changing to purple, large, handsome; stalks few-flowered; segments of calyx lance-shaped, hardly as long as the tube; style very broad, a character which Sweet thought sufficient to separate it from the genus *Orobus*. *Leaves*, composed of 2 or 3 pairs of closely-set, narrowly lance-shaped, acute leaflets; stem simple, striped. Caucasus. —— The rock-garden and borders, in deep and well-drained sandy loam. Division and seed.

Orobus lathyroides (*Lathyrus-like O.*) —A showy species with broad, smooth leaflets, and black roots; 1 ft. to 1½ ft. high. *Flowers*, early in summer; fine blue, small, numerous, in close spikes, 3 or 4 in number, springing from the axils of the upper leaves; teeth of calyx shorter than the tube. *Leaves*, composed of two leaflets, which are nearly 2 in. long and 1 in. across, oval-lanceolate, acute, with straggling nerves; stipules half-arrow-shaped, toothed at the base. *Stem* rigid, bent near the top, slightly winged, not branching. Siberia.——Borders, in ordinary soil. Division and seed.

Orobus luteus (*Yellow O.*) — A good but not showy kind, 1 to 1½ ft. high. *Flowers*, early in summer; yellowish, the back of the standard purplish-brown, in axillary clusters of from 6 to 8 blooms. *Leaves*, usually of 4 or 5 pairs of oval, pointed leaflets, which are about 1½ in. long, and nearly ½ in. broad; stipules large, half-arrow-shaped, toothed near the base. Siberia. —— Borders and naturalization in ordinary soil. Division or seed.

Orobus variegatus (*Variegated Bitter Vetch*).—An attractive perennial, with two firm and opposite wings on its wiry, zigzag stems, which ascend to about 1 ft. in height. *Flowers*, in early summer; small, beautifully variegated, the standard a fine rose with a network of purplish-crimson veins, the points of the side petals being blue; segments of calyx narrow, acute, as long as the tube. *Leaves*, with 2 or 3 pairs of lance-shaped leaflets, with almost parallel nerves; stipules ovate, entire, acute, much smaller than the leaflets. Southern Italy and Corsica.——Borders, in ordinary garden soil. Division and seed.

Orobus vernus (*Spring Bitter Vetch*). —The most beautiful of its family at present known to us; 10 in. to 1¼ ft. high. *Flowers*, in spring; purple and blue, with red veins, the keel tinted with green, the whole changing to blue; freely produced on one-sided, nodding stalks, shorter than the leaves; segments of the calyx broad, hardly as long as the tube, lower one longest. *Leaves*, with 2 or 3 pairs of shining ovate leaflets; stipules semi-arrow-shaped, entire; stems zigzag. Roots black; *O. flaccidus* is a variety with very narrow flaccid leaflets. Southern and Central Europe.—— Borders, fringes of shrubberies, etc., in any soil, but best in a deep, rich, and moist loam. It thrives perfectly either in exposed, shady, or half-shady places, and is eminently suitable for naturalization in almost any position. Division and seed.

Othonna cheirifolia (*Barbary Ragwort*).—A low-spreading evergreen perennial, with pleasing, glaucous foliage; 8 to 12 in. high. *Flowers*, in early summer; rich yellow, about 1½ in. across, on thick succulent stalks, at the ends of the branches; rays sharp-pointed, rather longer than the calyx, which is cut equally into eight segments. *Leaves*, greyish, thick, lance-shaped, 3-nerved, stalkless, narrow at the base, broad and rounded at the apex; stems half-shrubby, spreading. N. Africa.—— Borders and rocky banks, in any soil. In cold soils it rarely flowers, in warm loams it does so abundantly. Division or cuttings.

Ourisia coccinea (*Scarlet O.*)—A handsome creeping plant, with flower-stems from 6 to 8 in. high. *Flowers*, in summer; scarlet, axillary, pendent, in panicled clusters. *Leaves*, almost all radical, oval or oblong, notched. Chili.—— Rockwork, in half-shady positions, in moist, well-drained, peaty soil. Division.

Oxalis atropurpurea (*Hort.*) (*Purple-leaved O.*)—A densely-tufted, dark-leaved plant; 3 in. high. *Flowers*, in summer; small, golden-yellow, in an umbel. *Leaves*, of 3 obcordate leaflets, purplish. South Europe.—— Edgings, tufts, in borders, and as a bedding plant, best in light, sandy soil. Seed and division.

Oxalis Bowiei (*Bowie's Wood Sorrel*). —A brilliant dwarf bulbous perennial 6 to 10 in. high. *Flowers*, in autumn; fine rose-red, yellowish at the base inside; large and handsome, in umbels on peduncles about equal in length to the leaves. *Leaves*, of 3 obtuse leaflets,

almost sessile, handsome green above, slightly pubescent underneath, ciliated. Cape of Good Hope.——Warm flanks of the rock-garden or on sunny borders. In cold soils this seldom or never flowers; on warm well-drained and very sandy ones it does so abundantly, and where this is the case it may be used with effect as an edging-plant round beds of autumn-blooming plants. Division.

Oxalis floribunda (*Many-flowered O.*) —A tufted, abundantly-blooming kind. *Flowers*, in summer, continuously; rose-coloured, with dark veins; scape many-flowered; sepals obtuse, greyish, roundish-egg-shaped, concave at the apex, and hairy; root tuberous. There is a variety with white flowers. Native of South America.——Borders, in ordinary sandy soil. Division.

Oxalis lasiandra (*Woolly-stamened O.*)—A singular and handsome species, 9 to 18 in. high. *Flowers*, in summer; large, developed in succession, crimson, especially on the inside, the outside paler and finely pubescent, borne in umbels of about twenty flowers; sepals linear-elliptical, blunt, green, hairy, and marked with 4 orange-coloured lines, which meet at the apex. *Leaves*, all radical, digitate; leaflets 3 in. long, and 1 in. broad, 7 to 9 in number, on the top of the stem, oval-spoon-shaped, wavy at the edges, dark green, paler underneath, and spotted with crimson. Mexico. ——Borders, and the rock-garden, in warm, sandy soil. Division.

Oxalis Valdiviana (*Chilian Wood-sorrel*). — A handsome species, with a very branching stem, forming low tufts about 6 or 8 in. high. *Flowers*, in summer; deep yellow with a reddish streak particularly on the outside, very much resembling those of *Linum flavum*, in small clusters on the ends of very long flower-stalks. *Leaves*, trifoliate; leaflets heart-shaped reversed, with very rounded lobes. Chili.——This plant in good soils and favourable positions is perennial, but when exposed is liable to be cut off in winter. Rockwork, front margin of mixed border, or naturalization on bare banks, in well-drained sandy loam. Seed.

Oxytropis campestris (*Field O.*)—A dwarf stemless herb allied to the Milk Vetch, but differing by the keel having a fine point at its extremity; about 6 in. high. *Flowers*, in summer; yellowish tinged with purple, erect, in a dense, short, oblong spike; point of keel short, straight and erect; scapes hairy, about equal in length to the leaves. *Leaves*, with many pairs of lance-shaped leaflets, more numerous, narrower, and much less silky than those of the Purple Oxytrope. Europe, America, and in Scotland.——Borders and the rock-garden, in sandy loam. Seed and division.

Oxytropis fœtida (*Fetid O.*) — A dwarf Vetch-like viscous fetid plant, from 4 to 6 in. high. *Flowers*, in summer; large, lemon-coloured, in loose roundish-oval heads. *Leaves*, of 15 to 20 pairs of linear or oblong hairy leaflets with revolute edges. Mont Cenis.——Rockwork, and the margins of the mixed border, in rich loam. Seed or division.

Oxytropis pyrenaica (*Pyrenean O.*)—A handsome rock-plant 4 to 6 in. high. *Flowers*, in summer; sky-blue, erect, 9 to 15 in a short crowded raceme which afterwards becomes elongated-oval; bracts oblong; calyx very hairy, with short lance-shaped teeth. *Leaflets*, lance-shaped or oblong, pointed, somewhat concave, covered with long silky hairs; flower-stems set with stellate hairs. Central Pyrenees.—— The rock-garden, and among dwarf plants in borders, in sandy loam. Seed and division.

Oxytropis uralensis (*Purple O.*)—An elegant little perennial, resembling *O. campestris* in habit, but more densely clothed with soft silky hairs in every part; about 6 in. high. *Flowers*, in summer; bright purple, in dense round heads; point of keel same as in *O. campestris*. *Leaves*, with 10 to 15 pairs of ovate, acute leaflets, and an odd one. Scotland and other parts of Europe.——The rock-garden and borders, in moist sandy loam. Division and seed.

Pæonia albiflora (*White-flowered Pæony*).—A fine showy species, allied to *P. officinalis;* 1 to 3 ft. high. *Flowers*, in early summer; white; petals 8, large, oval, concave; carpels recurved, smooth. *Leaves*, ternate, alternate; leaflets 3-parted, ovate-lance-shaped, smooth, shining; differs chiefly from *P. officinalis* by its stems being nearly round, scarcely grooved, and more slender, and by its larger leaves. There are numerous varieties of this species. Native from Siberia to China.——Beds, borders, naturalization, groups on the grass in the picturesque garden, or isolated specimens in the same position, in rich, deep, sandy loam. Division.

Pæonia arietina (*Ram Pæony.*)—A distinct kind, 2 ft. high. *Flowers*, in summer; purple. *Leaves*, with three-lobed pinnatifid segments, decurrent, oval-oblong, flattish, hairy underneath. There are 2 varieties: *P. Andersonii* which has deep rose-coloured petals, less crisp than in the type; and *P. carnea* with flesh-coloured ragged-edged petals. Supposed to be a native of the East.——Borders or fringes of shrubberies, in deep rich soil. Division.

Pæonia edulis (*Edible P.*)—A very ornamental species, 2½ to 3¼ ft. high. *Flowers*, in May and June; rosy-flesh-colour in the bud, pure white when expanded, 1 to 7 on each stem, the terminal one being the largest; fragrant with a rose-like odour; calyx with 6 divisions, the 3 interior ones larger than the others, entire or notched; the outer one ending in a leafy point. *Leaves*, alternate, ternate, or biternate, with irregular division, plane or concave, oval-lanceolate, of a deep glistening green on the upper side; stems often tinged with violet, slightly branching above. There are many varieties of this species. China.——The same positions and treatment as for *P. albiflora*.

Pæonia lobata (*Lobed P.*)—A compact kind, 20 in. to 2 ft. high. *Flowers*, in May; deep rose, handsome. *Leaves*, numerous; segments nearly linear, smooth, decurrent, pinnate, three-lobed at the point. Seed-vessels woolly, somewhat erect. Native of Spain and Portugal. —— Treatment the same as for *P. albiflora*.

Pæonia officinalis (*Officinal Pæony*). —A showy and popular kind; 1 to 3 ft. high. *Flowers*, in early summer; red or crimson; carpels recurved, tomentose. *Leaves*, composed of several unequal lobes, which are cut into various segments, hairy beneath; stems unevenly 6- or 7-grooved. There are several varieties, one (*P. corallina*), considered as a species by some, is naturalized in the rocky clefts of the "Steep Holme" Island in the Severn. Native of many parts of Europe.——The same positions and treatment as for *P. albiflora*.

Pæonia tenuifolia (*Fine - leaved Pæony*).—Very distinct in aspect, from its fine thin leaflets; 12 to 18 in. high. *Flowers*, in early summer; fine dark red, nestling among the finely-divided upper leaves; petals 8, oval, spreading; carpels tomentose, spreading. *Leaves*, alternate, divided into narrow many-parted leaflets, smooth, on round stalks, channelled above; stems round, obscurely grooved, smooth, naked at the bottom. The double form is the one most frequently seen in gardens.

Siberia and Tauria.—— The same positions and treatment as for *P. albiflora*.

Pancratium illyricum (*Illyrian P.*) —A fine hardy bulbous perennial; 16 in. to 2 ft. high. *Flowers*, in summer; very fragrant, of a dull white colour, with a greenish - yellow tube, numerous, 6 to 12 issuing from a 2-valved spathe at the top of the stem. *Leaves*, oblong, ribbon-shaped, glaucous. *Bulb*, very large, pear - shaped, with an elongated neck, 10 in. or 1 ft. long, and covered with numerous, close, striated, glistening, brownish-black coats. Southern Europe.——Borders, in deep sandy loam. Division in autumn; replanting immediately.

Panicum altissimum (*Tall P.*)— Resembles *P. virgatum*, and though of more elegant habit, is often confounded with it; 20 in. to 6½ ft. high, according to the climate, soil, etc. *Flowers*, from late in summer until the first frosts, in large branching panicles, which, as they become old, change to a dark red or maroon hue. *Leaves*, linear, arching, with finely-toothed edges. West Indies, Tropical America, and West Coast of Africa. ——Borders, groups, or beds of perennials, or isolated near the edges of shrubberies, etc., in deep rich soil, and in sunny positions. Division in spring, or from seed; the former method is preferable.

Panicum bulbosum (*Bulbous P.*)— An elegant grass; 3 to 4 ft. high. *Flowers*, in summer; panicle compound, oblong, about a foot long, composed of numerous, alternate, or opposite, erect, somewhat adpressed, spikelets ½ in. long. *Leaves*, linear, pointed, flat, striated, smooth on the outside, hairy within, rough at the edges; sheaths striated, very smooth. *Root*, bulbous, with thickish fibres. There is a variety with pubescent

o

sheaths, and narrower leaves. Native of S. America.——Soil, positions, etc. the same as those for the preceding kind.

Panicum virgatum (*Twiggy P.*)—A very ornamental grass, growing in large, handsome, lively-green tufts; upwards of 3 ft. high, in good soil. *Flowers*, from late in summer, up to the first frosts; in panicles, which are at first narrow and slender, and afterwards spread and branch very extensively. *Leaves*, linear, flat, 1 ft. or more in length. North America.—— The same positions and treatment as for *P. altissimum*.

Papaver alpinum (*Alpine Poppy*).— A beautiful mountain Poppy; 3 to 6 in. high, or more. *Flowers*, in summer; white, with yellow centres, solitary, on stalks springing from the roots; sepals pilose; capsule roundish, prickly. *Leaves*, smooth or hairy, bipinnate; segments finely cut into acute lobes. This plant varies a good deal, there being white, scarlet, and yellow forms in cultivation. *P. a. albiflorum* is a variety with white flowers spotted at the base, and *P. a. flaviflorum* is one with showy orange flowers, and hairy leaves and stem, growing about 4 in. high. The higher Alps of Europé.——The rock-garden, in moist sandy soil, and in cool spots. Seed.

Papaver croceum (*Golden P.*)—Resembles *Meconopsis cambrica* in habit, but is not so hardy; 8 to 15 in. high. *Flowers*, in summer; large, orange-yellow, sometimes saffron; petals slightly waved at the margin. *Leaves*, all radical, erect, of a delicate green on the upper side, glaucous underneath, rough, as is the stem, with spreading hairs; sepals equally hairy. Altai mountains in Siberia.——Borders, and the rougher parts of the rock-garden in sandy loam. Seed.

Papaver lateritium (*Orange Poppy*). —A handsome and large kind, densely clothed with rigid white hairs, 1½ to 2 ft. high. *Flowers*, in May; bright orange; rather more than 2 in. across; petals obovate, sepals covered on the back with long yellow hairs. *Leaves*, linear-elliptical, pinnatifid at the base; those of the root densely crowded together, 6 to 12 in. long (including the leaf-stalk), and from ½ in. to nearly 1 in. broad; lower segments much divided; upper ones few and coarsely serrated; stem-leaves much smaller and nearly sessile. Valley of the river Tscharuck, which separates Armenia from the mountains of Pontus.——Borders, or naturalization, in ordinary soil. Division or seed.

Papaver nudicaule (*Iceland Poppy*). —Allied to *P. alpinum*, 12 to 15 in. high. *Flowers*, in summer; rich yellow, scented somewhat like those of the Jonquil, especially in the morning and evening; solitary on naked stems springing from the root; sepals 2, beset with bristles; petals 4, two inner ones rather smaller than the outer ones; capsules roundish or oblong, hairy. *Leaves*, pinnately-lobed; lobes cut or toothed, acute. There are several varieties. Siberia and the northern parts of America.——The rock-garden, in cool moist spots, in sandy loam or peat. Seed.

Papaver orientale (*Oriental Poppy*). —The most showy of all perennials, 2 to 3 ft. high. *Flowers*, in early summer; 6 in. or more across, one on each stem, deep scarlet, usually with a dark purple spot at the base of each petal; calyx of 3 sepals (not 2, as in other Papavers); capsules smooth, somewhat globose. *Leaves*, pinnately-parted, about 1 ft. long, clothed with white bristly hairs; stem rough and leafy. *P. bracteatum*, from the Caucasus, by some considered a distinct species, is a variety of this differing by the hairs of the calyx and flower-stalks being adpressed and not spreading, by the bracts under the flowers, and by flowering rather earlier. Armenia. —— Borders, in ordinary soil, and naturalization in open spots in woods, copses, etc. Division or seed.

Papaver pilosum (*Pilose Poppy*).— A showy species, distinguished by its very hairy stems and pale green foliage; 1 to 2 ft. high. *Flowers*, in summer; brick-red or deep orange, with a whitish spot at the base of each petal; equal in size to those of *P. lateritium*, solitary on the tops of the naked stalks; sepals pilose. *Leaves*, of the root oblong; stem-leaves ovate-oblong with serrated lobes, pilose on both sides, cut, stem-clasping; stem densely clothed with spreading hairs. Bithynia, on Mount Olympus. —— Borders, in sandy soil. Division and seed.

Paradisia Liliastrum (*St. Bruno's Lily*). — *Czackia*.— *Anthericum*.— An elegant alpine meadow plant, with blooms large, pure, and white, like small white lilies, 1 to 1½ ft. high. *Flowers*, early in summer; fragrant, of a transparent white, with a delicate green spot on the point of each division, about 2 in. long, funnel-shaped, with six regular divisions, and arranged in a loose spike, from 5 to 10 blooms on each stem. *Leaves*, long, narrow and grooved, about 1 ft. long and 6 or 8 in number. Root fibrous, rather fleshy, white. Abundant in the meadows of the Alpine Valleys of Piedmont, and many other mountainous parts of Central and Southern Europe. ——Well suited for tufts on the lower parts of the rock-garden, or for the choice mixed border, in good sandy loam, and for naturalization in parts of the pleasure-ground or open glades in woods where the grass is not cut early in the year, or at all. It should be carefully protected from slugs. Division and seed.

Parnassia asarifolia (*Asarum-leaved Grass of Parnassus*). — A beautiful marsh perennial, with larger leaves and flowers than those of the British species; 6 in. to 2 ft. high. *Flowers*, in summer; white; petals 5, abruptly contracted into a claw at the base. *Leaves*, of the root kidney-shaped, those of the stem roundish, heart-shaped. North America.——The artificial bog, very moist spots near the rock-garden in peat, or in pots plunged nearly to their rims in water. Division and seed.

Parnassia caroliniana (*Large Grass of Parnassus*).—Like the preceding, but with heart-shaped leaves, 9 in. to 2 ft. high. *Flowers*, in summer; from 1 to 1½ in. across; white, with green or pale-purple veins; petals sessile; sterile stamens 3 in each set, instead of 9 to 15 as in *P. palustris*. *Leaves*, thick, leathery, roundish-heart-shaped; stem-leaves ovate, stalkless. North America.——Soil, position, etc., the same as for the preceding.

Parnassia palustris (*Grass of Parnassus*).—An interesting native bog or moist meadow plant, 4 to 12 in. high. *Flowers*, in summer; white; an inch or more across, marked very distinctly with greyish veins; petals slightly scalloped at the edges and notched at the apex; stamens only half as long as the petals. *Leaves*, from ¼ to 1½ in. long, smooth, those of the root heart-shaped, on grooved stalks about 1½ in. long, bright green above, greyish beneath; stem with a single embracing leaf below the middle. Britain and many other parts of Europe.——Positions and treatment as for *A. asarifolia*.

Parochetus communis (*Shamrock Pea*).—A beautiful creeping perennial, with Clover-like leaves, 2 to 3 in. high. *Flowers*, in spring; handsome blue, solitary, on long stalks; standard two-lobed, drooping; keel blunt, covered by the wing; each flower like a handsome blue Pea-flower. *Leaves*, trifoliate, like those of the common Shamrock; leaflets truncate, dentate-serrate. Nepaul.——The rock-garden and choice borders in warm positions, in light vegetable soil. Division or seed.

Paronychia serpyllifolia (*Thyme-leaved P.*)—An interesting little creeping plant, 1 to 2 in. high. *Flowers*, in summer; white, small, in terminal heads, hidden among the roundish bracts; sepals obtuse. *Leaves*, opposite, ovate, stipulate, rather fleshy, smooth, with ciliated margins; stipules in pairs; stems prostrate, knotted, branched. Southern Europe, in arid places.——The rock-garden, in any light soil. Division.

Pelargonium Endlicherianum (*Endlicher's P.*)—The only hardy *Pelargonium*, and a handsome plant; 1 to 1¼ ft. high. *Flowers*, late in summer; large, rose-coloured, veined with a darker shade, arranged in an umbel; the two upper petals only are fully developed, the three lower ones being almost rudimentary. *Leaves*, lower ones roundish, notched and toothed, of a greyish-green colour; those of the stem more or less deeply divided into from 3 to 5 lobes. Taurus mountains in Asia Minor.——Warm nooks on the lower flanks of the rock-garden, warm borders or banks, in well-drained, very sandy loam. Division and seed.

Pentstemon argutus (*Graceful Pentstemon*).—A half-shrubby perennial, covered with a short pubescence; 3 to 4 ft. high. *Flowers*, in summer; bright purple; tips of the divisions of the lower lip sky-blue. *Leaves*, opposite, nearly connate; upper ones lanceolate; lower ones spoon-shaped, obtuse, much and irregularly-serrated, dark green on the upper side, paler beneath.

Mexico.——Borders, in good, sandy loam. Division and seed.

Pentstemon barbatus (*Bearded P.*)—A tall and brilliant perennial, 2 to 6 ft. high. *Flowers*, in summer; showy scarlet outside, white within, drooping, in long loose panicles; lower lip of the corolla 3-parted, bearded with yellow hairs; sterile filaments smooth. *Leaves*, connate, narrowly lance-shaped, glaucous, very long, entire, channelled; root-leaves crowded, spoon-shaped; stems branched. There are several varieties, *P. Torreyi* being a very large and tall one. Mexico.——Borders, in sandy loam. Division, cuttings, or seed.

Pentstemon campanulatus (*Bell-flowered P.*)—A very leafy, tufted plant; 16 in. to 2 ft. and upwards, in height. *Flowers*, from May to the first frosts; light rose-colour, somewhat dull on the outside; light flesh-colour veined with violet-carmine within, the lower lip having a few scattered hairs; corolla tubular, swollen; flowers grouped unilaterally, in twos and threes, in the axils of the leaves, and forming spike-like panicles. *Leaves*, opposite, sessile, linear-lanceolate or acute, serrated, the upper ones slightly downy and viscid. Mexico.——Borders, in sandy loam; one of the kinds, from which some of our finest varieties have sprung. Seed and cuttings.

Pentstemon Digitalis (*Foxglove P.*)—A handsome free-growing perennial; 1 to 2 ft. high. *Flowers*, in summer; white, downy, in racemose panicles; corolla large, nearly bell-shaped; the upper lip shorter than the lower one, which is 3-lobed and widened; sterile stamen longer than the others, and bearded about half way down with white hairs. *Leaves*, smooth, glossy, slightly toothed, and covered with numerous small dots; root-leaves oblong-lance-shaped, gradually tapering at the base, and running down the stalk, strongly nerved beneath, and channelled above; stem-leaves heart-shaped, taper-pointed, stalkless. Arkansas.—— Borders, in ordinary soil. Division and seed.

Pentstemon gentianoides (*Common P.*)—*P. Hartwegi.*—A beautiful and well-known kind; 2 to 3 ft. high. *Flowers*, in summer; purplish-red, in panicles; peduncles bearing from 1 to 3 flowers each; corolla downy outside; tube short, throat large; upper lip 2-lobed, lower one trifid, beardless; sterile stamen smooth. *Leaves*, lance-shaped, about 4 in. long, and ½ to ¾ in. broad, smooth, entire; stem downy, slender in the upper part. There is a white and numerous coloured varieties of this species. Mexico.——Borders, in rich sandy loam. In cold soils it perishes in winter; in warm ones in mild districts it is perennial, and forms full handsome bushes, when in flower. Seed and cuttings.

Pentstemon glaber (*Dwarf-Blue P.*) —A beautiful dwarf alpine species; 6 to 12 in. high. *Flowers*, early in summer; exquisite blue-purple, varying in hue, in terminal racemes; corolla nearly bell-shaped; segments of calyx roundish, tapering to a point; sterile filament slightly bearded. *Leaves*, lance-shaped, entire, smooth, sessile, the margins slightly undulated; stems mostly decumbent, but occasionally more or less erect. *P. speciosus* is now considered a variety of this, growing taller and more erect, and *P. cyananthus* is another form. North America. —— The rock-garden, in sandy or peaty soil, and in well-drained warm spots, and on the margin of the choice mixed border, in well-drained free soil. Seed, cuttings, and division.

Pentstemon Jaffrayanus (*Gentianblue P.*)— A handsome, slightly-shrubby plant; 1 ft. to 16 in. high. *Flowers*, from July to August; handsome gentian-blue, bell-shaped, with a very wide tube and reflected lobes; anthers purplish; 1 to 2 flowers on each pedicel, arranged in an irregular cluster, 4 to 8 in. long. *Leaves*, opposite, glaucous, oblong-lanceolate; the lower ones narrowed into a footstalk; the upper ones stem-clasping and broader; stems tinged with a reddish hue. California.——In warm lower parts of the rock-garden or on warm borders, in well-drained very sandy loam. This plant is somewhat tender. Cuttings and seed.

Pentstemon procerus (*Whorled P.*)— A very pretty, hardy, dwarf and spreading kind; 8 to 15 in. high. *Flowers*, early in summer; pale blue veined with purple, small, very freely produced in little racemes, that stand so close to the stem as to seem in whorls; sterile stamen bearded at top. *Leaves*, lance-shaped, entire; lower ones stalked; upper ones stalkless, sub-connate. North-west America and the Rocky Mountains.—— Flourishes freely in borders, in almost any soil, and suitable also for the rock-garden, among the more easily grown plants, and also as an edging. Division.

Pentstemon Scouleri (*Scouler's P.*)— A neat shrubby kind; about 1 ft. high. *Flowers*, in summer; pale lilacpurple, in racemes; stalks oneflowered; corolla ventricose, nearly 2 in. long, spreading at the mouth; anthers downy; calyx downy, segments taper-pointed. *Leaves*, narrow, obovate-lance-shaped, sharply notched; upper ones entire; stems suffruticose; branchlets pilose. North West America.——The rock-garden, or borders, in free well-drained soil. Cuttings and division.

Petasites fragrans (*Winter Heliotrope*).—A weedy-looking plant, 4 to 12 in. high. *Flowers*, in December and January, unless the weather be very severe; pale dingy lilac, in a rather short racemose panicle, deliciously fragrant. *Leaves*, round, with a deeply heart-shaped base, 4 to 8 in. across, usually appearing early in January. *Rootstock* creeping. N. Europe and Great Britain.——Unfit for garden culture, as it runs very much at the root, and becomes a perfect weed, but may be planted in semi-wild places, lanes, and hedges, as it is very useful for bouquets in winter. Division.

Petasites vulgaris (*Common Butterbur*).—*Tussilago Petasites.*—A native herb, closely allied to the common Coltsfoot, but with great Rhubarb-like foliage, 2 to 2½ ft. high. *Flowers*, in spring; appearing before the leaves, dull pinkish-purple, in a compound raceme, on stems 6 to 12 in. high; flower-heads tubular. *Leaves*, very large, heart-shaped, pointed, irregularly toothed, downy beneath, on long fleshy footstalks. Rather common in England and other parts of Europe. ——Exotic plants with less effective leaves than this have been lately much used with us; it however should not be allowed to come nearer to the garden than the margins of some adjacent stream, or in a moist bottom among other large-leaved herbaceous plants. Division.

Petrocallis pyrenaica (*Rock Beauty*). —A small and beautiful alpine plant, when not in flower resembling a mossy Saxifrage; 2 or 3 in. high. *Flowers*, in April; pale lilac faintly veined, sweet-scented, in short few-flowered racemes. *Leaves*, small, wedge-shaped at the base, cut into three short narrow lobes at the apex; the lower ones often cut into 5 lobes; stems shrubby at the base, dividing into many small branches. Native of Northern Italy, the Tyrol, and other parts of Southern Europe.——The rock-garden, in light moist sandy soil, and among the choicest alpine plants. Careful division and seed.

Phlomis ferruginea (*Rusty P.*)—A half-shrubby plant, with branches clothed with rusty purple loose wool; 1 to 3 ft. high. *Flowers*, early in summer; yellow, downy on the outside, in partial whorls of 12 to 20 blossoms, with rough lance-shaped bracts; calyx tubular, velvety, with long hairs at the throat, and short, stiff, awl-shaped teeth. *Leaves*, 2 or 3 in. in length, oblong-lance-shaped, obtuse, very much wrinkled, heart-shaped at the base, green and velvety on the upper side, covered with woolly down underneath. Naples. —— Borders, and fringes of shrubberies, in sandy loam. Cuttings and seed.

Phlomis fruticosa (*Jerusalem Sage*). —A distinct-looking shrubby plant, with branches clothed with a yellowish down, 2 to 4 ft. high. *Flowers*, in summer; yellow, rather showy, in whorls of 15 to 30, either solitary or in pairs, at the tops of the branches; bracts broad. *Leaves*, lance-shaped, acute, greenish, ciliated, oval or oblong, entire or more or less crenated. Found in dry exposed places on mountains on the Mediterranean coast.—— Borders, fringes of shrubberies, or banks, in ordinary soil. Cuttings and seed.

Phlomis Herba-venti (*Wind-herb P.*) — A handsome, neatly - spreading, large perennial, with erect green or purplish stems, clothed with long hairs; 1 to 2 ft. high. *Flowers*, in summer; purplish-violet, in whorls of from 10 to 20; corolla downy outside; calyx hairy, with awl-shaped, stiff, spreading teeth; bracts awl-shaped, ciliated, prickly, longer than the calyx. *Leaves*, often 6 or 8 in. long, oblong-lance-shaped, crenated, rounded at the base, leathery, green on both sides, or greyish beneath, the upper surface shining, rough; stem square, much-branched. Southern Europe on the Mediterranean coast.——Borders, shrubberies, or rocky banks in ordinary soil. Division or seed.

Phlomis Russelliana (*Russell's P.*)— A vigorous herb, with nearly simple stems, the branches being clothed with a loose white down; 3 to 5 ft. high. *Flowers*, in summer; yellow, from 30 to 50 in a whorl; calyx green, pubescent; bracts narrow, very acute, ending in a rather prickly point. *Leaves*, of root large, 6-8 in. long, ovate, deeply heart-shaped at the base, wrinkled, green above and covered with greyish tomentum beneath. Syria.——Borders, fringes of shrubberies, wild banks, etc., in ordinary soil. Division and seed.

Phlomis Samia (*Samian P.*)—Allied to *P. Russelliana*, but with less tomentose stems; 2 to 3 ft. high. *Flowers*, in early summer; greenish cream-colour on the outside, and thickly set with hairs; pinkish inside, lower lip also pinkish inside with numerous darker coloured veins or streaks; in axillary and terminal whorls sometimes of 10 to 15 flowers each; corolla tomentose; bracts numerous, linear, very acute, prickly, as long as the calyx. *Leaves*, heart-shaped, acute, crenated, wrinkled, green above and clothed with grey tomentum beneath, on hairy stalks; root-leaves about 3 in. long and 1½ in. broad at the base; stem-leaves smaller; stems hairy, 4-cornered, erect. Island of Samos and Barbary.——Borders, or naturalization, in ordinary soil. Division and seed.

Phlomis tuberosa (*Tuberous P.*)—A handsome and vigorous perennial, 3 ft. high. *Flowers*, in summer; purplish-rose, overlaid with a downy hoariness, very numerous, in dense whorls; upper lip very hairy, and margined with a delicate white fringe; lower lip perfectly smooth; bracts numerous with long, thin, pointed divisions irregularly set with hairs. *Leaves*, of the root on long stalks, which are deeply furrowed on the upper side, oval-obtuse, deeply heart-shaped, notched, wrinkled, and rough with short hairs; stem-leaves opposite, decussate, oblong-lanceolate, growing from the base of the whorls. Eastern parts of Europe.——Borders, or naturalization in copses and shrubberies, in ordinary soil. Division and seed.

Phlox Carolina (*Carolina P.*)—A smooth species, with stems ascending often from a prostrate base; 6 in. to 2 ft. high. *Flowers*, in early summer; pinkish or purple, in crowded corymbs; corolla about 1 in. long, and the limb 1 in. broad; lobes round, entire; teeth of calyx short, triangular-lance-shaped. *Leaves*, ovate-lance-shaped, sometimes heart-shaped at the base, attenuated. North America.—— Borders, in light-soil. Division and cuttings.

Phlox decussata (*Cross-leaved P.*)— A beautiful kind, the parent of many of our dwarfer garden varieties; 20 to 30 in. high. *Flowers*, in summer; numerous, red, arranged in pyramidal corymb-like panicles; calyx with short, acuminate, bristle-like teeth. *Leaves*, opposite, oblong, or oval-lanceolate, acuminate, downy or whitish underneath, the upper ones faintly jagged at the base. There are numerous varieties, one of which has variegated leaves. North America. ——Borders, and beds, in deep sandy loam. Division and cuttings.

Phlox divaricata (*Straggling P.*)— *P. canadensis.*—Intermediate in size between the dwarf and tall kinds; 9 to 16 in. high. *Flowers*, in spring and early summer; pale lilac or bluish, in forked corymbs; lobes of corolla obcordate, notched at the end, equalling or longer than the tube; calyx 5-parted; teeth slender awl-shaped.

Leaves, oblong or ovate, opposite, stalkless; lower ones about 1½ in. long; upper ones alternate; stems downy, spreading, or ascending from a prostrate base. North America.——Borders and rockwork, in ordinary light soil. Division.

Phlox ovata (*Ovate-leaved P.*)—A dwarf, neat perennial, considered by some to be a variety of *P. Carolina*; 1 ft. high. *Flowers*, from July to August; few, large, fine rose-colour, with a short tube, which is much exceeded in length by the sepals. *Leaves*, opposite, broadly-oval, pointed, seldom heart-shaped at the base, sometimes tinged with red. North America.——Borders, and the rock-garden, in well-drained, fine sandy or peaty ground. Division.

Phlox paniculata (*Panicled P.*)—A showy and noble kind, the parent of many of our garden varieties, with smooth, erect stems; 2 to 4 ft. high. *Flowers*, in summer; very fragrant, varying from pale purple to white, in a pyramidal panicled corymb; lobes of the corolla entire, rounded; teeth of calyx awn-pointed. *Leaves*, opposite, broadly-lance-shaped, smooth, pointed, tapering at the base, 3 in. long, and 1 in. wide in the centre, the upper ones often heart-shaped at the base. North America.——Borders and beds, in good sandy loam. Division.

Phlox procumbens (*Procumbent P.*)—A dwarf, hardy alpine perennial, forming straggling tufts; 4 or 5 in. high. *Flowers*, in summer; about ¾ in. across, lilac, with violet marks near the eye, in clusters of 3 or 4 blooms on the upper part of the stems. *Leaves*, small, opposite, linear-lanceolate, sessile; stems slightly downy. North America.——Rockwork, front margin of mixed border, in sandy loam. Division.

Phlox reptans (*Creeping P.*)—*P. verna*, *P. stolonifera*.—A neat, dwarf, creeping, very showy kind; 4 to 8 in. high. *Flowers*, in spring, showy, reddish-purple, in few-flowered corymbs; tube of corolla 1 in. long; limb about 1 in. broad. *Leaves*, of root roundish-obovate, somewhat smooth and thick; those of the flower-stems oblong or ovate, obtuse, often clammy. North America.——Borders, the rock-garden, edgings, in tufts, round beds of shrubs, etc., in any rather moist soil. Division.

Phlox subulata (*Mossy P.*)— A pretty dwarf kind, with creeping, tufted stems, densely clothed with narrow moss-like leaves. *Flowers*, in April and May, in great profusion; pinkish purple, with a darker centre. (sometimes white), in few-flowered corymbs; lobes of corolla wedge-shaped, notched, rarely entire; tube of corolla arched. *Leaves*, from ¼ to ½ in. long, awl-shaped, or narrow-lance-shaped, fringed on the edges, pubescent, rigid. A variety, *P. setacea*, has smaller flowers, with a straight tube, and a paler centre; its leaves also are not ciliated on the margin; the white-flowered form is grown under the name of *P. Nelsoni*. North America.——The rock-garden, borders, in tufts, on the edges of beds of low shrubs, in the small rings at the base of standard Roses, and in many like positions, in rather moist, sandy loam. Division.

Phygelius capensis (*Cape P.*)— A tall and showy perennial; 1½ to 3 ft. high. *Flowers*, in summer and autumn; numerous, pendent, with a vermilion, elongated, rather curved tube, and a yellowish throat; limb of the corolla very oblique, divided into 5 small rounded lobes. *Leaves*, oval, or oval-lance-shaped, notched, resembling those of *Scrophularia nodosa*. Cape of Good Hope.——Borders, on the south sides of houses, walls, etc. It is generally rather tender, but thrives very freely in mild districts, in light, sandy loam, or vegetable soil; in warmer countries it thrives on walls, and stony or gravelly places. Division.

Physalis Alkekengi (*Winter Cherry*). —A curious perennial, bearing scarlet berries in winter; 12 to 18 in. high. *Flowers*, in summer; dull white, solitary, on slender stalks, springing from the axils of the leaves; corolla rotate; calyx ovate, coloured, enclosing the berries, which are the size of a small Cherry, smooth, and round. *Leaves*, in pairs, entire, acute, of various shapes, some ovate, others angled, on long footstalks; stem slightly branched at bottom; root creeping. Southern Europe.——In warm borders, among low shrubs, etc., in sandy soil. Division and seed.

Physostegia denticulata (*Toothed P.*) —A handsome perennial; 1 to 1½ ft. high. *Flowers*, in autumn; rosy-purple, spotted with red on the lower lip, arranged in opposite pairs; throat inflated. *Leaves*, opposite, decussate, obovate-lanceolate, distantly toothed. North America.——Borders, in ordinary soil. Division.

Physostegia imbricata (*Imbricate P.*)—A tall and handsome perennial; 3 to 6 ft. high. *Flowers*, in autumn; pale purple, the lower lip of a lighter colour, marked with purple spots; upper lip much arched; throat open; calyx globular and inflated when in fruit. *Leaves*, of the root oval-lance-shaped, toothed, reddish underneath-stalked, arranged in rosettes; stem leaves opposite, sessile, lance-shaped, acute; distinguished from *P. virginiana* by its stems being higher and slenderer, its leaves broader, its calyx globular, and not egg-shaped, and its flowers of larger size, and of a deeper

colour. Texas.——Borders and naturalization, in sandy loam. Division.

Physostegia virginiana (*Virginian P.*)—A smooth perennial, with erect stems, 1 to 4 ft. high. *Flowers*, in summer; flesh-coloured or purple, showy, crowded in terminal racemes; corolla 1 in. long, upper lip slightly arching, nearly entire, lower one 3-lobed, spreading, the middle lobe broadest, notched; calyx inflated when the fruit is ripe. *Leaves*, stalkless, lance-shaped, acute, or oblong-ovate, very sharply toothed or nearly entire. North America.——Borders, or naturalization, in moist loam. Division.

Phyteuma comosum (*Rock P.*)—A dwarf distinct alpine plant, with sea-green leaves and flattish heads of flowers, very large for the size of the plant; 2 to 8 in. high. *Flowers*, in summer; blue, on very short stalks, in simple terminal umbellate heads; bracts very large, oboval, coarsely toothed. *Leaves*, of the root, roundish - heart - shaped, on long stalks; stem-leaves short-stalked, oval-lanceolate, acute; stems smooth, procumbent, spreading. The Alps.——The rock-garden, in dry sunny spots, in well-drained, very sandy or calcareous soil. I have seen this plant growing from small chinks in arid cliffs, where probably no other plant could exist. Seed.

Phyteuma orbiculare (*Round-headed P.*)—A dwarf perennial, with small flowers in dense heads, 6 in. to 1 ft. high. *Flowers*, in summer; numerous, small, blue, in heads which are at first spherical, but become egg-shaped in the course of flowering. *Leaves*, alternate, leathery, smooth, or velvety, notched, obtuse; the lower ones stalked, almost heart-shaped, lanceolate or oval-oblong; the upper ones sessile, lanceolate, narrow. Southern Europe.——Borders, in ordinary soil. Division and seed.

Phyteuma spicatum (*Spiked P.*)—A species variable in the colour of its flowers and the smoothness or pubescence of its leaves and stems; 1 ft. to 20 in. high. *Flowers*, in summer; numerous, white in lowland districts, blue on the mountains, in a lengthened egg-shaped spike which often becomes somewhat cylindrical. *Leaves*, smooth or pubescent; root and lower stem-leaves stalked, oval-acute, broad, and heart-shaped at the base, notched; the upper ones narrower, some of them nearly linear. South of Europe, in woods and meadows.——Borders, in ordinary soil. Division.

Phytolacca decandra (*Pigeon Berry*). —A very vigorous and remarkable-looking plant, with a rather unpleasant odour, and a large fleshy root, often as thick as a man's leg; 3 to 10 ft. high. *Flowers*, in summer; white, with green ovary, in terminal racemes, succeeded by a long raceme of dark purple berries which ripen in autumn. *Leaves*, ovate, nearly 6 in. long, and about 2½ in. broad, changing to purple in autumn; stem often purple, erect, divided at top. Native of Southern Europe, Barbary, and North America.——Naturalization in woods, copses, and coverts, and also as isolated plants, or in groups in pleasure grounds, in deep sandy loam. Division.

Pinguicula grandiflora (*Irish Butterwort*).—A very handsome dwarf bog herb, the flower-stems attaining a height of from 3 to 6 in. *Flowers*, in early summer; fine violet-blue, on leafless stalks springing from the root; corolla 1 in. or more long, and about 1 in. wide, spurred like those of the Horned Violet, with a broad open mouth. *Leaves*, in rosettes, light green, fleshy, and glistening, oval or oblong, obtuse, broadest in the middle. Bogs and wet heaths in the South-West of Ireland.——Moist, half-shady spots, in the rock-garden, the artificial bog, or in pots or pans in a moist and cool frame, in peat or moist vegetable soil. Increased by means of small green bulb-like buds, which are thrown off freely at the bottom of the stem.

Pinguicula longifolia (*Long-leaved P.*)—A very ornamental variety of *P. grandiflora*, with flower-stems from 3 to 6 in. high. *Flowers*, in summer; large, violet (rarely rose), solitary, terminal, usually larger than those of the type. *Leaves*, all radical, elongated-elliptical, 4 to 5 in. long, attenuated towards the base, of a yellowish-green colour, fleshy and mucilaginous. Central Pyrenees.——Rockwork, on slopes and ledges with a northern aspect, in a slightly shaded position, in peat and grit, wet, but well-drained. Seed. Sows itself freely.

Pisum maritimum (*Sea Pea*).—*Lathyrus maritimus*.—An interesting and ornamental native prostrate plant, with sharply 4-angled stems; 1½ to 2 ft. long. *Flowers*, in summer; bluish-purple, in clusters of 6 or 8 on axillary stalks. *Leaves*, alternate, composed of 5 or 6 pairs of oval, obtuse, entire, sessile leaflets; stipules 2 together, acute, toothed at the base, smaller than the leaves. Southern coasts of England, of Kerry, in Ireland, and many other sea-coasts in Europe, Asia, and America.——Borders and fringes of shrubberies, in deep sandy soil. In the College Botanic Gardens, at Dublin, this forms a very free and handsome plant, perhaps from its proximity to the sea, and from its being rooted in a rich marine deposit. Division and seed.

Plumbago Larpentæ (*Hardy Blue P.*) — A very ornamental perennial; 1 to 1¾ ft. high. *Flowers*, in autumn; deep blue, changing to violet, in dense bouquets on the summit of the stem, and in the axils of the leaves; bracts oval, smooth, shining, ciliated. *Leaves*, oboval, pointed, attenuated at the base, finely fringed, covered with very small scales on both sides. Northern China. ——Borders and the rock-garden, in ordinary soil. It thrives everywhere and in any soil, but to fully enjoy its flowers where the soil is heavy, it is better to plant it in sandy loam and in a sunny position. Division.

Podophyllum Emodi (*Himalayan May Apple*).—A remarkable plant; about 1 ft. high. *Flowers*, in spring; cup-shaped, whitish, 1 in. or more across, not showy. *Leaves*, folded in bud, roundish in outline, from 6 to 12 in. across, cut in 3 great lobes; the lateral lobes again divided in 2, and the middle lobe in 3, all serrated. *Fruit*, very large, edible, about 2 in. long, bright coral red, fleshy inside, irregular in outline. Himalaya Mountains. ——In moist, deep, peaty soil, in warm and slightly sheltered positions. A fine plant for the margin of beds of American plants, and also in bog-beds associated with such plants as *Cypripedium spectabile*, etc. Division and seed.

Podophyllum peltatum (*May Apple*). —A curious plant with large leaves and flowers like those of small single Camellias, succeeded by round pale-yellow berries; 6 to 9 in. high. *Flowers*, in May; white, 1½ to 2 in. across, solitary between the two leaves; petals 9, rounded at the top, plaited at the edges. *Berry*, about the size of a good cherry, green at first, becoming yellow when ripe. *Leaves*, opposite, peltate, smooth, light green, irregularly 7- to 9-parted. North America.——In shady peat borders, or naturalized in woods, in moist vegetable soil, and in shady or half-shady positions. Division. The horizontally-spreading roots are the source of the now popular medicine, Podophyllin.

Polemonium cæruleum (*Jacob's Ladder*).—A well-known old border perennial; 16 in. to 2 ft. high. *Flowers*, in early summer; blue, in terminal corymbs or panicles; corolla with a short tube, and a 5-lobed limb; calyx bell-shaped, hairy, 5-cleft. *Leaves*, pinnate, with from 11 to 21 lance-shaped entire leaflets; root-leaves forming a dense tuft; stem-leaves few, and smaller; stems erect, stiff, smooth. There are several varieties of this species. *P. cæruleum variegatum* is one with beautifully variegated leaves, so graceful that it might be mistaken for a "variegated fern." Of other varieties the white-flowered one is perhaps the most worthy of culture. Siberia and Northern Europe, and apparently wild in several parts of Britain.——Borders, in ordinary soil. The variegated form is used for edgings, and also has an excellent effect here and there in the mixed border. It may be increased readily by the division of well-established tufts in early autumn; the common form by seed also.

Polemonium reptans (*Creeping P.*)-- A low spreading kind; 6 to 8 in. high. *Flowers*, in early summer; varying from blue to white, in a loose panicled corymb; lobes of corolla wedge-shaped; lobes of calyx rather shorter than tube. *Leaves*, pinnate; leaflets 7 to 11, ovate, acute, of a darker green than those of *P. cæruleum*; stems leafy, weak. N. America. —— Borders and the rock-garden, in sandy soil. Division or seed.

Polygala calcarea (*Chalk Milkwort*). —A very pretty, small, half-shrubby plant, 4 to 6 in. high. *Flowers*, in summer; blue, in terminal racemes. *Leaves*, large, obovate, blunt, chiefly in an irregular, large terminal rosette; those of the flower-stem short, smaller, lanceolate. Chalk hills in the Southeast of England, rare.——The rock-garden, in sunny spots, in calcareous soil. It is the easiest to cultivate of the British kinds, and well-established tufts of it look very pretty among early summer flowering alpine plants. Easily increased by careful division.

Polygala Chamæbuxus (*Box-leaved Milkwort*).—A small, neat, evergreen shrub, with Box-like leaves, attaining a height of nearly a foot, or even more, in fine, rich, moist soils, but in poor ones not more than an inch or two. *Flowers*, in early summer; cream-coloured or yellow, tipped with purple, emitting a pleasant odour, in few-flowered racemes springing from the axils of the upper leaves. *Leaves*, oblong-lance-shaped, sharp-pointed, stiff, smooth, and shining, closely arranged on the stems. Alps of Austria and Switzerland, and other parts of Europe.—— Borders, the rock-garden, or beds of small shrubs, best in peat or very sandy loam, kept moist throughout the growing season. Division of established tufts.

Polygala paucifolia (*Fringed P.*)—An interesting and handsome perennial, 3 to 4 in. high. *Flowers*, in summer; rosy-purple, sometimes, though rarely, white, large and handsome, about ¾ in. long, 1 to 3 on stems springing from the slender prostrate shoots which also bear concealed flowers. *Leaves*, of root small, scale-like; stem-leaves crowded at the tops of the stems, ovate, acute, smooth. North America.——The rock-garden, in leaf-mould and sand, associated with such plants as *Linnæa borealis*, *Trientalis*, *Mitchella*, etc., in half-shady places. Division.

Polygonatum multiflorum (*Solomon's Seal*).—A very graceful well-known plant, 20 to 26 in. high. *Flowers*, early in summer; small and numerous; pendent, white, spotted with green in the throat and bearded on the end of each of the 6 divisions of the corolla. *Leaves*, oval-oblong or elliptical, rather obtuse, glaucous underneath, sheathing the stem. Europe and Britain, in woods and stony places.——Thrives in almost any position in sandy loam, and is worthy of a place in the choicest border or group, but is, perhaps, seen to greatest advantage when leaning forth from beneath shrubs or low trees on the margin of a shrubbery or grove. It should be abundantly grown as a wild plant in woods. Division.

Polygonum Brunonis (*Indian Knotweed*).—A dwarf perennial, 6 in. to 1 ft. high. *Flowers*, in summer; handsome rose, in dense spikes, 2 or 3 in. long. *Leaves*, oblong-lance-shaped, acute, narrowing into the stalk, slightly turned back along the margin, and curiously marked there with cartilage, so as to present the appearance of being hemmed with white thread; stem-leaves small, alternate, shortly stalked, and marked; ocreæ large, completely surrounding the stem, brown and scarious in the upper half. Himalaya.—— Borders, in ordinary soil. Division.

Polygonum cuspidatum (*Giant Knotweed*).— *P. Sieboldi*.—A very large perennial of noble port, 3½ to 8 ft. high. *Flowers*, in late summer and autumn; white, disposed in slender axillary clusters, forming a kind of panicle, succeeded by very handsome pale rosy fruit. *Leaves*, alternate, in two rows, stalked, broadly-oval or oval-oblong, acute, truncate at the base; stems erect at first, afterwards, when laden with leaves and flowers, gracefully arched. Japan.——This is most effective when planted as an isolated specimen in the pleasure-ground, or in groups of two, three, or five tufts. It would also do well for association with the more vigorous, herbaceous plants in rough places, in deep rich soil. Division.

Polygonum vaccinifolium (*Rock Knotweed*). — A neat half-shrubby plant, with prostrate, woody, much-branching stems, 6 in. high. *Flowers*, late in summer and in autumn; bright rose, freely produced in nearly round spikes. *Leaves*, smooth, ovate, or elliptical, attenuated at both ends, the margin slightly rolled back, netted with numerous prominent nerves, bright green, sometimes tinged with red above, pale beneath. Mountains of Northern India.——Borders, and the rougher parts of the rock-garden, in ordinary soil. Division.

Pontederia cordata (*Pickerel-weed*).— An erect aquatic plant, 1½ to 2 ft. high, with shining leathery leaves and spikes of blue flowers. *Flowers*, in summer and autumn; numerous, small, of a handsome sky-blue, sometimes white, with a greenish spot on the inside of the upper lobe, arranged in a bold spike. *Leaves*, thick, long stalked, erect, oval - oblong or elongated-heart-shaped, of a lively green, on stalks dilated and sheathing at the base. Mexico and Brazil.——Margins of ponds, streams, etc., in any soil. Division.

Potentilla alba (*White-flowered Cinquefoil*).—A prostrate herb, 4 to 6 in. high. *Flowers*, in early summer; white, strawberry-like, with a dark orange ring at the base, nearly 1 in. across; petals obcordate, longer than the calyx. *Leaves*, green and smooth above, silvery with dense silky down underneath; lower ones quinate, upper ones ternate; leaflets oblong, closely serrated at the apex; stems branched. *P. Vaillantii* is a variety of this species with petals twice as long as the calyx. European Alps.—— Naturalization among dwarf plants, in ordinary sandy soil. Division.

Potentilla alpestris (*Alpine Cinquefoil*).—A rare native plant, allied to *P. verna*, but with leaves of a paler green and on footstalks twice as long, 6 to 12 in. high. *Flowers*, in early summer; bright yellow, about 1 in. across; petals heart-shaped; segments of the calyx acute. *Leaves*, of root on stalks about 6 in. long, cut into 5 wedge-shaped divisions, notched at the top, rather hairy; stem-leaves ternate; stems ascending. Found on ledges of rocks and elevated slopes in Scotland and Northern England, and also in Switzerland, Lapland, and Denmark.——The rock-garden and borders, in moist sandy loam. Division and seed.

Potentilla atrosanguinea (*Blood Cinquefoil*). — A large showy kind, clothed with silky hairs, 1½ to 2 ft. high. *Flowers*, in summer; beautiful dark crimson, petals obcordate, longer than the calyx. *Leaves*, ternate, stalked; leaflets obovate, deeply notched, clothed with white tomentum beneath; stipules ovate-lanceshaped, entire or 2-lobed; stems decumbent. There have been numerous splendid hybrids raised from this species. Nepaul.——Borders, in ordinary soil. Division.

Potentilla calabra (*Calabrian Cinquefoil*).—A very silvery kind, from 4 to 10 in. high. *Flowers*, in early summer; lemon-yellow, about ¾ in. across, petals longer than the calyx. *Leaves*, divided into 5 wedge-shaped segments, tomentose, particularly on the under sides; leaflets much cut into narrow segments; stem prostrate. Native of Italy and Southern Europe.—— Borders, and naturalized on rather bare banks, in sandy soil. Division and seed.

Potentilla fruticosa (*Shrubby P.*) — A low shrubby plant, growing in tufts, with reddish, downy stems, from 10 to 20 in. in height. *Flowers*, all the summer; small, yellow, numerous, in terminal bouquets. *Leaves*, shortly-stalked, of from 5 to 7 ovalacute leaflets, very downy underneath, erect. Pyrenees and Britain.—— Among small shrubs, in rougher parts of the rock-garden, or naturalization, in sandy loam. Division.

POTENTILLA — PRIMULA.

Potentilla nitida (*Shining Cinquefoil*).—A neat small-tufted plant; 2 or 3 in. high. *Flowers*, in early summer; delicate rose, the green sepals showing between the petals with a pretty effect; petals nearly oval in outline, notched at the apex, longer than the calyx. *Leaves*, ternate; leaflets obovate, or wedge-shaped, toothed at the apex, clothed on both surfaces with shining, silvery, silky down; stems ascending. Alps of Dauphiny.——The rock-garden and borders, in sandy soil. Division.

Potentilla pyrenaica (*Pyrenean Cinquefoil*).— A fine showy species; 8 to 16 in. high. *Flowers*, in autumn; large, deep golden yellow; petals very round and overlapping, twice as long as the calyx. *Leaves*, the radical ones on long stalks, velvety, or nearly smooth, with oblong leaflets, toothed towards the end for about ⅔ of their length; stem-leaves 3- to 5-lobed, shortly-stalked, the upper ones entire; stipules united to the petiole for almost their entire length, the free part obtuse. The plant is sometimes very much covered with adpressed hairs, and sometimes almost smooth. Eastern and Central Pyrenees.——Margins of borders, and the rock-garden, in sandy loam. Division and seed.

Potentilla verna (*Spring Cinquefoil*).—A British plant, with short tufted stems, procumbent at the base, and ascending to the height of 6 or 8 in., sometimes prostrate. *Flowers*, in spring; bright yellow, in irregular panicles at the end of the stems; petals obcordate, longer than the calyx. *Leaves*, rigid, somewhat leathery, smooth, and marked with lines, which, with the stems, turn red as the season advances; lower ones on long stalks, with 5 or 7 oblong or wedge-shaped, toothed leaflets; upper ones quinate, or rarely ternate, nearly stalkless. The plant varies much in size and hairiness, and also in the size of the flowers. Found on rocks and dry banks in many parts of England and Scotland, but not plentifully.—— Borders and the rock-garden, in sandy loam. Division and seed.

[The many fine varieties of Potentillas now to be had in nurseries, are of more importance to the general cultivator of border flowers than any of the species. Lists of the best kinds will be found in the nurserymen's catalogues.]

Primula altaica (*Altaic Primrose*).— A handsome free-growing Primrose; 3 to 5 in. high. *Flowers*, numerous, large as those of Common Primrose, mauve or purplish crimson, with yellow centre. *Leaves*, obovate, younger ones lanceolate, sinuate-crenate, or nearly entire, obtuse, marked with narrow veins, and slightly mealy. —— The rock-garden, and choice, mixed borders, in moist, deep, sandy loam. Division and seed.

Primula amœna (*Caucasian Primrose*).—A handsome early kind, with somewhat the appearance of the Oxlip, and leaves somewhat like those of *P. denticulata*; 6 to 7 inches high. *Flowers*, in early spring; purple, larger than those of *P. denticulata*, in many-flowered umbels; limb of corolla smooth; tube longer than the ovate or oblong, angled calyx; involucre awl-shaped. *Leaves*, spoon-shaped or oblong, wrinkled, crenately toothed, hairy, woolly beneath. Caucasus.—— In the rock-garden, or warm borders, in deep loam and leaf-mould. Division or seed.

Primula Auricula (*Common Auricula*).— A well-known old garden-plant. *Flowers*, in spring; in various colours; stalks many-flowered, about the length of the leaves; tube of corolla gradually widening upwards, nearly 3 times the length of the bell-shaped calyx. *Leaves*, succulent, obovate, smooth, serrated, mealy at the edges. There are a great number of varieties. Alps of Switzerland.——Borders, in moist, open, rich soil. The fine variety, known as "alpine" in gardens, deserves to be abundantly grown on rockwork, and on the margins of the mixed border. Division and seed.

Primula cortusoides (*Cortusa P.*)—A rather tall and distinct kind; 6 to 10 in. high; with leaves like those of *Cortusa*. *Flowers*, in early summer; deep rose, in umbels. *Leaves*, large and soft, heart-shaped, almost lobed, crenated, wrinkled, on stalks 2 to 4 in. long. Siberia.——Borders, and the rock-garden, in sheltered positions, or among low shrubs and evergreen herbs, where it may not suffer much from winds, and in light vegetable soil. Division and seed.

Primula denticulata (*Toothed Primrose*).—A pleasing and distinct kind, not unfrequently seen cultivated in pots, but less so in the open air; 8 in. to 1 ft. high. *Flowers*, in spring and early summer; numerous, bright lilac, small, in neat, dense umbels; divisions of the calyx blackish. *Leaves*, oblong-lanceolate, wrinkled, toothed, hairy on both sides, and densely so underneath, where they are also more or less covered with a white mealiness. Mountains of Nepaul.——The rock-garden, in well-drained deep loam, and leaf-mould; also in pots in cold frames, for early blooming in the greenhouse. Division.

Primula erosa (*Fortune's Primrose*).—*P. Fortunei.*—Nearly related to *P. denticulata*, but distinguished from it by the smoothness of its leaves; 8 to 12 in. high. *Flowers*, in spring; purplish, with yellow eyes, in flattish heads, borne on stems usually very mealy, as is also the calyx. *Leaves*, obovate-lanceolate, obtuse, quite smooth and shining, generally without mealiness. Native of Nepaul.——The same treatment and positions as those for the preceding kind.

Primula farinosa (*Bird's-eye Primrose*).—A charming native species, with silvery leaves, in small rosettes, and flower-stems from 3 to 12 in. high, sometimes more. *Flowers*, in early summer; lilac-purple, with a yellow eye, in a compact umbel, on a stalk longer than the leaves; corolla small, tube about equalling the mealy calyx; lobes narrow, deeply notched. *Leaves*, obovate-lance-shaped, broadest near the top, toothed, small, often not more than 1 in. long, smooth above, and clothed beneath with a white, mealy down. *P. farinosa acaulis* is a diminutive variety of the preceding, with the flowers nestling down in the hearts of the leaves. Northern England and Scotland.——The rock-garden, or artificial bog, in moist peat, or fine sandy loam. It may also be grown to perfection in pots, plunged in sand, in the open air in fully exposed positions, supplied with plenty of water all through the spring and summer months. Division and seed.

Primula glutinosa (*Glutinous P.*)—A very beautiful and distinct species, deciduous in winter, growing about 4 in. high. *Flowers*, early in summer; brilliant bluish-purple, in clusters, nearly sessile. *Leaves*, lanceolate-wedge-shaped, erect, obtuse, smooth, margin serrated from the middle upwards. Styria, Carinthia, and the Tyrol.——Rockwork, in rich, moist, well-drained loam and grit; also in pots in cold frames, or plunged out of doors in beds of sand. Seed or division.

Primula integrifolia (*Entire-leaved P.*)—A neat kind, with glistening leaves, in rosettes close to the ground.

PRIMULA.

Flowers, in spring and early summer; rose, from 1 to 3 on stems 2 or 3 in. high, often so large as to hide the foliage; corolla deeply lobed; tube longer than the calyx. *Leaves*, elliptic or oblong, entire, smooth, shining, ciliate at the edge; margin of leaves and flower-stem villous. European Mountains.—— The rock-garden, in moist, fibry loam; also in pots. Division and seed.

Primula involucrata (*Creamy Primrose*).—A distinct and easily grown kind, 5 to 7 in. high. *Flowers*, in spring; of a creamy white, with a yellowish eye; lobes of the corolla roundish. *Leaves*, erect, oblong-lanceolate, of a bright green, narrowed into the leaf-stalk, disposed somewhat in the form of a rosette; stem surrounded near the top by a membranous, much-divided involucrum under the umbel of flowers. Nepaul.—— Moist spots in the rock-garden or bog-bed, in peat. This kind thrives freely in pots, plunged half way in water. Division.

Primula japonica (*Japan Primrose*). —A noble species recently introduced from Japan. *Flowers*, in May; deep crimson-rose with a wall-flower coloured ring round the mouth of the tube, arranged in whorls, many flowers in each, and from 3 to 6 whorls on a firm straight stem, from 12 to 20 in. high. *Leaves*, oval, obtuse, attenuated at the base, 6 to 10 in. long, and 3 to 4½ in. broad, thickly but somewhat irregularly toothed, hairless; midribs of leaves broad, succulent; veins very prominent below. Japan.——In the rock-garden, not among minute alpine species, but grouped with subjects growing a foot high or more, and in sheltered positions where its fine foliage would not be injured by harsh winds; also on warm sheltered borders and among dwarf shrubs, in sandy loam and leaf-mould. Seed, and division.

Primula latifolia (*Broad-leaved P.*)— A stout and handsome species, with from 1 to 20 flowers in an umbel, less viscid, larger, and more robust than *P. viscosa*; 4 to 8 in. high. *Flowers*, in early summer; violet, throat mealy, calyx also mealy. *Leaves*, obovate or oblong, sometimes 4 in. long, and nearly 2 in. broad; serrately toothed from the middle upwards, ciliate, and sprinkled with hairs on both sides. Pyrenees, Alps of Dauphiny, and other mountain chains in Southern Europe. ——The rock-garden, in moist sandy loam mixed with leaf-mould; also in pots, either in frames or plunged in sand in the open air. Division.

Primula longiflora (*Long-flowered P.*) — Closely allied to the Bird's-eye Primrose, but readily distinguished by its much longer flowers, which are also of a deeper colour than those of that species; about 4 in. high. *Flowers*, in early summer; purplish with white eye, 5 or 6 in a drooping umbel; tube of corolla 1 to 1¼ in. long, 3 times the length of the calyx; lobes narrower than in those of *P. farinosa*. *Leaves*, oblong or obovate, smooth, slightly crenate, pale but not mealy beneath. Mountains of Austria and Italy.—— The rock-garden, in moist places, in free loam. Division and seed.

Primula marginata (*Margined Primrose*).—Readily known by the white margins to its silver-grey leaves, 2 to 4 in. high. *Flowers*, in spring; violet-rose; scape many-flowered; throat of corolla mealy; calyx bell-shaped, slightly spreading, mealy within and on the margin. *Leaves*, oblong or obovate, deeply and unequally toothed, margins silvery from a bed of mealy dust lying on them. Alps of Tauria and Dauphiny. There is a very fine variety known as *P. marginata major*, deeper in colour and larger in all its parts.——The rock-garden and borders, in moist sandy loam. Division.

Primula minima (*Fairy Primrose*).—A most diminutive species, with very large and handsome flowers; about 1½ in. high. *Flowers*, in early summer; rose-coloured or sometimes white, large for the size of the plant, being often nearly 1 in. across, generally one on each short stem, but occasionally two. *Leaves*, about ½ in. long, smooth and shining, wedge-shaped, nearly square at the ends, stalkless, with 5 or 7 sharp teeth at the top, quite entire at the sides. *P. Floerkiana* is very nearly allied to this, if anything more than a variety, differing chiefly by the flower-stems bearing 2, 3, or more flowers, and by the leaves being roundish at the ends and toothed down the edges for a short distance. Mountains of Southern Europe.——The rock-garden, in rich moist loam, associated with *Eritrichium nanum*, *Ionopsidion acaule*, the Bavarian and other small Gentians, and like plants. Division.

Primula Munroi (*Munro's Primrose*).—Nearly allied to *P. involucrata*; 6 to 8 in. high. *Flowers*, in spring and early summer; white with a yellowish eye; corolla inflated about the middle, and with rounded, two-cleft lobes; calyx oblong, narrowed at the base, with 5 small teeth. *Leaves*, on long stalks, nearly heart-shaped, obtuse, slightly indented, smooth. Mountains of Nepaul, in the vicinity of water.——Same treatment, positions, etc., as those for *P. involucrata*.

Primula nivea (*Snowy Primrose*).—A neat kind, considered by some to be a variety of *P. viscosa*; 4 to 6 in. high. *Flowers*, in spring; pure white, freely produced in large trusses on stems as high again as the leaves; lobes of corolla obcordate; involucre small. *Leaves*, obovate or spathulate, ciliated, smooth, flat, sharply and irregularly toothed, rarely entire. Native of the Alps.——The rock-garden, choice border, or grown in pots in a cold frame, in light moist soil. Division.

Primula Palinuri (*Large-leaved Primrose*).—A vigorous kind, quite removed from all the other Primulas, inasmuch as it seems to grow all to leaf and stem; 6 to 9 in. high. *Flowers*, in April and May; bright yellow, in a drooping umbel at the top of the powdered stem; corolla funnel-shaped; calyx mealy, segments acute. *Leaves*, broad, spoon-shaped, smooth, sharply and unequally toothed, of a bright pale green, almost as large as those of young cabbages. Native of Southern Italy.——Borders, in deep soil, and also in the rock-garden, but not associated with the dwarf alpine kinds. Division.

Primula purpurea (*Purple Primrose*).—Allied to *P. denticulata*, but more ornamental; 6 to 10 in. high. *Flowers*, in spring and early summer; of an exquisite dark purple, in umbels about 3 in. across; mouth of the corolla very much dilated. *Leaves*, lanceolate, obtuse, very smooth, covered underneath with a yellow mealiness, notched and wavy on the margin; leaf-stalk winged, dilated at the base, rough, somewhat sheathing. High mountains of Nepaul.——Sheltered nooks in the rock-garden, at the base of large rocks and stones, in deep loam and leaf-mould. Division.

Primula scotica (*Scotch Bird's-eye P.*)—An exquisite kind, like the Bird's-eye P., but smaller and neater; 2 to 4 in. high. *Flowers*, in April or May; rich purple with yellowish eye; tube of the corolla about equalling the calyx and twice as long as the lobes. *Leaves*, obovate-lance-shaped, broadest near the middle, shorter and less indented than those of *P. farinosa*; very powdery on the underside. In damp

P

pastures in the counties of Caithness and Sutherland, and also the Orkney Isles.——The rock-garden, in moist sandy loam, in mossy spots, and in pots or pans. Seed; it frequently comes up from self-sown seeds in mossy places.

Primula sikkimensis (*Sikkim Cowslip*).—Like a tall and noble Cowslip, 1¼ to 2 ft. high. *Flowers*, in summer; pale yellow, nearly 1 in. long and more than ¼ in. across; in large umbels sometimes containing more than five dozen flowers each. *Leaves*, rough, wrinkled, obovate-oblong, obtuse, twice dentate, attenuated into a footstalk of equal length. Sikkim, Himalayas.——Moist deep soil, in the rock-garden; and when plentiful enough it should be tried as a border plant, and also in rich moist soil near the margins of streams or ponds. Division.

Primula Stuartii (*Stuart's Primrose*).—A vigorous, handsome, and very rare Primrose, about 16 in. high. *Flowers*, in summer; rich golden yellow, numerous, in umbels; stem mealy at the top. *Leaves*, nearly 1 ft. long, broadly-lanceolate, mealy below, smooth above, and sharply serrated. Native of Northern India.—— The rock-garden, in good light and deep soil. Till more plentiful it should be given favourable positions in the lower parts of the rock-garden, and where it would not be liable to suffer from strong cold winds. Division.

Primula Veitchii (*Veitch's Primrose*).—*P. cortusoides amœna*, Hook.— A handsome plant, allied to *P. cortusoides*, but distinct, and much larger and handsomer; 8 to 12 in. high. *Flowers*, in April and May; fine deep rose with white eye, but varying a good deal, the white in some forms spreading nearly over the petals, 1 to 1¾ in. across, 6 to 10 in an umbel. *Leaves*, ovate, the larger ones somewhat heart-shaped at the base, coarsely and irregularly toothed, 2 to 3 in. long, and 1 to more than 2 in. across, sometimes larger when grown under glass; seed-vessel grooved; seed roundish, flattened. *Root* creeping. Japan. As this plant is quite distinct, both in a botanical and horticultural point of view, from *P. cortusoides*, I venture to name it after its introducer, the late John Gould Veitch. —— In the rock-garden, on sheltered sunny places where the plant will escape injury from winds, and also in sheltered borders, and among dwarf shrubs, etc., in light, rich, sandy loam with leaf-mould. Seed and division of established tufts.

Primula veris (*Cowslip*).—Our well-known old friend of the early summer meadows; 4 in. to 1 ft. high. *Flowers*, in spring and early summer; bright yellow, in terminal umbels, hanging more or less to one side. *Leaves*, generally smaller than those of the Primrose, contracted immediately below the broadest part, and thickly pubescent with short stiff hairs. Europe and Britain.—— The numerous varieties of this plant, usually known as Polyanthuses, and many of which may be raised so easily from seed, are of great beauty, and should be grown abundantly, not only in beds in the flower-garden, but naturalized in semi-wild places. —— The Polyanthuses thrive best in a rich, light, and moist soil, but do well in ordinary garden earth. Division and seed.

[The true, or Bardfield Oxlip (*P. elatior*) is readily distinguished by its funnel-(and not saucer-)shaped corolla, which is also quite destitute of the bosses which are present in the Primrose and Cowslip. The common Oxlip (*P. officinali-vulgaris*) is a hybrid from *P. vulgaris* and *P. officinalis*, and differs from *P. elatior* in having larger flowers on much longer pedicels, triangular calyx-teeth, the limb of the corolla of a brighter colour and more spreading, the segments much broader and rounder, and the throat somewhat contracted, with 5 bilobed bosses, as in the Primrose and Cowslip. The Common Oxlip and its varieties are well worthy of being encouraged in the rougher parts of our pleasure-grounds, copses, etc. The Bardfield Oxlip is not so ornamental.]

Primula viscosa (*Viscid Primose*).— *P. villosa.*—A very handsome Primrose, very common on the Alps; 2 to 4 in. high. *Flowers,* in early summer; rosy-purple, with white eye, in umbels, on viscid stems; lobes of corolla heart-shaped, gashed; tube twice as long as the bell-shaped calyx. *Leaves,* obovate or suborbicular, with closely-set teeth, dark green, covered with glandular hairs, and viscid on both sides. The two handsome purple Primroses, known in gardens as *P. ciliata* and *P. ciliata purpurea,* are varieties of this, the latter said to be a hybrid between it and an Auricula. Alps and Pyrenees. —— The rock-garden and choice borders, in moist rich soil. It will be the better of being divided and replanted every autumn, or at least every alternate autumn. Division.

Primula vulgaris (*Common Primrose*). Our common Primrose; 3 to 6 in. high. *Flowers,* in spring; yellow, large, solitary, on peduncles, apparently radical, but which really spring from an umbel, the stalk of which is hidden by the base of the leaves. *Leaves,* obovate or oblong, tapering to the base, veined and wrinkled, smooth above and hairy beneath. There are many varieties of various colours, all of which are well worthy of cultivation. Very abundant in Britain. —— It is needless to say in how many ways this beautiful native plant may be grown in wild-wood or in garden. The charming coloured varieties now obtainable should be abundantly naturalized in pleasure-grounds, and the lovely old double kinds should be in every garden.' They enjoy partial shade, and light, rich, moist soil, and are easily propagated by division.

Prunella grandiflora (*Great Self-heal*). — A showy perennial; 6 to 12 in. high. *Flowers,* in summer; violet or purple, in 6-flowered whorls, densely spiked; corolla large, more than an inch long, above twice the length of the calyx; tube a little contracted at the throat; calyx tubularly bell-shaped, somewhat 10-nerved. *Leaves,* rather soft, ovate, entire or toothed; lower ones about 2½ in. long with channelled footstalks longer than the leaves; upper ones smaller, pinnatifid, and on footstalks shorter than the leaves. There is a white-flowered variety. Europe. —— Borders, in sandy loam, and naturalization in copses, etc. This plant frequently perishes in winter on stiff clay soils. Division and seed.

Prunella pyrenaica (*Pyrenean Self-heal*).—Allied to the preceding, and considered a variety of it; 8 in. to 1 ft. or more high. *Flowers,* in summer; larger than those of *P. grandiflora;* of a beautiful violet - purple above, much lighter within and white beneath, in large terminal cylindrical heads; upper part of the calyx deep purple. *Leaves,* hastate, irregularly lobed; radical ones nearly entire, oval-obtuse in outline, with a truncate base; lower stem-leaves often arrow-shaped, sometimes toothed at the base; upper ones oval, entire, toothed or pinnatifid. Pyrenees.——The same positions and treatment as those recommended for the preceding kind.

Pulmonaria dahurica (*Siberian P.*) —A graceful and slender perennial, with erect stems, smooth at the base, hairy above; 1 ft. to 16 in. high. *Flowers,* in May; beautiful blue, tubular, in panicled clusters, drooping at first, afterwards erect and elongated; corolla much longer than the calyx, which is hairy, and has acute sepals. *Leaves*, soft, smooth underneath, and covered with rough adpressed hairs on the upper side; root-leaves oval, stalked; stem-leaves linear-lanceolate, acuminate, sessile. Siberia. —— In the rock-garden, in sheltered nooks, or in borders or beds among dwarf shrubs, etc., which may prevent its being injured by high winds, in sandy peat and loam. Division.

Pulmonaria officinalis (*Lungwort*).— A British plant, much grown in gardens under various names. *Flowers*, in spring; rose changing to blue, in small terminal clusters, on stems 6 to 12 in. high. *Leaves* of root, in distinct tufts, ovate-oblong, on long stalks, about 6 in. long and 2½ in. broad, dark green on the upper side marked with many whitish spots, pale and not spotted beneath; stem-leaves smaller, almost stalkless, alternate. *P. angustifolia*, with blue flowers and narrow leaves that are rarely spotted, is by some botanists united with this species, and there is also a white-flowered and a spotless variety in cultivation. Woods in Central and Southern Europe, also found in Hampshire and the Isle of Wight in Britain. —— Borders, beds in the spring garden, and allowed to run wild in shrubberies, etc., in ordinary soil. Division.

Puschkinia scilloides (*Striped Squill*). —A beautiful spring-flowering bulb; 3 to 6 in. high. *Flowers*, in spring; whitish, striped with a delicate blue; divisions of equal length, lanceolate, rather blunt; tube short, of a deeper hue than the limb; arranged in a raceme of 4 to 10 blooms. *Leaves*, small, linear-lanceolate, concave. The Caucasus, especially the eastern parts. —— The rock-garden, bulb-garden, and choice borders, in deep sandy loam and leaf-mould. Separation of the bulbs every second or third year.

Pyrethrum achilleæfolium (*Narrow-leaved P.*)—A silky species; 2 ft. high. *Flowers*, in summer; few, golden yellow, almost globular, on long stalks, arranged in loose corymbs; inner scales of involucrum round, white and transparent at the top. *Leaves*, pinnatifid, with pinnate segments, covered with a white silky down when young, pubescent when full-grown. A variety named *pubescens* has numerous heads, arranged in broad corymbs. The Caucasus. —— Borders, in ordinary soil. Not very ornamental in its flowers, but with graceful leaves. Division.

Pyrethrum carneum (*Rosy P.*) — *Pyrethrum roseum.*—A very ornamental composite plant, 1½ to 2 ft. high. *Flowers*, in summer; solitary, larger than the Ox-eye Daisy, with a yellow disk, and rays of rose-colour more or less deep. *Leaves*, twice pinnate, with decurrent, lanceolate, incised segments, of a vivid green. The Caucasus. There are now many double varieties of this plant, many of them of great beauty. —— Borders, and beds, in good sandy loam. Division and seed.

Pyrethrum lacustre (*Marsh P.*)— *Chrysanthemum lacustre.* — A hardy herbaceous perennial, 2 to 2½ ft. high. *Flowers*, late in summer; 2 in. across, pure white with a yellow centre, solitary, terminal and axillary. *Leaves*, alternate, numerous, sessile, oval-lance-shaped, coarsely and irregularly toothed. Portugal.— Borders, and naturalization in deep moist soil. Division.

Pyrethrum Parthenium (*Feverfew*). — A well-known native plant, 1 to 2 ft. high. *Flowers*, in summer; ¼ to ¾ in. across, in a terminal corymb; florets of the ray white, disk yellow. *Leaves*, pinnate; leaflets ovate or oblong, pinnatifid and toothed; stalk shortly branched. There is a fine double-flowered variety popular in gardens: the *Pyrethrum* known as Golden Feather, and much used as an edging plant, is a yellowish-leaved sport from this. Europe and Caucasus, and rather freely dispersed over many parts of Britain, but probably not truly indigenous.——The double variety is a pretty border-plant, sometimes, too, used in mixed bedding arrangements, and will grow in any soil. Division.

Pyrethrum serotinum (*Late-flowering P.*)—A showy tall perennial, growing from 4 to 6 ft. high. *Flowers*, in autumn; 3 in. across, pure white with a yellow centre, solitary on the ends of the corymbose branches; scales of the involucrum brown on the margins, and terminated by an obtuse, transparent appendage. *Leaves*, smooth, sessile, lance-shaped, coarsely toothed; upper leaves entire. North America.—— Borders, among tall Asters, etc., shrubberies, or naturalization in ordinary soil. Division.

Pyrethrum Tchihatchewii (*Turfing Daisy*). — A dwarf hardy evergreen species, forming a dense turf, a little over 2 in. high. *Flowers*, early in summer; pure white with a yellowish disk, solitary, on axillary flower-stalks, 3 to 6 in. in length. *Leaves*, elegantly divided, with linear segments, of a fine dark-green colour; stems very numerous, rooting. Asia Minor.—— Useful for carpeting slopes, or even for making small turf-plats, on very arid soil where little else will grow. Division.

Pyrola rotundifolia (*Larger Wintergreen*).—A rare native evergreen herb. *Flowers*, in summer; pure white, fragrant, from 10 to 20 in a drooping raceme on an erect stem 6 to 12 in. high. *Leaves*, roundish or broadly oval, slightly toothed, or serrate. A variety, *P. arenaria*, found on sandy sea-shores, differs from the preceding in being dwarfer, deep green and smooth, and generally with several empty scale-like bracts below the inflorescence. Britain, in damp bushy places and reedy marshes.——Moist and half shady parts of the rock-garden and hardy fernery, in peaty soil, mixed with decaying moss, etc. Division.

Pyxidanthera barbulata (*Pine-Barren Beauty*). — A minute prostrate evergreen shrub, closely allied to the *Diapensia*, and singularly pretty; about 2 in. high. *Flowers*, in early summer; white, rose-coloured in the bud, solitary, stalkless, very numerous; corolla bell-shaped, 5-lobed, lobes rounded; calyx of 5 concave sepals. *Leaves*, narrow, awl-shaped, densely crowded, bearded at the base, mostly alternate on the sterile branches. Sandy "pine barrens" from New Jersey to North Carolina. ——The rock-garden, in very sandy soil and in sunny spots. Division.

Ramondia pyrenaica (*Rosette Mullein*).—A handsome stemless herb, with leaves in rosettes spreading flat on the ground; about 3 in. high. *Flowers*, in early summer; purple-violet, with orange-yellow centre, somewhat like that of the Potato, 1 to 1½ in. across, usually solitary, (rarely 2-5-flowered), on naked stalks 2 to 6 in. high. *Leaves*, ovate, tapering into the stalk, broadly and deeply crenated, deeply wrinkled and densely covered with short hairs, quite shaggy beneath and on the leaf-stalk. In groves on the Pyrenees and in Piedmont.——The rock-garden, in warm nooks and in moist, free, peaty, and gritty soil. Seed and careful division.

Ranunculus aconitifolius (*Fair Maids of France*).—A beautiful old border plant, usually seen in the double form, 8 in. to 3 ft. high. *Flowers*, in early summer; white, sometimes few, sometimes numerous; calyx smooth. *Leaves*, palmately 3- or 5-lobed, with the partitions deeply toothed; those of the stem cut into narrow lance-shaped lobes; stem branched. The flowers of the variety with double flowers, are so neat and pretty that they might almost be taken at first sight for miniature double white *Camellia* blossoms. Moist parts of valleys and woods in the Alps and Pyrenees.——The double kind in borders, in deep moist and free soil. The single one is best suited for naturalization in grassy places. Division.

Ranunculus acris (*Upright Meadow Buttercup*).—A very common, more or less hairy, native herb, with erect stems, varying in height from about 6 in. to 2 ft. or more. *Flowers*, most of the summer and autumn; bright yellow, large, on long terminal stalks, forming a large loose panicle; sepals of a yellowish-green, concave, shorter than the notched or entire petals. *Leaves*, nearly all stalked, 3- 5- or 7-parted, the lobes cut into 3 lance-shaped, acute, toothed segments; black or deep-purple at the points; stem not very leafy, round, hollow, much branched at top.——This plant is so very common in meadows and pastures throughout Europe, that it would not have been mentioned here were it not for the beauty of its fine double form, *R. acris, fl. pl.*, which is worthy of a place among the best medium-sized plants in borders, and grows freely in any soil. Division.

Ranunculus alpestris (*Alp Crowfoot*).—A pretty and diminutive species, 1 to 3 or 4 in. high. *Flowers*, in April; white; 1 to 3 on a stem; petals obcordate or 3-lobed; calyx smooth. *Leaves*, of a dark glossy green; root-leaves roundish or heart-shaped, 3-lobed, lobes deeply crenate, blunt at the apex; stem-leaves lance-shaped, entire. The leaves are sometimes trifid, sometimes hardly trifid, and sometimes 3-parted. Carpathian mountains, Pyrenees, Alps of Jura.——The rock-garden, in moist, sandy, or gritty soil; also in choice borders, in the same kind of soil, or naturalization by the margins of mountain rivulets, etc., in unshaded places. Division and seed.

Ranunculus amplexicaulis (*Snowy Crowfoot*).—A very graceful and showy kind, readily known by its handsome undivided leaves clasping the stem; 3 to 9 in. high. *Flowers*, in spring; white, with yellow centres, from 1 to 6 on each stem; scape and peduncles smooth. *Leaves*, ovate or lance-shaped, taper pointed, glaucous, smooth, or with a few deciduous hairs on the edges. *Roots* in bundles. Alps, Pyrenees, and other European mountain ranges.——The rock-garden and borders, best in moist loam, with plenty of vegetable matter and sand, though it thrives in ordinary garden soil; also a charming subject for naturalization in moist sandy soils, amid dwarf vegetation. Division.

Ranunculus bulbosus (*Bulbous Buttercup*). — A native British plant, common in meadows, and distinguished by the swollen or bulb-like base of the stem; about 1 ft. high. *Flowers*, in early summer; bright yellow, with hairy reflexed calyces, and furrowed peduncles. *Leaves*, of the root 3-lobed, lobes 3-parted, stalked; upper leaves cut into narrow segments.——Only mentioned here for the sake of recommending its double variety, (*R. b. fl. pl.*) which is a very pretty border plant, thriving in ordinary soil, and suitable for association with dwarfer plants than the double var. of *R. acris*, as it seldom grows more than half a foot high. Division.

Ranunculus chærophyllus (*Chervil Buttercup*).—A hardy, tuberous-rooted kind, 8 in. to 1 ft. high. *Flowers*, in early summer; brilliant glistening yellow, more than 1 in. across; divisions of calyx persistent, not reflexed. *Leaves*, stalked, much divided; segments very narrow; stem slightly downy. Portugal.——The rock-garden, and the margins of the mixed border, in fine sandy soil. Division.

Ranunculus glacialis (*Glacier Crowfoot*).—A very high alpine species; 3 to 6 in. high. *Flowers*, in summer; white, tinted with purplish rose on the outside, from 1 to 5 on a stem; calyx soft, with shaggy, brownish hairs; petals roundish, slightly notched, as long as the calyx. *Leaves*, usually smooth, the upper ones sometimes villous, palmately 3-parted or ternate, the lobes deeply cut, and of a dark brownish-green. Alps of Europe, among rocks near the limits of perpetual snow.——Cool and very moist spots in the rock-garden, in deep, gritty, peaty soil. Division.

Ranunculus Gouani (*Gouan's Buttercup*).—A large, robust, and very showy kind, about 1½ ft. high. *Flowers*, in May; bright yellow, nearly 2 in. across; sepals oval-acute, thinly covered with weak, longish hairs. *Leaves*, slightly downy; those of the root long-stalked, roundish in outline, 3- to 5-parted; segments deeply toothed; stem-leaves irregularly lobed, sessile; stem and peduncles more or less downy. Pyrenees.——Borders, in sandy soil, and naturalization in rough places. Division or seed.

Ranunculus gramineus (*Grassy Crowfoot*).—Easily known by its narrow grass-like leaves; 6 to 16 in. high. *Flowers*, in May; yellow, not numerous; petals triangular, wedge-shaped at the base; sepals smooth. *Leaves*, linear-lanceolate, entire, striated, smooth; stem and peduncles also smooth. There is a double variety, but it is seldom seen. Southern Europe.——Borders, in ordinary soil, and naturalization in grassy places. Division.

Ranunculus Lingua (*Large Marsh Buttercup*).—A vigorous marsh and brook-side plant; 2 to 3 ft. high. *Flowers*, in summer; bright yellow, 1½ in. across, usually not more than 2 or 3, erect on the top of the stem. *Leaves*, 8 or 9 in. long, and about 1 in. broad, smooth, lance-shaped, pointed, entire, sessile, embracing the stem. Britain and Europe.——In tufts on the margins of lakes, or streams, or in bogs. Division.

Ranunculus monspeliacus (*Montpellier R.*)—A large and handsome species, covered with silky down, 8 to 18 in. high. *Flowers*, in early summer; bright golden yellow, glistening, more than 1 in. across, with a broad wedge-shaped scale at the base of each petal; sepals very downy, reflected. *Leaves*, of the root ternate, or deeply 3-cleft, with segments more or less stalked, and subdivided into oval-lance-shaped or linear-lance-shaped divisions, which are sometimes bluntly toothed; stem-leaves narrow, with lance-shaped segments. *Root* composed of a closely-set bundle of small knobs, ending in, and interspersed with, fibres. Montpellier, and all the southern parts of France.——Borders, in sandy loam, and naturalization in grassy places. Division.

Ranunculus montanus (*Mountain Buttercup*).—A diminutive erect kind, with a creeping underground stem; 3 to 6 in. high. *Flowers*, in early summer; brilliant golden yellow, rather larger than those of the Common Buttercup, each little stem bearing one flower; calyx nearly smooth, spreading. *Leaves*, smooth; root-leaves roundish in outline, 3-parted, with trifid blunt segments; those of the stem stalkless, usually only two, 3- to 5-parted into linear, entire lobes. Alpine pastures on the principal great mountain chains of Europe.——The rock-garden and borders, in sandy soil, and associated with dwarf and compact plants. Division and seed.

Ranunculus parnassifolius (*Parnassia-leaved R.*)—A distinct and attractive kind, with leathery roundish leaves, somewhat like those of a *Cyclamen*; 2 to 8 in. high. *Flowers*, in early summer; snowy white, sometimes tinted with pink, about the size of those of *R. amplexicaulis*, from 1 to 12 on each stem; stems velvety, and of a purplish hue; peduncles hairy; calyx pinkish. *Leaves*, of a dark brownish green, entire, sometimes slightly woolly along the margins and nerves; root-leaves stalked, rather heart-shaped, ovate or roundish; those of the stem stalkless, ovate-lance-shaped. Abundant in many parts of the Pyrenees and Alps.——The rock-garden, in moist sandy soil; and also among the dwarf plants in the choice mixed border. Division and seed.

Ranunculus rutæfolius (*Rue-leaved Crowfoot*).—*Callianthemum rutæfolium.* —Known at once by its much divided leaves; 3 to 6 in. high. *Flowers*, in early summer; white, with orange centres, about 1 in. across; the stems usually bearing but 1 flower, but occasionally 2 or 3; petals 8 or 10, oblong; calyx smooth. *Leaves*, much and deeply divided; root-leaves twice divided. The higher Alps of Europe, near the limits of perpetual snow.—— The rock-garden, in moist sandy, or gritty soil. Division and seed.

Ranunculus spicatus (*Spiked Crowfoot*).—A large and handsome kind; 1 to 1½ ft. high. *Flowers*, in spring; yellow, on erect, few-flowered stems; calyx reflexed; carpels in a long spike. *Leaves*, somewhat hairy, stalked, roundish, 3-lobed; upper ones 3-parted; lobes linear, entire. Sicily and N. Africa.——Borders, in sandy soil. Division and seed.

Rhaponticum cynaroides (*Artichoke R.*)—A sturdy perennial, with graceful leaves; about 3 ft. high. *Flowers*, late in summer; few, erect, purple; scales of the involucrum toothed. *Leaves*, broad, oblong or oval, narrowed at the base, pointed at the apex; the lower ones pinnate; the upper ones hardly pinnatifid, the divisions all fringed with sharp teeth. Pyrenees. —— Among hardy plants having fine foliage, isolated in groves, near margins of shrubberies, in borders, and in rough places, in any deep soil. Division and seed.

Rhaponticum pulchrum (*Pretty R.*) —Another ornamental species; 2 ft. or more high. *Flowers*, late in summer; purplish, solitary, on the summits of the stems, which are leafless in the upper part. *Leaves*, the radical ones stalked; those of the stem sessile, all pinnately-cut, smooth above, covered with white down underneath, with oval, toothed segments which become confluent at the end. Caucasus. —— Similar positions and treatment to those recommended for the preceding kind.

Rheum Emodi (*Red-veined Rhubarb*). —A noble herbaceous plant, with very handsome foliage; about 5 ft. high. *Flowers*, in summer; very numerous, small, yellowish-white, arranged in long branching clusters. *Leaves*, alternate, very large, long-stalked, with a slightly wrinkled surface, large red veins and somewhat wavy edges; those of the stem gradually diminishing in size towards the top. Tartary. —— Isolated in the grass near the margins of shrubberies in the picturesque garden, or grouped with other fine-leaved hardy plants, in deep rich soil. Division and seed.

Rheum palmatum (*Palmate Rhubarb*).
—Known at once by its deeply-cut leaves; 6 to 8 ft. high. *Flowers*, in early summer; greenish-white, surrounding the branches in numerous clusters, and forming a sort of spike. *Leaves*, of root, numerous, large, rough, deeply cut into lobes, the lobes cut into irregular pointed segments, on long, round footstalks, becoming gradually smaller near the top. *Stem* erect, round, hollow, jointed, branched near the top. China and Tartary.
—— In groups of fine-leaved hardy plants; also suited for isolation with such subjects as the Ferulas, in deep rich soil. Division and seed.

Rhexia virginica (*Meadow Beauty*).
—A brilliant perennial, forming neat little bushes; 6 to 12 in. high. *Flowers*, in summer; bright rosy-purple, in cymose corymbs; petals 4, heart-shaped, spreading in the form of a cross, inserted with the 8 ochre-yellow stamens at the top of the tube of the calyx, which is urn-shaped and 4-cleft at the apex. *Leaves*, oval or lance-shaped, acute, opposite, entire, hairy, 3-nerved, about 2 in. long and ½ in. broad; stems square, with wing-like angles. North America.——In the artificial bog, or moist spots in the lower part of the rock-garden, always in very moist peat. Careful division.

Rhododendron Chamæcistus (*Thyme-leaved R.*)—A dwarf, tufted, evergreen, much-branched shrub, with small fleshy leaves about the size of those of *Helianthemum*; 6 in. high. *Flowers*, in early summer; of a beautiful pink colour, 3 or 4 together, about the size of those of *Kalmia latifolia*; peduncles 1 in. long, reddish-brown; corolla wheel-shaped, 5-cleft, segments ovate; calyx 5-cleft, of the same colour as the peduncles, segments acute; stamens 10. *Leaves*, oblong, stiffish, ciliated at the edge, on short reddish stalks. Calcareous rocks in the Tyrol.

——The rock-garden, in limestone fissures, in a mixture of equal parts of peat, loam, and sand; also in beds of choice dwarf shrubs. Seed and layers.

Rosa alpina pyrenaica (*Small Pyrenean Rose*).—A beautiful little mountain Rose, a variety of the Alpine Rose, but much smaller. *Flowers*, in summer; of a fine rosy lake, each bloom more than 2 in. across; calyx and flower-stalks covered with glandular hairs. *Leaves*, oblong-elliptical, toothed; teeth glandular, distant. Pyrenees.——The rock-garden, in dry poorish soil. Cuttings and seed.

Rudbeckia californica (*Californian Cone-flower*).—A vigorous hardy perennial, with a stout branching stem; 5 to 6 ft. high. *Flowers*, in summer; golden-yellow, about 5 in. across, with a dark brown conical centre more than 2 in. high. *Leaves*, oval, pointed, with an occasional lobe or tooth, rough; the lower ones 1 ft. long, and 6 in. across, attenuated into a stalk; the upper ones smaller and sessile. California.—— Back margins of the mixed border, shrubberies, or naturalization, in sandy loam. Seed or division.

Rudbeckia Drummondi (*Drummond's Cone-flower*). — *R. columnaris.— Obeliscaria pulcherrima.*—A showy perennial, 16 in. to 2 ft. high. *Flowers*, from June to September; florets of the ray citron-yellow at the base and point, purplish-brown in the middle, broadly obovate, slightly notched at the end, about 1¼ in. long, concave, twisted, and reflexed; in the place of the disk is a cylindrical-conic receptacle more than 1 in. long, closely covered with a great number of brownish florets. *Leaves*, alternate, pinnate, with linear toothed divisions; root-leaves not so deeply cut. Whole plant rough, slightly pubescent, of a greyish-green tint. Mexico.——Borders, in sandy loam. Division and seed.

Rudbeckia fulgida (*Glowing Cone-flower*).—Another showy kind, 2 ft. and upwards in height. *Flowers*, late in summer; 2 to nearly 3 in. across; florets of the ray nearly ½ in. long, orange-yellow, darker in the middle, unequal, spreading, 3-toothed; disk conical, purplish. *Leaves*, alternate, rough, those of the root oblong-lanceolate; lower stem-leaves toothed, upper ones entire and almost sessile. Stems rough, branching, tinged with red. North America.——Warm borders, in good dry loam. Division and seed.

Rudbeckia hirta (*Hairy Cone-flower*). —A showy, rough, hairy herb, 2 to 3 ft. high. *Flowers*, in summer; yellow, 3 to 4 in. across; disk dark purplish-brown. *Leaves*, lower ones spoon-shaped or oval, 3-nerved; upper ones stalkless, oblong or lance-shaped, toothed. North America. —— Borders, bare banks, naturalization in thin woods or margins of shrubberies, in ordinary soil. Division or seed.

Rudbeckia laciniata (*Cut-leaved Cone-flower*).—A showy perennial, 2 to 3½ ft. high. *Flowers*, in summer; bright pale yellow, 3 to 4 in. across; disk greenish - yellow, conical. *Leaves*, rough, clothed with small hairs, particularly at the edges, lower ones 5- to 7-parted; divisions 3-lobed, or sometimes cut; upper ones irregularly parted. *R. digitata* (*Newmanii, Hort.*) is a variety with the divisions of the lower leaves pinnatifid. North America.——Borders, and naturalization, in sandy loam. Division and seed.

Rudbeckia speciosa (*Showy Cone-flower*).—A rough, hairy, and showy plant, 1½ to 3 ft. high. *Flowers*, late in summer; orange-yellow, 3 to 4 in. across; disk blackish-purple,somewhat globose in fruit, about two-thirds of an inch long. *Leaves*, roughish, hairy, irregularly toothed, upper ones stalkless, lance-shaped; lower ones oval-lance-shaped, stalked, 3-nerved; root-leaves somewhat like the common Plantain. North America.——Borders, margins of shrubberies, or naturalization in thin woods or copses, in any rather sandy soil. Division and seed.

Rudbeckia triloba (*Three-lobed Cone-flower*).—A vigorous kind, 3 to 5 ft. high. *Flowers*, in summer; yellow, 2 to 3 in. across, 8 florets in a head; disk blackish-purple or deep brown. *Leaves*, lower ones 3-parted, coarsely toothed, upper undivided; root-leaves on slender stalks; those of the stem stalkless, somewhat hairy. North America.——Borders, bare banks, by wood-walks, or naturalization in open woods, in ordinary soil. Division or seed.

Rumex Hydrolapathum (*Water Dock*). —A huge plant, common in ditches and by the edges of streams in many parts of Britain; stem 4 to 5 ft. high, slightly branched. *Flowers*, in summer; greenish, in a long, dense panicle, leafy at the base. *Leaves*, lance-shaped or oblong, usually pointed, flat or slightly curled at the margins; root-leaves 2 to 3 ft. long, and 4 in. broad in the middle, narrowing into a long erect footstalk. Europe and Russian Asia.——An isolated tuft of this looks very well on the margin of a stream, pond, or lake, and may be effectively introduced in any marshy or wet place in or near the subtropical garden. Division.

Sagina glabra, *var.* **corsica** (*Lawn Pearlwort*). — *Spergula pilifera.* — A neat little alpine plant, moss-like in size and well-known from having been much recommended and often tried as a lawn plant, 2 or 3 in. high. *Flowers*, in summer; small, white, double the size of the calyx; sepals oblong, obtuse. *Leaves*, linear-awl-shaped, pointed. *Stem* half woody, sending out a great number of prostrate creeping branches from which spring erect flower-stalks. Alps of Dauphiny and

Corsica.——The rock-garden and borders, chiefly in wide-spreading tufts as a verdant carpet beneath taller subjects. Generally it is a failure in lawns. Unless great attention is given, no perfect lawn can be made with one kind of plant. Seed and division.

Salix reticulata (*Netted-leaved Willow*).—A prostrate, much branched, native alpine shrub, 3 to 6 in. high. *Flowers*, in early summer; catkins solitary, on longish stalks, at the ends of the short branches, purplish-red, as are also the buds. *Leaves*, about 1 in. long and broad, roundish, somewhat elliptical, entire, leathery, with netted veins, green and smooth above, white beneath. Scotch Highlands and mountains of Europe, Asia, and America. ——The rougher parts of the rock-garden, and on the margins of beds of dwarf shrubs, in light moist soil. It is only worth cultivating by those who take some interest in native plants. Division and cuttings.

Salix serpyllifolia (*Thyme-leaved S.*) —A curious little shrub, only 1 or 2 in. high. *Flowers*, in May; catkins oblong, few-flowered. *Leaves*, ovate, or ovate-lance-shaped, acute, entire, smooth, shining above. High mountains of France, Italy, and Switzerland. —— An interesting species for botanical and curious collections, the rock-garden, or borders, in moist, sandy soil. Cuttings and division.

Salvia argentea (*Silver Clary*).—*S. patula.*—A noble silvery-leaved biennial, 2 to 3 ft. high. *Flowers*, in early summer; in large whorls forming a panicled raceme; corolla white with the upper lip purplish and pubescent, the lower one yellowish; calyx bell-shaped, striped, villous; teeth rather spiny. *Leaves*, very large, ovate, 6 to 12 in. long, and 4 to 6 in. broad, clothed with loose white wool on both surfaces, stalked, wrinkled, sinuately lobed; stems erect, villous. Considerable variation may be observed among the plants, particularly as regards the size and hoariness of the leaves. Southern Europe and Africa. ——Borders, beds, and groups of silvery-leaved plants, in light sandy loam. As this plant is chiefly valuable for the beauty of its leaves, and these are seen to greatest perfection when spread flat on the ground in great rosettes before the plants flower, it is desirable to sow some of the seed every spring.

Salvia officinalis, *var.* tricolor (*Variegated Sage*).—A pretty variegated form of the common Sage, 1 ft. to 16 in. and upwards in height. *Flowers*, in summer; small, rosy-blue or whitish, not ornamental, in rather close groups of 4 to 6, forming a simple cluster. *Leaves*, oval-oblong, narrowed or rounded at the base, stalked, finely reticulated, of a greyish-green, often tinged with yellowish-white or flesh-colour, changing afterwards to rose-colour and sometimes to red; stems much branched, reddish. Whole plant covered with soft hairs, and diffusing a penetrating aromatic odour. Southern Europe. —— Borders, as a bedding plant, and on the margins of shrubberies, in any light soil. Cuttings.

Salvia patens (*Spreading Sage*). — The handsomest flowered *Salvia*, if not the handsomest labiate plant we have, 1½ to 2 ft. high. *Flowers*, in summer; fine blue, large and showy, in distant whorls. *Leaves*, heart-shaped or hastate, hairy above, pubescent below; stems somewhat shrubby at the base. Roots tuberous. Mexico. ——Warm borders, beds, and groups of fine perennials, in light, rich, and moist soil. It is unfortunately somewhat tender, and will, except in mild districts and in very favourable soils and positions, require protection at the root in winter; but, even if it perishes in spite of this precaution, it is sufficiently attractive to deserve being annually propagated from cuttings to ensure a good supply for planting annually. Cuttings and seed.

Salvia pratensis, *var.* **lupinoides** (*Lupin Salvia*).—A handsome form of a common British plant, 1¼ to 2 ft. high. *Flowers*, in summer; numerous, handsome; the upper lip, and the two lateral lobes of the lower one, light blue, while the large central lobe of the lower lip is white. *Leaves*, opposite, reticulated, wrinkled, those of the root spreading, stalked, oval-lance-shaped, with a heart-shaped base; the upper leaves sessile, clasping the stem; all irregularly and slightly toothed. France.——Borders, in any soil; also in a wild state in rough open places. Division and seed.

Sanguinaria canadensis (*Bloodroot*).—A singular and pretty plant, with thick creeping rootstocks; 3 to 6 in. high. *Flowers*, in spring; white, 1 on each stem; petals 8 to 12, spoon-shaped, inner ones narrower; sepals 2, ovate. *Leaves*, of root, kidney-shaped, lobed like those of the Fig. North America.——*S. grandiflora* is a variety with larger flowers; planted here and there under the branches of deciduous trees on lawns, this will be found to spread about, and without any attention become a charming naturalized plant. It prefers rather moist soil. The tubers of this plant purchased from the seedsmen are often dead before they are sold, as the plant does not bear being taken up and stored as some bulbs do. Division.

Santolina Chamæcyparissus (*Lavender Cotton*).—A grey shrubby plant, 2 to 2½ ft. high. *Flowers*, in summer; yellowish, in rounded heads. *Leaves*, alternate, linear, arranged in 4 to 6 rows, almost overlapping each other, somewhat fleshy, toothed; teeth oboval. Central Europe, in dry and arid places.——Among low shrubs, in borders, for forming low silvery hedges, on rough rock- or root-work, or naturalized on banks or rocky places, in any kind of soil. Division and cuttings.

Santolina incana (*Woolly Lavender Cotton*).—Dwarfer, neater in habit, and whiter than the common Lavender Cotton. *Flowers*, in summer; rather small, pale greenish-yellow. *Leaves*, linear, covered, as is the entire plant, with dense white down. Native of Central Europe.——Edgings, borders, and the rougher parts of the rock-garden, in ordinary soil. Division and cuttings.

Santolina viridis (*Green Lavender Cotton*).—With the habit of the common Lavender Cotton, but of a dark green hue, 2 to 2½ ft. high. *Flowers*, in summer, white slightly tinged with yellow, roundish, on long stalks. *Leaves*, of a deep green, those on the fertile branches distant from each other; those on the barren ones very close together, serrated with sharp-pointed teeth. South of France.—— Suited for the same positions, etc., as the Lavender Cotton, but is not so distinct-looking, nor likely to be so much employed. It would be interesting on rocky or stony banks, among the more easily grown rock shrubs, and grows in any soil.

Saponaria cæspitosa (*Tufted Soapwort*).—A neat alpine plant, with its leaves in dense tufts; 2 to 6 in. high. *Flowers*, in June or July; handsome; bright rose, scentless, on very short stalks, arranged on the top of the stem in a close, few-flowered cluster; petals obovate, entire, with two awl-shaped scales at the throat. *Leaves*, rather thick, leathery, short, linear, acute, sometimes bluntish, rough at the edges, keeled on the back, disposed in rosettes. Pyrenees and South-west of France.——The rock-garden, in exposed spots, and the margins of the mixed border, in sandy loam. Seed and division.

Saponaria ocymoides (*Rock Soapwort*).—A beautiful dwarf alpine herb with prostrate stems, forming dense roundish spreading tufts from 6 to 12 in. high. *Flowers*, in early summer; rosy-pink, freely produced in panicled clusters; petals 5, spreading horizontally, oblong-elliptic; calyx tubular, purple, villous, with 5 small erect blunt teeth. *Leaves*, opposite, entire, ovate or lance-shaped, generally 1-nerved. Southern and Central Europe, in rocky and stony places.—The rock-garden, borders, fringes of shrubberies, and naturalized on banks and slopes amidst dwarf plants, in any soil if the plants are elevated; if on the level ground, in ordinary sandy garden soil. Seed.

Saponaria officinalis (*Common Soapwort*).—A stout, vigorous, and showy perennial, 1 to 2 ft. high. *Flowers*, in summer; flesh-coloured or rose, varying to white, in dense panicled bundles; calyx cylindrical, nearly 1 in. long, yellowish, villous. *Leaves*, elliptic or lance-shaped, acute or obtuse, 2 or 3 in. long, opposite, connate, entire, 3- or 5-nerved, smooth. There is a variety with variegated leaves and a double-flowered one, common in gardens. Europe, North America, and Britain. ——Naturalized in any not very shady rough places, where little else will grow, and in borders, in ordinary soil. Division.

Sarracenia purpurea (*American Pitcher-plant*).—A very remarkable plant, known at once by its pitcher-like leaves; 8 to 15 in. high. *Flowers*, in June; globose, nodding, solitary, deep purplish-red, the fiddle-shaped petals arching over the greenish-yellow style. *Leaves*, pitcher-shaped, ascending, curved, broadly winged, veined with purple; the hood erect, open, round-heart shaped, clothed on the inner side with stiff bristles pointing downwards. There is a rare variety with greenish-yellow flowers, and without purple veins in the foliage. North America.——Though invariably treated as a house-, and usually a stove-plant, this curious subject will thrive in most parts in the artificial bog, in wet peat, and it is a very desirable plant to associate with *Cypripedium spectabile*, *Rhexia virginica*, the Parnassias, and other ornamental bog plants. Careful division of well-established tufts.

Saxifraga aizoides (*Streamlet Saxifrage*).—A low tufted evergreen herb, abundant by streams on our northern mountains. *Flowers*, in summer and autumn; yellow, and dotted with red towards the base, ½ in. across, from 3 to 12 or more in a loose panicle, on ascending stems, 3 to 6 in. high; calyx spreading, adherent at the base, segments hardly shorter than the petals, and often narrow and yellow like them. *Leaves*, about ½ in. long, alternate, narrow, rather thick, entire or sometimes finely notched with 1 or 2 teeth. When the leaves are sparsely ciliated, it is, according to Dr. Syme, the *S. autumnalis* of Linnæus. Europe and Britain.——The rock-garden, moist borders, and bog-bed; should be introduced near streams in the rock-garden. Division or seed.

Saxifraga Aizoon (*Everlasting Saxifrage*).—The silvery kind most commonly seen on the European mountains. *Flowers*, in early summer; cream-coloured, marked with small rose-coloured dots, in corymbs on stems 6 to 15 in. high; petals nearly round; peduncles lengthened, usually two-flowered; calyces smooth, with acute segments. *Leaves*, short, silvery, serrated; root-leaves in rosettes, wedge-shaped, ciliated at the base;

those of the stem obovate and mucronate; stems erect, simple, leafy, shining, with a few scattered gland-bearing hairs. *S. recta* is a variety of this, with 3- or 4-flowered peduncles, and petals without any dots. Europe and North America.——As hardy and easily grown in gardens as it is common and unfastidious in its native haunts, growing freely in any open soil, and forming handsome silvery tufts 1 ft. or more in diameter, and quite firm when fully exposed. It is useful for the rockwork or mixed border, and is also one of the kinds of which neat silvery edgings may be made. Division or seed.

Saxifraga Andrewsii (*Andrews's S.*) —An interesting and handsome hybrid kind, 8 in. to 1 ft. high. *Flowers*, in early summer; larger than those of *S. umbrosa*, conspicuously dotted with red; petals broadly-oval, very slightly notched at the end. *Leaves*, long, spoon-shaped, obtuse, smooth, rather thick, narrowed at the base into a slightly-fringed stalk, and having a membranous margin. Found in South-Western Ireland.——Borders, and the rock-garden, in sandy loam. Division.

Saxifraga aretioides (*Aretia Saxifrage*).—This forms cushions of little silvery rosettes almost as small and dense as those of *Androsace helvetica*, about ¼ in. high. *Flowers*, in April; golden-yellow, in dense, few-flowered corymbs; pedicels and calyces clothed with clammy down; stem covered with viscid hairs; petals with small round notches at the apex; segments of calyx ovate, acute. *Leaves*, linear-tongue-shaped, upright, very finely pointed, keeled, greyish, imbricate, ciliately toothed at the base, with a few perforated dots near the margin. Pyrenees.——Rather scarce at present, and worthy of a choice fully exposed position on the rockwork, in sandy or calcareous soil perfectly drained. Thus treated it forms dense tufts, sometimes more than a foot across, and from its very distinct appearance and yellow flowers, contrasts well with most of the other choice dwarf kinds. Division or seed.

Saxifraga aspera (*Rough Saxifrage*). —A small, grey, tufted, and prostrate kind. *Flowers*, in summer; dull white, rather large; peduncles longish, stiff, 1-flowered, clothed with glanduliferous hairs. *Leaves*, flat, lance-shaped, ciliated, lower ones closely imbricated, upper ones somewhat scattered; stems branched, reddish, brittle, hispid with short hairs. *S. bryoides* is considered a variety of this, but it does not send out runners like the preceding, and has yellow flowers. European Alps.——The rock-garden and borders, in moist sandy soil. Division.

Saxifraga biflora (*Large Purple Saxifrage*).—A beautiful species, allied to the British *S. oppositifolia*, but larger in all its parts and looser in habit. *Flowers*, in spring; rose-coloured at first, changing to violet, in heads of 2 or 3. *Leaves*, flat, spoon-shaped, small, ciliated, thinly scattered on the stem, not packed as in *S. oppositifolia*, imbricated in 4 rows. Alps and Pyrenees, near the limits of perpetual snow.——The rock-garden, in exposed spots, and in very sandy or gritty loam. Seed, cuttings, and division of well-established plants.

Saxifraga cæsia (*Silver Moss*).—A minute kind, forming dense silvery tufts, often less than ½ in. high. *Flowers*, in early summer; white, about ⅓ of an inch across, in a small panicle, on thread-like smooth stems, about 3 in. high; petals roundish, tapering at the base, 3- to 5-nerved, the side ones curved; pedicels and calyces with a few short glandular hairs; segments of calyx very blunt. *Leaves*, linear-oblong, recurved, 3-

sided, keeled, margined with white crustaceous dots. Alps and Pyrenees. ——Well-exposed spots in the rock-garden, in moist and firm sandy loam. Careful division, and seed.

Saxifraga cæspitosa (*Tufted S.*)—A green, densely tufted species, very nearly allied to *S. hypnoides*, but not emitting weak prostrate barren shoots like that species. *Flowers*, in spring or early summer; white, smaller than those of *S. hypnoides*, the flowering-stems mostly covered with a short glandular down, and bearing 1 to 4 flowers each; petals oval, twice as long as the obtuse divisions of the calyx, 3-nerved, the side ones curved. *Leaves*, of the root, 3- to 5-parted, or undivided; segments linear or lance-shaped, obtuse; lower stem - leaves palmate; upper ones mostly 3-parted. Plant beset with glandular hairs. Europe and the British Isles.——Borders, rockwork, and banks, in any soil. Division.

Saxifraga ceratophylla (*Horn-leaved S.*)—A very showy and vigorous species, with dark green leaves, forming compact wide-spreading tufts; 3 to 8 in. high. *Flowers*, in early summer; pure white, abundantly produced in loose branched panicles; petals oblong; calyx brownish, smooth; pedicels and calyces covered with clammy juice. *Leaves*, deeply 2- or 3-parted, stalked, stiff, smooth; segments awl - shaped, with horny points; stalks naked, channelled above; stems reddish at the base, covered with clammy juice. Spain. —— Borders, the rock - garden, or naturalized on bare banks, slopes, or rocky places, in ordinary soil. Division or seed.

Saxifraga coriophylla (*Early Silver Saxifrage*).—A sturdy and very ornamental little silvery species, nearly 3 in. high. *Flowers*, early in spring; few, large, pure white; petals obovate-oblong, marked with three straight veins; sepals oblong, obtuse, half as long as the petals. *Leaves* of the stem very small; those of the rosette entire, shortly oblong, obtuse, rigid, spreading, slightly concave on the upper side, convex and keeled beneath, carved on the margin into a series of 5 to 7 pits or depressions; stem glandular, downy. Alpine regions of Northern Albania.——The rock-garden, the margin of the choice mixed border, or even for diminutive edgings in the select spring garden, thriving in any free and rather cool soil. Division and seed.

Saxifraga cordifolia (*Heart - leaved S.*) — *Megasea cordifolia*. — A very large-leaved, evergreen perennial, entirely distinct in aspect from the small Saxifrages. *Flowers*, in spring, somewhat later than *S. crassifolia*; clear rose, large, in thyrsoid panicles; petals roundish, clawed, inserted in the calyx; calyx bell - shaped, 5-parted. *Leaves*, large, fleshy, roundish-heart-shaped, on long thick stalks, serrated, smooth; stalks furnished on both sides at the base with entire membranous stipules. *Roots*, thick, fleshy. Siberia. —— Borders, rough rockwork, rootwork, etc., and naturalized on sheltered sunny banks, where its early-flowering tendency would be encouraged, in ordinary soil. Division.

Saxifraga Cotyledon (*Pyramidal S.*) —A noble silvery-leaved kind; 1 to over 2 ft. high. *Flowers*, in early summer; white, in a large, elegant pyramidal panicle on a stem from 6 in. to a yard high; petals oblong or spoon-shaped, conspicuously 3-nerved; calyx densely beset with glands. *Leaves*, in large rosettes, flat, fleshy, spoon-shaped, silvery-edged, and margined with finely pointed serratures. Great mountain chains of Europe, from the Pyrenees to Lapland. *S. pyramidalis* is a variety having a more erect habit, narrower leaves, and somewhat larger flowers.——The rock-garden, borders, and naturalization in open rocky places, in any soil. Division.

Saxifraga crassifolia (*Thick-leaved S.*) —*Megasea crassifolia.*—A stout large-leaved perennial, very closely allied to *S. cordifolia*. *Flowers*, in spring; red, in a thyrsoid panicle, on a thick stalk about 9 in. high; petals elliptic-oblong, erect; calyx bell-shaped, half as long as the petals, 5-parted to about the middle, somewhat wrinkled on the outside, green. *Leaves*, alternate, spreading, about 9 in. long, flat, leathery, obovate or oblong, sub-retuse, very smooth, veined; stalks half the length of the leaves, roundish, channelled, smooth, with an ovate membranous stipule at the base. Native of Siberia.——Similar uses to those given for *S. cordifolia*, to which this is on the whole superior. Around Paris I have seen it used with good effect in beds in the spring-garden. It will prove much finer in warm and sheltered positions, for, though very hardy, the blooms are far better developed in sunny sheltered spots. Division and seed.

Saxifraga Cymbalaria (*Ivy S.*)—A distinct abundantly-blooming little annual species, with shining leaves somewhat like those of the Wall Linaria; 3 in. to 1 ft. high. *Flowers*, continuously from early spring to autumn; bright yellow, in dense masses, on numerous, weak, sprawling stems; petals obovate, much longer than the calyx; sepals oblong. *Leaves*, kidney-shaped, with crenate lobes, stalked. The Caucasus.——The rock-garden or borders, in ordinary soil. It is easily increased by seed, and often sows itself abundantly.

Saxifraga diapensioides (*Diapensia S.*)—A dense-growing and diminutive kind, and one of the most ornamental. *Flowers*, in early summer, white, bell-shaped, 3 to 5 in a terminal head on leafy stems, rarely exceeding 2 in. high, densely covered with viscid hairs; petals oblong, narrowed at the base, with a 5-nerved limb. *Leaves*, grey, 3-edged, linear, obtuse, with cartilaginous margins, ciliated at the base and with one or two perforated dots at the points, packed into dense cylindrical rosettes. Alps of Switzerland, Dauphiny, and the Pyrenees.——The treatment and positions recommended for *S. aretioides* will suit this perfectly. It may also be freely grown in pans. Seed and division.

Saxifraga Geum (*Kidney S.*)—Very like the London Pride, and differing chiefly in its leaves. *Flowers*, in early summer; pink, with darker spots, about ¼ in. across, in a loose, slender panicle. *Leaves*, roundish, heart-shaped at the base, with scattered hairs on both sides, on long stalks, which are usually very hairy, and less flattened than those of *S. umbrosa*. There are several varieties of this. *S. hirsuta* is very closely allied to it, if anything more than a variety, differing chiefly by its leaves being longer than broad, less heart-shaped, and more hairy. South-western Ireland, and other parts of Europe.——Borders, edgings, and the rougher parts of the rock-garden, in ordinary soil; also wild in woods and copses. Division.

Saxifraga granulata (*Meadow S.*)—A rather common native species, distinct in aspect from the alpine kinds, with several small scaly bulbs in a crown at the root; 6 to 12 in. high. *Flowers*, in spring and early summer; white, about ¾ in. across; 3 to 6 together in a branched terminal panicle; petals obovate, much longer than the calyx, marked with 3-branched veins. *Leaves*, somewhat fleshy, kidney-shaped, crenate or lobed, thickly clothed with shaggy glandular hairs; root-leaves on long stalks;

SAXIFRAGA.

those of the stem alternate and nearly stalkless; stem erect, round, leafy, pubescent, somewhat viscid. There is a double-flowered variety. Britain, in meadows and gravelly places.—— The double variety is the form worthy of general cultivation, and it is very pretty among low border - plants, thriving in any soil. Division.

Saxifraga Hirculus (*Yellow Marsh S.*) — A very distinct and attractive native kind; 6 to 10 in. high. *Flowers*, in summer; clear rich yellow, with orange dots on the lower half of each petal, about ¾ in. across, usually 1 to 3 on each ascending stem; petals 5, obovate, nerved; calyx reflexed. *Leaves*, in tufts, obovate, quite entire, smooth on both sides, sometimes ciliate at the margin with soft hairs; stem leafy, simple, upright, thinly clothed with brownish hairs. Europe, Asia, and Britain.——The bog-bed, moist spots in the rock-garden, in peaty soil, or in a wild state in bogs or marshes. Division and seed.

Saxifraga hypnoides (*Mossy Saxifrage*). — A well-known plant, very variable in its stems, leaves, and flowers, forming mossy tufts of deep fresh green. *Flowers*, in early summer; greenish-white, rather large; 1 to 8 on a stem with but few leaves, 3 to 6 in. high; petals elliptic-oblong, obtuse, with 3 green lines; segments of calyx not ½ so long as petals and more or less pointed. *Leaves*, narrow, pointed, sometimes entire, but often 3- to 7-cleft, the larger ones particularly so, smooth or more or less ciliated with glandular hairs. Root-stock usually shortly creeping, much branched, throwing out numerous decumbent barren shoots, which in moist places are 3 or 4 in. long, but sometimes contracted into a short tuft. Under this species may be grouped the following, which exhibit differences which some think sufficient

to mark them as species, *S. hirta, affinis, incurvifolia, platypetala*, and *decipiens*. Native of several parts of Britain, and Western Europe generally.——Margins of borders, rootwork, among quickly-spreading and easily-grown subjects in the rock-garden, and in a naturalized state among dwarf plants, in almost any position and soil. Division.

Saxifraga juniperina (*Juniper Saxifrage*).—A very distinct species, with sharp-pointed leaves in dense firm cushions. *Flowers*, in spring; yellow, in a 6- to 10-flowered spike; petals obovate, triple-nerved; pedicels short, clothed with clammy down. *Leaves*, deep green, awl-shaped, 3-edged, spine-pointed, densely set in cushioned masses, finely serrulated at the base; stems numerous, crowded with leaves and branching at the apex. The Caucasus.——The rock-garden, raised beds or borders, in moist sandy loam, also in pots or pans. Careful division and seed.

Saxifraga ligulata (*Great Strap-leaved S.*)—A handsome plant, allied to *S. crassifolia;* from 6 to 9 in. high. *Flowers*, in spring; large, rosy-white, in spreading panicles; petals obovate, somewhat notched, much longer than the calyx; sepals finely fringed at the ends. *Leaves*, obovate or somewhat heart-shaped, wavy, slightly toothed, expanded at the base into a fringed sheath. Nepaul.——Borders, sunny banks, and rough rockwork, in sandy soil. Division.

Saxifraga longifolia (*Long-leaved Saxifrage*). — The noblest species known. *Flowers*, in summer; white, in a large pyramidal panicle, on stems 1 to 2 ft. high, clothed with short, stiff, gland-tipped hairs. *Leaves*, linear, crenate, very long (sometimes 6 in.) greyish-green, arranged in magnificent rosettes sometimes 1 ft. in diameter. Pyrenees.——So much admired that until very common it is likely to be confined to the rockwork, on which its silvery rosettes are conspicuous ornaments, even in the depth of winter. It however thrives in the mixed border, in soil of ordinary quality, and like other kinds will grow in poor soil, but has been proved to grow much faster and better in soil enriched by decomposed stable manure. It is easily raised from seed, which should be gathered at intervals of two or three days, as the seeds on the lower branches of the panicle ripen some time before those towards the apex. The seeds should be sown at once in pans of fine sandy loam and peat, the soil firmly compressed, the seeds covered very slightly, and placed in a shallow cold frame. When well up they should be potted in small pots, and with liberal treatment they soon form strong plants, which may be placed in the open air in summer, and left there afterwards. The old rosettes do not perish after flowering, but do not always flower every year. Rabbits sometimes destroy it.

Saxifraga oppositifolia (*Purple Saxifrage*).—A brilliant native species, 2 in. high. *Flowers*, in early spring; purplish-rose, large for the size of the plant. solitary on short erect stems, but sometimes so freely produced as to completely hide the foliage; segments of calyx ovate, green, not half so long as the 5-nerved petals. *Leaves*, small, opposite, densely crowded, ovate or obovate, flat, obtuse, ciliated. There are the following varieties in cultivation : *pallida*, pale pink ; *alba*, white ; *major*, large. A very fine variety (*S. opp. pyrenaica*) has dense *erect* rosettes of leaves, and flowers ¾ in. across, varying in colour from flesh-pink to deep purple-crimson. Europe and Britain, on high mountains.——The rock-garden, and margins of borders, in moist sandy loam. When in borders it will be better to surround the specimen with half-buried stones, and if broken sandstone is mixed with the soil to a depth of 18 in., so much the better. Division.

Saxifraga pectinata (*Comb-leaved S.*) —A neat silvery species. *Flowers*, in summer; rather small, white spotted with purple in the centre; divisions of the calyx ovate-triangular, obtuse. *Leaves*, linear-spoon-shaped, pointed, sharply serrated with triangular teeth ; terminal tooth rather blunt, large, and prominent. Carniola.—— The rock-garden, in moist sandy soil. Division.

Saxifraga purpurascens (*Purple Himalayan S.*)—The handsomest of the large-leaved species, 3 to 6 in. high. *Flowers*, in April and May ; handsome reddish-purple, large, of an elegant bell-shape, in dense corymbose panicles. *Leaves*, nearly round or round-ovate, glossy green margined with red. Sikkim, Himalayas, at very high elevations.——Allied to the other Saxifrages of the large-leaved or *Megasea* section, it is very distinct from any of them, and, being dwarfer and more beautiful, deserves a choice spot in the rock-garden, in moist sandy peat and loam, with plenty of water, and a position fully exposed to the sun ; also on warm borders. I have only seen this in the open air at Glasnevin. It is very uncommon in gardens, but deserves a place in every collection. Seed and division.

Saxifraga retusa (*Retuse S.*) — A pretty kind, allied to the Purple Saxifrage. *Flowers*, in spring or early summer ; purple, 2 or 3 together on erect, few-leaved stems ; petals lance-shaped, acute; segments of calyx oblong-ovate, obtuse ; pedicels and calyces clothed with short glandular down. *Leaves*, small, fleshy, smooth, imbricated, oblong, 3-angled, acute, full of perforated dots above ; ciliated at the base and retuse at the apex. Alps and Pyrenees.——The rock-garden and borders, in moist sandy soil. Division.

Saxifraga Rocheliana (*Rochel's Saxifrage*).—A very compact and dwarf kind, allied to *S. cæsia*, forming dense silvery rosettes of white-margined leaves, with distinctly impressed dots. *Flowers*, in spring; white, large, freely produced in corymbs on stems 3 or 4 in. high; petals lance-shaped or ovate, twice the length of the calyx; sepals ovate. *Leaves*, of the rosettes tongue-shaped, smooth, ciliated at the base; those of the stem clothed with clammy hairs, pale green. Alps of Central Europe.——The rock-garden, in fully exposed spots, in firm, sandy soil; also for the margins of choice mixed borders, in the same kind of soil, surrounded by a few half-buried stones. Division or seed.

Saxifraga sarmentosa (*Creeping Saxifrage*).—Distinct in aspect from the alpine or any other cultivated kinds, having rather large, round, blotched leaves, and graceful, slender, and long runners. *Flowers*, in early summer; white, dotted with rose, on stems 6 to 10 in. high; petals 5, the two outer ones 3-nerved, much larger than the others. *Leaves*, roundish-heart-shaped, pilose, mottled above, red beneath, on roundish stalks longer than the leaves; creeping runners, which terminate in rooting offsets, proceed from the axils of the root-leaves. *S. cuscutæformis* is a variety of this, with much smaller leaves, petals more equal in size, and its stolons or runners like those of a Dodder. China.——The rock-garden, hardy fernery, or edges of raised beds. It is usually grown in greenhouses, but it is hardy in all but the coldest districts. Division.

Saxifraga tenella (*Slender Saxifrage*).—A handsome prostrate plant, forming tufts of delicate fine-leaved branches, which root as they grow; about 4 or 5 in. high. *Flowers*, in summer; numerous, whitish-yellow, arranged in a loose panicle. *Leaves* linear, pointed, very numerous, arranged in dense rosettes. Austrian Alps.——Rockwork and slopes, in moist soil, and in cool positions. Division in the end of summer or in spring

Saxifraga valdensis (*Vaudois S.*).— A diminutive species, growing in extremely dense and rigid glaucous tufts; 3 or 4 in. high. *Flowers*, late in spring; white, in a corymb of 6 to 10 blossoms; calyx and stem covered with blackish glandular hairs. *Leaves*, more or less triangular, slightly recurved at the end, where they widen and become almost spoon-shaped. Mont Cenis and other parts of the Alps.——In well-drained ledges on rockwork, in a mixture of loam and grit. Division and seed.

Scabiosa caucasica (*Caucasian Scabious*).—A large and handsome perennial; 18 in. to 3 ft. high. *Flowers*, in summer; pale blue, in a large head; corolla 5-cleft; limb of calyx sessile, with exserted bristles. *Leaves*, somewhat resembling those of a *Scorzonera*; those of the root lance-shaped, taper-pointed, entire, glaucous; involucrum very villous. The Caucasus and Armenia, in arid places.——Borders and naturalization, in ordinary soil. Division.

Scabiosa graminifolia (*Grass-leaved S.*).—A very distinct dwarf kind, with stems slightly woody at the base; about 1 ft. high. *Flowers*, in summer; pale blue, resembling those of *S. caucasica* but smaller; bristles of calyx 5, equal in length to the crown. *Leaves*, silvery white, about 4 in. long, and ¼ in. broad, lance-shaped. Mountains of Dauphiny, Italy, and Switzerland.——The rock-garden and margins of warm borders, in sandy loam. Division.

Scabiosa ochroleuca (*Yellow Scabious*).—A hardy perennial, with a furrowed stem, 1 ft. to 16 in. high. *Flowers*, in summer; pale sulphur-yellow, more than 2 in. across. *Leaves*, pinnate; radical ones a foot long; leaflets increasing in size from below upwards, coarsely toothed; stem-leaves pinnatifid, with linear divisions. Germany.——Naturalized in rough and half-wild spots, in ordinary soil. Seed or division.

Scabiosa Webbiana (*Webb's Scabious*).—A rather dwarf, silvery-leaved species, not growing more than from 6 to 10 in. high. *Flowers*, in summer; cream-coloured, in small heads, inconspicuous. *Leaves*, obovate; upper ones divided; lower ones toothed. Phrygia.—— The rock-garden, and warm borders, in sandy loam. Seed and cuttings.

Schivereckia podolica (*Podolian S.*) —*Alyssum podolicum.*—A small alpine herb, nearly white with starry down; 3 or 4 in. high. *Flowers*, in spring; small, white, in terminal racemes; petals slightly notched at the apex. *Leaves*, of the root in rosettes, oval-oblong, toothed; stem-leaves few, clasping. Podolia, Volhynia, and the Ural mountains.—— The rock-garden and borders, in light sandy soil. It has few claims for any but large and botanical collections. Seed and division.

Schizostylis coccinea (*Crimson S.*)— A handsome bulbous plant, with the habit of a *Gladiolus;* 2 to 3 ft. high. *Flowers*, in summer and autumn; of a bright crimson, 2 in. across, resembling in form those of *Tritonia aurea*, in a one-sided spike, and opening from below upwards. *Leaves*, sword-shaped, dark green, sheathing at the base. Caffraria.——Borders, fringes of beds of shrubs, associated with *Gladioli* and other autumn-flowering bulbs, in sandy peat and loam. Division.

Scilla amœna (*Star-flowered Squill*). —A charming, spring-flowering, bulbous plant, about 1 ft. high. *Flowers*, in April and May; dark indigo-blue, with a darker line through the middle of each petal; ovary conspicuous in the star-like bloom. *Leaves*, of a lively green colour, linear-lance-shaped, about ½ in. across, channelled. South of Europe.——Sheltered positions in borders, in light sandy soil. Increased by separation of the bulbs every second or third year.

Scilla bifolia (*Early Squill*).—A beautiful, early-flowering, dwarf species, from 6 to 10 in. high. *Flowers*, in March and April; dark blue, 4 to 6 on a spike, forming rich masses. *Leaves*, linear-lance-shaped, channelled, 2 in number (occasionally 3), of a delicate green colour, with reddish lines. There are numerous varieties. Southern and Central Europe.——Borders; flowers best in warm sunny spots, in light sandy soil. It is also well fitted for naturalization in sunny openings in woods where the ground vegetation is scant, and the soil of an open texture. Separation of the bulbs.

Scilla campanulata (*Large Bluebell*). —A vigorous and handsome kind, 8 to 18 in. high. *Flowers*, late in spring or early in summer; bell-shaped, of a light violet-blue, on short stalks, pendent from the axils of whitish bracts, and arranged in a pyramidal cluster. *Leaves*, broadly lanceolate, acute, about as long as the stem, and spreading in a broad rosette. *Bulb*, large, solid, rounded-oval, egg-shaped, or oblong, of various forms when young—depressed, elongated, cylindrical, oblong, or club-shaped. There are several varieties, much the largest and finest being *S. campanulata major*, which appears to be the plant figured by Redouté. The white and rose varieties are particularly well worthy of culture. S. Europe.——Fringes of shrubberies, mixed borders, and naturalization. It will grow in any position or soil in which the Common Bluebell thrives. Separation of the bulbs as occasion may require.

Scilla patula (*Spreading Bluebell*).—Nearly allied to our Common Bluebell; 10 to 15 in. high. *Flowers*, in early summer; larger and more open than those of the Common Bluebell, blue, pendent, of a cylindrical bellshape, arranged in an erect loose cluster, scentless. *Leaves*, numerous, broadly - linear, spreading on the ground. *Bulb*, elongated-pear-shaped, depressed or oblique, sometimes clubshaped. South of France, Spain, and Portugal.——Borders, fringes of shrubberies, and naturalization when it can be spared for this purpose, in ordinary soil. Division.

Scilla peruviana (*Pyramidal Squill*).—A noble and distinct species, 6 to 16 in. high. *Flowers*, in summer; numerous, of a brilliant blue, with white stamens, which form a charming contrast, arranged on long slender stalks in a large, regular, dense, pyramidal cluster, which is elongated during the period of flowering. *Leaves*, longer than the flower-stem, broadly linear, of a deep, glistening green, finely ciliated at the edges. *Bulb*, large, elongated-pear-shaped, covered with yellowish-white coats. South of Europe and Barbary.——Level but sunny and sheltered spots in the lower parts of the rock-garden, or warm sheltered borders, and occasionally on the fringes of shrubberies, always in a thoroughly-drained and free soil. The crown of the bulb to be at least five or six inches below the surface. This will guard it against any injury from cold. Of course, when large bulbs are planted in this way, there must be plenty of good soil beneath their base.

Separation of the bulbs every second or third year.

Scilla sibirica (*Siberian Squill*).—The brightest and bravest of all known early blue-flowered spring bulbs; 3 to 6 in. high. *Flowers*, early in spring; of a fine clear porcelain-blue, gracefully pendent, one to six on each stem, arranged in a loose, irregular cluster. *Leaves*, broadly linear, acute, slightly hollowed near the point, somewhat shorter than the flower-stem. *Bulb*, of the size of a chestnut, roundish, with dark-coloured, dry, transparent coats. Southern Russia and the Caucasus. —— Tufts in borders, or as edgings round choice beds of shrubs, either alone or alternated with other dwarf flowers; also indispensable for the rock-garden, and a charming subject for naturalization on sloping ground with a dwarf turf. Grows and increases freely in good sandy loam. Separation of the bulbs every second year, soon after the leaves have decayed.

Scutellaria alpina (*Alpine Skullcap*).—A neat perennial, with spreading pubescent stems, forming large round tufts 1 ft. high in the centre. *Flowers*, in summer; purplish, or with the lower lip white or yellow, in terminal 4-angled, oblong heads, short at first, afterwards lengthening; corolla 1 to 1¼ in. long. *Leaves*, nearly stalkless or very shortly stalked, ovate, roundish or heart-shaped at the base, notched, green, pubescent or pilose; floral leaves membranous, imbricated. *S. lupulina* is a variety of this with showy yellow flowers. Europe and Asia, on mountains. —— Borders, banks, and naturalization, in sandy soil. Division.

Scutellaria macrantha (*Large-flowered S.*)—A rather showy perennial, forming compact bushy tufts, 8 in. to 1 ft. high. *Flowers*, in summer; fine blue, in closely-set unilateral clusters. *Leaves*, opposite, lanceolate, obtuse, rounded at the base, finely ciliated on the margin, pale underneath. Siberia. ——Borders, in good soil. Division and seed.

Sedum acre (*Stonecrop*).—A well-known and diminutive inhabitant of old thatched roofs and sandy and gravelly places; 2 to 4 in. high. *Flowers*, in early summer; yellow, in small terminal cymes; sepals much shorter than the narrow-oblong petals. *Leaves*, small, thick, alternate, stalkless, ovate, sometimes nearly round, smooth. *S. acre variegatum* is a variety of which the tips of the shoots in spring become of a showy yellow. Europe and Britain, on walls or dry places.——Walls and bare sandy or gravelly places, borders, rough rockwork, etc. The variegated form is useful for edgings, etc., in the spring garden. Division.

Sedum album (*White Stonecrop*).—A distinct and pretty species, 4 to 6 in. high. *Flowers*, in summer; white or pinkish, freely produced in elegant corymbs; petals oblong and obtuse, almost three times the length of the oval sepals. *Leaves*, scattered, oblong, cylindrical, ¼ to ½ in. long, of a brownish green, stalkless, smooth. This, like the common Stonecrop, occurs on old roofs and rocky places in many parts of Europe.——The rock-garden, borders, walls, and wild in bare gravelly places. Division.

Sedum Anacampseros (*Evergreen Orpine*). — Readily distinguished by the leaves being arranged in pyramidal rosettes on the barren, prostrate branches; 6 to 8 in. high. *Flowers*, in summer; rose-coloured or purple, in very dense corymbs; petals flat, oboval, obtuse, one-third longer than the calyx; sepals lance-shaped. *Leaves*, wedge-shaped, obtuse, alternate, entire, glaucous, smooth, nearly stalkless. Alps, Pyrenees, and mountains of Dauphiny.——Borders and rough rockwork, in any soil. Division.

Sedum anglicum (*English Stonecrop*). —A small and pretty kind, 2 to 5 in. high. *Flowers*, in summer; white, sometimes tinged with pink, in a short few-flowered cyme; petals taper-pointed, awned, more than twice as long as the sepals. *Leaves*, crowded, alternate, short, ovate, gibbous, spurred at the base, smooth. Britain and various other parts of Europe. ——Similar positions, etc., to those given for *S. album*.

Sedum brevifolium (*Short-leaved Stonecrop*). — A very distinct and pretty species, allied to *S. dasyphyllum*, but readily distinguished from it by its pinkish mealy tone; 2 to 4 in high. *Flowers*, in summer; white, in loose, terminal, smooth cymes; petals bluntish, sepals thin (in *S. dasyphyllum*, thick). *Leaves*, ovate, obtuse, short, thick, opposite; stems smooth, twisted, and rather woody at the base. Southern Pyrenees and Corsica. ——The rock-garden, on warm spots, in firm dry soil; also on sunny parts of old walls and ruins, and in pots. It is somewhat tender. Division.

Sedum dasyphyllum (*Thick-leaved Stonecrop*).—A very dwarf and neat kind, 4 or 5 in. high, of a glaucous colour and not unfrequently of an amethystine blue tone. *Flowers*, in summer; dull white tinged with rose, in a spreading, glutinous panicle; petals bluntish, three times the length of the calyx, which is downy and clammy. *Leaves*, mostly opposite, densely packed, very thick and fleshy, swollen on the lower side, nearly flat on the upper side. *S. corsicum* is nearly allied to this but smaller. A native of Southern and South-western Europe, and a few localities in Southern England.——The rock-garden, or on ruins, old walls, etc. When planted out in the garden it should have poor, dryish, firm, sandy soil. Division.

Sedum Ewersii (*Ewers's Stonecrop*).—Somewhat like *S. Sieboldi*, but smaller and more compact in habit; 2 or 3 in. high. *Flowers*, in summer; purplish, in terminal corymbs; petals lance-shaped, acute, a little longer than the stamens. *Leaves*, glaucous, smooth, opposite, irregularly toothed; lower ones broadly elliptic, upper ones heart-shaped; stem rooting at the base. Altai Mountains.——The rock-garden, and margins of the mixed border, in open soil. Division.

Sedum glaucum (*Glaucous Stonecrop*).—A minute species of a greyish hue, forming dense tufts of short stems, 2 or 3 in. high, densely clothed with fat leaves. *Flowers*, in early summer; white, inconspicuous; petals, 6, mucronate, 1-nerved. *Leaves*, short, thick, and fleshy, alternate, glaucous; stems covered with spreading down. There are various other Sedums allied to this, and probably all are forms of one kind. Native of Hungary.——The rock-garden, sometimes in spreading masses as a glaucous "carpet plant," borders, edgings, lines, masses, etc., in the flower-garden, associated with other dwarf plants, in light soil. Division.

Sedum kamtschaticum (*Orange Stonecrop*).—A showy kind, somewhat resembling *S. spurium* in habit; 3 to 5 in. high. *Flowers*, in summer; dark orange-yellow, in terminal cymes; bracts much longer than the cymes. *Leaves*, oboval-lance-shaped, bluntly toothed, alternate or opposite. Eastern Siberia. ——Borders, edgings, and the rock-garden, in ordinary soil. Division.

Sedum Nevii (*Nevius's Sedum*).—A rather showy kind, with spreading simple stems, 3 to 5 in. high. *Flowers*, late in summer; white, with pointed petals and purplish anthers, in dense branching cymes. *Leaves*, all alternate; those of the sterile shoots wedge-shaped-obovate or spathulate: those of the flowering stems linear, spathulate and flattish. North America. ——Rockwork, in gravelly or sandy loam. Division.

Sedum populifolium (*Shrubby Stonecrop*).—More curious than beautiful, forming a small, much-branched plant, 6 to 10 in. high. *Flowers*, late in summer; white, in terminal corymbs. *Leaves*, scattered, smooth, stalked, flat, coarsely toothed; lower ones heart-shaped; upper ones ovate; stems erect, much branched, shrubby. Native of Siberia.——Borders, or the rougher parts of the rock-garden; chiefly suited for botanical and curious collections. Division.

Sedum pulchellum (*Bird's-foot Stonecrop*).—A handsome and distinct kind, 4 to 10 in. high. *Flowers*, in summer; purplish-rose, crowded in umbellate spikes, spreading or recurved when in flower, but straight and somewhat erect when in fruit. *Leaves*, very numerous, linear, obtuse, flattish, closely sessile, more or less jointed at the base; stems rising, often branched from the base. North America.——Borders, the rock-garden, and as an edging plant, in ordinary sandy soil. Division.

Sedum purpurascens (*Purple Stonecrop*).—Considered by some to be a variety of *S. maximum*, which it very much resmbles; 10 to 18 in. high. *Flowers*, late in summer and in autumn; purplish, arranged in an elongated and irregular corymb. *Leaves*, flat, fleshy, lengthened-oblong, toothed, rounded at the base, opposite or whorled, the upper ones almost clasping the stem, and of a dark purplish colour. France.——Borders, or naturalization, in ordinary soil. Division.

Sedum rupestre (*Rock Stonecrop*).—A greyish densely-tufted species, with numerous spreading shoots, usually rooting at the base and erect at the apex; 3 to 5 in. high. *Flowers*, in summer; yellow, larger than in any other British species; petals twice as long as broad; sepals short, ovate. *Leaves*, glaucous, narrow, cylindrical, with a short point, closely imbricated before flowering in 5 or 6 rows. There are several varieties or subspecies; notably the British *S. elegans*, and the green-leaved *S. Forsterianum*. Britain and other parts of Europe.——Borders, and the rougher parts of the rock-garden or banks, in any soil. Division.

Sedum sexangulare (*Six-angled S.*)—Allied to the Common Stonecrop, and by some considered a mere variety of it; 3 to 6 in. high. *Flowers*, in early summer, usually rather later than *S. acre*; yellow, in a trifid cyme; petals lance-shaped, taper-pointed. *Leaves*, sub-cylindrical, longer, more numerous, and usually much redder than those of *S. acre*, 3 in a whorl, on barren branches, imbricated in 6 spiral rows, those on the flowering-stems usually in threes; stems branching at the base, flowering-stems erect. Europe and Britain, in dry sandy soil, and on walls.——Borders, rough rockwork, or bare banks, in any soil. Division.

Sedum Sieboldi (*Siebold's Stonecrop*).—A prostrate and elegant plant with stems 6 to 8 in. long. *Flowers*, in autumn; small, rose-coloured, sometimes slightly tinged with purple, in a dense roundish cyme. *Leaves*, in whorls of 3, nearly round, coarsely toothed, very glaucous, almost grey, slightly tinged with rose, especially in autumn. There is a variegated variety. Japan.——The rock-garden, edges of raised borders or beds, vases, and in pots, in good sandy loam. Division and cuttings.

Sedum spectabile (*Noble Stonecrop*).—Remarkable for its full handsome habit and showy bloom, 1 ft. to 16 in. high. *Flowers*, late in summer and in autumn; rosy flesh-colour or purplish-carmine, very numerous, and forming a large, regular, spreading cyme often more than 6 in. across. *Leaves*, oval, pointed, opposite, large, fleshy, smooth, very glaucescent or greyish-green. Japan.——Borders, beds and groups of the finer autumn-flowering perennials, isolated specimens in the pleasure-ground, and naturalization in any soil. Division.

Sedum spurium (*Showy Sedum*).—A showy species, 4 to 8 in. high. *Flowers*, in summer; pale purplish-rose, sometimes rosy flesh-colour, numerous, in a compound corymb; petals lance-shaped, acute. *Leaves*, alternate or opposite, oboval or roundish, unequally toothed, slightly hairy and pale underneath. There is a variety which differs only in having flowers of a deep carmine hue. Caucasus. ——Borders, edgings, and the rougher parts of the rock-garden, in any soil. Division.

Sempervivum arachnoideum (*Cobweb Houseleek*).—A small and singular species of Houseleek, the tiny globose rosettes of which are covered at the top with a thick white down, like a close spider's web. *Flowers*, in summer; pretty, purple or rose-coloured, on stems 3 to 5 in. high; petals 8 or 9, spreading; scales bluntly notched. *Leaves*, lanceolate, acute, with glandular hairs on both sides. Alps and Pyrenees.—— The rock-garden, in sandy soil, and in chinks of old walls, ruins, etc. Division.

Sempervivum arenarium (*Sand Houseleek*).—A small kind, remarkable for the great number of stolons which it sends out from the axils of the leaves, bearing young rosettes, which, after a little time, detach themselves, and fall on the ground where they readily take root; 2 or 3 in. high. *Flowers*, in summer; light yellow, almost bell-shaped. *Leaves*, in medium-sized rosettes,

SEMPERVIVUM.

lance-shaped, acute, erect, smooth, fringed, tinged in autumn with red on the ends, and also on the lower side. European Alps.——The rock-garden and borders, in fully exposed positions, and in ordinary sandy soil. Division.

Sempervivum barbulatum (*Bearded Houseleek*).— A profusely - flowering kind, 3½ to 6 in. high. *Flowers*, in summer; bright rose-colour. *Leaves*, in small rosettes, velvety, glandular, terminating in a small pencil of white cobwebby hairs. European Alps.—— The rock-garden and borders, in fully exposed positions and in ordinary sandy soil. Division.

Sempervivum Boutignianum (*Boutigni's Houseleek*).—A medium-sized kind, 6 to 8 in. high. *Flowers*, in summer; of a very pale rose-colour, marked with a few darker lines, especially at the base. *Leaves*, in rather compact rosettes, often more fully developed on one side, smooth, of a very pale glaucous green, often marked on the outside with reddish lines, brownish-red at the top, and pale rose at the base. The rosettes emit a large number of short runners terminated by young rosettes, globular in form and with smooth leaves. Alps of Dauphiny.——The rock-garden and borders, in ordinary soil. Division.

Sempervivum calcareum (*Purple-tipped H.*)—*S. californicum, Hort.*—A large and handsome species now becoming very popular. *Flowers*, in summer; pale rose-colour, in panicled cymes, smaller than those of the Common Houseleek, on stems 6 to 10 in. high. *Leaves*, in dense rosettes, glaucous at the base, and marked on the upper part with a purplish spot. Alps of Dauphiny. This is the plant often grown under the name of *S. californicum* in gardens. A variety of the Common Houseleek is also grown under that name.——The rock - garden, borders, edgings, lines and panels in the flower - garden, and naturalized on walls, ruins, or any position where the Common Houseleek thrives. Division.

Sempervivum fimbriatum (*Fringed Houseleek*).—One of the most profusely-flowering kinds. *Flowers*, in summer; dark rose-colour, on stems 6 to 10 in. high. *Leaves*, in small rosettes, smooth on both sides, strongly fringed on the edges, and marked with a large purple spot on the end which terminates in a long point. European Alps.——The rock-garden or borders, in any sandy soil. Division.

Sempervivum flagelliforme (*Long-runnered H.*) — Allied to *S. montanum*, but larger, and readily distinguished from that species by its rosettes being produced at the ends of long runners. *Flowers*, in summer, purple, on stems 8 or 9 in. high. *Leaves*, ovate, finely pointed; stem-leaves narrower; those of the offsets terminated by a stiff brown point. Siberia.—— Borders and the rock-garden, in ordinary soil. Division.

Sempervivum Funckii (*Funck's House-leek*).—A medium-sized kind, light-green in colour. *Flowers*, in summer; rose-coloured, on stems 3½ to 6 in. high. *Leaves*, numerous, somewhat glandular on both sides, and strongly fringed, pointed, and of a light-green colour even in autumn, in small compact rosettes. Tyrolese Alps.——The rock-garden and borders, in sandy soil. Division.

Sempervivum glaucum (*Glaucous Houseleek*).—A large and vigorous kind. *Flowers*, in summer; nectaries clawed, acute; stamens 12 to 18; pistils the same number. *Leaves*, broadly obovate-wedge-shaped, glaucous, ciliated; runners spreading. Mount Simplon.—— Margins of borders, the rougher parts of the rock-garden, and as an edging or panel plant. Division.

Sempervivum globiferum (*Proliferous*

S.)—A neat kind growing in firm dense sheets. *Flowers,* in summer; pale yellow, in a dense corymb, on stems 6 to 8 in. high. *Leaves,* in spreading rosettes, smooth, fringed, pointed, inflected about the centre, with numerous stolons growing from the axils, terminated by young rosettes which detach themselves after a time. In autumn the outside leaves of the rosettes assume a reddish tinge. European Alps.——The rock-garden and the margins of borders fully exposed to the sun, in ordinary soil. Division.

Sempervivum heterotrichum (*Hair-tipped S.*) — An interesting kind. *Flowers,* in summer; rose-coloured, on stems 2½ to 3½ in. high. *Leaves,* in small and very closely-set rosettes, and of various forms and colours, furnished at the end with white cobweb-like hairs. Tyrolese Alps.—— The rock-garden, in sandy soil. Division.

Sempervivum Heuffeli (*Heuffel's Houseleek*). — Easily known by its deep-chocolate hue. *Flowers,* in summer; yellow, nearly bell-shaped, in a spreading corymb on stems 8 to 10 in. high. *Leaves,* in irregular rosettes, not round, long, smooth, fringed only at the end which preserves, even in summer, a deep red tint, especially on the fringed portion. Hungary.—— The dark hue of this species makes it attractive for edgings, panels, etc., while it is also more valuable than most of the species for the rock-garden or borders. Ordinary sandy soil. Division.

Sempervivum hirtum (*Hairy Houseleek*).— Distinguished by its fringed leaves and flowers. *Flowers,* in summer; yellowish, almost campanulate, forming a dense corymb, on stems 6 to 8 in. high; petals erect and narrow-lance-shaped, almost obtuse, with a long fringe on their margin. *Leaves,* in spreading rosettes, oblong-lanceolate, acute, strongly fringed. Alps of Provence.——Borders and the rock-garden, in ordinary soil and in fully exposed positions. Division.

Sempervivum Laggeri (*Lagger's Houseleek*).—Larger than the Cobweb Houseleek and whiter from its 'more abundant silvery cobweb-like down. *Flowers,* in summer; dark rose-coloured. *Leaves,* velvety - glandular, covered with cobweb-like down exceedingly abundant and cottony. European Alps.——Being very silvery, this is one of the best for the rock-garden, in firm sandy loam and in sunny positions. Division.

Sempervivum Mettenianum (*Metten's Houseleek*).—A species which flowers many times. *Flowers,* in summer; rosy-white, on stems 4½ to 6 in. high. *Leaves,* in medium - sized rosettes, fringed, pointed, assuming in autumn a reddish tinge, which is deeper on the upper side. European Alps.—— The rock-garden or borders, in sandy loam. Division.

Sempervivum montanum (*Mountain Houseleek*).—A dark green kind much smaller than the Common Houseleek, with an almost geometrical arrangement of leaves. *Flowers,* in summer; dull red, on stems 3½ to 6 in. high; petals 10—14, lance-shaped, taper-pointed, 3 times longer than the calyx; scales square, nearly entire. *Leaves,* forming neat rosettes, obovate or oblong, entire, shortly pointed, pubescent and glandular on both surfaces, ciliated; offsets rather contracted. European Alps.—— Borders and the rougher parts of the rock-garden, in ordinary soil. Division.

Sempervivum piliferum (*Hairy-tufted Houseleek*). — Distinguished by the hairy appendage to its leaves. *Flowers,* in summer; rose-colour, in panicled cymes, on stems 4 to 6 in. high. *Leaves,* in medium - sized rosettes. smooth, glaucous, very slightly fringed on the edges, but terminated by a bundle of small white hairs; in autumn the tops become somewhat reddish. Alps.——The rock-garden and borders, in sandy soil. Division.

Sempervivum ruthenicum (*Russian Houseleek*).—A very profusely-flowering and well-marked kind. *Flowers*, in summer; rosy-white, large, on stems 6 to 8 in. high. *Leaves*, in large rosettes, downy underneath, and often very much fringed with silvery hairs, pointed, and turning red at the ends in autumn. Caucasus.——The rock-garden and the margins of borders, in sandy loam. Division.

Sempervivum tectorum (*Common Houseleek*).—A well-known plant, grown for ages on housetops, old walls, etc. *Flowers*, in summer; pink, on stems 1 ft. high; petals 5 to 9, linear, pointed, entire, downy on the outside, ciliated on the edges. *Leaves*, thick and fleshy, oblong or obovate, taper-pointed, ciliated; the upper ones more or less clothed with short viscid down. It varies somewhat, a glaucous form with broad rosettes called *rusticum* being one of the most distinct. Britain and various parts of Europe.——Borders and the rougher parts of the rock-garden, in any soil. Division.

Sempervivum tomentosum (*Woolly Houseleek*). — Resembles *S. arachnoideum*, but has much smaller rosettes. *Flowers*, in summer; bright rose-colour. *Leaves*, in diminutive rosettes, like those of *S. arachnoideum*, furnished with numerous white cobweb-like hairs, which are fewer in the autumn and when the plant is grown in the shade. European Alps.——The rock-garden, in well-drained sandy loam and in sunny spots. Division.

Sempervivum Wulfeni (*Wulfen's Houseleek*).—Forms compact rosettes of medium size. *Flowers*, in summer; sulphur-yellow; on stems 6 to 8 in. high. *Leaves*, glaucous, oblong, long-pointed, fringed only at the base; the part not fringed is bordered sometimes in autumn with a reddish line. Tyrolese Alps. —— Borders and the rock-garden, in ordinary sandy soil. Division.

Senecio adonidifolius (*Adonis-leaved S.*)—A neat little perennial, 4 to 6 in. high. *Flowers*, in summer; small, deep yellow, in small terminal clusters. *Leaves*, much and deeply cut; segments almost thread - like; stem simple. Central Europe. —— Rockwork, or front margin of mixed borders, in sandy soil. Division.

Senecio argenteus (*Silvery Groundsel*). — Like a miniature of *Centaurea ragusina*, about 2 in. high. *Flowers*, in summer; yellow. *Leaves*, of silvery whiteness, from $\frac{1}{2}$ to $1\frac{1}{2}$ in. long, cut into rounded lobes, growing in dense, compact rosettes, 4 to 6 in. across; stem woody, branching and rooting. Pyrenees. —— The rock-garden, margins of the mixed border, and as a very dwarf silvery edging-plant, in sandy loam. Division.

Senecio campestris (*Woolly Groundsel*).—A pretty British Composite, 6 to 8 in. high. *Flowers*, in summer; yellow, 1 to 6 in a simple corymb. *Leaves*, woolly; those of the root oblong, nearly entire, narrowed below; stem-leaves lanceolate. In very wet seasons and near the sea this plant is often thrice as large, with many larger heads, and dentate lower leaves, when it is the *S. maritima* of some authors. Chalk downs, and on maritime rocks near Holyhead.——Borders, and the rock-garden, especially where an interest is taken in native plants; in light or calcareous soil. Seed or division.

Senecio incanus (*Hoary Groundsel*).— A small silvery species, but not so valuable or so easily grown as *S. argenteus*; 3 to 5 in. high. *Flowers*, in summer;

yellow, very closely-set, in simple corymbs; scales of involucrum woolly, obtuse and marked on the end with a black spot. *Leaves*, pinnatifid; lobes linear, obtuse, slightly toothed. South of France.——The rock-garden, in sandy or gritty well-drained soil. Division.

Senecio uniflorus (*One-flowered S.*) —A very dwarf silvery species about 1 in. high. *Flowers*, in summer; small, insignificant, yellow; scales of involucrum acute, downy, marked with a black spot on the end. *Leaves*, lower ones oblong, toothed or cut, narrowed into a footstalk; upper ones sessile, linear; whole plant covered with a white down. Swiss and Piedmontese Alps.——The rock-garden, in sandy loam. Division.

Serapias cordigera (*Heart-shaped S.*) —A curious Orchid, 1 ft. high. *Flowers*, in summer; large, brownish-red, 4 or 5 in a loose spike; lip large, red, nearly heart-shaped, hairy, furnished with two prominences at the base; bracts exceeding the flower in length; sepals, oval, pointed. *Leaves*, oblong-lanceolate, gradually diminishing into bracts. *S. Lingua* is distinguished by having bracts only as long as the flowers, and only one prominence at the base of the lip. Damp meadows and forests in the South and South-west of France.—— On the sunny slopes of the rock-garden or in the select border, in deep and good moist soil. Separation of the root-knobs.

Seseli gummiferum (*Gem Seseli*).— A handsome silvery plant, 18 in. to 3 ft. high. *Flowers*, in summer; rose-coloured, in terminal, convex, many-rayed umbels; involucrum few-leaved. *Leaves*, thrice pinnate, glaucous, with wedge-shaped, trifid segments; stems covered with fine down. Crimea.—— Warm banks and sunny slopes and nooks on the southern side of the rock-garden, in dry well-drained soil. This frequently perishes in winter on cold clay soils and on such should be planted on banks. It is probably a biennial and more likely to be useful in the subtropical garden, for which purpose it should be annually raised from seed, to be sown as soon as ripe.

Sida incarnata (*Pink-flowered Sida*). —A showy perennial, from 1½ to 2 ft. high. *Flowers*, in summer; very showy, pink, nearly 1½ in. across, in a close pyramidal spike. *Leaves*, smooth, long-stalked, deeply cut or lobed with very fine short hairs on the edges; lobes from 5 to 7, variously toothed or lobed. Brazil.——Borders and naturalization, in warm sandy loam. Division or seed.

Sidalcea malvæflora (*Mallow-flowered S.*) — A vigorous perennial with a branching stem nearly 3 ft. high. *Flowers*, in summer; very handsome, pale rose, about 1½ in. across, in clusters on the tops of the erect branches. *Leaves*, stalked, deeply divided, the segments again divided or lobed; stem and branches of a light green colour with a few scattered short white hairs. Oregon and New Mexico. ——Borders, in any soil. Division and seed.

Sideritis syriaca (*Syrian Ironwort*). —A dwarf herb densely clothed with white wool, with short woody stems 6 to 15 in. high. *Flowers*, in summer; yellow, 6 to 10 in a whorl; corolla clothed with silky down outside, twice the length of the calyx. *Leaves*, thick, lance-shaped, narrowed at the base; lower ones stalked, unequally toothed; floral ones stalkless, entire, heart-shaped at the base, equalling the calyces. Candia and Palestine.—— Warm borders, or in the drier and rougher parts of the rock-garden, in light sandy soil. In warm sandy loams this would probably form a useful edging-plant. Seed, cuttings, or division.

Silene acaulis (*Cushion Pink*).—A very dwarf alpine herb tufted into light-green masses like a wide-spreading moss, but quite firm. *Flowers*, in summer; pink-rose or crimson, on short stalks barely peeping above the leaves; petals obovate, slightly notched; calyx bell-shaped or tubular, quite smooth, with rather blunt teeth. *Leaves*, short, linear, smooth, crowded. There are several varieties: *alba*, with white flowers; *exscapa*, with the flower-stems shorter than in the usual form, and *muscoides*, dwarfer still; but none of them are far removed from the common plant, or of greater importance. Native of the mountains of Scotland, Ireland, North Wales, the lake district of England, and many other parts of Europe; found also in Asia and America.—— The rock-garden, in exposed parts, in any open moist soil. Division.

Silene alpestris (*Alpine Catchfly*).—A dwarf and beautiful alpine herb, about 6 in. high. *Flowers*, in early summer; white, shining, rather large, panicled; petals 4-toothed; calyx erect, with blunt teeth, as long as the petals. *Leaves*, linear-lance-shaped, bluntish, tufted, smooth, erect; stem simple, few-leaved. Some varieties of this species are quite sticky from viscid matter, and others perfectly free from it. Alps of Europe.——The rock-garden, borders, edgings, or naturalization in open, bare, or rocky spots, in ordinary soil, and always in a fully exposed position. Seed and division.

Silene Elisabethæ (*Elizabeth's Catchfly*).—A beautiful species, the flowers of which look more like those of some handsome but dwarf *Clarkia* than those of the commonly grown Silenes; 3 or 4 in. high. *Flowers*, in summer; large, bright-rose, the base of the petals white; from 1 to 7 borne on each stem. *Leaves*, oval-oblong, acutely pointed, about ⅙ in. broad, viscid, pubescent, and shining, growing in tufts. Tyrolese Mountains.——The rock-garden, in warm spots, in well-drained sandy loam, and on the margin of the choice mixed border. Seed.

Silene maritima (*Sea Catchfly*).—A dwarf herb with short spreading stems forming level glaucous tufts; 2 to 4 in. high. *Flowers*, nearly all the summer; white, usually solitary, about 1 in. across; petals bifid, crowned at the base; anthers deep purple; calyx purple, inflated, netted with veins. *Leaves*, connate, smooth, glaucous, lance-shaped, 1 to 2 in. long and about ⅙ in. broad. The double variety is the handsomest and is the kind generally seen in gardens. Sea-coast in several parts of Britain and Norway.——Borders, edges of raised beds, etc., in ordinary soil. Division.

Silene orientalis (*Umbel-flowered S.*)—A very showy perennial, about 2 ft. high. *Flowers*, in summer; very handsome, deep rose-colour, in dense umbel-like heads 3 in. across. *Leaves*, glaucous, oval, pointed, opposite, nearly erect, clothing the entire stem very densely. Native country unknown.——Borders, in sandy loam. Seed or division.

Silene pennsylvanica (*Pennsylvanian Catchfly*).—A very pretty and showy kind with numerous stems from the same root; 8 to 12 in. high. *Flowers*, in summer; light purple or pink, in a many-flowered cyme; petals oboval, very obtuse and hollowed at the tips; calyx gradually thickening, very clammy. *Leaves*, more or less sharp-pointed; radical ones spoon-shaped, gradually tapering into the stalks; stem-leaves lance-shaped. North America.——Rockwork, or margin of the mixed border, in very sandy loam. Seed and division.

Silene Pumilio (*Pigmy Catchfly*).—A densely-tufted species, 2 or 3 in. high, resembling the Cushion Pink. *Flowers*, in summer; much larger than those of *S. acaulis*, rose-coloured, 1 on each short stalk; petals obcordate, crowned; calyx inflated, hairy, many-nerved. *Leaves*, linear or spoon-shaped, somewhat succulent and obtuse, slightly pubescent. Alps of Germany.—— The rock-garden, and the margin of the choice mixed border, in moist sandy loam. Seed and careful division.

Silene Schafta (*Autumn Catchfly*).—A dwarf, neat, and pretty species, 4 to 8 in. high. *Flowers*, late in summer; large, purplish-rose-colour, erect, in branching elongated cymes; calyx slightly swollen in the upper part. *Leaves*, opposite, the lower ones oblong; the upper ones oval, acute, of a light-green colour. Caucasus.—— Borders and the rock-garden; best in light warm sandy loam. Seed and division.

Silene virginica (*Fire Pink*).—A clammy and rather tall kind with simple stems, usually of a dark brown hue; 1 to 2 ft. high. *Flowers*, early in summer; crimson, very large; petals deeply 2-cleft, lobes sometimes toothed; stamens projecting. *Leaves*, of the root spoon-shaped, with fringed stalks; stem-leaves oblong-lance-shaped, upper ones very short, pubescent. North America.——Rockwork, or borders, in sandy loam. Seed and division.

Silphium laciniatum (*Compass Plant*).—A vigorous Composite, rough with white spreading hairs; 6 to 10 ft. high. *Flowers*, in summer; yellow, few, in large heads 3 to 5 in. across, forming racemose spikes; terminal heads opening earliest. *Leaves*, pinnately divided, mostly stalked and clasping at the base; segments lance-shaped with wavy margin, or pinnatifid, sometimes entire; lower leaves 1 to 2½ ft. long; veins of the leaves, and the young heads clothed with long white hairs. North America.—— Naturalized among tall plants in half-wild spots, in any soil. Division.

Silphium perfoliatum (*Cup Plant*). — Another very stout perennial, 4 to 7 ft. high. *Flowers*, in summer, yellow, in corymbose heads, the middle one on a long stalk. *Leaves*, opposite, 6 to 12 in. long, 4 to 7 in. broad, oval, or oval-oblong, thin, coarsely toothed, on winged connate stalks; stem stout, square. North America. —— The same positions etc., as for the preceding kind, and occasionally in groups of the larger perennials. Division.

Silphium terebinthinaceum (*Prairie Dock*).—A smooth and vigorous species, 4 to 8 ft high. *Flowers*, late in summer; yellow, about 3 in. across, in a loose irregular panicle; scales of the involucre smooth. *Leaves*, oval or oval-oblong, mostly heart-shaped at the base, sharply toothed, often 2 ft. or more long, on long stalks, and somewhat like those of the Burdock but stiffer; stem smooth, roundish, leafless except near the base. North America.——Similar treatment etc., to that for the preceding kind.

Silybum eburneum (*Ivory Milk-thistle*).—A variety of *S. marianum*, distinguished from it by the ivory whiteness of its spines. It is also more tender and more liable to perish in winter. It is more decidedly a biennial than *S. marianum*, and when sown in spring seldom flowers before the following year, so that, during the first year, its fine rosettes of leaves continue in good condition for a much longer time. Britain.——In groups of fine-leaved hardy plants, or naturalized in light warm soils on rough banks, etc. Seed.

Silybum marianum (*Milk-thistle*).—A native biennial or annual plant, with large and handsome shining green leaves, brilliantly variegated with white; 4 to 5 ft. high. *Flowers*, in summer; purple, in large globose heads; involucrum formed of leafy, spiny scales. *Leaves*, alternate, very large, oblong-lance-shaped, spiny, clasping; those of the root pinnatifid, of a lively shining-green, usually variegated with large white marblings. Britain, in waste places.——In groups of fine-foliaged hardy plants, and in a wild state in rough and waste places, in ordinary soil. Seed.

Sisyrinchium grandiflorum (*Spring Satin-flower*). — A beautiful early spring-flowering perennial; 6 to 10 in. high. *Flowers*, in spring; deep purple, with red style and filaments, and yellow anthers (or pure white, with transparent style and white filaments), issuing from a 2-flowered spathe with a thin transparent margin. *Leaves*, shorter than the flower-stem, the upper ones linear-sword-shaped, sheathing at the base, erect and spreading at the ends; lower leaves reduced to the dimensions of mere scales. *Root*, fibrous, creeping. N.W. regions of North America.—— The rock-garden, and borders, in light peaty soil or very sandy loam, and in warm positions; also a charming subject for growth in pots in cold frames, whence it may be removed to the greenhouse when in flower in early spring. Careful division.

Soldanella alpina (*Alpine S.*)—A beautiful dwarf alpine plant, 2 to 4 in. high. *Flowers*, in spring; of a vivid blue, bell-shaped, with five divisions, finely fringed, and having in the throat five incised scales, from 2 to 6 blossoms gracefully drooping from the top of each stem. *Leaves*, rounded, kidney-shaped, entire, leathery, faintly and broadly crenated, of a lively green. Stems reddish and downy. Tyrol and Switzerland. —— The rock-garden, in fine, moist, and very sandy loam, also in pots or pans, and in raised borders, surrounded by half-buried stones. Division. The same treatment will do for all the kinds, the two largest—*S. alpina* and *S. montana*—being those most suited for choice borders.

Soldanella minima (*Small Soldanella*). — Another alpine gem about 1¼ in. high. *Flowers*, late in spring; solitary, dark lilac, streaked with purple on the inside; corolla divided for one-third of its length into spreading segments, naked at the throat, or furnished with very small scales. *Leaves*, roundish. Stems covered with a very short glandular down. Alps of Switzerland, Tyrol, and Carinthia. ——Culture, etc., as for *S. alpina*.

Soldanella montana (*Large S.*)— This plant very much resembles *S. alpina*. It is, however, larger in all its parts; the flower-stalks and calyx also are covered with down of greater or less length, instead of glandular tubercles as in *S. alpina*; the scales of the corolla are equal in length to the filaments of the stamens and not joined to them, are of oval-oblong form, as long as they are broad, indented, and with entire lobes. The Pyrenean plant is moreover paler in hue, and rather more villous than that of the Tyrol. Lower Pyrenees.——Culture, etc., as for *S. alpina*.

Soldanella pusilla (*Fragile S.*) — Another beautiful and minute kind about 2 in. high. *Flowers*, late in spring; solitary, blue, divided into a fringe for only ⅓ of its length, and without scales in the throat. *Leaves*, kidney-shaped, with a heart-shaped base; pedicels tubercled. Alps of Dauphiny and the Pyrenees.——Culture, etc. as for *S. alpina*.

Solidago canadensis (*Canadian Golden Rod*).—A vigorous Composite, from

3 to 5½ ft. high. *Flowers*, late in summer; golden yellow, in small heads, forming very numerous recurved racemes arranged in a large pyramidal panicle. *Leaves*, lance-shaped, usually unequally toothed, downy beneath and roughish above. Stems rough, hairy, or downy. Widely distributed in North America where it varies much.——Amidst vigorous herbs in shrubberies and semi-wild places, in any soil. Not worthy of a place in gardens. Easily increased by division of the tufts.

Solidago grandiflora (*Large Golden Rod*).—One of the most ornamental Golden Rods, about 2½ ft. high. *Flowers*, in August and September; large, yellow, arranged in dense spike-like clusters. *Leaves*, oval - lanceolate, toothed. Whole plant slightly villous. N. America. —— Similar treatment etc., to that for preceding kind.

Solidago nutans (*Nodding Golden Rod*).—About 5 ft. high. *Flowers*, from August to September; yellow, in numerous clusters, which are somewhat reflected at the end, and form a large panicle. *Leaves*, alternate, linear-lanceolate, slightly wrinkled. Whole plant somewhat villous. N. America. ——Similar positions etc., to those for *S. canadensis*.

Solidago multiflora (*Many-flowered S.*) — A stout much-branched herb, from 3 to 4 ft. high. *Flowers*, late in summer and in autumn; yellow, small, in very short spike-like racemes arranged in large erect panicles. *Leaves*, smooth, or the upper ones sometimes downy, sessile, lance-shaped, serrate. Resembles *S. canadensis*, but the racemes are short and in more erect panicles. A plant of uncertain origin, cultivated in the Paris garden and said to have been received from America——The same uses etc., as for *S. canadensis*.

[There is a crowd of other species of *Solidago*, but scarcely one of them is fitted for garden culture; any that may be received will do for naturalization in woods and copses. Indeed from a horticultural point of view they are all about of equal value. In borders they merely serve to exterminate much more valuable plants and to give a coarse and ragged aspect to the garden.]

Sorghum halepense (*Aleppo S.*)—A very handsome hardy grass, about 3½ ft. high, with an erect stem and broad leaves more than 1 ft. long. *Flowers*, in August; when it is most attractive, the inflorescence consisting of a dense panicle of purplish, awned flowers. Southern Europe, N. Africa, and Syria.——Borders, and isolation on the grass in the picturesque garden, in sandy loam. Seed and division.

Sparaxis pulcherrima (*Drooping S.*) —A plant of exquisite brilliancy of colour and much grace of habit; 5 to 7 ft. high. *Flowers*, in summer; large, bell-shaped, 1½ to 2 in. long, of a delicate pink, rose-colour, or ruby crimson, suspended on long fine stalks from gracefully arched and drooping stems, on which they form a very lax panicle of 1½ to 2 ft. in length. *Leaves*, sword - shaped, dark green, about 3 ft. long. Cape of Good Hope. ——Suited for fringes of shrubberies, and for dotting here and there in small tufts in openings in beds of American plants or other choice shrubs; it thrives best in deep sandy soil, but also does well in rather stiff moist soil. Division and seed.

Spigelia marilandica (*Worm-grass*). —A brilliant perennial with erect, simple, 4-angled stems from 6 to 18 in. high. *Flowers*, in summer; deep red outside, and deep yellow within, borne in a short terminal one-sided spike, either simple or forked; corolla 1½ in. long. *Leaves*, opposite, smooth, entire, stalkless, ovate, or

SPIRÆA — STATICE. 241

lance-shaped, acute. North America.
—— Bog-bed, peat borders, margins of beds of American plants, or in the lower parts of the rock-garden, always in moist deep peat soil. Division.

Spiræa Aruncus (*Goat's-beard S.*)—A vigorous perennial, 3 to 5 ft. high. *Flowers*, in summer ; white, small, freely produced in long spikes forming a terminal panicle. *Leaves*, tripinnate ; leaflets in 3 or 4 pairs with an odd one, about 2 in. long and about 1 in. broad, oblong, acute, serrate ; the terminal one ovate. Europe, Asia, and America.——Associated with the more vigorous herbaceous plants by wood-walks or banks, etc., and also grouped with the finer herbaceous plants having fine foliage. Division.

Spiræa Filipendula (*Dropwort*).—A rather common native herb, with pinnate leaves and erect stems, 1 to 2 ft. high. *Flowers*, in summer ; yellowish-white, often tipped with red, rather larger than those of *S. Ulmaria*, in loose terminal corymbs. *Leaves*, mostly radical or on the lower part of the stem, alternate, smooth, divided into numerous oblong-linear segments, deeply toothed ; roots swelling into small oblong tubers here and there. The double variety, *S. Filipendula, fl. pl.*, is a very pretty border-plant. Common in meadows throughout Europe.
——Borders, in ordinary soil, or as a fern-like edging-plant, the flowers to be pinched off. Division.

Spiræa palmata (*Palmate Spiræa*).— A new and handsome kind, 1½ to 2 ft. high. *Flowers*, in June and July ; crimson, in a terminal panicle which is many times divided. *Leaves*, 4 in. long, alternate, stalked, palmate, with 5 to 7 lobes, smooth, veined and reticulated, pale underneath ; lobes oblong, pointed, sharply and twice serrate. Stem herbaceous, striated, erect, smooth. Japan.—— Borders,

and beds of the finer perennials, in deep sandy loam. Division.

Spiræa Ulmaria (*Meadow-sweet*).—A common British plant with erect, reddish, angular, and furrowed stems 2 to 4 ft. high. *Flowers*, in summer ; yellowish-white, sweet-scented, small, numerous, in a large very compound cyme, the outer branches of which rise much above the central one. *Leaves*, large, pinnate ; leaflets 5 to 9, ovate, coarsely serrated, terminal one largest and 3-lobed ; stipules roundish, joined to the stalk. There is a variegated variety, and also a double-flowered one. Europe and Britain.
——Borders, in any soil, and in waste places. Division.

Spiræa venusta (*Queen of the Prairie*).—A handsome hardy perennial, 1½ to 3 ft. high. *Flowers*, in summer ; deep rosy-carmine, in large terminal compound cymes. *Leaves*, large, pinnate ; leaflets palmate-lobed ; lobes pointed and irregularly toothed. North America and Siberia.——Borders, margin of shrubberies, beds of the finer perennials, or naturalization, in sandy loam. Division.

Stachys lanata (*Woolly Woundwort*). —A densely woolly perennial, 12 to 18 in. high. *Flowers*, in summer ; purple, small, in whorled spikes, 30 flowers or more in a whorl ; corolla woolly outside, with an inclosed tube. *Leaves*, thick, wrinkled, oblong-elliptic, narrowed at both ends, densely clothed with silky hairs ; floral ones smaller. Tauria and the Caucasus.
——Borders, and as an edging-plant, in any soil ; also suited for naturalization. Division.

Statice angustifolia (*Narrow-leaved Sea Lavender*).—Considered a fine variety of the British Sea Lavender, *S. Limonium* ; 1 ft. to 16 in. high. *Flowers*, from July to September or October ; small, bluish-lilac, very numerous, in

R

long corymbose panicles. *Leaves*, oval-lanceolate, rather acute, of a deep green, smooth and glossy, numerous, about ½ or ¼ the height of the stems, which are also numerous, and grow in tufts. Resembles *S. latifolia* somewhat in its flowers, but is at once distinguished from it by the difference of the leaves. Various parts of Europe.——Borders, and beds of the finer perennials, preferring a deep, stiffish, moist soil. Careful division and seed.

Statice elata (*Tall Sea Lavender*).—*Goniolimon elatum*, Boiss.—A handsome plant of a lively green colour, growing in tufts 2 to 3½ ft. across at the top, and 20 to 30 in. high. *Flowers*, from July to September; blue or bluish-violet, in long panicles. *Leaves*, 1 ft. to 16 in. long, and 4 to 6 in. or more broad, almost all radical, oboval, very obtuse, with a short sharp point at the end, narrowed into a foot-stalk, twisted and wavy at the edges. Stems much-branched above; branchlets hairy, triangular. Southern Russia.—— Borders, in good deep loam. Seed or careful division of well-established plants in autumn.

Statice eximia (*Rosy Sea Lavender*).—A handsome kind, 1 to 2 ft. high. *Flowers*, in summer; numerous, small, white at first, afterwards rosy-lilac, in a large branching panicle. *Leaves*, glaucescent, almost all radical, oblong or obovate, obtuse, shortly mucronate, abruptly contracted into a long foot-stalk, with a narrow margin slightly crisped or waved. Central Asia.—— The mixed border, and the lower parts of the rock-garden, in good sandy loam. Seed and careful division.

Statice globulariæfolia (*Globularia-leaved Sea Lavender*).—A dwarf neat species, 8 to 18 in. high. *Flowers*, from May to September; white, arranged in threes in loose unilateral spikes, and surrounded by pointed bracts membranous at the edges.

Leaves, slightly glaucous, oboval-spoon-shaped, acute, rarely bluntish, with a short point at the end, and narrowed into the leafstalk. France.——Borders, in ordinary sandy soil; also among the less delicate plants in the rock-garden. Careful division and seed.

Statice incana (*Hoary Sea Lavender*). —*Goniolimon callicomum*, Boiss.— A handsome much branching perennial, from 1 to 1½ ft. high. *Flowers*, in summer; crimson, with a white calyx, in numerous short two-rowed spikes. *Leaves*, radical, oval, pointed, smooth, tinged with reddish-purple on the upper side, arranged in a rosette. Central Asia. —— The rock-garden among the stouter plants, or borders, in deep sandy loam. Seed.

Statice latifolia (*Great Sea Lavender*). —A noble species growing 20 in. to 2½ ft. high. *Flowers*, late in summer; blue, in an elegant broad panicle, the colour of which is a light blue with a greyish tinge from the numerous membranous bracts and scarious calyces. The inflorescence forms a dense round mass, composed of countless ramifications of flowering branchlets, and is most ornamental and peculiar in aspect. *Leaves*, radical, very broad, oblong-elliptical, obtuse, disposed in a rosette or tuft from 8 to 10 in. high and as much across. Russia. —— Borders, and as isolated tufts on the turf, or in beds of the finer autumn-flowering perennials. Careful division and seed.

Statice Limonium (*Common Sea Lavender*).— A British plant, found in salt marshes by the sea; 6 to 18 in. high. *Flowers*, late in summer; purplish, in densely imbricated spikelets arranged in a corymbose panicle. *Leaves*, nearly all radical, smooth, oblong or oblong-lance-shaped, attenuated at the base. There is a variety with white flowers (*S. L. flor. alb.*).

Europe and Britain.——Borders, preferring a deep, stiffish, moist soil. Seed and division.

Statice oleæfolia (Pour.) (*Olive-leaved Sea Lavender*).—*S. virgata.*—A dwarf kind, 4 to 16 in. high. *Flowers*, late in summer; blue, in a small, very loose, oval or oblong panicle, slightly branched and much shorter than the rest of the scape; spikelets very distant from each other. *Leaves*, rather leathery, one-nerved, flat or slightly convex on the upper side, smooth, narrow, oblong-wedge-shaped, rounded or blunt at the end. S. Europe, on the coasts of the Mediterranean.——Borders and the rock-garden, in well-drained light soil. Seed and division.

Statice speciosa (*Showy Sea Lavender*).—A very handsome and neat species, of a glaucous green hue; 1 ft. to 16 in. high. *Flowers*, in summer; rose-coloured, arranged in dense corymbs. *Leaves*, stalked, almost all radical, roundish or oblong-oval, abruptly narrowed to a point at the end, and narrower at the base. Stems stiff, flattened or 3-sided, much branched above. Southern Russia.——Lower parts of the rock-garden, and in borders, in well-drained sandy loam. Seed.

Statice tatarica (*Tartarian Statice*). —A very handsome and dwarf kind, 10 in. to 1 ft. high. *Flowers*, late in summer; rose-coloured or reddish, small, very numerous, arranged in pairs on two-rowed spikelets, in the axils of small dry bracts. *Leaves*, almost all radical, somewhat leathery, smooth, of a dark green colour, stalked, broadly obovate, or oblong-lance-shaped, acute. Tartary.——The rock-garden and the margin of the choice mixed border, in sandy and well-drained loam. Seed.

Stevia purpurea (*Purple S.*)—A somewhat fragrant, slender-stemmed perennial, covered with a velvety pubescence; 16 in. to 2 ft. high. *Flowers*, late in summer; of a rosy-purple, in a dense corymb, each head containing 5 florets with projecting stigmas. *Leaves*, alternate, lance-shaped, slightly toothed at the end; the lower ones oblong, all more or less aromatic. Mexico.——Warm borders, in ordinary soil. Division and seed.

Stipa pennata (*Feather Grass*).—A very graceful perennial grass, with flowering-stems 16 to 20 in. high, bearing in summer a narrow feathery panicle of great beauty. *Leaves*, long, stiff, erect, rush-like, shorter than the flower-stem, growing in a tuft. France, and other parts of Europe; found also in Siberia.——Borders and naturalization; best in good deep sandy loam. Division and seed.

Stokesia cyanea (*Stokes's Aster*).—A stout, free, but late-flowering herb, 1½ to 2 ft. high. *Flowers*, in September and October; blue, showy, and somewhat like those of the China Aster, 3 or 4 in. across when well opened, but in this country the plants are often injured by the frosts before the flowers open. *Leaves*, alternate, somewhat lance-shaped, smooth and of a slightly glaucous colour. South Carolina. ——Warm sheltered borders, facing the south, in well-drained sandy loam. The plant does but poorly in cold soils and positions, but, grown in pots, it flowers very well in a cold house or conservatory in autumn. Division.

Stylophorum diphyllum (*Celandine Poppy*).— A dwarf perennial somewhat resembling the Celandine in foliage and flowers; 1 ft. high. *Flowers*, in April or May; deep yellow, about 2 in. across, the buds nodding; sepals 2, bristly; petals 4. *Leaves*, pale beneath, smoothish, deeply cut into 5 or 7 oblong unevenly-lobed divisions, those of the root often with a pair of distinct leaflets. Damp woods in North America.

R 2

——Borders, and fringes of shrubberies, or the rougher parts of the rock-garden, in ordinary soil. Division.

Swertia perennis (*Marsh Swertia*).— A singular-looking perennial with erect, simple, slightly 4-cornered stems, about 1 ft. high. *Flowers*, in summer; dull greyish-purple, in erect spikes; corolla rotate, 5-parted, dotted with black, and with bristly pores at the edge. *Leaves*, stalked, ovate or elliptic, entire, smooth. Europe and Siberia, in mountain bogs.——One of the most interesting subjects for the artificial peat-bog; also in moist spots near the rock-garden, or naturalized in marshy places. Division.

Symphyandra pendula (*Pendulous S.*) —A dwarf Campanula-like herb with large flowers almost hidden amongst the leaves; about 1 ft. high. *Flowers*, in summer; cream-coloured, drooping, in a loose panicle; peduncles 1- to 3-flowered; corolla funnel-shaped, velvety, 5-lobed at the apex. *Leaves*, ovate, acute, toothed, velvety; stems branched, pendulous, pilose. Caucasus, in rocky places.—— Borders and among the more easily-grown plants in the rock-garden, in ordinary soil. Seed and division.

Symphytum asperrimum (*Rough S.*)— A tall and vigorous perennial clothed with short sharp prickles; 4 to 6 ft. high. *Flowers*, in summer; red before expanding, afterwards blue, in terminal twin racemes; corolla downy outside, bell-shaped; calyx 5-parted; sepals sharply pointed. *Leaves*, broad, very rough, hairy, ovate-heart-shaped, taper-pointed, upper ones nearly opposite. Caucasus and Tauria.——One of the most suitable plants for naturalizing in rough places and among the coarsest herbaceous vegetation. Almost too rampant in habit for borders. Division and seed.

Symphytum bohemicum (*Bohemian Comfrey*).—A very handsome and brilliantly coloured perennial, probably a variety of *S. officinale*; 1 to 1½ ft. high. *Flowers*, in early summer; brilliant reddish-purple, in erect twin racemes. *Leaves*, alternate, ovate-lance-shaped, decurrent; stems winged. Bohemia.——Borders, and fringes of shrubbery, in ordinary soil, also a pretty subject for naturalization in rather open sunny places. Division.

Symphytum caucasicum (*Caucasian Comfrey*).—A beautiful free-growing perennial, 1½ to 2 ft. high. *Flowers*, in spring and early summer; handsome blue, in terminal twin racemes; corolla cylindrically bell-shaped; calyces hispid, obtuse. *Leaves*, clothed with soft hairs, greyish beneath, slightly decurrent, ovate-lance-shaped, gradually narrowing at the base; upper ones opposite; stem hairy, angular, branched at the apex. Native of the Caucasus.—— An admirable plant for naturalization in shrubberies, copses, or in almost any position, and in any soil; also good for borders, but seen to far greater advantage in the positions first named. Division.

Symphytum officinale (*Comfrey*).—A branching, rough-leaved plant, from 1 to 2 ft. high. *Flowers*, in summer; yellowish-white or purple, tubular, about 1 in. long, in pendent clusters. *Leaves*, alternate, oval-lance-shaped, rough; stem-leaves decurrent. Britain and Europe.——The variegated form is the only one fitted for the garden proper; the purple variety will be worth planting in wild places, copses, or hedgebanks, in any soil. Division.

Tanacetum vulgare (*Tansy*). — A well-known native plant, 2 to 4 ft. high. *Flowers*, in summer; yellow, numerous, in corymbose heads. *Leaves*, smoothish, twice-divided. Europe and Britain; also found in America. This is only described here in consequence of its variety, *T. vulgare crispum*, which has leaves more finely divided and curled, and is a graceful fern-like plant.——Borders, and groups of fine-leaved hardy plants, in any soil. It is better to pinch off the flowers when they appear. Division.

Teucrium Chamædrys (*Wall Germander*).—A compact perennial with shining foliage; 6 to 10 in. high. *Flowers*, in summer; reddish-purple, from 2 to 6 in a whorl, forming a short loose terminal raceme. *Leaves*, ovate or oblong, deeply toothed, wedge-shaped at the base, smooth and shining above, sometimes villous; stems procumbent at the base, almost woody. Throughout Europe, on walls, rocks, etc.——Borders and naturalization on ruins, stony banks, etc., in any light soil; it is sometimes used as an edging-plant on the Continent. Division.

Teucrium Marum (*Cat Thyme*).—A small grey wiry-branched shrub with somewhat the habit of the common Thyme. *Flowers*, in summer; bright red, in loose whorled spikes at the ends of the branches. *Leaves*, greyish above, tomentose beneath, ovate, small, stalked; floral leaves smaller. Spain.——Only likely to prove hardy in the southern parts of these islands, and then only on ruins, old walls, or in dry chinks in chalk or gravel-pits. If planted out, the soil should be of the driest and poorest description, brick-rubbish, etc., with sand and a little poor dry loam, and in positions where cats cannot get at it, as they usually destroy it. Cuttings.

Teucrium Polium (*Poly Germander*).—A curious dwarf whitish herb, 3 to 5 in. high. *Flowers*, in summer; small, pale yellow, whitish or purplish, in small roundish terminal heads; calyces densely covered with short yellow down. *Leaves*, narrow, notched, thickly covered with soft white or yellowish down, as are also the stem and branches. Southern Europe.——The rock-garden, in sunny spots, and in light free soil. Probably not hardy except in the milder southern districts and in favourable spots in the rock-garden, where it grows freely. Seed, cuttings, and division.

Teucrium pyrenaicum (*Pyrenean Germander*).—A dwarf hardy perennial, 3 to 7 in. high. *Flowers*, in summer; purplish and white, in dense terminal clusters. *Leaves*, nearly round, notched at the margins, and thickly covered with soft down, as are also the stem and short branches. Pyrenees.—— The rock-garden and borders, in ordinary soil. Seed, cuttings, or division.

Thalictrum anemonoides (*Rue Anemone*).—A delicate, diminutive, and interesting American wood-plant, with the habit and foliage of *Isopyrum*, and the inflorescence and fruit of an *Anemone*; 6 in. high. *Flowers*, in April and May; white, nearly 1 in. across, several in an umbel; sepals 5, oval, $\frac{1}{2}$ in. long; stamens yellowish. *Leaves*, of the root on long stalks, 2- or 3-ternate; leaflets roundish, somewhat 3-lobed, on long stalks; floral leaves 2 or 3 in number, wedge-shaped, stalked. There is a pretty double variety, with the flowers smaller than those of the single form. Common in the woods of North America.——The rock-garden, margins of beds of choice dwarf American shrubs, etc., in fine sandy or peaty soil. Division.

Thalictrum aquilegifolium (*Columbine Meadow Rue*).—In flower the handsomest of its numerous family, 1 to 3 ft. high. *Flowers*, in early summer; purplish, in large terminal panicles; sepals deciduous, recurved, much shorter than the stamens, which are alone conspicuous. *Leaves*, like those of Columbine, tripinnate, with roundish, smooth, deeply-toothed leaflets; stems hollow, purple, covered with a mealy bloom. Native of Germany and other parts of Central Europe.——Borders or naturalization, in any soil. Division and seed.

Thalictrum fœtidum (*Fetid Meadow-Rue*).—A dwarf herb, resembling *T. minus* but somewhat larger and with a fetid smell; about 1 ft. high. *Flowers*, in early summer; small, nodding, in an erect spreading panicle; sepals reddish on the outside; anthers yellow. *Leaves*, decompound, clothed with a clammy pubescence; segments 2- or 3-pinnate; leaflets roundish, heart-shaped, 3- to 5-lobed at the apex. Europe and Asia.——Borders, rough rockwork, or naturalization for the sake of its graceful leaves. Thrives in any soil. Division.

Thalictrum minus (*Maidenhair Meadow-Rue*).—A very graceful fern-like plant, 1 to 1½ ft. high. *Flowers*, in early summer; insignificant, greenish-yellow, drooping, in a loose panicle; sepals pale purple, with white edges. *Leaves*, finely dissected into numerous small, smooth, roundish, glaucous leaflets, toothed at the apex; stem zigzag. Europe, Britain, and Russian Asia.——The rock-garden, borders, edgings to flower-beds, or in wild places for the effect of its elegant habit and leaves. It thrives in any garden soil. Division.

Thermopsis barbata (*Shaggy T.*)— An interesting perennial of the pea-flower tribe; 6 to 18 in. high. *Flowers*, in June; large, of a peculiar, dull very dark violet, in short axillary racemes, which together form a thick, dense, elongated, compound raceme; standard erect, roundish, 2-lobed. *Leaves*, in whorls of 3 to 7, sessile, lanceolate, pointed, smooth, sometimes ciliated and hairy; stems stout, erect, branching, villous with soft-spreading white hairs, as are also the bracts, pedicels, calyx, and leaf-stalks. Himalayas.—— Borders, in good loam. Division.

Thermopsis fabacea (*Bean-like T.*)— A showy perennial clothed with silky hairs; 1 to 2 ft. high. *Flowers*, in early summer; yellow, alternate, in terminal racemes. *Leaves*, trifoliate, stalked; leaflets broadly oval; stipules ovate, obtuse, shorter than the leaf-stalk. Kamtschatka.—— Borders, in good sandy loam. Division and seed.

Thlaspi latifolium (*Showy Bastard Cress*).—A dwarf but vigorous perennial, with large indented root-leaves, and flowers somewhat like those of *Arabis albida*, but larger; 6 to 12 in. high. *Flowers*, in spring; white, in terminal racemes. *Leaves*, of the root on long stalks, heart-shaped, unevenly toothed; those of the stem on short stalks, ovate-heart-shaped. Caucasian and Iberian mountains.—— Borders, the spring-garden, in beds, and naturalized in association with the dwarfer flowers of spring and early summer; thrives in ordinary garden soil. Division and seed.

Thymus Serpyllum (*Wild Thyme.*)— A long-trailing, much-branched, spreading plant, common in the grass in many places, with slender stems 2 or 3 in. high, hard but scarcely woody at the base. *Flowers*, in summer; purple, 6 or more in a whorl, forming short terminal leafy heads. *Leaves*, small, flat, ovate, obtuse, on short stalks, more or less ciliated, sometimes smooth and sometimes covered with short stiff hairs. *T. lanuginosus* is a very woolly variety and there is also a white-flowered one. The woolly variety is best worthy of a place in gardens. Europe and Northern Asia, and abundant in Britain. —— Borders and the rock-garden, in ordinary garden soil. Division.

[There are sundry other species of Thyme in cultivation, but few of them are ornamental, though they are interesting subjects for planting on very dry banks or borders.]

Trachelium cæruleum (*Blue Throatwort*).—An attractive perennial, 1 to 3 ft. high. *Flowers*, in early summer; azure blue, small, numerous, forming a wide-spreading corymb. *Leaves*, ovate, acute, flat, on short stalks, coarsely serrate, smooth or ciliated; stem smooth. There is a white variety. Mediterranean region, among rocks.——Dry borders, or rocky banks, old ruins, or walls. Seed.

Tradescantia virginica (*Virginian Spiderwort*).—A distinct and valuable perennial, 1 to nearly 2½ ft. high. *Flowers*, in summer; abundantly and continuously, of a deep violet-blue with anthers of a golden-yellow, arranged in umbels on the tops of the stem and branches. *Leaves*, linear-lance-shaped, alternate, sheathing at the base, slightly fringed at the edges. There are several varieties: one with double violet, one with single rose-coloured, one with single lilac, and one with white flowers. The last is particularly pleasing from the contrast afforded by the violet-bearded stamens. North America, especially in Virginia.——Borders, fringes of shrubberies, and naturalization. It grows in the wettest clays as well as in ordinary garden soil. Division.

Trichonema Bulbocodium (*Bulbocodium T.*)—An interesting little bulbous plant, 3 to 5 in. high. *Flowers*, early in spring, solitary, violet, yellow at the bottom of the corolla, in the type, but displaying various shades under culture, on very slender stems which fall on the ground after the plant has flowered; segments of the flower lance-shaped. *Leaves*, very narrow, grass-like, channelled and furrowed, longer than the flower-stem. *Bulb* about the size of a Hazel-nut. South of Europe.——Borders, in light deep soil. Division.

Trientalis europea (*Starflower*).—An interesting and graceful plant, 3 to 6 in. high. *Flowers*, in spring and early summer; white or pink-tipped, star-shaped, 1 to 4 on slender stalks springing from the centre of the whorl of leaves; corolla mostly 7-parted, flat, without any tube. *Leaves*, lance-shaped, entire; arranged in a whorl of 5 or 6 at the top of the simple stems, the largest nearly 2 in. long; below the whorl are 2 or 3 small ones. Northern and Arctic Asia, America, and Europe, and found in the Scotch Highlands and the North of England.—— Peat borders, and the lower fringes of the rock-garden among low shrubs, in peaty soil; also on the margins of beds of American shrubs. Division.

Trifolium alpinum (*Alpine Trefoil*). —A stout spreading kind, with large but not brilliant flowers; 3 to 6 in. high. *Flowers*, in early summer; large, purple, in an umbel; the upper petal flesh-coloured and streaked with purple. *Leaves*, trifoliate, on long stalks; leaflets lance-shaped or linear, bluntish, toothed; stipules very long and narrow, acute. *Roots*, having the taste of Liquorice. Higher mountains of Europe.—— Margins of borders, in ordinary soil. Division and seed.

Trifolium repens var. **purpureum** (*Four-leaved Shamrock*).—A variety of the common White or Dutch Clover with brown or purplish leaves; 3 to 5 in. high. *Flowers*, from the end of May or beginning of June to the end of summer; small, white, faintly fragrant, in globular heads or clusters. *Leaves*, long-stalked, each consisting of 4 or 5 leaflets with a broad purplish spot on the upper side; this spot sometimes fills the entire surface, but more commonly it is surrounded by a green margin. Europe.——Edgings, tufts in the mixed border, the rougher parts of the rock-garden, edges of vases, etc. in ordinary garden soil. Division.

Trifolium rubens (*Red T.*)—An ornamental perennial, 1 ft. to 16 in. high. *Flowers*, from June (sometimes earlier) to August; large, carmine-rose or purplish-red, in long, oblong, or cylindrical heads which usually grow in pairs, and after flowering present a downy appearance from the fringed divisions of the numerous calyces. *Leaves*, lower ones alternate, stalked; upper ones sessile; all trifoliate, with leathery, oval-oblong, or oblong-lanceolate leaflets. There is a variety (not ornamental) with white flowers. Europe.——Will grow almost anywhere, seeming to prefer dry, calcareous, marly, or gravelly soil, and is therefore well adapted for naturalization on arid declivities with a southern aspect. Division or seed.

Trifolium uniflorum (*One-flowered Trefoil*).—A rare and singular, creeping, tufted kind, with very short stems, 1 or 2 in. high. *Flowers*, in early summer; brilliant rose, solitary, on short axillary stalks; corolla very long, much longer than the cylindrical striped calyx. *Leaves*, trifoliate; leaflets ovate, toothed; stipules sheathing, ending in a short taper point. Southern Europe.——The rock-garden or choice border, in very fine moist loam. Division.

Trillium cernuum (*Nodding T.*)—A curious tuberous-rooted plant, having its parts arranged in threes; 1 ft. to 20 in. high. *Flowers*, late in spring; 1 to 1½ in. across; sepals 3, narrow, oval-oblong, almost pointed and reflected, green, ½ to ¾ in. long; petals 3, similar in shape and size to the sepals, but white. *Leaves*, 3, in a whorl, roundish - lozenge - shaped, abruptly pointed, narrowing into a wedge-shape at the base, nearly sessile, of a dark green colour. North America.—— Among shrubs in moist peat borders, or in moist spots in the hardy fernery, or rock-garden. Division.

Trillium grandiflorum (*White Wood Lily*).—A remarkably beautiful plant, 6 in. to 2 ft. high. *Flowers*, in spring; pure white, 2 to 5 in. broad, pendent; sepals 3, oblong, spreading, green; petals 3, white, oblong - elliptical, ¼ longer than the sepals. *Leaves*, 3, in a whorl, lozenge - shaped, pointed, from 4 to 6 in. long, on short stalks,. North America, from Canada to Carolina.——In moist, quite shady, thoroughly sheltered spots by the side of wood-walks, in moist shady hollows of the rock-garden, and in the hardy fernery with the Osmundas and moisture-loving Ferns, always in deep, moist, very sandy loam, and leaf-mould or peat soil. Division of well-established tufts.

Triteleia uniflora (*Spring Star-flower*). — A delicately-coloured free-flowering bulbous plant, 4 to 6 in. high. *Flowers*, in spring; solitary, of an iridescent white with bluish reflections, and marked through the middle of the divisions on the outside with a violet streak which is continued down the tube. *Leaves*, broadly-linear, of a glaucous green, spreading on the ground. *Bulb*, small, elongated-egg-shaped, nearly solid, with whitish coats, and exhaling (as does the whole plant) an odour of Garlic. South America and Southern States of North America. —— Borders, edgings, the rock-garden and naturalized among spring flowers, growing in any soil. Division.

Tritoma Burchelli (*Burchell's Flame-flower*).—A noble and showy perennial, distinguished from the better known *T. Uvaria* by its flower-stem being marked with black spots, and also by the colour of its flowers, which have a scarlet base passing into carmine, and then into pale yellow and green at the extremities. The leaves are of a light green. A variety of this has leaves ribboned with white and green, but it is very tender. South Africa.——Borders, in well-drained and deep sandy loam, slightly protected about the roots in winter. Careful division.

Tritoma Uvaria (*Flame-flower*).—A noble and brilliant perennial, of late years popular in gardens; 3 to 4 ft. high. *Flowers*, late in summer; large, tubular, of a handsome coral-red, changing as they fade to orange and then to a greenish-yellow, arranged in a dense, oval-oblong spike. *Leaves*, very long and narrow, channelled and keeled, with very fine teeth on the edges and on the keel. *Root*, yellowish and occasionally swollen. South Africa.——Borders, beds, or groups of the finer autumn-flowering perennials, or as isolated tufts on the grass, in deep, free, and rich loam. It is desirable to protect the roots of this a little in winter. Division.

[There are sundry other fine varieties of Tritoma, such as *glauca*, *grandis*, *Rooperi*, *glaucescens*, and *recurvata*, all noble plants worthy of cultivation, and of which *grandis* (*Uvaria major*) is the tallest and the latest-flowering kind, often blooming till Christmas.]

Trollius asiaticus (*Asiatic Globe-flower*).—A handsome free-blooming perennial, 1½ ft. high. *Flowers*, in early summer; deep yellow; sepals somewhat more open than those of the common Globe-flower; petals longer than the stamens. *Leaves*, deeply divided and cut, larger than those of *T. europæus*, of a paler green, the segments also fewer and larger. Siberia.——Borders, and naturalization among medium-sized perennials, in ordinary soil. Division.

Trollius europæus (*Globe-flower*).—A native species, 1½ to 2 ft. high. *Flowers*, in early summer; pale yellow, large; sepals concave, forming a kind of globe, and almost concealing the petals and stamens. *Leaves*, of the root not unlike those of the Meadow Crowfoot; segments 3 or 5, lobed and cut; those of the stem few, smaller, and almost stalkless. Europe and Britain.——Borders, in ordinary soil, or associated with the exotic kinds in semi-wild places. Division.

Trollius napellifolius (*Napellus-leaved Globe-flower*). — More showy than either of the two preceding kinds, fine as they are; 1 ft. to 20 in. high. *Flowers*, early in summer; of a fine orange-yellow, terminal, large, fragrant, globular. *Leaves*, alternate, stalked, chiefly radical, of a dark green, paler underneath, with a palmate limb of 5 to 7 lobes, deeply toothed. Considered by some a variety of *T. europæus*, from which it appears to differ in its colour, in not being quite so tall, and in having a greater number of lobes in its leaves. Various parts of Europe.——Borders, beds, groups of the finer perennials, and naturalization, in ordinary soil. Division.

Tropæolum pentaphyllum (*Five-leaved T.*)—A rapidly-growing climber, 6 to nearly 10 ft. high. *Flowers*, in summer; yellowish-red; petals shorter than the calyx. *Leaves*, divided into 5 shortly-stalked, oval-oblong, entire, smooth segments. *Root* tuberous; stems smooth, climbing. Fruit almost berry-shaped, of a dark violet colour. Chili.——For covering pillars, walls, chains, bowers, etc.; best in light and warm loams or calcareous soils. Division or seed.

Tropæolum polyphyllum (*Yellow Rock T.*)—A peculiar creeping species, with pale glaucous-green leaves, and shoots 20 in. to 2 ft. long. *Flowers*, in summer ; light orange, with obtuse entire petals, as long as the calyx. *Leaves*, small, peltate, with from 5 to 10 obcval-oblong segments, slightly toothed. Chili.——The rock-garden, and banks where its creeping shoots may be seen to advantage, in deep and good sandy loam. Division.

Tropæolum speciosum (*Flame Nasturtium*).—A very brilliant climbing plant, 6 to 10 ft. high. *Flowers*, in summer ; brilliant vermilion ; petals obcordate, upper ones narrowly wedge-shaped, lower ones roundish, all longer than the long-spurred calyx. *Leaves*, nearly peltate, 6-lobed ; lobes oblong-obtuse, downy underneath ; stem and three-cleft stipules also downy. Chili.——Against warm walls, in which position it may be allowed to scramble over the adjoining wall-plants, on half shrubby banks, or the fringes of the hardy fernery, in rich, light, moist and deep soil. It is seen to greatest advantage running wild over shrubs, and is so beautiful when seen in good condition that it should be tried in several different positions, and under slightly different conditions. Seed or careful division.

Tropæolum tuberosum (*Tuberous T.*) —A distinct kind with tuberous roots ; 20 in to 2 ft. high. *Flowers*, late in summer ; deep yellow, on stalks much longer than the leaves ; petals entire, or notched at the end, furrowed on the claw, a little longer than the calyx ; calyx crimson, shorter than the spur. *Leaves*, heart-shaped at the base, 5-lobed ; lobes entire, notched, sometimes two-cleft ; leaf-stalks twice as long as the leaf, tendril-like. Peru.——Sunny borders beneath walls, in very sandy loam. Separation of the tubers.

Tulipa Celsiana (*Crocus-like Tulip*). —A pretty species, resembling a large yellow Crocus when expanded ; 4 to 6 in. high. *Flowers*, in early summer ; solitary, erect, yellow on the inside, and generally orange on the outside. *Leaves*, linear-lanceolate, folded or doubled, smooth. *Bulb*, small, producing its cloves at the end of long filaments, and covered with a smooth coat. South of Europe and North of Africa.——Borders, beds, and the bulb-garden, in deep sandy loam. Separation of the bulbs soon after flowering, every second or third year.

Tulipa Clusiana (*Clusius's Tulip*).— A delicately coloured and very desirable kind, about 14 in. high. *Flowers*, in spring and early summer ; tolerably large, white inside, with a purple claw, white on the outside with a bright rosy longitudinal stripe in the middle of each of the divisions. *Leaves*, linear, pointed, the lower ones sheathing. *Bulb*, small, covered with a coat woolly on the inside. The South of France (particularly about Toulouse) and other parts of South Europe.—— Similar positions, etc., to those for the preceding kind.

Tulipa Gesneriana (*Gesner's Tulip*). —The parent of the many fine varieties of the florists' Tulip ; 6 to 18 in. high. *Flowers*, in spring and early summer ; solitary, fine crimson, and of various colours, excepting blue, the nearest approach to that colour being a purplish-violet. *Leaves*, sessile, smooth, glaucous, the lower ones oval-acute, flat, sometimes slightly wavy, clasping the stem at the base ; the upper ones narrower. *Bulb*, of medium size, oblong or egg-shaped, covered with a dry and thin coat, of a chestnut-brown colour. N. Asia.—— Some make a speciality of this, and cultivate it as a florists' flower, sheltering the bloom with canvas and placing the bulbs in fresh soil every year ; but it thrives well in any ordinary light soil, and should be abundantly grown. The bulbs may be taken up every year, or, in the case of the less rare kinds, allowed to remain several years in the ground. Deep and rich sandy loam suits it best. Separation of the bulbs.

Tulipa Oculus-solis (*Sun's Eye*).—An interesting and showy kind, 1 ft. to 14 in. high. *Flowers*, in early summer; solitary, very large, open, with pointed petals, scarlet on the inside, paler without, marked on the base of each division with a large eye (or elongated spot) of a purplish black, surrounded by a small yellowish margin. The three external divisions larger and more pointed than the internal ones. *Leaves*, large, undulating, and recurved, longer than the flower-stem. *Bulb*, of medium size, oblong, rather elongated, with the coat covered on the inside with long, buff-coloured, woolly and felted hairs. Southern Europe.——Warm borders, and the bulb-garden, in sandy loam. Increased as the preceding kind.

Tulipa præcox (*Large Sun's Eye*).— Very like *T. Oculus-solis*, but flowering earlier; 1 ft. to 18 in. high. *Flowers*, late in spring; scarlet, like those of *T. Oculus-solis*, but much larger and rounder, with the external divisions of a yellowish hue, less pointed and rather pubescent at the top. *Leaves*, also larger and more undulating. South of France.——The bulb-garden, and borders and beds in the spring garden, in deep sandy loam. Division.

Tulipa sylvestris (*Wood T.*) — A native species, 1 ft. to 16 in. high. *Flowers*, early in summer; 1, rarely 2 on a stem, yellow, fragrant, rather drooping, bearded on the tips of the divisions, expanding fully only in the sunshine. *Leaves*, lance-shaped, acute, smooth. *Bulb*, rather small, covered with a smooth coat, lined on the inside with buff-coloured hairs. Most parts of Europe and of Britain. ——Naturalization by wood-walks and in rough grassy places. Scarcely desirable for the spring garden, as there are many fine yellow varieties now in cultivation. Increased like preceding kinds.

Tulipa turcica (*Parrot Tulip*).—A very showy kind, known at once by its large irregular petals; 8 to 16 in. high. *Flowers*, in May; singularly varied in colour, from the brightest red to the deepest yellow, sometimes one-coloured, sometimes streaked, margined, or flushed with one or other of these tints, or with bright green or orange; corolla large; petals spreading widely, irregular. more or less wavy, sometimes deeply cut into unequal segments, sometimes merely jagged or fringed at the edges, sometimes accompanied with spurs, or little horns, or sharp beaks. *Leaves*, broadly-oval, very wavy, glaucous. *Bulb*, large, its coat covered on the inside with adpressed tawny hairs. Thrace, Turkey.——The spring garden and borders, in good deep soil. Increased like preceding kinds.

Tunica Saxifraga (*Rock Tunica*).— A neat mountain plant with somewhat the aspect of a *Gypsophila*, having much-branched stems, about 9 in. long, and forming tufts a few inches high. *Flowers*, in summer; pale rose-coloured, small, but freely produced in terminal panicles on thread-like stems. *Leaves*, narrow, linear, stiff, those on the younger stems crowded. Stony places on the Alps and Pyrenees.——Borders, the rock-garden, and naturalization on ruins, old walls, and bare sandy or stony banks, in light sandy soil. Seed and division.

Umbilicus chrysanthus (*Houseleek Umbilicus*).—Resembles a small Houseleek; about 4 in. high. *Flowers*, in summer; yellowish, in short panicles; petals lance-shaped, acute, with a line of purplish-red prominences on the back, smooth on the other parts, twice the length of the calyx. *Leaves*, greyish, oblong-spoon-shaped, flat, densely covered on both sides and on the edges with small prominences, and arranged in rosettes. Flower-stem springing from the centre of the rosette, leafy, erect, furnished with ovate-oblong, bluntish leaves, closely-set. Western parts of Mt. Taurus. ——The rock-garden, and borders, in dryish soil; also in pots wherever *Sedums* and *Sempervivums* are grown in this manner. Division.

Umbilicus spinosus (*Spiny U.*)—A very singular looking plant with somewhat the appearance of a small *Apicra* or *Haworthia*. *Flowers*, in early summer; yellow, on short stalks collected into a terminal cylindrical spike. *Leaves*, pointed by a spine at the apex; root-leaves in rosettes, oblong, convex towards the points; stem-leaves, lance-shaped, flat. Siberia, China, and Japan.——The rock-garden, in very sunny dry spots. I am not sure that it is hardy everywhere; it will be safer to keep a reserve in frames. Seed and division.

Uvularia grandiflora (*Large-flowered U.*)—An interesting but not showy plant, 1 ft. high. *Flowers*, in early summer; light yellow, oblong-bell-shaped, drooping. *Leaves*, alternate, sessile, perfoliate, oblong-acute, slightly undulating at the base, somewhat downy underneath, of a delicate green, becoming drooping and wrinkled at the period of flowering. N. America, on shady hills.——Peat borders, in sheltered half-shady positions; it is chiefly valuable for botanical collections. Division.

Vaccinium macrocarpum (*American Cranberry*).—An interesting trailing shrub, with stems 1 to 3 ft. long. *Flowers*, in early summer; pale rose, on thread-like stalks, nodding; corolla deeply 4-parted; segments lance-shaped. *Leaves*, oblong, obtuse, about ½ in. long, glaucous beneath, and scarcely rolled downwards at the edge, downy at the points when young; stems very slender, trailing; flower-bearing branches erect. Berries from ½ to 1 in. long, much larger than those of the Red Whortleberry. North America, in peaty bogs.——The artificial bog and among dwarf American shrubs, in moist peat soil. Seed, division, and layers.

Vaccinium Vitis-idæa (*Red Whortleberry*).—A small evergreen shrub with Box-like leaves, 6 to 8 in. high. *Flowers*, in early summer; white or rose-coloured, small, in short terminal drooping clusters, succeeded by red berries about the size of red currants, very like those of the Cranberry: corolla bell-shaped, with 4 spreading lobes. *Leaves*, obovate, rolled downwards, minutely toothed, dotted beneath; stems tufted, creeping, branched, the branches erect. Europe, Russian Asia, and North America, and plentiful in several parts of Britain. —— Borders, and among low shrubs, in peat or sandy soil. Division.

Valeriana montana (*Mountain Valerian*).—A dwarf, smooth, or slightly hairy herb with simple stems; 6 to 14 in. high. *Flowers*, in early summer; white, tinged with red, in a panicled corymb; corolla with an obconical or cylindrical tube, not spurred as in *Centranthus*, and a bluntly 5-cleft limb. *Leaves*, lower ones oblong or obovate, obtuse, slightly toothed and on long stalks; upper ones lance-shaped, acute, and on short stalks; roots horizontal. Mountains of Europe.——Borders, and the rougher parts of the rock-garden, in ordinary soil. Division.

Veratrum album (*White V.*)—A remarkable looking perennial, 3 to 5 ft. high. *Flowers*, in summer; whitish within, greenish on the outside, forming dense and elongated clusters arranged in a large, nearly pyramidal panicle. *Leaves*, large, alternate, sessile, broadly - oval, acute, regularly folded, 1 ft. or more long. *V. viride* differs from the above only in the colour of its flowers, which are green. Europe, the Caucasus, and Altai Mts., in high pastures.——Among groups of perennials with fine foliage, in deep, rich, and light soil. Division.

Veratrum nigrum (*Black V.*)—Allied to the preceding, and useful for like purposes, but not so fine in foliage; 3 ft. high. *Flowers*, in summer; numerous, of a blackish purple, with 6 oblong spreading segments, and arranged in an almost pyramidal downy panicle. *Leaves*, oval, broad and large, the upper ones narrower and pointed, all of a dark green, plaited, and narrowed at the base. Central Europe and Siberia, in woods on mountains. —— Similar positions and treatment to those given for the preceding.

Verbascum Chaixii (*Nettle-leaved V.*) —A very handsome perennial, with large pyramids of flowers; 2 to 5 ft. high. *Flowers*, in summer; small, flat, yellow, with a violet throat, arranged in a large pyramidal panicle with spreading, ascending, slender branches, which bear the flowers in groups distant from each other. *Leaves*, slightly downy and green above, woolly and greenish-white underneath; the lower ones lance-shaped, with toothed lobes on the edges; sides unequal at the base which is usually incised-lyrate; middle stem-leaves with shorter stalks, oval, rounded at the base; the upper ones only sessile, not clasping. Eastern Pyrenees.——Borders, in groups of the finer perennials, isolation in tufts, and naturalization, in deep free soil. It, unlike most of its cultivated brethren, is a true perennial. I have seen a plant like this, but much larger, grown in the Paris botanical garden, under the name of *V. vernale*. Division or seed.

Verbena venosa (*Veined V.*) — A rigid-growing ornamental perennial, 10 to 16 in. high. *Flowers*, in summer; bluish - violet, arranged in terminal spikes, which are at first umbel-like, and afterwards elongated, usually in threes, the lateral spikes stalked and smaller. *Leaves*, oblong-wedge-shaped, opposite, nearly clasping, entire, toothed, wrinkled, rough above, bristly underneath. Brazil.—— Borders, and as a bedding-plant, in free soil. Division and seed.

Vernonia noveboracensis (*N. York Vernonia*).—A very large and vigorous perennial, 5 to 8 ft. high. *Flowers*, in late summer and autumn, purple, about ¼ in. across, in terminal cymose clusters. *Leaves*, almost sessile, lance-shaped, pointed, finely serrated, with strongly-marked veins on the under side; stem furrowed, branching above. N. America.—— Naturalization among the tallest perennials, in any soil. Division.

Veronica alpina (*Alpine Speedwell*). —A tufted, smooth, evergreen herb, with stems shortly creeping, not woody as in *V. saxatilis*, the flowering branches ascending; from 2 to 5 in. high. *Flowers*, in early summer; blue, varying to pale pink, small, borne in short slightly hairy racemes, 4 or 5 blooms in each; calyx hairy; stamens shorter than the corolla. *Leaves*, small, opposite, stalkless, elliptic-ovate, obtuse, entire or somewhat serrated. Great mountain chains of Europe, Asia, and America, and also on some of the higher Scotch mountains.—— The rock-garden, and borders, in free loam. Division, cuttings, or seed.

Veronica amethystina (*Amethyst V.*) —*V. paniculata.*—*V. spuria.*—A very pretty kind, 1 ft. to 16 in. high.

Flowers, in summer; amethyst-blue, arranged in branching pyramidal clusters. *Leaves*, opposite, often in threes, stalked, the upper ones nearly sessile, all lance-shaped, acute, notched or indented. A variety with rosy flowers is also in cultivation. South of Europe. ——Borders, in ordinary soil. Division.

Veronica austriaca (*Austrian Speedwell*).—A slightly downy kind, forming compact masses of shoots covered with sheets of bloom; 1 ft. high. *Flowers*, in early summer; blue, in loose lateral racemes; pedicels longer than the entire bracts; calyx 4-parted, somewhat hairy. *Leaves*, lance-shaped, stalkless, deeply serrated, and pinnatifid. Central and Southern Europe. ——Borders, in any soil, and naturalization on somewhat bare banks and slopes. Division.

Veronica Buchanani (*Buchanan's Speedwell*).—A diminutive grey shrub, much and neatly branched; from 4 to 8 in. high. *Flowers*, in summer; dull white, in short, dense, terminal heads, ¼ to ½ in. long. *Leaves*, small, about ¼ in. long, roundish, in fours, closely imbricated, spreading or recurved, sessile. Stem and branches marked with annular scars. New Zealand. ——The rock-garden, in warm well-drained spots, in light loam. Cuttings.

Veronica candida (*Silvery Speedwell*).—A valuable kind, dwarf in habit, and with silvery leaves; 1 ft. high. *Flowers*, in June and July; purplish-blue, in a dense, pointed spike. *Leaves*, mostly radical, in tufts, ovate, strongly veined underneath, densely covered with short white down; stem-leaves few, ovate-lanceolate, decussate, the upper ones with axillary buds. Russia. ——Borders, edgings, and the rock-garden, in ordinary free soil. When employed as an edging the flower-shoots should be pinched off as soon as they appear. Division.

Veronica caucasica (*Caucasian Speedwell*).—A pretty, delicately-coloured, medium-sized kind, 4 to 10 in. high. *Flowers*, in early summer; few, large, of a very pale flesh-colour streaked with carmine. *Leaves*, opposite, almost sessile, pinnate, with oblong or linear-wedge-shaped segments, entire or cut. Stems smooth, spreading. The Caucasus. ——Borders, in ordinary soil. Division.

Veronica Chamædrys (*Germander Speedwell*).—A very pretty and common British plant, remarkable from having hairs curiously arranged in two opposite lines down the stem, while the other portions are smooth; 6 in. high. *Flowers*, in spring and summer; bright blue, freely produced in axillary racemes one from each pair. *Leaves*, ovate or heart-shaped, unequally serrated, hairy, lower ones slightly stalked, upper ones stalkless. Very common throughout Europe. ——Although a very frequent plant in Britain, we grow numbers of exotics much less worthy of a place on borders, or even on rockwork, than this. Seed and division.

Veronica corymbosa (*Many-spiked Speedwell*).—A slightly downy greyish species and one of the most ornamental; 2 ft. high. *Flowers*, in summer; nearly sessile, small, pale blue, arranged in racemes which together form a large and heavy corymb; lower bracts longer than the flowers. *Leaves*, nearly sessile, ovate, acute, serrated towards the end, downy. Native country unknown. ——Borders, in rich sandy loam. Division.

Veronica foliosa (*Many-leaved Speedwell*). — A free-growing perennial, 3 ft. high. *Flowers*, in summer; lilac-blue, very numerous, in dense, erect, panicled spikes. *Leaves*, oval, pointed, coarsely serrated, more than 2 in. long and nearly 1 in. across, shortly stalked, in whorls of three. Stem thick, straight, smooth, and round. Hungary.——Borders, among dwarf shrubs, or naturalization, in ordinary soil. Division.

Veronica fruticulosa (*Fruticulose Speedwell*). — Very closely allied to *V. saxatilis* and perhaps only a variety of it; 3 to 6 in. high. *Flowers*, in summer; flesh-coloured, with deeper veins, in loose many-flowered racemes; segments of calyx obtuse. *Leaves*, small, opposite, upper ones oblong, obtuse, entire or nearly so; stems erect, slightly woody, and rather downy. Alps and Pyrenees, and one or two places in Scotland, but rare.——The rock-garden and the margins of borders, in sandy loam. Division, cuttings, or seed.

Veronica gentianoides (*Gentian-leaved Speedwell*).—A somewhat showy and pleasing kind, with simple ascending stems smooth below, forming a carpet of shining leathery leaves; 1 to 2 ft. high. *Flowers*, in early summer; pale blue with darker blue streaks, in a loose terminal spiked raceme; upper segment of the corolla smaller than the side ones; calyx hairy, 4-parted, segments equal. *Leaves*, of root, resembling those of *Gentiana acaulis*, but longer, often 6 in. long, opposite, lance-shaped, acute, crenated, 3-nerved, sheathing at the base, pale green, with cartilaginous margins, smooth; uppermost stem-leaves quite entire, hairy. There is a handsome variegated variety. Tauria, Cappadocia, and Armenia.——Borders, in any soil. Division.

Veronica incarnata (*Flesh-coloured Speedwell*).—An elegant kind, 15 to 22 in. high. *Flowers*, in summer; flesh-coloured, in a dense terminal spike, surrounded by several smaller axillary spikes. *Leaves*, opposite, oval-lance-shaped, acute, coarsely and irregularly serrated, rough on both sides with very short fine hairs. Stem also hairy.

This plant is a variety of *V. paniculata*.——Borders, or naturalization, in ordinary soil. Division.

Veronica incisa (*Cut-leaved Veronica*). —A graceful kind, 1½ to 2 ft. high. *Flowers*, in summer; lilac, small, very numerous, in dense panicled spikes. *Leaves*, nearly 2 in. long, varying very much in width, and very deeply and irregularly cut and toothed, stalked, opposite, with smaller leaves in the axils. Stem erect, slender, round. Siberia.——Borders, or naturalization, in sandy loam. Division.

Veronica laciniata (*Fern-leaved Speedwell*).—An elegant species, singular in foliage and with pretty blooms; 20 to 30 in. high. *Flowers*, in the end of June or beginning of July; delicate lilac, in dense spikes forming a handsome panicle of 12 or 15 spikes, each from 2 to 4 in. long, springing from beneath the base of a strong central spike more than twice as long. *Leaves*, 1½ to 3 in. long, deeply and irregularly cut into lobes, sometimes deeply toothed, sometimes entire, deeply and narrowly channelled. Siberia. —— Borders, beds of summer-flowering perennials, or naturalized in uncultivated places, in ordinary soil. Division.

Veronica maritima (*Maritime V.*)— A species of which there are several varieties in cultivation, 20 in. to 2 ft. high. *Flowers*, in summer; blue, on short stalks, grouped in terminal, solitary, or panicled clusters, the central one from 6 to 10 in. long. *Leaves*, opposite, oval-lanceolate, finely toothed. Southern Europe.——Borders, in any soil. Division.

Veronica multifida (*Narrow-leaved V.*) —A pretty species with branching stems, about 1 ft. high. *Flowers*, in summer; ½ in. across, lavender-blue, marked with lines of a darker colour, in long spikes. *Leaves*, nearly sessile, narrow, pointed, irregularly cut and toothed. Siberia.——- Borders, or naturalization, in ordinary soil. Division.

Veronica neglecta (*Greyish Speedwell*).—A hoary species resembling, but not so good as, *V. candida*; 12 to 15 in. high. *Flowers*, in June or July; dull purplish-blue, in solitary spikes, each bloom a little more than ⅓ in. across when fully expanded, the yellow stamens projecting; buds dull purple before bursting; calyx downy. *Leaves*, greyish from down, lanceolate or oval, rather acutely pointed, gradually narrowed at the base, and regularly serrated in all but the leaves just beneath the bracts. Siberia.——Borders, in any soil. Scarcely worth growing where *V. incana* can be obtained, being less attractive both in foliage and flowers. Division at any season.

Veronica pectinata (*Scallop-leaved V.*) —A dwarf and pretty early kind with prostrate ascending stems, 3 or 4 in. high. *Flowers*, in spring; small, vivid gentian-blue with a white eye, in close spikes. *Leaves*, small, spoon-shaped, stalked, deeply notched round the margin. Italy.——The rock-garden, or front margin of mixed border, in sandy loam. Division and seed.

Veronica prostrata (*Prostrate Speedwell*).—A dwarf, greyish, spreading kind, forming tufts 6 in. high. *Flowers*, in early summer; deep blue but varying a good deal, there being several white and rose-coloured varieties, in opposite axillary racemes; calyx unequal, nearly smooth. *Leaves*, stalkless, oblong, obtuse, serrated; upper ones lance-shaped, flat; barren stems prostrate, flowering ones ascending. Central and Southern Europe.—— The rock-garden and the margin of the mixed border, in light loamy soil. Seed and division.

Veronica satureiæfolia (*Savory-leaved V.*)—A neat and attractive species, with more or less decumbent sinuous stems, about 1 ft. high. *Flowers*, early in summer; bright blue, in handsome spikes. *Leaves*, opposite, sessile, oval-oblong, irregularly toothed; uppermost ones very narrow, entire, fascicled. South of Europe.——Borders, in well-drained soil. Division.

Veronica saxatilis (*Rock Speedwell*).— A dwarf and pretty, spreading, bush-like evergreen herb, with procumbent stems slightly woody at the base, the flowering branches ascending; 3 to 6 in. high. *Flowers*, in early summer; blue, striped with violet, with a narrow ring near the bottom of the corolla, the base being pure white, freely produced in corymbose racemes. *Leaves*, opposite, smaller than those of *V. fruticulosa* and of a deeper green, oblong-obovate or elliptic, with small round notches. Alpine rocks in various parts of Europe and a few places in the Highlands of Scotland.——The rock-garden, in ordinary soil; also in borders. Division and seed.

Veronica spicata (*Spiked Veronica.*) —A native species, with erect stems branching at the base; 8 in. to 1 ft. high. *Flowers*, early in summer; blue, numerous, in dense spikes. *Leaves*, ovate, serrate at the sides, entire at the end; lower ones blunt, stalked, with a wedge-shaped base. There is a white-flowered variety, and one with variegated leaves.—— Borders, or rougher parts of rockwork, in any soil. Seed or division.

Veronica taurica (*Taurian Speedwell*).—A beautiful evergreen kind with prostrate, almost woody stems, forming neat dark green tufts less than 2 in. high. *Flowers*, in early summer; gentian-blue, freely produced in axillary racemes. *Leaves*, crowded, linear, entire, about ½ in. long, somewhat wedge-shaped, and 3-toothed at the tip. Tauria.——The rock-garden and the margins of the mixed border, in light loam. Division and seed.

Veronica virginica (*Great Virginian Speedwell*).—*Leptandra virginica.*—A very tall and vigorous kind, 3 to nearly 5 ft. high. *Flowers*, in the end of summer; small, white, very numerous, with reddish anthers, and arranged in erect spikes, of which the central one is often more than 8 in. in length and is surrounded by a whorl of 3 or 4 smaller ones. *Leaves*, oval-lanceolate, toothed, stalked, disposed in whorls of 4 to 6, sometimes more, at the top of the stem. N. America. —— Naturalization in half-wild places among tall perennials. Division.

Vesicaria utriculata (*Bladder-podded V.*)—A showy rock-plant not unlike the Alpine Wallflower in its flowers, but easily known by its bladder-like seed-pods; about 1 ft. high. *Flowers*, from April to June; very showy, sulphur-yellow, produced abundantly in terminal racemes; petals entire. *Leaves*, oblong, entire, smooth; lower ones ciliated; stems woody and branching at the base, leafy to the top. Mountains in France, Italy, and Southern Europe.——The rock-garden, on dry banks, and in warm borders. Seed.

Vicia argentea (*Silvery Vetch*).—A handsome perennial of prostrate habit, with silvery and downy leaves; 8 to 12 in. high. *Flowers*, in summer; whitish, spotted with purple in the lower and veined with violet in the upper part, on axillary many-flowered stalks, all turning the same way. *Leaves*, of from 4 to 10 pairs of oblong-linear finely-pointed leaflets without tendrils; stems 4-angled, never climbing. Pyrenees.—— Borders and the rock-garden, or naturalized on open banks, in sandy soil. Seed or division.

Vicia Cracca (*Tufted Vetch*). — A neglected British climbing perennial of the highest merit, with branched tendrils; 2 to 4 ft. high. *Flowers*, in summer; bluish-purple, nearly ½ in. long, abundantly produced in one-sided racemes, on stalks rather longer than the leaves. *Leaves*, terminated by a tendril, pinnate; leaflets numerous, oblong or lance-shaped, finely-pointed, alternate or opposite; stipules linear, entire. Plant clothed with greyish down or smooth. There is a white variety. Europe, and plentiful throughout Britain. —— Borders, banks, hedgerows, rootwork, and in any position where a dwarf climbing plant may be desired. It will grow in any soil. Division or seed.

Villarsia nymphæoides (*Common Villarsia*).—An attractive British aquatic, with simple leaves (like those of a Water-lily but smaller) floating on the surface of the water. *Flowers*, in summer; yellow, borne singly on stalks as long as those of the leaf. *Leaves*, heart-shaped or roundish, on long stalks; stems creeping and rooting at the base, dichotomous, and ascending to the surface of the water, with a single leaf at each of the upper branches, and a terminal tuft. Europe and Asia, and many places in England and Ireland. —— Lakes, ponds, and quiet bays in streams. Division.

Vinca herbacea (*Herbaceous Periwinkle*).—An elegant perennial with creeping and rooting herbaceous stems. *Flowers*, in spring and early summer; purplish - blue, solitary, axillary; corolla salver - shaped, tube longer than the calyx, throat bearded. *Leaves*, oblong-lance-shaped, opposite, minutely ciliated on the edges while young. Hungary.——Being much less rampant in habit, this is more suitable for the rock-garden than the common kinds. It does best in a sunny position, in light but good soil, rather dry than moist. Division.

Vinca major (*Larger Periwinkle*).— A well - known evergreen trailing plant with large and handsome flowers; 1 to 2 ft. high, or more. *Flowers*, in spring and early summer, and sometimes a second time in autumn; blue, large, borne singly on axillary stalks; tube of corolla nearly bell-shaped, slightly contracted at the mouth; lobes broad; calyx deeply divided into 5 narrow segments, ciliated on the edges. *Leaves*, broadly-ovate, shining, ciliated, opposite; barren stems trailing, flowering ones erect, simple. There are several varieties. Europe, common in Britain.——Naturalization in almost any position; fully exposed tufts look well when in flower in early summer, on the fringes of shrubberies. The variegated kinds are well fitted for edgings and vases etc., and, like the common form, may be naturalized. Division.

Vinca minor (*Lesser Periwinkle*).—Another well-known kind, smaller in every part than the previous one, and usually with a more trailing habit; the flowering shoots short and erect. *Flowers*, in spring and nearly all the summer; blue, small; tube of corolla more open than in *V. major ;* calyx quite smooth, with shorter and broader segments. *Leaves*, narrowly ovate, quite smooth. This, like the preceding, varies much in the colour of the flowers, and there are also variegated and double varieties. Europe, and Britain, but probably not truly indigenous.——Similar positions etc., to those given for the preceding; the double and prettily-coloured varieties of this are however worthy of a position in borders and as edgings to beds of small shrubs, etc., where their pretty blossoms may be seen in spring.

Viola altaica (*Altai Violet*). — A showy species with the habit of our Pansies. *Flowers*, from May to July; yellow, or deep violet with a small eye of bright yellow; spur very short, scarcely longer than the appendages of the calyx; sepals acute, toothed. *Leaves*, oval; stipules oblong-lance-shaped, incised. Altai Mountains, near China.——Borders, or among the free-growing plants in the rougher parts of the rock-garden, in sandy loam. Division or cuttings.

Viola biflora (*Two-flowered Violet*).— A singularly pretty little yellow Violet, 3 or 4 in. high. *Flowers*, in early summer; yellow, with the lip streaked with black, small, usually borne in pairs; petals smooth; spur very short; sepals linear; stigma bifid. *Leaves*, kidney-shaped, serrated, smooth. *Roots* creeping. There is a variety bearing only one flower on each stem. Widely distributed throughout Europe, Asia, and America.——Chinks between stones in the steps in moist parts of the rock-garden; in this and like positions it will run about freely and look as pretty as it does between and under the rocks in its native alpine valleys. Division.

Viola calcarata (*Spurred Violet*).— Closely allied to the now common *V. cornuta*, but easily known by the stipules and by its habit of increasing by runners under the earth, instead of forming strong leafy tufts above it; 3 to 6 in. high. *Flowers*, in early summer; light blue; sepals oblong, glandularly toothed; spur awl-shaped, longer than the calyx. *Leaves*, roundish or spoon-shaped, crenate; stipules, in the shape of a spatula elongated and widened at the top, entire towards the base and trifurcate at the top, never crenated or widened like the limb of a leaf. There is a yellow-flowered variety, *V. c. flava* (*V. Zoysii*). Alps.——The rock-garden and borders, in sandy loam. Division and seed.

Viola canadensis (*Canadian Violet*).— A free-growing kind, 6 in. to nearly 2 ft. high. *Flowers*, in early summer; whitish inside; petals slightly twisted, the upper ones often tinged with violet beneath, the side ones bearded. Leaves, alternate, broadly heart-shaped, tapering to a point, serrate, the nerves pubescent, on stalks half their length, the upper ones shorter. North America.——Naturalized, on the fringes of woods or shrubberies, in any soil. Division.

Viola cornuta (*Horned Violet*).—A very ornamental and popular species, 6 to 10 in. high. *Flowers*, nearly all the summer ; pale blue, but darker than those of *V. calcarata;* spur awl-shaped ; sepals awl-shaped. *Leaves*, heart-shaped-ovate, crenated, ciliated; stipules incise-dentate, not pinnatifid, with a triangular terminal lobe larger than the lateral ones. Alps and Pyrenees.——Beds, edgings, borders, etc. ; best in sandy loam, though it will grow almost anywhere. Division, cuttings, or seed.

Viola delphinifolia (*Delphinium-leaved Violet*).—An interesting and distinct kind. *Flowers*, in spring ; fine sky-blue, rather smaller than those of *V. pedata*, on stems that are at the time of flowering a little longer than the leaves, the 2 upper petals pubescent, the lower ones notched at the ends ; spur pouched, short. *Leaves*, pubescent on the margins and nerves, pedately 7- to 9- parted ; segments narrow, 2- to 3-divided ; stipules ovate - lance - shaped, nearly entire. Prairies of Missouri.——Rockwork, or borders, in sandy loam. Division and seed.

Viola lutea (*Yellow Violet*).—A very pretty dwarf Violet considered by Mr. Bentham a variety of *V. tricolor*, but it is certainly distinct enough for garden purposes. *Flowers*, nearly all the summer; yellow, with blackish lines, larger than those of *V. tricolor;* petals wedge-shaped, bearded at the base, the lateral ones paler, the 2 upper ones sometimes purple; sepals lance-shaped, acute ; spur as long as the calyx. *Leaves*, ovate or oblong, crenate, fringed ; stipules palmatifid ; stems simple, triangular. Britain. —— Beds, borders, edgings, or the rock-garden, in any good garden soil. Division, seed, or cuttings.

Viola obliqua (*Large American Violet*). —*V. cucullata*).—A large and showy kind, 4 to 10 in. high. *Flowers*, in early summer ; fine cobalt blue, scentless, very numerous, large ; upper divisions rayed and streaked with white or violet ; the lower one tinged with white at the base ; sometimes the flowers are one-coloured. *Leaves*, erect, numerous, smooth, long-stalked, heart-shaped, pointed, slightly folded or hollowed like a spoon, serrated. North America.——Borders and the rock-garden, or naturalized in copses, in ordinary light soil. Division.

Viola odorata (*Sweet Violet*).—Probably more grown than any other plant for the sake of its grateful odour ; about 6 in. high. *Flowers*, in spring and early summer ; readily known from the other kinds by their odour. *Leaves*, roundish-heart-shaped, crenate, smoothish ; runners long, rooting. There are numerous varieties of this plant, some of the most important being the double blue, double purple, double white, double pale blue, single white, and also a striped one. Europe, Asia, and frequent in Britain. —— Borders, beds, edgings, etc., preferring a warm sandy loam. Although a native plant, it is not found in many districts. Where it does not occur wild in the pleasure-grounds or woods, it should be abundantly naturalized therein, preferring at first warm banks and slopes where it might be encouraged to bloom well in early spring. Division.

Viola palmata (*Palmate-leaved V.*)— An interesting kind, distinct in the shape of its leaves ; about 6 in. high.

s 2

Flowers, early in summer; bright violet- or lilac-blue, rarely white; spur short and thick; stigma triangular; lower petals bearded; sepals ovate-lance-shaped, fringed, the claws keeled. *Leaves*, heart-shaped in outline, divided like the hand into five parts or lobes; lobes toothed, the middle one much the largest. North America.——Borders, or the rock-garden, in common soil. Division.

Viola pedata (*Bird's-foot Violet*).—A very handsome and profuse flowering kind, 3 to 6 in. high. *Flowers*, in early summer; usually deep blue, sometimes pale, large, scentless, on naked stalks; petals all smooth; stigma large and thick. *Leaves*, pedately 7-parted; segments sometimes very narrow, and cut; stipules fringed; rhizome thick. Dry sandy hills and woods in North America.——The rock-garden and borders, in very sandy and cool soil. Seed and division.

Viola pinnata (*Pinnate-leaved V.*)—Rather smaller than *V. pedata*, which it somewhat resembles. *Flowers*, in early summer; pale blue with darker veins, the two lateral petals bearded; sepals ovate; spur broad, as long as the calyx, nearly straight. *Leaves*, deeply divided into 4 or 5 segments, which are either 3-parted or pinnatifid, jagged and very narrow. Mountains of Southern Europe, and Siberia. ——The rock-garden and borders, in any moist soil. Division.

Viola pubescens (*Downy Yellow Violet*).—A pretty yellow kind, 6 to 12 in. high. *Flowers*, in spring and early summer; yellow, lower petal streaked with purple; spur very short; sepals oblong-lance-shaped; stigma bearded with 2 tufts of hairs. *Leaves*, broadly heart-shaped, somewhat pointed, toothed; stipules large, ovate, entire or serrated at the top; stem somewhat decumbent, simple, naked below. Woods in North America.——Margins of borders, and in the rock-garden, in ordinary soil. Division or seed.

Viola rostrata (*Long-spurred Violet*). —An interesting and uncommon kind, 4 to 6 in. high. *Flowers*, in early summer; dingy purple or lavender, with dark streaks; petals beardless; spur slender, rather acute, ½ in. long, longer than the petals; stigma beakless. *Leaves*, roundish-heart-shaped, serrate; upper ones acute; stipules lance-shaped, fringed, toothed, large; stems ascending, leafy from base to summit. North America.——Borders, and the rock-garden, in light soil. Division.

Viola tricolor (*Heartsease*).—The well known Pansy or Heartsease. *Flowers*, in early summer; very variable in colour and size; spur thick, obtuse. *Leaves*, ovate or heart-shaped, obtuse, slightly crenated; stipules large, leaf-like, deeply divided into several lobes, the middle one largest. Europe, Siberia, and North America, plentiful in Britain.—— The garden varieties of Heartsease are very numerous and diverse in colour and habit; it is however very doubtful if they have all sprung from this plant. Beds, borders, edgings, and among the free-growing kinds in good garden soil. Seed, cuttings, and division.

Vittadinia australis (*New Holland Daisy*).—*V. triloba*.—A small, much-branched, spreading perennial forming neat little bushes 6 to 12 in. high, covered with numerous Daisy-like flowers. *Flowers*, all the summer; rays white, tipped with pink, disk yellowish. *Leaves*, wedge-shaped or narrow-spoon-shaped, 3- to 5-lobed at the apex; ¼ to ½ in. long. Australia and New Zealand.——Dry borders and banks, the rock-garden, in well-drained free soil, or naturalized in chalk-pits or on warm rocky banks in the southern and milder parts of the country. Seed and cuttings.

Wahlenbergia hederacea (*Ivy Harebell*). — *Campanula hederacea*. — A small, graceful, creeping perennial, far from showy in aspect, with very slender branches. *Flowers*, in summer and autumn; pale blue, on long thread-like stalks, drooping in the bud, almost erect when fully expanded; corolla narrow-bell-shaped, less than ½ in. long, 5-lobed at the mouth. *Leaves*, small, on long stalks, heart-shaped or roundish, bluntly angled. Moist places in Western Europe, North America, and various parts of Britain. —— The artificial bog, margins of rivulets, and moist spots in the rock-garden. Division.

Waldsteinia geoides (*Geum W.*)— A dwarf tufted perennial, 4 to 6 in. high. *Flowers*, in spring and early in summer; small, yellow, numerous, usually in terminal pairs. *Leaves*, numerous, long - stalked, palmate-lobed; lobes 3 to 5, sharply toothed; leaf-stalks hairy, especially at the base, where they are dilated, sheathing the short erect root-stock. Hungary, in shady woods in moist peaty soil.——Scarcely ornamental enough for the mixed border but pretty as an edging-plant to beds of herbaceous plants, or in the spring garden, in ordinary soil; also good for naturalization on sunny banks among dwarf plants. Division and seed.

Waldsteinia fragarioides (*Strawberry W.*)—A showy perennial, with creeping, bright-red, hairy stems; about 6 in. high. *Flowers*, in early summer; numerous, bright yellow, about ½ in. across; petals oblong-ovate; sepals acute, hairy and spreading, with here and there a little segment between the others, showing a disposition to become 10-cleft. *Leaves*, ternate, on long channelled stalks, dilated and ciliated at the base; leaflets obovate, irregularly serrated and cut into lobes with ciliated edges, smooth and green, fading to a lurid colour. N. America, on wooded hill - sides. —— Borders, fringes of shrubberies, or naturalization, in any soil. Division.

Waldsteinia trifolia (*Running W.*)— A dwarf but vigorous plant, spreading about with stout but stubby running stems; 3 to 5 in. high. *Flowers*, late in spring; rich golden-yellow, with a dense brush of golden filaments and stamens in the centre; petals rounded at the base. *Leaves*, trifoliate, very deeply cut, rounded at the base. Transylvania.——A thoroughly hardy kind, good for any kind of rockwork, or the margin of the mixed border, in any soil, or for running about in a half-wild state in shrubberies. Division.

Wulfenia carinthiaca (*Carinthian W.*) — A dwarf, almost stemless, evergreen herb; 12 to 18 in. high. *Flowers*, in summer; blue, drooping, solitary on short stalks, in the axils of the bracts; stem many-flowered, erect; corolla tubular, limb 4- or 5-cleft; segments roundish, upper one notched, lower one crenated; tube with a swelling above the base. *Leaves*, oblong, narrowed at the base, doubly crenated, stalked. Carinthia. —— Borders, and the rock-garden, in light moist sandy loam. Division and seed.

Xerophyllum asphodeloides (*Asphodel-like X.*)—A tuberous-rooted plant with the aspect of an Asphodel, and a simple stem 1 to 4 ft. high, with a bulbous base. *Flowers*, in summer; white, showy, in a compact simple raceme. *Leaves*, of the stem needle-shaped, very numerous, thickly covering the stem, the upper ones reduced to mere bristle-like bracts; radical leaves 1 ft. or more long, and 1 in. wide below, rough on the margin, remarkably dry and rigid, very numerous, in a dense tuft. North America.—— Borders, in very sandy soil, or the drier parts of the artificial bog. Seed.

Yucca aloifolia (*Aloe-leaved Y.*)—A fine kind, usually grown in the greenhouse, but hardy, at least in the warmer parts of the country; 2 to nearly 10 ft. high. *Flowers*, in autumn; white, with a purplish spot at the base, becoming afterwards slightly tinged with violet on the middle of the petals. *Leaves*, pale green, in a dense tuft, very stiff, linear-lanceolate, thick, rough and toothed at the edges. There are in cultivation four varieties—one with drooping leaves, one with leaves streaked with rose-colour, one with white and yellow leaves, and one with narrow ones. Jamaica, Mexico, Carolina, and Florida.——On warm rocky banks, or sunny nooks on mounds, in perfectly-drained light loam. Fine specimens of the variegated varieties, kept in the conservatory during winter, are valuable for placing in the flower-garden in summer. This kind seeds pretty freely in Southern Europe, and is easily raised from seed.

Yucca angustifolia (*Narrow-leaved Y.*)—A narrow-leaved, distinctly habited kind, as yet but seldom seen in cultivation in this country, though not rare in Continental collections; 6½ ft. or more high. *Flowers*, in summer; numerous, white, slightly tinged with yellow. *Leaves*, very narrow, sharp-pointed, and fringed on the edges with long, silvery filaments. North America. —— Warm banks, open parts of rockwork, or sunny but sheltered nooks on fringes of shrubberies, in sandy and well-drained soil. Seed and stem-cuttings.

Yucca filamentosa (*Thready Y.*)— Like the Flaccid Yucca, chiefly valuable from its free-flowering tendency, though it has not this in a degree equal to *Y. flaccida*; 3½ to 5 ft. high. *Flowers*, late in summer, of a yellowish white, greenish at the base externally, arranged in a large panicle of about 200 blooms. *Leaves*, lanceolate-oblong, hollowed into a very broad channel, ending in a small point, erect and recurved, with very strong, twisted, whitish or buff-coloured marginal filaments 2½ to 3½ in. long. Carolina and Virginia.——Positions and uses similar to those given for the Flaccid Yucca. The fine variegated variety, *Y. filamentosa variegata*, is of slow and difficult growth, and when planted in the open air is best placed in some sunny spot on rockwork or a rocky bank, in thoroughly-drained and light soil. Increased by cuttings of the short stem, or by division.

Yucca flaccida (*Flaccid Y.*)—Not an imposing species, nor so valuable for the effect of its foliage as other kinds, but exceedingly so for its flowers, which are annually produced in great abundance; 3 to 4 ft. high. *Flowers*, in summer; pure white. *Leaves*, narrow, erect, often furnished with filaments on the edges. North America. ——The outer fringes of groups of Yuccas on mounds, banks, etc., as isolated specimens near the walks in the picturesque garden, or in the larger kinds of rock-garden; associated with Tritomas, Lilies, and the nobler herbaceous plants in irregular groups, or in the mixed border, flowering most profusely in good open soil. Division.

Yucca gloriosa (*Adam's Needle*).— Perhaps the best known, and certainly one of the finest, of its noble family, lacking the grace of *Y. recurva*, but of bolder port; 3½ to 7 ft. high. *Flowers*, late in summer and in autumn; large, almost pure white, in an immense pyramidal panicle. *Leaves*, numerous, stiff, and pointed. There are several varieties: *Y. longifolia*, *Y. plicata*, *Y. maculata*, *Y. glaucescens*, and *Y.*

minor. North America.——On rocky banks or mounds in the picturesque garden, isolated or grouped with fine herbaceous plants and other Yuccas; also on margins of shrubberies, in open glades, by wood-walks, or in almost any position, in ordinary garden soil, flourishing best, however, in good, well-drained, sandy loam. Increased by suckers, and by division of the buried part of the stem, also from seed; it varies a good deal when raised in the last way.

Yucca recurva (*Weeping-leaved Y.*) —A well-known and graceful species, easily distinguished by its elegant habit; 3 to 8 ft. high. *Flowers*, in summer and autumn; large, numerous, pure white, in a large branching panicle. *Leaves*, at first erect and glaucous, afterwards of a deep green and gracefully bending downwards. North America.——A noble plant for almost any position in any style of garden, either as isolated specimens, or grouped with other Yuccas or hardy plants, thriving in ordinary garden soil. When very fine isolated specimens are desired, it is best to commence with vigorous and simple-stemmed young plants, planting them in deep, well-drained sandy loam. In winter some tie the leaves carefully together in a bundle, to guard against injury from snow or excessive frost. Division of the suckers, which spring up freely round old plants.

Yucca Treculeana (*Rigid Y.*) — A noble Yucca, about 4 ft. high when well grown, with very rigid and deeply channelled leaves. *Flowers*, in summer; with long narrow petals of a yellowish white, shining, and as it were glazed; buds of a rusty red externally, densely covering the erect branches on the top of the flower-stalk. *Leaves*, in a dense tuft sometimes 6 ft. through, large, straight, thick, deeply concave, ending in a stiff, very sharp point, very finely toothed on the edges, which are of a brownish red and scarious. Texas. ——This fine kind, as yet but rarely seen in this country, is probably quite as hardy, if not quite as free, as any kind commonly grown; but being so rare, and somewhat slow in growth, it should be placed in sunny and warm positions, always in open and well-drained soil. Slightly elevated warm banks are among the best positions for it. Increased by cuttings from the stems of old plants, and by seed ripened in warmer climes than ours.

Zapania nodiflora (*Creeping Vervain*). —A pretty and modest-looking, compactly spreading, trailing plant, with prostrate stems 2 or 3 ft. or more in length. *Flowers*, in late summer and autumn; small, purplish, in small roundish heads, on long stalks springing from the axils of the leaves. *Leaves*, spoon-shaped, coarsely and irregularly notched, with a wedge-shaped base attenuated into a stalk; upper and axillary leaves small and pointed. Asia and America.——Borders, edgings, the rougher parts of the rock-garden, or naturalized on bare banks, in any rather warm soil. Division.

Zauschneria californica (*Vermilion Z.*)—A showy and distinct perennial, 8 to 16 in. high. *Flowers*, late in summer; bright vermilion, gracefully drooping, in a loose, erect, almost one-sided spike; petals small, 4 in number, 2-cleft at the end and reflected, inserted into the end of the calyx, which is long, funnel-shaped, and of a scarlet colour, so as frequently to be taken for the corolla. *Leaves*, alternate, small, sessile, linear-lance-shaped, the upper ones oval, acute. California.——Borders and the rock-garden, in sandy and fibry loam. It will require a little protection at the root in cold parts. Division in early spring and seed.

Zephyranthes Atamasco (*Atamasco Lily*).—*Amaryllis Atamasco.*—A dwarf and very handsome Lily-like plant, 6 to 12 in. high. *Flowers*, in spring or early summer; bright red outside and when in bud, white after expansion, 3½ in. across, one on each stem. *Leaves*, strap-shaped, concave, fleshy, appearing with or before the flowers. *Bulb*, small, oval-oblong. There is a variety with smaller flowers. Abundant in the pastures of Virginia and Carolina. ——In well-drained positions on rockwork, or sunny borders, in sandy warm loam. Division in winter or early spring.

Zephyranthes candida (*Peruvian Swamp-lily*).—An evergreen bulbous plant, 4 to 8 in. high. *Flowers*, late in summer and in autumn; white, resembling a large white Crocus, and expanding fully only in the sunshine. *Leaves*, rush-like, linear, fleshy, permanent, and freely produced. *Bulb*, small, round, and black. Lima and Buenos Ayres.——Warm spots on rockwork, or at the foot of a south wall, or warm borders, in rich sandy loam. Seeds freely, but is best propagated by division of the offsets, which are abundantly produced.

Zietenia lavandulæfolia (*Lavender-leaved Z.*)—An evergreen, spreading, half-shrubby perennial, of a greyish hue, with a stem 6 to 12 in. high. *Flowers*, in summer; purple, in whorls forming a spike about 6 in. long, with a very slender, downy stalk; each whorl having two long-pointed bracts underneath. *Leaves*, lance-shaped, rather obtuse, long-stalked, fascicled; the stalks very downy and overlapping each other. Bark of stem brown and rugged. Caucasus. —— Margins of borders, and the rougher parts of the rock-garden, or naturalized in any soil, wet or dry. Division.

ADDENDA.

New species, or those omitted in preceding part.

Alisma Plantago (*Water Plantain*).—A common British aquatic plant, rather stately in habit and with large panicles of pretty flowers; 2 to 3 ft. high. *Flowers*, late in summer; pale rose-colour, in a large, handsome, whorled panicle. *Leaves*, all radical, ovate-heart-shaped or lanceolate, on long stalks; submersed leaves linear. Europe and Britain, Asia, Egypt, N. America and New Holland.——Margins of lakes and streams or ponds. Sows itself freely.

Anthemis Aizoon (*Everlasting A.*)—A very neat silvery plant, 2 to 4 in. high. *Flowers*, early in summer; resembling a white daisy; florets of the ray 14 to 18 in number, trifid, twice as long as the breadth of the disk. *Leaves*, lanceolate or tongue-shaped, sharply and deeply serrated, narrowed towards the base, covered with white down, lower ones crowded; stem-leaves rather acute, gradually decreasing in size. Sub-alpine parts of Northern Greece.——The rock-garden, in sandy loam. Division and seed.

Arethusa bulbosa (*Bulbous A.*)—A beautiful hardy orchidaceous plant, about 9 in. high. *Flowers*, in May; solitary (very rarely two), bright rosy-purple, 1 to 2 in. long; lip dilated and recurved, spreading towards the summit, and bearded-crested down the face. *Leaf*, solitary, linear, nerved, hidden in the sheaths of the scape, protruding after flowering. North America.——In the artificial bog, or moist spots in the rock-garden, in peaty soil.

Asperula tinctoria (*Three-lobed Woodruff*). — A free-flowering and pleasing perennial, 8 to 10 in. high. *Flowers*, in summer; white with a faint rosy tinge, in small terminal cymes; petals frequently 3 in number; bracts oval. *Leaves*, linear, smooth, the lower ones in whorls of 6, the upper ones in pairs, and the intermediate ones in whorls of 4. France.——Borders, or the rougher parts of the rock-garden, in ordinary soil. It may be easily naturalized in shrubberies or copses. Division.

Buphthalmum salicifolium (*Willow-leaved B.*)—A showy perennial, 1 to 2 ft. high. *Flowers*, late in summer; yellow, large, solitary on the tops of the branches. *Leaves*, of a lively green, thin, downy or slightly rough on both sides, ciliated with long hairs, faintly sinuate-toothed; the lower ones lance-shaped, attenuated into a long stalk; the upper ones sessile, linear-lance-shaped; stem erect, rigid, slightly branched above. South of Europe.——Borders, in sandy loam. Division and seed.

Buphthalmum speciosum (*Heart-leaved B.*)—A stout and distinct-looking plant, 4 to 6 in. high. *Flowers*, late in summer; pale yellow with a flat, purplish disk; each flower more than 2 in. in diameter. *Leaves*, very large, alternate, broadly oval, acute, twice toothed, somewhat villous underneath; the whole plant pubescent.——Among hardy plants grown for the effect of their foliage, in rich glades in woods and the rougher parts of pleasure-grounds. Division.

Butomus umbellatus (*Flowering Rush*).—An ornamental aquatic perennial, 2 to 3 ft. high. *Flowers*, in summer; rose-coloured, in an irregular many-flowered umbel, which stands erect on the top of the flower-stalk. *Leaves*, all radical, linear, acute, triangular, channelled, erect. There is a variety with variegated leaves, but it is rather tender. Europe, S. W. Asia, and Britain.—— Margins of lakes and streams, large fountain basins, etc., in any soil. Division.

Calla æthiopica (*African Lily*).—A graceful and beautiful plant of the *Arum* family, much grown as a greenhouse and window plant, 2 to 3½ ft. high. *Flowers*, in summer and autumn in the open air in Britain; large, pure white, with orange spadix. *Leaves*, all radical, large, arrow-shaped, nearly erect, on long stalks. There are two varieties, one of which has the leaves spotted with white, and the other with yellow. Cape of Good Hope.—— In the southern, western, and milder parts of England and Ireland this thrives well as an aquatic plant, and would doubtless also do well in rich soil in borders, as I have noticed it doing in the gardens in San Francisco. Division.

Callisace dahurica (*Siberian C.*)—A large and ornamental umbelliferous plant, 8 to 10 ft. high. *Flowers*, late in summer; white, in umbels which are frequently 2 ft. each in diameter. *Leaves*, lower ones about 6 ft. long and 4 ft. wide, much divided; stem-leaves reduced to a mere stalk with a large sheath. Siberia.——Isolation on the turf, or in groups in the picturesque garden, in deep rich loam. I have not seen this plant, but Mr. A. Perry, who saw it on the Continent, informs me that it is the most imposing of herbaceous plants. Seed and division.

Chrysanthemum indicum (*Common Chrysanthemum*).—The well-known ornament of our gardens and greenhouses in autumn; 3 ft. high or more. *Flowers*, in autumn; varying very much in colour under culture, the original plant having purplish-red flowers with a yellow disk, in corymbose panicles. *Leaves*, alternate, varying much in shape, usually oval-heart-shaped, more or less regularly incised, toothed or lobed, sometimes pinnatifid. East Indies, China, and Japan.—— It is needless to speak of the culture of this plant, so abundantly seen in every greenhouse in autumn; but as an out-door ornament against walls and in warm positions where it may flower before being destroyed by severe weather, it does not receive enough of attention. The best kinds are enumerated in the catalogues of most nurserymen. Cuttings.

Colchicum chionense (*Chion Meadow Saffron*).—I have not seen this species, but Mr. P. Barr describes it as the finest he has seen. *Flowers*, in autumn; like those of *C. variegatum*, but handsomer, more firm in texture, and lasting longer. *Leaves*, small, undulated at the margin, lying on the ground. Island of Chios.——The rock-garden, in spots where there is a deep soil, and in borders in ordinary sandy soil. Separation of the bulbs.

Cirsium Douglasii (*Brilliant Thistle*).—A handsome and showy Thistle. *Flowers*, in summer; purple, in subcorymbose heads scarcely rising above the leaves; scales of the involucrum smooth, purplish and spiny at the point. *Leaves*, pinnatifid, the lateral lobes lance-shaped, often bifid, terminal lobe elongated, all more or less spiny. California.——Warm borders, in well-drained sandy loam. Seed.

Doronicum Clusii (*Clusius's Doronicum*).— *Aronicum Clusii.— Arnica Clusii.*—A showy plant about 1 ft. high. *Flowers*, in early summer; yellow, solitary on the top of the stem, on long stalks which are thickened towards the top and covered with long hairs. *Leaves*, soft, those of the root entire or scarcely toothed, oblong, obtuse, attenuated into a stalk; stem-leaves sessile, half clasping, lance-shaped, toothed in the lower half, entire towards the top. Alps of Dauphiny, in moist places at high elevations.——Borders, in sandy loam. Division and seed.

Fuchsia coccinea (*Scarlet F.*)—A graceful bushy species, with slender downy branches, which are reddish when young; 3 ft. or more high. *Flowers*, in summer and autumn; petals violet, oboval-oblong; calyx purple at the base, with oblong, acute, scarlet sepals. *Leaves*, small, oval or roundish-oval, obtuse, scarcely toothed, heart-shaped at the base, covered with white down underneath, nearly smooth above, turning purplish-scarlet in autumn. Mexico.—— Borders, and fringes of shrubberies, in ordinary garden soil. Division and cuttings.

Fuchsia conica (*Conical-tubed F.*)— A vigorous species, 3 to 6 ft. high. *Flowers*, in summer, solitary; petals violet-purple, notched, about equal in length to the calyx; sepals lance-shaped, scarlet. *Leaves*, 3 or 4 in a whorl, ovate, flat, toothed, smooth, on downy stalks 3 times as long as the leaves. Chili.——Borders, in ordinary garden soil. Cuttings.

Fuchsia corymbiflora (*Corymbose F.*) —A showy species with 4-angled branches, which are reddish and downy when young, and growing 6 ft. or more high in warm countries: *Flowers*, in summer; in long terminal clusters; petals violet-red or carmine, oblong-oval, or oblong-lance-shaped, bifid; sepals, same colour as the petals, lance-shaped, acute. *Leaves*, very large, opposite, oblong-lance-shaped, with a rosy-violet midrib. There are several fine and distinct vars. of this. Peru. —— Warm borders, in rich, light, and well-drained soil, in the milder parts of the southern counties. Cuttings.

Fuchsia fulgens (*Brilliant F.*)— Distinguished by its swollen, almost tuberous, roots; over 6 ft. high in warm countries. *Flowers*, in summer, the upper ones in pendent clusters; petals, blood-red, acute, shorter than the calyx; sepals vermilion-red, oval-lance-shaped, acute, tube about 2 in. long. *Leaves*, very large, opposite, stalked, oval-heart-shaped, acuminate, toothed, smooth. A variety (*F. f. d'Arck*) has violet-tinged leaves and flowers of a vivid scarlet, finer than those of the type. Mexico.——On warm borders, in rich, well-drained, and light soil. Thrives well in the South of England. Cuttings.

Fuchsia globosa (*Globe-flowered F.*) —A neat shrub, 5 or 6 ft. high. *Flowers*, freely all the summer; globular in shape; petals purplish-violet; calyx purplish-red. *Leaves*, oval, acute, smooth, toothed. Chili.——Near the coast in many parts of both England and Ireland, but chiefly in Ireland, this plant is quite hardy, and forms very handsome bushes, usually escaping being cut down by frost. Admirable among the taller plants at the back of the herbaceous border, and on the margins of shrubberies. Cuttings: grows freely in ordinary garden soil.

FUCHSIA — FUMARIA.

Fuchsia gracilis (*Slender F.*)—A handsome species, with finely pubescent branches; 6 to 10 ft. high. *Flowers*, from early summer to October; petals purple, convolute and retuse; calyx scarlet; sepals oblong, acute, exceeding the petals; stigma undivided. *Leaves*, opposite, glabrous, long-stalked, remotely denticulated. A variety (*F. g. multiflora*), has smaller and glaucous leaves and a conical stigma. Mexico.—— Warm borders, and fringes of shrubbery, in sandy loam. Cuttings.

Fuchsia magellanica (*Fuegian F.*) *Magellan F.*—A rather robust glabrous plant, 3 to 6 ft. high. *Flowers*, in summer and autumn; petals violet, obovate, convolute; sepals scarlet, oblong, acute. *Leaves*, ovate-oblong, or oblong-lance-shaped, acute or rounded at the base, toothed, smooth, or minutely pubescent underneath. Tierra del Fuego and Chili.——Warm borders, or against sunny walls, in rich light loam. Cuttings.

Fuchsia microphylla (*Small-leaved F.*)—A neat little species, 15 in. to 2 ft. high. *Flowers*, in autumn; petals bright rose-colour, irregularly incised; sepals oval, acuminate, dark-purple or violet-carmine. *Leaves*, opposite, small, thick, oblong-elliptical, smooth, irregularly-toothed, dark-green on the upper side, paler underneath. Mexico. ——Warm borders, and on the margins of beds of choice shrubs, etc., in light well-drained soil. Thrives in the open air in the South of England and Ireland. Division and cuttings.

Fuchsia serratifolia (*Saw-leaved F.*) —A very handsome species with furrowed branches, which, as well as the leaf-stalks and midribs of the leaves, are of a carmine red colour; 6 to 8 ft. high in warm countries. *Flowers*, in summer, large; petals oval-oblong, orange-red or poppy-red, slightly wavy on the margin; sepals lance-shaped, pointed, deep rose-colour, tinged with green at the points, longer than the petals. *Leaves*, in whorls of 3 or 4, narrow, oblong, acute, edged with glandular teeth. Peru. —— In the southern counties of England and Ireland, in rich, light, and well-drained soil. Cuttings.

Fuchsia thymifolia (*Thyme-leaved F.*) —A dwarf, tufted species, with slender downy branches, which when young are of a reddish colour. *Flowers*, in summer; petals rose-coloured, oboval-oblong, entire. *Leaves*, nearly opposite, small, oval or roundish-oval, obtuse, hardly toothed, covered with white down above, nearly smooth underneath. There is a variety with large flowers. Mexico.——The same treatment and positions as those recommended for *F. microphylla*.

[Little or no mention is made in botanical or gardening books as to the Fuchsia's merit as a hardy plant, and over the greater part of the country it is only known as a greenhouse plant, with the exception perhaps of one neglected kind in the borders. But near the sea all round our coasts, and especially in the southern and western parts of England and Ireland, several species of Fuchsia are hardy, and are perhaps the most beautiful objects in the gardens. Some varieties, such as *Ricartoni*, and many others, thrive perfectly also. *F. Dominiana* succeeds well in Cornwall. Frequently the species and varieties are cut down by frost, but spring up again vigorously and live the life of herbaceous plants in fact. Hence they find a place in this book. But in mild districts, and near the sea-coast, they frequently escape being cut down for years, and become large and handsome bushes].

Fumaria densiflora (*Dense-flowered Fumitory*).—A glaucous, much-spreading species, about 6 in. high. *Flowers*, from May to July; of an intense purple colour, sometimes rose-coloured, and occasionally white, in dense racemes. *Leaves*, twice-divided, with linear, acute, channelled segments. South of France, in stony fields and on walls.——Borders, and the rougher parts of the rock-garden, in ordinary light soil. Division.

Globularia vulgaris (*Common G.*)—A pleasing perennial, 6 in. to 1 ft. high. *Flowers*, in summer; bright blue (rarely white), in dense heads surrounded by an involucre of 9 to 12 imbricated leaflets. *Leaves*, of the root numerous, leathery, obovate, notched or 3-toothed at the point, and arranged in a rosette; stem-leaves much smaller, lance-shaped, acute, sessile; stems herbaceous, erect, simple. Alps of Europe. ——Borders, and the rock-garden, in free, sandy, and cool loam. Division.

Heracleum eminens (*Blunt-lobed Cow-Parsnip*).—A peculiarly distinct species, 3 to 4 ft. high. *Flowers*, in summer; in large umbels. *Leaves*, trifoliate, with blunt or roundish lobes, of a thick texture and finely covered with velvety down, which gives them a slightly glaucous appearance.—— Among fine foliaged hardy plants in the subtropical garden, either isolated or grouped with its relatives the other Cow-parsnips. Seed.

Jaborosa integrifolia (*Mandrake J.*) —An interesting perennial, allied to the Mandrake, 9 to 12 in. high. *Flowers*, from July to September; large, pure white, tubular, about 2 in. long, very fragrant. *Leaves*, all radical, entire, oval, obtuse, stalked, about 6 in. long, rising slightly above the flowers. Buenos Ayres. —— Warm borders, or sunny spots on the warmer and lower flanks of the rock-garden, in sandy well-drained loam. Seed.

Lathyrus roseus (*Rosy-flowered L.*)— A very glabrous plant, allied to *L. tuberosus;* about 2 ft. high. *Flowers*, from June to August, of a beautiful rose-colour, rather smaller than those of *L. tuberosus*, usually growing in pairs. *Leaves*, with one pair of ovate-roundish leaflets; tendrils very short; stipules small, subulate; stem slender, not winged. Iberia, rare.——Borders and banks, in sandy loam. Division.

Lewisia rediviva (*Bitter-root Plant*).— A very singular and ornamental plant, allied to the Mesembryanthemums, 3 to 4 in. high. *Flowers*, in summer; opening only during sunshine, rose-coloured, large, solitary on a fleshy stalk jointed in the middle; calyx elegantly veined with red, and of a consistency like paper. *Leaves*, all radical, linear, bluntish, succulent, growing in tufts from the crown of the root, and beginning to wither as soon as the flower opens. *Root*, tapering, fleshy, edible, largely used as food by the Indians. North America, particularly in Washington Territory and in Oregon. —— Warm spots in the rock-garden, in dryish soil. Seed.

Lilium Washingtonianum (*Washington Lily*).—A noble white Lily recently introduced, 3 to 5 ft. high. *Flowers*, in summer; white more or less tinged with purple or lilac, fragrant, drooping, in a long erect raceme. *Leaves*, smooth, oblanceolate, acute, 4 or 5 in. long, in whorls of 10 to 12. Sierra Nevada, California.—— As it has been only recently introduced nothing is known of the conditions under which this will best thrive. I saw it on the Sierra Nevada, but not in flower, growing abundantly in sunny but not warm regions in light dark loam, and in or near open woods. A warm sandy or peaty loam, and warm position, should be given it in this country. Separation of the bulbs and by scales.

Lunaria biennis (*Honesty*).—A beautiful early summer flower of the Wall-flower order, 1½ ft. to 3 ft. high.

LIMNOCHARIS — ORONTIUM.

Flowers, in spring and early summer; purplish-violet with deep yellow stamens, numerous, in loose clusters which form a large panicle. *Leaves*, alternate; oval-heart-shaped, irregularly toothed, the lower ones stalked, upper ones sessile. *Fruit*, remarkable for its size, consisting of a flat, very broadly-oval seed-vessel, rounded at both ends, and with a shining, satiny, permanent dissepiment, which is very ornamental for a long time after the seed is shed. Central Europe.—— Although a biennial this is included here because it will sow itself abundantly on banks, or in shrubberies or copses; certainly on all light warm soils. No plant is more worthy of naturalization, while it is also excellent for the spring garden and for borders. Seed.

Limnocharis Humboldtii (*Humboldt's L.*)—A handsome aquatic plant, with long, slender, creeping rootstocks, and floating leaves. *Flowers*, from July to September; of a lively golden yellow colour, marked with a broad dark spot at the base of each of the 3 petals; sepals 3, green, persistent, shorter than the petals. *Leaves*, oval, long-stalked, fleshy, smooth, of a lively green colour. S. America.—— In fountain basins and clear rather still waters, where the plant will be fully exposed to the sun. It thrives and flowers freely during the summer months in the open air, grown in rather large pots placed on the bottom of the tank or pond. It will probably not survive out of doors in winter except in the mildest districts, and placed at least 18 in. below the surface. It might, however, escape in water that does not freeze. Plants put out of a warm aquatic house in May soon begin to grow in the open air. Division.

Mitchella repens (*Variegated Partridge Berry*).—A very neat, trailing, small, evergreen herb, 2 or 3 in. high. *Flowers*, in summer; white, often tinged with purple, funnel-shaped, 4-lobed, densely bearded inside, fragrant, growing in pairs. *Leaves*, small, opposite, roundish-ovate, smooth and shining, stalked, often variegated with whitish lines. North America, in dry woods.——In shady spots near the rock-garden or hardy fernery, in sandy peat and leaf-mould. Division.

Muscari armeniacum (*Armenian Grape Hyacinth*).—A strikingly beautiful and scarce species, 6 in. high. *Flowers*, in May; fine cobalt-blue with 3 small yellow dots near the mouth of the corolla, in a dense spike about 2½ in. long, agreeably fragrant. *Leaves*, ribbon-like, concave, pointed, about 9 in. long and ¼ in. broad. Armenia. ——The bulb-garden, and on level spots in the rock-garden; also in borders, when sufficiently plentiful, in light soil. Division.

Onopordon acaule (*Stemless Cotton Thistle*).—A singular and interesting fine-foliaged biennial, with a very short stem, from 2 to 4 in. high. *Flowers*, in July; dull white, globose, solitary on the top of the stem; involucre of narrowly lance-shaped, green or yellowish scales ending in sharp spines. *Leaves*, very large, all radical, stalked, sinuate-pinnatifid, with triangular toothed spiny lobes, covered with white down on both sides, and forming a rosette 4 ft. or more in diameter, and 12 to 18 in. high; stem, thickened at the base, woolly, not winged, frequently emitting from the base one or two short ascending branches. Pyrenees.——In the picturesque garden, isolated on the turf, or naturalized on sunny banks or slopes in the rougher parts of the pleasure-ground; also in groups of fine-foliaged hardy perennials. Seed.

Orontium aquaticum (*Golden Club*). —A handsome aquatic perennial of the *Arum* family, 1 ft. to 18 in. high. *Flowers*, early in summer; yellow, densely crowded all over the narrow spadix, and emitting a singular odour. *Leaves*, lance-shaped-ovate, entire, long-stalked, floating, of a peculiar glaucous tone. North America, in rivulets and stagnant waters.——Margins of ponds and fountain basins, or in the very wettest part of the artificial bog. I have never seen this plant really well-grown, except in the late Mr. Borrer's garden, at Henfield; but from what I saw of it in the bogs of New Jersey in 1870, I have no doubt it will prove of easy culture in marshy soil with us. Division.

Pentstemon crassifolius (*Thick-leaved P.*)—A neat, spreading, bushy kind, about 1 ft. high. *Flowers*, in May; lilac-rose, about 1 in. long, in few-flowered, terminal racemes; anthers very villous; sterile filament villous at the extremity. *Leaves*, obovate-lance-shaped, much broader and shorter than those of *P. Scouleri*, entire, leathery, keeled underneath; those on the flowering branches gradually diminishing in size. N.W. coast of North America.——The rock-garden, among dwarf shrubs and vigorous alpine plants, or in the mixed border, in ordinary soil. Cuttings.

Phormium tenax (*New Zealand Flax*).—A stately plant with sword-like leaves, 4 ft. to over 6 ft. high. *Flowers*, early in autumn; lemon-coloured, in a unilateral spike scarcely higher than the foliage. *Leaves*, long, leathery, broadly sword-shaped, gracefully recurved at the top, and forming noble tufts of foliage. New Zealand. ——As isolated tufts in the pleasure-ground, and by wood walks; or in groups of hardy foliage-plants. Also as an aquatic. I have seen it growing freely in water nearly 2 ft. deep, and its effect on the surface of water is very fine. It is only suited for the above-named positions near the sea-coast and in the south and west of England and Ireland, where it thrives remarkably well. About London and in many northern and inland districts, it is only seen in perfection grown as a pot-plant. The handsome variegated variety will no doubt also prove hardy out of doors in the south. Division.

Phyllostachys bambusoides (*Bamboo-like P.*)—A noble fine foliaged plant, nearly allied to the Bamboos; 10 to 12 ft. high. *Flowers*, in a broad and shining panicle nearly 2 ft. long. *Leaves*, oblong-lance-shaped, rounded or attenuated at the base, very acute at the point, 3 to 4 in. long and ⅜ to ¾ in. across, smooth above, pale and pubescent underneath. *Stems* smooth, yellowish, with prominent nodes. Japan.——In the picturesque garden, in sheltered but sunny positions, in deep sandy well-drained loam; most likely to succeed in the southern counties.

Polygonum sachalinense (*Sachalin P.*)—A tall and vigorous species, with the aspect of a giant Dock, said to exceed the height of a man in its native habitats, and differing from *P. cuspidatum* in having an angular striated stem, leaves glaucous underneath and covered on the ribs with slender hairs. *Flowers*, late in summer; of a delicate greenish colour, in axillary clusters; bracts ovate, long-pointed. *Leaves*, broadly ovate, or ovate-oblong, acuminate, the lower ones sub-cordate at the base, upper ones truncate, all with glaucous and prominently veined under-sides. Island of Sachalin, and North Eastern Asia.——So recently introduced that nothing can be said of its cultivation, but it may be tried in the same position as *P. cuspidatum*, and also by river-banks, etc., where a vigorous type of vegetation is desired.

Saxifraga umbrosa (*London Pride*).—A well-known and popular old favourite, 4 to 12 in. high. *Flowers*, in summer; small, white delicately dotted with red and yellow, drooping in the bud, and arranged in dense panicles. *Leaves*, oboval, crenate, with a cartilaginous margin, attenuated into a ciliated stalk, arranged in a broad rosette, and persistent for several years. There is a variety with variegated leaves, not often met with in gardens. Europe and Ireland: a variety occurs in Yorkshire, but is considered a doubtful native.—— Borders, rough rocky places, or banks, or naturalized in woods or copses. Although coming from the pure moist air of the Killarney hills, it thrives perfectly in small gardens in London and other cities. Division.

Scilla nutans (*Blue-bell*). — Our common Blue-bell, 14 to 30 in. high. *Flowers*, in May; blue, bell-shaped, cylindrical, in a nodding raceme. *Leaves*, narrow, channelled, smooth, dull green, shorter than the flower-stem. *Bulb*, white, elongated-pear-shaped, oblong, or club-shaped. There are varieties with white, flesh-coloured, and rosy flowers. Europe and Britain. ——The common form should be seen abundantly in rough grassy places, while the pink and white forms are among the most attractive spring bulbs we have, and will grow in any soil. Division.

Scolymus grandiflorus (*Large-flowered S.*)—A rather showy Thistle-like herb, 12 to 18 in. high. *Flowers*, in summer; large, orange-yellow, terminal and axillary, sessile, each surrounded by 3 leathery, spiny, lance-shaped bracts, except the terminal one which has 6. *Leaves*, oblong-lance-shaped in outline, deeply cut into oval-lance-shaped segments, dentate-spiny, slightly pubescent, and traversed by white veins; stem-leaves decurrent: stem more or less downy. South Europe and North Africa.——Borders and naturalization, in sandy loam. Division and seed.

Senecio Doronicum (*Large-flowered S.*)—The most showy-flowered of its family, 8 in. to 3 ft. high or more. *Flowers*, in summer; bright yellow or orange, very large, short-stalked, 1 to 5 on the top of the stem. *Leaves*, thick, leathery, woolly underneath; the lower ones oblong-oval, with a winged stalk; upper ones lance-shaped or linear-lance-shaped, sessile, half-clasping; stem somewhat angled near the top. S. of Europe.——Borders, in ordinary light soil. Division.

Smilacina stellata (*Star-flowered Lily of the Valley*).—An interesting perennial, 1 to 2 ft. high. *Flowers*, early in summer; white, numerous, closely-set in an erect terminal cluster about 2 in. long. *Leaves*, 7 to 12 in number, sessile, oblong-lance-shaped, of a lively green, covered with minute down when young, slightly clasping. Berries blackish. N. America.—— Naturalization in open woods, copses, or on bushy banks. It thrives in ordinary soil, best however in a deep vegetable one. Although scarcely worthy of a position in borders, it would be very desirable in moist shrubberies. Division.

Tigridia Pavonia (*Peacock T.*)—A dwarf but magnificent bulbous plant, 1 to nearly 2 ft. high. *Flowers*, late in summer; very showy, nearly 6 in. across, 1 to 3 on each stem; petals fiddle-shaped, yellow, spotted with purple; sepals larger than the petals, of a violet colour in the lower part, marked with bands of yellow spotted with purple, and with brilliant scarlet points. *Leaves*, sword-shaped, acute, sheathing at the base, and of a lively green colour. Mexico. —— Borders and the bulb-garden, in very sandy and well-drained loam, or in sandy peat, the bulbs to be planted with their crowns 3 or 4 in. beneath the surface of the soil. Separation of the small bulbs.

Verbascum phœniceum (*Blue-flowered Mullein*).—A handsome South European Mullein, 3 ft. or more high. *Flowers*, all the summer; large, somewhat variable in colour, but usually of a violet blue overlying a yellow ground striped with violet, and with purple stamens, arranged in a very long spike. *Leaves*, of the root, stalked, oval-lance-shaped, slightly toothed, somewhat hairy above, and forming a wide-spreading rosette; stem-leaves alternate, sessile. South Europe.—— Borders, in well-drained sandy loam. Does not live through the winter on very cold and wet soils. Seed.

Vicia sylvatica (*Wood Vetch*).—A handsome native free-trailing Vetch, with a climbing stem, 2 to 4 ft. long. *Flowers*, in summer; numerous, cream-coloured, streaked with blue or purple. *Leaves*, of 6 to 10 pairs of oval or broadly-elliptical leaflets, rounded or truncate and mucronate at the apex, and of a bright pea-green colour. Stipules very broad, lunate, deeply toothed at the base. Britain, in woods and thickets. —— In hedgerows, fringes of shrubberies, etc., allowed to trail over low bushes, etc. Seed.

Vieusseuxia glaucopis (*Blue-eyed Peacock Iris*).—*Iris Pavonia*, Linn.—An exquisitely beautiful bulbous plant, 9 to 15 in. high. *Flowers*, in the end of May or beginning of June; about 2 in. across, pure white, with a beautiful porcelain-blue stain nearly ¼ in. broad at the base of each of the three larger divisions; the spot is margined with dark purple teeth, and is of a fine deep violet at the base; the throat hirsute. *Leaves*, slender and grass-like, glaucous, 15 to 18 in. long. *Bulb* small, about ¼ in. in diameter. Cape of Good Hope.——On warm sheltered borders, in sandy peat, or sandy loam and leaf-mould; the bulbs to be planted rather deep, say about four inches of firm soil above the crest. Separation of the bulbs in autumn.

ADDENDA (SUPPLEMENT).

Anagallis tenella (*Bog Pimpernel*). —A beautiful, delicate, creeping native bog-plant. *Flowers*, in summer; very pretty, delicate pink with deeper veins, on slender stalks; corolla bell-shaped, deeply 5- or 6-cleft. *Leaves*, roundish, very small, opposite; stems very slender, a few inches long. Wet mossy banks and bogs throughout Western Europe and in Britain.—— In wet parts of the artificial bog, or in any position where sphagnum moss thrives. The leaves of the plant are scarcely discernible, woven here and there through the moss, and the delicate rose flowers, large for the size of the plant, just rise above the moss in profusion.

Goodyera pubescens (*Silvery Rattlesnake Plantain*).—An interesting and pretty hardy Orchid, with silvery-veined leaves; 6 to 12 in. high, when in bloom. *Flowers*, in summer; greenish-white, small, numerous, in a crowded spike. *Leaves*, in a tuft, ovate, with thickish stalks, and silvery veins, which give the plant an attractive appearance at all times. North America.——Shady moist parts of the rock-garden or hardy fernery. Also in the bog bed, and naturalized in shady ditches and in narrow moist lanes; it grows freely in sandy vegetable soil. Division.

Onopordon Acanthium (*Scotch Thistle*).—A stout, vigorous, and stately native biennial, quite silvery from cottony wool; 6 to 8 ft. high. *Flowers*, in late summer; light purple, in large globular heads. *Leaves*, very prickly; of root sessile, deeply sinuated and of noble outline; stem - leaves smaller and decurrent; stems much-branched and winged to the top. Europe and Asia.—— Margins of shrubberies, or naturalized in rough places; also in groups of fine-foliaged plants and in large borders. Comes up readily from self-sown seeds.

PART III.

SELECTIONS

OF

HARDY FLOWERS FOR VARIOUS PURPOSES,

INDEXES AND GLOSSARY.

SELECTIONS OF HARDY PLANTS.

In the opening chapters of the book I endeavoured to give a comprehensive view of the various ways in which hardy flowers may be grown, but the reader who glances over the headings of the following selections will obtain a much fuller one. They are intended to act as guides to the inexperienced in carrying out every kind of embellishment with hardy flowers. Some plants are named that are not described in the body of the book, as for example, climbing shrubs, for covering bowers, rustic wigwams, etc., in the list for that purpose. Some perennials, too, have a place in the list for special purposes that were not sufficiently important for description in the body of the book, and annuals are also associated with perennials for various special purposes. Considerable care has been bestowed on making each selection suitable for its purpose, and as comprehensive as the plants in cultivation will admit of. These are respects in which garden literature has always seemed to me to be deficient, and they are very important ones.

A Choice Selection of the very finest Herbaceous Perennials.

Bulbs are omitted from this selection.

Acanthus	Alstrœmeria	Anemone	Arundo
latifolius	aurea	palmata	Donax
longifolius	chilensis	Pulsatilla	Asclepias
spinosissimus	Anchusa	stellata	tuberosa
Achillea	italica	sylvestris	Asphodelus
asplenifolia	Anemone	Aquilegia	luteus
Eupatorium	alpina	alpina	ramosus
Ptarmica, fl. pl.	angulosa	cærulea	Aster
Aconitum	apennina	glandulosa	Amellus
japonicum	coronaria	truncata	elegans
variegatum	fulgens		lævis
Adonis	Hepatica	Arum	Novæ Angliæ
vernalis	japonica	italicum	Novi Belgii

HARDY FLOWERS.

Aster
  pyrenæus
  Reevesi
  turbinellus
  versicolor
Astragalus
  monspessulanus
Baptisia
  australis
Betonica
  grandiflora
Calceolaria
  Kellyana
Calla
  palustris
Callirhoe
  involucrata
Calystegia
  dahurica
  pubescens
Campanula
  alpina
  carpatica
  grandis
  macrantha
  nobilis
  persicifolia
  rotundifolia
  turbinata
Carduus
  eriophorus
Cassia
  marilandica
Catananche
  cærulea
Centranthus
  ruber
Chelone
  glabra
  obliqua
Commelina
  cœlestis
Convallaria
  majalis
Convolvulus
  Soldanella
Coreopsis
  lanceolata
  tenuifolia

Coronilla
  iberica
  montana
  varia
Corydalis
  lutea
  nobilis
Crambe
  cordifolia
Cynara
  Scolymus
Cypripedium
  Calceolus
  spectabile
Delphinium in fine
  variety
Dentaria
  laciniata
Dicentra
  eximia
  spectabilis
Dictamnus
  Fraxinella
Dodecatheon
  integrifolium
  Jeffreyanum
  Meadia
Doronicum
  caucasicum
Dracocephalum
  argunense
  austriacum
  grandiflorum
  Ruyschianum
Echinops
  ruthenicus
Epilobium
  angustifolium
  rosmarinifolium
Epimedium
  pinnatum
Eranthis
  hyemalis
Erigeron
  speciosum
Erodium
  Manescavi
Eryngium
  alpinum
  amethystinum

Erythronium
  Dens-canis
Ferula
  communis
  glauca
  tingitana
Funkia
  grandiflora
  Sieboldi
Gaillardia
  aristata
  grandiflora
Galega
  officinalis
Gentiana
  Andrewsii
  asclepiadea
Geranium
  ibericum
  Lambertianum
  platypetalum
  sanguineum
  striatum
Geum
  chilense
  montanum
Gypsophila
  paniculata
  Steveni
Hedysarum
  obscurum
Helenium
  atropurpureum
  autumnale
Helianthus
  orgyalis
  rigidus
Helichrysum
  arenarium
Helleborus
  atrorubens
  niger and its
    varieties
  olympicus
  purpurascens
Hemerocallis
  disticha
  flava
  fulva
  graminea

Hesperis
  matronalis, fl
    pl.
Hibiscus
  militaris
  palustris
  roseus
Iris
  flavescens
  florentina
  germanica
  Monnieri
  nudicaulis
  ochroleuca
  pallida
  sambucina
  subbiflora
  variegata
Lathyrus
  grandiflorus
  latifolius
  maritimus
  rotundifolius
Leucanthemum
  lacustre
Liatris
  elegans
  spicata
  squarrosa
Linaria
  dalmatica
  vulgaris
Linum
  alpinum
  arboreum
  flavum
  narbonnense
  perenne
Lobelia
  cardinalis
Lupinus
  polyphyllus
Lychnis
  diurna fl. pl.
  chalcedonica
    and vars.
  Haageana
  Lagascæ
  vespertina fl. pl.

SELECTION OF HERBACEOUS PERENNIALS.

Lychnis
  Viscaria
Lythrum
  Salicaria roseum
Malva
  campanulata
  moschata
Meconopsis
  cambrica
Medicago
  falcata
Melittis
  Melissophyllum
Menyanthes
  trifoliata
Mertensia
  virginica
Monarda
  didyma
  Kalmiana
Myosotis
  dissitiflora
  palustris
  sylvatica
Nepeta
  Mussini
Œnothera
  fruticosa
  Jamesii
  macrocarpa
  marginata
  riparia
  speciosa
Omphalodes
  verna
Onobrychis
  montana
Ononis
  arvensis
  rotundifolius
Orobus
  cyaneus
  flaccidus
  lathyroides
  variegatus
  vernus

Pæonia in great variety
Papaver
  bracteatum
  lateritium
  nudicaule
  orientale
  pilosum
Phlomis
  herba-venti
  Russelliana
  Samia
  tuberosa
Phlox
  Carolina
  decussata and vars.
  ovata
  paniculata
Phygelius
  capensis
Physostegia
  denticulata
  imbricata
  virginiana
Phytolacca
  decandra
Platycodon
  autumnale
  grandiflorum
Plumbago
  Larpentæ
Polygonatum
  multiflorum
Polygonum
  cuspidatum
Potentilla in var.
Primula
  denticulata
  sikkimensis
  Stuarti
  Veitchii
  veris
  vulgaris
Prunella
  grandiflora
Pyrethrum
  carneum

Pyrethrum
  serotinum
Ranunculus
  aconitifolius
  acris fl. pl.
  amplexicaulis
  monspeliacus
  montanus
  spicatus
Rhexia
  virginica
Rudbeckia
  californica
  Drummondi
  fulgida
  hirta
  laciniata
  speciosa
Salvia
  argentea
  patens
Saponaria
  ocymoides
Saxifraga
  cordifolia
  crassifolia
Scabiosa
  caucasica
Scutellaria
  alpina
  lupulina
Sedum
  kamtschaticum
  Sieboldi
  spectabile
  spurium
Silene
  alpestris
  Elizabethæ
  maritima
  Schafta
Sisyrinchium
  grandiflorum
Spigelia
  marilandica
Spiræa
  Aruncus

Spiræa
  palmata
  venusta
Statice
  latifolia
  speciosa
  tatarica
Symphyandra
  pendula
Symphytum
  bohemicum
  caucasicum
Thermopsis
  fabacea
Thlaspi
  latifolium
Tradescantia
  virginica and vars.
Tritoma
  Uvaria
Trollius
  asiaticus
  europæus
  napellifolius
Tropæolum
  pentaphyllum
  polyphyllum
  speciosum
Verbascum
  Chaixii
Veronica
  candida
  corymbosa
  gentianoides
  incarnata
  incisa
Vicia
  argentea
  Cracca
Vinca
  herbacea
Viola
  calcarata
  cornuta
  lutea
  odorata
  pedata

HARDY FLOWERS.

A Selection of the finest Hardy Bulbs, including Rhizomatous Plants like the Irises and Hardy Orchids.

Acis
  autumnalis
Agapanthus
  umbellatus
Allium
  azureum
  ciliatum
  fragrans
  Moly
  neapolitanum
Amaryllis
  Belladonna
Anomatheca
  cruenta
Arum
  crinitum
  Dracunculus
  italicum
Brodiæa
  coccinea
  congesta
  grandiflora
Bulbocodium
  vernum
Calla
  palustris
Calliprora
  lutea
Calypso
  borealis
Camassia
  esculenta
Colchicum, all the kinds
Crinum
  capense
Crocosmia
  aurea
Crocus
  Aucheri
  biflorus
  Imperatonius
  luteus
  nudiflorus
  Orphanidis

Crocus
  reticulatus
  Sieberi
  speciosus
  vernus
  versicolor
Cypripedium
  acaule
  Calceolus
  guttatum
  spectabile
Epipactis
  palustris
Erythronium
  americanum
  Dens-canis
Fritillaria
  imperialis
  Meleagris
Galanthus
  nivalis
  plicatus
Gladiolus in great variety
Gymnadenia
  conopsea
Hyacinthus
  amethystinus
  orientalis
Iris
  cristata
  flavescens
  florentina
  germanica
  graminea
  iberica
  ochroleuca
  pallida
  pumila
  reticulata
  sambucina
  Susiana
  xiphioides
  Xiphium

Leucojum
  æstivum
  vernum
Libertia
  magellanica
Lilium
  auratum
  bulbiferum
  canadense
  candidum
  chalcedonicum
  croceum
  eximium
  japonicum
  longiflorum
  speciosum
  tenuifolium
  tigrinum
  venustum
  Washingtonianum
Merendera
  Bulbocodium
Muscari
  armeniacum
  botryoides
  comosum monstrosum
  Heldreichii
Narcissus
  bicolor
  Bulbocodium
  incomparabilis
  Jonquilla
  juncifolius
  maximus
  minor
  odorus
  poeticus
  tenuior
  triandrus
Ophrys
  apifera
  arachnites
  aranifera

Ophrys
  muscifera
  Scolopax
Orchis
  foliosa
  latifolia
  maculata
  militaris
  Morio
  nigra
  papilionacea
  pyramidalis
Ornithogalum
  montanum
  narbonnense
  nutans
  pyramidale
  umbellatum
Pancratium
  illyricum
Puschkinia
  scilloides
Scilla
  amœna
  bifolia
  campanulata
  nutans
  patula
  peruviana
  sibirica
Serapias
  cordigera
  Lingua
Sparaxis
  pulcherrima
Sternbergia
  lutea
Tigridia
  Pavonia
Trillium
  grandiflorum
Triteleia
  uniflora
Tritoma
  Burchelli

A SELECTION OF CHOICE ALPINE PLANTS. 281

Tritoma	Tulipa	Tulipa	Vieusseuxia
præcox	Clusiana	sylvestris	glaucopis
Uvaria	cornuta	turcica	Zephyranthes
Tulipa	Gesneriana	viridiflora	Atamasco
Celsiana	Oculus-solis		candida

A Selection of Choice Alpine and Rock Plants suitable for the Margins of Mixed Borders, etc.

This is a most important selection, inasmuch as the appearance of all garden borders may be improved very much by being fringed with choice alpine plants. In this simple way, which may be practised without expense in the humblest cottage-garden, numbers of lovely kinds may be grown, all of which, from personal experience, I can testify will thrive in this way. All kinds are omitted that are liable to perish when grown on the level ground, also all kinds that grow too tall to be used on the margin.

Acæna	Antennaria	Campanula	Dianthus
microphylla	dioica	alpina	deltoides
Acantholimon	tomentosa	cæspitosa	dentosus
glumaceum	Anthyllis	carpatica	neglectus
Achillea	montana	Cenisia	petræus
Clavennæ	Antirrhinum	fragilis	annulatus
tomentosa	rupestre	garganica	Dielytra
umbellata	Arabis	muralis	eximia
Adonis	albida	pulla	Diotis
vernalis	petræa	Raineri	maritima
Æthionema	Arenaria	turbinata	Dryas
saxatile	montana	Cerastium, in var.	Drummondi
Ajuga	purpurascens	Colchicum, in var.	octopetala
genevensis	Armeria	Convolvulus	Eranthis
Alyssum	vulgaris rosea	lineatus	hyemalis
alpestre	Astragalus	Soldanella	Erica
saxatile	monspessulanus	Cornus	carnea
Andromeda	Aubrietia, in var.	canadensis	Erodium
tetragona	Bellis	Coronilla	Manescavi
Anemone	hortensis aucu-	iberica	Erysimum
angulosa	bæfolia	minima	ochroleucum
apennina	double vars.	varia	Erythronium
blanda	Bulbocodium	Crocus, many spe-	Dens-canis
coronaria	vernum	cies and va-	Euonymus
fulgens	Calandrinia	rieties	radicans varie-
Hepatica	umbellata	Cyclamen	gata
palmata	Calceolaria	europæum	Fragaria
pavonina	Kellyana	hederæfolinm	indica
Pulsatilla	Callirhoe	repandum	Galanthus
ranunculoides	involucrata	Daphne	nivalis
stellata	pedata	Cneorum	plicatus

Gaultheria
  procumbens
Genista
  prostrata
  sagittalis
Gentiana
  acaulis
Geranium
  argenteum
  cinereum
  lancastriense
Geum
  montanum
Gypsophila
  prostrata and
  others
Helianthemum in
  var.
Helichrysum
  arenarium
Hutchinsia
  alpina
Hyacinthus.
  amethystinus
Iberis
  corifolia
  correæfolia
  Garrexiana
  gibraltarica
  sempervirens
  Tenoreana
Iris
  cristata
  nudicaulis
  pumila
  reticulata
Isopyrum
  thalictroides
Leucojum
  vernum
Linaria
  alpina
Linum
  alpinum
  arboreum
Lithospermum
  prostratum
Muscari
  botryoides

Muscari
  Heldreichii
Myosotis
  alpestris
  dissitiflora
  palustris
Narcissus
  Bulbocodium
  juncifolius
  minor
Nierembergia
  rivularis
Œnothera
  marginata
  missouriensis
  taraxacifolia
Omphalodes
  verna
Orobus
  cyaneus
  vernus
Oxalis
  Bowiei
  floribunda
Pentstemon
  procerus
Phlox
  divaricata
  reptans
  subulata
Plumbago
  Larpentæ
Polygala
  Chamæbuxus
Polygonum
  vaccinifolium
Potentilla
  alpestris
  pyrenaica
Primula
  amœna
  Auricula
  integrifolia
  marginata
  officinalis,
  in var.

Primula
  Veitchii
  viscosa
  vulgaris, in var.
Prunella
  grandiflora
Pulmonaria
  officinalis
Puschkinia
  scilloides
Ranunculus
  alpestris
  amplexicaulis
  montanus
  rutæfolius
Sagina
  glabra, var. cor-
    sica
Salix
  reticulata
  serpyllifolia
Sanguinaria
  canadensis
Santolina
  incana
Saponaria
  ocymoides
Saxifraga
  Aizoon
  Andrewsii
  cæspitosa
  Cotyledon
  granulata plena
  hypnoides
  juniperina
  ligulata
  longifolia
  oppositifolia
  pectinata
Scilla
  bifolia
  sibirica
Scutellaria
  alpina
Sedum
  album
  Ewersii

Sedum
  glaucum
  kamtschaticum
  pulchellum
  rupestre
  Sieboldi
  spectabile
  spurium
Sempervivum
  arenarium
  calcareum
  glaucum
  globiferum
  hirtum
  montanum
  soboliferum
  tectorum
Senecio
  argenteus
Silene
  acaulis
  alpestris
  Elisabethæ
  maritima
  Pumilio
  Schafta
Smilacina
  bifolia
Sternbergia
  lutea
Symphyandra
  pendula
Thalictrum
  anemonoides
  minus
Thlaspi
  latifolium
Thymus
  lanuginosus
Triteleia
  uniflora
Tunica
  Saxifraga
Vaccinium
  Vitis-idæa
Veronica
  candida
  fruticulosa

ORNAMENTAL ANNUAL AND BIENNIAL PLANTS. 283

Veronica
  prostrata
  saxatilis
  taurica
Vicia
  argentea
Vinca
  minor
Viola
  calcarata
  cornuta
  lutea
Viola
  odorata
  pedata
Waldsteinia
  geoides
  trifolia
Zapania
  nodiflora
Zauschneria
  californica
Zietenia
  lavandulæfolia

A Selection of the most Ornamental Annual and Biennial Plants.

As no annual and but few biennial plants are described in this book, and as many of them, however, have claim to a high place among "hardy flowers," a choice selection of good kinds is given here.

Acroclinium
  roseum
Alyssum
  maritimum
Amberboa
  moschata
  odorata
Arabis
  arenosa
Asperula
  azurea setosa
Brachycome
  diversifolia
  iberidifolia
Calandrinia
  discolor
  grandiflora
Campanula
  Loreyi
  Medium
  sibirica
  strigosa
Cenia
  turbinata
Centaurea
  cyanus
Centauridium
  Drummondi
Centranthus
  macrosiphon
Chrysanthemum
  coronarium
Clarkia
  elegans
  pulchella
  and vars.
Clintonia
  pulchella
Collomia
  coccinea
Convolvulus
  tricolor
Coreopsis
  aristosa
Cosmidium
  Burridgeanum
  Engelmannii
  filifolium
Delphinium, annual varieties
Digitalis
  purpurea in var.
Dimorphotheca
  pluvialis
Emilia
  sagittata
Erysimum
  arkansanum
  Peroffskianum
Eschscholtzia in var.
Eucharidium
  grandiflorum
Eutoca
  viscida
Gaillardia
  bicolor
  picta
Glaucium
  Fischeri
  fulvum
Godetia
  insignis
  Lindleyana
  reptans
  rosea-alba
  viminea
  Whitneyi
Gypsophila
  elegans
  muralis
  viscosa
Helianthus
  annuus
Helichrysum
  bracteatum
  macranthum
Heliophila
  araboides
Iberis
  coronaria
  umbellata
Ionopsidium
  acaule
Ipomopsis
  elegans
Kaulfussia
  amelloides
Kochia
  scoparia
Lasthenia
  californica
Lathyrus
  magellanicus
  odoratus
Lavatera
  trimestris
Leptosiphon
  androsaceus
  densiflorus
  luteus
  roseus
Limnanthes
  Douglasi
Linaria
  bipartita
  multicaulis
  saxatilis
  spartea
  speciosa
Linum
  grandiflorum
Lunaria
  biennis
Lupinus
  affinis
  Hartwegi
  luteus
  Menziesii
  mutabilis
  nanus
  pilosus
  subcarnosu
Malcolmia
  maritima
  and var. alba
Malope
  grandiflora
  trifida
Matthiola
  annua in var.
  incana in var.

HARDY FLOWERS.

Michauxia campanuloides	Palava flexuosa	Rhodanthe atrosanguinea	Tropæolum majus
Monolopia major	Papaver croceum	maculata Manglesii	minus peregrinum
Nemesia versicolor	Rhæas double vars.	Saponaria calabrica	Venidium calendulaceum
Nemophila atomaria	somniferum double vars.	Schizanthus pinnatus	Verbascum floccosum
discoidalis insignis	Phacelia tanacetifolia	retusus Senecio	phœniceum pulverulentum
maculata	Pharbitis	elegans	Thapsus
Nigella damascena	hispida and vars.	Silene Armeria	Veronica
Fontanesiana	Phlox	pendula	syriaca
Œnothera in var.	Drummondi	Specularia	Viscaria
Omphalodes linifolia	in var. Platystemon	speculum Sphenogyne	oculata Whitlavia
Oxalis rosea	californicus Polygonum	speciosa Statice	grandiflora Xeranthemum
Oxyura chrysanthe- moides	orientale Reseda odorata	spicata Trifolium incarnatum	annuum cylindraceum

A Selection of the finest Hardy Flowers that bloom in Spring.

Adonis vernalis	Antennaria dioica	Cardamine trifolia	Cyclamen in var. Dentaria
Allium neapolitanum	Arabis albida	Cheiranthus Cheiri	digitata Dicentra
Alyssum alpestre	arenosa blepharophylla	Marshallii Chelidonium	eximia spectabilis
montanum saxatile	petræa procurrens	grandiflorum japonicum	Doronicum caucasicum
Androsace in var.	purpurea	Convallaria	Clusii
Anemone alpina	Arenaria verna	majalis Corydalis	Columnæ Draba in var.
apennina coronaria	Armeria vulgaris	Marschalliana nobilis	Epimedium, all the kinds
fulgens nemorosa	Asperula odorata	tuberosa Crocus	Eranthis hyemalis
palmata Pulsatilla	Aubrietias, all the kinds	biflorus Imperatonius	Erica carnea
ranunculoides stellata	Borago orientalis	luteus and vars. reticulatus	Erysimum ochroleucum
sulphurea sylvestris	Bryanthus erectus	Sieberi	Erythronium Dens-canis
trifoliata vernalis	Bulbocodium vernum	vernus and vars. versicolor	Ficaria grandiflora

AUTUMN-BLOOMING HARDY FLOWERS. 285

Fritillaria, all the kinds
Galanthus
  nivalis
  plicatus
Gentiana
  acaulis
  alpina
  verna
Helleborus, all the kinds
Hepatica
  angulosa
  triloba
Hutchinsia
  alpina
Hyacinthus
  amethystinus
  orientalis
Iberis, all perennial kinds
Iris
  nudicaulis
  pumila
  reticulata
Jeffersonia
  diphylla
Leucojum
  æstivum

Leucojum
  vernum
Lithospermum
  prostratum
Lunaria
  biennis
Meconopsis
  cambrica
Muscari, all the kinds
Myosotis
  alpestris
  dissitiflora
  palustris
  sylvatica
Narcissus, all the kinds
Omphalodes
  verna
Orobus
  cyaneus
  flaccidus
  vernus
Petrocallis
  pyrenaica
Phlox
  divaricata
  procumbens

Phlox
  reptans
  setacea
  subulata
Primula, many species
Pulmonaria, all the kinds
Puschkinia
  scilloides
Ramondia
  pyrenaica
Ranunculus
  aconitifolius
  acris
  alpestris
  amplexicaulis
  chærophyllus
  Gouani
  gramineus
  monspeliacus
  montanus
  spicatus
Sanguinaria
  canadensis
Saponaria
  calabrica
Saxifraga, most of the kinds

Scilla
  amœna
  bifolia
  rosea
  sibirica
Silene
  pendula
Soldanella, all the kinds
Thlaspi
  latifolium
Trientalis
  europæa
Triteleia
  uniflora
Tulipa, all the kinds
Veronica
  pectinata
Vesicaria
  utriculata
Viola
  odorata
  suavis
  tricolor in var.
Waldsteinia
  geoides
  trifolia

A Selection of Autumn-blooming Hardy Flowers.

The greater number of hardy flowers bloom in spring and early summer, but as numbers of persons having large gardens live in town at these seasons, it is desirable to indicate the kinds that bloom late in summer and autumn. As the number of perennials that flower in autumn is somewhat limited, annuals and biennials are included.

Acæna
  microphylla
Acanthus in var.
Achillea
  ægyptiaca
  Eupatorium
  Millefolium roseum
  Ptarmica plena
Acis
  autumnalis

Aconitum
  autumnale
  chinense
Adenophora
  Lamarckiana
Alstrœmeria
  in var.
Althæa in var.
Alyssum
  maritimum

Amberboa
  moschata
  odorata
Anagallis
  arvensis
Anemone
  japonica and vars.
  vitifolia
Antirrhinum
  majus and vars.

Arundo
  conspicua
Asclepias
  tuberosa
Aster in var.
Astilbe
  rivularis
Calandrinia
  umbellata

HARDY FLOWERS.

Calla
  palustris
Calliopsis in var.
Callistephus
  chinensis
Cassia
  marylandica
Chrysanthemum in
  great variety
Clematis in var.
Colchicum in var.
Commelyna
  cœlestis
Convolvulus
  mauritanicus
Coreopsis
  lanceolata
  tenuifolia
Corydalis
  lutea
Crocosmia
  aurea
Crocus
  nudiflorus
  speciosus
Daphne
  Cneorum
Delphinium in
  var.
Erodium
  Manescavi
Erpetion
  reniforme
Erysimum
  arkansanum
  Peroffskianum
Eschscholtzia
  californica

Eucharidium
  concinnum
Eupatorium
  ageratoides
  purpureum
Fuchsia in var.
Funkia
  grandiflora
Galatella
  hyssopifolia
Gaura
  Lindheimeri
Geranium
  lancastriense
  sanguineum
Gladiolus in var.
Godetia in var.
Gynerium
  argenteum
Helenium
  autumnale
Helianthus in var.
Hibiscus in var.
Humulus
  Lupulus
Hutchinsia
  alpina
Ionopsidium
  acaule
Lavatera
  trimestris
  unguiculata
Lobelia
  Tupa, and many
    hybrid vars.
Lupinus in var.
Malope
  trifida

Malva
  Alcea
  campanulata
  Morenii
Matthiola in var.
Merendera
  Bulbocodium
Mirabilis
  Jalapa
Myosotis
  palustris
Nolana in var.
Œnothera in var.
Oxalis
  Bowiei
  floribunda
Pentstemon in var.
Phlox
  Carolina
  decussata
    and vars.
  paniculata
    and vars.
Phygelius
  capensis
Platycodon
  autumnale
Plumbago
  Larpentæ
Polygonum
  cuspidatum
  orientale
  vaccinifolium
Pyrethrum Par-
  thenium
  pleno
  serotinum
  carneum

Reseda
  odorata
Saponaria
  calabrica
Scabiosa
  caucasica
Schizostylis
  coccinea
Sedum
  Ewersii
  Sieboldi
  spectabile
Silene
  Schafta
Silphium in var.
Sparaxis
  pulcherrima
Statice in var.
Sternbergia
  lutea
Stevia
  ovata
  purpurea
Stokesia
  cyanea
Tradescantia
  virginica
Tritoma in var.
Verbena
  venosa
Veronica, shrubby
  kinds in var.
Viola
  cornuta
  lutea
  tricolor
Xeranthemum
  annuum

A Selection of Edging Plants.

This selection includes not merely edging plants in common use, but many seldom or never employed yet equally suitable, and may serve to show how great is the variety that may be produced in this way. It is not confined to silvery plants, or those that flower brilliantly, as, in a tastefully disposed garden, edgings of very various hues would be required, and none would prove more beautiful round beds of dwarf evergreens in winter than the Saxi-

A SELECTION OF EDGING PLANTS.

fragas of the *Hypnoides*, or mossy section. These are of the most vivid and refreshing green in winter.

Acæna
 microphylla
 Millefolium
Achillea
 ægyptiaca
 tomentosa
 umbellata
Acorus
 gramineus va-
  riegatus
Adonis
 vernalis
Æthionema in var.
Ajuga
 reptans varie-
  gatum
Alyssum
 montanum
 saxatile varie-
  gatum
 spinosum
Andromeda
 tetragona
Androsace
 lanuginosa
Andryala
 lanata
Anemone
 apennina
 coronaria
Antennaria
 dioica
 hyperborea
 tomentosa
Anthemis
 nobilis plena
Anthyllis
 montana
Arabis
 albida variegata
 lucida variegata
 procurrens va-
  riegata
Arctostaphylos
 Uva-ursi
Arenaria
 balearica

Arenaria
 montana
Armeria
 cephalotes
 vulgaris rosea
Artemisia
 frigida
Astragalus
 monspessulanus
 pannosus
Aubrietia in var.
Bellis in var.
Bellium
 bellidioides
 crassifolium
 minutum
Bulbocodium
 vernum
Calandrinia
 umbellata
Callirrhoe
 involucrata
Campanula
 barbata
 Barrelieri
 cæspitosa
 carpatica
 alba
 bicolor
 fragilis
 garganica
 hirsuta
 isophylla
 pulla
 Raineri
 rotundifolia
 turbinata
Cerastium
 alpinum
 Bibersteini
 Boissieri
 grandiflorum
 tomentosum
Cheiranthus
 Cheiri nana
Colchicum in var.
Collinsia in var.

Convolvulus
 lineatus
Coronilla
 iberica
 montana
Crocus in var.
Crucianella
 stylosa
Dactylis
 glomerata va-
  riegata
Daphne
 Cneorum
Dianthus in var.
Dicentra
 eximia
Diplotaxis
 tenuifolia varie-
  gata
Dodecatheon
 integrifolium
 Jeffreyanum
 Meadia
Dracocephalum
 grandiflorum
 Ruyschianum
Epigæa
 repens
Erica in var.
Erodium
 alpinum
 caruifolium
 macradenum
 Manescavi
Erysimum
 ochroleucum
Erythronium
 americanum
 Dens-canis
Euphorbia
 Cyparissias
Festuca
 glauca
Funkia
 grandiflora
 and all the va-
  riegated forms

Galanthus
 nivalis
 plicatus
Genista
 prostrata
 sagittalis
Gentiana
 acaulis
 gelida
 verna
Geranium
 argenteum
 cinereum
Godetia in var.
Gypsophila
 prostrata
 repens
Helianthemum in
  var.
Helichrysum
 arenarium
Hepatica
 angulosa
 triloba
Hippocrepis
 comosa
Houstonia
 cærulea
Hutchinsia
 alpina
Hypericum
 humifusum
 nummularium
 verticillatum
Iberis in var.
Iris
 nudicaulis
 pumila
Isopyrum
 thalictroides
Lamium
 maculatum al-
  bum
Leptosiphon in
  var.
Leucojum
 vernum

Linum
  arboreum
Lithospermum
  prostratum
Lobelia
  Erinus
  ramosa
Lotus
  corniculatus
    plenus
Lychnis
  alpina
  Lagascæ
  lapponica
  Viscaria fl. pl.
Lysimachia
  Nummularia
    ,, aurea
Malcolmia
  maritima
Matthiola in var.
Menziesia
  cærulea
  polifolia
Muscari in var.
Myosotis in var.
Narcissus
  Bulbocodium
  juncifolius
  nanus
  tenuifolius
  tenuior
  triandrus
Nemophila in var.
Nierembergia
  rivularis
Œnothera
  marginata
  taraxacifolia
Omphalodes
  Luciliæ
  verna
Onosma
  taurica
Ophiopogon
  japonicus variegatus

Orobus
  cyaneus
  vernus
Oxalis
  Bowiei
  corniculata
  Valdiviana
Oxytropis
  uralensis
Paronychia
  serpyllifolia
Pentstemon
  procerus
Phlox
  procumbens
  reptans
  subulata
  ,, alba
Phyteuma
  comosum
Polemonium
  cæruleum variegatum
Polygonum
  vaccinifolium
Portulaca in var.
Potentilla
  calabra
Primula
  veris
  viscosa
  vulgaris
Prunella
  grandiflora
Pulmonaria
  officinalis vars.
Puschkinia
  scilloides
Ranunculus
  asiaticus in var.
  bullatus, fl. pl.
  chærophyllus
  gramineus
  montanus
Rhexia
  virginica
Rhodanthe in var.

Sagina glabra var. corsica
Salvia
  argentea
Sanguinaria
  canadensis
Santolina
  alpina
  Chamæcyparissus
  incana
  viridis
Saponaria
  ocymoides
Saxifraga in var.
Scabiosa
  graminifolia
  Webbiana
Scilla in var.
Sedum in var.
Sempervivum in var.
Senecio
  argenteus
Sideritis
  syriaca
Silene
  alpestris
  maritima plena
  pendula
  Schafta
Sisyrinchium
  grandiflorum
Smilacina
  bifolia
Spiræa
  filipendula plena
Statice
  bellidifolia
Sternbergia
  lutea
Symphyandra
  pendula
Tagetes
  signata
Thalictrum
  minus

Thymus
  citriodorus
  aureus
  lanuginosus
  Serpyllum albus
  vulgaris variegatus
Trifolium
  repens pentaphyllum
Triteleia
  uniflora
Venidium
  calendulaceum
Veronica
  alpina
  Buchanani
  candida
  Chamædrys variegata
  fruticulosa
  gentianoides variegata
  saxatilis
  spicata variegata
Vesicaria
  utriculata
Vicia
  argentea
Vinca
  major variegata
  media
Viola
  cornuta
  lutea
  obliqua striata
  papilionacea
  pedata
  suavis
Waldsteinia
  geoides
  trifolia
Zapania
  nodiflora
Zietenia lavandulæfolia

A Selection of Plants for forming " Carpets" beneath larger Subjects.

Very little reflection suffices to show that a much more beautiful effect may be obtained from a mingling of several distinct types and sizes of vegetation than from an array of any one species or even plants of one size. On the mountain-sides Violets and Lilies of the Valley bloom beneath Hazel and Mezereon, and below the golden showers of the Laburnum, while the forest vegetations reign over all. One of the most successful ways of getting like effects in the rock-garden and on the choice border is by covering the ground with small spreading plants, which heighten the effect of the taller objects placed among them, and indeed often benefit them by keeping the ground in a more open and natural condition. Besides, the highest effect is not possible in any garden where there are bare surfaces in spring or early summer. I should strongly advise the reader to "carpet" his choice mixed border as well as his rock-garden with any dwarf spreading plants he may think suitable. It is obvious that almost all herbaceous plants may be used in this way under certain conditions. A species that might seem a giant compared to some of those in the following list, would form a "carpet" far beneath the branches of forest trees. This list, however, is confined to things of dwarf stature suitable for beds, borders, and the rock-garden. Those requiring plants to form "carpets" in woods may consult the list of plants that will grow in woods and copses. Subjects, however, as large as the Vincas, Common Forget-me-Not, and Creeping Forget-me-Not (*Omphalodes verna*) are included, as they would answer well for placing beneath Rhododendrons and other shrubs, and also in permanent arrangements of the stronger perennials. Not a few plants may be enjoyed in this way better than in any other, as, for example, such as Mentha Requieni and Ionopsidium acaule, which are not usually considered ornamental enough for cultivation, but used as "carpets" in the ground occupied by choice bulbs, or alpine plants, their effect will be of the happiest kind. Annuals are included in this selection in consequence of their freedom of growth and the facility with which they may be raised and grown, for at once forming a turf. Somewhat slow-growing things are also included, as, for example, the Æthionemas, but these could be used with the best effect as surface plants for groups or small beds of neat shrubs, or other subjects that thrive best when planted permanently.

Acæna	Antennaria	Artemisia	Campanula
microphylla	dioica	frigida	hederacea
Æthionema in var.	hyperborea	Asperula	pulla
Agrostis	tomentosa	odorata	Raineri
nebulosa	Anthyllis	Aubrietia in var.	Cenia
Alyssum	montana	Brachycome in var.	turbinata
maritimum	Arabis	Calandrinia	Cerastium in var.
montanum	albida	discolor	Claytonia
Anagallis in var.	Arenaria	grandiflora	sibirica
Anemone	balearica	Campanula	Clintonia
apennina	montana	cæspitosa	elegans
Antennaria	purpurascens	fragilis	pulchella
alpina	verna	garganica	Collinsia in var.

HARDY FLOWERS.

Convolvulus
  althæoides
  mauritanicus
  Soldanella
  tricolor
Cornus
  canadensis
  suecica
Coronilla
  varia
Cosmidium
  filifolium
Crucianella
  stylosa
Dianthus
  deltoides
Draba in var.
Dryas
  Drummondi
  octopetala
Erinus
  alpinus
Erpetion
  reniforme
Fragaria in var.
Galium
  verum
Genista
  prostrata
  sagittalis
Gilia in var.
Godetia in var.
Gypsophila
  dubia
  elegans
  muralis
  prostrata
  viscosa
Hedera in var.
Helianthemum in var.
Helichrysum
  arenarium
Hepatica in var.
Hippocrepis
  comosa
Hutchinsia
  alpina
Hypericum
  humifusum

Ionopsidium
  acaule
Jasione
  humilis
Lamium
  maculatum album
Lathyrus
  tuberosus
Leptinella
  scariosa
Leptosiphon in var.
Linaria
  alpina
  Cymbalaria
  Elatine
  repens
Linnæa
  borealis
Linum
  alpinum
Lithospermum
  prostratum
Lotus
  corniculatus
Lysimachia
  Nummularia
Malcolmia
  maritima
Malva
  campanulata
Medicago
  elegans
Mentha
  Requieni
Mesembryanthemum in var.
Mimulus in var.
Myosotis in var.
Nemophila in var.
Nertera
  depressa
Nierembergia
  rivularis
Nolana in var.
Œnothera
  acaulis
Bistorta
  marginata
  taraxacifolia

Oxalis
  Acetosella
  Bowiei
  corniculata var.
  floribunda
  Valdiviana
Parochetus
  communis
Paronychia
  serpyllifolia
Pentstemon
  procerus
Phlox
  canadensis
  Drummondi
  procumbens
  reptans
  subulata
Platystemon
  californicus
Polygonum
  vaccinifolium
Polypogon
  monspeliensis
Potentilla
  alba
  calabra
  gracilis
  reptans
  verna
Pyrethrum
  Tchiatchewi
Ranunculus
  repens
Reseda
  odorata
Rhodanthe in var.
Sagina
  glabra var. corsica
Santolina
  alpina
Sanvitalia
  procumbens
Saponaria
  calabrica
  ocymoides
Saxifraga in great var.

Schizopetalon
  Walkeri
Sedum in great var.
Selaginella
  denticulata
Sempervivum in var.
Senecio
  argenteus
Sibthorpia
  europæa
Silene
  acaulis
  alpestris
  maritima
  pendula
  Schafta
Smilacina
  bifolia
Specularia
  pentagonia
  speculum
Symphyandra
  pendula
Symphytum
  caucasicum
Thymus
  lanuginosus
Tropæolum in var.
Tunica
Saxifraga
Umbilicus
  chrysanthus
Venidium
  calendulaceum
Veronica
  alpina
  Chamædrys
  fruticulosa
  repens
  saxatilis
  syriaca
Vicia
  argentea
Vinca in var.
Viola in var.
Waldsteinia
  fragarioides
Zapania
  nodiflora

PLANTS WITH SILVERY OR VARIEGATED FOLIAGE. 291

Hardy Plants with Silvery or Variegated Foliage.

Achillea
  ægyptiaca Clavennæ
  Millefolium variegata
  umbellata
Aconitum
  Napellus variegatus
Acorus
  gramineus variegatus
  "japonicus" variegatus
Ægopodium
  Podograria variegata
Agapanthus
  umbellatus variegatus
Agrostis
  vulgaris variegata
Aira
  cæspitosa variegata
Ajuga
  reptans variegata
Alyssum
  olympicum
  saxatile variegatum
  spinosum
Androsace
  lanuginosa
Andryala
  lanata
Antennaria
  alpina
  dioica
  tomentosa
Anthyllis
  montana
Bahia
  lanata

Barbarea
  vulgaris variegata
Bellis in var.
Betonica
  officinalis variegata
Cacalia
  suaveolens variegata
Calluna
  vulgaris
  tomentosa
Calystegia
  sepium variegata
Carduus
  eriophorus
  Marianus
Carex
  muricata variegata
  riparia   ,,
Centaurea
  babylonica
Cerastium
  alpinum
  Biebersteini
  Boissieri
  grandiflorum
  tomentosum
Chamæpeuce
  diacantha
Cheiranthus
  Cheiri variegatus
Chelidonium
  majus variegatum
Chrysanthemum
  Leucanthemum variegatum
Cineraria
  maritima
Colchicum
  autumnale variegatum

Comarum
  palustre variegatum
Convallaria
  majalis variegata
Convolvulus
  Cneorum
  lineatus
Cynanchum
  Vincetoxicum variegatum
Cynara
  horrida
  Scolymus
Dactylis
  glomerata variegata
Dianthus
  barbatus variegatus
Diotis
  maritima
Diplotaxis
  tenuifolia variegata
Dorycnium
  sericeum
Elymus
  arenarius
Epilobium
  hirsutum variegatum
Euphorbia
  Myrsinites
Festuca
  glauca
Fragaria
  chilensis variegata
Fritillaria
  imperialis variegata
Funkia
  albomarginata
  aurea maculata
  lancifolia variegata

Funkia
  ovata variegata
  univittata
Galeobdolon
  luteum variegatum
Geranium
  macrorrhizum variegatum
  pratense variegatum
Glaucium in var.
Glechoma
  hederacea variegata
Helianthemum
  vulgare variegatum
Helichrysum
  Stœchas
Hemerocallis
  fulva variegata
Heracleum
  Sphondylium variegatum
Hoteia
  japonica variegata
Humulus
  Lupulus variegatus
Hypericum
  humifusum variegatum
  tomentosum
Iberis
  semperflorens variegata
Iris
  fœtidissima variegata
  Pseudacorus variegata
Juncus
  conglomeratus variegatus,

Lamium
  album variegatum
  maculatum
Leontodon
  Taraxacum variegatum
Ligularia
  Kæmpferi aureo-maculata
Ligusticum
  Levisticum variegatum
Lilium
  candidum variegatum
Linaria
  Cymbalaria variegata
Luzula sylvatica variegata
Lychnis
  coronaria Flos-Jov's
Lysimachia
  Nummularia aurea
Marrubium
  candidissimum
Matthiola
  tristis variegata
Melissa
  grandiflora variegata
  officinalis variegata

Mentha
  piperita variegata
  rotundifolia variegata
  sylvestris variegata
Molinia
  cærulea variegata
Onopordon in var.
Ophiopogon
  japonicus variegatus
Othonna
  cheirifolia
Ranunculus
  repens variegatus
Reineckia
  carnea variegata
Rosmarinus
  officinalis variegatus
Rubus
  fruticosus variegatus
Rudbeckia
  hirta variegata
  laciniata variegata
Rumex
  Acetosa variegatus
  sanguineus variegatus

Ruta
  graveolens variegata
Salvia
  argentea
  officinalis variegata
Santolina
  alpina
  Chamæcyparissus
  incana
Saponaria
  officinalis variegata
Saxifraga
  granulata variegata
  sarmentosa
  umbrosa variegata
  and the silvery species
Scabiosa
  graminifolia
  Webbiana
Scrophularia
  mellifera variegata
  nodosa variegata
Sedum
  carneum variegatum
  dasyphyllum glaucum
  sempervivoides
  Sieboldi variegatum

Sedum
  Telephium variegatum
Sempervivum
  arachnoideum
  Laggeri
Senecio
  argenteus
  incanus
  Jacobæa variegatus
  uniflorus
Sideritis
  syriaca
Solanum
  Dulcamara variegatus
Solidago
  ambigua variegata
Spiræa
  Ulmaria variegata
Stachys lanata
  sylvatica
Symphytum
  officinale variegatum
Tanacetum
  vulgare variegatum
Veronica
  candida
Vicia
  argentea
Vitis
  heterophylla

HARDY FLOWERS FOR NATURALIZATION. 293

A Selection of Hardy Flowers suitable for Naturalization in Woods, Copses, Hedgerows, on Ruins, Rocky Banks, and in various other wild or half-wild places.*

Acanthus
  mollis
  spinosissimus
Achillea
  asplenifolia
  Eupatorium
Aconitum in var.
Actæa
  racemosa
Adiantum
  pedatum
Adonis
  vernalis
Ajuga
  genevensis
Allium
  ciliatum
  Moly
  neapolitanum
Alstrœmeria
  aurea
Alyssum
  saxatile
  Wiersbeckii
Anchusa
  italica
  paniculata
Anemone
  alpina
  apennina
  fulgens
  japonica
  sylvestris
  trifoliata
Anthericum
  Liliago
  Liliastrum (Paradisia)
Anthyllis
  montana
Antirrhinum
  majus

Aquilegia
  alpina
  cærulèa
  canadensis
Arabis
  albida
Arenaria
  balearica
  graminifolia
  laricifolia
  montana
Artemisia
  anethifolia
  cana
Arum
  Dracunculus
Asclepias
  Cornuti
  Douglasii
Asphodelus
  ramosus
Aster in great var.
Astragalus
  galegiformis
  monspessulanus
  ponticus
Astrantia
  major
Athamanta
  Matthioli
Aubrietia in var.
Baptisia
  australis
Betonica
  grandiflora
Bulbocodium vernum
Calla
  palustris
Campanula
  cæspitosa
  carpatica

  garganica
  grandis
  nobilis
  persicifolia
Centranthus
  ruber
Cerastium in var.
Clematis
  campaniflora
  Flammula
  montana
Colchicum in var.
Coreopsis
  alata
Cornus
  canadensis
Coronilla
  montana
  varia
Corydalis
  nobilis
Crambe
  cordifolia
Crocus in var.
Cyclamen
  hederæfolium
Cypripedium
  spectabile
Delphinium in var.
Dianthus
  neglectus
  petræus
Dicentra
  eximia
  spectabilis
Digitalis in var.
Dodecatheon in var.
Doronicum in var.
Dryas
  Drummondi
Echinops in var.

Epimedium
  pinnatum
Eranthis
  hyemalis
Erigeron
  speciosus
Erinus
  alpinus
Erodium
  Manescavi
Eryngium in var.
Erythronium
  Dens-canis
Eupatorium in var.
Ferula in var.
Ficaria
  grandiflora
Fritillaria in var.
Funkia Sieboldii
Galanthus
  plicatus
Galega
  officinalis
Gaultheria
  procumbens
Genista
  sagittalis
Gentiana
  acaulis
  Andrewsii
  asclepiadea
Geranium
  affine
  cinereum
  ibericum
  platypetalum
Geum
  montanum
Gypsophila in var.
Hedysarum
  obscurum

---

* Full details of the naturalization of hardy exotic flowers will be found in my "Wild Garden."

HARDY FLOWERS.

Helianthemum in var.
Helianthus multiflorus rigidus
Helichrysum arenarium
Helleborus in var.
Helonias bullatus
Hemerocallis in var.
Hepatica in var.
Heracleum in var.
Hesperis matronalis
Heuchera, in var.
Hyacinthus amethystinus
Hypericum, in var.
Iberis in var.
Iris in var.
Lathyrus grandiflorus latifolius
Lavatera in var.
Leucojum in var.
Liatris in var.
Lilium in var.
Linaria Cymbalaria purpurea
Linum alpinum arboreum narbonnense
Lithospermum prostratum
Lunaria biennis

Lupinus polyphyllus
Lychnis Lagascæ
Lythrum diffusum virgatum
Malva in var.
Matthiola in var.
Mertensia virginica
Mimulus in var.
Monarda in var.
Muscari in var.
Myosotis dissitiflora
Narcissus in var.
Nuphar advena
Œnothera in var.
Omphalodes verna
Onobrychis montana
Ononis in var.
Onopordon in var.
Ornithogalum in var.
Orobus in var.
Oxalis Bowiei floribunda
Pæonia in var.
Papaver bracteatum lateritium
Phlomis Herba-venti Russelliana tuberosa

Phlox canadensis paniculata reptans
Physostegia in var.
Phytolacca decandra
Podophyllum peltatum
Polygonum alpinum cuspidatum vaccinifolium
Pontederia cordata
Potentilla in var.
Prunella grandiflora
Pyrethrum roseum serotinum
Ranunculus aconitifolius amplexicaulis spicatus
Rosa in var.
Rudbeckia hirta Newmanni
Salvia argentea
Sanguinaria canadensis
Saponaria ocymoides
Saxifraga in var.
Scilla in var.
Scutellaria alpina
Sedum in var.

Sempervivum in var.
Sida in var.
Silene alpestris Elisabethæ Schafta
Silphium in var.
Solidago in var.
Spiræa Aruncus venusta
Sternbergia lutea
Symphytum bohemicum caucasicum
Telekia speciosa
Teucrium Chamædrys
Thalictrum in var.
Thermopsis fabacea
Tradescantia virginica
Trillium grandiflorum
Trollius in var.
Tulipa in var.
Verbascum Chaixii
Vernonia in var.
Veronica in var.
Vicia in var.
Vinca in var.
Viola in var.
Waldsteinia in var.
Yucca filamentosa flaccida

A Selection of Fragrant Hardy Plants.

In this selection are included annuals and biennials, and also kinds of which it is in the leaves the fragrance is most evident, as in the Balm and Thymes, or in the roots, as in Iris florentina.

Abronia
  umbellata
Acorus
  Calamus
Adenophora
  liliifolia
Allium
  fragrans
  odorum
  suaveolens
Alyssum
  maritimum
Amberboa
  moschata
  odorata
Anthoxanthum
  odoratum
Asclepias
  Cornuti
  Douglasii
Asperula
  odorata
Boussingaultia
  baselloides
Calamintha
  glabella
Cedronella
  cana
  triphylla
Centaurea
  Cyanus
Centranthus
  angustifolius
  ruber
Cheiranthus in var.
Clematis in var.
Convallaria
  majalis
Crambe cordifolia
Crinum
  capense
Cyclamen in var.

Daphne
  Cneorum
Datura
  ceratocaula
Dianthus in great
  var.
Dictamnus
  Fraxinella
Dracocephalum
  altaicense
  moldavicum
Erysimum in var.
Funkia
  grandiflora
Galium
  verum
Gilia
  tricolor
Gymnadenia
  conopsea
Gypsophila
  viscosa
Hedysarum
  coronarium
Hemerocallis
  in var.
Hesperis in var.
Hyacinthus
  orientalis
Hyssopus
  officinalis
Iberis
  odorata
Ionopsidium
  acaule
Iris
  florentina
  germanica
  pallida
  persica
  plicata
  Xiphium

Lathyrus
  odoratus
Lavandula in var.
Leucojum
  vernum
Libertia
  magellanica
Lilium in var.
Lindheimeria
  texana
Lophanthus
  anisatus
  urticæfolius
Lunaria
  rediviva
Lupinus
  affinis
  Cruikshankii
  hybridus
  luteus
  Menziesii
  mutabilis
  polyphyllus
  pubescens
Lychnis
  vespertina
Malcolmia
  maritima
Malva
  moschata
Martynia
  fragrans
  proboscidea
Matthiola in var.
Melilotus
  suaveolens
Melissa in var.
Mentha in var.
Mimulus
  cardinalis
  moschatus

Mirabilis
  Jalapa
  longiflora
Monarda in var.
Moscharia
  pinnatifida
Muscari
  moschatum
  racemosum
Myrica
  Gale
Myrrhis
  odorata
Narcissus
  Jonquilla
  major
  odorus
  poeticus
Nycterinia
  capensis
  selaginoides
Nymphæa
  odorata
Œnothera in var.
Orchis
  pyramidalis
Origanum in var.
Pæonia in var.
Pancratium
  illyricum
  maritimum
Pectis
  angustifolia
Phlox
  paniculata
  pyramidalis
Primula
  elatior
  veris
  vulgaris
Ptarmica in var.
Pyrethrum in var.

296 HARDY FLOWERS.

Reseda odorata	Saponaria officinalis	Schizopetalon Walkeri	Vesicaria utriculata
Rosmarinus officinalis	Scabiosa atropurpurea	Thymus in var. Tussilago fragrans	Viola odorata

A Selection of Herbaceous Plants, etc., that will Grow in the shade of Trees, and in Copses, etc.

Acanthus in var.
Aconitum in var.
Actæa in var.
Anemone in var.
Aquilegia vulgaris
Aralia edulis
 nudicaulis
 racemosa
Arctium in var.
Aristolochia in var.
Artemisia in var.
Arum Dracunculus italicum
Aruudinaria falcata
Asclepias in var.
Asparagus Broussonetti
Asperula odorata
Asphodelus ramosus
Aster in great var.
Astilbe in var.
Astrantia in var.
Athyrium in var.
Balsamita vulgaris
Baptisia in var.
Betonica grandiflora
Borago orientalis
Bromus in great var.

Bupthalmum grandiflorum salicifolium
Calystegia in var.
Campanula, tall kinds
Carex pendula
Centaurea montana
Chelidonium majus
Clematis in var.
Crambe cordifolia
Datisca cannabina
Delphinium in var.
Dentaria in var.
Digitalis in var.
Doronicum Pardalianches plantagineum
Echinops in var.
Elymus arenarius
Epigæa repens
Epilobium angustifolium
Epimedium pinnatum
Equisetum sylvaticum Telmateia
Eryngium alpinum
Eupatorium in var.
Ferula in var.

Fragaria in var.
Fritillaria in var.
Funkia in var.
Galanthus nivalis plicatus
Gaultheria in var.
Geranium in var.
Geum in var.
Gynerium argenteum
Hedysarum in var.
Helianthus in var.
Heuchera in var.
Hieracium boreale corymbosum
Humulus Lupulus
Hypericum in var.
Inula Helenium
Iris in var.
Lamium in var.
Lastrea in var.
Lathyrus in var.
Lavatera in var.
Leucojum in var.
Lilium, vigorous and hardier kinds in variety
Linnæa borealis
Lupinus polyphyllus
Luzula in var.
Lychnis diurna

Lupinus vespertina
Lysimachia in var.
Lythrum in var.
Malva in var.
Medicago in var.
Melilotus in var.
Milium effusum
Mimulus moschatus
Mitchella repens
Monarda in var.
Myosotis in var.
Narcissus in var.
Œnothera, taller and stronger kinds in var.
Omphalodes verna
Onopordon Acanthium
Ornithogalum in var.
Osmunda in var.
Panicum altissimum bulbosum capillare
Phlomis in var.
Phormium tenax
Physostegia in var.
Polygonatum in var.
Polygonum alpinum cuspidatum
Polypodium in var.

SELECTION OF HARDY PERENNIALS. 297

Polystichum in var.	Sanguinaria canadensis	Smilacina stellata	Uvularia grandiflora
Pyrola in var.	Saxifraga cordifolia	Spiræa in var.	Valeriana dioica
Rubus in var.	crassifolia	Symphytum in var.	officinalis
Rudbeckia californica	Geum umbrosa	Thalictrum in var.	Phu pyrenaica
hirta	Scilla in var.	Tradescantia virginica	Veratrum in var.
laciniata	Sedum	Trollius in var.	Vernonia in var.
triloba	spectabile	Tulipa in var.	Vinca in var.
Ruscus aculeatus	Smilacina bifolia	Tussilago fragrans	Viola in var.
racemosus			

A Selection of Hardy Perennials, etc., suitable for Exhibition when Grown in Pots.*

Acæna microphylla	Arabis albida	Callirhoe involucrata	Coronilla minima
Achillea ægyptiaca	blepharophylla	Caltha palustris plena	montana varia
Clavennæ	Armeria cephalotes	Camassia esculenta	Corydalis nobilis
Ptarmica plena serrata plena	Asclepias tuberosa	Campanula in great var.	Crocosmia aurea
Æthionema in var.	Asphodelus luteus	Centranthus ruber	Cyclamen in var.
Alyssum alpestre	Astragalus monspessulanus	Cheiranthus Cheiri, fl. pl.	Cypripedium in var.
montanum olympicum saxatile	Aubrietia in var.	Marshalli	Daphne
Amaryllis Belladonna	Begonia Veitchii	Chrysobactron Hookeri	Cneorum Delphinium in var.
Andromeda fastigiata tetragona	Betonica grandiflora	Convallaria majalis	Dentaria in var. Dianthus in var.
Androsace in var.	Brodiæa coccinea	Convolvulus mauritanicus	Dicentra cucullaria
Anemone in great var.	grandiflora Bryanthus	Coreopsis auriculata`	spectabilis Digitalis
Anthyllis montana	erectus Bulbocodium	lanceolata tenuifolia	purpurea in var. Thapsi
Antirrhinum majus	vernum Calceolaria	Coronilla iberica	Dodecatheon in var.
Aquilegia in var.	Kellyana	juncea	Draba in var.

* The way in which herbaceous and alpine plants are generally shown has frequently been a source of regret to me, knowing, as I do, that no plants in existence are capable of forming more brilliantly attractive and neat specimens. It is quite common to see such poor ragged specimens shown even by large growers of these plants, that one might suppose the prize had been offered for the worst specimens that could be found. (See chapter ix. p. 27 in Part I.)

Dracocephalum in var.
Dryas
  Drummondi
  octopetala
Edraianthus
  Pumilio
Epimedium in var.
Erica in var.
Erinus alpinus
Erodium
  alpinum
  macradenum
  Manescavi
  petræum
  Reichardi
Eryngium in var.
Erysimum
  ochroleucum
  pumilum
Ficaria
  ranunculoides
  plena
Fritillaria in var.
Gaillardia in var.
Genista
  prostrata
  sagittalis
  tinctoria
Gentiana in var.
Globularia in var.
Hedysarum
  obscurum
Helichrysum
  arenarium
Helleborus in great variety
Hesperis
  matronalis, fl. pl.
Hoteia
  japonica
Houstonia
  cærulea
Hutchinsia
  alpina
Hypericum
  nummularium
  verticillatum
Iberidella
  rotundifolia

Iberis in var.
Iris in var.
Leucanthemum
  alpinum
  lacustre
Leucojum
  vernum
Liatris in var.
Libertia
  magellanica
Lilium in var.
Linaria
  alpina
Linum
  alpinum
  arboreum
  flavum
  narbonnense
Lithospermum
  prostratum
Lychnis in var.
Lysimachia
  Nummularia
Lythrum
  alatum
  Salicaria var.
    roseum
  virgatum
Mazus
  Pumilio
Melittis
  Melissophyllum
Menziesia
  cærulea
  empetriformis
  polifolia
Mertensia
  virginica
Michauxia
  campanuloides
Monarda in var.
Muscari in var.
Myosotis in var.
Narcissus in var.
Omphalodes
  Luciliæ
  verna
Onobrychis
  montana

Ononis
  arvensis albus
  rotundifolia
Onosma
  taurica
Ophrys in var.
Orchis in var.
Orobus
  cyaneus
  vernus
Ourisia
  coccinea
Oxalis in var.
Pæonia in var.
Pancratium
  illyricum
Paradisia Liliastrum
Parochetus
  communis
Pentstemon in var.
Petrocallis
  pyrenaica
Phlox, both the tall and the alpine kinds in var.
Pinguicula
  grandiflora
Platycodon
  autumnale
  grandiflorum
Plumbago
  Larpentæ
Polygala
  calcarea
  Chamæbuxus
Polygonum
  vaccinifolium
Potentilla in var.
Primula in var.
Prunella
  grandiflora
Puschkinia
  scilloides
Pyrethrum
  carneum in great var.
Pyxidanthera
  barbulata

Ranunculus in var.
Rhexia
  virginica
Rudbeckia
  hirta
  speciosa
Salvia patens
Santolina
  Chamæcyparissus
  incana
Saponaria
  cæspitosa
  ocymoides
Saxifraga in var.
Scabiosa
  graminifolia
  Webbiana
Scilla in var.
Scutellaria
  alpina
  lupulina
Sedum
  kamtschaticum
  pulchellum
  Sieboldi
  spectabile
  spurium
Silene
  acaulis
  alpestris
  Elisabethæ
  maritima plena
  pennsylvanica
  Pumilio
  virginica
Sisyrinchium
  grandiflorum
Smilacina
  bifolia
Soldanella in var.
Sparaxis
  pulcherrima
Spigelia
  marilandica
Spiræa
  Filipendula plena
  palmata

AQUATIC AND MARSH PLANTS.

Spiræa
  venusta
Statice
  incana
  latifolia
  speciosa
  tatarica
Symphytum
  bohemicum
  caucasicum

Thermopsis
  fabacea
  lanceolata
Thlaspi
  latifolium
Tradescantia
  virginica and vars.
Trillium
  grandiflorum

Triteleia
  uniflora
Tritoma in var.
Trollius in var.
Tropæolum
  speciosum
Tulipa in var.
Verbascum
  Chaixii

Veronica in var.
Vicia
  argentea
Viola in var.
Vittadinia
  triloba
Zephyranthes
  Atamasco

A Selection of Ornamental Aquatic Plants.

Acorus
  Calamus
  gramineus
Actinocarpus
  Damasonium
Alisma in var.
Aponogeton
  distachyon
Aster
  Tripolium
Butomus
  umbellatus
Calla æthiopica
  palustris
Caltha
  palustris
Carex
  paniculata
  pendula
  Pseudo-cyperus
Cyperus
  longus

Epilobium
  hirsutum
Equisetum in var.
Glyceria
  aquatica
Hippuris
  vulgaris
Hottonia
  palustris
Houttuynia
  cordata
Hydrocharis
  Morsus-ranæ
Iris
  Pseudacorus
  sibirica
Limnanthemum
  nymphæoides
Lobelia
  Dortmanna
Lysimachia
  thyrsiflora

Lythrum
  Salicaria
Menyanthes
  trifoliata
Myosotis
  palustris
Myriophyllum in var.
Nuphar
  advena
  Kalmiana
  lutea
  pumila
Nymphæa
  alba
  minor
  odorata
Œnanthe
  fistulosa
Orontium
  aquaticum
Osmunda in var.

Phormium
  tenax
Polygonum
  amphibium
  Hydropiper
Pontederia
  cordata
Ranunculus
  aquaticus
  Lingua
Rumex
  Hydrolapathum
Sagittaria
  sagittifolia fl.pl.
Scirpus
  lacustris
Sparganium in var.
Stratiotes
  aloides
Thalia
  dealbata
Typha, all the kinds

A Selection of Plants thriving in Marshy or Boggy Ground.

Butomus
  umbellatus
Calla
  palustris
Caltha in var.
Carex
  pendula
Chrysobactron
  Hookeri

Coptis
  trifoliata
Cornus
  canadensis
Crinum
  capense
Cypripedium
  spectabile
Drosera in var.

Epilobium
  hirsutum
Epipactis
  palustris
Equisetum in var.
Eriophorum in var.
Eupatorium in var.
Ficaria in var.

Galax
  aphylla
Gentiana
  Pneumonanthe
Gunnera
  scabra
Helonias
  bullatus
Hibiscus in var.

300   HARDY FLOWERS.

Hydrocotyle bonariensis	Linnæa borealis	Petasites vulgaris	Sagittaria in var. Sarracenia
Iris graminea	Lobelia syphilitica	Phormium tenax	purpurea Spigelia
Monnieri ochroleuca	Lycopodium in var.	Pinguicula in var.	marilandica
Pseudacorus sibirica	Lysimachia thyrsiflora	Primula Munroi	Swertia perennis
Leucanthemum lacustre	Lythrum in var. Narcissus in var.	sikkimensis Pyrethrum	Symplocarpus fœtidus
Leucojum æstivum	Nierembergia rivularis	serotinum Rhexia	Tofieldia in var. Tradescantia
Hernandezii	Orchis in var.	virginica	virginica

Herbaceous and Alpine Plants, etc., that may with advantage be Raised from Seed.

Of course nearly all plants may be raised from seed, but in many cases it is undesirable to do so, from the plants being easier to increase in other ways, and in some cases it is very difficult to raise them. Therefore this list chiefly comprises those it is expedient for the amateur to raise in this way.

Acanthus, scarce kinds	Brodiæa coccinea	Coronilla, all Corydalis, good and	Eremostachys, all Erigeron in var.
Achillea in var.	Calamintha	rare kinds	Erinus in var.
Aconitum rare kinds	glabella Callirhoe, good	Crambe cordifolia	Eriogonum in var. Erodium, good
Adenophora in var.	kinds	Craspedia	kinds
Æthionema, all	Camassia	macrocephala	Eryngium, rare
Allium, rare kinds	esculenta	Crinum	kinds
Alyssum in var.	Campanula in var.	capense	Erysimum
Anchusa in var.	Carlina	Crucianella	ochroleucum
Anemone in var.	acanthifolia	stylosa	pumilum
Antirrhinum in var.	Cassia marilandica	Delphinium in var. Dentaria in var.	Erythræa littoralis
Aquilegia, all	Centaurea in var.	Dianthus in var.	Euphorbia
Arabis in var.	Cerastium, good	Dicentra in var.	Myrsinites
Arenaria in var.	and rare kinds	Digitalis in var.	Ferula in var.
Armeria, rarer kinds	only Chelone in var.	Dorycnium sericeum	Ficaria grandiflora
Aster, good and rare kinds	Chrysobactron Hookeri	Draba in var. Dracocephalum in	Fritillaria, rare kinds
Astragalus in var.	Cistus, rare kinds	var.	Gaillardia in var.
Athamanta Matthioli	Commelyna cœlestis	Dryas Drummondi	Galega in var. Gaura
Aubrietia, all	Convolvulus, rare	Echinacea in var.	Lindheimeri
Baptisia, all	kinds	Echinops, good dis-	Genista, all
Bellium, all	Coreopsis in var.	tinct kinds.	Geranium, good
Betonica grandiflora	Coris monspeliensis	Epilobium, rare kinds	kinds Geum in var.

DWARF PERENNIAL AND ALPINE PLANTS.

Globularia
Gypsophila in var.
Hedysarum, good kinds
Helenium in var.
Helianthemum in var.
Helichrysum arenarium
Heracleum in var.
Hesperis in var.
Heuchera, good kinds
Hibiscus in var.
Hippocrepis comosa
Horminum pyrenaicum
Hutchinsia alpina
Hypericum in var.
Iberidella rotundifolia
Iberis in var.
Inula, good kinds
Iris, rare and good kinds
Isopyrum thalictroides
Jasione, all
Kitaibelia vitifolia
Lathyrus, all
Leucanthemum, in var.
Liatris in var.

Lilium, good rare kinds
Linaria in var.
Linum in var.
Lobelia, herbaceous kinds in var.
Lunaria, all
Lupinus in var.
Lychnis in var.
Lythrum, rarer kinds
Malva in var.
Matthiola semperflorens
Melianthus major
Meum in var.
Michauxia campanuloides
Mimulus in var.
Molopospermum cicutarium
Monarda, good kinds
Morina longifolia
Myosotis in var.
Nierembergia in var.
Odontarrhena carsinum
Œnothera in var.
Onobrychis, good kinds
Ononis, good kinds

Onosma taurica
Orobus in var.
Oxytropis, all
Papaver, all
Parnassia, all
Pentstemon in var.
Petrocallis pyrenaica
Peucedanum in variety
Phlomis in var.
Phlox, rare species
Physostegia, all
Phyteuma in var.
Phytolacca decandra
Platycodon in var.
Polemonium rare kinds
Polygonum, good and rare kinds
Potentilla in var.
Primula in var.
Prunella, best sorts
Pyrethrum in var.
Ranunculus, good rare kinds.
Rhaponticum in var.
Rheum, best kinds
Rudbeckia in var.
Salvia in var.
Santolina in var.
Saponaria in var.

Saxifraga in var.
Scabiosa, best kinds
Scutellaria in var.
Sedum in var.
Sempervivum, rare kinds
Seseli in var.
Sidalcea malvæflora
Sida incarnata
Silene in var.
Spiræa, rare kinds
Statice in var.
Teucrium, good rare kinds
Thermopsis in var.
Thlaspi latifolium
Trifolium, good kinds
Trollius, rarer kinds
Tropæolum in var.
Tunica Saxifraga
Verbascum in var.
Veronica in var.
Vesicaria utriculata
Vicia, good kinds
Viola, rare kinds
Vittadinia triloba

List of Dwarf Hardy Perennial and Alpine Plants, with Fern-like or graceful Leaves, and suitable for Association with those distinguished by beauty of Flower in borders, the rock-garden, etc.

Acæna Millefolium
Achillea ægyptiaca
Anthriscus fumarioides
Asparagus tenuifolius

Astragalus pannosus
Athamanta Matthioli
Centaurea dealbata
Coreopsis tenuifolia

Corydalis lutea
Dicentra eximia
Erodium carnifolium Manescavi

Erodium trichomanefolium
Geranium anemonæfolium
Helleborus fœtidus

Isopyrum
  thalictroides
Melianthus
  major
Meum
  adonidifolium
  athamanti-
    cum
	Molopospermum
	  cicutarium
	Peucedanum
	  involucratum
	  longifolium
	  Petteri
	Polemonium
	  cæruleum
		Pyrethrum
		  achilleæfolium
		  tanacetoides
		Seseli
		  elatum
		  globiferum
		  gummiferum
			Spiræa
			  Filipendula
			Tanacetum vulgare
			  crispum
			Thalictrum
			  fœtidum
			  minus

A Selection of Hardy Perennials affording the finest effects in the Picturesque or "Sub-tropical" Garden.

Acanthus in var.
Aralia
  edulis
  nudicaulis
Astilbe
  rivularis
Arundo
  Donax
  ,, versicolor
Bambusa in var.
Bocconia
  cordata
Carex
  paniculata
  pendula
Carduus
  eriophorus
	Carlina
	  acaulis
	Cassia
	  marilandica
	Centaurea
	  babylonica
	Crambe
	  cordifolia
	Cynara
	  Scolymus
	Datisca
	  cannabina
	Echinops
	  ruthenicus
	Eryngium
	  alpinum
	  amethystinum
		Gynerium
		  argenteum
		Gunnera
		  scabra
		Helianthus
		  orgyalis
		Hemerocallis
		  fulva
		Heracleum in var.
		Inula
		  Helenium
		Melianthus
		  major
		Meum
		  athamanticum
		Molopospermum
		  cicutarium
			Morina
			  longifolia
			Panicum
			  bulbosum
			  virgatum
			Phytolacca
			  decandra
			Polygonum
			  cuspidatum
			Rhaponticum
			  cynaroides
			  pulchrum
			Rheum in var.
			Statice
			  latifolia
			Tritoma in var.
			Yucca in var.

A Selection of Hardy Plants of Vigorous Habit and Distinct Character suited for Planting in Semi-wild places, in Pleasure-grounds, or near Wood-walks.

Acanthus in var.
Althæa in var.
Aralia
  canescens
  edulis
  nudicaulis
  spinosa
Arum
  Dracunculus
Asclepias
  Cornuti
Asparagus
  Broussoneti
	Astilbe
	  rivularis
	  rubra
	Arundo
	  Donax
	  ,, versicolor
	  Phragmites
	Bambusa
	  falcata
	Bocconia
	  cordata
	Buphthalmum
	  speciosum
		Callisace
		  dahurica
		Carex
		  pendula
		  paniculata
		Carduus
		  eriophorus
		Centaurea
		  babylonica
		Crambe
		  cordifolia
		  juncea
			Cucurbita
			  perennis
			Cynara Scolymus
			Datisca
			  cannabina
			Dipsacus
			  sylvestris
			Echinops
			  ruthenicus
			Elymus
			  arenarius
			Erianthus
			  Ravennæ

A SELECTION OF ORNAMENTAL GRASSES.

Eryngium
  alpinum
  amethystinum
Ferula in var.
Gunnera
  scabra
Helianthus
  lætiflorus
  Maximiliana
  multiflorus
  ,,   fl. pl.
  occidentalis
  orgyalis
  rigidus
Hemerocallis
  fulva
Heracleum in var.
Hibiscus
  moscheutos
  palustris
  roseus

Inula
  Helenium
Lavatera
  arborea
  thuringiaca
  unguiculata
Ligularia
  macrophylla
Molopospermum
  cicutarium
Morina
  longifolia
Mulgedium
  alpinum
  Plumieri
Onopordon
  Acanthium
Pæonia in var.
Panicum
  bulbosum
Papaver
  bracteatum

Petasites
  vulgaris
Phytolacca
  decandra
Poa
  aquatica
Polygonatum
  multiflorum
Polygonum
  cuspidatum
Rhaponticum
  cynaroides
  pulchrum
  scariosum
Rheum in var.
Rudbeckia
  digitata
  laciniata
  californica
Rumex
  Hydrolapathum
Silphium in var.

Silybum
  eburneum
  marianum
Spiræa
  Aruncus
Statice
  latifolia
Tanacetum
  vulgare var.
  crispum
Thalictrum in var.
Tritoma in var.
Veratrum
  album
Verbascum in var.
Verbesina
  persicifolia
Vernonia
  noveboracensis
Yucca in var.

A Selection of Ornamental Grasses.

Mixed borders, groups, and beds of the finer perennials may be much improved by being varied with tufts of the finer ornamental grasses.

Agrostis
  nebulosa
  spica-venti
  Steveni
Arundo
  conspicua
  Donax
  ,,   versi-
    color
  festucoides
  Phragmites
Bambusa in var.
Elymus
  arenarius
  condensatus
Erianthus
  Ravennæ
Gynerium
  argenteum and
  its vars.

Calamagrostis
  argentea
Poa
  aquatica
  fertilis
Saccharum
  ægyptiacum
  cylindricum
  Maddenii
Stipa
  pennata
Zea
  Mays in var.
Andropogon
  argenteus
  bombycinus
  formosus
  Sorghum
  strictus
  squarrosus

Chloropsis
  Blanchardiana
Gymnothrix
  latifolia
Holcus
  saccharatus
Erianthus
  strictus
  violascens
Chloris
  myriostachys
Panicum
  bulbosum
  altissimum
  capillare
  gongyloides
  miliaceum
  maximum
  virgatum

Panicum
  violaceum
Penicillaria
  spicata
Sorghum
  cernuum
  halepense
  melanocarpum
  nankinense
  tataricum
Tripsacum
  dactyloides
  monostachyum
Milium
  nigricans
  multiflorum
  effusum
Bromus
  brizopyroides

HARDY FLOWERS

Briza	Pennisetum	Stipa	Echinochloa
gracilis	longistylum	capillata	Zenkowski
geniculata	Piptatherum	Chascolytrum	Paspalum
maxima	multiflorum	erectum	elegans
rufiberbis	Setaria	Leptochloa	Phyllostachys
Hordeum	germanica	gracilis	bambusoides
jubatum			

Selection of Alpine and Rock Plants of Prostrate or Drooping Habit suited for placing so that they may Droop over the Brows of Rocks and Like Positions.

Alyssum	Cerastium	Fragaria	Lysimachia
montanum	tomentosum	indica	Nummularia
saxatile	Clematis (the new	Galium	Malva
Androsace	varieties of	verum	campanulata
lanuginosa	the lanugi-	Genista	Medicago
Antirrhinum	nosa section,	prostrata	falcata
rupestre	and many	sagittalis	Œnothera
Arabis	species).	tinctoria	acaulis
albida	Convolvulus	Gypsophilas (seve-	missouriensis
procurrens	arvensis	ral)	taraxacifolia
purpurea	mauritanicus	Helianthemum (in	Ononis
Artemisia	Cornus	variety)	arvensis
frigida	canadensis	Hippocrepis	albus
Astragalus	Coronilla	comosa	Orobus
monspessulanus	iberica	Hypericum	roseus
Aubrietias in var.	varia	humifusum	Pentstemon
Boussingaultia	Cyananthus	Iberis	procerus
baselloides	lobatus	corifolia	Phlox
Callirhoë	Dianthus	sempervirens	reptans
involucrata	deltoides (and	Tenoreana	subulata
pedata	others)	Lathyrus	Plumbago
Calystegia	Diotis	grandiflorus	Larpentæ
dahurica	maritima	latifolius	Polygonum
pubescens pl.	Dracocephalum	,, albus	complexum
Campanula	argunense	tuberosus	vaccinifolium
Barrelieri	Dryas	Linaria	Potentilla
cæspitosa	octopetala	alpina	alpestris
,, alba	Empetrum	Cymbalaria	calabra
fragilis	nigrum	Linnæa	Hopwoodiana
garganica	Epigæa	borealis	McNabiana
muralis	repens	Lithospermum	Tonguei
rotundifolia	Erica	prostratum	verna (and nu-
,, alba	carnea	Lotus	merous vars.
Cerastium	Euphorbia	corniculatus	and hybrids)
Biebersteinii	Myrsinites	Lysimachia	Rubus
grandiflorum		nemorum	arcticus

Salix	Saxifraga	Thymus	Vicia
lanata	sarmentosa	Serpyllum	argentea
reticulata	Scabiosa	Trifolium	Cracca
Santolina	graminifolia	repens	Vinca
incana	Webbiana	pentaphyllum	herbacea
Saponaria	Sedum	Tropæolum	major
ocymoides	Ewersii	polyphyllum	minor
Saxifraga	kamtschaticum	speciosum	Zapania
biflora	reflexum		nodiflora
ceratophylla	Sieboldi	Tunica	Zauschneria
hypnoides	spurium	Saxifraga	californica
oppositifolia	Thymus	Veronica prostrata	Zietenia
and vars.	lanuginosus	taurica	lavandulæfolia

Trailers, Climbers, etc., for Covering Bowers, Trellises, Railings, Old Trees, Stumps, Rockwork, Banks, etc. etc.

Ampelopsis	Clematis	Clematis	Menispermum
bipinnata	Flammula	Viticella alba	canadense
cordata	florida	,, venosa	virginicum
hederacea	,, pl.	Cynanchum	Passiflora
tricuspidata	,, Standishi	acutum	cærulea
Apios	Fortunei	monspeliacum	Periploca
tuberosa	Francofurtensis	Hablitzia	græca
Aristolochia	Hendersoni	tamnoides	Smilax hardy kinds
Sipho	insulensis	Hedera (all the	Tamus
tomentosa	Jackmani	finer varieties	communis
Asparagus	lanuginosa	of Ivy, both	Vitis
Broussoneti	montana	green and va-	æstivalis
Boussingaultia	nivea	riegated)	amooriensis
baselloides	patens Amelia	Jasminum	cordifolia
Calystegia	,, Helena	nudiflorum	heterophylla
dahurica	,, insignis	officinale	variegata
pubescens	,, Louisa	revolutum	Isabella
pleno	,, mon-	Lathyrus in var.	Labrusca
Cissus	strosa	Lonicera	laciniosa
orientalis	,, Sophia	Caprifolium	riparia
pubescens	,, violacea	confusa	Sieboldi
Clematis	pubescens	flava	vinifera
azurea grandi-	rubro-violacea	japonica	apiifolia
flora	Shillingii	Periclymenum	vulpina
calycina	Sieboldi	Lycium	Wistaria
campaniflora	tubulosa	europæum	sinensis and
elliptica	Viticella		vars.

x

Selection of Alpine and Rock Plants for Growing on Old Walls, Ruins, Chalk-Pits, Stony Banks, etc.

Acæna
  microphylla
Achillea
  tomentosa
Adiantum
  Capillus-Veneris
Alyssum
  montanum
  saxatile
  spinosum
Antennaria
  dioica minima
Antirrhinum
  majus
  Orontium
  rupestre
Arabis
  albida
  arenosa
  blepharophylla
  (old mossy
  walls)
  lucida
  ,, variegata
  petræa (old
  mossy walls)
Arenaria
  balearica
  cæspitosa
  ciliata
  graminifolia
  montana
  verna
Asperula
  cynanchica
Asplenium
  Adiantum-nigrum
  fontanum
  germanicum
  lanceolatum
  Ruta-muraria
  Trichomanes
  and vars.
  viride

Astragalus
  monspessulanus
Aubrietia, all the
  vars.
Bellium
  bellidioides
  crassifolium
  minutum
Campanula
  Barrelieri
  cæspitosa
  fragilis
  garganica
  rotundifolia
Centranthus
  ruber
  ,, albus
  ,, coccineus
Ceterach
  officinarum
Cheiranthus
  Cheiri
  ,, pleno in
  var.
Coronilla
  minima
  varia
Corydalis
  lutea
Cotyledon
  Umbilicus
Dianthus
  cæsius
  deltoides
  monspessulanus
  petræus
Draba
  aizoides
  bœtica
Erinus
  alpinus
Erodium
  romanum (old
  walls)
  Reichardi

Gypsophila
  muralis
  prostrata
Helianthemum
  (many of
  the varieties
  might be
  grown upon
  old ruins,
  stony banks,
  &c.)
Iberis in var.
Ionopsidium
  acaule
Iris
  germanica and
  vars.
  pumila
Koniga
  maritima
Linaria
  Cymbalaria
Linum
  alpinum
Lychnis
  alpina
  lapponica
Malva
  campanulata
Matthiola
  tristis
  garden kinds in
  var.
Ononis
Petrocallis
  pyrenaica
Polypodium
  vulgare
Reseda
  odorata
Sagina
  procumbens
Santolina
  incana
Saponaria
  ocymoides

Saxifraga
  bryoides
  cæsia
  crustata
  cuscutæformis
  diapensioides
  Hostii
  intacta
  lingulata
  longifolia
  pectinata
  pulchella
  retusa
  Rhei
  Rocheliana
  rosularis
  sarmentosa
Sedum
  acre
  ,, variegatum
  Aizoon
  album
  anglicum
  brevifolium
  cæruleum
  dasyphyllum
  elegans
  Ewersii
  farinosum
  glaucum
  kamtschaticum
  multiceps
  pulchellum
  sempervivoides
  sexangulare
  sexfidum
  spurium
Sempervivum
  arachnoideum
  arenarium
  calcareum
  globiferum
  Heuffellii
  hirtum
  montanum

Sempervivum piliferum soboliferum tectorum Silene acaulis alpestris	Silene Schafta Symphyandra pendula Thlaspi alpestre	Thymus citriodorus Tunica Saxifraga Umbilicus chrysanthus	Veronica fruticulosa saxatilis Vesicaria utriculata

List of Ferns that may be Grown with Advantage away from the Fernery Proper.

Even should any of these thrive better in shade, it is usually easy to secure this for them in groups by wood-walks, and they may be associated with hardy flowers in many positions.

Adiantum pedatum Asplenium Adiantum nigrum Filix - fœmina and vars. fontanum germanicum Halleri lanceolatum monanthemum Ruta-muraria septentrionale Trichomanes viride Ceterach officinarum Cystopteris alpina fragilis	Cheilanthes odora Cyrtomium caryotideum falcatum Dennstædtia punctilobula Diplazium thelypteroides Lastrea Filix-mas and vars. Goldieana ,, assurgens intermedia marginalis noveboracensis atrata erythrosora opaca Standishii	Lomaria magellanica (in warm districts) Onoclea sensibilis Osmunda cinnamomea Claytoniana gracilis regalis ,, cristata spectabilis Platyloma atropurpurea Polypodium hexagonopterum Phegopteris vulgare Polystichum acrostichoides	Polystichum aculeatum angulare vestitum venustum Pteris aquilina Scolopendrium vulgare and vars. Struthiopteris germanica pennsylvanica Woodsia hyperborea ilvensis polystichoides Woodwardia areolata aspera japonica orientalis radicans

x 2

HARDY FLOWERS CLASSED ACCORDING TO THEIR COLOURS.

For various obvious reasons it is desirable to have a colour classification, so to speak, of hardy plants.

A Selection of Hardy Plants with White Flowers.

Achillea
  Clavennæ
  Ptarmica pl.
  serrata pl.
  umbellata
Aconitum
  Napellus albus
Actæa
  spicata
Allium
  ciliatum
  neapolitanum
  ursinum
Androsace
  Chamæjasme
Anemone
  alba
  alpina
  japonica
  ,, Honorine Jobert
  narcissiflora
  nemorosa
  sylvestris
  thalictroides
  trifolia
  vitifolia
Antennaria
  dioica
Anthemis
  nobilis plena
Antirrhinum
  majus albus
Aquilegia
  vulgaris alba
Arabis in var.
Arenaria
  montana
  verna

Argemone
  grandiflora
Asperula
  odorata
Asphodelus
  ramosus
Astilbe
  rivularis
  rubra
Astragalus
  hypoglottis
  albus
Bellium in var.
Calla
  æthiopica
  palustris
Campanula
  cæspitosa alba
  carpatica alba
  glomerata alba
  lactiflora
  lamiifolia
  latifolia alba
  Medium alba
  nitida
  persicifolia alba
  pyramidalis alba
  rotundifolia alba
  Trachelium alba
  urticæfolia alba
Cardamine
  trifolia
Centranthus
  ruber albus
Cerastium in var.

Chrysanthemum
  Leucanthemum sinense, numerous white-flowered vars.
Clematis
  erecta
  Flammula
  montana
Crambe
  cordifolia
  maritima
Crocus, white vars.
Dianthus
  Caryophyllus, white vars.
  deltoides albus
  plumarius albus
Dryas
  octopetala
Epilobium
  angustifolium album
Erinus
  alpinus albus
Erythronium
  Dens-canis album
Eupatorium
  ageratoides
  aromaticum
Fritillaria
  Meleagris alba
Funkia
  grandiflora
Galanthus
  nivalis
  plicatus

Galega
  officinalis alba
Gentiana
  asclepiadea alba
Geranium
  pratense alba
  sylvaticum album
Hepatica
  triloba alba
Hesperis
  matronalis alba plena
Hutchinsia
  alpina
Iberis
  corifolia
  correæfolia
  saxatilis
  semperflorens
Iris
  florentina
  germanica alba
  pumila alba
Isopyrum
  thalictroides
Jeffersonia
  diphylla
Lamium
  maculatum album
Lathyrus
  latifolius albus
Leucanthemum
  lacustre
Leucojum
  æstivum
  vernum

HARDY PLANTS WITH WHITE FLOWERS. 309

Libertia
  magellanica
Lilium
  Browni
  candidum
  japonicum
  longiflorum
  speciosum al-
    bum
  Washingtonia-
    num
Linum
  monogynum
  perenne album
Lupinus
  polyphyllus al-
    bus
Lychnis
  vespertina fl. pl.
Malva
  moschata alba
Michauxia
  campanuloides
Muscari
  botryoides alba
Myosotis
  sylvatica alba
Narcissus
  angustifolius
  poeticus
Nierembergia
  rivularis
Nymphæa
  alba

Œnothera
  marginata
  speciosa
  taraxacifolia
Ononis
  arvensis alba
Oxalis
  Acetosella
Pæonia in var.
Pancratium
  illyricum
Paradisia
  Liliastrum
Phlox, numerous
  white hy-
  brids
  subulata alba
Platycodon
  grandiflorum
  album
Potentilla
  alba
Primula
  involucrata
  Munroi
  nivea
  Veitchii alba
Prunella
  grandiflora alba
Pyrethrum
  carneum album
  Parthenium
  fl. pl.
  serotinum

Ranunculus
  aconitifolius
  plenus
  alpestris
  amplexicaulis
Sagittaria
  sagittifolia
  plena
Sanguinaria
  canadensis
Saxifraga
  affinis
  ajugæfolia
  cæspitosa
  ceratophylla
  diapensioides
  granulata, fl. pl.
  hirta
  hypnoides
  longifolia
  palmata
  pectinata
  Rocheliana
  Stansfieldii
Scilla
  bifolia alba
  campanulata
    alba
  nutans alba
Sedum
  album
Silene
  alpestris
  maritima

Silene
  Zawadskii
Sisyrinchium
  grandiflorum
  album
Smilacina
  bifolia
Spiræa
  Aruncus
  Filipendula
  Ulmaria
Statice
  Limonium ai-
    bum
Stevia
  ovata
Thlaspi
  latifolium
Tradescantia
  virginica alba
Trillium
  grandiflorum
Triteleia
  uniflora
Verbascum
  phœniceum
  album
Vinca
  minor alba
Viola
  cornuta alba
Zephyranthes
  Atamasco
  candida

A Selection of Hardy Plants with Red, Crimson, Scarlet, or Pinkish Flowers.

Acæna
  microphylla
Achillea
  asplenifolia
  Millefolium ro-
    seum
Æthionema in var.
Allium
  roseum
Althæa
  rosea and vars.

Amaryllis
  Belladonna
Androsace
  carnea
Anemone
  coronaria
  fulgens
  hortensis
  japonica
  pavonina

Anomatheca
  cruenta
Antennaria
  rosea
Anthyllis
  montana
Antirrhinum
  majus
Apocynum
  androsæmifo-
    lium

Aquilegia
  canadensis
  Skinneri
  truncata
Arabis
  blepharophylla
Armeria
  cephalotes
  vulgaris rosea
Asclepias
  tuberosa

Aster
  coccineus
  Novæ Angliæ
  roseus
Astragalus
  monspessula-
  nus
Begonia
  Veitchii
Bellis
  hortensis rubra
Betonica
  grandiflora
  officinalis
Brodiæa
  coccinea
Bryanthus
  erectus
Butomus
  umbellatus
Calandrinia
  umbellata
Callirhoë
  digitata
  involucrata
Calystegia
  pubescens pl.
Colchicum in var.
Coronilla
  varia
Cortusa
  Matthioli
Daphne
  Cneorum
Delphinium
  nudicaule
Dianthus in var.
Dicentra
  eximia
  spectabilis
Dictamnus
  Fraxinella
Digitalis
  purpurea

Dodecatheon, all
Epilobium
  angustifolium
Erica in var.
Erinus
  alpinus
Erodium
  Manescavi
Erythyræa
  littoralis
Fuchsia in var.
Geranium
  Lambertianum
  sanguineum
Geum
  coccineum
Gladiolus in var.
Hedysarum
  coronarium
  obscurum
Helianthemum in
  var.
Hepatica
  triloba rubra
Hibiscus
  militaris
  moscheutos
  roseus
Lathyrus in var.
Lavatera
  Olbia
  thuringiaca
Liatris in var.
Lilium
  chalcedonicum
  tenuifolium
  Thunbergia-
  num
  tigrinum
  umbellatum
Linum
  grandiflorum
Lobelia
  Tupa

Lunaria
  biennis
Lychnis in var.
Lythrum in var.
Malva in var.
Matthiola in var.
Menziesia
  empetriformis
Mirabilis
  Jalapa
Modiola
  geranioides
Monarda in var.
Ononis
  arvensis
  rotundifolia
Ourisia
  coccinea
Oxalis in var.
Pæonia in var.
Papaver in var.
Pelargonium
  Endlicheria-
  num
Pentstemon
  barbatus
  gentianoides
Phlox in var.
Phygelius
  capensis
Potentilla in var.
Primula
  cortusoides
  japonica
  viscosa
  Veitchii
Pulmonaria in var.
Pyrethrum
  carneum in var.
Rhexia
  virginica

Saponaria
  cæspitosa
  calabrica
  ocymoides
  officinalis
Saxifraga
  biflora
  cordifolia
  crassifolia
  lingulata
  oppositifolia
  purpurascens
Schizostylis
  coccinea
Sedum
  Ewersii
  pulchellum
  Sieboldi
  spectabile
  spurium
Silene
  Armeria
  Elisabethæ
  pendula
  pennsylvanica
  Pumilio
  Schafta
  virginica
Sparaxis
  pulcherrima
Spigelia
  marilandica
Spiræa
  palmata
  venusta
Symphytum
  bohemicum
Tigridia
  Pavonia
Tritoma in var.
Tropæolum
  speciosum
Tulipa in var

HARDY PLANTS WITH YELLOW FLOWERS. 311

A Selection of Hardy Plants, with Blue, Bluish, or Purplish Flowers

Aconitum in var.
Adenophora in var.
Agapanthus
  umbellatus
Allium
  azureum
Anchusa in var.
Anemone
  apennina
  blanda
  Pulsatilla
Aquilegia in var.
Aster
  alpinus
  altaicus
  Amellus
  lævis
  Shortii
  turbinellus
Aubrietia in var.
Baptisia
  australis
  exaltata
Borago
  orientalis
Brodiæa
  congesta
  grandiflora
Camassia
  esculenta
Campanula in great variety
Catananche
  cærulea

Centaurea
  Cyanus
  montana
Cichorium
  Intybus
Clematis in var.
Commelyna
  cœlestis
Crocus in var.
Cyananthus
  lobatus
Delphinium in great var.
Dracocephalum in var.
Echinops
  ruthenicus
Edrianthus
  Pumilio
Erigeron
  speciosum
Eryngium
  alpinum
  amethystinum
Galega
  orientalis
Gentiana in fine var.
Geranium
  affine
  ibericum
  pratense
  sylvaticum
Globularia in var.

Hepatica
  angulosa
  triloba
Hyacinthus
  amethystinus
  orientalis in var
Iris in fine var.
Linaria
  alpina
  purpurea
Linum in var.
Lithospermum in var.
Lobelia in var.
Lupinus in var.
Mertensia
  virginica
Mulgedium
  alpinum
  Plumieri
Muscari in var.
Myosotis in var.
Nepeta
  Mussini
Omphalodes
  Luciliæ
  verna
Ophiopogon
  spicatus
Orobus
  cyaneus
  flaccidus
  vernus
Parochetus
  communis

Pentstemon
  glaber
  Jaffrayanus
Phyteuma in var.
Pinguicula in var.
Platycodon
  autumnale
  grandiflorum
Plumbago
  Larpentæ
Polemonium in var.
Polygala
  calcarea
Prunella in var.
Pulmonaria
  angustifolia
Puschkinia
  scilloides
Salvia
  patens
Scilla in var.
Stokesia
  cyanea
Symphytum
  caucasicum
Tradescantia
  virginica
Trichonema
  Bulbocodium
Columnæ
Verbena
  venosa
Veronica in fine var.
Vicia in var.
Vinca in var.

A Selection of Hardy Plants with Yellow Flowers in Various Shades, or in which Yellow Predominates.

Achillea
  ægyptiaca
Eupatorium
  tomentosa
Adonis
  vernalis

Allium
  Moly
Alstrœmeria
  aurantiaca
Alyssum in var.

Anemone
  palmata
  ranunculoides
  sulphurea
Asphodelus
  luteus

Barbarea
  vulgaris plena
Bupthalmum
  grandiflorum
  salicifolium

Calceolaria
　Kellyana
Cassia
　marilandica
Cheiranthus
　Cheiri
　Marshallii
Chelidonium
　grandiflorum
　japonicum
Chlora
　perfoliata
Chrysobactron
　Hookeri
Cistus
　formosus
　ocymoides
　Tuberaria
Coreopsis in var.
Coronilla
　iberica
　juncea
　minima
　montana
Corydalis in var.
Crepis
　aurea
Crocosmia
　aurea
Crocus in var.
Dondia
　Epipactis
Doronicum in var.
Draba
　aizoides
　Aizoon
　ciliaris
　cuspidata
Dryas
　Drummondi

Epimedium
　pinnatum
Eranthis
　hyemalis
Erysimum
　ochroleucum
Ficaria
　grandiflora
　ranunculoides
　plena
Fritillaria
　imperialis lutea
Gaillardia in var.
Genista in var.
Geum
　montanum
Helenium
　autumnale
　Hoopesii
Helianthemum in
　　var.
Helianthus in var.
Helichrysum
　arenarium
Hemerocallis · in
　　var.
Hypericum in var.
Inula in var.
Iris
　De Bergii
　flavescens
　germanica, yellow var.
　Monnieri
　ochroleuca
　Pseudacorus
　xiphioides, vars.
　Xiphium
Lathyrus
　pratensis

Limnanthemum
　nymphæoides
Lilium
　excelsum
　monadelphum
Linaria
　vulgaris
Linum
　arboreum
　campanulatum
　flavum
Lotus
　corniculatus
Lupinus
　luteus
　Menziesii
Lysimachia
　angustifolia
　Nummularia
Medicago
　falcata
Narcissus in fine
　　var.
Nuphar
　lutea
Œnothera in var.
Onosma
　taurica
Orobus
　aurantius
Oxalis
　Valdiviana
Papaver
　alpinum flaviflorum
　croceum
　nudicaule
Phlomis
　fruticosa
　Russelliana
Potentilla in var.

Primula
　Auricula lutea
　elatior
　Palinuri
　sikkimensis
　vulgaris
Ranunculus in var
Rudbeckia in var.
Saxifraga
　Cymbalaria
Scutellaria
　lupulina
Sedum acre
　kamtschaticum
Senecio in var.
Silphium in var.
Solidago in var.
Statice
　Fortunei
Sternbergia
　lutea
Thermopsis
　fabacea
　lanceolata
Trollius in var.
Tropæolum
　polyphyllum
Tulipa in var.
Verbascum
　Chaixii
　Thapsus
Vesicaria
　utriculata
Viola
　lutea
　pubescens
　tricolor in var.
Waldsteinia
　fragarioides
　geoides
　trifolia

INDEX

TO

THE NATURAL ORDERS OF THE PLANTS NAMED IN PART II.

Acæna	Rosaceæ,	Rose	Family.
Acanthus	Acanthaceæ,	Acanthus	,,
Achillea	Compositæ,	Aster	,,
Acis	Amaryllidaceæ,	Amaryllis	,,
Aconitum	Ranunculaceæ,	Buttercup	,,
Acorus	Araceæ,	Arum	,,
Adenophora	Campanulaceæ,	Harebell	,,
Adonis	Ranunculaceæ,	Buttercup	,,
Æthionema	Cruciferæ,	Wallflower	,,
Agapanthus	Liliaceæ,	Lily	,,
Agrostemma	Caryophyllaceæ,	Pink	,,
Ajuga	Labiatæ,	Salvia	,,
Alfredia	Compositæ,	Aster	,,
Alisma	Alismaceæ,	Water Plantain	,,
Allium	Liliaceæ,	Lily	,,
Alstrœmeria	Amaryllidaceæ,	Amaryllis	,,
Althæa	Malvaceæ,	Mallow	,,
Alyssum	Cruciferæ,	Wallflower	,,
Amaryllis	Amaryllidaceæ,	Amaryllis	,,
Ammobium	Compositæ,	Aster	,,
Amsonia	Apocynaceæ,	Periwinkle	,,
Anchusa	Boraginaceæ,	Borage	,,
Andromeda	Ericaceæ,	Heath	,,
Androsace	Primulaceæ,	Primrose	,,
Andryala	Compositæ,	Aster	,,
Anemone	Ranunculaceæ,	Buttercup	,,
Anomatheca	Iridaceæ,	Iris	,,
Antennaria	Compositæ,	Aster	,,
Anthemis	,,	,,	,,
Anthericum	Liliaceæ,	Lily	,,
Anthyllis	Leguminosæ,	Pea	,,
Antirrhinum	Scrophulariaceæ,	Snapdragon	,,
Aphyllanthes	Liliaceæ	Lily	,,
Apios	Leguminosæ,	Pea	,,

Apocynum	Apocynaceæ,	Periwinkle	Family
Aponogeton	Alismaceæ,	Water Plantain	,,
Aquilegia	Ranunculaceæ,	Buttercup	,,
Arabis	Cruciferæ,	Wallflower	,,
Aralia	Araliaceæ,	Ginseng	,,
Arctostaphylos	Ericaceæ,	Heath	,,
Arenaria	Caryophyllaceæ,	Pink	,,
Argemone	Papaveraceæ,	Poppy	,,
Aristolochia	Aristolochiaceæ,	Birthwort	,,
Armeria	Plumbaginaceæ,	Thrift	,,
Aronicum	Compositæ,	Aster	,,
Artemisia	,,	,,	,,
Arum	Araceæ,	Arum	,,
Arundo	Arundinaceæ,	Reed	,,
Asarum	Aristolochiaceæ,	Birthwort	,,
Asclepias	Asclepiadaceæ,	Silkweed	,,
Asparagus	Liliaceæ,	Lily	,,
Asperula	Rubiaceæ,	Woodruff	,,
Asphodelus	Liliaceæ,	Lily	,,
Aster	Compositæ,	Aster	,,
Astilbe	Saxifragaceæ,	Saxifrage	,,
Astragalus	Leguminosæ,	Pea	,,
Astrantia	Umbelliferæ,	Fennel	,,
Athamanta	,,	,,	,,
Aubrietia	Cruciferæ,	Wallflower	,,
Bahia	Compositæ,	Aster	,,
Bambusa	Gramineæ,	Grass	,,
Baptisia	Papilionaceæ,	Poppy	,,
Barnardia	Liliaceæ,	Lily	,,
Begonia	Begoniaceæ,	Begonia	,,
Bellis	Compositæ,	Aster	,,
Betonica	Labiatæ,	Salvia	,,
Bocconia	Papaveraceæ,	Poppy	,,
Borago	Boraginaceæ,	Borage	,,
Boussingaultia	Basellaceæ,	Basella	,,
Briza	Gramineæ,	Grass	,,
Brodiæa	Liliaceæ,	Lily	,,
Bromelia	Bromeliaceæ,	Pine Apple	,,
Bryanthus	Ericaceæ,	Heath	,,
Buphthalmum	Compositæ,	Aster	,,
Bulbocodium	Melanthaceæ,	Meadow Saffron	,,
Butomus	Alismaceæ,	Water Plantain	,,
Calamagrostis	Gramineæ,	Grass	,,
Calamintha	Labiatæ,	Salvia	,,
Calandrinia	Portulaceæ,	Purslane	,,
Calceolaria	Scrophulariaceæ,	Snapdragon	,,
Calla	Araceæ,	Arum	,,
Calliprora	Liliaceæ,	Lily	,,
Callirhoe	Malvaceæ,	Mallow	,,
Calluna	Ericaceæ,	Heath	,,

INDEX TO THE NATURAL ORDERS. 315

Calopogon	Orchidaceæ,	Orchid	Family
Caltha	Ranunculaceæ,	Buttercup	,,
Calypso	Orchidaceæ,	Orchid	,,
Calystegia	Convolvulaceæ,	Bindweed	,,
Camassia	Liliaceæ,	Lily	,,
Campanula	Campanulaceæ,	Harebell	,,
Cardamine	Cruciferæ,	Wallflower	,,
Carduus	Compositæ,	Aster	,,
Carlina	,,	,,	,,
Cassia	Leguminosæ,	Pea	,,
Catananche	Compositæ,	Aster	,,
Centaurea	,,	,,	,,
Centranthus	Valerianaceæ,	Valerian	,,
Cerastium	Caryophyllaceæ,	Pink	,,
Cheiranthus	Cruciferæ,	Wallflower	,,
Chelidonium	Papaveraceæ,	Poppy	,,
Chelone	Scrophulariaceæ,	Snapdragon	,,
Chimaphila	Pyrolaceæ,	Wintergreen	,,
Chrysanthemum	Compositæ,	Aster	,,
Chrysocoma	,,	,,	,,
Chrysopsis	,,	,,	,,
Cichorium	,,	,,	,,
Cineraria	,,	,,	,,
Cirsium	,,	,,	,,
Clematis	Ranunculaceæ,	Buttercup	,,
Colchicum	Melanthaceæ,	Meadow Saffron	,,
Commelina	Commelinaceæ,	Spiderwort	,,
Convallaria	Liliaceæ,	Lily	,,
Convolvulus	Convolvulaceæ,	Bindweed	,,
Coptis	Ranunculaceæ,	Buttercup	,,
Coreopsis	Compositæ,	Aster	,,
Coris	Primulaceæ,	Primrose	,,
Cornus	Cornaceæ,	Dogwood	,,
Coronilla	Leguminosæ,	Pea	,,
Cortusa	Primulaceæ,	Primrose	,,
Corydalis	Fumariaceæ,	Fumitory	,,
Cotyledon	Crassulaceæ,	Stonecrop	,,
Cousinia	Compositæ,	Aster	,,
Crambe	Cruciferæ,	Wallflower	,,
Crepis	Compositæ,	Aster	,,
Crinum	Amaryllidaceæ,	Amaryllis	,,
Crocosmia	Iridaceæ,	Iris	,,
Crocus	,,	,,	,,
Crucianella	Rubiaceæ,	Woodruff	,,
Cucurbita	Cucurbitaceæ,	Cucumber	,,
Cyananthus	Polemoniaceæ,	Phlox	,,
Cyclamen	Primulaceæ,	Primrose	,,
Cynara	Compositæ,	Aster	,,
Cypripedium	Orchidaceæ,	Orchid	,,
Daphne	Thymelaceæ,	Garland-flower	,,

Datisca	Datiscaceæ,	Datisca	Family
Delphinium	Ranunculaceæ,	Buttercup	,,
Dentaria	Cruciferæ,	Wallflower	,,
Dianthus	Caryophyllaceæ,	Pink	,,
Diapensia	Diapensiaceæ,	Phlox	,,
Dicentra	Fumariaceæ,	Fumitory	,,
Dictamnus	Rutaceæ,	Rue	,,
Digitalis	Scrophulariaceæ,	Snapdragon	,,
Diotis	Compositæ,	Aster	,,
Diphylleia	Berberidaceæ,	Barberry	,,
Diplopappus	Compositæ,	Aster	,,
Dodecatheon	Primulaceæ,	Primrose	,,
Dondia	Umbelliferæ,	Fennel	,,
Doronicum	Compositæ,	Aster	,,
Draba	Cruciferæ,	Wallflower	,,
Dracocephalum	Labiatæ,	Salvia	,,
Dryas	Rosaceæ,	Rose	,,
Dyckia	Bromeliaceæ,	Pine Apple	,,
Echinacea	Compositæ,	Aster	,,
Echinops	,,	,,	,,
Edraianthus	Campanulaceæ,	Harebell	,,
Empetrum	Empetraceæ,	Crowberry	,,
Epigæa	Ericaceæ,	Heath	,,
Epilobium	Onagraceæ	Evening Primrose	,,
Epimedium	Berberidaceæ,	Barberry	,,
Epipactis	Orchidaceæ	Orchid	,,
Equisetum	Equisetaceæ,	Mare's Tail	,,
Eranthis	Ranunculaceæ	Buttercup	,,
Eremostachys	Labiatæ,	Salvia	,,
Erica	Ericaceæ,	Heath	,,
Erigeron	Compositæ,	Aster	,,
Erinus	Scrophulariaceæ,	Snapdragon	,,
Eritrichium	Boraginaceæ,	Borage	,,
Erodium	Geraniaceæ,	Crane's Bill	,,
Erpetion	Violaceæ,	Violet	,,
Eryngium	Umbelliferæ,	Fennel	,,
Erysimum	Cruciferæ,	Wallflower	,,
Erythræa	Gentianaceæ,	Gentian	,,
Erythronium	Liliaceæ,	Lily	,,
Eupatorium	Compositæ,	Aster	,,
Euphorbia	Euphorbiaceæ,	Spurge	,,
Ferula	Umbelliferæ,	Fennel	,,
Ficaria	Ranunculaceæ,	Buttercup	,,
Fragaria	Rosaceæ,	Rose	,,
Frankenia	Frankeniaceæ,	Sea Heath	,,
Fumaria	Fumariaceæ,	Fumitory	,,
Funkia	Liliaceæ,	Lily	,,
Fuchsia	Onagraceæ,	Evening Primrose	,,
Gaillardis	Compositæ,	Aster	,,
Galanthus	Amaryllidaceæ,	Amaryllis	,,

INDEX TO THE NATURAL ORDERS.

Galatella	Compositæ,	Aster	Family
Galega	Leguminosæ,	Pea	,,
Gaultheria	Ericaceæ,	Heath	,,
Gaura	Onagraceæ,	Evening Primrose	,,
Genista	Leguminosæ,	Pea	,,
Gentiana	Gentianaceæ,	Gentian	,,
Geranium	Geraniaceæ,	Crane's Bill	,,
Geum	Rosaceæ,	Rose	,,
Gillenia	,,	,,	,,
Gladiolus	Iridaceæ,	Iris	,,
Glechoma	Labiatæ,	Salvia	,,
Globularia	Globulariaceæ,	Globularia	,,
Gnaphalium	Compositæ,	Aster	,,
Gymnadenia	Orchidaceæ,	Orchid	,,
Gynerium	Gramineæ,	Grass	,,
Gypsophila	Caryophyllaceæ,	Pink	,,
Hedysarum	Leguminosæ,	Pea	,,
Helenium	Compositæ,	Aster	,,
Helianthemum	Cistaceæ,	Sunrose	,,
Helianthus	Compositæ,	Aster	,,
Helichrysum	,,	,,	,,
Heliopsis	,,	,,	,,
Helleborus	Ranunculaceæ,	Buttercup	,,
Helonias	Melanthaceæ,	Meadow Saffron	,,
Hemerocallis	Liliaceæ,	Lily	,,
Heracleum	Umbelliferæ,	Fennel	,,
Hesperis	Cruciferæ,	Wallflower	,,
Heuchera	Saxifragaceæ,	Saxifrage	,,
Hibiscus	Malvaceæ,	Mallow	,,
Hieracium	Compositæ,	Aster	,,
Hippocrepis	Leguminosæ,	Pea	,,
Hoteia	Rosaceæ,	Rose	,,
Hottonia	Primulaceæ,	Primrose	,,
Houstonia	Cinchonaceæ,	Madder	,,
Humulus	Cannabinaceæ,	Nettle	,,
Hutchinsia	Cruciferæ,	Wallflower	,,
Hyacinthus	Liliaceæ,	Lily	,,
Hypericum	Hypericaceæ,	St. John's-Wort	,,
Iberidella	Cruciferæ,	Wallflower	,,
Iberis	,,	,,	,,
Inula	Compositæ,	Aster	,,
Iris	Iridaceæ,	Iris	,,
Isopyrum	Ranunculaceæ,	Buttercup	,,
Jasione	Campanulaceæ,	Harebell	,,
Jeffersonia	Berberidaceæ,	Barberry	,,
Kitaibelia	Malvaceæ,	Mallow	,,
Lachenalia	Liliaceæ,	Lily	,,
Lactuca	Compositæ,	Aster	,,
Lamium	Labiatæ,	Salvia	,,
Lathyrus	Leguminosæ,	Pea	,,

Lavatera	Malvaceæ,	Mallow	Family
Leiophyllum	Ericaceæ,	Heath	,,
Leontopodium	Compositæ,	Aster	,,
Leptinella	,,	,,	,,
Leucanthemum	,,	,,	,,
Leucojum	Amaryllidaceæ,	Amaryllis	,,
Lewisia	Mesembryaceæ,	Ice Plant	,,
Liatris	Compositæ,	Aster	,,
Libertia	Iridaceæ,	Iris	,,
Lilium	Liliaceæ,	Lily	,,
Limnocharis	Alismaceæ,	Water Plantain	,,
Linaria	Scrophulariaceæ,	Snapdragon	,,
Lindelofia	Boraginaceæ,	Borage	,,
Linnæa	Caprifoliaceæ,	Honeysuckle	,,
Linosyris	Compositæ,	Aster	,,
Linum	Linaceæ,	Flax	,,
Lithospermum	Boraginaceæ,	Borage	,,
Lobelia	Lobeliaceæ,	Lobelia	,,
Loiseleuria	Ericaceæ,	Heath	,,
Lophanthus	Labiatæ,	Salvia	,,
Lotus	Leguminosæ,	Pea	,,
Lunaria	Cruciferæ,	Wallflower	,,
Lupinus	Leguminosæ,	Pea	,,
Lychnis	Caryophyllaceæ,	Pink	,,
Lycopodium	Lycopodiaceæ,	Club-moss	,,
Lysimachia	Primulaceæ,	Primrose	,,
Lythrum	Lythraceæ,	Loosestrife	,,
Malva	Malvaceæ,	Mallow	,,
Mazus	Scrophulariaceæ,	Snapdragon	,,
Meconopsis	Papaveraceæ,	Poppy	,,
Medicago	Leguminosæ,	Pea	,,
Melianthus	Zygophyllaceæ,	Honeysuckle	,,
Melissa	Labiatæ,	Salvia	,,
Molittis	,,	,,	,,
Mentha	,,	,,	,,
Menyanthes	Gentianaceæ,	Gentian	,,
Menziesia	Ericaceæ,	Heath	,,
Merendera	Melanthaceæ,	Meadow Saffron	,,
Mertensia	Boraginaceæ,	Borage	,,
Meum	Umbelliferæ,	Fennel	,,
Michauxia	Campanulaceæ,	Harebell	,,
Mimulus	Scrophulariaceæ,	Snapdragon	,,
Mirabilis	Nyctaginaceæ,	Marvel of Peru	,,
Mitchella	Rubiaceæ,	Madder	,,
Modiola	Malvaceæ,	Mallow	,,
Mœhringia	Caryophyllaceæ,	Pink	,,
Molopospermum	Umbelliferæ,	Fennel	,,
Monarda	Labiatæ,	Salvia	,,
Morina	Dipsacaceæ,	Teasel	,,
Mulgedium	Compositæ,	Aster	,,

Muscari	Liliaceæ,	Lily	Family
Myosotis	Boraginaceæ,	Borage	,,
Myrrhis	Umbelliferæ,	Fennel	,,
Narcissus	Amaryllidaceæ,	Amaryllis	,,
Nepeta	Labiatæ,	Salvia	,,
Nertera	Cinchonaceæ,	Madder	,,
Nierembergia	Solanaceæ,	Potato	,,
Nuphar	Nymphæaceæ,	Water-lily	,,
Nuttallia	Rosaceæ,	Rose	,,
Nymphæa	Nymphæaceæ,	Water-lily	,,
Œnothera	Onagraceæ,	Evening Primrose	,,
Omphalodes	Boraginaceæ,	Borage	,,
Onobrychis	Leguminosæ,	Pea	,,
Ononis	,,	,,	,,
Onosma	Boraginaceæ,	Borage	,,
Ophiopogon	Liliaceæ,	Lily	,,
Ophrys	Orchidaceæ,	Orchid	,,
Opuntia	Cactaceæ,	Cactus	,,
Orchis	Orchidaceæ,	Orchid	,,
Ornithogalum	Liliaceæ,	Lily	,,
Orobus	Leguminosæ,	Pea	,,
Orontium	Araceæ,	Arum	,,
Othonna	Compositæ,	Aster	,,
Ourisia	Scrophulariaceæ,	Snapdragon	,,
Oxalis	Oxalidaceæ,	Wood Sorrel	,,
Oxytropis	Leguminosæ,	Pea	,,
Pæonia	Ranunculaceæ,	Buttercup	,,
Pancratium	Amaryllidaceæ,	Amaryllis	,,
Panicum	Gramineæ,	Grass	,,
Papaver	Papaveraceæ,	Poppy	,,
Paradisia	Liliaceæ,	Lily	,,
Parnassia	Droseraceæ,	Sundew	,,
Parochetus	Leguminosæ,	Pea	,,
Paronychia	Illecebraceæ,	Paronychia	,,
Pelargonium	Geraniaceæ,	Crane's Bill	,,
Pentstemon	Scrophulariaceæ,	Snapdragon	,,
Petasites	Compositæ,	Aster	,,
Petrocallis	Cruciferæ,	Wallflower	,,
Phlomis	Labiatæ,	Salvia	,,
Phlox	Polemoniaceæ,	Phlox	,,
Phormium	Liliaceæ,	Lily	,,
Phygelius	Scrophulariaceæ,	Snapdragon	,,
Physalis	Solanaceæ,	Potato	,,
Physostegia	Labiatæ,	Salvia	,,
Phyteuma	Campanulaceæ,	Harebell	,,
Phytolacca	Phytolaccaceæ,	Pokeweed	,,
Pinguicula	Lentibulariaceæ,	Butterwort	,,
Pisum	Leguminosæ,	Pea	,,
Plumbago	Plumbaginaceæ,	Thrift	,,
Podophyllum	Berberidaceæ,	Barberry	,,

Polemonium	Polemoniaceæ,	Phlox	Family
Polygala	Polygalaceæ,	Milkwort	,,
Polygonatum	Liliaceæ,	Lily	,,
Polygonum	Polygonaceæ,	Dock	,,
Pontederia	Pontederaceæ,	Pickerel-weed	,,
Potentilla	Rosaceæ,	Rose	,,
Primula	Primulaceæ,	Primrose	,,
Prunella	Labiatæ,	Salvia	,,
Pulmonaria	Boraginaceæ,	Borage	,,
Puschkinia	Liliaceæ,	Lily	,,
Pyrethrum	Compositæ,	Aster	,,
Pyrola	Ericaceæ,	Heath	,,
Pyxidanthera	Polemoniaceæ,	Phlox	,,
Ramondia	Cyrtandraceæ,	Potato	,,
Ranunculus	Ranunculaceæ,	Buttercup	,,
Rhaponticum	Compositæ,	Aster	,,
Rheum	Polygonaceæ,	Dock	,,
Rhexia	Melastomaceæ,	Melastoma	,,
Rhododendron	Ericaceæ,	Heath	,,
Rosa	Rosaceæ,	Rose	,,
Rudbeckia	Compositæ,	Aster	,,
Rumex	Polygonaceæ,	Dock	,,
Sagina	Caryophyllaceæ,	Pink	,,
Salix	Amentiferæ,	Willow	,,
Salvia	Labiatæ,	Salvia	,,
Sanguinaria	Papaveraceæ,	Poppy	,,
Santolina	Compositæ,	Aster	,,
Saponaria	Caryophyllaceæ,	Pink	,,
Sarracenia	Sarraceniaceæ,	{ American Pitcher Plant	,,
Saxifraga	Saxifragaceæ,	Saxifrage	,,
Scabiosa	Dipsaceæ,	Teasel	,,
Schivereckia	Cruciferæ,	Wallflower	,,
Schizostylis	Iridaceæ,	Iris	,,
Scilla	Liliaceæ,	Lily	,,
Scolymus	Compositæ,	Aster	,,
Scutellaria	Labiatæ,	Salvia	,,
Sedum	Crassulaceæ,	Stonecrop	,,
Sempervivum	,,	,,	,,
Senecio	Compositæ,	Aster	,,
Serapias	Orchidaceæ,	Orchid	,,
Seseli	Umbelliferæ,	Fennel	,,
Sida	Malvaceæ,	Mallow	,,
Sidalcea	,,	,,	,,
Sideritis	Labiatæ,	Salvia	,,
Silene	Caryophyllaceæ,	Pink	,,
Silphium	Compositæ,	Aster	,,
Silybum	,,	,,	,,
Sisyrinchium	Iridaceæ,	Iris	,,
Smilacina	Liliaceæ,	Lily	,,

INDEX TO THE NATURAL ORDERS.

Soldanella	Primulaceæ,	Primrose	Family.
Solidago	Compositæ,	Aster	,,
Sorghum	Gramineæ,	Grass	,,
Sparaxis	Iridaceæ,	Iris	,,
Spigelia	Loganaceæ,	Worm-grass	,,
Spiræa	Rosaceæ,	Rose	,,
Stachys	Labiatæ,	Salvia	,,
Statice	Plumbaginaceæ,	Thrift	,,
Stevia	Compositæ,	Aster	,,
Stipa	Gramineæ,	Grass	,,
Stokesia	Compositæ,	Aster	,,
Stylophorum	Papaveraceæ,	Poppy	,,
Swertia	Gentianaceæ,	Gentian	,,
Symphyandra	Campanulaceæ,	Harebell	,,
Symphytum	Boraginaceæ,	Borage	,,
Tanacetum	Compositæ,	Aster	,,
Teucrium	Labiatæ,	Salvia	,,
Thalictrum	Ranunculaceæ,	Buttercup	,,
Thermopsis	Leguminosæ,	Pea	,,
Thlaspi	Cruciferæ,	Wallflower	,,
Thymus	Labiatæ,	Salvia	,,
Tigridia	Iridaceæ,	Iris	,,
Trachelium	Campanulaceæ,	Harebell	,,
Tradescantia	Commelinaceæ,	Spiderwort	,,
Trichonema	Iridaceæ,	Iris	,,
Trientalis	Primulaceæ,	Primrose	,,
Trifolium	Leguminosæ,	Pea	,,
Trillium	Liliaceæ,	Lily	,,
Triteleia	,,	,,	,,
Tritoma	,,	,,	,,
Trollius	Ranunculaceæ,	Buttercup	,,
Tropæolum	Tropæolaceæ,	Nasturtium	,,
Tulipa	Liliaceæ,	Lily	,,
Tunica	Caryophyllaceæ,	Pink	,,
Umbilicus	Crassulaceæ,	Stonecrop	,,
Uvularia	Melanthaceæ,	Meadow Saffron	,,
Vaccinium	Ericaceæ,	Heath	,,
Valeriana	Valerianaceæ,	Valerian	,,
Veratrum	Melanthaceæ,	Meadow Saffron	,,
Verbascum	Scrophulariaceæ,	Snapdragon	,,
Verbena	Verbenaceæ,	Verbena	,,
Vernonia	Compositæ,	Aster	,,
Veronica	Scrophulariaceæ,	Snapdragon	,,
Vesicaria	Cruciferæ,	Wallflower	,,
Vicia	Leguminosæ,	Pea	,,
Vieusseuxia	Iridaceæ,	Iris	,,
Villarsia	Gentianaceæ,	Gentian	,,
Vinca	Apocynaceæ,	Periwinkle	,,
Viola	Violaceæ,	Violet	,,
Vittadinia	Compositæ,	Aster	,,

Wahlenbergia	Campanulaceæ,	Harebell	Family.
Waldsteinia	Rosaceæ,	Rose	,,
Wulfenia	Scrophulariaceæ,	Snapdragon	,,
Xerophyllum	Liliaceæ,	Lily	,,
Yucca	,,	,,	,,
Zapania	Verbenaceæ,	Verbena	,
Zauschneria	Onagraceæ,	Evening Primrose	
Zephyranthes	Liliaceæ,	Lily	,,
Zietenia	Labiatæ,	Salvia	,,

A CONCISE GLOSSARY

OF

THE DESCRIPTIVE TERMS USED IN THIS WORK.

Achene, a hard dry one-seeded superior seed-vessel.
Acuminate, drawn out into a long point.
Acute, sharp; forming an angle less than a right angle at the tip.
Adpressed, pressed close to anything.
Albumen, nutritious matter contained in the seed to feed the young plant.
Alternate, placed successively on the opposite side of an axis; opposed to opposite.
Amplexicaul, clasping the stem with the base.
Annular, forming a ring.
Anther, the part of the stamen which contains the pollen.
Apex, the end furthest from the point of attachment.
Apical, at or relating to the apex.
Apiculate, having a very small hard point at the end.
Approximate, close together.
Arborescent, growing into a tree.
Arching, curved into the form of an arch.
Arcuate, curved so as to form a considerable part of a circle.
Arrowshaped (Sagittate), shaped like the head of an arrow.
Ascending, curving upwards into a vertical position.
Attenuate, narrowing gradually to a point.
Auricled, having *auricles*, or appendages at the base of the leaves.
Awn, a long-pointed bristlelike appendage, as the beard of many kinds of grasses.
Awned, having awns.
Axil, the upper angle formed by the union of the stem and leaf.
Axillary, placed in an axil.
Axis, the line passing through the centre of anything; the common stalk of the flowers in a spikelet of Grasses, etc.
Base, the end nearest to the point of attachment.
Beak, a long pointed projection.
Bearded, having long hair like a beard.
Berry, a pulpy fruit containing several seeds.
Bifid, divided half-way down into two parts.

Bipartite, divided nearly to its base into two parts.
Bipinnate, when the divisions of a pinnate leaf are themselves pinnate.
Bipinnatifid, when the divisions of a pinnatifid leaf are themselves pinnatifid.
Biternate, when the divisions of a ternate leaf are themselves ternate.
Bracteoles, minute bracts.
Bracts, small leaves somewhat different from the others, seated on the peduncles.
Bulb, a leaf-bud with fleshy scales, usually placed underground.
Bulbiferous, bearing bulbs.
Bulbils, small bulbs, produced in the axils of the leaves of some plants, as in *Lilium bulbiferum*.
Bulbous, having radical bulbs.
Cæsius, with a fine pale blue bloom.
Cæspitose, in close dwarf tufts.
Calyx, the outer whorl of leaf-like organs forming the flower.
Campanulate, bell-shaped.
Capillary, like very slender threads.
Capitate or *Capitular*, growing in heads or close clusters.
Capsule, a dry usually many-seeded seed-vessel.
Carpel, the divisions of the ovary or capsule.
Catkin, a spike of closely crowded flowers of one sex, in which the perianths are replaced by bracts.
Chaffy, covered with minute membranous scales.
Channelled, hollowed somewhat like a gutter.
Cilia, hairs placed like eyelashes on the edge of anything.
Ciliate, with cilia.
Circinate, rolled up from the top towards the base like the unfolding leaves of ferns.
Clavate, clubshaped.
Claw, the narrow base of a petal.
Clawed, having a claw.
Cleft, deeply cut, but not to the midrib.
Clubshaped, a body which is slender at the base and gradually thickens upwards.
Cluster, a close head of flowers.
Cohering, the attachment together of similar parts, as the petals forming a monopetalous corolla.
Compound, formed of many similar parts, as the leaves of many acacias.
Compressed, flattened laterally.
Conical, narrowing to a point from a circular base.
Connate, when two similar parts, as leaves, are slightly connected round the stem.
Connivent, converging.
Converging, their points gradually approaching.
Convolute, rolled together lengthwise.
Cordate, with two rounded lobes at the base, heart-shaped.
Coriaceous, leathery, tough.
Corm, a fleshy bulb-like, solid, not scaly, underground stem.
Corolla, the whorl of floral leaves between the calyx and stamens, usually coloured, called petals.
Corymb, a raceme with the peduncles becoming gradually shorter as they approach the top, so that all the flowers are nearly on a level.

Corymbose, in the form of a corymb.
Cotyledons, the seed lobes, often forming the first leaves of the plant.
Crenate, with rounded marginal teeth.
Crenulate, minutely crenate.
Crested, having an appendage like a crest.
Cruciform, four parts, as petals, arranged so as to form a cross as in *Arabis*.
Cuneate, like a wedge, but attached by its point.
Cuspidate, abrupt, but with a little point at the end.
Cuticle, the external skin.
Cylindrical, nearly in the form of a cylinder.
Cyme, inflorescence formed of a terminal flower, beneath which are lateral branches each having a terminal flower and lateral branches again similarly dividing, and so on.
Cymose, arranged in a cyme.
Deciduous, falling off.
Declining, straight, but pointing downwards.
Decompound, subdivided more than three times, as the leaves of many Umbelliferous plants.
Decumbent, lying on the ground, but tending to rise at the end.
Decurrent, when the limb of a leaf is prolonged down the stem, below the point of attachment of the midrib, as in the case of the common Comfrey.
Decussate, opposite leaves in four equal rows.
Deflexed, curved downwards or towards the back.
Dehiscence, the mode in which an organ opens.
Deltoid, fleshy with a triangular transverse section.
Dentate, with short triangular teeth.
Denticulate, finely toothed, like the Camellia leaf.
Depressed, when flattened vertically or at the top, like an orange or a flat onion.
Dichotomous, when a branch or stem is much forked, as in the Mistletoe.
Diffuse, widely spreading.
Digitate, fingered leaves or lobes all starting from the top of the petiole, as the leaves of the Lupin.
Diœcious, with the different sexes on different plants.
Disk, a fleshy surface from which the stamens and pistils spring.
Distichous, arranged in two rows, as the leaves of the common *Taxodium*.
Divaricate, spreading at an obtuse angle.
Diverging, gradually separating.
Dorsal, attached to, or on the back.
Elliptic, oval but acute at each end.
Elongate, much lengthened.
Emarginate, slightly notched at the end.
Entire, not toothed nor lobed nor divided at the edge.
Equitant, overlapping each other, as the leaves of the Iris.
Erose, irregularly cut, as if gnawed.
Equalling, when the ends of organs rise to the same height, even though their relative lengths are different.
Falcate, sickle-shaped, as the leaf of *Rochea falcata*.
Fascicle, a cyme which is rather crowded with flowers placed on short pedicels of nearly equal length, as in the Sweet William and some other Pinks.

Fasciculate, when several similar parts are collected into a bundle and spring from the same spot.
Feathery, like a feather in structure, sometimes used to express very gracefully divided leaves as those of the Ferulas.
Fibrous, having many threadlike parts.
Filament, the stalk usually found supporting an anther.
Filiform, like a thread, as the stamens of maize
Fistular, hollow like a pipe, as the fruiting stems of onions.
Flaccid, weak, flabby.
Flexuose, zigzag, usually changing its direction at each joining.
Floccose, with little tufts like wool.
Florets, the small flowers of Composite plants.
Follicle, an inflated 1-celled carpel, opening by a suture to which several seeds are attached.
Forked, like a fork of two prongs.
Frond, the leaf-like part of Ferns.
Fruit, the seed-vessel with its ripe contents and any external appendages.
Fruticose, shrubby.
Fugacious, soon falling off, like the cap on the flower bud of Eschscholtzia.
Funnel-shaped, tubular below, but gradually enlarging upwards, like the flowers of Brugmansias.
Furcate, forked.
Fusiform, spindle-shaped; thick tapering to each end, like the root of a long radish.
Gibbous, swollen on one side, like the flower of Valerian.
Glabrous, without hairs or other clothing, as the Camellia leaf.
Gland, a wartlike cellular secreting organ usually raised above the surface, as on the leaves of many peaches.
Glandular, having glands.
Glandular-hairy, having hairs tipped with glands.
Glandular-serrate, having short teeth tipped with glands.
Glaucous, green with a whitish-blue lustre, like *Echeveria secunda*.
Globose, round like a globe, like the heads of flowers of *Echinops*.
Glumes, the scales enclosing the spikelet of flowers in Grasses.
Habit, the port or aspect of a plant.
Hastate, enlarged at the base into two lobes directed nearly horizontally, as in leaf of sheep's sorrel,
Head, a close terminal collection of flowers surrounded by an involucre, as in composite flowers.
Helmet, the hooded upper part of some flowers, as in the monkshood.
Helmet-shaped, arched and concave like a helmet.
Herbaceous, the parts of plants which are not woody; also organs, or parts of them, of a green colour.
Hermaphrodite, having both sexes in one bloom, as in most common plants.
Hispid, covered with stiff hairs, as in the Borage and like plants.
Hoary, with greyish-white down, like *Cerastium incanum*.
Hooded, flowers formed into a hood at the end, like the Aconites.
Hybrid, a cross between two species.
Imbricate, arranged over each other like the scales of a fir cone.
Impari-pinnate, pinnate, with an odd terminal leaflet, as the leaves of the French Honeysuckle.

GLOSSARY.

Incise, deeply cut, as the leaves of the Hawthorns.
Included, not extending beyond the organs surrounding it.
Incurved, curved inwards.
Indefinite, many but uncertain in number, like the stamens of some Cactuses.
Indehiscent, not bursting.
Indeterminate, inflorescence having always a terminal leaf bud.
Induplicate, when the edges of organs arranged in a valvate manner are folded inwards.
Inferior, beneath.
Inflexed, curved inwards.
Inflorescence, arrangement of the flowers.
Internode, the space between two nodes.
Interruptedly pinnate, when pairs of small alternate with large pinnæ.
Involucels, the involucres of secondary umbels.
Involucre, the whorled bracts at the base of an umbel, head, or single flower.
Involute, rolled from the back of anything, as towards the upper side of a leaf.
Keel, a prominent ridge, also applied to the union of the two lower petals of pea-flowers.
Laciniate, divided into narrow irregular lobes.
Lanceolate or *lance-shaped*, narrowly elliptic and tapering to each end.
Lancet-shaped, shortly and bluntly lanceolate.
Lax, loosely arranged.
Leaflets, the subdivisions of compound leaves.
Legume, a one-celled and two-valved seed vessel with the seeds arranged along the inner angle, as in the Pea.
Ligulate, strapshaped.
Ligule, a membrane at the base of the blade of the leaf of Grasses.
Limb, the flattened expanded part of a leaf or petal.
Linear, very narrow and long.
Lingulate, tongueshaped; long, fleshy, convex, blunt.
Lipped, a corolla or calyx of two lips, like the Snapdragon.
Lobate, cut into rather large divisions,
Lobule, a small lobe.
Lozenge-shaped, obliquely quadrangular, attached by one of the more acute angles.
Lunate, shaped like the new moon.
Lyrate, a pinnatifid leaf with the lobes successively and gradually enlarging from the petiole, and ending in one still larger lobe, like that of the Turnip.
Marcescent, withering but remaining in its place.
Membranous, of the texture of membrane; thin and flexible.
Midrib, the large vein extending along the middle of a leaf from its petiole nearly or quite to the other end.
Monocotyledonous, having one sheathing cotyledon.
Monœcious, with the sexes in separate flowers on the same plant.
Monosepalous; monopetalous, when the sepals or petals are joined by their edges so as apparently to form one.
Mucronate, abruptly tipped with a short point of the same texture.
Multifid, divided into many parts.
Muricate, covered with short sharp points.
Nectary, an organ which secretes honey.
Netted, covered with lines connected together like network.

Node, a point in a stem where a leaf is produced; a joining.
Nut, a hard dry 1-seeded seed-vessel.
Ob, in conjunction with terms means inverted; thus *obovate* means ovate with the attachment at the narrow end.
Oblong, long oval, equally broad at each end.
Ocrea, a tubular membranous stipule surrounding the stem.
Opaque, not shining.
Opposite, when two similar organs grow one on each side of some body; or different organs are opposed to each other with a stem between them.
Orbicular, nearly round and flat.
Oval, an ellipse; a figure rounded at each end, not broader at one end than at the other, and about twice as long as broad.
Ovary, the young seed-vessel.
Ovate, eggshaped; a short flat figure rather broader below the middle of its length.
Palate, the prominent part of the base of the lower lip which closes the mouth of a ringent corolla.
Palea, the leaf-like parts of the flower of Grasses, inclosing the stamens, pistils, and hypogynous scales.
Palmate, spreading like the fingers of a hand from the same point.
Palmatifid, palmate, with the divisions extending to the middle of the leaf, as in the Castor-oil plant.
Palmate-lobed, palmate with rounded lobes, as in the leaves of the Maple.
Palmatisect, palmate, with the divisions extending to the bottom of the leaf, as in the leaves of *Potentilla reptans*.
Panicle, a raceme with branching pedicels.
Papilionaceous, like the flower of a Pea.
Pappus, the crest of the fruit in Composites, formed of the altered limb of the calyx.
Patent, spreading widely.
Pectinate, scalloped, crenately incised.
Pedate, palmate with three lobes and the lateral lobes having similar large lobes on their outer edge, as the leaves of *Helleborus*.
Pedate-lobed, pedate, with rounded divisions or lobes.
Pedatifid, pedate, with the divisions reaching to the middle of the leaf.
Pedatisect, pedate, with the divisions extending nearly to the midrib.
Pedatipartite, pedate, with the divisions nearly reaching to the bottom of the leaf.
Pedicel, the branch of a peduncle.
Peduncle, flowerstalk.
Peltate, when its point of attachment is on the face, not at the edge, of a leaf or other organ.
Pentagonal, with five angles having convex spaces between them.
Pentangular, with five angles and five flat or concave faces.
Perfoliate, when the leaf completely surrounds the stem so that the latter seems to pass through it.
Perianth, the floral whorls when the calyx and corolla are not distinguishable.
Pericarp, seed-vessel, including adhering calyx if present.
Persistent, not soon falling off.
Personate, a monopetalous two-lipped corolla of which the lower lip is pressed upwards so as to close the opening, as in the Snapdragon.

Petals, the divisions of the corolla.
Petal-like, resembling petals in texture and colour.
Petiolate, having a petiole.
Petiole, the stalk of a leaf; *petiolule*, of a leaflet.
Phyllaries, the scales or bracts of the involucre of Composites.
Pilose, with scattered rather stiff hairs.
Pinnæ, the segments of a pinnate leaf.
Pinnate, when leaflets are arranged on opposite sides of a common stalk. A leaf is bi- or tri-pinnate when its primary or secondary divisions are pinnate.
Pinnatifid, a leaf deeply cut into segments nearly to the mid-rib, as in the leaves of the Artichoke. A 2- or 3-pinnatifid leaf is analogous to a 2- or 3-pinnate leaf.
Pinnati-partite, pinnate, with the divisions acute, and almost free as in the leaves of the Corn-poppy.
Pinnati-sect, pinnate, with the divisions reaching nearly to the mid-rib, as in the leaves of Water-cress.
Pinnules, the segments of a bipinnate leaf.
Pistil, the ovary, style, and stigma taken together.
Pitted, covered with small depressed spots.
Pod, a 1-celled and 2-valved seed-vessel with the seeds arranged along the inner angle.
Pollen, the dust in the anther.
Polygonal, with many angles.
Polypetalous, with many separate petals.
Polysepalous, with many separate sepals.
Pores, small, often roundish, holes.
Prickles, hardened epidermal appendages resembling thorns, but not woody.
Procumbent, prostrate; lying on the ground.
Pubescence, closely adpressed down.
Pubescent, with pubescence.
Pulverulent, covered with fine powdery matter.
Punctate, having minute spots like pin-holes, real or apparent.
Pyramidal, nearly in the shape of a pyramid.
Pyriform, pear-shaped.
Quadrifoliate, with four leaflets diverging from the same point.
Quinate, arranged in fives.
Raceme, a spike with stalked flowers, as that of the Laburnum.
Racemose, flowering in a raceme.
Rachis, the central stem of some kinds of inflorescence. The stalk of the frond of Ferns above the lowest pinnæ.
Radical, springing from just above the root.
Ray, parts diverging in a circle from a central point.
Receptacle, the dilated top of the stalk bearing the flowers in Composites; the common support of the parts of a flower.
Recurved, bent moderately backwards.
Reflexed, bent considerably backwards.
Reniform, transversely oval, but broadly cordate at the base; kidney-shaped.
Reticulate, forming a network.
Retuse, abruptly blunt with a notch in the middle.
Revolute, rolled back, as towards the underside of a leaf.

Rhizome, a prostrate more or less subterranean stem producing roots and leafy shoots.
Rhomboidal, approaching a quadrangular, not square, figure attached by one of its more acute angles.
Ringent, a 2-lipped, widely open corolla, like that of the Dead-nettle (*Lamium*).
Rootstock, a thick short rhizome or tuber.
Rosette, a collection of leaves growing close together, like the petals of a double rose.
Rotate, a monopetalous corolla with a short tube and very spreading limb.
Rugose, covered with a net of lines inclosing convex spaces.
Rugulose, finely rugose.
Runcinate, where the lobes of leaves are directed towards the base.
Runner, a prostrate shoot rooting at its end.
Sagittate, like the barbed head of an arrow, the auricles or lobes pointing backwards.
Salvershaped, a corolla with a long slender tube and flat limb.
Scabrous, rough.
Scales, minute rudimentary leaves.
Scape, a leafless radical peduncle.
Scarious, with a thin, dry, and shrivelled appearance.
Secund, all turned towards one side.
Sepals, the divisions of the calyx.
Serrate, toothed like a saw.
Serratures, teeth like those of a saw.
Serrulate, with very small saw-like teeth.
Sessile, without a stalk.
Seta, a bristle; a bristle tipped with a gland; a slender straight prickle.
Setaceous, like a bristle.
Setose, bearing bristles or setæ usually ending in glands.
Sheath, the lower part of a leaf or its petiole, which forms a vertical sheath surrounding the stem.
Silicle, a silique about as long as it is broad.
Silique, a long pod-like fruit of *Crucifers* having its edges connected by an internal membrane.
Simple, not compound; not branched.
Sinuate, having many large blunt lobes.
Slashed, with deep tapering incisions.
Smooth, free from all kinds of roughness.
Solitary, growing singly.
Spadix, a succulent spike bearing many sessile closely placed flowers.
Spathe, a large bract often inclosing a spadix.
Spathulate, oblong, with a long and narrow base.
Spike, a long simple axis with many sessile flowers.
Spikelet, the small group of flowers in Grasses inclosed within one or more glumes.
Spine, a stiff sharp woody persistent thorn.
Spinose, furnished with spines.
Spinulose, with small, often very minute spines or prickles.
Spur, a tubular extension of the lower part of a petal or monopetalous corolla; a loose prolongation of the base of a leaf beyond its point of attachment.

GLOSSARY.

Spurred, furnished with a spur.
Squarrose, rough with projecting or deflexed scales.
Stamen, the male organ of a flower, usually formed of a filament and anther.
Standard, the upper or posterior petal of a Pea-flower which is outside the others in the bud.
Starlike, applied to flowers of which the petals are narrow and distant and radiate like the rays of a star.
Stellate, radiating from a centre like a star.
Stellulate, like minute stars.
Stigma, the cellular part at the top of a carpel or style to which the pollen adheres.
Stipe, the stalk of Ferns up to the lowest pinnæ.
Stipules, leaf-like appendages at the base of the petiole.
Strapshaped, not very narrow nor long, and with nearly parallel sides.
Streak, a straight line of peculiar colour or structure, or a furrow.
Striate, with slender streaks or furrows.
Striped, having coloured streaks.
Style, the space between the ovary and stigma.
Sub, in composition means a near approach to; thus *subrotund* means nearly round.
Subulate, awl-shaped, tapering from the base to a fine point, a long narrow triangle.
Sucker, a stem produced at the end of an underground shoot.
Suffruticose, half-shrubby.
Superior, above anything; a calyx is superior when its tube is wholly attached to the ovary, half-superior when attached only to the lower half of it; an ovary is superior when wholly free from the calyx.
Supra-decompound, subdivided many times.
Tailed, having a long slender point.
Tendril, a twisting slender organ for laying hold of objects.
Terete, applied to round or nearly round stems.
Ternate, growing in threes.
Tetragonous, with four angles and four convex faces.
Thorn, an abortive branch with a sharp point; distinguished from a prickle by being woody.
Throat, the orifice of the tube of a monopetalous corolla or monosepalous calyx.
Thyrsoid, having a close-branched raceme of which the middle is broader than the ends.
Tomentose, covered with cottony entangled hairs, forming a matted shagginess called *tomentum;* felted.
Triangular, with three angles and three flat faces.
Trichotomous, in forks of three prongs successively repeated.
Trifid, dividing about halfway down into three parts.
Trifoliate, composed of three leaflets, as the leaves of Clover.
Trigonous, with three angles and three convex faces.
Tripartite, divided into three parts nearly to its base.
Tripinnate, three times pinnately subdivided.
Triquetrous, having three angles and three concave faces.
Truncate, blunt as if cut off at the end.
Tube, the pipe formed by the cohesion of the parts of a floral whorl.

Tuber, a thickened and underground fleshy part of the stem.
Tubercles, little round knobs.
Tubercular, tubercled; covered with little knobs.
Tuberous, like a tuber, but not part of the stem.
Tubular, hollow and nearly cylindrical.
Turbinate, topshaped, conical and attached by its long point.
Umbel, when many stalked flowers spring from one point and reach about the same level. *Partial* umbels are umbels seated upon the branches of an umbel, the whole forming a *compound* umbel.
Unilateral, turned to one side.
Urceolate, like a pitcher contracted at the mouth.
Veins, bundles of vessels in leaves and their modifications.
Ventricose, swelling unequally on one side.
Verticillate, arranged in whorls.
Villous, shaggy with loose long soft hair.
Viscous, clammy.
Wedgeshaped, like a wedge, but attached by its point.
Whorl, similar organs arranged in a circle round an axis, as the leaves of *Galium* and of some Lilies.
Whorled, arranged in whorls.
Winged, having leaf-like or membranous expansions.
Wings, the lateral petals of a Pea-flower; the flat membranous appendages of some seeds.

When two terms are combined, as *ovate-lanceolate*, it means that the form or structure is compounded of the two, or lies between them.

INDEX TO ENGLISH NAMES.

A BCHASIAN Christmas Rose, 141
Aconite, winter, 120
African Lily, 265
Alpine Alyssum, 49
„ Barrenwort, 118
„ Erinus, 121
„ Erodium, 122
„ Eryngo, 123
„ Hutchinsia, 146
„ Lychnis, 169
„ Pink, 106
„ Sanicle, 97
„ Toadflax, 165
„ Wall-flower, 125
American Cowslip, 112
„ „ Jeffreys', 111
„ Cranberry, 252
„ Senna, 87
Amethyst Hyacinth, 146
„ Eryngo, 124
Amoor Pink, 107
Artichoke, French, 103
Asarabacca, 67
Asphodel, yellow, 68
„ great, 68
Atamasco Lily, 264
Auricula, common, 206
Autumnal Acis, 43
Avena, Chiloe, 135
„ creeping, 135
„ Drummond's, 115
„ Mountain, 115

B ABYLONIAN Centaury, 87
Balm, common, 174
„ Melittis, 175
Bamboo, common hardy, 75
„ dark-stemmed, 76
„ Fortune's, 76
„ greyish, 76

Bamboo, Metake, 76
„ yellow stemmed, 75
Barbary Rag-wort, 190
Barrenwort, alpine, 118
Bastard Cress, showy, 246
Bearberry, 63
Bearded Pentstemon, 196
Bears' Breech, common, 42
„ „ armed, 42
„ „ spiny, 42
„ „ stately, 41
Bee Balm, 178
„ Orchis, 188
Bell-flower, great, 83
„ „ wall, 84
Bell-flowered Mallow, 173
„ „ Pentstemon, 196
Bergamot, wild, 178
Betony-leaved Dragon's-head, 114
Bindweed, blue Rock, 95
„ Bryony-leaved, 94
„ Cantabrian, 94
„ Mallow, 94
„ silvery, 94
„ sea, 95
Bitter-root Plant, 268
Bitter Vetch, blue, 190
„ „ variegated, 190
„ „ spring, 190
Black Crow-berry, 117
Black-eyed Erodium, 122
Bloodroot, 220
Blue-bell, 228, 270
Blue Daisy, 68
„ Dandelion, 155
„ Sow-thistle, 178
„ Spiderwort, 93
Blue-eyed Peacock Iris, 270
Bluets, 146
Bog Arum, 80

Bohemian Comfrey, 244
Borage, early, 77
,, Fairy, 122
Border Fly-trap, 60
Bristly Gaillardia, 129
Brown's Lily, 159
Buban's Candytuft, 147
Buckbean, 175
Buff Lily, 164
Burchell's Flame-flower, 248
Bush Pink, 108
Butter-bur, common, 198
Buttercup, upright Meadow, 214
,, bulbous, 214
,, chervil, 215
,, Gouan's, 215
,, large marsh, 215
,, mountain, 215
Butterwort, Irish, 202
Button Snake-root, 158

CALAMINT, Tom Thumb, 79
Californian Cornflower, 217
Californian Everlasting Pea, 156
Canadian Golden Rod, 239
,, Lily, 160
Candytuft Buban's, 147
,, Lebanon, 46
,, rock, 148
,, window, 148
Cape Crinum, 99
Caraway-leaved Erodium, 122
Cardinal-flower Lobelia, 168
Cardinal Mimulus, 177
Carmine Lysimachia, 172
Carnation, 107
Catchfly, 237
Cat Thyme, 245
Celandine, greater, 89
,, lesser, 128
,, Poppy, 243
Chamomile, 59
Cheddar Pink, 107
Chicory, 90
Chiloe Avens, 135
Christmas Daisy, 70
,, Rose, 141
,, Rose, Abchasian, 141
Cinquefoil, alpine, 205
,, blood, 205

Cinquefoil, Calabrian, 205
,, Pyrenean, 206
,, shining, 206
,, spring, 206
,, white-flowered, 205
Clammy Ononis, 187
Cobweb Houseleek, 232
Columbine, alpine, 60
,, Canadian, 61
,, common, 61
,, glandular, 61
,, large scarlet, 61
,, Pyrenean, 61
,, sweet, 61
Columna's Doronicum, 112
Comfrey, Bohemian, 244
,, Caucasian, 244
,, common, 244
Compass Plant, 238
Coneflower, 217
Coris-leaved Iberis, 147
Coris, Montpellier, 96
Cornel, dwarf, 96
Cornfield Gladiolus, 136
Cotton-weed, sea, 111
Cotyledon, wall, 98
Cow-parsnip, downy, 144
,, ,, Persian, 144
,, ,, Wilhelm's, 144
,, ,, yellowish, 143
Cowslip, 210
,, American, 112
,, Virginian, 176
Cranberry, American, 252
Crane's-bill, dwarf, 135
,, Endress's, 134
,, grey, 133
,, Iberian, 134
,, Lambert's, 134
,, silvery, 133
Creeping Avens, 135
,, Bugle, 47
,, Forget-me-not, 186
,, Gromwell, 168
,, Jenny, 172
,, Vervain, 263
,, Winter-green, 131
Crimean Snowdrop, 130
Crimson Malva, 80
Crinum, Cape, 99

INDEX TO ENGLISH NAMES. 335

Crocus, Cartwright's, 100
,,   Cloth of gold, 101
,,   common yellow, 100
,,   Imperati's, 100
,,   Large autumn, 101
,,   Mount Athos, 100
,,   naked-flowered, 100
,,   Orphanides', 100
,,   saffron, 101
,,   spring, 101
,,   various-coloured, 101
,,   white autumn, 99
Crocus-like Tulip, 250
Crowfoot, Alp, 214
,,   glacier, 215
,,   grassy, 215
,,   Rue-leaved, 216
,,   snowy, 214
,,   spiked, 216
Cuckoo Flower, 86
Cucumber, perennial, 102
Cudweed, pearl, 137
Cup Plant, 238
Currant-leaved Heuchera, 145
Cushion Pink, 237
Cyclamen-leaved Anemone, 57
Cypress Spurge, 126

DAFFODIL, golden, 181
,,   incomparable, 181
,,   least, 182
,,   Rush-leaved, 182
,,   twisted, 182
,,   two-coloured, 182
Daffodil-Allium, 48
Daisy, common, 77
,,   Michaelmas, 72
,,   blue, 68
,,   New Holland, 260
Dame's Violet, 144
Dandelion, blue, 155
Dandelion-leaved Œnothera, 186
Day-lily, Dumortier's, 143
,,   tawny, 143
,,   two-rowed, 143
,,   yellow, 143
Dead-nettle Gargano, 155
Dielytra, 109
Dog's-tooth Violet, 125
,,   ,,   yellow, 125

Dragon's Arum, 66
,,   mouth, 66
Dropwort, 241
Drummond's Avens, 115
,,   Coneflower, 217
Dwarf blue Pentstemon, 197
,,   Flag, 252
,,   Libertia, 159
,,   Mazus, 174
Dyer's Genista, 131

ELECAMPANE, 148
   Elizabeth's Catchfly, 237
Epipactis, 112
Eryngo, alpine, 123
,,   amethystine, 144
,,   Bourgati's, 124
,,   flat-leaved, 124
,,   giant, 124
,,   Pine-apple, 124
Evening Primrose, large, 185
,,   ,,   Rock, 186
,,   ,,   tall white, 186
Evergreen Alkanet, 51
,,   Orpine, 230
Everlasting, yellow, 140
,,   pea, 156

FAIR MAIDS OF FRANCE, 212
   Fairy Borage, 122
,,   Wall-flower, 125
Feather Grass, 243
Fetid Hellebore, 141
Feverfew, 212
Fire Pink, 238
Fischer's Pink, 107
Flame-flower, Burchell's, 248
,,   common, 249
,,   Nasturtium, 250
Flea-bane, large-flowered, 121
,,   showy, 121
Flax, alpine, 166
,,   evergreen, 166
,,   Narbonne, 167
,,   perennial, 167
,,   viscid, 167
,,   yellow herbaceous, 166
Fleur-de-lis, the Iris, 150
Flowering Rush, 265
Fly Orchis, 188

INDEX TO ENGLISH NAMES.

Forget-me-not, alpine, 180
,, Azorean, 180
,, common, 180
,, creeping, 186
,, early, 181
,, wood, 181
Fortune's Tiger Lily, 164
Fox-glove, common, 111
,, Gladiolus, 136
,, large-flowered, 110
,, Pentstemon, 196
,, yellow, 110
Fragrant Orchis, 137
Fraxinella, 110
French Artichoke, 103
,, Honeysuckle, 138
,, Willow, 117
,, ,, Rosemary, 118
Fringed Pink, 109
Fruiting Duck-weed, 183
Fuchsia, 266

GARGANO DEAD-NETTLE, 155
Garland Flower, 104
Geneva Bugle, 47
Gentian, Andrews's, 132
,, Asclepias-like, 132
,, Bavarian, 132
* crested, 133
,, marsh, 132
,, Pyrenean, 133
,, vernal, 133
,, yellow, 132
Gentianella, 131
German Catch-fly, 171
Giant Eryngo, 124
Giant Fennel, common, 127
,, ,, glaucous, 127
Gibraltar Iberis, 148
Glacier Pink, 108
Globe-flower, 249
Goat's-rue, officinal, 130
,, oriental, 130
Golden Club, 269
,, Tuft, 50
,, Drop, 187
,, Rod, Canadian, 239
Goldilocks, 166
Gold-striped Lily, 159
Goldthread, 95

Grape Hyacinth, 179
,, ,, Armenian, 269
,, ,, changeable, 179
,, ,, feathery, 179
,, ,, Greek, 179
,, ,, yellow, 179
Grass of Parnassus, 195
,, ,, Asarum-leaved, 195
,, ,, large, 195
Grass Rose, 108
Great Pilewort, 128
Great Reed, 67
Greek Grape Hyacinth, 179
Gromwell, creeping, 168
,, rock, 167
Ground Ivy, 136
,, Laurel, 117
,, Pine, 171
Groundsel, silvery, 235

HAREBELL, alpine, 81
,, bearded, 82
,, Carpathian, 82
,, common, 85
,, Elatine, 82
,, fragile, 83
,, Gargano, 83
,, Ivy, 83
,, Ligurian, 84
,, long-flowered, 84
,, Mont Cenis, 82
,, noble, 83
,, pyramidal, 85
,, Rainer's, 85
,, shining, 84
,, showy, 85
,, tufted, 82
,, vase, 86
,, Wanner's, 86
,, Zoysi's, 86
Heartsease, 260
Heath, ciliated, 120
,, Cornish, 121
,, cross-leaved, 121
,, Scotch, 120
,, Sea, 128
,, St. Daboec's, 175
,, Winter, 120
Heliotrope, winter, 197
Hellebore, dark purple, 141

INDEX TO ENGLISH NAMES. 337

Hellebore, fetid, 141
,, Olympian, 142
,, oriental, 142
,, purple-flowered, 142
,, sweet, 142
Hemp Agrimony, Aromatic, 126
,, ,, purple, 126
Heron's-bill, fairy, 123
,, rock, 123
,, Roman, 123
,, showy, 122
Hollyhock, common, 49
,, Mallow, 173
Honesty, perennial, 169
Honey-flower, large, 174
Honeysuckle, French, 138
Hoop-petticoat Narcissus, 181
Hop, Common, 146
Horse-shoe Vetch, 145
Horse-tail, dwarf, 119
,, giant, 119
,, variegated, 120
,, wood, 119
Houseleek, 232
Hyacinth, Amethyst, 146
,, common, 147
Hybrid Alkanet, 51

INDIAN KNOTWEED, 204
Iris, Blue-eyed Peacock, 270
,, common, 150
,, crested, 149
,, dwarf, 152
,, early bulbous, 152
,, Elder-scented, 152
,, English, 154
,, Florentine, 149
,, Gladdon, 149
,, golden, 151
,, Grass-leaved, 150
,, Iberian, 150
,, long-petalled, 151
,, marsh, 151
,, mourning, 153
,, naked-stemmed, 151
,, pale-flowered, 151
,, pleasing, 149
,, Rush, 150
,, Russian, 152
,, Siberian, 152

Iris, Spanish, 154
,, spurious, 153
,, squalid, 153
,, Swert's, 153
,, variegated, 154
,, yellowish, 149
Ironwort, Syrian, 236
Italian Alkanet, 51
,, Arum, 66
Ivy Harebell, 261

JACOB'S LADDER, 203
Jerusalem Sage, 198
Jonquille, 182
,, large, 182

KNOT-WEED, giant, 204
,, Indian, 204
,, rock, 204

LADY'S SLIPPER, common, 103
,, noble, 104
,, spotted, 104
,, white, 103
Larkspur, bee, 104
,, elegant, 105
Lavender Cotton, 220
Lawn Pearlwort, 218
Lebanon Candytuft, 46
Leopard's-bane, 113
,, Caucasian, 112
Lesser Celandine, 128
Lily, African, 265
,, Atamasco, 264
,, Belladonna, 50
,, black, 162
,, Brown's, 159
,, buff, 164 ·
,, bulb-bearing, 160
,, Canadian, 160
,, Carolina, 160
,, Fortune's Tiger, 164
,, giant, 161
,, gold-striped, 159
,, great American, 163
,, Japan, 162
,, Martagon, 162
,, of Carniola, 160
,, of the Valley, common, 94
,, of the Valley, star-flowered, 270

z

Lily, orange, 161
,, Peruvian Swamp, 264
,, scarlet Martagon, 161
,, spotted, 163
,, St. Bruno's 195
,, Tiger, 164
,, Tom Thumb, 163
,, transparent trumpet, 161
,, Trumpet, 162
,, Turban, 163
,, Washington, 268
,, white, 160
Ling, common, 80
Lion's-foot, 157
London Pride, 270
Loosestrife, 173
Lotus, common, 169
Lungwort, 212
Lupine, large-leaved, 169
,, perennial, 169

MAIDEN PINK, 107
Mallow, Rose, 145
Marsh Marigold, 80
,, Vetchling, 156
Martagon Lily, 162
Marvel of Peru, 177
May Apple, 203
,, ,, Himalayan, 203
Meadow Beauty, 217
,, Geranium, 134
,, Rue, 245
Meadow-saffron, alpine, 93
,, common, 93
,, spring, 79
,, variegated, 93
Meadow-sweet, 241
Michaelmas Daisy, 72
Milk-thistle, common, 239
,, ivory, 238
Milkwort, Box-leaved, 204
,, chalk, 203
Monkey-flower, coppery, 177
,, yellow, 177
Monkshood, autumn, 43
,, common, 44
,, Japan, 44
,, panicled, 44
,, northern, 44
Moren's Mallow, 173

Mountain Avens, 115
,, everlasting, 58
,, Valerian, 252
Musk, common, 177
,, Hyacinth, 179
,, Mallow, 173

NEW Holland Daisy, 260
,, Violet, 123
New Zealand Flax, 269
Night-scented Rocket, 144

ORANGE LILY, 161
Orchis, Bee, 188
,, Fly, 188
,, fragrant, 137
,, Guernsey, 189
,, leafy, 188
,, marsh, 188
,, spotted Hand, 189
Orpine, evergreen, 230
Oxlip, 210
Oyster Plant, 176

PÆONY, EDIBLE, 192
,, fine-leaved, 193
,, lobed, 193
,, officinal, 193
,, Ram, 192
,, white-flowered, 192
Pampas-grass, 137
Panic-grass, bulbous, 193
,, tall, 193
,, twiggy, 194
Partridge Berry, variegated, 268
Pasque-flower, common, 57
,, mountain, 57
Peacock Anemone, 57
Pearl Cudweed, 137
Pennyroyal, Requien's, 175
Perennial Cucumber, 102
Periwinkle, 257
Persian Assafœtida, 127
Peru, Marvel of, 177
Peruvian Swamp-lily, 264
Phlox, Carolina, 199
,, creeping, 200
,, cross-leaved, 199
,, mossy, 200
,, ovate-leaved, 200
,, panicled, 200

INDEX TO ENGLISH NAMES.

Phlox, procumbent, 200
,, straggling, 199
Pickerel-weed, 205
Pigeon Berry, 202
Pilewort, Great, 128
Pine-apple Eryngo, 124
Pine Barren Beauty, 213
Pink, alpine, 106
,, Amoor, 107
,, blood-scarlet, 107
,, bush, 108
,, Cheddar, 107
,, cushion, 237
,, fire, 238
,, Fischer's, 107
,, fringed, 109
,, garden, 108
,, glacier, 108
,, maiden, 107
,, rock, 108
,, sweet, 108
Pitcher-plant, American, 221
Plumy Dielytra, 109
Poet's Narcissus, 183
Poppy, alpine, 194
,, golden, 194
,, Iceland, 194
,, orange, 194
,, oriental, 194
,, pilose, 195
,, prickly, 174
,, Welsh, 174
Poppy Anemone, 56
Portland Spurge, 126
Prairie Dock, 238
Prickly Poppy, 174
,, Thrift, 41
Primrose, Altaic, 206
,, Bird's-eye, 206
,, broad-leaved, 208
,, Caucasian, 206
,, common, 211
,, Cortusa, 207
,, creamy, 208
,, entire-leaved, 207
,, Fairy, 209
,, Fortune's, 207
,, glutinous, 207
,, Japan, 208
,, large-leaved 20

Primrose, long-flowered, 208
,, margined, 208
,, Munro's, 209
,, purple, 209
,, Scotch Bird's-eye, 209
,, snowy, 209
,, Stuart's, 210
,, toothed, 207
,, Veitch's, 210
,, viscid, 211

QUAKING-GRASS, common, 78
Quamash-root, 81
Queen of the Prairie, 241

RAGGED ROBIN, 170
Rag-wort, Barbary, 190
Red Campion, 170
,, Valerian, 88
,, Whortleberry, 252
Red-veined Rhubarb, 216
Reed, great, 67
Requien's Pennyroyal, 175
Rest-harrow, hairy, 187
,, Ram, 187
,, round-leaved, 187
,, shrubby, 187
Rhubarb, red-veined, 216
Rock Beauty, 198
,, Candytuft, 148
,, Gromwell, 167
,, Jasmine, 52
,, Pink, 108
,, Strawberry, 128
Rock cress, rosy, 62
,, white, 62
Rocket, night-scented, 144
,, yellow, 124
Rose Campion, 47
Rosemary, French Willow, 118
Rosette, Mullein, 213
Round-leaved Vetchling, 157
Rue, Anemone, 245
,, meadow, 154

SAND-MYRTLE, 157
Sandwort, Balearic, 63
,, fringed, 63
,, mountain, 64
,, vernal, 64

INDEX TO ENGLISH NAMES.

Sanicle, alpine, 97
Satin-flower, spring, 239
Saxifrage, 221
Scabious, 227
Scarlet Lychnis, 169
Sea Cotton-weed, 111
,, Heath, 128
,, Holly, 124
,, Lavender, common, 242
,, ,, narrow-leaved, 241
,, Pea, 202
Self-heal, great, 211
,, Pyrenean, 211
Senna, American, 87
Shamrock Pea, 195
Sickle Medick, 174
Silkweed, 67
Silver Clary, 219
Silvery Vetch, 257
Skull-cap, alpine, 229
,, large-flowered, 229
Snap-dragon, great, 59
,, rock, 60
Sneezewort, 43
Snowdrop Anemone, 58
Snowdrop, common, 130
,, Crimean, 130
,, Imperati's, 129
Snowflake, spring, 158
,, summer, 157
,, small, 158
Soapwort, common, 221
,, rock, 221
,, tufted, 220
Solomon's Seal, 204
Sow-thistle, blue, 178
Speedwell, 253
Spider-wort, blue, 93
,, Virginian, 247
Spignel, 176
Spiked Button Snake-root, 158
,, Snake's Beard, 188
Spikenard, 63
Spring Satin-flower, 239
Spurge, Cypress, 126
,, glaucous, 126
,, Portland, 126
Squill, 228
St. Bruno's Lily, 195
St. Daboec's Heath, 175

Starflower, 247
Star-flowered Lily of the Valley, 270
Star of Bethlehem, tall, 189
Starwort, 69
Stokes's Aster, 243
Stonecrop, 230
Strawberry, rock, 128
Striped Squill, 212
Sundrops, 185
Sunflower, dark-red, 140
,, graceful, 140
,, rigid, 140
Swamp-lily, Peruvian, 264
Sweet Cicely, 181
,, Hellebore, 142
,, Pink, 108
,, William, 106
,, Woodruff, 68
Syrian Ironwort, 236

TANSY, 244
Thistle, dwarf, 87
,, woolly, 87
Thrift, common, 64
,, great, 64
Throat-wort, blue, 247
Tiger Lily, 164
Toad-flax, alpine, 165
,, common, 166
,, thick-leaved, 165
Tom Thumb Lily, 163
Trefoil, alpine, 247
Tufted Soapwort, 220
Tulip, 250
,, Crocus-like, 250
Turban Lily, 163
Turfing Daisy, 213
Twin-flower, 166
Twin-leaf, 155

VALERIAN, red, 88
Variegated Partridge Berry, 263
,, Sage, 219
Vervain, creeping, 263
Vetch, Horse-shoe, 145
,, silvery, 257
,, tufted, 257
Violet, 258
,, Dame's, 144
,, Dog's-tooth, 125

INDEX TO ENGLISH NAMES.

Violet, New Holland, 123
,, water, 146
Virginian Cowslip, 176

WALL-FLOWER, alpine, 125
,, common, 89
,, fairy, 125
Wall Germander, 245
Washington Lily, 268
Water-dock, 218
Water Lily, common yellow, 184
,, small yellow, 184
,, sweet-scented, 185
,, white, 185
,, yellow American, 184
Water Plantain, 265
Water-Violet, 146
Welsh Poppy, 174
White Cup, 184
,, Lily, 160
Whorl-flower, 178
Whortleberry, red, 252
Wild Bergamot, 178
,, Thyme, 246
Windflower, alpine, 55
,, apennine, 55
,, Japan, 56
,, scarlet, 56
,, vine-leaved, 58

Window Candytuft, 148
Winter Aconite, 120
,, Cherry, 201
Winter-green, creeping, 131
,, larger, 213
Winter Heliotrope, 197
Wolf's-bane Aconite, 44
Wood Anemone, common, 57
,, yellow, 57
Wood Lily, white, 248
Woodruff, sweet, 68
Wood-sorrel, Bowie's, 191
,, Chilian, 191
Worm-grass, 240
Wormwood, alpine, 65
,, graceful, 65
,, sea, 65
,, silky, 65
Woundwort, woolly, 241

YARROW, common, 43
,, dwarf silvery, 43
,, Egyptian, 42
,, noble, 42
,, silvery, 42
,, woolly, 43
Yellow Everlasting, 140
,, Grape Hyacinth, 179
,, Rocket, 124

THE END.

www.ingramcontent.com/pod-product-compliance
Lightning Source LLC
Chambersburg PA
CBHW030318240426
43673CB00040B/1206